WITHDRAWN

Austria, Great Britain, and the Crimean War

The Destruction of the European Concert

Austria, Great Britain, and the Crimean War

The Destruction of the European Concert

PAUL W. SCHROEDER

Cornell University Press | Ithaca and London

First published 1972 by Cornell University Press.
Published in the United Kingdom by Cornell University Press Ltd., 2-4 Brook Street, London W1Y 1AA.

International Standard Book Number 0-8014-0742-7
Library of Congress Catalog Card Number 72-3451

Printed in the United States of America by Vail-Ballou Press, Inc.

Librarians: Library of Congress cataloging information appears on the last page of the book.

TO MY PARENTS

Contents

Appendixes

Maps

Illustrations

(following page 104)

Preface

The events of the Crimean War served to destroy for a significant period the existing international system in Europe and the prevailing rules by which foreign policy was conducted and peace maintained. The war undermined the Concert of Europe, the complex of practices and arrangements whereby the five great powers cooperated to settle dangerous European problems and to avoid great-power confrontations. It broke up the so-called Holy Alliance (the conservative front of Austria, Prussia, and Russia) and isolated Austria. It created a major new alignment (Britain, France, and Sardinia), and raised the possibility of others (France and Russia, Prussia and Russia, or a combination of all three). It paved the way for the unification of Rumania, the Polish revolution of 1863 and the attendant European crisis, and the wars of Italian and German unification. Above all, it changed the spirit and style of European diplomacy. As Gordon Craig writes, "National self-restraint, respect for the public law as defined in treaties, and willingness to enforce its observance by concerted action were, then, the conditions which made possible the maintenance of peace and the balance of power in the period 1830–1854. The most notable thing about the Crimean War which broke out in 1854 was that it destroyed these conditions." *

The main purpose of this book is to indicate to what extent these results were unforeseen and unintended, or anticipated and even deliberate, and to show that, whether intended or not, they flowed naturally from the kind of diplomacy practiced during the war, particularly by the Western powers. I have concentrated on Austria

* "The System of Alliances and the Balance of Power," in the *New Cambridge Modern History*, X (Cambridge, 1960), 267.

and Britain because their respective policies and actions represent a clash between two opposed diplomatic systems and modes of behavior: the traditional Concert approach held by Austria—which sought to avert war and check Russia by restraining her within the established Concert and compelling her to deal with Turkey through it, thereby preserving the existing treaties and boundaries in Europe —and the Whig-Palmerstonian tactics of confrontation—which sought to force Russia to back down before an overwhelming coalition and to create a new Western-led league of states in Europe to promote progress and ordered liberty. The main reason war was not averted, this book contends, was that the Western powers, especially Britain, frustrated every hopeful effort at a diplomatic solution, primarily because no such solution could bring the defeat for Russia and the victory for Britain and her principles that Palmerston and liberal opinion demanded.

Austria's policy, the work argues further, aimed during the war not primarily to exploit it for Austrian gains, nor simply to avoid war for herself, but to achieve a European solution * to the Eastern question through cooperation with the West. Again it was the sea powers, with Britain in the lead, who frustrated the efforts by Austria to reach a negotiated peace, even though such a peace would have been distinctly favorable to them, because only a decisive military victory would give them the prestige and leadership in a new European system they wanted. Austria contributed indispensably to ending the war, against British desires and efforts, and to reaching a relatively moderate peace settlement. Britain, however, had by then succeeded in undermining the existing Concert and opening the path to future changes in Europe, above all at Austria's expense—although British statesmen had no clear idea as to what these were to be, and no intention of taking responsibility for the ultimate results of Britain's policy.

This is a controversial interpretation, here stated very baldly. In trying to present the evidence fully and fairly, with the necessary nuances, I have followed a conventional pattern for diplomatic history—giving a narrative account of international developments concentrating upon the strategies and actions of leading statesmen,

---

* Here and later I use the word "European" to mean "in accordance with the established practices and ideals of European Concert diplomacy."

rather than analyzing the decision-making process or the policy-making elites, studying pressure groups, dissecting internal political or social structures, or employing psychodynamic theory to explain policy. There are serious scholars who contend that even if a work of diplomatic history contains new information and interpretations, as this one claims to, the story still should not be told in this traditional fashion, for at best it deals only with a surface phenomenon. Foreign policy is always the expression of deeper forces within a country. Therefore diplomatic history should always be viewed and written as part of general political history, or as part of socio-economic or intellectual or even psychological history—but not any longer on its own terms, as if the old principle of the primacy of foreign policy still held good, and the manipulations of cabinet ministers and ambassadors constituted the real story.

This view is widespread and plausible enough to deserve a brief answer here—an explanation, highly condensed, of why I consider the traditional method and materials not only still worthwhile for the purposes of this study, but in fact the only way for the diplomatic historian to carry out his primary responsibility (though not his sole one) in writing the history of international relations.

Diplomatic history is of course intimately connected with many other kinds of history. International relations in the narrow sense are only part of the various political, social, economic, and ideological relationships between governments and peoples. The methods urged to broaden and reinterpret diplomatic history (some of them not nearly so modern as their proponents suggest), used properly, yield valuable insights. The now fashionable principles of the primacy of domestic politics in foreign policy and the inextricable interweaving of foreign policy and economic interest are, I believe, often valid, and as often not, depending on the circumstances. During the Crimean War, domestic politics clearly shaped foreign policy in Britain and perhaps in France, but not, I think, in Austria, Prussia, or Russia. Much of what is called traditional diplomatic history does give the impression of unreality and narrowness.

But if these points are granted, the key questions remain whether this unreality and narrowness actually derive from concentrating on the diplomatic narrative and on traditional sources, and whether expanding the scope of the investigation would cure the problem.

Those who answer these questions affirmatively assume that the diplomatic historian's primary responsibility is to analyze foreign policy in terms of the determinants of decisions and actions—the mixture of intentions, purposes, and pressures behind them. By doing this, the historian not only can show the deeper reasons why statesmen acted as they did, but also demonstrate how these are connected with the life of the nation and the culture and thought of the time—in short, he can expose the roots of foreign policy and fit it into the organic unity of history.

If this is the diplomatic historian's primary task and goal, then undoubtedly he must branch out into other areas, use other materials, and extend his investigation. But the assumption is open to challenge. To put it simply, I do not believe that analyzing foreign policy in terms of the determinants of decisions is the most important or satisfactory way of understanding what happens in international relations and why. The dynamics of international relations operate to a considerable degree autonomously, independent of decisions and their determinants. It is less important to know why statesmen took certain actions than to know what reactions and results those actions produced in the international arena, and why under the prevailing system they led to these results and not others, and how these actions affected the system itself. If this is the case, an attempt to integrate diplomatic history into other broader kinds of history before one has dealt with it adequately in terms of its own rules and dynamics distorts and obscures rather than illuminates the nature of international politics.

Why is the analysis of the determinants of decision less important than is often supposed? First, because often the determinants do not really determine—statesmen do not usually act mainly because of motives, aims, and influences, even when they think they do. Very much of what statesmen present and historians discuss as reasons for their actions involves covering their tracks, consciously or subconsciously finding reasons plausible to themselves and others for doing what they were bound to do anyway.* Nor does it usually help much to try to peel away layer upon layer of subterfuge in the hope of getting down to the bedrock of genuine motive; often there

---

* Metternich's explanations of his actions usually provide good examples of this, as the writings of Professor Bertier de Sauvigny on Metternich show particularly well.

is none. The statesman is acting within, and reacting to, a situation over which he has little or no control, playing a game in which some fairly elemental rules and strategy largely dictate what he can and must do. The best practitioners of statecraft have always recognized that opportunities, capabilities, contingencies, and necessities take precedence over motives and intentions. No one excelled Bismarck at divining the aims of his opponents or at devising ways of killing five birds with one stone. The deciphering of his aims and strategy has provided historians with endless material for debate. Yet he repeatedly insisted that one could not conduct or understand foreign policy on the basis of fixed aims and intentions, that practicing the art of statecraft was like listening for the rustle of the skirts of Providence as she hastened by in the night and groping blindly to seize them and follow where they led. Many others have said the same thing in a less colorful way.

Moreover, even if these supposed determinants of decision explain, as they sometimes do, the actions of statesmen or nations, they only explain their input into the process of international relations. The outcome depends mainly not on what the actors are trying to do, but upon the system of relationships within which they act, and how it transmits and transmutes these actions and the reactions of others. There are virtually no simple, unambiguous actions in diplomacy, no signs and signals that cannot carry a variety of meanings, no moves that cannot have opposite effects under differing circumstances, no way to get directly and certainly from means to ends. Therefore every attempt to depict diplomatic history primarily in terms of determinants of decisions, by old methods or new, introduces a false rationality into the process. It overstresses motives and influences at the expense of results; it ignores the imperfect, often nonexistent, correspondence between what an actor tries to do and what he actually succeeds in doing; and it obscures the most salient features of international politics. These are the facts that it combines a high degree of rationality and purposiveness in the use of means, so that every move must be assumed to have some hidden significance or purpose,* with a great uncertainty and incalculability of outcomes; and that there is little or no relationship among

---

* This is aptly illustrated by what Metternich is supposed to have said when his old rival, the Russian diplomat Pozzo di Borgo, died: "Now why do you suppose he did that?"

the various actors between what they need to do and what they can do—between power and responsibility, problems and resources, merits and rewards, crimes and punishments. Foreign policy must be seen as a marketplace in which Lazarus may have to bid against Croesus; a play in which the stupidest actor may play Hamlet and the wisest Rosencrantz or Guildenstern; a system of justice in which, to quote the Spanish proverb, one man can steal horses to great applause while another is hanged for looking over the fence.

Ignoring these facts not only makes for unreality in diplomatic history, but also for unfairness—for the ethics of success that pervades much of it. One continually encounters diplomatic history, traditional and modern, which proceeds by analyzing a statesman's aims, expounding the strategy used in pursuing them, and concluding that if the aims were achieved, the policy was a realistic one. If not, then not. Yet not only are statesmen often no more responsible for the success of their policies than farmers are for the success of their crops, but frequently the least important thing to be said about a policy is that it achieved its purposes. The most important outcomes in foreign policy are often unintended and unanticipated results, and the best diplomatic history (for example, that of George F. Kennan) continually shows the discrepancies between what international actors think they are doing and what they are really bringing about in the way of results. The main goal of diplomatic history ought to be accounting not for the determinants of policy, but for the results—all the results, for the whole system, as only the historian from his perspective can detect and portray them. This is the purpose of this book, and the traditional narrative and materials provide the best means to try to fulfill it.

It is a pleasure to acknowledge the help of many individuals and institutions. My research in Austria in 1965 and in Britain, France, and Austria in 1967 was supported by grants-in-aid from the American Council of Learned Societies, with a supplementary grant in 1965 from the American Philosophical Society. The Graduate Research Board, the Center for Advanced Study, the History Department, and the Library of the University of Illinois also aided my research generously in many ways, particularly through granting a half-year's sabbatical leave and another semester's research leave, giving subvention for travel abroad in 1967 and 1970 and for the purchase of research materials, and providing research assistants.

In Vienna, Fräulein Ursula Baudisch (now Frau Dr. Ursula Baudisch Schulmeister) helped me greatly in getting through the materials in the Vienna archives. Dr. Waltraud Heindl, of the Austrian Institute for Eastern and Southeastern Europe, very kindly made available to me materials that she secured from the Buol Nachlass in Salzburg and the Depôt Burckhardt in the Library of the University of Geneva. I also benefited from discussing Buol and Austrian diplomacy with her. A number of scholars have read all or parts of this study in various stages of completion. They include Professors R. John Rath of Rice University, Robert A. Kann of Rutgers University, Enno E. Kraehe of the University of Virginia, John S. Curtiss of Duke University, Keith A. Hitchins of the University of Illinois, Winfried Baumgart of the University of Bonn, and Dr. Heindl. Their helpful suggestions have always been welcome, although I have not always followed them. My research assistants, especially Dr. Roy A. Austensen and Miss Christine Holden, often did more than was required of them. The staffs of the various archives and libraries at which I worked were pleasant and helpful. I am particularly thankful to the personnel of the repository most important to my study, the Haus-Hof-und Staatsarchiv in Vienna, for their patient dealing with my many questions and requests. I acknowledge with gratitude the gracious permission of Her Majesty the Queen to make use of materials in the Royal Archives at Windsor; the kind permission of the seventh earl of Clarendon to quote from the Clarendon Papers on deposit at the Bodleian Library at Oxford; that of the Trustees of Broadlands to use the Palmerston Papers; and that of Count Ludwig Plaz of Salzburg, descendant of Count Buol, to use the papers from the Buol Nachlass in his keeping, given to me by Dr. Heindl.

PAUL W. SCHROEDER

Urbana, Illinois

Abbreviations Used
in Notes

Ab. Corr.: Aberdeen Correspondence (1846–1862). Privately printed by Lord Stanmore. State Papers Room, British Museum.

Add. ms.: Additional manuscripts. Manuscript Division, British Museum.

AMAE: Archive du Ministère des Affaires Etrangères. Paris. The main correspondence consulted was the Correspondance politique, Autriche, cited as AMAE, Autr. Other citations refer to various sections of Mémoires et documents, cited as AMAE, Mem. et doc. Turquie, Roumanie, etc.

AMG: Archive du Ministère de la Guerre. Vincennes.

AOK: Armee Oberkommando, Kriegsarchiv. Vienna.

ASV, NV: Archivio Segreto Vaticano. Nunziatura di Vienna.

Clar. dep.: Clarendon deposit. Bodleian Library, Oxford.

FA: Feldakten. Kriegsarchiv, Vienna.

FO: Foreign Office. London.

GA Berlin: Gesandschaftsarchiv Berlin. Haus-Hof-und Staatsarchiv, Vienna.

GSA, MA: Geheimes Staatsarchiv, Ministerium des Aeussern. Munich.

3 Hansard: *Hansard's Parliamentary Debates.* 3d series. Vols. CXXIV–CLXVII (1853–1856). London, 1853–1856.

HHStA: Haus-Hof-und Staatsarchiv. Vienna.

KA: Kriegsarchiv. Vienna.

Kab. Arch. Geh. Akt.: Kabinettsarchiv, Geheimakten. Haus-Hof-und Staatsarchiv, Vienna.

MKSM: Militär-Kanzlei Seiner Majestät. Kriegsarchiv, Vienna.

MR Prot.: Ministerrats-Protokolle. Haus-Hof-und Staatsarchiv, Vienna.

Nistor: Nistor, Ion I., ed. *Corespondența lui Coronini din Principate: Acte și rapoarte din Iunie 1854–Martie 1857.* Cernauți, 1938.

PA: Politisches Archiv. Haus-Hof-und Staatsarchiv, Vienna.

Palm. Papers: Palmerston Papers. At the time I used them, these were temporarily under the care of the Historical Manuscripts Commission, London.

PAP: Manteuffel, Otto, Baron von. *Preussens auswärtige Politik, 1850–1858: Unveröffentlichte Dokumente aus dem Nachlasse Manteuffels.* Ed. by Heinrich Ritter von Poschinger. 3 vols. Berlin, 1902.

PRO: Public Record Office. London.

QVL: Victoria, Queen of Great Britain. *The Letters of Queen Victoria: A Selection from Her Majesty's Correspondence between the Years 1834 and 1861.* Ed. by Arthur Christopher Benson. 1st series. 3 vols. London, 1907.

RA: Royal Archives. Windsor.

Rel. dipl. Aust.-Sard.: Istituto Storico Italiano per l'Età moderna e contemporanea, *Le relazione diplomatiche fra l'Austria e il Regno di Sardegna.* 3d series: 1848–1860. Vols. III–IV (1849–1857). Ed. by Franco Valsecchi. Rome, 1968.

Rel. dipl. Aust.-Tosc.: Istituto Storico Italiano per l'Età moderna e contemporanea. *Le relazioni diplomatiche fra l'Austria e il Granducato di Toscana.* 3d series: 1848–1860. Vol. IV (1853–1856). Ed. by Angelo Filipuzzi. Rome, 1968.

Rel. dipl. Fr.-Tosc.: Istituto Storico Italiano per l'Età moderna e contemporanea. *Le relazioni diplomatiche fra la Francia e il Granducato di Toscana.* 3d series: 1848–1860. Vol. II (1851–1857). Ed. by Armando Saitta. Rome, 1959.

Rel. dipl. GB-Sard.: Istituto Storico Italiano per l'Età moderna e contemporanea. *Le relazioni diplomatiche fra la Gran Bretagna e il Regno di Sardegna.* 3d series: 1848–1860. Vols. I–V (1848–1856). Ed. by Federico Curato. Rome, 1955–1968.

Sess. Papers: Great Britain, House of Commons, Sessional Papers.

tg: Telegram.

A Note on Documentation and Quotations

To keep the notes manageable in size, I have cited published letters and documents only by page number in the particular collection. For unpublished letters and documents, I have omitted the place of origin except where I thought this point of some particular importance. I have also reluctantly omitted such designations as "private," "secret," "reserved," and "confidential," and the particular numbers of the dispatches, except where I felt that these numbers in addition to the date would be necessary for identifying a particular dispatch. For published works listed in the Selected Bibliography, I have given only the author and an abbreviated title in the initial footnote citation; full bibliographical information is given in the footnotes for items not in the bibliography. After the initial citation, works are referred to only by the author's name, unless more than one work appears under that name, in which case a short title is added. All translations in the direct quotations are mine. Lord Clarendon and other British statesmen resorted to many conventional abbreviations in their private letters ("&" for "and," "wd" for "would," and the like). The usual scholarly procedure of filling in the missing letters within brackets would be irritating to the reader and wholly unnecessary, since in no case was there any doubt as to the word indicated by the abbreviation. I have therefore written out the abbreviated words in full.

The Great-Power Representatives

This chart of the more prominent diplomats and their posts is intended merely to help the reader follow the narrative by reminding him who served where. Diplomatic representatives who do not figure importantly in the story are omitted, as are all government officials not in the diplomatic service. No distinction is drawn here between regular representatives and chargés. Full names are given in the Index.

Great Britain

Foreign Secretary: Clarendon
Paris: Cowley
St. Petersburg: Seymour
Vienna: Westmorland, Elliot, Seymour
Constantinople: Redcliffe
Berlin: Bloomfield, Loftus
Turin: Hudson
Special mission: Russell

Austria

Foreign Minister: Buol
Undersecretary: Werner
Paris: Hübner
St. Petersburg: Lebzeltern, V. Esterházy
Berlin: F. Thun, G. Esterházy
London: Colloredo
Constantinople: Klezl, Bruck, Koller, Prokesch
Munich: Apponyi
Frankfurt: Prokesch, Rechberg
Special mission: Leiningen

France

Foreign Minister: Drouyn, Walewski
London: Walewski, Persigny
St. Petersburg: Castelbajac
Vienna: Bourqueney, De Serre
Constantinople: LaCour, Baragueys d'Hilliers, Thouvenel
Berlin: Moustier

Russia

Foreign Minister: Nesselrode
Paris: Kiselev
London: Brunnow
Vienna: Meyendorff, Gorchakov
Berlin: Budberg
Special missions: Menshikov, Orlov

Prussia

Foreign Minister: O. Manteuffel
Paris: Hatzfeldt
London: Bunsen, Bernstorff
Vienna: Arnim
Frankfurt: Bismarck
Special missions: E. Manteuffel, Alvensleben, Groeben, Usedom, Münster, Wedell

Austria, Great Britain, and the Crimean War

The Destruction of the European Concert

I

Illusion of Recovery: Austria and Europe after 1848

Historians of the Austrian Empire commonly contrast the strong leadership of Prince Felix zu Schwarzenberg, premier from 1848 to 1852, with the weak policy of Count Karl von Buol-Schauenstein, foreign minister from 1852 to 1859. Under Schwarzenberg, Austria survived revolutions and war and emerged with her international position strengthened. Under Buol, the international assets rescued by Schwarzenberg were frittered away. As the great historian Heinrich Friedjung remarked, Buol in antagonizing Russia in 1854 risked all of Metternich's and Schwarzenberg's hard-won gains for a soap bubble.[1]

There were differences between Schwarzenberg and Buol, but not simply those of decisiveness versus failure. Schwarzenberg's hard-won gains were themselves in good part a soap bubble; Austria's international position when Buol took over was far from solid. This does not deny Schwarzenberg's achievement. He brought Austria through one of the worst crises in her long crisis-ridden history, and left her at his death on April 5, 1852, in far better shape than when he had taken office in November 1848, with only the army seeming to stand between her and dissolution. By 1852, the internal revolts had been suppressed, foreign attacks defeated, alliances renewed, and the governmental lethargy of Metternich's last years and the paralyzing indecision of his immediate successors replaced by a spirit of apparent unity and energy. In other words, Austria survived under Schwarzenberg. But she only survived. Schwarzenberg merely arrested the decline in Austria's relative power, and even this success cost Austria heavily in terms of missed opportunities and foreclosed possibilities for far-reaching reform.

Foreign policy was Schwarzenberg's specialty, and Germany the area in which he most hoped to improve Austria's position. His colleague as Minister of Trade, the energetic entrepreneur and economic statesman Baron Karl Ludwig von Bruck, aspired to create a great central European trade and customs union centered in Austria. Schwarzenberg supported this, but had a political dream in addition: uniting the rest of Germany with Austria into an "Empire of seventy millions." This slogan gave Schwarzenberg enduring fame, making him a hero or a villain to generations of proponents and opponents of a Greater Germany. It helped establish his reputation as the Austrian Bismarck, the first of the mid-century *Realpolitiker,* the one who started the struggle for mastery of Germany that ended at Königgrätz in 1866, the cynical power politician who tried to solve all political problems with cannons.[2]

This picture is at least exaggerated. Schwarzenberg was certainly more ready to fight than Metternich had been. His tactics were often aggressive and sometimes cynical (though hardly worse than average for his time). One can see why he was termed an "army diplomat," and why Tsar Nicholas I described him as Palmerston in a white coat. But Schwarzenberg never forgot Austria's limitations and the essentially conservative nature of her interests. On the whole, his policy shows more caution and continuity with Metternich's ideas than it does brashness or new initiatives.

Even in dealing with Germany, where Metternich criticized him for trying the impossible, his actual aims were less expansive than the phrase "Empire of seventy millions" suggests. What he sought concretely was to reform and strengthen the existing German Confederation, set up in 1815; to include all of Austria within it, bringing in the non-German provinces left out in 1815; to centralize power within the Confederation in the hands of the two German great powers, Austria and Prussia; and to set up the central European customs union proposed by Bruck. These would certainly have meant major gains for Austria. But all these aims, theoretically at least, could have been realized by negotiation, and Schwarzenberg did not intend to use violence to achieve them.

In fact, Prussia, not Austria, started the struggle for mastery in Germany and pushed it to a conclusion. Although the story is too long and complicated to be related here, it is clear enough that from

1848 on Austria waged a basically defensive fight to retain her traditional leadership in Germany. Prussia meanwhile repeatedly tried to oust her entirely from Germany or to gain overall parity with her, with Prussia in control of everything north of the Main River. Schwarzenberg countered these moves, moreover, not with armed force, but with the Metternichian devices of delay, maneuver, conciliation, and attempts to isolate his opponent politically and morally. When a war with Prussia finally seemed inevitable in November 1850, Schwarzenberg dismayed some of his colleagues and Austria's German allies by drawing back from the brink. Various factors contributed to Austria's failure to push the quarrel to a military decision —Prussia's desire to retreat from danger, the fact that the Austrian minister at Berlin, Count Prokesch, helped Prussia escape, the reluctance of Emperor Francis Joseph to start his reign with a German war, Russian advice against war, and the unfavorable attitude of other European powers. Yet the basic fact remains that Schwarzenberg opted for an essentially conservative policy out of concern for Austria's vulnerable position. She could accept a war to defend her traditional rights and interests, but she would not launch one to create a new position of strength. Schwarzenberg therefore returned perforce to efforts to gain Austria's essential goals by negotiation, which he thought might be more possible with the conservative Prussian regime headed by Baron von Manteuffel.[3]

Thus the Olmütz Punctation that Austria and Prussia signed in November, often described as a humiliation for Prussia, really represented a lucky escape for her and an ultimate defeat for Austria, wasting her last apparent good chance to render Prussia harmless. Austria's efforts at the Dresden Conferences of early 1851 to strengthen the Confederation and bring all Austrian territory within it proved abortive. Prussia's skillful obstruction, the jealous particularism of other German states, and the opposition of other European powers ruined the schemes for reform and centralization. Accepting the advice of Buol, his envoy to the Dresden Conferences, Schwarzenberg returned to the old Confederation, commenting that a threadbare cloak was better than none. The only fruit of Austrian efforts to reach an agreement with Prussia was a three-year defensive alliance signed in 1851, which covered up but did not end their stalemated contest for supremacy in Germany.

Buol, who succeeded Schwarzenberg as foreign minister, made no change in Austria's German policy. Though he opposed provoking a war to cut Prussia down to size, Buol, keenly conscious of the fragile basis of Austrian leadership, remained dead set against any concessions to Prussia touching Austria's rights and dignity as head of the Confederation. This prevented any reform of it.[4] Austria did gain a small improvement in position during Buol's first year in office. Bruck, who quit the government in 1851 in disgust over Schwarzenberg's indecisive policy, was empowered to negotiate a trade treaty with Prussia, concluded in February 1853. Among other things, the treaty allowed Austria a period of twelve years to negotiate her entrance into the Prussian-dominated German Zollverein. The great benefits Bruck and his successor, Trade and Finance Minister Ritter von Baumgartner, hoped for from the treaty never developed, however. Prussia's economic lead continued to grow, as Austria remained unable to meet German competition in industry and agriculture and therefore unwilling to risk entering the Zollverein.[5]

In dealing with France, Schwarzenberg followed Metternich's old script more closely than in Germany, and enjoyed greater success. Both he and Baron Hübner, Austrian minister at Paris, had few illusions about Louis Napoleon, elected president of the Republic in December 1848. They knew everything about him that made him dangerous and hostile to Austria—his revolutionary conspiratorial activity against her in his youth, his name, his ambition, his program, his fatalistic belief in his destiny, his bent for adventure, his hatred for the Vienna system. Especially after his coup d'état of December 2, 1851, overthrowing the Second French Republic, it became obvious that, just as his uncle had done, Napoleon would govern by appealing simultaneously to the French desire for peace and glory, order and revolution. All things to all men at home, he would also hold open all possibilities for conservatism or adventure in foreign policy. Repeatedly Austrian diplomats reported French attempts at blackmail, suggestions that unless Austria conciliated France with political or territorial concessions, Napoleon would be forced to adopt a revolutionary policy in order to stay in power. Austria saw how France encouraged Prussia's ambitions in Germany and flirted with Sardinia and the revolutionary and liberal factions in Italy.

Nevertheless, Schwarzenberg still believed along with Metternich that the only possible stable government for the restless and demoralized French people was a Napoleonic regime minus Napoleon I's principle of conquest. Besides, Napoleon had some conservative advisers, especially his shrewd half-brother, the Duc de Morny, and Schwarzenberg felt that Napoleon's instinct for self-preservation and his desire to found a dynasty eventually would lead him to join Austria on the conservative path. Schwarzenberg also did not want to drive France into Britain's arms. Therefore he courted Napoleon just as Metternich had wooed Guizot, especially by cooperating with France in Italy. At Austria's invitation, France took the lead in overthrowing Mazzini's Roman Republic and restoring Pius IX in 1849–1850. Austria and France worked together for reform in the Papal States in the abortive Gaëta conferences. French soldiers occupied Rome, and Austrian troops the Legations. Schwarzenberg encouraged Napoleon to overthrow the Republic; Napoleon in turn encouraged Austria to return to absolutism.[6]

Buol, who was basically more pro-Western than Schwarzenberg, wanted to continue the policy of conciliating France. It was his misfortune to inherit a delicate problem with which Schwarzenberg was contending at his death, and which, though basically trivial, caused considerable stir. It concerned what policy to follow when Napoleon declared himself Emperor of France, as he plainly intended to do. Austria preferred an empire to the republic, but she did not want to encourage French imperial ambitions, weaken the European treaty system, or alienate Austria's conservative friends and allies, especially Russia. Although the Tsar did not hate Napoleon personally, he considered his claim to emperorship outrageous and regarded Schwarzenberg's original proposal of virtually unconditional recognition as cowardly and unprincipled. To satisfy Russia, Buol adopted a compromise proposal by Schwarzenberg, which led to a protocol signed with Russia in May 1852, to which Prussia later acceded. It called for the three powers jointly to recognize Napoleon as emperor, at the same time requiring France to guarantee the territorial status quo and reserving the powers' freedom of action should Napoleon designate his successor or found a hereditary dynasty. (This proviso enabled them to uphold the letter, if not the spirit, of Article 2 of the Quadruple Alliance of November 20, 1815, excluding a Napoleonic dynasty from the throne of France.)

Unfortunately, Britain declined to join them. At the time of the coup d'état, Lord Palmerston, British Foreign Secretary, wanting to steal a march on the Holy Alliance in dealing with France, immediately congratulated Napoleon on his successful action. Palmerston's unauthorized move roused a political storm in Britain. Under pressure from the Queen, Lord John Russell, head of the Whig ministry, forced Palmerston to resign, whereupon Palmerston soon thereafter brought down the Whig government. But the Tory government under Lord Derby that succeeded it in February 1852 was at first little more inclined than the Whigs to adopt a joint policy with the Eastern powers.

Later in 1852, however, it became clear that Napoleon intended to proclaim himself Emperor Napoleon III (i.e., the scion of a legitimate dynasty derived from Napoleon I through Napoleon II, King of Rome). This added a new complication; the numeral III implicitly denied the legitimacy of the intervening Bourbon and Orleanist regimes and challenged the whole Vienna system. For a time the great powers seemed united in opposition. The Tsar warned Napoleon against adopting the numeral III; the Tory Foreign Secretary Lord Malmesbury denounced it and called for its repudiation. Buol, seeing a chance to save appearances and to keep the powers united without seriously alienating France, worked out with Russia and Prussia a compromise agreement for recognizing Napoleon without using the offending numeral or the customary address of "Sire Mon Frère." As Buol had hoped, Britain also seemed ready to a degree to support the stand of the Eastern powers. In a four-power memorandum of late November, postdated December 3, she joined in calling on France to confirm her treaty obligations.

But the conservative entente collapsed almost immediately. Lord Cowley, ambassador at Paris, persuaded Malmesbury to recognize Napoleon without conditions just four days after he proclaimed himself emperor on December 2, so as to take advantage of Napoleon's dislike of the Holy Alliance and to make him lean toward Britain. Smaller states followed suit, including even the Kingdom of the Two Sicilies, a citadel of Bourbon reaction. Russell, Foreign Secretary pro tem in the Aberdeen ministry that took office in late December, refused even to transmit the four-power memorandum to France, arguing that it would offend her needlessly and cause parliamentary difficulties at home. Prussia, frightened by the British stance, informed her allies she intended to follow Britain's example and recognize Napoleon unconditionally. Buol now saw that his proposed mode of action, instead of solidifying a united four-power front, was likely to isolate Austria and Russia and make Austria the prime target of French anger, while Prussia gained the friendship of the sea powers. He tried to get Russia to agree to unconditional recognition, but Nicholas refused, denouncing Austria and Prussia as cowards. Thereupon Austria joined Prussia, leaving only Russia to attach conditions to her recognition and to refuse Napoleon the courtesy title of "Mon Frère."

This caused a brief but fairly serious crisis in January. France refused to accept the Russian ambassador N. D. Kiselev's letters of credence unless they conformed to the standard usage. Hübner and the Prussian minister Count Hatzfeldt were then ordered not to extend theirs until Russia's were accepted. But on Cowley's advice Napoleon finally instructed his foreign minister, Drouyn de Lhuys, to accept Kiselev's credentials as they stood, thus ending the crisis.[7]

As usual in foreign affairs, the repercussions of the recognition question were more important than the issue itself had ever been. Napoleon keenly resented the supposed slight, new evidence of his status as parvenu among European crowned heads (a status also demonstrated by his failure to find a consort among the leading royal houses, and by the disdain that greeted his marriage to the Spaniard Eugénie de Montijo). The affair showed how hard it was to achieve any concerted action with Britain if it cost her some advantage abroad or caused her trouble at home. It proved Buol's lack of skill and luck. Nicholas became further convinced that with Austria and Prussia so spineless, Russia would have to rely on herself alone. At the same time, the British concluded that the German powers were servile satellites to Russia.[8]

But these results should not be overestimated. The main point is that France emerged the winner. Napoleon gained virtually universal recognition on his terms. The path was open to an entente with Britain, while the conservative front collapsed in disarray. Austria, moreover, immediately set out to conciliate France, and the French responded in kind. The French envoy at Vienna, Baron Lacour, was transferred to Constantinople, to be replaced by one of France's ablest diplomats, Baron Bourqueney, as ambassador. Austria and France tried jointly to curb press attacks on them in Sardinia and Belgium. The abortive Mazzinian rising in Milan on February 6, 1853, and the attempted assassination of Francis Joseph in Vienna later that month shocked the French. Though Austro-French rivalry in Italy persisted, in early 1853 there seemed a good prospect for an entente between the two powers.[9]

Anglo-Austrian relations, in contrast, still suffered from the estrangement begun during Palmerston's reign at the Foreign Office in 1846–1851. Some of the causes for estrangement were specific and fairly superficial. A mob attacked the Austrian General Haynau on his visit to London in 1850, while Louis Kossuth and other revolutionary leaders received an enthusiastic welcome. Austria responded to the insults by refusing to send a suitable delegation to the Duke of Wellington's funeral in 1852. Austrians denounced as scandalous the attacks in the British press on Francis Joseph and the Austrian government, and held the British ministry partly to blame. The British accused Austria of waging a calculated campaign of harassment of British travelers, journalists, and Protestant missionaries, especially in Lombardy-Venetia.

Besides being cumulative in effect, these quarrels pointed to fundamentally divergent views, above all over Italy. Austrians believed that Palmerston and the Whigs had deliberately helped promote revolution in Italy before 1848, had sided with Sardinia-Piedmont in her two attacks on Austria, and had finally tried to protect Sardinia from suffering any consequences from her defeat. The Austrian view was exaggerated, but had some foundation. Palmerston, like many other Englishmen, believed Austria had no right to be in Italy at all. While he did not try to promote war or revolution, once they broke out in Italy he did his best by diplomatic means to induce Austria to leave. No doubt anti-Austrian feeling was not his main motive. He acted more out of general Whig convictions, a desire for popularity at home, the fear of a French intervention and of a Franco-Austrian war in Italy, a concern for British trade and maritime interests, and a hope of forming a North Italian buffer state that would keep France and Austria apart and lean toward Britain. Still, his policy encouraged Sardinia to aggrandize herself at Austria's expense, and Austria resented it. Many Englishmen disagreed with Palmerston's Italian policy, but the British condemned

Austria's Italian policy almost unanimously, especially after the revolutions were overthrown. They viewed her occupation of the Papal Legations, the stationing of auxiliary forces in the Po Duchies and Tuscany, Austria's special military conventions with these states, and the imposition of a military government on Lombardy-Venetia as tyrannical repression of the Italian people and as an extension of Austria's power that menaced the peace and the European balance.[10]

In 1850, Palmerston made good for his failure to remove Austria from Italy with a triumph over her and Russia in the Near East. Despite sharp personal rivalries between Metternich and such British leaders as George Canning and Palmerston, prior to 1848 Austria and Britain had usually cooperated in sustaining the Ottoman Empire. The British normally viewed Austria as a bulwark against Russian expansion. Partly for this reason, Palmerston favored Austria's suppression of the Hungarian revolution in 1848–1849 and even approved of Russia's intervention on Austria's behalf. But the British public and leaders reacted sharply to Austria's allegedly brutal subjugation of Hungary after her defeat,* while Austria's appeal to Russia convinced many that Austria now served only to spread Russian power and despotism into Central Europe. Sensitive to popular feeling, Palmerston joined with Stratford Canning, Lord Redcliffe, ambassador at Constantinople, to support Turkey vigorously against Russo-Austrian demands for the extradition or internment of Hungarian and Polish refugees in Turkey. The British fleet was even sent into the Straits to stiffen Turkish resistance. Russia and Austria had to back down, leaving an unsettled refugee problem that continued to anger Austria.[11]

Another refugee question was equally troublesome—the plots of Italians and Hungarians in England against Austria and other governments, and Austria's charge that Britain failed to meet her re-

---

* The charges of special Austrian brutality in Hungary are really a good example of the effectiveness of Magyar propaganda and of the double standard the British then, and liberal historians since, used in judging Austrian policy. Given the seriousness of the Hungarian revolt, Austria's measures were milder than those she used in Prague and Vienna, and nothing like what the British did to suppress Irish revolutions. The same policy Austria followed in Hungary, to punish the leaders (who were certainly guilty of high treason) and to let the lesser culprits and ordinary followers go, would earn the British Governor-General of India in 1858 the soubriquet "Clemency Canning."

sponsibility to curb them. While Buol was ambassador in London in 1851–1852, he exchanged bitter words with the Foreign Office over this issue, especially during the brief tenure of Palmerston's immediate successor, Lord Granville.[12]

Ideological rivalries and popular passions worsened all these issues. In the militantly Protestant England of the 1850's, still aroused by the "Papal Aggression" of 1850, it was easy to believe that Austria, the Pope, and other reactionary states and leaders were united in an ultramontane conspiracy to destroy liberty, with Britain the main target. There was no ground for the charge. Although Austria drew closer to Rome on Church polity, their political ties in the 1850's were not especially close. Buol, who had no use for Austrian ultramontanes, was particularly careful to keep foreign policy and ecclesiastical polity separate.[13] But the British belief that Austrians hated and feared Britain because of her system of constitutionalism and free trade had some basis. Many Austrians genuinely believed that Britain deliberately protected and exported revolution and that she exploited the resultant unrest. Palmerston was particularly hated for this, not only in Austria but over much of the Continent.* Austrians were also prone to believe that free trade was Britain's way of destroying native European industry and fastening economic peonage on the Continent—the message of the influential economist Friedrich List.

Yet if there were exaggerated passions and baseless beliefs on both sides, Britain could afford to indulge hers, and Austria could not. Like Prussia and Russia, Austria knew that Britain could do her far more harm than she could do Britain in return. For this reason Austria's policy toward Britain was basically cautious and appeasing. Schwarzenberg and Buol certainly contributed something to the

---

* Metternich illustrated the popular feeling about Palmerston with this supposedly true story: two small boys in Vienna were fighting over a toy, when the older and stronger finally tore it away and ran down the street with it. The younger screamed after him, "You swindler! You thief! You good-for-nothing! You Palmerston!!" (Carl J. Burckhardt, ed., *Briefe des Staatskanzlers Fürsten Metternich an . . . Graf Buol, 1852–1859*, 62–63). Princess Lieven reported something similar in St. Petersburg early in the war: cabmen would call each other "Palmerston" after exhausting all other epithets (Geneviève Gille, ed., "Au temps de la guerre de Crimée: Correspondance inédite du Comte de Morny et de la Princesse de Lieven," *Revue des deux mondes* [Feb. 1966], 332–33).

quarrel. Schwarzenberg resolved to answer Palmerston's intermeddling blow for blow, and once tried to form a united continental front against Britain on the refugee issue. Buol, though basically an Anglophile, was overly sensitive about his own dignity and Austria's.[14] Both Granville and Malmesbury were amateurs in diplomacy, and the lectures they received on fundamental points of international law and practice from Buol and Schwarzenberg were not apt to improve Anglo-Austrian relations.[15] Nonetheless, the initiative in the quarrel lay with Britain; she alone could afford it, and she alone, as long as Palmerston was conducting her policy, saw profit in it. Everywhere save in Hungary he was involved in the opposition to Austria: in Italy; in Switzerland, where Austria was engaged in another dispute over revolutionary refugees; in Germany, where Palmerston cautiously encouraged Prussia in her ideas for German unification while opposing Schwarzenberg's plans by all diplomatic means; in the Near East, where he worked to prevent even the smallest face-saving concessions to Austria on the refugees. Palmerston's opposition to despotic Austria not only raised his prestige and Britain's aboard and suited his ideas of promoting liberty and progress, but also contributed to his popularity at home.[16]

Still, Palmerston was not England; Austria and Britain did not have to remain estranged simply because some of their leaders and people detested each other. Despite the Francophobia and Russophobia common in Britain,[17] her relations with France and Russia in early 1853 were cordial enough. The Derby ministry, to Buol's relief, helped clear up old quarrels and avoided new ones.[18] Aberdeen, head of the ministry formed in December 1852, was an old Austrophile eager to heal the rift, and the Foreign Secretary–designate, Lord Clarendon, professed the same sentiments.[19] Britain's parliamentary system and public opinion ruled out any alliance or close entente with Austria, but good relations seemed quite possible.

The main obstacle to realizing this possibility proved to be the instability of the new Cabinet, because it increased the influence of dissident elements within it who happened to be anti-Austrian. Weeks of patient negotiation had been needed to bring the Peelites and Whigs together. The Whig leader Russell, obstructionist in the formation of the Cabinet, remained dissatisfied with the posts assigned to his party and determined to force Aberdeen out of the premiership in his own favor. Foreign policy differences, though never raised during the process of cabinet formation, were likely to provide Russell handy weapons. Like Aberdeen, most of the Peelites (William E. Gladstone, Chancellor of the Exchequer, Sir James Graham, First Lord of the Admiralty, the Duke of Newcastle, Colonial Secretary and Secretary for War, the Duke of Argyll, Lord Privy Seal, and Sidney Herbert, Secretary at War) were essentially noninterventionists, eager to avoid involvement in European quarrels. But Palmerston, Home Secretary, had long opposed Aberdeen on foreign policy, especially his alleged appeasement of Russia and Austria. Other Whigs, especially Russell and the Marquis of Lansdowne, both ministers without portfolio, strongly advocated somehow helping Italy. Clarendon, inexperienced in foreign affairs, was strongly influenced by Russell.[20]

The Court exercised a moderating influence in foreign policy. Victoria and Albert were anti-Austrian and pro-Prussian on German questions, but opposed Palmerston's aggressive activism and Russell's eagerness for action in Italy.[21] Abroad, Britain was competently represented by Cowley at Paris, Sir G. Hamilton Seymour at St. Petersburg, and Lord Bloomfield at Berlin. Two trouble spots loomed, however, precisely where Anglo-Austrian relations were most likely to be affected. At Vienna, Lord Westmorland was retained as ambassador despite his advanced age, High Tory principles, and Russell's and Clarendon's utter lack of confidence in him. He was a better envoy than they gave him credit for, but the fact that they would allow Britain to be represented by someone they repeatedly termed a foolish old woman indicates the slight value they placed on a rapprochement with Austria. Even more dangerous was the decision to send Redcliffe back to Constantinople. His ability was unquestioned, but his autocratic temperament and his long-standing quarrel with Nicholas were likely to get Britain into trouble with Russia. However, he could be expected to promote British prestige at the Porte, and if left at home he might make himself still more troublesome to the ministry by entering Parliament.[22]

In contrast, Austria's relations with Russia seemed harmonious on every issue. The Tsar took a paternal and protective interest in Francis Joseph's welfare; the two monarchs met frequently and corresponded on intimate terms. But this façade of close friendship concealed serious problems. The Russian intervention in Hungary had really caused bitterness on both sides. Austria was chagrined at having to ask for assistance and humiliated at seeing the Russians pose as conquerors, claim all the credit for the victory, fraternize with rebel officers, and openly display their contempt for the Austrian army. Nicholas, irritated at the outset by the conditions Austria tried to impose on his assistance, was further angered when Austria ignored his advice to treat the rebel leaders with clemency—advice he himself failed to follow in Poland. Schwarzenberg in turn resented Russian interference in a purely internal affair like the treatment of conquered Hungary. Elsewhere mistrust and differences emerged. Russia's foreign minister, Chancellor Count Nesselrode, considered Schwarzenberg's tactics needlessly brusque, especially toward Britain, while both Schwarzenberg and Buol, ambassador at St. Petersburg from 1848 to 1850, thought the Russians were too eager to appease Britain at Austria's expense. The Austrians distrusted some of the Tsar's advisers, especially his favorite General Paskevich, Prince of Warsaw, the commander of the Russian Army in Hungary. Nicholas in turn disliked the new modernizing and centralizing leaders of Austria and, with his penchant for military men, had no respect for the civilian Buol. Realizing how valuable the German buffer was to them, the Russians deliberately tried to keep alive and unresolved a certain amount of tension between Austria and Prussia; even under Austrian leadership, a united Germany might be uncomfortable for Russia.[23]

Such differences and irritations occur in the best of friendships. But Schwarzenberg's prophecy that Austria would some day astound the world by the magnitude of her ingratitude toward Russia indicated a deeper source of potential trouble. The more other countries, Russia included, considered Austria dependent on Russia, the more Schwarzenberg and Francis Joseph were determined to prove the contrary. The feudal aristocrats and military men who continued to plead for a close alliance with Russia against revolution were no longer listened to. Buol also took up Metternich's old theme of the Russian menace in the Balkans, repeatedly warning that Russia's remorseless pressure and encroachments ultimately would break up the Ottoman Empire even without a direct attack. Emerging with the lion's share of the spoils, Russia would hem in Austria and reduce her to complete subservience.

This was a realistic appraisal of the situation. Already the Danubian Principalities of Moldavia and Wallachia, nominally Turkish, seemed lost to Russia. Through concessions wrung from Turkey in the treaties of Kuchuk-Kainarji, Bucharest, and Adrianople (1774, 1812, and 1829), the Tsar had become their protector and suzerain more than the Sultan. Russia's occupations of them in 1829–1834 and 1848–1851 had strengthened her influence. She had already annexed them once (1809–1812) and repeatedly contemplated the step since; she could use any rising or other trouble as a pretext for an occupation that could easily be turned into annexation. This would give her direct control of the whole lower Danube, Austria's prime commercial artery, and surround Austria on her whole southeastern frontier. Russia's control of the western Balkans would be almost as complete. The principalities of Serbia and Montenegro and the Turk provinces of Bosnia-Hercegovina would be at her door—Slav (Serbo-Croat), mainly Orthodox, and open to Russian penetration.[24]

One more shadow had just arisen over Austro-Russian relations— popular national rivalry and hatred. Slavophiles in Russia were now beginning to see Austria, not Turkey, as the chief barrier to the unity and cultural development of all the Slavs. Similarly, the idea long current among German liberals, that Russian barbarism was the great enemy of German *Kultur* and its civilizing mission to the east, was starting to take root in Austria alongside the old Austrian fear of Russia's patronage of the Austrian Slavs.[25]

If Austria's relations with Russia were far from ideal, they were no better with the lesser German states often considered Austria's satellites. They generally followed Austria, but only reluctantly, out of fear of Prussia and each other. Italy was a source of acute danger, with Sardinia at the center of it. Purely in terms of power politics, Austria had let Sardinia escape in 1849 just like Prussia in 1850. The Truce of Vignale in April and the Peace of Milan in August, which ended the Austro-Sardinian conflict pretty much on the *status quo ante*, although denounced as harsh by patriotic Italians, really represented Austria's failure to exploit her last chance to render Sardinia harmless.[26] Her reasons were cogent enough—the foreign pressure on Austria, distraction with other critical problems, and a faint hope that a mild peace might induce the new king, Victor Emmanuel II, to become friendly with Austria in order to save his throne. The hope naturally went unfulfilled. Under the leadership of Count Cavour, Sardinian premier, Sardinia waged a skillful and implacable anti-Austrian campaign in press and parliament. Meanwhile, Tuscany, Modena, Parma, and the Papal States, weak and inept, were unable to live comfortably with Austrian armed support or to survive without it. The Austrian auxiliary forces, for which they paid dearly in money and popularity, safeguarded them only against revolution, not possible conquest. For if a major war broke out in Italy between France and Austria, Austria, as these governments were aware, would probably withdraw north of the Po and let them shift for themselves.

Austria's internal situation in 1853 was even more discouraging than her international position. Schwarzenberg's mission had been to construct a new, stronger Austria out of the ashes of revolution. His ideas for a modernized, centralized, more powerful government clashed with the popular demands for liberalism and federalism aroused in the revolution and represented in the Kremsier Constituent Assembly. But there could have been some compromise even between these polar ideals. Schwarzenberg initially accepted the need for a constitution and some guaranteed civil liberties. Contemptuous of the feudal aristocracy he belonged to, he favored careers open to all talents and equality under the law for all the nationalities. His ministry not only was talented but contained some genuine liberals —for example, Justice Minister Count Stadion and Finance Minister Philip Krauss—who wanted to reconcile the peoples with their monarch and government by granting them ordered freedom and more participation in the government. Bruck, less liberal politically, showed great vision and energy as an economic statesman. Interior Minister Alexander Bach, though having renounced his earlier revolutionary liberalism, was a very able administrator and not a dogmatic centralist, despite the reputation his "Bach System" would later give him. He recognized that the root weakness of the Austrian bureaucracy was its lack of contact with the masses of people, and he wanted to attack the evil by humanizing the bureaucracy and providing for local elections of some officials and for communal self-government. Progressive army leaders, especially Radetzky's chief of staff Major General Baron Hess, proposed a fundamental reorganization of the army. In short, there was no chance of a liberal-democratic or federalist 1789 for Austria under Schwarzenberg, but some chance for an 1807, that is, for the kinds of reforms that had revived Prussia during the Napoleonic wars.

By 1853, even this hope was dead. The interim had not been fruitless. Agrarian reform, which Friedjung calls the great monument of neoabsolutism in Austria, had been carried through and proved beneficial, especially in Hungary. Bruck's economic reforms, though incomplete, were valuable—a Ministry of Trade, chambers of commerce, a single customs system for the monarchy, and new commercial regulations. But the central problem of reconciling the peoples and the dynasty, the provinces and Vienna, local freedom and central power had not been confronted, much less solved. The Kremsier Assembly had been dispersed and its promising constitutional project rejected. A substitute constitution written by Stadion had been proclaimed but was never put in force, then was suspended and finally discarded entirely, giving the inescapable (though incorrect) impression that the government had always intended to break its promises and return to absolutism. Discarded with the constitution were Bach's carefully formulated plans for organizing the local and district governments and conducting local elections. Peoples who were loyal in 1848–1849 got the same centralized bureaucratic rule from above as the rebellious Magyars and Italians. Nor did neoabsolutism and the treatment of people simply as the object of government bring real efficiency or strength. As in Metternich's day, a clumsy bureaucracy administered rather than governed Austria; the concentration of authority and responsibility in the Emperor's hands stifled initiative.[27] Though the army had been extensively reorganized along neoabsolutist lines, with the Emperor assuming supreme command and the War Ministry losing ground steadily to his Central Military Chancellery and to the Army Supreme Command, little had been done to eliminate the army's defects in equipment or tactical readiness, of which Hess had complained years before.[28] Still uncured were the economic troubles that had helped cause the revolution and the financial distress that perennially plagued the state treasury. While Austrian censorship was no longer so stultifying as under Metternich, the government now relied for internal security more than ever on its secret police and on a new elite military corps, the gendarmerie.[29]

No revolt was imminent, but any war or serious crisis raised the danger of it. Hungary was sullenly quiescent under military occupation, but Lombardy-Venetia still stirred restlessly, and Fieldmarshal Radetzky's military government fed the discontent because of its arbitrariness and because of constant friction between military and civilian authorities.

Even in Lombardy, however, revolution had to be incited from abroad. The rising in Milan on February 6, 1853 was Mazzini's work, promoted from the canton of Ticino in Switzerland. It failed completely and was universally condemned in Europe, also by Cavour, who feared and hated Mazzini almost as much as Austria did. Austria's reaction was prompt and severe. The reprisals in Milan (fifteen executed, in reply to the killing of twelve Austrian soldiers and the wounding of seventy-four, twenty-five seriously) were hardly disproportionate to the crime and would by themselves have caused little stir in Europe, though there were protests from Paris. But Francis Joseph and Bach, without Buol's prior knowledge, now decided to strike at the supposed heart of the revolutionary movement—the Lombard émigrés who had taken refuge in Piedmont in 1848–1849 and who now as Sardinian citizens drew revenues from their Lombard estates and continued their anti-Austrian activities. On February 18, Radetzky proclaimed the Emperor's decree of the thirteenth sequestering the estates of all Austrian subjects who had left Lombardy illegally in 1848–1849, whether or not they were now Sardinian citizens. To most Austrians, even Metternich, the move seemed a suitable minimal measure of reprisal and self-protection. Radetzky wanted much stronger action, including preventive war if necessary. Nevertheless, the sequestrations were clearly illegal, since Austria had recognized the Sardinian citizenship of the émigrés in a trade treaty of 1851. Moreover, the measure made no distinction between innocent and guilty (Austria's argument that Sardinia would not seriously investigate the complicity of the émigrés or extradite them if guilty was probably true, but did not alter the case). Moreover, Austria took this step precisely when Sardinia, for reasons of its own, complied with Austrian requests for a crackdown on Maz-

zinian agitators and sympathizers. In short, having surrendered the
weapon of reprisal against the émigrés in her previous abortive efforts to normalize relations with Sardinia, Austria now tried to re-
claim and use it anyway. It was a blunder that would cost Austria
dearly in her cold war with Sardinia.[30]

The Emperor himself must be blamed for very much of the failure
of neoabsolutism. At twenty-three Francis Joseph displayed many of
the qualities needed in a ruler—maturity, coolness under fire, courage, determination, conscientiousness in duty. As his adjutant and
chief of the Military Chancery General Count Grünne remarked,
he would have made an excellent minister of police (Grünne meant
this as a compliment). But he had all the defects of his qualities. Early
matured, he developed little; his mental and spiritual horizons remained contracted. Self-controlled, he lacked passion, imagination,
and breadth of mind. Much of his industry was spent on bureaucratic routine. Self-willed and secretive, he suspected ministers who
gained too much fame and popularity and was determined to concentrate power in his own hands. He distrusted the feudal conservatives, as Schwarzenberg did, because they were incompetent and
potential *frondeurs;* but like Schwarzenberg he was also instinctively
averse to every popular force. Though he adapted himself during his
long reign to all sorts of constitutional changes, at heart he remained
an absolutist, most at home with the military, the police, and ministers who were strictly his servants and advisers.[31]

A number of persons close to the Emperor encouraged his absolutist tendencies—his mother the Archduchess Sophia and other
members of the court; Grünne; Cardinal Rauscher, Archbishop of
Vienna; and Baron Kempen, chief of the state police and head of the
gendarmerie, a corps in which Francis Joseph took keen interest.[32]
Most influential in encouraging him to be the actual, not symbolic,
center of power and decision was Baron Kübeck, President of the
Reichsrat. The so-called Bach system of neoabsolutism, as Friedrich
Walter says, would be better called the Kübeck system (although
finally it was simply Francis Joseph's system). While honest in his
own lights, not personally power-hungry or a social climber, and
thoroughly *kaisertreu,* Kübeck was also a bitter, jealous man and a
good hater. His patient mining and sapping succeeded where feudal
aristocrats like Metternich and Prince Windischgrätz, Schwarzen-

berg's brother-in-law, had failed, in overthrowing both the Stadion constitution and Bach's plans for communal reorganization and self-government. Hoping to make the *Reichsrat* supplant Schwarzenberg's *Ministerrat* (ministerial council) at the Emperor's side (actually Francis Joseph used them both as tools in a policy of divide and rule), Kübeck promoted the fatal collegial system for the ministry, in which the ministers were only imperial advisers with no unity or authority, and endless papers and questions were funneled to the Emperor's desk for decision. Kübeck helped make sure that Francis Joseph appointed no successor to Schwarzenberg as Minister-President. The Emperor ruled directly, the individual ministers served at his pleasure, and Buol enjoyed, besides the Foreign Ministry, only the empty title of presiding officer in the ministerial conference. Moreover, Kübeck's style of subterranean opposition to his many enemies and collaboration with a conservative camarilla to oust them from favor and to gain influence over Francis Joseph contributed to a poisoned atmosphere in Vienna, where intrigues and struggles for power went on constantly behind the apparently untroubled façade of neoabsolutism.[33] *

The atmosphere inevitably affected Buol and his diplomacy. Buol is a difficult person to appraise or characterize. He seems colorless, his personal attributes and talents subject to widely differing interpretations, his previous career unremarkable though not unimportant, his relation to the Emperor and his colleagues unclear. The offhand denigrating judgments on him common in the literature, seldom based on good evidence,[34] could be ignored were it not that close contemporaries judged him very diversely. Some, such as Nesselrode and Buol's brother-in-law Baron Meyendorff, Russian

---

* A glaring example of such intrigue was the Debraux affair. Alois Debraux, section councillor and director of the Austrian Consulate General at Paris, sent Kübeck secret reports from November 1852 to early 1854 on Austrian policy toward France. Kübeck relayed them to the Emperor. In his reports, Debraux, a venal and unsavory character evidently in French pay, constantly attacked both Hübner and Buol, grossly misrepresenting their positions and actions. Hübner, finding out about Debraux's activity, finally succeeded in getting Debraux removed from the Consulate, but the next year he was sent back to Paris in another capacity and resumed his secret reports. (The correspondence is in Kab. Arch. Geh. Akt. 3.) The whole business sheds a lurid light on Kübeck's methods, and speaks even worse of the Emperor, who encouraged him in it.

minister at Vienna, who liked him at first and praised his work, learned to dislike him later. Others such as Clarendon and the British diplomat Lord Loftus were to change their minds in the other direction. With Bourqueney and Drouyn he always got along well, and he was to impress Russell very favorably; but other diplomats and colleagues detested him cordially, considering him haughty, stiff, and sarcastic, or talentless, indecisive, and shallow. Metternich called him a knife with a sharp point but no edge, that is, better at starting a quarrel than ending it, aware of immediate problems but not of long-range consequences. The charge has some basis, but it came only when Metternich believed Buol was ignoring his advice during the Crimean War. During the eleven years Buol had served with him, Metternich had never complained seriously about Buol's work; they became close friends and remained so, even after the Crimean War. Schwarzenberg was equally satisfied with Buol's work and proposed him as his successor, and Francis Joseph seems to have had no doubts about following his advice.[35]

Leaving the final judgment on Buol's personality and talents in abeyance, one can say that though he had wide diplomatic experience (Stuttgart, Turin, St. Petersburg, Dresden, London) and fully satisfied his superiors, he also often became involved in disputes, not usually of his own making, and when he left Turin and St. Petersburg he was extremely unpopular. He was always purely a diplomat, showing little interest in either Austrian domestic affairs or those of other states. Though *kaisertreu* and conservative by general European standards, he counted in Austria as a liberal and Westerner, because he believed it possible for Austria to get along with Britain, France, and even Sardinia, despite differing ideologies, on the basis of mutual respect and regard for common interests. He was mainly suspicious of Prussia's hegemonic aspirations in Germany and Russia's tendency to dominate her neighbors and to expand in the Near East. Buol's attitude made him unpopular with the Austrian feudal and military proponents of the Holy Alliance, and their distrust was greatly strengthened by Buol's close friendship with Bach, against whom Windischgrätz, Kübeck, Grünne, Kempen, and the Minister of Public Worship and Education Count Leo Thun waged a running battle. Nor did he enjoy the confidence of all of his subordinates in the foreign service; Hübner at Paris and Count Friedrich

Thun at Berlin considered him ill suited for the post, while Prokesch disdained him as a civilian. This points to one of Buol's greatest handicaps: unlike Schwarzenberg, he did not wear a uniform and therefore encountered added difficulty in fighting the military and maintaining the aura of success and power, partly spurious, that Schwarzenberg had left behind. Buol's greatest asset was the Emperor's confidence and the fact that criticism of him tended only to make Francis Joseph more determined to show that he was in charge by retaining him. But of course that confidence could be withdrawn or Buol's policy overruled at any time.[36]

Buol's assistants at the Foreign Office—Under-Secretary of State Baron Werner, Count Biegeleben, and Baron Meysenbug—were able advisers. Werner was one of the few Austrians who could be called friendly toward Prussia, though even he gave up on her in time. Biegeleben and Meysenbug leaned toward an entente with France, but there is no evidence that they strongly influenced Buol in this direction.

Some serious problems existed in Austria's representation abroad. Hübner, regarded as a parvenu and social climber, was neither liked nor respected at Paris. Prokesch, though talented in many directions and a leading orientalist, was a fish out of water in Germany. Prussia virtually forced Austria to remove him from Berlin, and his transfer to Frankfurt as presidial delegate proved equally unfortunate. His reputation for slipperiness and intrigue was also no asset. Count Friedrich Thun, his successor at Berlin, was less hostile to the Prussians than Prokesch had now become, but his superior attitude toward them hardly helped improve relations. Count Alexander Mensdorff's illness created an important vacancy at St. Petersburg, in addition to the one at Constantinople caused by the quarrel with Turkey over the refugees; neither Count Valentin Esterházy at St. Petersburg nor Bruck at Constantinople were to prove satisfactory. At London, Count Colloredo, one of Buol's few loyal friends, worked faithfully, but had neither the social standing nor the experience to make a great impact. The sequestrations issue would soon force the removal of the able Count Rudolph Apponyi from Turin to the second most important German post, Munich. At Rome, Count Maurice Esterházy slid from apathy into torpor; his political reports dwindled from few and far between to none at all.[37]

These problems were not unique to Austria and could have been solved or lived with. The worst difficulty Buol's diplomacy would face was a development almost entirely outside Austria's control—a change in the European public mind. A postrevolutionary malaise had spread over Europe—a sickening of the peace, an impatience with the old conservative restraints that preserved peace but also seemed to throttle all progress. Because of this malaise, essentially minor questions of prestige like the recognition question or Austria's quarrels with Britain or even the sequestrations issue assumed major proportions. The old Europe was visibly dying, the new not ready to be born; conservative conviction declined, liberal belief was shaken by the failures and excesses of the revolution. Leaders and governments wanted to break loose from old paths, without knowing where the new paths might lead. The restless spirit was most evident in France, but other powers also felt it; even Austria was not immune. How hard it would be for the old diplomacy to contain the desire for change and adventure, the developing crisis in the East would show.

The Leiningen
and Menshikov Missions:
Dangerous Success and Failure

The quarrel over the Holy Places in Jerusalem out of which the Crimean War eventually arose can be summed up for our purposes in a few words.[1] It began as a dispute between Greek Orthodox and Roman Catholic clerics over the control of certain shrines, and became an international issue when France and Russia backed the claims of their respective confessions. The Turks, who owned Palestine but cared nothing about the quarrel between Christians, did their best to avoid trouble by their usual dodging and procrastination. But strong pressure first from France and then from Russia forced them into contradictory promises and concessions which finally antagonized both sides.

The bullying of Turkey by European great powers was normal. It was harder to understand why France and Russia should challenge each other over so petty a stake. The question has given rise to a number of plot explanations, but these have long been discredited. Louis Napoleon did not plan to provoke a war in the East in order to destroy the Holy Alliance and escape isolation, The French initiative was lauched by an overzealous ambassador in 1850; Napoleon then took it up largely for domestic reasons and personal prestige. By the time the international issue grew serious, he was tired of it. Even Drouyn, anti-Russian as he was, wanted by 1853 mainly to save face.[2] In Russia's case there is more substance to the plot theory, that is, that the Tsar seized on the religious dispute as a pretext to break up the Ottoman Empire. The thought of Turkey's demise and Russia's policy in dealing with it was never far from his mind. Nevertheless, he acted primarily from the conviction that Orthodox privileges in Turkey were his special concern and that an expansion of French influence at Constantinople was dangerous to Russia and personally insulting to him.[3]

At first none of the other powers took the quarrel very seriously. Britain, whose only religious concern was to protect Protestant interests, blamed France for putting Turkey in danger by baiting Russia. Still trusting Nicholas's peaceful assurances, the British in early 1853 had no intention of intervening except with friendly advice to Turkey.[4] Austria, interested in reviving her influence in the East, had earlier backed France's claims and vigorously asserted her own treaty rights to protect Catholics in the Ottoman Empire. But by 1853, Austria's stand had become conciliatory and moderately pro-Russian. Urging caution on both sides, Buol suggested solving the religious question by getting Europe as a whole to press Turkey for equal privileges to all Christians alike. He also told France that a return to the status of 1740, on which she based her claims, was impossible, and that she could not expect Turkey to keep promises France had coerced from her, which contradicted others she had made. Buol's advice carried no great urgency, however; like many others, he and Hübner were surprised by the serious turn the issue took later in 1853.[5]

One reason for this surprise was that in January 1853 the conflict between Montenegro and Turkey seemed far more important and dangerous. This conflict, which had erupted in November 1852, was different from the common troubles caused by banditry or Montenegrin raids into Bosnia or Albania. At stake now was the fundamental relation of Montenegro to Turkey. The tiny mountainous principality had long been independent of the Sultan in fact, though not in law. The prince-bishop of Montenegro, Danilo, already enjoying a Russian pension and the Tsar's protection, had gained Russia's consent to secularize his rule and had proclaimed himself prince. The Turks, rightly viewing this step as a move toward complete independence for Montenegro, decided to intervene. The Montenegrins anticipated Turkish intervention by seizing the Turkish fortress of Zabliak on Lake Scutari, whereupon the Ottoman government ordered one of its best commanders, Omer Pasha (a Croat and a renegade from the Austrian Army), to crush the insurrection. The position of Montenegro, invaded by land and threatened by sea from Albania, seemed critical, and Danilo called Austria and Russia to the rescue.[6]

Austria had many reasons for responding favorably to this appeal. She did not want to let the revolt spread to Serbia and Bosnia or to allow Russia to enjoy exclusive influence in Montenegro. Army leaders in particular sympathized with the Montenegrins, and Francis Joseph considered himself their protector. The Turks were not only generally despised in Austria, but considered dangerous. Turkey might try to establish more garrisons like those she now occupied in Serbia near the Austrian border, or she might try to use Klek and Sutorina, two enclaves of hers on the Bay of Cattaro, for military purposes, breaking Austria's exclusive military control of the Dalmatian coast.[7] The fighting had already, as usual, caused a massive flight of refugees onto Austrian soil, which had to be stopped or controlled; so did Turkey's attempt to assert her full sovereignty over Montenegro.[8] The many Polish and Hungarian émigrés in Omer's army represented a danger to Austria. Kossuth hoped to use them to promote an Austro-Turkish conflict that could touch off new revolutions in Austria and lead to war between her and a Western coalition of powers.[9] While these dangers alone sufficed to make Austria want to intervene, her ambitions were also involved. For some time Francis Joseph had anticipated and even looked forward to a military reckoning with Turkey;[10] many Austrian military men were tempted by territorial gains in the western Balkans at Turkey's expense.

Austria's chargé at Constantinople, Baron Klezl, took up Austria's griefs with the Porte, but the main task of bringing the Turks to terms over Montenegro and other issues fell to Lieutenant Field Marshal Count Leiningen, sent on a special mission to the Porte in late January. He was to demand that Turkey promptly suspend hostilities and evacuate Montenegro; give a satisfactory explanation for her armaments near Austria's frontier; stop harassing Austrian merchants in Turkey and repay them for their losses; intern or remove the refugees in Omer's army; and either cede Klek and Sutorina against a money compensation or at least recognize that the waterways surrounding them belonged to Austria and could not be used for Turkish naval purposes. If Turkey refused, Leiningen was to threaten the Sultan with joint Austro-Russian armed intervention. Only on the Holy Places was Leiningen instructed to be conciliatory—to urge the Porte to call on Austria to help mediate a solution based on equality for all Christians alike.[11]

An imposing show of military force backed Leiningen's mission. Border patrols were strengthened, Austrian troops in Dalmatia under Governor-General Baron Mamula put on a war footing, and orders given to the Banus of Croatia, General Jellačić, to assemble his forces on the Bosnian frontier. At the same time, the Ninth Army Corps was mobilized, while Hess threw himself into plans for possible operations in Bosnia. As a precautionary measure, two Austrian army officers were sent directly to Omer to warn him against violating the Austrian frontier and to demand assurances regarding Klek and Sutorina and the removal of refugees from his forces and entourage.[12] Yet neither these measures nor the energetic representations of Leiningen sufficed at first to frighten the Turks into acquiescence. Leiningen rejected the inital evasive Turkish reply of February 10 and 11, declared his mission at an end and boarded ship, ready to break relations and to sail for home. This was no bluff; all the political and military preparations were made at Vienna for crossing the Unna into Bosnia. Only when Turkey yielded at the last minute were the marching orders sent to Jellačić on February 25 recalled.[13]

Austria had won a striking victory. Even though she still had to put pressure on Turkey to carry out her promises, by the end of March, Montenegro was evacuated and the military measures in Croatia-Slavonia could be liquidated.[14] A failure of the Leiningen mission could have had incalculable results—probably an Austro-Russian war on Turkey which, since Britain and France were just drawing together in Turkey's defense, could have led to a general European conflict.

Austria's victory caused repercussions as it was. Buol portrayed the mission to other powers as intended to preserve Turkey's integrity and to restore good Austro-Turkish relations, explaining Austria's troop movements as purely defensive and precautionary. Only very late did he admit that a Turkish refusal would lead to major coercive measures. The British were not deceived; Aberdeen and Russell, though convinced that the Turks had provoked Austrian intervention, were deeply disturbed by the peremptory tone Austria took with Turkey. Redcliffe told Colloredo in London that Turkey was entitled to use her sovereign rights to Klek and Sutorina if she chose.[15] France, less concerned by Austria's browbeating of Turkey, at first supported the Leiningen mission diplomatically. However, Austria's ultimatum and her threat to occupy Bosnia worried Drouyn, primarily because they indicated a close Austro-Russian cooperation that would isolate France in Europe and ruin her influence in the East.[16] At Constantinople, both Western representatives, especially the British chargé, took the Sultan's side against Austria. Leiningen and Klezl blamed them for the Porte's first unsatisfactory answer, and Buol answered Western criticism of Austria's tactics with complaints about their representatives' conduct at Constantinople.[17]

But once the crisis passed, tension quickly disappeared. Cowley and Clarendon agreed that it was better for Turkey to be bullied and humiliated than for Britain to get in trouble on her account. Discounting reports of an Austro-Russian plot to dismember Turkey, Clarendon and Russell defended Austria on this score in Parliament. Prussia, meanwhile, supported Austria at Constantinople despite Manteuffel's suspicions of her.[18]

The most important impact of the Leiningen mission was its effect on Russia. Metternich and Francis Joseph later traced the whole Eastern crisis to Russia's reaction to it.[19] It was common at that time and later to interpret the Menshikov mission Nicholas sent to Turkey in late February as his answer to Austria's success, his proof that Russia could outdo Austria in aggressive diplomacy.[20] Many facts contradict this view, however, the main one being that Russia and Austria cooperated over Montenegro. Austria did not clear the Leiningen mission with St. Petersburg in advance, just as Russia did not clear the visit of Colonel Kovalevskii to Montenegro in late January with Austria. But the two missions ran parallel in purpose and presupposed close cooperation. Austria at Russia's request provided arms and supplies to the Montenegrins, declined Russia's offer of payment, and turned the money that Kovalevskii had brought along for the purchase of arms over to Montenegro for restoring churches and homes. Russia, which had long encouraged Austria's support of Montenegro, urged her to occupy Bosnia and Montenegro if necessary, and told the Turks that an attack on Austria would constitute one on Russia also. Buol kept Russia better informed than any other power; Leiningen confided only in Russia's representative at Constantinople.

The Menshikov mission, rather than being an answer to Leiningen's, was planned before it and only delayed by accidental circumstances. Though Nicholas may have been sorry that the Turks yielded instead of fighting, he always knew that Austria could act more effectively than Russia on Montenegro's behalf.[21] Certainly Austria's gain in prestige delighted Francis Joseph and other Austrians, and it probably irritated and aroused jealousy in some Russians.[22] But Nesselrode and Nicholas do not seem to have felt this resentment. The Tsar even decorated Buol with the Grand Cross of St. Alexander Nevsky. Buol thanked Russia warmly for her support, indicating, according to Meyendorff, that Austria would repay it if Russia's quarrel with Turkey grew serious.[23]

Here lies the real harm of the Leiningen mission: encouraging Nicholas to believe that Austria was united with Russia in dealing with Turkey by ultimatums and threats to occupy her territory, regardless of the consequences. The Tsar had more evidence for his belief that Austria was bound to support his program than merely the Leiningen mission. In late February, Buol told St. Petersburg that Austria wanted a protectorate over Bosnia similar to Russia's over the Danubian Principalities and asked for Russia's help in preventing the rising in Bosnia that an Austrian occupation might provoke.[24]

But Nicholas's hubris and ambitions antedated the Leiningen mission and arose independently of Austrian encouragement. As the Tsar's famous conversations with the British Ambassador Hamilton Seymour in January 1853 show, he now contemplated partitioning Turkey among the great powers, abandoning Russia's policy since 1829 of maintaining her intact as a safe, inoffensive neighbor.[25] In late 1852 he began seriously planning a seaborne attack on Constantinople. Persuaded that the risks were too great, he only moved the proposed invasion to Varna and Burgas in Bulgaria. Most dangerous of all was the fact that the Tsar really did not know what he wanted from Turkey or how to get it. Canvassing the various possibilities for action before the Menshikov mission, he ended up determined to settle issues with Turkey, though not sure what the issues were; insistent on getting reparations and guarantees, though unable to define them or assess their worth; ready for strong measures and confident Turkey would collapse under pressure, though convinced the status quo was still desirable and anxious about the final outcome. In short, Nicholas was ready to open up and solve the Eastern question without believing that a really good solution was available. The best possible bad solution was a peaceful partition compensating all the great powers except Prussia, which wanted nothing. Russia and Austria would jointly control and garrison the Straits, and Russia would gain some territorial annexations and new client states in the Balkans.[26]

Plainly such ideas, however vague and tentative, were criminally rash and completely broke with the conservative spirit of the Austro-Russian Münchengrätz Agreement of 1833, calling for upholding Turkey's integrity. But Francis Joseph's ideas also diverged from this, and the Tsar did not intend to wreck the European Concert or defy the other powers. Though he feared Western influence in Turkey and deeply distrusted Palmerston, Redcliffe, and the Whigs, he hoped to cooperate with Britain, as his frankness with Seymour and the friendly reception he gave Russell's evasive reply show.[27] He thought that his gentlemen's agreement on Turkey reached with Robert Peel and Aberdeen in 1844–1845 was still valid (which was incorrect), and that the British government, like others in Europe, trusted his word (which was partly true).[28] Though he opposed French influence at Constantinople, he did not want to exclude France from a final settlement and a share in the spoils. Understandably though mistakenly, he supposed Austria's interests and his were identical. The overconfidence and illusions of Nicholas about other powers' reactions to his policy are easy to explain, if not excuse.

Much the same can be said for the reckless and aggressive aspects of the Menshikov mission—the choice of Menshikov, who was an admiral, not a diplomat, and a member of the Orthodox party, to represent Russia; the armaments and military display accompanying his mission; his instructions, arrogant and peremptory in tone, if not immoderate in substance by Russian standards; and his bullying methods. All these derived from Russia's belief that Turkey would only yield to intimidation and that Europe would not interfere or be seriously disturbed by it.[29] One cannot assume that the Tsar wanted Menshikov to fail. He could conceivably have succeeded, as Leiningen did, and Nicholas would have been temporarily satisfied. The Russian demands were vaguer than Leiningen's, and the main one, for a convention or note confirming Russia's right of intervention on behalf of the religious rights of Turkey's Orthodox subjects, was in principle dangerous for Turkey. But the Russians genuinely believed their argument that Russia had possessed and exercised this right ever since the Treaty of Kuchuk-Kainarji in 1774.

As for Redcliffe, who arrived at Constantinople in April, he was not determined to defeat Menshikov. Within the limits of saving Turkey's independence and upholding his own influence, he wanted to see Russia satisfied, especially in regard to the Holy Places, and he nearly succeeded. Had a better negotiator than Menshikov been sent, or had he presented his compromise proposals before Redcliffe arrived, or had the Grand Vizier Mehemet Ali not been overthrown in favor of Redcliffe's protégé Reshid Pasha, or had Russia simply been clearer from the outset on what guarantees she wanted, the outcome could have been different.[30]

Nevertheless, by late May, Turkey had rejected Menshikov's final note and Menshikov had departed, breaking relations between Russia and Turkey. Where Leiningen had succeeded within three weeks, Menshikov failed after almost three months (February 28 to May 20), over issues that had been simmering for nearly three years. Positions had now hardened, Russia's honor was committed, Turkey's resentment and Europe's suspicions of Russia were aroused.

Buol's attitude showed the effects of the prolonged tension. Even though he too initially thought Turkey was on the point of collapse, and went along reluctantly with the idea of territorial compensations for Austria, he always feared a crisis. He encouraged the sea powers to take an interest in the Russo-Turkish dispute (though he disapproved of France's sending her fleet into eastern waters in March), and he told Britain and France that all five great powers should cooperate to maintain Turkey's integrity. But in the main he adhered to the Austro-Russian partnership, assuring Turkey and the other powers that Austria was confident of a peaceful solution.[31]

By mid-April his confidence was badly shaken. Dismayed at Menshikov's demands and insisting that they violated Russian promises of moderation to Austria, Buol said he would be willing to sacrifice the results of the Leiningen mission if such sacrifice would avert the probable results of Menshikov's. By early May he was pressing Russia to deny reports that she wanted a protectorate over the whole Orthodox church in Turkey. When the Russo-Turkish break came,

Buol, though still unwilling to join an entente against Russia, urged a five-power understanding in favor of Turkey's integrity.[32] Buol's change in attitude was not simply a return to his normal suspicions of Russia, for Klezl went through the same transition, beginning staunchly pro-Russian and later convinced that Menshikov's kind of protectorate would be fatal for Turkey. He finally joined Redcliffe and other representatives in declining to urge the Sultan to accept Menshikov's last note, advice tantamount to telling him to reject it.[33]

Unlike Austria, which gradually awakened to the danger, France first made a bold demonstration over the Menshikov mission and then fell back into passive expectancy. Though weary of the Holy Places issue by this time, she officially insisted for the sake of her honor on retaining the remaining scraps of Turkish concessions granted her. Drouyn's anger over Menshikov's overbearing conduct at Constantinople reinforced this attitude. The French decision to send her fleet from Toulon to Salamis, however, was prompted by other motives than checking Russia. Drouyn and other ministers advised against it, but Count Persigny, Napoleon's close friend, argued that the Emperor needed a more active foreign policy to enhance his prestige. Besides, the move would draw Britain along with France and cement their entente. When the fleet sailed on March 22, Drouyn authorized Lacour to call the ships into the Dardanelles and even to Constantinople under certain conditions. He also unleashed a calculated indiscretion at Brussels, aimed at Britain and other powers. The French minister His de Butenval hinted unmistakably that if Austria and Russia aggrandized themselves at Turkey's expense, France would make a move against Belgium. Hübner quickly warned Buol that Austria must be strong in Italy, "for the first blows, if blows there are, will come from that side." [34]

Britain, however, still declined to be drawn or frightened into active cooperation with France. When the British fleet stayed at Malta, the French demonstration lost its main impact, and France began insisting on her purely defensive, European purposes. Both Cowley and Hübner reported that France was eager to have the Holy Places issue settled at almost any cost, and France accepted the Turkish firmans conceded to Menshikov on May 8 with the declaration that they left France's concessions of 1852 intact. Menshikov's abrupt departure caused shock rather than satisfaction at

Paris; "they are very pacific and very accommodating here," Hübner reported.[35]

Theoretically, at least, Britain held the key to stopping potential Russian aggression. Austria and Prussia were closely tied to Russia and vulnerable to her pressure; France was involved in the religious dispute. Britain, invulnerable to attack herself, was the only power Nicholas feared and wished to appease. Divided counsels, however, plagued her government. While Palmerston was anti-Russian and pro-Turk, Aberdeen and the Peelite contingent abhorred the Turks, trusted the Tsar, and considered his proposals to Seymour well meaning and the Menshikov mission relatively harmless. Victoria and Albert were less sanguine about Russia, while Russell was the first to warn of possible war between Russia and the sea powers.[36]

Clarendon epitomized Britain's ambivalence. Throughout April and May he repeatedly expressed trust in Nicholas and confidence in a peaceful outcome, rejecting reports of aggressive Russian aims. Yet simultaneously he showed profound distrust of Menshikov, viewed Nicholas as bent on humiliating the French and the Turks, complained of his lack of honesty, and felt that Britain should have returned a stiffer answer to the Tsar's proposals to Seymour. He worked to defuse a possible crisis, trying to get France to recall her fleet to Toulon and urging Redcliffe to pursue a Russian suggestion for a mutual five-power pledge against unilateral interference in Turkey's affairs. But he also came increasingly to feel that Britain and France would have to meet Russia's challenge by force, telling Palmerston that if she was trying to impose another treaty of Unkiar-Skelessi on Turkey, making Russia dominant at Constantinople, "it would be the greatest fraud and insult towards us and France that one power ever attempted toward another and no casus belli in modern times would be more complete." [37]

The ambivalence reflected not only Clarendon's uncertainty and impressionable character, but also the diverse requirements of British foreign and domestic policy. Britain wanted to maintain peace and good relations with Russia, but also to support Turkey and be ready for trouble. She needed an entente with France, but feared that France might drag Britain along on dangerous initiatives. Redcliffe had to be watched and restrained at Constantinople, but could not be recalled or made too angry. Clarendon wanted to be moderate, but dreaded being thought soft on tsarism by the public and Parliament in comparison to Palmerston. Russell knew that a foreign crisis might interfere with his cherished plans for electoral reform; but it might also help him to unseat Aberdeen and take his place.[38]

In such a situation, the device most apt to overcome doubts and hesitation is an appeal to national honor. This was the note Palmerston sounded consistently and robustly. Russia was challenging Britain and France in the East, and they must respond by aiding Turkey and sending their fleets into the Straits or be utterly disgraced. To Aberdeen's scruples about allying with beastly Turks, Palmerston replied that Britain's contest was with Russia; Turkey's character was irrelevant to the issue, and far better than Russia's character anyway. Liberated from Russia's pressure, unhampered by Russian treaties, supported and guided by the West, Turkey could become a model of progress and religious equality.[39] Clarendon, the swing member who often decided the outcome in the Cabinet between the forward party and the peace group, resisted these arguments until late May. Menshikov's final note, interpreted in Britain as a violation of the Tsar's solemn promises to respect Turkey's independence, rendered Western support of Turkey justified and a requirement of national honor. When Turkey rejected the note, Clarendon changed his mind and called for sending the fleet East, though conceding that he did not know whether the Tsar had really broken his word or Menshikov had exceeded his instructions. As he told Redcliffe, the note put Russia *"in the wrong, and there we must endeavour to keep her."* Aberdeen still insisted that Menshikov's demand did not menace Turkey's integrity, and Graham argued that effective protection of Turkey would require an occupation of the Black Sea, which meant war. But Clarendon pointed out that a prompt fleet move was "the least measure that will satisfy public opinion and save the government from shame if, as I firmly expect, the Russian hordes pour into Turkey on every side." So Aberdeen yielded to the pressure exerted by Clarendon, Palmerston, Russell, and Lansdowne; Admiral Dundas received his orders to sail to Besika Bay outside the Dardanelles, where the British and French fleets arrived June 13 and 14.[40]

The Anglo-French naval action should have paved the way for joint diplomatic intervention by the European Concert. Even Prussia, reluctant though she was to commit herself, was sufficiently afraid of Britain and aware of the serious nature of the problem to be willing to take part. But the most important requirement for successful Concert action in the East was missing—cooperation between Austria and Britain. When these two powers in recent decades had worked together to guide and restrain Russia (e.g., 1821–1823, 1839–1841), Russia had proved not only moderate but actively cooperative. Whenever the British either refused to commit themselves at all or tried to control Russia without Austria's help (e.g., 1825–1829, 1831–1833), Russia had emerged with important gains. The two powers complemented each other in checking Russia, with Britain supplying the deterrent of her navy and her invulnerability to Russian pressure, and Austria providing the ideological rationale for Russian restraint and cooperation. But in 1853 there was little enthusiasm in Britain for Concert diplomacy. Palmerston wanted Britain and France to control the solution and impose terms on Russia. The Whigs favored a close entente with France. The Peelites talked of Concert action, but mainly as a means of avoiding any British involvement or commitments. And if Britain was indifferent to Concert diplomacy, she was positively hostile to cooperation with Austria, which represented in British eyes a worse enemy to Britain and a greater menace to European peace than Russia.

This attitude did not stem from the Eastern question. The British sometimes suspected an Austro-Russian conspiracy to carve Turkey up, because of the Leiningen mission and Nicholas's statements that his interests and Austria's were identical.[41] But this was a minor theme. British suspicions of Austro-Russian collusion were far less active at this early stage, when there was some basis for them, than they would be later when all the evidence disproved them. The causes of British-Austrian hostility were those old issues that arose after 1848 and were recently exacerbated—first of all, the Hungarian and Italian political refugees in Britain. Austrians, frantic with fear and rage over the rising in Milan and the attempted assassination of the Emperor in Vienna in 1853, charged that Britain had knowingly granted asylum to assassins and sheltered the Central Committee at London that was behind all the conspiracies. The charges were of course grossly exaggerated. Kossuth and Mazzini had followers and organizations in Britain, but they were less united and formidable than Austria believed; Switzerland was a worse center of subversion.[42]

Nonetheless, Clarendon could not simply brush the accusations aside, for he himself was morally certain that the refugees were abusing their asylum. British agents and travelers reported that all of Germany and most of the Continent joined Austria in condemning Britain. Many of Aberdeen's friends among the elder statesmen of Europe appealed to him to do something; even Victor Emmanuel and the French thought some action was called for.[43] Aberdeen himself, Prince Albert, and Charles Greville, Clarendon's old friend and Clerk to the Privy Council, saw some justification for Austria's attitude and admitted that there were deficiencies in British law. Worse still, Clarendon knew that Britain rejected Austria's demands not because remedial action was legally or constitutionally impossible, but because it would be politically unpopular. As Aberdeen conceded, even administrative measures against the refugees would be politically suicidal, to say nothing of a new law.* "Foreign powers have some cause for complaint," Clarendon admitted, "and we can do nothing, absolutely nothing, to remove it." "The English government," Colloredo commented, "is faithful to its ancient practice of doing nothing for foreign governments which could cause it the least embarrassment at home." [44]

Palmerston, with typical resilience and easy conscience, dismissed Austria's complaints as a silly fuss over nothing. Clarendon, however, listened uneasily as Austria quoted Blackstone to back up her demands and proved from British blue books that she asked only what Britain claimed from the United States in regard to Irish revolutionaries on American soil, and what the British earlier had granted France.[45] So Clarendon suppressed his doubts and counterattacked, denouncing Austria's charges as utterly baseless. Their

---

* The McHale incident illustrates the helplessness of the government before public opinion. On Palmerston's orders, the police raided McHale's armaments factory, seizing a quantity of munitions ordered for Kossuth. But instead of the discovery's serving to discredit Kossuth with the advanced British liberals, as Clarendon hoped, it only brought them to his defense and to attacks on Palmerston in Parliament (Clarendon to Palmerston, 14 April 1853, Palm. Papers GC/CL/505; Clarendon to Aberdeen, 27 April, Add. ms. 43188; 3 Hansard, 125, 1208–16; 126, 797–804, 1142–67).

only purpose was to discredit Britain, the main obstacle to Austro-papal schemes for fastening a uniform despotism on Europe, and to promote Buol's organized program of opposition to Britain and harassment of British travelers. Clarendon rejected as absurd West-morland's reports that Buol deeply regretted the rift and was hold-ing out against intense pressure from the Austrian public and others in the government for a far stronger anti-British course, Buol notori-ously hated England, Clarendon insisted, and had himself whipped up the outcry over Kossuth and Mazzini in order to form a con-tinental league against Britain. To Aberdeen's pleas for more under-standing of Austria's feelings, he replied that with Vienna "quite mad about the refugees," there was little chance of better re-lations.[46]

The British counterattack was facilitated by an issue that in their eyes put Austria wholly in the wrong: the sequestrations in Lom-bardy. Britain's violent reaction to this measure, which in no way directly affected her, may surprise a modern observer,* but its gen-uineness cannot be doubted. Austria was attacking the rights of private property; she refused to presume the émigrés innocent until proved guilty; she threatened the livelihood of nobles and respect-able members of society. Even Aberdeen denounced the sequestra-tions as "an odious exercise of arbitrary power." Greville, normally moderate and skeptical, believed everything that the Marquis Ema-nuele d'Azeglio, Sardinian minister at London, told him about Aus-tria's crimes and tyranny. Clarendon and Russell saw the decree as one more proof that Austria was the world's worst enemy of orderly freedom. The British did not deny that some émigrés might be im-plicated in the Milan rising—Azeglio had tacitly admitted as much—but insisted that Austria's medieval methods of reprisal would only promote revolution in Italy and a war with Sardinia that could easily engulf all of Europe.[47]

Clarendon believed, in fact, that Austria intended "to try a war by way of increasing her power and improving her finances." Rus-sell agreed, and he urged bringing France and Prussia into an anti-

---

* A. J. P. Taylor remarks: "In that civilized age it was thought a reasonable demand that political refugees should be allowed to draw enormous revenues from their estates while conducting revolutionary propaganda against the rule of the country in which the estates lay" (*Struggle for Mastery*, 71, n. 3).

Austrian coalition to defend Sardinia at all costs. Cowley warned that Austria planned not only to start a war in Italy but also to occupy the Swiss canton of Ticino. Russell's father-in-law, Lord Minto, living in Florence in supposed political retirement under the suspicious eye of the Tuscan authorities, constantly inflamed Russell's Austrophobia with reports of Austrian schemes, insisting that only British firmness had thus far restrained Austria from preventive war.[48]

Thus for Britain, Austria, not Russia, menaced the European peace in the spring of 1853. Clarendon not only stated this repeatedly, but appealed from March to mid-May for Russian help in checking Austria's headlong plunge toward war and revolution. Nesselrode, whom Clarendon urged "to give a lesson to Austria" about "her insane policy," tried intervening on behalf of Britain at Vienna, without noticeable effect.[49] Clarendon also recurrently urged Austria to take Britain's policy of confident trust in Russia as a model for her own stance toward Piedmont and Switzerland. "Generosity and confidence," he argued, "are quite as likely to beget good actions in Piedmont and Switzerland as in Russia." Unfortunately, he complained, Buol and the Austrians simply did not understand human nature.[50]

The British promised Sardinia only moral support and made no official protest to Vienna over the sequestrations (Colloredo was instructed to reject any protest as an interference in Austria's internal affairs). Within these limits, however, Britain tried every available means to get Austria to abolish them. Russell denounced the Austrian decrees in the House of Commons, to thunderous applause. Clarendon commended Sardinia for recalling her envoy at Vienna, though commenting that it would "probably make Buol more spiteful." On the urging of Sir James Hudson, British minister at Turin, he pressed Austria to adopt Hudson's proposed settlement as perfectly fair, honorable, and safe: Austria should lift the sequestrations as soon as the émigrés gave their word of honor as gentlemen that they had not supported the insurrection. Throughout 1853 (in fact, throughout the war) Clarendon denounced the measure as hateful persecution, wholly pointless since Sardinia only wanted to live in peace with her neighbors.[51]

Above all, Britain tried to rally France to her side against Austria.[52] This was not a simple task. Napoleon and Drouyn were not aroused by the sequestrations; they even urged moderation on Britain. Drouyn merely suggested a modification of the decree to Austria, and Hübner soon saw that Drouyn avoided the issue or handled it gingerly. The French attitude was understandable. Napoleon was a usurper ruling autocratically in a country with a history of revolutions and attentats; neither he nor his followers, dependent on him for their political lives, had any desire to encourage or condone insurrection and assassination. Drouyn did not consider the émigrés blameless or Piedmont innocent over against Austria. Besides, Buol had a neat riposte to any French representations: if you will agree not to talk about our sequestrations, we will not mention your confiscations of the goods and estates of Orleanists in France, and their deportation without trial.[53] But the British repeatedly complained of France's slackness and refusal to see Piedmont as the innocent injured party. Even when Drouyn did denounce Austria in late May, Cowley rightly suspected that he did so from fear of Austro-Russian collusion in the East, not from hatred of Austrian crimes in the West.[54]

Austria's crimes extended to Switzerland as well, and the British found France's attitude unsatisfactory here also. Incensed not only that the canton of Ticino harbored Italian political refugees and conspirators near the Austrian frontier, but also that the Ticino expelled Austrian Capuchin friars, Austria in early 1853 ousted Ticinese subjects living and working in Lombardy, closed the Ticinese-Lombard frontier, and withdrew her envoy from the federal capital of Bern. She also tried with little success to get France, Prussia, and the south German states to join her in this severe pressure, all (as Austria claimed) to get the Federal and Ticinese governments to live up to their international obligations. Drouyn expressed sympathy with Austria's claims and promised diplomatic support at Bern; the British merely saw that Austria was again bullying a peaceful neighbor. Clarendon insisted that Buol's spitefulness alone had created and maintained the quarrel, and he was delighted when British pressure kept France from actually supporting Austria, leaving her isolated.[55]

The main device Britain used to isolate Austria, and to some extent the price she paid to do so, was to agree to an entente with

France in the East. The most important point about the origins of this entente was that neither power originally intended it primarily as a means of protecting Turkey against encroachment. France desired it mainly to gain an ally and to counter and possibly break up the Holy Alliance. Britain wanted it so as to control and appease France, preventing her from causing trouble by challenging Russia and turning her against Austria instead.[56] Russell enthusiastically endorsed Clarendon's idea of joining with France "as a security to Piedmont, Switzerland, etc., etc." But like Clarendon and Cowley he wanted France to back down in the East, if necessary ungracefully. Drouyn initially made no headway in arousing Britain to a united policy and action in the East. Drouyn proposed converting the Preamble of the 1841 Straits Convention into a European guarantee of Turkey. Clarendon replied that Russia and Austria would find some way to escape any such obligations and that Austria was no fit partner in such an endeavor. Drouyn complained of Britain's failure to respond to his overtures; Cowley replied that any threat to Turkey's integrity was the fault of France and Austria. Privately, he and Clarendon laid the blame for the danger of war wholly on France—like irresponsible children, "they and they alone are the authors of this mischief in the East," seeing Russian designs for conquest in a mere religious quarrel where Russia upheld the status quo. But just as the British were irritated by France's ardor over the Eastern question, they were elated by any sign that France disapproved of Austria's policy and was willing to defend Sardinia.[57]

To be sure, by late May, Clarendon no longer was talking about Britain's confident trust in Russia and was glad of French help to block her. But the British remained suspicious of French designs in the East. Cowley complained that France's language was designed to irritate Russia, while Russell feared that Russia might lure France into a partition of the Ottoman Empire by offering her Egypt and Crete.[58] In any case, Britain's growing opposition to Russia only increased her animosity toward Austria as Russia's subservient ally.

Buol tried for cooperation with Britain in the East, suggesting to Clarendon in late March that they coordinate their efforts to uphold Turkey's integrity. Clarendon replied that Austria could best contribute to this end by ceasing to incite the Sultan's subjects to discontent and refraining from more Leiningen missions.[59] Buol also tried to moderate Austria's policy in Italy in response to Western pressure. Though he agreed at a ministerial conference of March 29 that it was necessary to maintain the sequestrations, he argued for keeping them provisional in character and for conciliating Sardinia. His instructions to Count Rechberg, named civil adlatus to Radetzky in April, emphasized the importance of improving conditions in Lombardy-Venetia as a means to this end. No doubt this was merely a meager treatment of symptoms, but it was probably as much as could be achieved in the face of the Emperor's sympathy with military demands and the constant appeals of Grünne, Radetzky, Kempen, and others for even stronger measures of repression.[60] Besides, Sardinia would have played the role of the injured party no matter what Austria did, as the later history of the sequestrations issue was to show. Nothing but Austria's disappearance from Italy could have purchased her good relations with Cavour. Nor would Britain have been appeased by greater Austrian flexibility, for the basic obstacles to Anglo-Austrian friendship were emotional and ideological rather than political. The British could be partners with France, despite Napoleon's autocratic regime, because France was an advanced Western country, Napoleon was openly pro-British, and the French, as Drouyn assured London, admired British institutions.[61] Prussia was a possible ally because she was Protestant and potentially liberal. Russia at least had to be respected for her strength. No Whig could see any sound basis for partnership with Austria —Catholic, reactionary, oppressive, and decadent.

The Prussians, for one, saw this fact and played upon it. Manteuffel, determined neither to support Austria in Italy nor to give up the long-range contest with her in Germany, worked assiduously to blacken Austria's reputation in the West, and his tactics bore fruit especially in Britain. Already Prince Albert and others hoped that the Eastern crisis and Austria's other troubles would enable Prussia to shake off Austrian hegemony and reorganize herself and Germany along liberal nationalist and constitutional lines.[62] Thus Menshikov's failure not only increased the danger of war and awoke Europe to it, but also accentuated the isolation and other dangers that threatened Austria.

The Vienna Note:
The Concert Mobilized

Instead of declaring war on Turkey after Menshikov's failure, as he was tempted to do, the Tsar settled for an ultimatum threatening to occupy the Danubian Principalities if Turkey did not immediately accept the unaltered Menshikov note. Field Marshal Paskevich persuaded Nicholas that this was a superior strategy; an occupation of the Principalities would cause Christian revolts in the Balkans that would bring Turkey down with little or no fighting by Russia. Paskevich probably did not believe this himself, but fearful as he was of insurrections in Poland and Lithuania and distrustful of Austria and Prussia, he preferred promoting Christian risings in Turkey, even if they proved abortive, to exposing the Russian army to the perils of a Balkan campaign. In mid-May, even before Menshikov's final failure, the Tsar developed Paskevich's proposal into a three-stage program for coercing Turkey: first the occupation of the Principalities; then, if necessary, an Austrian occupation of Bosnia-Herçegovina and Serbia and a Russian blockade of the Bosporus and naval war with Turkey; and finally, if Turkey still did not yield, a joint Austro-Russian recognition of the independence of Moldavia, Wallachia, and Serbia, launching Turkey's disintegration.[1]

The brashness of this program needs no comment; but again it is plain that there was more stubbornness and hubris in it than clear military or political aims. Russia had little to gain by occupying the Principalities. She already virtually controlled them; annexing them would be impossible to justify legally and could bring serious international complications, while making them independent might cause Russia real trouble. The same points applied to the rest of the Balkans. Nicholas already had, or thought he had, the sort of religious-political protectorate that suited him. He did not want more territory, and independent small states would probably be trouble-makers, as independent Greece had been. Even while he referred to Constantinople as "Tsargrad," he clearly recognized that no problem caused by Turkey's collapse would be more thorny and dangerous than the fate of Constantinople and the Straits, and even his pro-posal of Russian annexation of the capital and joint Austro-Russian occupation of the Straits was only a *pis aller*. Though he courted war, he also wished and hoped that Turkey would meet his demands and avoid it. His only unequivocal aim was the vague and dangerous one of teaching the Turks (and indirectly the French and British) not to trifle with Russia.[2] It was the Tsar's own foolish pride that led him into trouble, but Russia's conservative diplomats helped by fail-ing to warn him sufficiently about the likely attitude of the Euro-pean powers. They even shared his basic illusions: that Russian dom-inance over Turkey rested on unalterable facts of geography, ethnic distribution, religion, and history; that Turkey was a negligible fac-tor militarily; that an anti-Russian coalition was impossible; and that Russia could force Europe to back her demands on Turkey by oc-cupying the Principalities.[3]

Nowhere did Russia's naive arrogance show more clearly than in her attitude toward Austria. Nicholas not only supposed that his help in 1849 entitled him automatically to Austrian support, and told Francis Joseph so, but even set the timetable for Austrian action in his three-stage program. He was willing to share the spoils, offering Austria a joint protectorate over the newly independent Balkan states and consultation over the disposition of the Straits, but he assumed that the only question to discuss was what to do with the remains of Turkey after she had collapsed under Austro-Russian pressure. Meyendorff, who favored maintaining the Ottoman Em-pire, knew that Russia's policy contravened Austria's interests, but dismissed the possibility of serious opposition. If Austria acted at all, he reported, she would do so at Russia's side.[4] The Russians brushed aside Francis Joseph's argument that inflammatory appeals from St. Petersburg to the Balkan Christians would subvert his own subjects as well as the Sultan's. His warnings that joint Austro-Russian pro-tectorates in the Balkans would be impractical and would endanger Austro-Russian friendship, while independent states would breed rev-olution as in Cracow and Switzerland, went equally unheeded. Mey-endorff commented privately that Austria might well dislike the fact that Orthodox believers everywhere looked to the Tsar for protection, but that this fact remained Russia's strongest asset and would be exploited whether Austria liked it or not. By early summer, reports reached Vienna of revolts brewing in Bulgaria, Serbia, Thessaly, and Epirus, and of tacit or overt Russian encouragement of them.[5]

To mitigate the danger of revolution, Buol pleaded with Nesselrode to delay occupying the Principalities or at least to do it without fanfare. Helpless to control policy, Nesselrode replied by blaming Buol, Klezl, and the new internuncio to the Porte, Bruck, for not supporting Russia and ending the crisis long ago. An intimation by Buol that Austria could not refuse Western demands for a four-power conference indefinitely brought Nesselrode's reply that this threat ruined the good impression made on Nicholas by the Leiningen mission.[6] Instead of 25,000–30,000 troops occupying the Principalities, as the Austrian chargé Baron Lebzeltern had been led to expect, 50,000 began marching in on July 5, accompanied by proclamations stressing the sweeping religious and political claims of Russia toward Turkey which Austria could not accept. Russia promptly broke her promise not to interfere with the internal administration of the Principalities, ordering the hospodars to suspend communication with the Sultan, to stop paying him tribute, and to place the sums collected for it at the Russian commander's disposal. Spurred on by Redcliffe, the Sultan in turn ordered the hospodars, Princes Barbu Ştirbei of Wallachia and Gheorghe Ghica of Moldavia, to leave their territories—a decision Buol and Bruck admitted was legally justified, but which increased the danger of disorder and of a permanent Russian occupation.[7] * Moreover, while the Tsar demanded that Austria help him coerce Turkey, Nesselrode and other conservatives wanted her to help save Russia from Nicholas's policy and its dangers—that is, Austria should compel the sea powers to make Turkey yield before Russia was led to do something still more drastic. As Lebzeltern reported, the Russians always insisted that peace and war lay entirely in Austria's hands, as if Austria had no other great powers to deal with.[8]

Basically, Buol tried to do what Russia wanted—to save Russia

---

* As it turned out, the hospodars delayed their departure till October, but only at the cost of trouble with the Porte and the Western representatives leading to later complications, as will be seen.

from herself by obtaining for her the substance of her demands, if not the form. Rejecting the complaints of Austrian lethargy, he ordered Bruck to support Nesselrode's ultimatum (though without hope or real desire for success). Bruck tried hard to combine the Menshikov note and the Turkish premier Reshid's reply into a compromise satisfactory to Russia. Buol rejected the contention of the Turks and Redcliffe that Turkey would endanger her independence by any further agreement with Russia over the rights of Ottoman Christians. There was danger in making unilateral concessions under threats, he conceded, but in substance Russia's demands were not new or menacing, and a refusal to promise her anything at all would be suicidal.[9]

At the same time, however, Buol warned Russia that Austria considered the Tsar's claim to protect the Sultan's Orthodox subjects indefensible and the occupation absolutely unjustified. To try to forestall or limit it, Major General Count Gyulai was sent to confer with Nicholas in early July. Buol emphasized in Gyulai's instructions that Austria would not occupy Bosnia or Serbia, which would now constitute an "invasion," nor join in a war on Turkey, which would bring the sea powers down on Austria's back and promote general revolution. Instead, if war came, Austria, like every other power, would act according to her interests, and this might require very different kinds of military measures than Russia expected. The fact that Russia had helped Austria in 1849 and in the Leiningen mission, where both powers were united in a conservative cause, did not oblige Austria to aid Russia in a revolutionary policy now. Gyulai's main task, Buol told him in a confidential dispatch, was to find out whether the Tsar would really push his aggressive policy to the point of war. Buol supposed that he was now beginning to doubt his earlier assumptions and to look for a way out. If so, Austria would do everything possible to help him. But Russia must do her share by either suspending the occupation, this "new *false move* in Russian policy," or by preparing to withdraw quickly. For Austria would be forced when questioned by the sea powers to condemn it herself. Moreover, once Russia entered the Principalities, she lost control of the maintenance of peace; it became dependent on the moderation of other powers and on circumstances out of her hands.[10]

Other dispatches of Buol's were equally outspoken, provoking violent outbursts from Nicholas and a thinly veiled appeal to Francis Joseph to disavow him. Nesselrode and Meyendorff took to toning down Buol's "stiff and unpleasant" language to avoid arousing the Tsar and thus to save Buol's position—Nesselrode because he still liked Buol, Meyendorff because he feared any successor to Buol would be as bad or worse. Yet Buol's intent was not to denounce Russia's policy, but to plead with her to stop short of the brink. "Does no one," he wrote Lebzeltern, "comprehend the danger there is in arousing the fanaticism of a barbaric people [the Turks]?" Could not St. Petersburg see that the Balkan peoples, once "liberated" from Turkey, would not turn to Russia for protection, but become all-out revolutionaries instead? [11]

What prevented these warnings from having any effect, besides Nicholas's anger and pride, was the Russian conviction that they did not really represent Austria's policy—that, as Meyendorff reported, Francis Joseph, Hess, and Grünne had given assurances that Austria would stand by Russia in a pinch, and that the Emperor would discard Buol rather than break with Russia.[12] Unfortunately, there was some basis for the Russian view. Francis Joseph was not attached to the Tsar in grateful devotion, as St. Petersburg imagined, but his ideas did diverge from those of Buol. He agreed with Buol that Russian expansion in the East was a menace to Austria and that Nicholas's ideas for disposing of the Ottoman Empire were wholly unacceptable, but he still leaned toward the solution Prokesch, Bruck, and some Austrian military men suggested—a secret agreement with Russia to divide the Balkans outright in a manner favorable to Austria. On July 25–26, Grünne secretly instructed Gyulai delicately to take this idea up with the Tsar and to discuss whether it should be done with or without the prior consent of the Western powers and how to meet the dangers of war in Italy and on the Rhine that would result. Fortunately, Gyulai found no occasion to raise the point with Nicholas and Francis Joseph quickly withdrew the idea.[13]

Detaching himself from Russia, Buol cautiously approached the Western powers. He admitted much of their case—that Turkey had a right to view the occupation as a casus belli, that there was no analogy between the occupation and the sea powers' move to Besika

Bay, that they had a right to intervene if war came, that Russia, once she occupied the Principalities, would have to answer to Europe and accept European mediation. But he carefully accompanied each admission with qualifications and pleas for moderation and peace.[14] His policy looks like the temporizing of a power caught in the middle and unwilling to choose sides, and this it was; Buol told Thun at Berlin that this was Austria's reason for gaining time and mediating "to the farthest limits." [15] But there was principle as well as short-range expedient involved. Russia was just beginning to back down from her more exaggerated claims. If Europe could succeed in making Russia retreat without humiliating her or resorting to an overt anti-Russian coalition, this success could also serve to deter future Russian aggression, to reestablish a balance of influence at Constantinople, and to strengthen the European Concert. Should the effort fail, an anti-Russian entente might prove necessary—but only after the chances of a direct Russo-Turkish agreement had disappeared and when Russia had justified it by plainly putting herself in the wrong. Even then the entente should not flaunt its anti-Russian character; hence Vienna was a better center for it than London.[16] Prokesch, author of the Balkan partition scheme that tempted Francis Joseph, began, already in June, to urge Buol to choose which side Austria would join in the coming war, recommending Russia because she seemed to promise Austria better gains. Buol rejected this advice, not only because he feared Russian hegemony, but also because he knew that the combination of antirevolutionary ideology and crude *Realpolitik* represented by Prokesch and many other military men presented no adequate basis for the policy of a conservative power.[17]

Meanwhile the debate in Britain persisted even after the fleets sailed to Besika Bay. Aberdeen, promptly regretting having given his consent, wanted to reassure Russia that it was not a hostile move. But Russell insisted that Britain had already reached the limits of conciliation, and Palmerston called constantly for stronger measures, like putting British, Polish, and Hungarian officers in charge of the Turkish army, occupying the Black Sea as soon as Russia moved into the Principalities, and annulling Russia's religious treaty rights vis-à-vis Turkey. Redcliffe warned that measures like this would surely promote war.[18] On June 19, Russell proposed that Britain should not forcibly oppose a Russian annexation of the Principalities. Turkey, he argued, could afford to lose them (he did not apparently consider the effects of such an annexation on Austria or the European balance worth mentioning). But if Russia crossed the Danube, the British fleet must intervene, though of course it could not enable the Turks to stop the Russian advance. If Constantinople fell to Russia, Britain and France would have to declare war, forcing Austria through pressure in Italy to give them moral support.

Lansdowne and Graham approved this program, but Aberdeen protested against any further British commitments, and Palmerston attacked it as far too weak. Russia, he argued, must be forced out of the Principalities, and this could be done if Turkey protested strongly, the sea powers made a bold naval demonstration, and Austria and Prussia lent moral support. Should pressure short of war fail, the sea powers could sustain Turkey in a Russo-Turkish war indefinitely, meanwhile undermining Russia's hold on the eastern Black Sea coast by aiding the Circassian leader Shamil against Russia. The contest, Palmerston said, was a great chess game; "as we have the most pieces we are sure to win if we do not make any false moves," like continuing the present feeble policy.[19] Clarendon meanwhile still leaned toward peace and caution, but the diplomatic expedients he tried or proposed, as will be seen, uniformly broke down. When the Cabinet decided on June 29 to take no initiative at all, Clarendon confessed himself baffled. He could find no middle ground between Britain's policy and France's, that is, between offering Russia too much and not enough. At the same time he repeatedly insisted that British patience was being exhausted; if success did not come soon she would abandon her mediation and stand solidly with France against Russia.[20]

Britain's general policy was thus ambivalent and indecisive. Far more bewildering, however, was Clarendon's attitude toward Austria. His basic views and aims on the Eastern question seemed identical to Buol's. In fact, Clarendon still trusted the Tsar more than Buol did and was more sympathetic to what he called "the great *desideratum*," an honorable retreat for Russia. On numerous points of diplomatic strategy Buol and Clarendon were in agreement against Drouyn or others. The Foreign Secretary professed fully to understand Austria's dangerous position, insisting that Britain did not expect Austria "to say or do anything that might be repugnant or inconvenient to her" or to give the West active support against Russia. She only hoped Austria would not sanction Russia's acts. Clarendon even worried that France might press Austria too hard and drive her out of a neutrality that could be very useful to the sea powers. The Austrians, he told Cowley, "should be the *peace agents* of England and France," instruments for negotiation and diplomatic exploration.[21]

Warnings and doubts, to be sure, accompanied Britain's assurances of friendship and cooperation. Like the Russian moderates, Clarendon expected Austria to save Britain from herself. England relied on Austria to prevent war, he told Westmorland, "and if she is to have any success there is no time to be lost, for we are getting very warlike here." [22] Austria ought to press Russia more and Turkey less, he argued, for Austria stood to lose most in a general conflict. Clarendon suspected that Austria's language at St. Petersburg was not as firm as Buol claimed, and heard complaints from Redcliffe about Bruck and stories of an Austro-Russian plot from Manteuffel. But Buol and Westmorland had little difficulty combatting these reports, and Clarendon several times told Cowley that Austria's conduct was surprisingly brave and as good as it was possible to expect.[23] Seymour also insisted that Austria was Britain's best instrument for peace, telling Clarendon, "You may make her I think put down our Kaiser's [Nicholas's] throat what he would not swallow if presented by English hands." [24]

But this general harmony on the Eastern question had no visible effect on other aspects of Anglo-Austrian relations. British pressure on Austria over Italy and Switzerland was kept up and the quarrel over mistreatment of British travelers grew much worse, especially in the Sichel case. The details of the affair are not germane here.* The point is that from late May into September, all the while Clarendon was supposedly seeking Austria's help in settling the worsening Eastern crisis, he was also threatening to break relations with her unless she met Britain's stiff demands for political and monetary reparations for the arrest of this British citizen traveling in Lombardy. Neither Aberdeen's moderate advice nor Westmorland's and Buol's explanations that the trouble lay with the Austrian military authorities in Italy, over which Buol had little or no control, affected Clarendon at all. The contradictions in his attitude toward Austria

* See Appendix A.

are clearly illustrated by two private dispatches to Westmorland on July 12. In one, Clarendon wrote, "We rejoice to find ourselves going hand in hand with Austria." The whole Cabinet was delighted with her conduct in the Eastern crisis; she should feel free to promote any peace project, British, French, or Austrian, she thought best. In the other, Clarendon violently denounced Austria over the Sichel case, concluding, "We must now prepare to go further [i.e., to a diplomatic break] whatever be the consequences." [25]

This was not the only inconsistency. On June 11, Palmerston urged Clarendon to summon the other three powers (without Russia) to a London Conference. Here the four powers would sign a protocol pledging them to support Turkey's integrity and to refrain from interfering between the Sultan and his Christian subjects, and making Austria and Prussia endorse the move of the Western fleets to Besika Bay. Obviously Palmerston wanted to isolate Russia, deal her a diplomatic defeat, break up the Holy Alliance, and assert Britain's leadership in the Eastern question. Equally plainly, his proposal was incompatible with Clarendon's oft-expressed desire to use Austria for peacemaking and mediation without requiring her openly to take sides against Russia, so as to help the Tsar retreat with honor. Clarendon had agreed with Buol that even a five-power entente based at Vienna would be premature until hopes of a direct Russo-Turkish agreement were exhausted. Yet he immediately pronounced Palmerston's idea excellent and proposed it to Colloredo and Buol, apparently without reference to Aberdeen or the Cabinet. Though Austria promptly rejected it, neither Palmerston nor Clarendon abandoned the plan.[26] Moreover, however readily Clarendon spoke of cooperating with Austria, he carried on his real diplomacy, not merely on the Eastern question, but also on Italy and Switzerland, with France. As Colloredo remarked, Clarendon talked with him and the Russian ambassador Baron Brunnow, but he treated only with the French ambassador Count Walewski.[27]

Clarendon's inconsistencies no doubt can be explained in various ways; the important point is the connection between his attitude and that of other British statesmen toward Austria and their general view on peace or war. Aberdeen wanted peace almost unconditionally, and really desired cooperation with Austria to achieve it. Palmerston was not necessarily in favor of war, but was determined to win the contest with Russia whatever the cost, and disdained Austria. Clarendon was ambivalent on both scores. Though he still thought a war unnecessary and foolish, public opinion was becoming more aroused and he feared that he and the government would look bad in the public eye when the crisis was over. Therefore he wanted to use Austria for purposes of peace, but not to trust her far or to employ her too long,[28] and he anticipated shunting her aside if and when Britain and France had to take command and act decisively.

This outlook accounts for the puzzling aspects of Britain's attitude toward Austria as it developed in July. Austria's policy, as will be seen, became steadily more pro-Western, and Clarendon acknowledged the fact. "I have always and at all times thought that Austria and England were natural allies," he assured Westmorland on July 19; the whole Cabinet had "the warmest feelings" toward her.[29] Yet the more Austria cooperated, the less London really seemed to be satisfied; new demands were raised, pressure and complaints abounded not merely in regard to Russia, but also concerning Italy, Switzerland, Bosnia, Serbia, Montenegro, the case of the Hungarian refugee Martin Koszta,* and the treatment of British travelers.[30] A climax was reached in late July when, just as Austria was ranging herself with the West against Russia far more closely than Clarendon had earlier thought possible, British leaders identified her with Russia and denounced her as treacherous and hostile. Clarendon wrote Berlin on July 26, "The moment is good for emancipating Prussia from the thraldom of Austria exercised through the king which of course is that of Russia." Prince Albert warned that Austria was too despotic and dependent on Russia to be worth anything as an ally; Russell was profoundly suspicious of her precisely because she was so ready to come to an agreement with the sea powers. Though he could not say what Austria's strategy was, he was certain the Austrians were "playing a game which may ruin the peace, themselves, and Turkey." Significantly, the next day he told Clarendon that a successful war would prolong Turkey's life by twenty years.[31]

Probably the British genuinely believed that Austria had sinister purposes; reports from Berlin, Turin, and elsewhere constantly en-

---

* The Koszta affair involved a clash between Austrian and American consuls and naval officers at Smyrna in Turkey over the fate of Koszta. A very full, though one-sided, account of it is Andor Klay, *Daring Diplomacy* (Minneapolis, Minn., 1957).

couraged this belief. But the explanation of British suspicions of Austria lies not so much in what the British thought Austria was doing, as in what the British were thinking of doing themselves. The changes in British attitudes toward Austria were dependent upon changing British ideas on how to deal with Russia, what to do with the fleets in Besika Bay, and how to exploit the four-power negotiations that started in late July at Vienna. Originally Britain had reacted to Russia's occupation of the Principalities much more mildly than Austria. Clarendon, agreeing with Greville that "nobody here would care one straw about the Russian occupation," was confident that diplomacy could solve the problem. Austria would help build the golden bridge for Nicholas's retreat. The Cabinet generally shared this view; Clarendon and Russell helped Aberdeen defeat two efforts by Palmerston to have the fleets sent into the Straits. This would promote war, they agreed, and the public wanted more efforts at negotiation.[32]

But by late July, Palmerston's relentless pressure, a growing anti-Russian public opinion, and increasing doubts about the possibility of preserving peace had brought Clarendon around to Palmerston's line. He now agreed with Russell that "a successful war would give new life to Turkey." [33] This meant that the four-power note just being drawn up at Vienna, a means of joint European mediation long sought by Britain and France, now was viewed by Clarendon in advance as only a final, probably useless diplomatic prelude to some form of Western action against Russia. On July 26, Clarendon wrote Westmorland that even if a diplomatic settlement was reached, Russia would surely play the sea powers false, and Britain had to take decisive measures if there was any delay or bullying. At the same time, reversing his earlier stand, he tried to persuade Aberdeen to let the fleets go immediately into the Straits, arguing that the Tsar was bound to perpetrate some treachery, which Britain ought to counter in advance. Besides, adverse weather would soon render Besika Bay untenable as an anchorage (actually, the autumnal storms were still three months away), and withdrawing the fleets before Russia evacuated the Principalities was impossible because of public opinion.[34] In short, Clarendon had joined Palmerston, and the hard line was winning out in the Cabinet—which accounts in turn for increased British suspicion of Austria.

France's policy, both in general and toward Austria, was more consistent and needs less explanation. Though determined to remain linked with Britain, she chafed at British hesitations and often called for a stronger anti-Russian stance. Some of Drouyn's ideas resemble Palmerston's (like sending the fleets into the Dardanelles, or developing the Preamble of the 1841 Straits Convention to eliminate Russia's right of intervention in Turkey),[35] but with an important difference. Palmerston's larger goal was to destroy Russian influence, to replace it with British at Constantinople, and to construct in Europe a British-led bloc of states to paralyze the Eastern powers. The plan was reminiscent of his Quadruple Alliance of 1834 and, like it, anti-Austrian as well as anti-Russian. This made Vienna for Palmerston as inappropriate as St. Petersburg as the center for a diplomatic settlement on the Eastern question; only London or Constantinople would do. Drouyn aspired to wipe out the memory of 1815 and make France the leader of the European Concert. For this purpose he needed most of all to detach Austria from Russia and attach her to France. To this end, and because of his distrust of Redcliffe, he wanted Vienna to be the center for the Concert against Russia and tried by every means possible to get Austria to take the lead. He frequently hinted at the trouble France could cause Austria in Lombardy, he pleaded with her to help defend the Catholic cause, and above all he insisted that unless Austria helped France, France would abandon her conservative course and turn revolutionary. What Drouyn and Bourqueney urged in more concrete terms was that Buol call a four-power conference at Vienna which would draw up terms for a settlement and impose them on both sides. But Drouyn also pressed Austria to propose her own terms for a settlement to St. Petersburg, hoping for a failure that would alienate her from Russia. Austria, he contended, ought to threaten Russia's flank with troops in Transylvania and the Bukovina, or occupy Little Wallachia or all of Wallachia to forestall Russia; but an Austrian occupation of Bosnia or Serbia would be intolerable, for it would mean a joint Austro-Russian partition of Turkey.[36]

Prussia was the one power whose concrete aims in the East did not differ from Austria's. Both hoped to avoid involvement and feared that either a victory or a serious defeat for Russia would endanger them. Manteuffel even contemplated going to Vienna to discuss with Buol how they might escape war and revolution. But he decided against it, feeling that Austria's position was far weaker and that Austria's trouble was Prussia's opportunity. Prussia was not, like Austria, vulnerable in Italy or directly involved in the Eastern question; besides, Austria simply wanted to use Prussia for her purposes at Constantinople and would betray Prussia to either side if she had the chance. Buol's suspicions of Prussia ran along similar lines, and he also supposed that Berlin was too afraid of both Britain and Russia to take any concrete action. Insofar as Frederick William had a positive policy on the Eastern question, it was the fantastic one of using the Concert of Europe to try to restore Christian rule to Constantinople on this four hundredth anniversary of Byzantium's fall to the Turks. In addition, Manteuffel was so uncommunicative and Prussian politics so riddled with faction and intrigue that it was almost impossible to deal with Berlin; every secret was betrayed overnight. At Frankfurt, meanwhile, any hope of Austro-Prussian cooperation was killed by the bitter duel between Prokesch and the Prussian delegate Count Bismarck.[37]

With this background of the purposes of the different powers it becomes possible to understand how the Vienna Note, the first joint European proposal for a settlement, emerged and what it really meant. The exact course of its development and its precise language are not important; it was an attempt to mediate the dispute, not adjudicate it, to make Turkey feel safe enough and Russia satisfied enough to end this crisis and set a precedent for European intervention in any future ones. What counts is how each power behaved, what purposes it was really pursuing, and what effect these had on the efforts of Concert diplomacy.

Austria's aim quite simply was mediation. Though Bruck was formally instructed to support Nesselrode's ultimatum, his real assignment on leaving for Constantinople in early June was to persuade the Turks to follow Austria's advice for escaping their troubles. Meanwhile, Vienna worked on St. Petersburg to accept her good offices for mediation, which Russia did. The ideas behind Austria's mediatory efforts were simple enough. On the one hand, Turkey had to save the essential elements of her independence, which could be jeopardized by Russia's original demands; on the other hand, she had to concede something to Russia to avoid a suicidal war. The way out was to offer Russia sweeping assurances about the protection of Ottoman Christians, while preserving the responsibility for such protection strictly for the Sultan (where even Menshikov had admitted it belonged). Anyway, what really menaced Turkey, according to Buol, was not Russia's treaties or notes, but the fact that Turkey stood in an isolated one-to-one relation to Russia, and that Russia wanted to keep things that way. The answer to this basic danger was for the European powers, intervening at Turkey's request, to "group" Russia and require her to act in concert with them in regard to Turkey. Let Turkey, relying on the advice of the European ambassadors, draw up a compromise note for Russia, offering to send it to St. Petersburg by a special envoy and asking the powers to support it. Austria would then take the lead in getting Russia to accept the note, evacuate the Principalities, and restore normal relations.[38]

Buol saw the risks involved in making Constantinople the main center of the European action. Redcliffe might encourage the Turks to be intransigent; his protégé Reshid's reputation was blackened for Austria by his role in the refugee question in 1849–1850. But Buol believed Redcliffe would try for peace and was willing to forget Reshid's past. Bruck threw himself with his customary energy into the quest for a compromise note to send to St. Petersburg, and though Redcliffe and Reshid accused him of trying to force a sugar-coated Menshikov note down the Sultan's throat, he seemed to have a chance of success. Buol, resisting French pressure on Austria to bypass Constantinople and produce her own note, urged him to persist and gave him wide room for his own initiative.[39]

The sea powers tried persistently to drag Austria out of her cautious mediatory role. Drouyn called constantly for a Vienna conference. As soon as Russia accepted Austria's good offices, he and Cowley tried to get Austria to propose her own terms; Cowley vigorously criticized Buol to Hübner for not convening all the Vienna envoys, Meyendorff included, to work out a note to send to Constantinople. Neither Redcliffe nor the Sultan would dare reject it, said Cowley. Buol, conceding to Hübner that Austria's position seemed colorless, insisted that Austria was not ready to accept the whole responsibility for peace or war.[40]

But while pressing Austria for a solution, the sea powers produced a wealth of proposals of their own in late June and July. Clarendon, more suspicious of Redcliffe than Buol was, and convinced with Drouyn and Cowley that anything coming from Constantinople would be too distasteful for St. Petersburg, drew up proposals for a Russo-Turk convention to be approved by France and then sent to Redcliffe. Drouyn rejected the convention as worse than the Menshikov note, Britain rejected his counternote as too meager for Russia, and a stalemate resulted. Then Drouyn proceeded to send his note to the French minister at St. Petersburg, General Castelbajac, for Russia's approval. Clarendon responded by deciding to put forward his projected convention whether or not France approved it. Drouyn's note, though clever, would not do because it provided no golden bridge for the Tsar, he said, and there was no reason "why we should not fly our own kite just as they have done theirs." In the meantime, Bourqueney, adapting a suggestion of Drouyn's, launched a new initiative through Meyendorff, according to which the Turks were to accept the Menshikov note essentially unaltered, in exchange for satisfactory assurances from the Tsar against interference in Turkish internal affairs. The Russians of course seized on this suggestion with both hands, and Drouyn, though unwilling to grant Russia the Menshikov note under any circumstances, found Russia's favorable response useful for promoting his own note at St. Petersburg. It also enabled him to tell London, insincerely, that France did not object to Clarendon's convention, but was somewhat committed to following up the Bourqueney project.[41]

What is plain in all this confusion is that despite their frequent calls on Austria for cooperation and leadership, neither of the sea powers cooperated with her at all. Buol's pleas for pressure on Turkey in favor of a compromise note went largely ignored. Drouyn went directly to St. Petersburg through Castelbajac and Bourqueney through Meyendorff, with no concern for the diplomatic efforts being made at Constantinople or the angry protests of Redcliffe and Bruck. However annoyed Clarendon became with the French, he carefully avoided alienating them, telling Cowley he would approve Bourqueney's project or any proposal made by Redcliffe and Lacour if the Porte was satisfied with it. He was equally careful not to cross Redcliffe, insubordinate though he considered him, or to bypass Turkey, which he termed sardonically "our *independent* ally." But the subordinate role Austria played in his plans is shown by the words with which he conveyed his proposed convention to Cowley: "If Drouyn has no objections to offer to it I shall send it to Constantinople and let them *know* of it at Vienna." That is, Austria would receive the text of the proposal at the same time Russia did. Austria, "the peace making machine," was supposed to make Russia adopt what Britain and France had concluded and Turkey had agreed to in advance.[42]

Austria was also proposed for tasks or responsibilities the sea powers preferred not to take upon themselves. If any difficulty arose in regard to his convention or the Bourqueney proposal over whether Russia or Turkey should go first in proposing a settlement, Clarendon said, Austria should assume "the charge of exchanging the notes and thus saving the dignity of both sides." Drouyn, hearing that Austria found Russia's reception of the Bourqueney project encouraging, immediately wired Bourqueney, "Leave to the Court of Vienna the initiative and the responsibility of the expedient which is attributed to you." When he learned that Buol approved the contents of his note, Drouyn similarly wanted Austria to take it over and repress his authorship, and Cowley hinted to Hübner that Britain also would support a note coming from Vienna provided that if Russia rejected it Austria would join the sea powers.[43]

Buol was dismayed not only at the confusion produced by all these initiatives but also the likelihood that Turkey, faced with too many proposals, would agree to none of them. Since Drouyn's note represented the kind of compromise between the Menshikov and Reshid notes Buol had long advocated, he welcomed it in substance, but regretted that France had sent it to St. Petersburg and not to Constantinople, where it might have ended the hesitations of the Turks. Falsely informed by the French that Russia had accepted Drouyn's note, Buol immediately ordered Bruck to support it at Constantinople, only to earn Nesselrode's acid rebuke that Russia wanted the unaltered Menshikov note, as in Bourqueney's project, or nothing. As for Clarendon's proposed Russo-Turkish convention, Buol objected that it really did not say anything, that Russia probably would reject it, and that since it was in the form of a new treaty Redcliffe and the Turks were almost certain to do so. Yet so desperate (or as Meyendorff said, fanatical) was Buol for peace that he would have gladly supported Clarendon's expedient if it would work. The only thing he said he could not do was to support any new projects until the fate of the old ones was decided, and he still wanted precedence given to what Turkey would produce under European influence.[44]

Buol adhered to this position until late July. But Bruck's dispatches of July 18 made him fear that the Constantinople efforts would not produce a workable settlement, and Turkey's actual proposals of July 20 and 25 (usually termed, misleadingly, the "Turkish ultimatum") confirmed his fears. The Turks offered Russia only a firman confirming the privileges of the Greek Church instead of a note, and they accompanied their offer of a special mission to St. Petersburg with a violent denunciation by Reshid of the occupation of the Principalities. Though Bruck defended the proposal and even took credit for it, it was plainly Redcliffe's work, did not even try to meet Russia's demand for a note, and contained language so insulting and compromising that Buol declined to transmit Reshid's letter to Nesselrode.[45]

Convinced that the Constantinople mediation was breaking down and that further delay would be fatal, Buol yielded to French pressure and convened a conference at Vienna to draw up a note that the powers could compel Turkey to accept and persuade the Tsar to agree to. Drouyn's note, already sent by Buol to Bruck for use at Constantinople, became the basis for negotiations in the Vienna conferences of July 24–28. Though Bourqueney and Buol worked well together at these talks, the differences in their motivation and tactics were clear. The French wanted the conference to be a coalition against Russia, with Austria being responsible for ensuring that Russia accepted its decision. Buol still wanted to group Russia within the Concert, and only Meyendorff's declining to take part kept it from being a five-power meeting. In any case, both he and the Turkish representative were kept fully informed throughout.

Thus Drouyn's note, with small changes proposed by Britain and Austria (Austria's all intended to sweeten the pill for Russia) was adopted on July 28, ratified in Paris and London, signed July 31 at Vienna, and transmitted by Austria to St. Petersburg for the Tsar's acceptance. Buol also sent it to Bruck to begin selling it to the Sultan.[46] This procedure has often been criticized, most formidably by H. W. V. Temperley, on the ground that the powers rejected Redcliffe's argument that the Turkish ultimatum represented the absolute limit of Turkey's concessions, and wounded Turkish pride by submitting the note first to the Tsar.[47] The argument certainly has weight; Bruck agreed with Redcliffe that no amount of diplomatic pressure could have induced Turkey to swallow the Vienna Note. Buol had always seen the danger of trying to force down her throat a note concocted abroad, and for this reason he held out as long as he did against a Vienna Conference. It was Bourqueney who insisted on sending the note first to St. Petersburg, while Buol's rejection of Turkey's proposals as unsatisfactory and his refusal to transmit Reshid's letter were fully approved by the other powers.[48]

There is also another side to the problem. If it was unlikely that Turkey would accept the Vienna Note, it was still more unlikely that the Tsar could agree to Turkey's proposal. In fact, it was not clear that he would even agree to the Vienna Note; as late as July 30, Nesselrode was still insisting on the unaltered Menshikov note. Had a European solution been proposed first to the Sultan and then to St. Petersburg, Nicholas's pride would have been wounded at least as much as the Sultan's was by the actual procedure. Nicholas actually accepted the Vienna Note only because he considered it Austria's ultimatum, which Europe would force on Turkey. Europe thus had to choose which stubborn power primarily to persuade and which to coerce. Russia may have deserved coercion where Turkey did not, but Turkey evidently had more to lose by intransigence, and Russia would be more difficult and dangerous to coerce as a great power and member of the Concert. In any case, Britain and France were just as convinced as Austria that Turkey had to be made to accept the Vienna Note for her own good. Russell, for example, proposed that the Tsar be given a choice between the English and French projects, and then his choice be "imposed" upon the Turks—a procedure far more humiliating than that actually followed. Clarendon promised Aberdeen to write Redcliffe that Turkey must accept the note, remarking rather naively, "I begin to think we shall have as much trouble with the Turks as with the Russians." [49]

Thus, though the best course cannot be clearly determined even by hindsight, Austria's policy was a reasonable one, and Buol certainly strove for peace with virtually no hidden motives. A rift opened between Buol and Bruck at this time mainly over Buol's refusal to prepare for the coming war by securing strategic positions and occupying territory, chiefly Bosnia and Serbia.[50] France's policy also was fairly consistent, though her aims were more diverse than Austria's and her will to peace more conditional. But the contradictory impulses of British policy showed up again in her handling of the Vienna Note. Clarendon had helped defeat the Turkish proposals Redcliffe sponsored; Britain fully agreed to the Vienna Note and the procedure for using it, and accepted joint responsibility. Indeed, Clarendon's main fear was that Russia would reject it and make Europe look ridiculous. Yet knowing how Redcliffe opposed any compromise note, especially one coming from Vienna, and fully realizing that only strong pressure by Redcliffe on the Porte could possibly gain acceptance of it at Constantinople, Clarendon still told Redcliffe that a *sine qua non* for any plan was that the Turks should consider it "perfectly safe for the Porte"—something the Turks and Redcliffe certainly would not consider it to be.[51]

One might suspect deliberate sabotage, in view of Clarendon's last-minute ambivalence about the note and his insistence that the Tsar was about to perpetrate some treachery, but Clarendon was not clever and consistent enough to be Machiavellian. What this does show, however, is that the Vienna Note, soon to be denounced as a Buol-Meyendorff trap laid for the West, really trapped Austria. She was drawn reluctantly out of her cautious, noncommittal mediation into taking the main responsibility for imposing on both sides a diplomatic solution that she did not originate, involving a procedure about which she had grave doubts. Meanwhile France had designs of her own behind the *démarche*, while leading British statesmen were half-prepared to abandon it before it was even launched and did not wholeheartedly support it before their own ambassador at Constantinople.[52]

IV

Buol's Project Rejected: The Concert Bypassed

Buol, who never shared the supposition common in Europe that the crisis was virtually over once the Vienna Note was signed, immediately set out not only to sell it to Russia and Turkey, but also to persuade all the powers involved to take some concrete step away from direct confrontation.[1] At St. Petersburg, Austria had some success. Nicholas refused Buol's plea to set a date for starting the evacuation of the Principalities, but he did accept the Vienna Note and promised again that as soon as Turkey did likewise, Russia would begin evacuation.[2] At Constantinople, however, Bruck's energetic browbeating of the Turks proved useless.[3] Encouraged by Redcliffe's private disapproval of the note, the Porte on August 19 demanded amendments to it and a four-power guarantee against further Russian interference in Turkish affairs. This demand for amendments and a guarantee may have been the best reply obtainable at this time; Bruck agreed with Redcliffe on this score. Nonetheless, it was tantamount to a rejection and blocked any settlement, while Redcliffe's attitude encouraged the Turks to expect more Western support.[4]

Meanwhile, Buol's efforts for a detente got a mixed reception in London. Clarendon appreciated his aims and recognized that his proposal for an informal agreement tying the withdrawal of the Western fleets to the start of Russian evacuation would be the most suitable and amicable procedure. The trouble, he told Cowley, was that "we have had enough of treating matters in a gentlemanlike manner." But while refusing to commit Britain on this score, he indicated to Buol that the sea powers would order the fleets moved once Russia began to evacuate, if Austria would guarantee the completion of the evacuation. This was some help.[5] Yet Clarendon greeted Russia's acceptance of the Vienna Note in a puzzlingly negative fashion. He refused at first to acknowledge it as genuine, insisting that she had probably agreed to something else or that Russian troop movements made the acceptance meaningless. He also raised new demands, insisting that Russia set her date for evacuation immediately, without even waiting to see if Turkey accepted the note, and he now urged four-power action, with or without Russia's consent, to convert the 1841 Straits Convention Preamble into a guarantee of Turkey (the same Palmerston-Drouyn idea that Clarendon had earlier rejected).[6]

Plainly Clarendon was again wavering under uncertainty and diverse pressures. His most important concern was fear over Britain's position if Turkey should reject the British-sponsored Vienna Note after Russia accepted it. The peace party insisted that Britain would then have to turn her back on Turkey and recall Redcliffe. Russell even proposed letting Russia remain all winter in the Principalities, as long as she did not cross the Danube, to bring the Turks to their senses. If the Turks rashly provoked war, he said, "Russia can hardly be kept on a leash—and we must take fresh counsel with our three allies."[7] Clarendon claimed to agree with Russell entirely, telling Redcliffe that the Vienna Note was really a humiliation for Russia. Privately he repeatedly expressed the hope that Redcliffe would resign.[8] Yet all the while he knew that no matter what Turkey did, Britain would not abandon her; neither Britain's strategic position nor the power of Palmerston, Parliament, and public opinion would permit it.

If we abandon Turkey [he told Cowley] which we should have a right to do so [sic] on her rejection of our advice we make her at once the prey of Russia which Austria would then join, if we support her it will be in her wrong and against our own advice. This may be a terrible fix but it is not an improbable one and I have at no time felt more uneasy about the final solution than I do at this moment.

Thus the hedging against Russia's acceptance and the raising of new demands was in preparation (how consciously so, it is hard to say) for blaming Russia for the failure of the four-power effort, so that Britain could continue to back Turkey. Clarendon soon argued that the "terrible fix" he anticipated was part of a cunning Russian trap. Nicholas had accepted the Vienna Note only because he knew the Turks would refuse it. The Turk refusal would improve his diplomatic position, enable Russia to remain in the Principalities, and weaken Turkey by causing internal disturbances at Constantinople.[9]

Turkey's actual demand for amendments brought the rift in the British Cabinet into the open. Aberdeen, convinced Britain should not even ask the Tsar to accept Turkey's demands, called for withdrawing the fleets to coerce Turkey. Clarendon, though venting his rage unstintingly on the Turks and Redcliffe, proposed nothing concrete.[10] Palmerston, while critical of Turkey's stubbornness, urged delay, arguing that the weather would not necessitate moving the fleets from Besika Bay for weeks or months to come. But Russell now suddenly changed his mind. Where he had as late as August 27 damned the Turks for their suicidal policy, he insisted on August 28 and 29 that the sea powers must support Turkey, though they should still try to maintain the status quo and gain the winter for negotiations, for Turkey was wholly in the right against Russia. Turkey no doubt wanted war, he told Aberdeen, and had made her demands for amendments simply to incite the Tsar; but she was not necessarily wrong for doing so.[11]

The decision was further complicated by advice from France. The French agreed with Austria in wanting to put more pressure on Turkey, but also wished to improve the West's position vis-à-vis Russia by sending the fleets inside the Dardanelles, on the pretext of saving them from bad weather. Cowley found himself in the position of defending to the French the Turks' right to demand amendments to the Vienna Note, but at the same time resisting France's idea for giving Turkey support with the fleets. Clarendon saw no good solution. The plea of weather would not do for moving the fleets, because there were other anchorages as safe as the Dardanelles; yet sending the fleets farther away from the Straits would look like a retreat and make Britain a laughing stock. Entering the Straits, on the other hand, was illegal except when the Porte was at war; it would create the very *status belli* the sea powers had warned Turkey against. And how could they justify the move now, when Russia had done what the powers asked and Turkey was defying them? As he wrote to Cowley on August 30: "This would make our position still more false and it can be only upon some new act on the part of Russia further [*sic*—evidently a word was omitted here] hostile intentions against Turkey that we would be justified in this onward movement." The right policy for the moment was therefore to "wait a few days and see when we can get *a locus standi for a policy*"—that is, to wait to see whether Russia might soon do something to justify Britain's going into the Straits.[12]

Very soon, however, Clarendon came to feel that British prestige at home and abroad necessitated moving into the Dardanelles, and on September 3 he supported Russell and Palmerston on seeking firmans from Turkey for this purpose. Aberdeen, with help from Graham and Lansdowne, successfully resisted this in a stormy meeting on September 4, proving by expert Admiralty opinion that the weather would not require a fleet movement until November at the earliest.[13] * Clarendon seemed temporarily to go back to supporting Aberdeen in advocating a cruise in the Archipelago for the fleet. But by September 12, Aberdeen ruefully recognized that Clarendon was again leaning, with Palmerston and Russell, toward sending the ships into the Dardanelles.

The situation was graver than Aberdeen knew; Clarendon had renounced all thought of getting Turkey to accept the Vienna Note, because, as he wrote Redcliffe, Turkey was bent on war and "however foolish the Turks may be we cannot abandon Turkey." Disagreeable though Britain's fix was, he told Cowley, she could not compel Turkey to accept the unmodified note, even if the Turks deserved it. For public opinion in Britain and France would not permit it, "and if the Turks persisted in refusing and defied us we should look very foolish in continuing to support them quand même or in withdrawing (as in ordinary case we should be entitled to do) and thus leaving them a prey to Russia." Britain would look just as foolish if the Turkish ministry swallowed the note under Western

* Kingsley Martin's charge that Aberdeen and Graham here abused expert naval advice in the interest of their political decision (*Triumph of Palmerston*, 81–82) is natural but mistaken. What happened is that Palmerston and Russell, who wanted for political reasons to send in the fleets, argued (in direct contradiction to what Palmerston had maintained just a week before) that the weather made it unsafe to keep the fleets at Besika Bay much longer. Aberdeen, who knew already from Graham that the Admiralty experts denied this, simply asked Graham to obtain written confirmation of their opinion (Graham to Aberdeen, 9 Sept. 1853, and Aberdeen to Graham, 12 Sept., Graham Papers Reel 18). In other words, it was the war party, not Aberdeen, who chose to alter the known facts about the weather to suit their political wishes.

pressure and then was overthrown by a revolution at Constantinople, bringing the war party to power. Therefore the fleets had to go into the Straits to support Turkey right or wrong, though this must not be admitted yet. Painful and serious as it was to violate a treaty, "that is far preferable to anything like a retreat." [14]

Clarendon's renewed change of position virtually decided the contest within the Cabinet. What the forward party still desired was only a better moral justification for openly supporting Turkey— some clearer proof of Russia's continued aggressive intentions than her acceptance of the Vienna Note provided (though Russell, Clarendon, and Cowley already agreed that this was a Russian trick to advance her sinister plans). Russell, who had earlier condemned the Turkish amendments as senseless and provocative, now proposed requiring Russia to accept them. If she refused, she should be summoned to accept Turkey's ultimatum of July 20, and if she refused again, it meant the Tsar wanted war. Palmerston claimed that the Turkish amendments were perfectly justified, and Russia's rejection of them would prove her aggressive designs. Clarendon, unable to agree that the amendments were any use (in fact, he insisted that if Russia really wanted to interfere in Turkey's internal affairs, she would find half a dozen good pretexts for doing so even in the Vienna Note as amended by Turkey), argued that if the changes were merely insignificant, Russia ought to be willing to accept them. If she refused, it must be because the amendments would hamper her plans. By mid-September, Clarendon and Russell were anticipating a Russian declaration "that the modifications do alter the sense of the note," which they said would compel the four powers to drop the note and would even justify an Anglo-French declaration of war.[15]

All these details about the maneuvers within the Cabinet add up to a significant point. The reason usually assigned for Britain's abandoning the Vienna Note in late September and deciding along with France to order the fleets to Constantinople is that Russia issued a "violent interpretation" of the Vienna Note which apparently proved that she still had aggressive aims. This violent interpretation, reviving and deepening Britain's and France's mistrust of Russia, destroyed their confidence in the Vienna Note and four-power diplomacy as the way to peace and led them to support Turkey more fully instead. The mistrust the violent interpretation engendered also contributed to the failure of all later efforts for peace.[16]

This thesis, though plausible, does not fit the facts just laid out. Those leaders whose policy finally prevailed in Britain had decided well in advance of the violent interpretation that the Vienna Note could not be forced on Turkey; the sea powers would have to support her right or wrong. France had long advocated sending the fleets into the Dardanelles, and Palmerston, Russell, and Clarendon already pressed for it, not because of their reading of Russia's deeds and intentions, most certainly not because of the violent interpretation that they had not yet even heard of, but out of concern for public opinion, the French alliance, the maintenance of the Cabinet in power, and Britain's prestige and strategic position. Had no violent interpretation come along from Russia, they would have invented one and were in fact in the process of inventing or provoking one in order to justify the move they intended to make anyway.

Certainly the British distrusted Russia, as they also distrusted Turkey, France, Austria, and other powers; the point is to determine what role, if any, that distrust actually played in the formation of policy, not to assume that it was the cause. It is here sounder to see British distrust of Russia as a consequence of British policy than a determinant of it. Both before and after the violent interpretation, Clarendon and Russell wavered back and forth between trusting the Tsar (i.e., believing he was only trying to escape from his predicament with honor) and distrusting him; their position depended largely on whether or not they considered some new forward move against Russia desirable at a particular time. Indeed, sometimes the trust or distrust British leaders showed toward Russia was in direct contradiction to the direction of the policy they followed. Clarendon sometimes distrusted the Tsar profoundly as early as April 1853, when he certainly was working for peace; he still trusted in the Tsar and blamed the Turks for all the trouble as late as January 1854, when he had clearly opted for war. Russell was no different. In this case, Britain did not decide to support Turkey and drop the Vienna Note because she distrusted Russia; she distrusted Russia chiefly because she had decided to support Turkey and drop the Vienna Note.

This attitude helped frustrate Buol's efforts to save the Vienna

Note; he failed either to get the Tsar to accept some of the Turkish modifications or to get the Turks to withdraw them.* With a calmness that surprised Meyendorff, he turned to an earlier French proposal: let the Sultan, while accepting the unaltered note, write an autograph letter to the Tsar stating Turkey's objections to it and her interpretation of what she was agreeing to. Austria would get the Tsar to reply with reassurances on the points raised by Turkey, and the four powers would back up Russia's reply with a separate declaration on the meaning of the note. Thus Turkey's honor would be preserved and the powers would have an authentic interpretation of the note for the future.[17]

Buol's proposal was similar to ideas broached apparently independently at Constantinople by Bruck and Redcliffe; it seemed a hopeful device both for overcoming the present crisis and preventing its recurrence.† The Vienna Conference fully supported Buol's efforts. Even Meyendorff cooperated, and Prussia used her influence in favor of moderation at St. Petersburg and Constantinople. France supported Austria's views, though with important qualifications.[18] The main difficulty remained the absence of either support or consistent policy from Britain. While she refused to press the unaltered note on the Turks, she also hindered Buol's efforts to persuade the Tsar to accept Turkey's amendments. Aberdeen assured both Brunnow and Colloredo that England would never give Turkey the guarantees she wanted and that the Turks would have to yield, which prompted Brunnow to advise a wait-and-see policy for Russia. Simultaneously Clarendon curtly dismissed Buol's suggestion for some form of Western-Russian agreement on reciprocal

---

* There is some ground for believing that Buol's efforts to force Turkey to accept the unaltered note for her own good need not have been hopeless, or even wholly unwelcome at the Porte, had Europe united behind them. The Turkish ambassador at Paris, Vely Pasha, told Cowley that his instructions were that the Porte would not sign the unaltered note "with its consent." Asked by Cowley what this phrase meant, Vely replied, "The Porte would sign if there was greater danger in persisting in her refusal, than in signing" (Cowley to Clarendon, 2 Sept. 1853, No. 656, FO 519/2).

† When Drouyn suggested expanding the 1841 Preamble into a European guarantee of Turkey, Buol replied that he would be delighted to continue the Vienna Conference for this purpose after the crisis was past; but let the powers first snuff out the flames and then confer on fire prevention measures (Bourqueney to Drouyn, 1 Sept. 1853, No. 80, AMAE Autr. 451; Buol to Hübner, 8 Sept., PA IX/44).

withdrawal from the Principalities and Besika Bay as an inducement to the Tsar to swallow the Turkish amendments.[19]

But one British initiative in mid-September appeared constructive, and to some extent was so—her proposal to offer the unaltered Vienna Note to Turkey with a four-power declaration guaranteeing Turkey against any Russian misinterpretation of it. Several versions of this idea were current; this particular one came from Redcliffe. Clarendon first called it judicious but impractical because of Turkey's determination to go to war. But after Cowley urged the same idea and France sponsored it, and when Clarendon received the news on September 13 of Russia's rejection of Turkey's amendments (though Russia's reasons were not yet known), he agreed that a four-power guarantee of the note seemed the next logical step. He still hesitated to propose it, anticipating a Russian "violent interpretation" and insisting that the Turks and Redcliffe would make the effort useless, until Palmerston, delighted at the martial ardor Turkey was displaying, also proposed such a guarantee on September 14. This move fit Palmerston's strategy of making Austria and Prussia guarantee Turkey's integrity against Russia, thus creating an anti-Russian coalition under British leadership.[20]

The proposal also promised to help solve some of Clarendon's current difficulties. He was mortified at the prospect of England's being dragged into war by the Turks. He knew that he had no substitute for the Vienna Note as a basis for a settlement and that a move into the Straits would still cause trouble in the Cabinet. The proposed guarantee might give Britain some control over Turkish policy, without which fanatics at Constantinople might overthrow the Sultan, plunge Turkey headlong into war, and start massacring Christians—all of which would make it still more embarrassing to support Turkey against Russia, and even more dangerous to leave her to her fate. Finally, this proposal might enable Clarendon to meet some of the strong criticism coming from France over Britain's negative and vacillating policy.*

* The most forceful example of this criticism was Drouyn's dispatch to Walewski of September 15, demanding that Britain decide which course she wanted: a diplomatic compromise, or a defense of Turkey with France at all costs. Her refusal to send in the fleets seemed to prove she wanted the former; in that case the sea powers must in strict honor and duty press Constantinople to accept the settlement the four powers had worked out and Russia had ac-

Therefore Clarendon, together with Palmerston and Aberdeen, drafted a dispatch to Redcliffe on September 15 containing the collective guarantee proposal, to be sent for approval also to Paris and the Vienna Conference. For Aberdeen and the royal couple the proposed guarantee represented a real effort to reassure Turkey without humiliating Russia. Clarendon's motives were more mixed. He would have liked to see the *démarche* succeed, but repeatedly declared that it could not possibly do so because the Turks were bent on war. What he hoped it would do was to hold the Cabinet together, satisfy France, and head off France's and Austria's extremely annoying efforts to get Turkey to accept the unaltered note with lesser guarantees. A four-power guarantee would also compel the other powers "to take part with Turkey in any future quarrel with Russia arising out of the Note" and would put Nicholas in an embarrassing position. He would hardly dare to reject a four-power interpretation of the note, which would give Europe a hold over him for the future, and if he did reject it he would place himself openly in the wrong now.[21] Thus Clarendon really expected the proposal to accomplish some good everywhere except at its destination, Constantinople, and except for its supposed purpose, peace.

Precisely at this moment, the "violent interpretation" became public and this *démarche* became connected with it. Nesselrode officially rejected the Turkish amendments on September 7 simply on the ground that Russia had accepted the proposal without conditions. But he also sent Meyendorff two other less official dispatches arguing in pettifogging legalistic fashion that Turkey's amendments tended to undermine Russia's existing rights to protect Turkey's Or-

cepted. Supposing Russia did give the Vienna Note a violent interpretation, as Britain anticipated, the four powers could then simply establish its true meaning in conference—it was after all *their* note. Nor was the British contention valid that the powers would have to abandon Turkey to her fate if she rejected their pressure; surely they did not have to help her reject their own advice in order to save her from being wiped out by Russia! As for the claim that pressure on Turkey would cause revolt at Constantinople, Drouyn pointed out that the surest way to promote anti-Christian risings was to allow Turkey to go to war. Besides, if this was the real problem, the best answer was material support for the Turkish government, not a "diplomatic abstention." The crucial issue remained: did the Western powers really want to encourage Turkey to reject their own advice? Out of fear of Parliament and Stratford, Drouyn concluded, the British Cabinet *did* want to do this, and could do so if it wished—but not too much at France's expense (AMAE Mem. et Doc. France 2120).

thodox Christians. The argument was not new and hardly violent; Russia had been saying something like this all along. Had she refused to give any concrete reasons at all for rejecting the amendments, British leaders planned to demand them of her and to accuse her of keeping Europe in crisis simply for the sake of Russian pride. Buol in any case kept quiet about the second dispatch, conveying only Russia's official answer to the conference on September 14 and urging the other powers to persuade Turkey to accept the unaltered note by giving her whatever assurances they thought best. He and Bourqueney still thought the best insurance policy would be the exchange of explanatory letters between the Sultan and the Tsar, with the four powers to take official note of them.[22]

Meanwhile the violent interpretation leaked out in the German press and was confidentially communicated by Russia to Britain and France on September 16. Drouyn, though not really aroused by it per se, saw in it a chance to force Austria either to oppose Russia's interpretation or to disavow her own assurances to the Turks. He ordered a bewildered Bourqueney to stop working in favor of Austria's proposed four-power declaration and instead to get Buol to adopt Britain's collective guarantee proposal, just approved at Paris. Thus both the sea powers pressed this guarantee proposal on Austria after they knew of the violent interpretation, as their answer to it.[23]

Neither Buol nor the Prussian minister Count Arnim favored the proposed collective guarantee as it stood. Having just urged the Vienna Note very strongly on Turkey in his September 13 instructions to Bruck, Buol argued he could not now adopt the much more lukewarm language of Britain's proposal. Besides, he still did not want to lead an openly anti-Russian coalition, and still less to give Turkey an unlimited promise of support in any future quarrel with Russia over the note. But his principal contention was that at this moment a collective guarantee of Turkey would increase the danger of war, which arose mainly (as Clarendon also said repeatedly) from Turkish belligerence and the Turks' *idée fixe* that "bon gré malgré the European powers whatever they may do will be forced to come to their aid." If and when Turkey yielded, Europe would have to give her moral support and even material aid; until then, Europe would at least have to appear ready to leave a recalcitrant Turkey to her fate.[24]

Despite these reasons, Buol and Arnim decided on September 18 under heavy Western pressure to join in a collective declaration that the Vienna Note contained nothing injurious to the Sultan's sovereignty, provided the sea powers would then seriously press Turkey to accept it. But no sooner had Bourqueney and Westmorland reported this achievement than their instructions were changed. On the nineteenth, Clarendon still urged a collective guarantee as the best way to get Turkey to accept the Vienna Note. On the twentieth he repudiated the note entirely, flatly refusing any longer to recommend it in any fashion to Turkey, but at the same time demanding that the Vienna Conference deny in a formal protocol that the note conferred any new rights on Russia. Drouyn, dragged along by the British action, ordered Bourqueney to secure the protocol Britain wanted, without mentioning any support for the Vienna Note at Constantinople.

Buol now dug in his heels. Professing his bewilderment to Francis Joseph as to why Britain wanted a protocol attesting the harmlessness of a note she was determined to repudiate, he and Arnim replied that they would sign both the proposed protocol and the declaration already decided upon, if the sea powers would support the note at Constantinople; if not, then not.[25] The conference was suspended in this impasse on September 22 and the next day Buol and the Emperor left for Olmütz to meet with Nicholas and Nesselrode to try to get Russia to repudiate the violent interpretation. Austria's alleged refusal to guarantee a safe interpretation of the Vienna Note was immediately exploited in Britain as proof that the note had been from the outset a Buol-Meyendorff trap, and the trip to Olmütz was seen as the prelude to an Austro-Russian partition of Turkey.[26]

The fact was that Austria had not rejected the Anglo-French guarantee proposal. The sea powers themselves had abandoned it along with the Vienna Note as a device to promote peace, instead trying to use it to entangle Austria and Prussia in a four-power front against Russia—and in this they had failed. Moreover, internal cabinet politics rather than foreign developments had once more been the main reason for Britain's change of course. Russell, being away from London, had not shared in formulating the guarantee proposal. Hearing of it, he denounced it as a shameful betrayal of Turkey, threatening to resign if it were actually sent to Constantinople. This was another of his abrupt changes in position (on Septem-

ber 12 he had been confident of the Tsar's moderation and hopeful
that a good Russian beating of the Turks would help promote new
negotiations). Obviously Russell was seeking a pretext to overthrow
the ministry; Aberdeen took pleasure in pointing out that Palmerston helped draft the proposal he considered a shameful surrender.
(To this, Russell replied that even a fully guaranteed Vienna Note
was unacceptable since, with the Turks now fanatically aroused,
Turkey would accept none but virtually triumphant conditions of
peace.) [27]

Unreasonable though Russell's protest was, it affected Clarendon
much more than did the concurrent communication of the "violent
interpretation" by Brunnow. While Brunnow's note deepened Clarendon's gloom over the prospects of peace, it did not lead him either
to give up his guarantee proposal or to believe that Nicholas's intentions really were aggressive. The next day he wrote Stratford that
the Vienna Note with a collective guarantee was still the great
desideratum. Nesselrode's dispatches to Meyendorff, he remarked,
were "in tolerably temperate language" and did not contain much to
object to; "*I have no doubt*," he emphasized, "that Russia wants to
get out of the affair." [28] Only after conferring with Russell to avert
a Cabinet crisis did Clarendon come to see the violent interpretation
as a good reason to discard the Vienna Note entirely, and even then
it was not because the violent interpretation had proved the Tsar
untrustworthy. His argument to Aberdeen on September 19 is worth
quoting:

> Here is the note [the collective guarantee proposal] as amended by
> Lord John. If it could be proposed to the Emperor at Olmütz by the
> Emperor of Austria he might possibly for the sake of peace accept it,
> but I really don't think we can press the Turks to sign the note upon
> our interpretation of it having before our eyes the notice of the Em-
> peror with whom the engagement is made that he understands it in
> quite a different sense. It would be offensive and hostile to him [i.e., to
> the Tsar!]. It would give Austria a pretext for disconnecting herself
> from us. And it would be useless with the Turks unless we declared
> that besides interpreting the Note we were prepared to take up every
> quarrel they might have hereafter with Russia about it.

Besides, he concluded, England would only suffer a humiliating rebuff if she tried to force the hated Vienna Note on the Turks.[29]

Plainly Clarendon was arguing *ad hominem* here, appealing to

Aberdeen's desire to conciliate Austria, his respect for Nicholas, and his aversion to commitments in favor of Turkey. Clarendon's contention that Austria would be given an excuse to break away from the West if the sea powers adhered to the Vienna Note shows how desperately he was straining for arguments. But in strategy and purport the letter is quintessential Clarendon; since the Vienna Note and the guarantee proposal promised merely to produce a Cabinet split and a failure at Constantinople, the sea powers should drop both of them, and the violent interpretation provided a good excuse for doing so.

Other developments at this same time helped impel Clarendon to discard the note and let matters take their course. Redcliffe warned that the Turkish ministry would fall if it were retained. Cowley after long wavering also gave up on it, warning Clarendon that the French might treacherously join Austria in using the note to force Turkey to surrender. At the same time he reported that France would soon send her fleet into the Straits, alone if necessary. Seymour emphasized the dangers of British isolation from France. The news of outbreaks at Constantinople and of Redcliffe's summoning four British and French steamships to the Bosporus strengthened Clarendon's impression of being caught up in an irresistible tide of events. He welcomed Redcliffe's action as proof that the sea powers did not wish to "violate treaty *more than they could help*," but it also helped make him throw up his hands. Nothing would work, he told Graham—everything tended toward war, there was no point to further negotiations at all. Aberdeen shared his despair.[30] Both Colloredo and Hübner understood the sea powers' decision better than many later historians, recognizing that the British had seized on the violent interpretation as a means to break off a negotiation they had never liked or believed in and which they now considered hopeless, and to go over to a policy in support of Turkey which would be less embarrassing and more popular. The French also abandoned the Vienna Note not on account of the violent interpretation, but to seal the entente with Britain by drawing her into more overt action, and at the same time to put more pressure on Austria to take the responsibility for preventing war.[31]

The main impact of the violent interpretation was felt in its side effects. It really convinced some waverers, such as the royal couple, that Russia's policy was underhanded and dangerous, and it gave those Peelites who remained unconvinced an excuse to yield.[32] When it became public, it made a change of policy easier and, once made, difficult or impossible to reverse. It provided valuable anti-Russian and anti-Austrian propaganda and paved the way for ordering the fleets into the Straits. Above all, it relieved Clarendon's anxiety, temporarily at least, by providing a justification for the pro-Turkish policy he had considered inevitable but impossible to justify. Time and again he expressed his immense satisfaction over the violent interpretation, by which, he said, Russia had done the British a great good turn. She had put herself in the wrong, thus sparing Britain the embarrassment of having to press Turkey for terms the Turks would surely have rejected, and enabling Britain to continue to support Turkey. As he told Palmerston, just after ordering Redcliffe to call the fleets into the Straits: "I think it is good that Nicholas should have thrown off the mask and that our action with Austria should be for a time at least suspended and I hope that things have been done pretty much as you point out." Russell concurred: "I am not sorry the bear has thrown off the mask. It simplifies the question wonderfully." [33]

Britain's first step to exploit her improved position was the instruction to Redcliffe on September 23 to summon the fleet to Constantinople. Though Clarendon and Aberdeen took this decision without consulting the Cabinet, Palmerston's bellicose advice and Russell's threat of resignation clearly played a large role in it.[34] Ostensibly the fleets were to go up to prevent anti-Christian riots at Constantinople. Aberdeen doubtless believed, or persuaded himself, that this danger demanded the presence of the fleets, for nothing else could justify to his conscience a step that he knew would overtly challenge Russia and tend to incite Turkey to war.

But few others believed this ostensible interpretation. Graham reluctantly accepted the move as something inevitable and valuable for protecting British interests when the Ottoman Empire collapsed. For Clarendon the humanitarian argument was a device to use with Russians, Austrians, and conscience-stricken colleagues. Westmorland was instructed to stress to Buol and Meyendorff the "entire truth," that Britain's "real and bona fide objects" were "stopping the effusion of blood." Only this could overcome her deep reluctance even to appear to be violating the Convention of 1841. Simultaneously Clarendon wrote Palmerston that the fleet would go in to protect British interests and to be ready for any development. Even Aberdeen, Clarendon claimed, now admitted "that necessity, which has no law, has likewise no treaty." [35] Britain and France had to make this move, he told Cowley, because the time for negotiations was over and the time for a clear stand had arrived. It amused him, he commented, that Drouyn had objected to dropping the Vienna Note even while he was urging sending the fleets into the Straits; "the *gentlemanlike* side of such a question evidently did not strike him." (I.e., it was ungentlemanly, not playing the game, to propose continued negotiations with Russia while standing up to her by sending in the fleets.) [36] Palmerston and Russell applauded the move as a first instance of the energetic policy they had long demanded; Cowley insisted that only this kind of forceful action would impress Austria and Prussia.[37] *

The developments of September 15–23 illustrate a pattern often encountered in the Anglo-French partnership. France, eager to seal the alliance by action and hopeful of gaining a position by which the sea powers could impose their terms on the contending parties, would urge Britain on in some forward move. Britain, at first hesitant, would finally make the move, but in such a way as to frustrate, not promote, the diplomatic settlement France wanted. The two powers, finding themselves in a supposedly stronger position, but really further from a settlement, would then decide that Austria was to blame for this outcome, and denounce her for it. Despite the suspension of the Vienna Conference, Buol continued his efforts to

---

* Clarendon's use of the humanitarian explanation even caused him some trouble—with France, because it obscured France's motives for the fleet move, to counter Russia's occupation of the Principalities and to gain control of Turkish policy, and with Palmerston, because he warned that if the Western fleets could go to Constantinople to prevent a rising, so could Russia's. Clarendon told Drouyn and Walewski that the humanitarian excuse was the only one available so long as the Porte had not declared war, and he reminded Palmerston that Aberdeen and the Cabinet needed some such humanitarian reason. Minto's objection was that "it is more *English* to tell the plain truth than to resort to the French and Russian and Austrian expedients of an unprofitable lie" (Cowley to Clarendon, 26 Sept. 1853, No. 715, FO 519/2; Clarendon to Cowley, 27 Sept., FO 519/169; Palmerston to Clarendon, 29 and 30 Sept., Clar. dep. c. 3; Clarendon to Palmerston, 30 Sept., Palm. Papers GC/CL/528; Minto to Russell, 8 Oct., PRO 30/22/11B).

gain the cooperation of the sea powers. Explaining frankly what he and Francis Joseph wanted to do at Olmütz, he urged the Western powers to discuss among themselves and with Austria what to do if Russia or Turkey declared war, so that the powers would not again be caught napping by events. Encouraging them to give Turkey any guarantees they thought suitable, he raised no objection to their sending in the fleets if it would serve to calm and restrain Turkey. Instead of wanting to break up the Anglo-French entente, as the British believed he did, Buol counted on France to guide Britain into a more consistent policy.[38]

The French, sorry to see the Vienna Conference suspended, promptly blamed Buol for its breakup and warned Austria that the sea powers would not let Austria stay neutral if war came.[39] The British, in contrast, were delighted to be rid of the Vienna Conferences and Austria's cooperation; this meant no more negotiations except on Western terms and under Anglo-French control. On September 21, Palmerston renewed his proposal to summon a London Conference, where Russia would be offered nothing but Turkey's spontaneous declaration that she intended to fulfill her treaty engagements. Even before this, Russell had declared the Vienna Conference very injurious to peace. Clarendon repeatedly expressed his satisfaction at the demise of the conference, telling Cowley that Austria "was not a fit companion to us" and might entrap the West in "fresh entanglements." [40]

Once again, the beliefs supporting the suspicious attitude toward Austria—the insistence that the Vienna Note was a Buol-Meyendorff trick and that the Olmütz meeting was a prelude to a partition of Turkey [41]—were doubtless sincerely held. But the question is *why* the British believed these ideas. The evidence on the Olmütz meeting went against this supposition, and the theory about the Vienna Note was absurd on its face. Quite apart from overwhelming proof available to Britain that refuted it, the British need only have asked themselves a simple question: if the Vienna Note was a cunning Austro-Russian trick, why did Russia give the game away with her violent interpretation? The fundamental reason for British distrust of Austria is that it fulfilled a functional purpose similar to that of British distrust of Russia. It justified an anti-Austrian policy, at this moment one of shunting Austria aside so that she could not drag the West into new negotiations on terms or under circumstances that Britain did not control.

Besides, the British expected that Austria would probably end up on Russia's side in the war many now considered virtually inevitable, mainly because of the kind of war Britain expected it to become. Palmerston told Clarendon that the best answer to the partition of Turkey which was likely to be agreed on at Olmütz would be for Britain "to play old gooseberry with both the would be partitionists" by liberating Georgia and Circassia from Russia and Italy from Austria. To Sidney Herbert, Secretary at War, Palmerston argued the same day that if war came it should be fought by supplying Turkey with British, French, Polish, and Hungarian officers, and by raising revolutions in Poland, Circassia, and Georgia.[42] No one could doubt where such methods of warfare would drive Austria.

In reality, both Russia and Austria were too worried about the coming war to be plotting the partition of the Ottoman Empire. Nesselrode, Meyendorff, and Brunnow were anxious and conciliatory; the Tsar, though still proud and stubborn, plainly was eager to find an honorable retreat. The trouble was that even Russia's caution did not eliminate the grave dangers of her policy for Austria. Paskevich, for example, continued to advocate his program of revolutionary propaganda in the Balkans, promising that it would raise 40,000 to 50,000 soldiers for Russia. Moreover, he wanted to establish Russia's defensive line across the Danube in Bulgaria, keeping the Principalities occupied by Russia.[43] The Tsar and Nesselrode blamed Russia's troubles on Austria and called on her to keep the Western powers in line, to get Redcliffe recalled, and to impose the Vienna Note on the Turks. Nicholas grew more angry than ever with Buol because of his requests for more assurances on Russia's aims and definite promises to evacuate the Principalities, for these demands implicitly challenged the Tsar's word.[44] *

---

* At Olmütz, Nicholas gave Prince William of Prussia a good example of just why his word was not trusted implicitly by other powers, and could not be. When William pressed him on the dangers of occupying the Principalities, pointing out that France threatened to occupy Belgium in reply, Nicholas answered that Belgium's neutrality was guaranteed by treaties. William retorted that there were also treaties respecting the Principalities. Nicholas replied, "But only between the Porte and me, and no European ones, and there one is his own interpreter of the treaties."

In Vienna, meanwhile, the danger of war led Windischgrätz, Kempen, and others to rally around Russia and the Holy Alliance, while Bruck urged Buol to secure either a secret agreement with Russia partitioning the Ottoman Empire, or her promise strictly to preserve the status quo, after which Austria, Prussia, Russia, and the German Confederation could combine to force terms on Turkey and prevent the sea powers from interfering. Buol was not at all tempted by such brash counsels. His goal at Olmütz would be simply to guide Nicholas away from his dangerous course and back to a safer policy.[45]

In three days of talks Buol obtained what he wanted: a solemn disavowal by the Tsar of any desire to secure new rights from Turkey or to interfere in her internal affairs. This formal declaration became the basis for a new Austrian peace initiative, the so-called Olmütz or Buol Project. The Tsar's declaration would be presented to the Vienna Conference, guaranteed collectively by the four powers, and transmitted to Turkey in a new note. The declaration would cancel the violent interpretation and enable Turkey to accept the Vienna Note on the basis of an authentic, safe interpretation. Incomplete though the records of the Olmütz discussions are, certain points are clear. While Nicholas and Nesselrode were both willing to disavow the violent interpretation, it took considerable effort to get the desired declaration from Nicholas, not because he objected to its content, but because he resented having to repeat pledges he felt he had already made. Buol would have preferred starting over with a new note, but Nesselrode insisted on retaining the Vienna Note because it was the only instrument tying Russia to an agreement with the European powers. Whether Nicholas would have agreed to a substitute note is not clear; he certainly wished to evacuate the Principalities and escape further trouble on any honorable basis, however, and he showered attention and assurances on the Western observers, Westmorland and General Count Goyon, the French military envoy.[46]

Temperley correctly terms the Buol Project "a very serious effort at peace," which failed largely on account of Britain's opposition to it. He explains this opposition as a result of British mistrust of Russia; except for Aberdeen, no one any longer considered Nicholas an honest man. "Clarendon," he writes, "recognized the sincerity of the Czar's desire for peace, but seems to have thought the 'violent interpretation' of Nesselrode a fatal objection to accepting other assurances from Russia." [47]

This is a natural and plausible explanation for Britain's rejection of Buol's proposal; many passages in the documents seem to fit in with it. But more closely examined, it proves unsatisfactory, first of all in regard to Clarendon's reasons. From September 17 to 21, Clarendon thought of using the Olmütz meeting to promote his own plan of settlement to replace the Vienna Note. On September 20, he instructed Westmorland to go to Olmütz to get Austria and Russia to approve a new British note designed to meet Turkey's objections. But once the instructions to Redcliffe regarding the fleets were sent out on September 23, Clarendon was determined in advance to reject any proposal from Olmütz, no matter what it might be. Hearing the news of Austria's proposal from Westmorland, but knowing no details, he told Cowley September 30, "I am sorry for this. It will probably be a fraud and will certainly be a botch." Since any proposal from Austria could not possibly satisfy Turkey, he said, he had already told Walewski and Colloredo it would have to be rejected. The next day, when Colloredo presented the proposal, Clarendon informed him that it was no use, for Russia had once for all revealed her aggressive aims. But at this same time he told Russell that it was Redcliffe who ruined the chances for peace, and that he (Clarendon) knew from three different sources that the Tsar in August had really wanted to accept Turkey's amendments to the Vienna Note, but Nesselrode had stopped him from doing so. Two days later Clarendon used the news of the Turkish Grand Council's resolution for war on September 26 as his reason for rejecting the Buol Project, without submitting it to the Cabinet. Palmerston approved heartily, applauding the Turks for resolving on war and insisting that no room was left for diplomacy. Britain must either surrender to Russia or give all out aid to the Turks.[48] *

This proves, to be sure, only that Clarendon had decided in advance to reject the Buol Project, that the ostensible reasons he gave for considering it harmful contradicted one another, and that he clearly did *not* believe that the violent interpretation rendered further assurances by Russia, like the Olmütz Declaration, unacceptable.

---

* Palmerston also urged Clarendon to confer with him, without going through the Cabinet, on how to provide British officers for the Turkish army.

On the contrary, he wrote Seymour that the Tsar at Olmütz "did eat dirt and went far to neutralize the dispatch of objections to the modifications." Seymour agreed; Nicholas was obviously trying to back down, and "the note cooked up by the Chancellor and Buol is a notable specimen of what can be done in the way of backing." [49]

The real reason why the Buol Project had to be rejected at London was first indicated by Cowley. He had the difficult task of persuading France to oppose a proposal which Napoleon, Drouyn, Morny, and the other great-power ministers at Paris all favored.[50] * Cowley himself had to confess, "I must say that I never expected to get as much out of the Czar"; if it were not for Redcliffe the conflict might still have been resolved. But having failed to convince Drouyn that the Olmütz scheme was obscure or unsatisfactory per se, Cowley came to his real objection: suppose the sea powers decided that the proposal was indeed adequate and safe for Turkey— would they be willing to *force* it on her, and to abandon her if she rejected it? Drouyn, according to Cowley, admitted that they would not, and this, Cowley said, was the crucial point. "The difficulty for us," Cowley warned Clarendon, "appears to me to avoid getting again into *the fix* out of which we have just escaped—that is finding ourselves advocating Russia against Turkey." Buol's plan might require this, and so it must not be approved.[51]

Clarendon argued this same point even more plainly to Walewski. Anglo-French acceptance, he said, would be a "fatal mistake" because

We would gratuitously replace Russia in the good position she had lost by Nesselrode's dispatch and resume the embarrassing position we were occupying previous to that dispatch, and secondly that we should expose ourselves to a certain refusal from the Porte and then find ourselves completely hampered, for by accepting the assurances of Russia

---

* In fact, as Buol pointed out to Drouyn, the Project was drawn from Drouyn's dispatch to Bourqueney on September 17. Bourqueney had therefore encouraged Buol to act as he did at Olmütz. Then when agreement was reached there, Bourqueney received a telegram on the twenty-eighth insisting that the violent interpretation had ruined the Vienna Note once for all. Britain, having previously compelled Drouyn to disavow the Vienna Note which he had authored, now made him oppose his own suggestion for saving it. Small wonder that Hübner found Drouyn reserved and irritable in discussing the Buol Project.

we should have shown ourselves satisfied with her and should find it extremely difficult it [sic] then to take active measures against her in support of the Turks who had a second time rejected our advice.

Walewski proposed that the four powers simply send the Tsar's assurances to the Sultan in a Vienna Conference protocol, with the sea powers recommending Turkish acceptance but exerting no pressure for it. Clarendon rejected this procedure as equally unsatisfactory. Even if Austria went along with it, which was doubtful, "France and England could not submit to having their *advice* rejected by the Porte." The sea powers must therefore "stick to our improved position and not impair it by vacillation"—must convince Russia and Austria that they were willing to go "the whole hog" in aid to Turkey.

Not that Clarendon was at all happy and sanguine about aiding the Turks. He continued to denounce them as the real warmongers, deplore the outrageous follies they would doubtless commit, and question whether Western sea power could really defend them against Russia. For a brief moment (or so he wrote Aberdeen on October 2) Clarendon hoped that Redcliffe would not actually summon up the fleets, but would "make the Porte decline the French fleet without the English." News of the Turkish war resolution of September 26, however, made Clarendon the next day call for sending in the fleets to Constantinople to defend Turkey; "*as yet*," he commented, "I don't see that we are required to take part in an offensive war." Without the Turkish action, he conceded, something might have been made of the Olmütz Project, but now it had to be rejected, for if Britain adopted it, "we would get a flat refusal [from Turkey] and thereby place ourselves in great difficulty about affording aid to the Turks hereafter." [52]

France went along with Britain readily enough in scuttling the Buol Project, partly to preserve the entente with her, partly because the Turkish war resolution seemed to render it nugatory, and partly because, despite Buol's insistence to the contrary, Russia's concessions led France to believe she could be forced to retreat still further. Otherwise, Bourqueney argued, Russia would not have tacitly swallowed the Western decision to send their fleets into the Straits; Buol's failure to protest against it indicated that Russia at Olmütz had given him orders not to protest. [53]

The one difficulty that remained was how to explain the rejection of the Buol Project to Austria, since intrinsically (as the British and French privately conceded) it satisfied the West's previous objections to the Vienna Note. France and Britain were not agreed on this point. Clarendon suggested that they condemn the Buol Project with the same arguments they had used against the violent interpretation (which, as he admitted, the Buol Project disavowed). The French balked at this; Cowley confessed his inability to get them to state that the project was intrinsically unsatisfactory. Drouyn explained to Vienna that France rejected it only because of Britain's attitude and the Turkish war resolution. To Cowley, Drouyn suggested that the sea powers, while thanking Buol for his efforts, should tell him he had ruined a good opportunity by waiting too long to bring his plan forward.

But London decided that the Buol Project must be another dishonest Austro-Russian trick. As Russell said, "Of course the proposition from Olmütz is intended only to deceive"; "if Nicholas, or Nesselrode, or Buol were to act honestly all might be settled in half an hour." [54] Clarendon therefore rejected the project with a mixture of quibbling and distortions (e.g., that the Vienna Conference had endorsed Turkey's amendments, and that the Tsar's declaration did not disavow the violent interpretation). Writing privately to Westmorland, Clarendon conceded that the Tsar's assurances were all very well. Buol, however, had spoiled them by trying to use them in behalf of the Vienna Note: "Buol is of course thoroughly Russian, and plays into the hands of his brother-in-law [Meyendorff],* but he seems to forget that England and France now united as one nation are not Russian." Buol wanted a patch-up peace only to save Russia; the West did not. Westmorland replied

* This common charge that Buol was pro-Russian and Meyendorff's tool may have been sincerely (though rather foolishly) held by some in Britain (e.g., Russell, Albert, and Victoria). Coming from Clarendon, however, it must be termed a deliberate falsehood. He had overwhelming testimony and evidence to the contrary from Westmorland, Bourqueney, and Seymour; he had often himself noted and rejoiced over the hatred the Tsar felt for Buol and his policy. As to Meyendorff, at the very moment Clarendon wrote this he had direct evidence of his feelings about Buol. On September 29, Cowley wrote Clarendon that he had talked with Meyendorff's son, who told him that his father had a very low opinion of Austria and its Emperor, and a still lower one of Buol, the worst anti-Russian of all (Clar. dep. c. 6).

plaintively: If you think everything was done wrong at Olmütz, why did you not give me different instructions in the first place? [55]

Buol's efforts to press the Olmütz Project on the Turks were obviously hopeless under these circumstances. But his instructions to Bruck do show the difference in spirit between his diplomacy and that of the sea powers. He adhered to the Vienna Note despite Turkey's objections, Russia's analyses of it, and its partial repudiation by other powers, he explained, because

The note is the work of the conference, and we grant to neither of the two sides the right to interpret it arbitrarily. We see in it neither the dangers which Turkey seeks in it nor the conclusions which Russia draws from it. We see in it still the best expedient for both sides to bring the ugly business to a close [*um den bösen Handel zu schlichten*].

No Constantinople concoction could serve to straighten out the conflict now; the Turkish government was even more disunited than the European cabinets, there was no unity among the representatives at Constantinople, and Redcliffe would never do anything that might reduce his own personal influence. The most important task, he urged Bruck, was to keep the Turks from believing that they could win more concessions by intransigence and delays, or that they could force Russia to evacuate the Principalities before Turkey negotiated a diplomatic settlement. This policy for Turkey would mean sacrificing the substance for a point of pride. After all, the goal both Turkey and the powers should be seeking was a Russo-Turkish reconciliation, and "coercive measures are not compatible with reconciliation." If the war party did force through a declaration of war at Constantinople, Bruck should openly condemn it.[56]

The Turkish war resolution (not yet quite a declaration of war) became known at Vienna the day this dispatch was written. It did not cause the Buol Project to fail, but it sealed its fate along with the Vienna Note. Now Austria had to try to localize and to end the Russo-Turkish conflict her efforts had failed to prevent.

V

The December 5 Protocol:
The Concert Compromised

The outbreak of Russo-Turkish war virtually forced Austria and Prussia to consider supporting each other in the East. Prince William, King Frederick William's brother and heir-apparent, urged a policy of joint neutrality at Olmütz and found Francis Joseph and Buol favorable to it. So was Nicholas; a guaranteed Austro-German neutrality was by now as much as he could hope for, and it would at least limit the number of his enemies and protect his most vulnerable frontier. But at a later meeting at Warsaw that the Tsar and Francis Joseph persuaded Frederick William to attend, Nicholas failed to get the guarantee of German neutrality he sought, and the Tsar's subsequent visit to Potsdam on October 8 failed as well.[1]

Manteuffel promptly took the credit for the Russian failure, telling London and Paris that he had defeated an Austrian proposal for a joint declaration of neutrality favorable to Russia. Buol vigorously denied this, pointing out that Prussia at the same time claimed at St. Petersburg that she had foiled an anti-Russian proposal by Austria. The Warsaw talks were secret, and so exactly what transpired is uncertain, but the participants' basic aims are fairly clear. Nicholas wanted the German powers by their neutrality to prevent the sea powers from intervening in his quarrel with Turkey. Buol wanted by joint neutrality to hold the Tsar to his promises to conduct a defensive, nonrevolutionary war and to respect the status quo. Francis Joseph, though angry about the trouble Russia was creating for Austria, feared mainly that the sea powers might promote war and revolution, and wanted Prussia to renew the 1851 defensive alliance, soon to expire, to meet this danger. He probably used Holy Alliance arguments with Prussia, though there is no reason to believe he had in mind holding the ring for Russia. As for Prussia, the

King in particular simply wanted to avoid involvement or giving offense to either side—hence his rejection of joint neutrality. But for once, paradoxically, the contradictory stories Prussia told the West and Russia may have been in a certain way true. That is, Prussia rejected simultaneously the neutrality based on the Holy Alliance that Francis Joseph envisioned and the neutrality directed implicitly against Russia desired by Buol.[2]

Undeterred, Austria announced her own neutrality on October 13, accompanying it by a large reduction in her standing army. This step had long been planned for financial reasons, but was reconsidered at a special ministerial conference on October 9 called by Francis Joseph at Kübeck's urging. The Emperor himself opposed the army reduction, arguing that the sea powers might adopt a policy that would force Austria to abandon her neutrality and to fight both them and the revolution. Kübeck argued similarly that the Eastern crisis might compel Austria to adopt armed neutrality. But Bach, Justice Minister Krauss, and Baumgartner favored the army reduction on financial grounds, and Buol defended it politically. With winter approaching, he foresaw little danger of general war or need for armed neutrality. The Tsar had given Austria satisfactory assurances; the sea powers really wanted peace. Moreover, the army reduction would help reassure and calm France, which seemed to believe that Austria somehow was threatening her. On this advice, Francis Joseph ordered the reduction.[3]

At first glance, Kübeck's and Francis Joseph's views seem far more prudent and farsighted than Buol's. Bruck later charged that the army reduction and neutrality proclamation ruined Austria's chances of decisively influencing the conflict, while Josef Redlich contends that they helped lull Russia into a false sense of security— both plausible criticisms.[4]

But they overlook one point. The Emperor, Kübeck, and the whole military establishment, though they disapproved of Russia's present policy, were not worried by the Russo-Turkish war per se. The only danger to Austria they saw was that France, intervening alone or along with Britain, would turn the conflict into a general revolutionary war, forcing Austria onto Russia's side.* Armed neu-

* This prevailing point of view was strikingly illustrated at a later ministerial conference of November 13, at a time when major fighting was going on

trality, therefore, was supposed to enable Austria to prevent or discourage any Western intervention, as well as Turkish incursions into Austria and Turkish- and Western-inspired revolutionary movements. It would thus be implicitly (for Bruck, explicitly) directed against the West and would serve to hold the ring for Russia, which Buol was determined not to do. While he hoped still to be able to mediate a peaceful settlement, he was convinced that Austria had no right to try to stop the sea powers if they chose to intervene on Turkey's side, and he knew that such an attempt would provoke the very revolutionary war the Emperor feared.

Thus Buol's argument that the army reduction would help reassure France was entirely sincere; the reduction would show that Austria was not going to attempt armed mediation, which the sea powers would not tolerate. Perhaps Buol should have tried harder to convince Francis Joseph and his fellow ministers of the Russian menace, but at the moment he had few concrete arguments to use. While Russia had recently done almost all Austria asked of her, Turkey had declared war and started the fighting, while the sea powers had ordered their ambassadors to summon the fleets into the Straits, had repudiated the Vienna Note and rejected the Buol Project, and were now trying to force Austria to take sides by bribes and threats.

In any case, Austria's neutrality proclamation and army reduction, reducing her effectives by 109,000 men, did not make a bad impression on Europe. Bourqueney interpreted the moves accurately as a demonstration of Austria's intent to remain genuinely neutral and to mediate. Hübner believed the measure helped calm war fever in France; Drouyn conceded that it was sensible as long as no large-scale fighting broke out, though Austria could not remain neutral in a general war. While the British viewed the proclamations as further proof of Austria's weakness and yearning for peace at any price,* it was not a bad idea to impress upon Britain that everyone in Austria wanted the war localized and ended. Meanwhile, Buol's

---

along the Danube. Francis Joseph and the military men present were concerned solely about possible Turkish incursions or the spread of Turkish-inspired revolts. Buol was the only one to mention a danger from Russia, and even he did this quite indirectly (MR Prot. 13).

* Count Mensdorff, former Austrian ambassador to England and a friend of Prince Albert, encouraged Albert in this view (Mensdorff-Albert, 17 and 25 Oct. 1853, RA G6/51 and 80).

proclamation and his instructions to Austrian envoys made clear that Austria's neutrality depended on the Tsar's keeping his promises on the conduct and aims of the war. When Drouyn complained that Austria's neutrality forced France to lean exclusively on England, Buol answered that if the Tsar broke his promises, Austrian neutrality would mean one hundred thousand men on Russia's flank and rear. The Tsar clearly saw the anti-Russian point of Buol's proclamation, but he tolerated it as the best to be hoped for then.[5]

Austria's neutrality declaration, in fact, was too anti-Russian for Prussia and Germany to support fully. A special mission by Prokesch to Berlin in October and an Austrian circular to the German courts on October 30 failed to gain Manteuffel's endorsement of it. Prokesch returned empty-handed to Frankfurt, advising Buol to drop the matter. But Buol went ahead with a unilateral Austrian declaration before the Diet on November 10, to which Bismarck replied by emphasizing Prussia's complete independence of decision.[6]

The Prussians presented plausible grounds for their refusal to join Austria: a joint declaration was premature, Austria's draft was too anti-Russian, it implied some commitment to Turkey, and it would impede joint four-power peace efforts. The real reasons lay deeper. Prokesch suggested that Prussia wanted to get Austria involved in war so that she could become the protector of Germany's neutrality. Buol knew that Manteuffel was trying to sell his refusal to join Austria as a favor to the West and a boon to Russia at the same time. But neither knew the main Prussian reason: Manteuffel, as will be seen, was secretly working with Britain to form a special three-power entente with the sea powers to isolate Austria and compel her either to follow their lead or go over to Russia.[7]

Meanwhile, Buol still tried to mediate in the Russo-Turkish conflict. When the Turks declared war and the Buol Project was rejected, he calmly turned to a new plan. On October 6, he wrote Nesselrode privately urging him to offer the Turks direct negotiations on the basis of the Olmütz Declaration and those parts of the Vienna Note both parties agreed on. Though the original Vienna Note had to be abandoned because of Turkish fanaticism and British prejudice, Buol argued, the sea powers might accept direct Russo-Turkish negotiations, and Austria would support such talks even if they did not. In any case, Russia had to move quickly before actual fighting broke out. Although the Tsar's initial reaction was cool, Nesselrode answered Buol on October 17 that Russia was willing to treat in spite of Turkey's declaration of war, though he posed unacceptable conditions, such as requiring the Turks to come to Russian headquarters at Bucharest for negotiations.[8] In hopes of a favorable reply, Buol had resisted Western demands for a new note to be pressed on Russia and Turkey, arguing that only a truce and direct negotiations would serve to stop the fighting that had already begun along the Danube.[9] Now that Russia had agreed to this in principle, Buol's main efforts would be directed for the next months to getting the sea powers, especially Britain, to go along.

Meanwhile, despite his instructions to Redcliffe to summon the fleets to Constantinople, Clarendon was still vacillating agonizingly over whether to press ahead with aid to Turkey regardless of the consequences or to try once more for a settlement through some new British version of the Vienna Note. His private letter of September 24 to Redcliffe, the day after the fateful instructions were sent, was a great jumble of confused griefs which ended in the conclusion that a new note would do no good because the Tsar could not be expected to submit to more humiliation and the Turks wanted war. Redcliffe should therefore advise London what kind of military help Turkey expected and how she could be aided by the fleets, a subject, Clarendon said, on which London was "entirely in the dark." [10] Russell, sympathizing with Clarendon on the evils and embarrassment involved in aiding Turkey, reminded him that Britain's honor was nonetheless at stake in it: "I know something of the English people and I feel sure they would fight to their stumps for the honour of England. To have held out such encouragement to the Turks as we have done, and afterwards to desert them would be felt as deep disgrace and humiliation by the whole country." [11]

But the argument of national honor, if it provided a sufficient rationale for helping Turkey, failed to answer questions about the means, efficacy, and extent of such aid. While Palmerston busily devised schemes for putting British and European officers in charge of the Turkish army, and Minto suggested forcing Austria to join the West on pain of having her Adriatic trade extinguished and her Italian territory liberated (good precautionary measures in any case, he advised), Russell's proposals of October 4 stimulated the most debate. Arguing that Turkey had a perfect right to declare war,* Russell proposed that the sea powers become Turkey's auxiliaries and enter the Black Sea, interdicting Russian supplies being sent elsewhere than into the Principalities. If Russia crossed the Danube, they should expand the naval war into the Baltic. The Sultan in exchange should agree in advance to equitable terms of peace (not defined) and immediately do something (not specified) to benefit his Christian subjects. If the sea powers became principals in the war, they should then reconsider the means and goals of their war effort.[12]

Palmerston applauded Russell's vindication of Turkey, but denounced the conditions and restrictions placed on Western aid, insisting that the fleets should immediately be sent into the Black Sea for unconditional assistance to her. Aberdeen, clinging to his post and his hope for peace, refused to make any commitments to Turkey. Gladstone and Graham supported him, but the most effective argument on their side came from Argyll, whose basic outlook, doubtless unbeknownst to him, was close to Buol's.† Though he despised the Turks, he admitted that they should be defended south of the Danube. But sending the fleets into the Black Sea now would appear to give British approval to the Turkish declaration of war; this would ruin British mediation, increase war fanaticism at Constantinople, and heighten the danger that the Turks would drag Britain in with them. Instead of bowing to Turkish pride or defending a theoretical Turkish independence that did not exist and could not be created, Britain should aim solely to make sure no one power gained an exclusive protectorate over Turkey. Any of the proposed notes would do this; they all demonstrated the right and determination of the four powers to act in united fashion to settle the Eastern

---

*In fact, said Russell, Turkey's *casus belli* against Russia was as good as Sardinia's against Austria.

†The British peace party often used arguments similar to those of Austria, yet they seldom mentioned this, either because they shared the prevailing British feelings about Austria, or because they were afraid of being accused of being soft on Habsburgism, or, most likely, because they simply were not aware of what Austria was doing and saying. For example, in a letter to Aberdeen on October 9, Graham asked plaintively: If the violent interpretation is the major reason for England's change of policy, would it not be possible to secure a retraction of it by diplomatic means? (RA G6/21). Obviously, Graham had no idea what the Buol Project had been all about.

question. With Turkey evidently now determined to fight on her own volition, but without relying on her own resources, the fleets ought to be restricted simply to saving Turkey *"from the extreme consequences of defeat."* If Britain insisted on doing more than this, she would have to cast off all restraints, and she ought at least first consider the costs, dangers, and incalculable consequences of fighting a European war for the sake of Turkey.[13]

Argyll's argument, which found considerable support at the Court, was harder to ignore or override than Aberdeen's hand-wringing hope-for-the-best counsel. In any case, on October 7 and 8, the Cabinet, in an uneasy compromise, evaded rather than solved the crucial questions of how far to aid Turkey, by what means, and to what end. Redcliffe, who had delayed summoning the fleets to Constantinople so as not to whip up war frenzy, would be strictly ordered to do so now. But the fleets, rather than either being sent directly into the Black Sea or confined solely to defending the Straits, would be empowered to enter the Black Sea to defend Turkey against a Russian attack if Redcliffe and the admirals decided the situation warranted it.

The compromise, undoubtedly another step toward war, really satisfied no one. Aberdeen, convinced the distinction between defensive and offensive action would soon break down, contemplated resignation. Victoria and Albert criticized him for agreeing without their sanction to a step that would compromise England.[14] Gladstone and Graham pleaded for peace and no commitments, Palmerston and Russell for all-out support of the Turks. Anything less, said Palmerston, "would be set down by all the world to an unworthy and abject fear of Russia"; the sea powers must win the contest with Russia, or sink into second class rank. Clarendon was pleased that his proposals had gone through and was sure that anything less would have outraged public opinion. But he still bewailed Britain's dependence on the "canaille" at Constantinople and he described the now certain prospect of European war over "a form of words" as "not only shocking but incredible."[15]

Meanwhile, Redcliffe had not attempted to stop the Turks from declaring war, but had tried to discourage them from waging it actively and to prepare them for a new note. He suggested to Clarendon either drawing up a truncated Vienna Note that the Turks would not object to, or making the four-power representatives at Constantinople, plus one other envoy, into an arbitral court to work out a new proposal based on the Olmütz Declaration and on the Vienna Note as amended by Turkey. Clarendon's many divergent reactions to these suggestions and to the Cabinet controversy make his real views and aims even harder than usual to decipher. He damned the Turks and defended the Russians to Redcliffe, urging him to make his proposed new note palatable to Russia and not to order the fleets into the Black Sea unless Russia was actually preparing a descent on Constantinople, so as not to ruin the reviving hope of negotiations.[16] Through Aberdeen, Clarendon informed Princess Lieven, socially prominent wife of the former Russian ambassador, that Britain had not rejected the Tsar's Olmütz Declaration; the Cabinet simply wanted to put it to better use. He secured Aberdeen's consent to a new version of the Vienna Note. It was drafted by the Turkish envoy Musurus Bey, but Clarendon seemed to agree with Aberdeen that the note had to contain some warning to the Turks. Moreover, he advocated both his version of the note and Redcliffe's project vigorously at Vienna, and thought of sending Granville to replace or assist Westmorland if any more important diplomatic business was to be done there—another sign of apparent seriousness about negotiation.[17]

Yet at the same time he adopted Palmerston's suggestions for the note, designed to make it unacceptable to Russia, and he agreed with Palmerston that the undertaking was really useless. Only Redcliffe's recommendations and the Cabinet's insistence on trying something, he argued, made it necessary.[18] What he told Cowley probably comes closest to his real thoughts: Britain had no quarrel at all with the Tsar, and therefore she should try to avoid or postpone a "gratuitous insult" like sending the fleets into the Black Sea. Peace was not absolutely impossible, for Redcliffe now seemed to be seeking it, but Austria's insincerity, Turkey's fanaticism, and the Tsar's understandable resentment of Turkey's challenge made it highly unlikely. In any case, this new note should be tried for appearances' sake: "Until the Turks get licked or frozen or drowned they won't discover the advantage of making peace. Still however this is Stratford's proposal and we should cut a bad figure in the blue book if we did not act upon this last chance for peace." [19]

All this would enable one to accept with reservations Temperley's view that Clarendon was sincerely trying to stem the drift toward war. Conciliating his colleagues and the public plainly was more important to him than settling the issues in dispute, and appearing to work for peace more vital than achieving it, but these attitudes, common enough in politics, do not necessarily disprove the genuineness of his attempt at a settlement through a new note and his desire at least to postpone a provocation of Russia in the Black Sea.

However, another little-noticed aspect of this peace effort, involving Austria in particular, does seem to call its genuineness into question. This is Clarendon's attempt with Palmerston and Russell to transfer the Vienna Conference to London, where a diplomatic solution worked out secretly with France and Prussia would be presented to Austria on a take-it-or-leave-it basis, and thereupon be imposed on Russia. The proposed transfer was originally Palmerston's idea, but Clarendon had earlier opposed it because he knew Austria would not consent to it and Russia would not accept a proposal reached without Austria. The Buol Project and the Tsar's Olmütz Declaration, however, convinced Clarendon that Russia was in retreat. On October 5, taking advantage of a vague hint from Manteuffel, he instructed Lord Loftus, chargé at Berlin, to get Prussia to propose moving the conference to London.[20]

This move was not due to the conviction that Austria was Russia's tool and advance guard or that she was useless in dealing with Russia. However much Clarendon talked about Russia and Austria as partners planning to partition the Ottoman Empire, the Olmütz meeting had again proved Clarendon's own thesis that Austria was the only possible mediator between Russia and the sea powers and was best able to extract concessions from Russia. Moreover, Clarendon was annoyed not by Austria's alleged pro-Russian sentiments, but by her eagerness to cooperate with the West. On October 7, he told Cowley that he would have to find a way somehow to reject Buol's Project without letting him know what the sea powers wanted in its stead, or "if we do, you may be sure that they [the Austrians] will take a stand upon that and renew it in some form or other which will only lead to disappointment and further waste of time." [21] The real reason Clarendon changed his mind and decided to get the conference moved to London was that he was now following Palmerston's direction, and Palmerston had always insisted that Britain must be seen to take the lead and control any settlement between Turkey and Russia.

Prussia was chosen to help execute this move not because her policy hitherto had been better than Austria's, for it had been clearly worse. In August, Clarendon complained sharply to Bloomfield that Manteuffel, Britain's favorite, lagged behind Buol on the Eastern question; all through September, Prussia's timidity and Russian leanings were constantly compared unfavorably with Austria's attitude. On October 8, Clarendon told Cowley he expected both Austria and Prussia to sign treaties with Russia at Warsaw.[22] Only after this move was launched did he hear of Manteuffel's claim to have frustrated an Austro-Russian plot, which like other Englishmen he believed without waiting for evidence.[23] Prussia was useful to Britain because she was Austria's rival and wanted to isolate her and gain the lead in Germany, and because Prussia fit at least potentially into Palmerston's plan for a great league of liberal constitutional states led by Britain against Russia, while Austria did not.

With Prussia supposed to take the initiative (actually Manteuffel proved shifty on this point as on most others), Clarendon tentatively broached the idea of a London conference to St. Petersburg and instructed Westmorland to get Austria to make the Tsar accept it. Of course, he said, he expected Austria to be unreasonable about it. But Buol must clearly understand that a London conference was the only hope of peace—Clarendon claimed he could whip up a note satisfactory to both sides there in no time—and if Austria did not abandon her own mediation efforts and cooperate wholeheartedly, the results would be war, alienation from France and Britain, and revolution all over Italy.[24] Russell drew up on October 16 a note for the London conference to endorse and submit to the Porte, to serve as a foundation for the peace treaty he now tardily recognized would be necessary. The note's basis would be either the Vienna Note, somewhat revised, or the Buol Project, or both.* As for the procedure to follow, Russell remarked: "I believe these views to agree with those of Drouyn and Manteuffel and Lord Stratford— If so we should easily carry them into effect in the Conference of

---

* Russell, here and at other times, based his own peace proposals on plans that he denounced as deceitful tricks when Austria proposed them.

London and Austria might conform or separate from the three as she pleased."

Clarendon agreed with Russell that Austria had to be presented with a *fait accompli*, but he had various objections to the proposed procedure. The chief one was that Redcliffe wanted all four powers to support the proposed note that he, Lacour, and Reshid would work out at Constantinople on the basis of Clarendon's and Musurus's suggestions. But Clarendon thought he saw a way to make Austria support Britain's terms both at St. Petersburg and Constantinople without letting her into any meaningful negotiations or decisions. Britain should inform Prussia in advance of what she wanted, since Manteuffel, Clarendon explained, wanted to break with Austria and have everything settled in partnership with Britain at London. Then Britain should send the proposed note to Redcliffe, simultaneously asking Berlin and Vienna to support it at Constantinople. This would satisfy Redcliffe's desire for four-power action, he told Palmerston; "otherwise I think the less we have to do with Austria the better." [25]

Palmerston cared little for these questions of procedure, and still less about how to justify the move to London.* His only concern was to get the conference away from Vienna and to control the settlement it would dictate to Russia. Russia's treaty rights vis-à-vis Turkey had to be completely eliminated; Turkey must have the right to change the proposed note, already pro-Turkish, in any way she wanted; and there must be no hint of withdrawing support from her if she refused. Once again Palmerston made his familiar argument about losing caste in Europe if the sea powers failed wholeheartedly to back Turkey because of the "shabby pretext" that she declined to follow their advice.[26]

Russell agreed entirely, repeatedly reminding Clarendon to discourage Buol and to prevent any revival of the Vienna Conference.

---

* Palmerston proposed that Austria and Prussia simply be told (to the latter's delight) that they had broken up the Vienna Conference and separated themselves from the sea powers, and so no more conferences could be held except at London. If a further reason was demanded, England should say that Olmütz and Warsaw had, fairly or unfairly, destroyed Austria's reputation for impartiality and therefore "the two powers who are prepared and who intend to support Turkey can negociate only in one or the other of their two capitals." That is, Vienna was unsuitable for mediation because Austria had allegedly compromised her impartiality as a mediator; London or Paris was suitable because the sea powers were openly partial to one side.

Clarendon and Bunsen meanwhile conferred on the note to be sent to Redcliffe and sprung on Austria, a note Bunsen told Manteuffel would be cast in the terms and spirit of the Buol Project. Clarendon, Bunsen confided to Albert, was uneasy about the secrecy practiced over against Austria, but recognized its necessity. Clarendon was nervous only because he feared his scheme might backfire on him; on October 18, he suggested to Cowley still another way of using Austria without letting her participate in negotiations. The sea powers should present their note alone to the Porte, get its consent first, and then ask Austria and Prussia to make Russia sign it. True, this would sacrifice the four-power action Redcliffe wanted at Constantinople, and Buol was eager to act with the West. But Austria and Prussia counted for nothing at Constantinople anyway, and Buol was really waiting for Russia's orders. He would learn while waiting, Clarendon told Palmerston, that Britain could do without him.[27]

Still, some answer had to be given to Buol's repeated and urgent offers of cooperation, and Clarendon supplied it in two private letters to Westmorland on October 19. The first proved by means of the Sichel case of the previous summer that Buol was pro-Russian, anti-British, and indifferent to every English desire expressed since Clarendon had taken office. The second blamed Austria for Turkey's declaration of war; her stand on the Vienna Note "drove the Sultan to convoke that Council which decided in favor of war, and left him no option about declaring it." Buol was also accused of trying to exclude the sea powers from a direct Russo-Turkish settlement (an exact parallel to what Clarendon was really doing to Austria) and of seeking an offensive-defensive alliance with Russia against the West.[28] It is perfectly obvious that Clarendon knew better than these charges.* Westmorland in his reply to Clarendon repeated Buol's previous denials of these accusations and developed further his point-by-point refutation. Finally the long-suffering Westmorland challenged Clarendon to send him the information on which he based his views, and though he (Westmorland) considered it

---

* On this same day he wrote Loftus offering to let Manteuffel, as a reward for his "frank and fair" conduct, see and consult in advance on the Anglo-French note, to be conveyed to Austria only after its conclusion. But he also told Loftus that Buol had swallowed Britain's rejection of the Olmütz Project very calmly and was extremely eager to work with Britain.

wholly erroneous, he would use it any way he was instructed to, acting in the meantime as if his own information was correct. Clarendon did not respond.[29]

Since the attempt to move the conference to London, as will be seen, ultimately failed, it could plausibly be dismissed as a minor episode not worth discussing. In fact, it says something significant about its sponsors. This was not merely an effort to move the conference to an allegedly more suitable site; it represented an attempt to exclude Austria from any effective or meaningful role in Concert diplomacy and to impose on Russia an Anglo-French-Turkish solution to the Eastern question. Hardly any step in nineteenth-century diplomacy was more serious or any affront graver than excluding a great power from the Eastern question. When Palmerston had led the three Eastern powers in July 1840 to sign with Britain a convention in support of Turkey without France's participation, France had armed and nearly gone to war, producing the worst crisis in Europe since 1815. Palmerston could then argue that France had excluded herself by failing to help negotiate and to sign the convention. Here in 1853, when Austria's interests were more directly affected than anyone else's, when her policy had run parallel to Britain's in recent months as in most of the recent decades, when she was desperately striving to cooperate with the powers to prevent war, maintain the European Concert, and uphold Turkey's integrity, Britain secretly conspired with her rival Prussia to concoct a settlement that Austria would either have to accept and help impose on Russia or to reject, joining Russia and suffering the consequences. It adds a certain touch to this proceeding, moreover, that the British intended to use the declaration Buol had secured from Nicholas at Olmütz as one of the weapons to isolate Austria and defeat Russia diplomatically—the declaration that they had denounced to Austria as useless and a trick, but that Clarendon had told Princess Lieven the British only wished to put to more suitable use.

A further point is still more important. Clarendon knew and stressed repeatedly that the only road to peace was a settlement that would both protect Turkey and enable Russia to retreat with her honor and vital interests intact. He also knew that Austrian participation in a settlement was indispensable to these ends; so did Redcliffe. The clear choice here was between Concert diplomacy including

Austria and an Anglo-French confrontation with Russia effectively excluding her, and Palmerston wanted the latter. His whole aim in moving the conference to London was to gain what a Vienna conference could never give him, a proposal that would if accepted by Russia publicly proclaim Britain's victory over her and destroy Russia's position in the East, and if rejected would mean European war. It is pointless to argue that Palmerston would have preferred to gain these ends by peaceful means; statesmen seldom prefer violence when they can gain what they want otherwise. To insist on ends impossible to achieve except by the political humiliation of one's opponent is to want war, and this is what Palmerston demanded. The only question about him is whether he wanted war with Austria as well as with Russia.

As for Russell, he was so erratic that it is hard ever to know what he really wanted. But it is clear enough that he would accept war and that he detested Austria at least as much as Russia.[30] One must also take Clarendon's capacity for inconsistency into account. Yet he surely knew, as his private correspondence shows, that the Tsar could not be expected to go to Canossa, accepting at a London Conference a proposal produced by Musurus Bey, Palmerston, Redcliffe, and Reshid. Seymour, who was extremely reluctant even to mention the idea of a London conference to Nicholas, warned repeatedly that this was out of the question; Aberdeen, hearing later of this effort carried on behind his back, called it "morbid" and said that only those who wanted to make peace impossible could sponsor it.[31]

The general Cabinet conflict over policy, as it happened, obstructed the plan for a London conference. Clarendon wanted to avoid Cabinet debate by drawing up his proposed note solely with Palmerston and Russell, but Aberdeen had to be consulted. Despite Palmerston's objections and Russell's renewed threat to resign, Aberdeen demanded that Turkey be required to accept the note without alterations and be warned that her response would affect future Western aid to her. The Court, Newcastle, Graham, Gladstone, and Argyll all agreed with him.[32] Nonetheless, at a Cabinet of October 20, Aberdeen, warned by Clarendon of an imminent breakup of the Cabinet and fearful himself of the public reaction to anything that appeared to be British bullying of Turkey, gave up his demand that the Turks would have to accept the note without changes. In its place, Aberdeen told Gladstone, he would try to insert in the note a requirement that Turkey accept an armistice during the negotiations the sea powers would undertake on her behalf. Clarendon would support this idea, Aberdeen believed, and the Turks would refuse it, leaving Britain's hands once again free.[33] *

But Aberdeen asked a price for allowing the Turks to demand changes in the proposed note—Austria must be included in the *démarche*. Clarendon now had to persuade Palmerston to accept this demand, which he said Aberdeen would take to the Cabinet if necessary. After setting out Aberdeen's arguments, Clarendon added his own reasons for considering Austria's participation relatively harmless. Buol's abandonment of the Vienna Note and the Olmütz Project proved that he had received the Tsar's orders "to agree to whatever we propose." It made little practical difference which powers presented the note at Constantinople anyway, since the Turks would surely reject it; but Redcliffe had called for four-power participation, and the public would not like it if this was ignored. Clarendon conceded that it was difficult to tell "whether we should stand better or not in the Blue Book for permitting Austria and Prussia to act with us." However, the concession would buy Aberdeen's agreement that the four powers could endorse any modifications Turkey proposed. Moreover, the *démarche* would not revive the Vienna Conference. The note would simply be communicated to Austria "to support it or not as they pleased at Constantinople." [34]

Though Russell grumbled about this wasted effort and "fresh attempts to please Austria," he and Palmerston agreed, providing this new step did not revive the Vienna Conference.[35] Controversy still arose over Aberdeen's desire to warn Turkey that her response

* Gladstone replied that he thought the best way to preserve Britain's free hand was simply to tell Turkey that she disapproved of Turkey's declaration of war and refused "to be bound by its results" (21 Oct. 1853, Add. ms. 43070). This reply, like Aberdeen's suggestion, shows that the Peelites, except for Argyll, had no constructive alternative to pose to Palmerston's policy of confrontation. They implied, even advocated, simply abandoning Turkey to Russia if she proved stubborn—a course equally rash for foreign and domestic policy. The sound alternative was Argyll's (and Austria's): to insist that the four European powers had a permanent right to intervene between Russia and Turkey to settle quarrels and prevent war. (See Argyll to Russell, 18 and 19 Oct., PRO 30/22/11B).

to the note would affect Britain's future support of her. For the Peelites this warning was to be an escape clause; for Albert and Argyll, it was a means to allow Britain to support strictly European interests rather than purely Turkish ones; for Palmerston it represented a cowardly abandonment of Turkey that would justify breaking up the government.[36]

Again Clarendon had to mediate frantically, agreeing with Aberdeen on an escape clause, and at the same time assuring Palmerston that it implied no abandonment of Turkey, but was only supposed to appease Aberdeen and the Court and to make the Sultan "believe we are masters of our own policy." [37] To Cowley, after pouring out his hatred of Austria, aversion to Concert diplomacy, humiliation at being unable to control the Turks, and fear lest the public discover that Russia's policy was really conciliatory and Britain's position a shameful one, Clarendon revealed his real intent in the note with its warning passage. Its purpose, he explained, was to delineate British policy better, to prevent the public from saying that Britain had "thrown away a glorious opportunity for making peace" and had let herself be dragged into war by the Turks. Without it, Britain would have to "bear the whole responsibility of the war which I look upon as inevitable." "These are not reasons to give to a foreign government," Clarendon reminded Cowley, "but you will understand their *domestic cogency*." Besides, "collateral advantages" might be gained if Turkey unexpectedly accepted the note. For Russia would then be trapped. If she accepted it in turn, Britain would have a complete victory over her; if she refused it, Britain would have "a real good case both at home and abroad for lustily aiding the Turks." [38] Ridden though Clarendon was by various fears, the main peril he dreaded was, as always, political trouble at home, and the best way to avoid it remained that of making Russia appear to be in the wrong. Like Palmerston, he now concentrated on winning the game. Although Britain, as he told Cowley, really had no quarrel with Russia, "France and England having embarked in this business *they must win* and we must not contemplate any other issue as possible." [39] With Clarendon in this mood, Palmerston could accept the final passage in the note, knowing that it still left the decision for peace and war in Turkey's hands and confident events would go his way.

On October 25, Clarendon sent the note to Stratford and dispatches to Westmorland and Bloomfield calling for immediate and unconditional Austrian and Prussian approval of it. By coincidence, Buol reconvened the Vienna Conference that same day to consider his proposal: let the four powers send Turkey the Russians' invitation to peace negotiations, along with a four-power note urging Turkey to accept negotiations at some neutral spot where her friends could support her (Vienna was meant but not mentioned). Buol pleaded for approval of his plan and for authorizing the conference to draw up the note to Constantinople. Clarendon immediately refused without waiting for details. Austria was heart and soul with Russia in wanting to destroy Turkey, he said; the Turks were far too righteously angry at Vienna to listen to anything that came from there.[40]

Paris reacted differently. Drouyn privately agreed with Buol that Britain's projects were unsuitable (though he dared not tell London so, and Bourqueney had to support them at Vienna). Besides, he still wanted Austria and Prussia to take the lead and responsibility in peacemaking. Baron Thouvenel, director of the Foreign Ministry's Political Department, viewed Buol's plan and the revived Vienna Conference as a great hope for peace; Bourqueney seconded Buol's pleas, underlining his hints that even an unsuccessful negotiation carried through together by the powers would tend to unite them for the future. So Drouyn, while criticizing Buol's proposal itself as inadequate and dangerous, told London that France wanted to exploit it.[41]

Austria's initiative became even harder to reject when Britain's proposed note began to collapse under Buol's polite but firm critique, to which Bourqueney and Westmorland could find no answer. A simple note would no longer suffice as a basis for settlement, he said, now that war had been declared and fighting begun. Moreover, Britain's note contained phrases Turkey had specifically objected to, it did not provide for an armistice or for the evacuation of the Principalities, and it did not even explain how Reshid was supposed to address and transmit a note to a power with whom Turkey had broken relations and was at war. In addition, the longer Turkey resisted Redcliffe's advice, the harder it became for Clarendon to insist that the Vienna Conference must simply endorse the terms

Redcliffe was going to send them from Constantinople.[42] Buol, who told Francis Joseph that the British proposal was "a washed-out copy of the Olmütz idea," [43] remained calm during the conferences. But the gulf between his spirit and aims and those of the sea powers, and his growing desperation, were made clear in his letter of November 1 to Hübner:

What can I tell you except that the time for notes seems to me past, at least that of imposing them on others. This was from the beginning an unfortunate idea of Russia which we perhaps should not have insisted on and which in any case we retained too long. The projects rain from all sides *et hinc illae lacrimae.* I hardly digested the Clarendon project when Lord Westmorland produced another one for me which arrived all hot from Constantinople, and I hear still a third cited (French), of which there is a rumor in Berlin. It seems to me impossible to find a way out except by bringing the two contending parties together to argue out their griefs. Does this mean that we have to abandon the fate of the negotiation to the play of intimidation and bribery? By no means! It is precisely up to us to watch over European interests and not to allow the weaker party to be unduly pressured. If only they would give the conference a certain power to act! But instead of leaving the lead to it, they act without consulting it, they make it take on the role of intermediary, and they paralyze its influence by setting it in contradiction with itself. From this conference *à quatre,* another *à six* would develop later by necessity. The Russo-Turk quarrel once ended, it would be necessary to reconvene if only to reestablish the treaty of 1841, which is today practically suspended. That would be precisely the moment to occupy ourselves jointly with the improvement of the lot of the Christians in Turkey.

But to arrive at these ends, it is essential first to end the state of war, and is it possible to imagine that one could ever arrive at that goal through the Clarendon project, which bears the stamp of the most inconceivable levity? It does not mention either the state of war or the evacuation of the Principalities. One would suppose then that if the Porte did not recoup this and if it declared itself satisfied, England would also drop the matter. But I am going to stop, I do not wish to bring out all its vices, this could bring me to the point of slander.

Out of consideration for the other powers, Buol continued—a consideration Britain had completely failed to show Austria—Austria had thus far waited to convey to Turkey the Russians' invitation to treat. But she could not wait forever, for the Turks' sake and for the sake of keeping her promise to Russia. She needed an answer to her proposal soon, and counted on Paris to help overcome the difficulties raised by London.[44]

Buol's belief that France's aims were fundamentally the same as Austria's, nourished by what Drouyn said to Hübner and Bourqueney rather than to Cowley, was quite mistaken. The French insisted on having any Russo-Turkish negotiations carried on in a way designed to humiliate Russia: the terms of peace were to be first worked out by the Vienna Conference, then passed to Turkey, and finally submitted to Russia in an open six-power session. Yet Drouyn did give Austria some support at London and agreed that the actual Russo-Turkish talks need not occur in the physical presence of the four-power representatives.[45] To meet France's requirements, Buol proposed on November 6 that the conference be authorized to draft a note to Turkey such as the French and, professedly, the British wanted. It would recall the 1841 Preamble, recapitulate the Tsar's Olmütz assurances and the Porte's promises to observe existing treaties, and invite the Porte to state its terms for treating with Russia. The recent serious battle of Oltenița on the Danube showed how dangerous further delay was, Buol pleaded; France must help overcome Britain's prejudices against any and every Austrian proposal and join in getting the belligerents to the conference table.[46]

Drouyn, still mainly interested in destroying the Holy Alliance, was immune to this appeal but at least refused to reject Buol's proposal outright. Cowley argued that it had to be followed up, even though Austria was doubtless Russia's advance guard, for it was the only idea "likely to lead to a practical solution," and there would be real trouble with France if Britain simply spurned it. Drouyn favored the idea with modifications and at least wanted so to revise it that Buol, not the sea powers, would repudiate it.[47] Clarendon was already under Drouyn's fire over the difficulties caused to France by Britain's "extreme prejudice" against Austria.[48] * Finally aware that his proposed note would not do, Clarendon conceded that Buol's plan looked good, though adding, "I distrust all that comes from

---

* Clarendon replied to Cowley that it was mean of Drouyn to complain in this way. Of course Britain distrusted Austria; Buol was simply trying to save Russia from defeat and rob Turkey of her victories by arranging an armistice. This made it all the more vital to move the conference to London. Cowley's main task would be "to persuade the Emperor . . . that Buol is Meyendorff,

Vienna." Palmerston suggested three conditions that would disarm this treacherous Austrian proposal. First, the conference must be moved to London or at least to a neutral site—Paris, Brussels, Frankfort, Dresden, or Prague.* Second, the peace terms must include the revision or nonrenewal of all Russo-Turkish treaties and the transfer of Russia's protectorate over the Principalities, Serbia, and the Orthodox Christians in Turkey to all five powers. Finally, in order to get an armistice and negotiations, Russia must first evacuate the Principalities while Turkey retired behind the Danube.[49]

Clarendon quickly fell into line, pressing for Palmerston's conditions at Paris, St. Petersburg, and Vienna,[50] despite his own grave doubts about these demands and his knowledge of what they implied for peace. While he insisted on a London conference as the price for Britain's participation in four-power mediation, he told Cowley that Nicholas would never accept Britain and France as mediators, and he had no answer when Colloredo reminded him of his own earlier arguments that Austria was the only suitable one.[51] He supported the idea of treaty revisions before the other powers and instructed Seymour to take this up with Russia, despite the fact that the Cabinet on November 10 decided against demanding them. He also persisted in calling for Russian evacuation prior to an armistice, assuring Aberdeen that this step "might suit the Emperor Nicholas" and should be tried. (Aberdeen replied that it would be taken as an insult by Russia and as hardly serious by Austria.) Yet Clarendon himself condemned such ideas to Redcliffe and told Palmerston that treaty revisions were impossible unless Russia suffered great military defeats and that, as Seymour repeatedly reported, evacuation of the Principalities as a precondition for negotiations was out of the question. "Nicholas," he wrote, "seems now prepared to eat a great deal of dirt and to swallow modifications and other things he would not look at 4 months ago but I suppose there must be a limit." [52]

It is most striking that while Clarendon was following the Home

---

that Meyendorff is Nicholas and that the Turks know it." Moreover, France and Britain were ignored and allowed to play only secondary roles at Vienna. To Westmorland, who also relayed French complaints, Clarendon wrote: "I am utterly at a loss to know what Drouyn means by our hatred and distrust of Austria. We have none."

*Clarendon's letter of 4 Nov. 1853 to Cowley (FO 519/169) indicates that the reason for mentioning Prague, also an Austrian city, was that there the sea powers would at least get rid of Buol and Westmorland.

Secretary's lead in foreign policy so closely that often Palmerston's very words to Clarendon on one day would be in Clarendon's dispatches the next, he at the same time condemned Palmerston's intention to tie Britain hand and foot to Turkey and bring her into war.* It is barely possible that Clarendon really believed that all-out aid to Turkey now, even though she was in the wrong, was the only way to prevent war.[53] But the bulk of the evidence suggests once more that, ridden by his fears, he was no longer trying to control events but only to save appearances.[54]

Drouyn was willing to join in demanding a Russian evacuation as a condition for an armistice, not to help the Turks—Napoleon despised them and wanted to force both sides to accept any terms the four powers proposed [55]—but in order to get Austria to commit herself further against Russia. To this end he had long urged Austria to occupy part of the Principalities and to send reinforcements to Transylvania. He had offered Austria Russia's protectorates on the Danube and territorial annexations at its mouth, and threatened to let Russia keep the Principalities along with Serbia and Bosnia if she failed to act. He charged Austria with subservience to Russian plans for a partition of Turkey and with plotting with Rome to destroy France's Catholic protectorate in the East. A principal reason why he wanted an Anglo-French occupation of the Black Sea was to make Russia's presence in the Principalities a menace to Austria rather than to Turkey. Now he hoped to make Austria help force Russia out of the Principalities before she could obtain the armistice Buol desired so desperately.[56]

France's chief threat all the while was that of unleashing revolution and war in Italy. Napoleon, Eugénie, Drouyn, and others frequently voiced it directly and indirectly; France even seemed to be preparing for some such move. Hübner thought he detected troop movements in Provence; Apponyi at Turin and the Austrian chargé Count Paar, who succeeded him, both reported rumors of secret treaties or understandings between Sardinia and the sea powers for

---

* For example, Clarendon denounced as the most impudent thing he had ever seen Reshid's request for an Anglo-French-Turkish military convention committing the sea powers to various kinds of military aid to Turkey. But he and others in England knew that this was Palmerston's doing as well as Redcliffe's; Palmerston had discussed this very idea with Clarendon four weeks before (Clarendon to Cowley, 8 Nov. 1853, FO 519/169; Albert's memorandum, 6 Nov., RA G6/113).

action against Austria in case of war.[57] The mission of Baron Brenier, former foreign minister and an Italophile liberal, to Italy in early December was a dangerous omen, reminding Austria of France's competition with her for influence and of Austria's great vulnerability in this theater.[58]

It is often supposed that France's pressure worked; Austria's pro-Western policy is seen as the result of fear of France, especially over Italy. Naturally Buol took this pressure and the danger in Italy seriously. He had his agents check out rumors of Western understandings with Sardinia or French encouragement to revolutionaries, and he tried to calm Austria's nervous client states. To promote good relations, he curbed attacks on Napoleon in the Austrian press.[59] Through constant pressure Bourqueney managed to extract from Buol some tentative, qualified promises of future action. If the war became prolonged and menaced the European status quo or balance, Buol would say, Austria would do her duty; or, Austria would not fire the first shot, but she would not necessarily remain inactive. The sea powers naturally tried to stretch and distort these statements, regularly connected with pleas for cooperation to help make the current peace efforts succeed, into hard-and-fast Austrian commitments.[60]

But in the main France's bribes and threats did not work. After a time Bourqueney gave up trying to tempt Buol with the Principalities, telling Drouyn that Vienna was not yet ready for this approach. Hübner, frightened by the menace of revolution, began hinting at an alliance with France in October. But Hübner's advice was not followed by Buol, while his indiscreet and disloyal language and conduct at Paris did both Buol and Austrian policy considerable harm.* At Vienna, France's overt threats proved counterproductive,

---

* According to Cowley, Hübner called Buol unfit for his position and said that Austria should long ago have told Russia that her crossing the Prut would be Austria's *casus belli*. He also claimed that Buol wanted to detach France from Britain and that he (Hübner) had accrued great unpopularity in Vienna for having forced Austria to work with the sea powers. The latter statements were of course flatly untrue; in fact, the policy of trying to separate France from Britain was Hübner's and Prokesch's, but not Buol's (Cowley to Clarendon, private, 7 and 30 Nov. and 8 Dec. 1853, Clar. dep. c. 7). For more evidence of Hübner's self-importance, superior attitude over against Buol, and belief that he was responsible for forcing him into a pro-Western policy, see Hübner, I, 142–43, 178–80, 193–94, and 213.

1. Count Buol. From an 1854 lithograph. Bild-Archiv der Österreichischen Nationalbibliothek, Vienna.

2. Emperor Francis Joseph in 1859. Bild-Archiv der Österreichischen Nationalbibliothek, Vienna.

3. Baron Prokesch. From an 1853 lithograph. Bild-Archiv der Österreichischen Nationalbibliothek, Vienna.

4. The Vienna Conference, 1855. Plenipotentiaries, from left to right: Westmorland, Bourqueney, Russell, Drouyn, Buol, Prokesch, Ali Pasha, Arif Efendi, Titov, Gorchakov. Bild-Archiv der Österreichischen Nationalbibliothek, Vienna.

5. Tsar Nicholas I. From an 1854 lithograph. Bild-Archiv der Österreichischen Nationalbibliothek, Vienna.

6. Count Nesselrode. Bild-Archiv der Österreichischen Nationalbibliothek, Vienna.

7. Emperor Napoleon III.
Bild-Archiv der Öster-
reichischen Nationalbib-
liothek, Vienna.

8. Count Walewski. From
a lithograph. Bild-Archiv
der Österreichischen Na-
tionalbibliothek, Vienna.

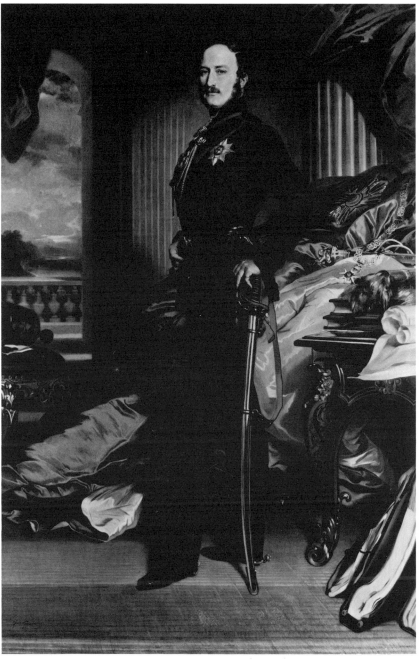

9. Prince Albert. Portrait by Franz Xaver Winterhalter. National Portrait Gallery, London.

10. Viscount Palmerston. Sculpture by E. E. Wyon. National Portrait Gallery, London.

11. The Aberdeen Coalition Ministry. Left to right: Wood, Graham, Molesworth, Gladstone, Argyll, Clarendon, Lansdowne, Russell, Granville, Aberdeen, Cranworth, Palmerston, Grey, Herbert, Newcastle. Artist, John Gilbert. National Portrait Gallery, London.

12. Lord John Russell. Portrait by Francis Grant. National Portrait Gallery, London.

13. The Earl of Clarendon. A detail from Plate 11. National Portrait Gallery, London.

14. The Paris Peace Congress, 1856. From a lithograph. From left clockwise: Bourqueney, Cowley, Djemil-Bey, Clarendon, Walewski, Orlov, Brunnow, Buol, Hübner, Villamarina, Cavour, Ali Pasha. Bild-Archiv der Österreichischen Nationalbibliothek, Vienna.

giving ammunition to Buol's opponents and making it harder for him to carry out his policy of cooperation with the West. When Buol heard of such threats he repudiated them in unmistakable terms.[61] Noting that Drouyn in private conversations with Hübner had shown "a certain tendency toward intimidation" and a desire to force Austria into war against Russia, Buol replied:

If the Minister was able really to believe that this language would produce an effect on us, it would be right and fair to undeceive him once and for all. The idea of wanting by threats (and what a threat indeed, for a good and honest war one could understand!) to entangle us in a fight which would not suit us, seems to me so *monstrous* that I refuse to credit it. We would believe, in addition, that this would not change our stand in any way. From that day on [i.e., of French-inspired revolution in Italy] there would be no more Eastern question for us. No doubt it is possible to force us into war, but to dictate to us against whom we will fight: never! If France wants to be on terms of good friendship with Austria, it will depend solely on her, but it will never be except on the basis of *perfect equality*. We respect the independence of action to which every foreign government has a right, but we ask that others show the same respect to us.

Besides, M. Drouyn de Lhuys proceeds from premises which are not sound. I do not believe that it was up to us to prevent the Emperor Nicholas from occupying the Principalities; still less do I believe that a tone of threat on our part would be timely today, and that it would produce the desired effect. He says that France and England have frankly made up their minds, and that it is up to Austria to declare herself. But it seems to me that our particular position is very clear in the eyes of Russia at least and that she knows what to believe. The feeling that she cannot count on us worries her perhaps more than the two fleets, which passed the Dardanelles when they could not any longer stay at Besika, and the sending of an Ambassador-General [Baragueys d'Hilliers] who is offered, in a pinch, as commander for *the Turk army*.

If then France wants to make war for the *Turks*, that is her affair, provided that she does not seem to want to force others to do the same. It is the Turks who have declared war, that is obvious, I do not deny that they may have been provoked into it; nevertheless, finally they decided to run the risks of war. The Russians, in consequence, have a right to accept the challenge and even to defeat their enemy if they can. As for us, we do not want to fight either for the crescent or for the Greek cross. We could never be forced into the struggle except for questions of a European scope that are connected with it. But even then we would not allow either the time or the field of our operations to be imposed on us. If we are obliged to penetrate into Wallachia or Serbia, the orders for it are not going to come from Paris. And let them set their minds at ease, we are not going to seize anything *as a security* ["Nous ne prendrons pas *de gage*"]. They would be wrong either to fear it or hope for it at Paris. Austria undoubtedly will have a major word to say in this question, it may even have the last word, but it will not be such a dupe as to fire the first cannon. . . .

Let us hope that we will not come to these extremities and that Europe will still escape the crisis that menaces it. We are finally, and not without difficulty, on the right path, for which the credit in great part belongs to the French cabinet. It has been able to reconquer a very necessary influence over the English ministers, who are too preoccupied with the blue book and with their portfolios to follow a reasoned and reasonable course. Let France act on London, we will try to make our influence good at St. Petersburg, and possibly everything can still be settled.[62]

This kind of language, of which this was not the only instance, had an immediate salutary effect. Drouyn promptly denied any intention of ever threatening Austria and urged Bourqueney to soothe Buol's feelings; he only wanted to point out the connection between the Eastern and Western questions and to show that France was sensitive to Austria's Danubian and other European interests as Britain was not.[63]

What frightened Buol most was not French threats, but the danger that Russia's offer to treat with Turkey would remain unexploited. His pleas ignored by the West, he finally sent Russia's invitation to Constantinople on November 11 himself, first notifying the other powers of this move, which he had warned them he would eventually have to take. He may have hoped to jar them into action, or the move may have represented an *acquit de conscience* toward Russia, for Buol knew that it could not succeed if the other powers did not support it.[64] Clarendon promptly denounced it as a Russian plot and ordered Stratford to oppose it. However, he decided to test Buol on his earlier proposal of November 6, which had suggested a four-power note to Turkey from the Vienna Conference requesting her to state her conditions for treating with Russia. Clarendon proposed that Britain and France should agree to such a note, provided that Russia, in order to obtain an armistice, be required to accept without alterations whatever terms Turkey advanced. If Buol, as Clarendon expected, rejected this proposal, it would show that he was obviously acting for Russia; if he accepted these conditions, it would prove that Russia had really backed down out of fear of war, in which case the sea powers could expect to make great gains at the negotiations. (Either way, of course, the test would prove that Buol was working for Russia.) Just in case Buol agreed to these conditions, Clarendon instructed Cowley to persuade Drouyn to support revision of the Russo-Turkish treaties, and he asked Stratford to tell him what kind of final peace treaty the West should demand.[65]

Drouyn also denounced Buol for sending Russia's invitation to treat to Turkey, and now he refused any longer to support the idea of an armistice. But he disliked Clarendon's conditions for the four-power note to Turkey, mainly because he foresaw that if given carte blanche the Turks would demand impossible terms the sea powers would have to endorse.[66] Nevertheless, Clarendon sent his proposal to Vienna with the by now normal hectoring; Austria's views were identical with Russia's, Russia's aims were as aggressive as ever, and if Austria rejected these minimal conditions the sea powers would proceed alone. To the West's astonishment, Buol promptly accepted, though he insisted that the note should at least contain a strong warning to Turkey against refusing reasonable terms of peace. Austria's acceptance provoked a flurry of speculation; had Russia completely backed down, or had Austria abandoned Russia out of fear? The British immediately chose the latter explanation; Buol had passed Britain's test, thus proving himself a coward. "Buol has taken fright," said Russell, "and is perhaps disposed to act cordially with us." "I own I had not expected such a complete assent," Clarendon told Cowley, adding that it must derive from Austria's fear of French threats and of being forced onto Russia's side to face war and revolution. In any case, the Vienna Conference must not be allowed again to interfere with Western diplomacy.[67]

Drouyn promptly proposed a way to exploit Austria's unexpected amenability. Let the Vienna Conference draw up the note to Constantinople as Buol wished; in return Austria and Prussia would have to sign a protocol that would declare Turkey's integrity and independence a European interest and that would require the maintenance of the territorial status quo. This protocol would isolate them still more from Russia and might later lead to an alliance with the West.[68] Clarendon saw the value of this—in fact, he initially thought of using Austria, "our best indeed only medium of communication with Russia," to extract further concessions from St. Petersburg—but the embarrassments and dangers of cooperation with Austria quickly outweighed its possible advantages. France might become too intimate with her; the French had proved suspiciously unwilling to move the conference to London. Association with Austria would strengthen France's inclination to put pressure on Turkey as well as on Russia—a sign, according to Clarendon, that the faithless French would throw Turkey over at the first opportunity.

But the worst danger in Drouyn's protocol was an indirect one. Drouyn argued that having guaranteed Turkey's integrity, the four powers should summon both belligerents to treat at a neutral site and should put pressure on whichever one declined. Moreover, he dodged Cowley's demand to know whether France intended to abandon Turkey if she stubbornly refused. Once again that danger arose that Clarendon always feared most, which had already led Britain to abandon the Vienna Note, spurn the Buol Project, and reject Buol's plea for direct Russo-Turkish negotiations: the likelihood that Russia would accept a European-sponsored settlement while Turkey would not, which would force Britain either to join the other powers in coercing Turkey, apparently on Russia's behalf, or to support Turkey alone in her resistance to Britain's own advice.[69] The remedy lay as usual in presenting Russia with terms she must reject; to this end Clarendon hoped to prevent Austria from helping draft the protocol and the note or from reviving the Vienna Conference.[70] But in the end he contented himself with ensuring that both documents were safe—that is, they would not put pressure on Turkey or entangle the sea powers, though they would engage Austria and Prussia. Apologizing to Redcliffe for going through Vienna at all, and assuring him that the *démarche* was "dependent of course upon no other arrangement being made by you," Clarendon explained that France had insisted upon including Austria and since the note was harmless Britain did not want to fall out with France over the issue.[71]

The draft note and protocol were conveyed to Vienna in Britain's usual fashion. Britain was delighted that Austria was now cooperating, said Clarendon—and she had better, with revolution in Italy hanging over her. If she proved herself pro-Russian by failing to sign, Britain would be forced to abandon her patient efforts to work with her. At the same time Clarendon spurred Prussia to greater efforts to win the West's favor. Two weeks before, Clarendon had expressed to Loftus his delight at "the improved position now occupied by Prussia, owing to the manner in which Austrian and Russian trammels have to a certain extent been shaken off." Prussia, he said, "cannot too often assert her independence" against Russia and Austria, "supposed to be her servile instrument." Now, on November 29, Clarendon simultaneously blamed Prussia's timidity on Austria's influence and hinted that Britain would not need Prussia "if we can keep Buol up to the anti-Russian mark, where he appears to be at present." Just as he threatened Austria with French-inspired revolution in Italy, so he menaced Prussia with French bayonets on the Rhine.[72] Cowley even used the Austrian danger to keep Redcliffe and the Turks in line, telling him that Austria wanted the Turks to refuse to negotiate because it would put Russia in a better position.

Still, all their precautions could not rid Clarendon and Cowley of the suspicion that they were being led into an Austrian trap. For this reason Clarendon rejected Drouyn's suggestion that the sea powers should sign their protocol alone if Austria and Prussia refused to. His argument was extremely confused, but the substance of it seemed to be that a refusal by the German powers (obviously on Russia's orders) and a separate signing by the Western powers would mean "a prodigious triumph to Russia." Moreover, Austria and Prussia must not be allowed to suggest changes, for Bourqueney was too Austrian and Westmorland too dull-witted to avoid the snares Meyendorff would suggest to Buol. Cowley insisted that Austria could not be sincere because she only hinted at Anglo-French help for her in Italy; she ought to ask for it openly.[73] In short, the British were willing to put any interpretation on Austria's acceptance of Britain's proposal, except the obvious one that Austria so desperately wanted united four-power action in bringing the belligerents to the peace table that she would pay heavily for it. Moreover, Britain put Austria's acquiescence to every possible use, except that of actually cooperating with her to achieve peace.

This holds, of course, only for those who finally determined policy. An opposition remained—the royal couple (now wavering) and the Peelites—but it grew steadily more silent and ineffectual. Aberdeen protested helplessly over a series of grievances. He complained about Redcliffe's sending a small squadron of steamers into the Black Sea in order, Aberdeen believed, deliberately to challenge Russia; about Russell's intrigues against him and lust for war; about the government's inexplicably chilly response to Buol's call for an armistice. He had supposed, he said, that an armistice was desirable as the first step to peace, but confessed, "I do not know what is thought of the matter." The renewed attempts to remove the conference to London caused him still keener distress. He had not been consulted; it would destroy the last hope of peace; now even Seymour was working for it. "All this," he complained, "is not quite fair." [74]

Only once, however, when he found out that Clarendon at Palmerston's behest had instructed Cowley to sound out Drouyn on seeking Russo-Turkish treaty revisions in the negotiations (though he did not know that Clarendon had also instructed Seymour to propose them and had asked Redcliffe to suggest what treaty revisions should be sought), did Aberdeen really become angry. He denounced this as something he had always opposed, as absurd and utterly destructive of chances for peace, and as bound to mislead France into thinking that this was Cabinet policy when it was not. Clarendon replied with several embarrassed and disingenuous disclaimers, and sent a prompt letter to Cowley ruling out treaty revisions for the present. [75]

At the Vienna Conference of December 5, Britain's note and France's protocol were adopted with no objections from Buol (prompting Westmorland to tell Clarendon that since Buol had now passed still another test Clarendon had predicted he would fail, Britain might try trusting Austria a little, as France did). [76] It was probably bad judgment for Buol so readily to accept the West's terms, but he was ready to do almost anything to get Turkey to the peace table and negotiations started, and he saw no other way to do so. He still argued for terms and conditions that would not be impossible for Russia to accept. Negotiations à six, he contended, might be desirable but were not essential; the four powers should regulate the final outcome, not dictate the course of the Russo-Turkish talks.

Though Russia had started the conflict, Turkey was lately more to blame for continuing it, and the only hope for peace lay in four-power united pressure exerted equally firmly on both sides. And if Turkey was to get a European guarantee, she ought also to accept some European restraints against her troublemaking proclivities. Drouyn, who really believed all these points himself, applauded Buol's stand, claimed credit for bringing Britain to accept a note signed at Vienna, and insisted that he had long urged Vienna as the best site for the coming Russo-Turkish negotiations. The military situation seemed to conduce to serious peace talks. After earlier successes, the Turks had again withdrawn south of the Danube, leaving the Danubian campaign more or less a draw—the best situation, Buol and Clarendon both felt, for four-power mediation.[77] Though Redcliffe would doubtless obstruct anything coming from Vienna, at least the four powers, Buol believed, were finally united.

Had he seen Palmerston's, Russell's, and Clarendon's correspondence at this time, his confidence would have disappeared. On November 25, four days before the draft note and protocol were sent to Vienna for adoption, Palmerston again urged an offensive occupation of the Black Sea to prevent Russian movements of troops or materiel anywhere, even from one Russian port to another. Russell promptly supported this. Claiming that Russia was preparing a great winter offensive, he suggested the Allied naval intervention of 1827 against Turkey and Egypt as a good precedent for action.* But Clarendon wanted to wait until after the present *démarche* failed; Britain ought not frighten Austria away "by abruptly declaring war against Russia." Besides, if Turkey's demands proved to be unreasonable, public opinion would be against the war. But if Turkey accepted Britain's proposals and Russia refused them (and she surely would, for "no man eats dirt willingly"), then the sea powers could send in their fleets and summon Austria to go along. Unconvinced, Lord John laid bare his real fear. Suppose Russia beats Turkey on

---

* Like many of Russell's historical parallels, this was not a happy choice. Quite apart from the immense difference between three great European powers coercing weak states like Turkey and Egypt, and two great powers coercing a third directly in her own back yard, Russell might have reflected that the fleet action he cited as a precedent had led to the battle of Navarino, a Russo-Turkish war, a Russian victory, the Peace of Adrianople, and the very Russian ascendancy over Turkey that Britain was now trying to overthrow.

land, he said, and then consents magnanimously to treat on our terms? This would be good for the Turks; "but how would it stand with England? I conceive very ill." For Britain, not Turkey, was involved in the real contest with Russia, and as she would have done nothing, "our reputation in the world would be seriously affected." Besides, with a little judicious help Turkey could wrest whole Asiatic provinces from Russia.[78]

None of this, of course, proves that the war party had clearly decided to scuttle the December 5 peace move in advance. It does show them contemplating insurance against its success, and it fits with the uniform pattern of their policy for the past two months, of which the complicated details are less important than the consistent spirit and tendency. Ever since the outbreak of the Russo-Turkish war, Buol had worked to end it by the most direct and rational means: getting an armistice proclaimed and bringing both sides together for direct negotiations under the watchful eye of the four powers, who would establish the general basis for the talks and control the final outcome. In seeking this he had made one concession after another to the sea powers, especially to Britain, to gain their indispensable support.

In contrast, every step they took or tried to carry through—the refusal of negotiations unless all six powers participated, the rejection of an armistice except upon impossible terms, the refusal to permit any pressure on Turkey, the attempt to move the four-power conference to London and exclude Austria from any meaningful participation, the demand for treaty revisions and a preliminary Russian evacuation of the Principalities, the insistence upon Russia's accepting Turkey's terms in advance without alterations, the calls by the war party for an offensive occupation of the Black Sea— went in the opposite direction. Each served to ensure that there would be no negotiations and no peace settlement except under conditions that Britain and France would control and that would clearly signify their victory over Russia and the destruction of Russia's position in the East. Again, this series of events does not prove that the sea powers were bent on seizing this favorable opportunity to wage a preventive war to break Russia's power, though this idea certainly cropped up and tempted many—not merely Palmerston and Russell, but also Cowley, Seymour, Loftus, and Clarendon (incidentally, Redcliffe seems to have come to it much later and more reluctantly than some of his colleagues).[79] But at least the conclusion is inescapable that both the sea powers considered defeating Russia, elevating their prestige, and (for Britain) avoiding Cabinet conflict much more important than preventing a European war.

Meanwhile Nicholas watched Austria's approach to the West and the deterioration of Russia's position with angry bewilderment, seeing Western policy as madness and Austria's and Prussia's as pure cowardice. Bravado alternated with anxious retreat in Russia; hard on the heels of Nesselrode's offer to treat with Turkey came the Tsar's war manifesto to his people on October 20. The Russian army in the Principalities was held strictly on the defensive in the face of Turkish attack, but Nicholas gave Prince Vorontsev in the Caucasus permission to invade Turkey if she tried an offensive. Nicholas swallowed the Allied occupation of the Straits, but he ordered Menshikov to resist an entrance of the fleets into the Black Sea as an act of war and to attack the Turkish fleet if it came out in support of the Turkish army.[80]

However Russia wavered, as far as Austria was concerned the key points in her policy remained the same. Rather than abandon Turkey to British domination, the Tsar intended to fight and to use the weapon of revolution, counting on Turkey's collapse from internal revolt and exhaustion regardless of Austrian protests. Despite Russia's efforts now to avoid overtly provoking Austria by such steps as arming the Serbs for revolt, her determination if war came to ride roughshod over Austrian interests remained the controlling element in Austro-Russian relations.[81] Moreover, any light on the diplomatic horizon or success on the battlefield revived Russia's hopes of victory. After minor Russian successes on the Danube and in Asia, Nesselrode, repudiating any participation by other powers in Russia's negotiations with Turkey, wrote Meyendorff that a "patched-up peace" could not satisfy Russia. He intended to draft a treaty fit to be imposed on Turkey after military victory; until this was achieved, no negotiations with the Porte or other powers could yield Russia an honorable result.[82]

Russia's measures in the Principalities continued to be extremely disquieting, bringing Western protests also down on Austria's head, and Russia's persistent ideas about setting up independent client states in the Balkans were still more so.[83] The same kind of pressures and demands on Austria came from Russia as from the West: all Austria had to do was be firm, and Turkey would yield and the sea powers cease to interfere; Austria must make the Turks accept Russia's terms at Russian headquarters, because Russia always dealt with the Turks after their wars in this way; Austria should remember 1849, the Holy Alliance, the cause of Christ, and the menace of England, and join Russia.[84] The December 5 Protocol was the worst blow yet to Russia—Austria and Prussia had de facto joined an anti-Russian coalition—and provoked the sharpest Russian response. Meyendorff worked day and night to get Buol replaced by Windischgrätz and warned him daily that Austria's policy at this time would determine Austria's relations with Russia for Francis Joseph's whole reign. If Russia did not get an honorable settlement with Turkey, she would retire from Europe, and Austria would be the helpless prey of France and the revolution.[85]

As for Prussia, her signature of the December 5 Protocol did not mean any change in attitude toward Austria. Buol, hearing Manteuffel often express the fear that the sea powers would force Austria and Prussia to abandon their neutrality, sent Berlin a secret proposal to renew their 1851 alliance against this danger and others. But Manteuffel evaded any commitment. He expected that ultimately Austria and Prussia would be forced into war; but he was sure the sea powers' pressure would hit Austria first and hardest. Austria would have to seek Berlin's help in her futile attempt to stay out of the war, and Prussia could then exact concessions from her in regard to Germany and gain control over Austria's policy in the East.[86]

Thus Austria took upon herself not only the chief efforts and concessions involved in promoting the December 5 peace move, but also the major risks. In binding herself to some extent to the West, she gravely compromised her relations with Russia without gaining Prussia's support. If the peace move failed, as most expected it would, all the other powers intended to exploit Austria's vulnerability, calculating that her isolation and the force of events would force her to their side. Only success could justify Buol's gamble, and it depended on factors outside his control.

VI

Descent into War:
The Concert Defeated

Buol promptly began campaigning for the December 5 peace move, though without great hope of success. He sent more exhortations and warnings to Russia and Turkey, more pleas to Prussia and Germany to support Austria at St. Petersburg, and more suggestions on practical steps that all the parties could take to facilitate peace. He especially pleaded that the sea powers not insist on presenting Russia with Turkey's eventual peace terms as a four-power demand in a collective note. Such a procedure would "compromise the whole business wantonly"; he proposed letting Austria present them to Russia instead.[1]

Drouyn, not worried about jeopardizing the peace move, promptly had the December 5 Protocol published in the *Moniteur*, parading before the world the anti-Russian coalition Buol wished not to stress. Both Austria and Prussia protested sharply, and Cowley had to agree with them. But Clarendon, though disclaiming any responsibility for Drouyn's action, noted privately that it would help alienate Russia and Austria; the latter was "not yet securely *nailed* though she has made great progress lately in the right direction."[2]

As for Buol's proposal, the French saw no reason why Austria should not bear the expected Turkish terms to Russia. As Bourqueney remarked, "Why should we not let the affront of a refusal fall on Austria's head?" But the British objected to making any distinction in procedure between Turkey and Russia. Since the powers had sent Turkey a collective note asking her to state her terms, Russia must get a collective note demanding that she accept them. To persuade the British, Drouyn suggested that Austria pay for this privilege of taking the terms to Russia by promising to sign a collective note blaming Russia for ruining Europe's peace efforts if

Russia refused them. Buol agreed, providing that the note remain secret and not be signed or sent unless it really proved necessary (elementary precautions in view of what Drouyn had just done with the December 5 protocol). But again the British, though recognizing the value of Drouyn's idea for estranging Austria and Russia, feared that a collective procedure for blaming Russia if she frustrated the December 5 peace move might entangle Britain in a collective procedure for blaming Turkey and putting pressure on her if she turned out, as Clarendon expected, to be the one to frustrate it. Buol's other suggestions for promoting a favorable reception at St. Petersburg made good sense, Clarendon privately granted, but they would look like concessions to Russia, and were therefore inadmissible.[3]

Buol's efforts to smooth the path for Concert diplomacy would thus have proved futile in any case in the face of France's determination to produce an Austro-Russian breach and Britain's refusal to do anything that might conceivably appear to be appeasing Russia or abandoning Turkey. But in fact something far more dramatic seemed to render the December 5 peace move an academic exercise—the news reaching Western capitals on December 11 that a Russian naval squadron had on November 30 virtually wiped out a Turkish squadron at Sinope on Turkey's Black Sea coast. Less than two weeks after news of this "massacre of Sinope" arrived, the sea powers took their last major step toward open conflict with Russia, a decision to occupy the Black Sea with their fleets, confining the Russian navy to port. The obvious and natural supposition is that this move was a response to Sinope. It served to recoup the prestige lost by the Allies in allowing Russia such a smashing victory while their own fleets were in the Straits, and to meet the strident public demand for action, especially in Britain. This view is not wrong, but too simple; the links between Sinope, the Western decision on the fleets, and the abortion of the December 5 peace move are more complicated and indirect than it suggests.

Drouyn did decide after some hesitation that Sinope demanded an offensive occupation of the Black Sea, and he renewed his earlier proposal of this to Britain on December 15–16. His concern, just as before, was both to raise Allied prestige and to gain a counterweight to Russia's control of the Principalities. Through controlling the Black Sea, the sea powers could either force Russia to evacuate them,

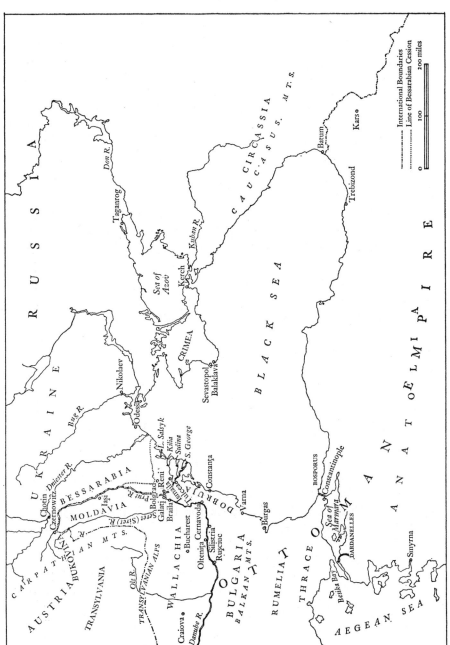

1. BLACK SEA AREA

or they could divert Russia's drive westward toward Serbia, Bosnia, and Montenegro, forcing Austria, as Cowley put it, to "attach herself body and soul" to the West. In addition, with their fleets in the Black Sea the Western powers might gain some control over Turkey's policy.[4]

The British ministry was again divided in its reaction both to Sinope and this French proposal. According to Temperley, the great public outcry over the battle swayed and finally swept the Cabinet along; Clarendon "nobly controlled his excitement" until the clamor for war and his fear that France would enter the Black Sea by herself overcame his scruples about undermining the current move for peace. In fact, at least initially the ministers, Clarendon included, did not display any great excitement over Sinope or any overriding concern about the public reaction. Aberdeen and Albert deplored the clamor, Albert suspecting the Turks of having courted disaster in order to drag the sea powers into war. Palmerston used Sinope to attack Aberdeen as a coward and to call for occupying the Black Sea, but he had been doing this for months. Cowley, surprisingly calm about Sinope, tried to dissuade Drouyn from sending in the fleets during the stormy winter.[5] Clarendon, though distressed at the blow to Allied prestige and the additional complications Sinope caused, blamed the Turks, not Russia, for the disaster at least up to December 17, and even later he was not sure who was at fault. The main thing, he told Cowley, was to prevent its recurrence.[6]

What still bothered Clarendon was not Sinope but the recurring problem of Britain's basically false diplomatic position. He feared that the Sultan, given virtual carte blanche at Britain's insistence in the December 5 peace move, would demand terms obviously "unwise for himself and unacceptable for Russia." If this happened, Clarendon wrote Redcliffe, England's position

will be one so false and embarrassing I will say so humiliating that I cannot contemplate it without horror, for we should then really be dragged in her wake against our own convictions and we could rely upon no support from the country in a war against Russia which by our own showing and our own recorded advice might have been prevented. I can fancy no greater diplomatic and political *fix* than such a state of things.

The only way he could see out of this predicament, he told Cowley, was for Russia to reject an apparently reasonable set of Turkish terms; this would give the sea powers the "pretext" needed for Drouyn's "extreme measures," that is, the occupation of the Black Sea.[7]

To add to Clarendon's woes, the news of Sinope arrived at a time when the Aberdeen coalition was actually breaking up. On December 10, Palmerston demanded an offensive occupation of the Black Sea in order to force treaty revisions on Russia; the news of Sinope the next day merely provided added ammunition for his demand. Aberdeen, supported by the Court, rejected it and Palmerston resigned on December 14, allegedly over Russell's proposal for electoral reform.[8] His resignation played into Russell's hands.* Russell had already secretly got Clarendon to instruct Seymour to warn Russia unofficially that if she crossed the Danube in force, the fleets would move into the Black Sea for offensive purposes. Anticipating Palmerston's secession, Russell told Aberdeen on December 10 that unless he secured a foreign policy he could defend in the House of Commons the ministry could not survive, nor would he stay in it.[9]

While Aberdeen, Graham, and Prince Albert tried to persuade Russell not to resign, Clarendon mediated desperately. To Aberdeen and Graham he contended that Lord John's proposal for sending in the fleets was a good answer to Sinope; peace was impossible anyway because of the Turks, and with Austria and Prussia terrified of Russia the sea powers had to act alone. Simultaneously he warned Russell that war now would destroy Turkey and questioned whether sending in the fleets was really necessary. If we could only agree, he pleaded, on what we would accept as evidence of Russia's peaceful intentions, what should be our *casus belli* with her, and what would require coercing her short of war, "we shall have something like a policy to meet Parliament with." [10] The peace party's pleas and Clarendon's frantic improvisations were no match for Russell's threat

---

* Aberdeen's staunch support for Russell on electoral reform did not seem to affect Russell's attitude at this time or later. When his reform project had to be dropped finally in April 1854 because of the war, Russell, though remarking that Aberdeen was the only one who had behaved with honor, still thought of resigning and breaking up Aberdeen's Cabinet (Ab. Corr. 1854–1855, 99).

to resign. On December 13, Aberdeen accepted Russell's proposal to send the fleets into the Black Sea if Russia crossed the Danube. Russell assured him he still wanted peace, and Aberdeen hoped that Russell would assume the office Palmerston had resigned. But mainly Aberdeen yielded in the belief that in saving his ministry he was preventing a real war cabinet from taking office.[11] *

Aberdeen's concession and France's proposal led on December 17 to a Cabinet decision to order the fleets into the Black Sea now, but solely for defensive action on behalf of Turkey, a step which seemed to go little beyond the Cabinet decision of October 8. Relieved, Aberdeen informed the Queen that if the Cabinet's present peaceful temper continued, he had hope for the future. His optimism was short-lived, for the agreement had been based upon misunderstanding and confusion. Aberdeen thought his colleagues had agreed to a simple defensive fleet action designed to keep the Russian and Turkish fleets separate until the fate of the December 5 peace plan was known. But Russell insisted on a declaration now that Russia's crossing the Danube would bring an offensive occupation, that is, the interdiction of Russian shipping. On December 14, Clarendon assured Russell that Aberdeen would not further obstruct this offensive move, provided that Russell did not tell him about Clarendon's unauthorized instructions to Seymour to warn Russia of it, and provided also "that crossing the Danube is not such a *casus belli* as to require a declaration of war." Russell reluctantly accepted this, insisting that Clarendon make sure that Russian shipping really would be interdicted and that he also somehow reconcile the lack of an official notice to Russia "with fairness and straightforward conduct toward the Emperor Nicholas."[12]

The December 17 Cabinet decision, instead of clearing everything up, compounded the confusion by providing for an actual fleet entry into the Black Sea for *defensive* action at this time, without providing for *offensive* action if Russia crossed the Danube. Lord John, insisting Aberdeen had betrayed his promise, demanded a clear decision for offensive action or he would resign. Graham

---

* Even Aberdeen, however, denied that he feared war with Russia. "I believe," he told Russell, "that we should ruin her in a very short time. Guarantee me from *further war* and I should not at all object to bringing Russia to her knees."

pleaded for him at least to wait to see whether the fleets had already gone in. But on December 20, Aberdeen again yielded, telling Graham that since Russell was adamant and the French proposal had somehow to be answered, he had agreed to offensive action now. He hoped that Russell would now be satisfied and that the new instructions for the admirals, providing for interdiction of shipping and confining the Russian navy to port, would not antagonize Russia or endanger peace more than further naval collisions would.[13]

This critical step toward war, formalized by the Cabinet on December 22, plainly resulted from the interaction of several factors. Intra-Cabinet politics came first and foremost, but the public outcry, French pressure, and simple confusion played a role. It would be a mistake to give too neat an explanation of it; the process by which the decision was reached bewildered some of the participants themselves. The decision, moreover, was plainly, as Temperley says, a compromise; one might add that it resembled the famous British naval compromise of 1909, in which the ministers wanted only four new dreadnoughts laid, the admirals demanded six, and they compromised on eight. Temperley's general explanation as to *why* this compromise was reached, however, is not entirely satisfactory. He explains that France's insistence on an offensive occupation, backed by her threat to go into the Black Sea alone if necessary, finally pushed Clarendon and Aberdeen into going along with it reluctantly, in the hope thereby of gaining France's support for the December 5 peace move.[14]

This explanation, adequate for Aberdeen, is wrong for Clarendon and misses the main point about the pressure France exerted on British policy. As Clarendon made clear to Cowley, he basically stood with Palmerston and Russell on foreign policy, not with Aberdeen. He had not for some time opposed an offensive occupation in principle; he cooperated with Russell secretly to pave the way for it, and worked to overcome the Peelites' objections. His scruples and hesitations arose only over the appearances of the move and the trouble it would cause in the Cabinet. Since November 25 he had objected that Britain should wait for the right pretext, that is, a Russian rejection of Turkey's peace terms. Immediately on learning of France's proposal for an offensive occupation, he wrote Cowley, "I like Drouyn's propositions very much but you must not say so until I have consulted the Cabinet." [15] Only after the Cabinet on December 17 decided on a purely defensive occupation did Clarendon argue to France than an offensive one was of doubtful legality, would spoil the current peace move, was inconsistent with British mediation, and should be preceded by a declaration of war. Temperley cites Clarendon's letter to Aberdeen on December 18 to show that Clarendon reluctantly accepted an offensive occupation because of the public outcry over Sinope. In fact, this very letter supports a different view. The whole passage, of which Temperley quotes just the first sentence, reads:

You think I care too much for public opinion but really when the frightful carnage at Sinope comes to be known we shall be *utterly disgraced* if upon the mere score of humanity we don't take active measures to prevent any more such outrages. This will be quite reason enough for Austria and if she does not admit it it will be because the Sinope affair inclines her more to Russia.

From the vast scale of the Emperor's [Nicholas's] preparations, the declaration of Persia, and the proceedings of the Russian fleet I infer that he has no real intentions of making peace even if the Turks propose reasonable terms so that by the time Parliament meets we shall find ourselves bamboozled and in a worse position than ever.

Pray remember also that both at home and abroad it will be thought that Palmerston has resigned on account of the Eastern question and that the policy of the Government is about to be still tamer than it has yet been.[16]

This passage gives Clarendon's reply to Aberdeen's three main objections to the proposed fleet move: that it would tend to promote war, would mean a break with Austria and the Concert, and would ruin the pending peace move. For these reasons Aberdeen wished at least to wait until Britain knew Russia's answer to the terms Turkey would propose. Clarendon here used every conceivable argument to persuade Aberdeen: that the move would actually prevent future bloodshed, that public opinion demanded it, that Palmerston's resignation made some strong action necessary to save the ministry, that there was no use waiting for Nicholas's answer because it would only be deceptive and treacherous anyway, and that the humanitarian justification would satisfy Austria, if she were not completely pro-Russian. It is impossible to discern what Clarendon really believed from this farrago or, for that matter, from anything he would tell Aberdeen. What matters is that in this argument Clarendon was trying to do what he regularly did: to avoid political embarrassment and possible disgrace at home and abroad by taking renewed offensive action against Russia, using Sinope as a convenient justification.

Precisely this same thinking determined his attitude in regard to France. It was not her threat to go alone into the Black Sea that worried him. As he told Cowley on December 21, while assuring him that he would support France's proposal before the Cabinet, he was certain Admiral Hamelin would never dare go in alone; "they [the French] would be nicely floored if they were taken at their word." Still less was he worried that the French would not support the December 5 peace move—he did not even want their kind of support, which meant pressing both Russia and Turkey to accept Allied terms. His real fear was that France might abandon Turkey or the British alliance, and this was the fear Drouyn played on. If Turkey rejected the December 5 overture, Drouyn warned Cowley, the sea powers would find themselves once again in the bad position of supporting Turkey when she had put herself in the wrong. Therefore they must not await the results of the collective overture, but exploit the pretext Sinope now gave them for strong action, before the Turks again proved intractable. Cowley warned Clarendon that Drouyn's threat to abandon the Eastern question to Britain and Austria seemed quite serious. Clarendon, already worried by reports from Loftus at Berlin that Austria's attempts to separate France from Britain [17] were making headway, promptly yielded to the warning from Cowley, conceding that France's proposal to go forward now while Sinope apparently put Russia in the wrong was "the least bad course open to us in our unavoidably false position." The proposal itself had never been objectionable, he told Cowley and Prince Albert, but only the way France pushed for it. Cowley agreed.[18]

One more point needs to be made about the Cabinet of December 22 in which Clarendon's instructions to Redcliffe concerning the fleets were adopted. Temperley calls the decision an unrealistic compromise, "a step which the pacifists hoped would not lead to peace, and which the forward party thought might not end in war." The instructions, he explains, "represented a real, though not an apparent, surrender to France," for while the British government still entertained the hope of restraining both Russia and Turkey, taking charge of negotiations, and achieving a settlement, the provisions for offensive naval action actually negated that hope.[19] This interpretation correctly reflects the hopes of Aberdeen and the peace party; the real issue, as Temperley rightly notes, was whether the sea powers, along with sending their fleets into the Black Sea, would also act by diplomacy to make the current peace move succeed.

But the opposition to doing this had never come from Paris. It had always been the British forward party which refused to restrain Turkey and put serious pressure on her for reasonable peace terms. With Palmerston out of the Cabinet and Russell ambivalent on the question of coercing Turkey, the burden of opposing any such coercion fell on Clarendon and Cowley. At Cowley's suggestion, Clarendon drafted the critical dispatches to Redcliffe precisely so as to enable the Turks to demand virtually any terms and to make any Russian refusal of them for any reason, or the breakdown of negotiations on any other grounds, the basis for full Western support of Turkey. Victoria, Albert, and Aberdeen protested that Clarendon's draft would tie Britain hand and foot to Turkey before she knew either the terms Turkey would propose or the reason why negotiations failed. The concession which Aberdeen believed he gained on December 22, in exchange for conceding the offensive occupation of the Black Sea, specifically covered this point. On the naval side, Turkey would be forbidden to attack Russia, the Turkish navy would be controlled by the Allied admirals, and Russia would be informed of this fact. On the political side, France and Britain would demand of Turkey, as a condition of their further assistance, that they refer the peace terms to the sea powers' discretion.[20] Essentially Aberdeen was calling for the kind of Anglo-French armed mediation France had often advocated. Turkey as well as Russia would be restrained and required *now* to rely on the sea powers for a diplomatic settlement on her behalf.

Whether such a plan could have succeeded is open to question. Turkey would no doubt have balked at surrendering her diplomatic independence and Russia at accepting Western armed mediation. But as events would show, the Turks were growing less bellicose at this time, and Russia would not have taken even an offensive occupation of the Black Sea as *casus belli,* were Turkey similarly restrained. Aberdeen's idea was thus not a foolish one. Unfortunately, he was right in quoting the words of King David in regard to it: "I labour for peace; but when I speak to them thereof, they make them ready for battle." Perhaps Aberdeen should not have quoted this passage to Russell, however, for though Russell worked for an occupation of the Black Sea, if his December 21 letter to Aberdeen is to be believed, he still hoped to bring both sides to a settlement and for some reason thought the *offensive* occupation would come only if Russia crossed the Danube.[21]

It was Clarendon who, barely conforming to the letter of the agreement with Aberdeen, made it something different in spirit and substance. On December 24, he did insist, in his private letter to Redcliffe accompanying the official dispatches, that Turkey undertake no naval action without the previous knowledge of the Allies. A Turkish attack on Russia under Western naval protection while the sea powers were still at peace would be too embarrassing and outrageous. He also pleaded with Redcliffe to persuade Turkey to be reasonable in her terms. But as to imposing this as a condition of further Allied aid and making Turkey accept a diplomatic settlement now, he wrote:

If the Porte has given an unfavorable answer to the last offer of the 4 powers we ought to insist now that we are about to run the chance perhaps I ought to say *face the certainty* of war with Russia that the Porte should agree to place itself in the hands of England and France for the negotiation of peace on the clear understanding that it will be asked to agree to nothing it has already objected to. As to the mode of pressing this and the extent to which the pressure should be applied great latitude must of course be left to you. It can't be made *quite* a sine qua non. Otherwise on being refused we ought to *recall* the fleets from the Black Sea, but unless we have some engagement from the Porte and some security that we are not to be at war for the beaux yeux of the Turks and that we are not perpetually to be begging them to assent to what we think for their advantage and to meet with nothing but repulse.*

---

* This last sentence is incomplete; Clarendon attached no conclusion to the conditional clause beginning, "unless we have some engagement etc." The grammatical error is trivial; the refusal to follow up warnings to Turkey with action was fundamental to British policy.

Though Clarendon's language is confused, this passage proves an important point. What made the Cabinet compromise of December 22 an unrealistic one, defeating Aberdeen's hopes of supporting the December 5 collective peace move and thus reaching a settlement, was the fact that Clarendon did not do what Aberdeen thought he did. In his secret instruction to Redcliffe he did not demand that Turkey turn over her cause diplomatically to the sea powers as a *sine qua non* for further Allied aid, and he would not consider withdrawing the fleets if Turkey refused. Thus the support given Turkey was, as far as terms of peace were concerned, essentially unconditional. Moreover, this letter hints, and later correspondence even more strongly suggests, that Clarendon, in urgently requesting Turkey to turn the peace terms over to the Allies, had in mind not imposing a diplomatic settlement on both sides now, but controlling a final peace settlement after the wider Anglo-French-Russian conflict, now considered inevitable, was ended. On December twenty-seventh he ordered Redcliffe to try for "some short form of convention" binding Turkey to accept any peace terms the sea powers thought honorable—which was exactly the price Palmerston on October 7 had proposed exacting from Turkey in exchange for the sea powers' becoming her auxiliaries in the war. His private letter to Cowley on the twenty-ninth confirms this interpretation.[22]

If the war party, moreover, supposed that the instructions to the fleets might not lead to war, they saw this possibility as a remote one. Clarendon expected and hoped that the Tsar would declare war as soon as he was notified of the admirals' orders; the Allies could then attack Sevastopol, "*finish up* Russia as a naval power in the East," and wipe out her Baltic fleet. Such a great coup, he told Cowley, "would be very gratifying to our respective *publics* and might have incalculable consequences for the future. . . . Having now arrived at a conviction that Emperor means and wants war I have no idea of his being allowed to declare it at his own time." Cowley predicted with delight that Russia would be set back twenty-five years in the Black Sea.[23] Clarendon did have worries about starting naval operations in the winter and still regretted having to use Sinope as the pretext for belligerent action, partly, as he told Redcliffe, because England still did not know if Russia really intended the battle as a challenge to her, and mainly because the Allied case would have looked better and stood a better chance of pulling Austria and Prussia along had the sea powers made war on Nicholas "as the obstacle to peace" rather than over Sinope. However, if war once began it would have to be waged with vigor.[24]

Two characteristic developments completed the drama in London. The first was the healing of the Cabinet schism. On December 23, Palmerston resumed his post, blandly assuring Aberdeen that his resignation had been a misunderstanding, while boasting to his friends over his foreign policy victory.[25] His self-congratulation was justified, not only on the naval issue, but also on the fundamental one of all-out aid to Turkey. The Peelites, especially Graham, had posed the question: Was Britain willing to fight Russia simply because Britain and France could not or would not control Turkey? In Palmerston's stead, Russell and Clarendon had answered "Yes" and had triumphed.[26] The second embellishment was Clarendon's discovery that Austria was in some way about to betray the West. The insight was not easily acquired. Despite more anti-Austrian stories from Berlin and Russell's constant warnings of some imminent Austrian treachery, Clarendon saw clearly that Austria (purely out of fear, of course) was eager to cooperate with the West. On December 24, he told Redcliffe that Buol's conduct far exceeded his expectations. But on the twenty-seventh he warned Cowley that Austria was evidently preparing to escape her obligations, and the next day he called for France to put pressure on her to nip her anticipated and unspecified betrayal in the bud.[27]

The crowning irony (there is a good deal of grim humor in Crimean War diplomacy) is that while Austria's efforts to make the four-power peace move of December 5 succeed were being wrecked by London and Paris, the peace move was also being discarded at Constantinople, for more defensible reasons. Though Redcliffe's will to peace was not nearly so strong as it had been two months earlier,[28] he still preferred a peaceful settlement and had really worked hard in October and November to keep Russo-Turkish hostilities from degenerating into general conflict. By early December, Turkey's internal troubles, an indecisive Danubian campaign, and the Sinope disaster had made the Porte more amenable to peace. Redcliffe began working out with Reshid and the other representatives a new four-power note for the Porte which, rather than simply inviting Turkey to state her own terms as Clarendon had insisted on doing in the December 5 note, laid down the actual bases for negotiation—the course Buol had advised.[29]

While this Constantinople note was being prepared, the December 5 collective note arrived. Redcliffe first delayed acting on it, gaining the agreement of his colleagues to his own collective note of December 15. Then two days later he persuaded them not to present the note from Vienna at all. Buol received the news of the December 15 *démarche* without protest, even though it violated his instructions to Bruck against joining more collective moves initiated at Constantinople. Accepting the action as conforming to the sense of Bruck's instructions of November 11, Buol wanted the Constantinople note used to give more precise content and emphasis to Europe's collective invitation to Turkey to treat. But he was painfully shocked by the refusal to use the December 5 note at all. It was unique in the annals of diplomacy, he told the Emperor, that four cabinets should be disavowed by their own representatives, an action all the more compromising for the powers since France had already publicized the documents. Although Buol blamed Redcliffe, the rebuke he administered to Bruck brought their relations near the breaking point.[30]

From his standpoint, Redcliffe's action can be defended. His desire to block a settlement coming from Vienna matched the wishes of his superior in London. Moreover, his note was superior to the one Clarendon had drafted for Vienna, and presenting the latter to the Porte first might have disrupted the whole effort. But Buol rightly contended that four-power mediation would work only if the peace plan presented at Constantinople and St. Petersburg clearly represented the united will of all four governments. No note concocted by Redcliffe and Reshid and signed only by four envoys could possibly have this impact. It is hard to see why the two *démarches* could not have been combined, as Buol wished.

In any case, Redcliffe's note, though later accepted by the Porte, also fell victim ultimately to the entry of the fleets into the Black Sea on January 4, while Buol's efforts to salvage and use the December 5 collective note proved another futile exercise. He got the Vienna representatives to seek their governments' authorizations to submit the note to the Porte through the Turkish ambassador at

Vienna. Drouyn, irritated at Redcliffe, agreed to this, demanding in exchange that Buol agree to send any Turkish reply as a collective note to St. Petersburg.[31] But Clarendon, delighted at what Redcliffe had done, bluntly refused the Vienna Conference request, warning Austria that her benevolent neutrality toward Russia was the real obstacle to peace. Aberdeen was disturbed by the obvious justice of Austria's complaints, but Clarendon insisted Buol was being extremely unfair—Redcliffe's note was the best peace plan yet. To Cowley, Clarendon wrote, "Buol always wants to be doing *something*, encouraged I suppose by repeated failures." What needed doing now, he remarked, was to destroy Sevastopol and the Baltic fleet.[32]

The same attitude dictated Britain's procedure in notifying Austria about the fleet movements and instructions to the admirals.* Buol did not oppose the fleets' entry into the Black Sea *per se*. Believing it would be valuable to have them in a position to defend and restrain Turkey, and supposing from Hübner's reports that a defensive occupation was all that was intended, he hinted that Austria would not object, and he disavowed a protest lodged against the move by Bruck at Constantinople.[33] The hints naturally further convinced the sea powers, especially Britain, that Austria was frightened and in their pocket, while his concurrent warnings about the results of refusing to consult with Austria and his complaints of the crude pressures of British diplomacy served to show London at the same time that he was still treacherous and pro-Russian.[34]

When the fleet decision was made, Drouyn tried to conceal its offensive nature until Austria and Prussia had first declared their support of it in the Vienna Conference. But Clarendon, intensely

---

* The British procedure in a way was a repetition of her presenting Austria with a *fait accompli* at the time the fleets moved into the Straits in October. Then Buol had lodged a mild protest over the fact that the sea powers had declared the Straits Convention of 1841 suspended without even notifying its cosignatories, Austria and Prussia. He also asked whether the Sultan had called for the entry of the fleets. Clarendon replied to the first point by telling Buol in effect that it was none of his business and simply refused to discuss the second. Aberdeen, pointing out that the Anglo-French action was at least a discourtesy to the German powers, urged Clarendon to modify his dispatch, to no apparent effect (Buol to Hübner, 16 Oct. 1853, PA IX/44; Clarendon to Westmorland, 27 Oct. and 2 Nov., No. 350 and confidential, FO 7/415; Aberdeen to Clarendon, 4 Nov., Add. ms. 43188).

fearful of any delay, refused to postpone the notification to Russia for any reason, and so Westmorland informed Vienna of the admirals' instructions just when they were being put into execution (as Buol had predicted).[35] Austria was greatly dismayed at the provocative character of the move. The Emperor reportedly cried, "C'est la guerre!" Hübner saw it as clearly throwing down the gauntlet to Russia. Buol was especially chagrined that it came when the negotiations on which Austria expended so much effort were still under way.[36] The attacks on Buol and his pro-West policy increased; Meyendorff argued forcefully that the sea powers, by acting thus without a word to Austria and Prussia, had liberated them from any commitments assumed on December 5. Yet Buol, though protesting sharply to the sea powers, refused to condemn the move publicly or change his policy.[37] Clarendon brushed aside Buol's complaints with the comment that "really we have had enough of child's play." It was time to teach Russia that the West was not afraid of her. Cowley added his own straightforward if cynical comment to Drouyn's explanations of why Austria had not been consulted: "Besides, what was the use of consulting other governments unless we intended to listen to their advice, a course clearly impossible so long as the intentions of the [Vienna] conference were pacific only." [38]

On December 31, Turkey gave her reply to Redcliffe's note of December 15 calling for a peace proposal. Out of this grew diplomatic developments in mid-January that, though they never had a chance to bring peace, fit the familiar pattern and should be mentioned. On January 13, the Vienna Conference endorsed Turkey's proposal, even though she had raised her terms somewhat and Reshid, at Redcliffe's instance, had written a supplementary note on January 3 demanding even stiffer concessions from Russia. Buol again tried desperately to make this conference resolution work for peace;[39] once again he obtained no support. Redcliffe, now entirely reconciled to war, was concerned only to vindicate British honor in the fight and to make sure France did not gain the lead in the East. Aberdeen still wished to use Turkey's reply for a last-ditch peace effort, but other British leaders either were waiting for Russia's declaration of war in response to the instructions of the Allied admirals or, fearing that Russia would still not be provoked into issuing one, urged precipitating it by an Anglo-French summons to evacuate the Principalities. The Turkish reply worried Clarendon because he feared Buol and Bourqueney might treacherously turn it into a proposal Russia would accept.[40] At the same time, the conference's endorsement of Turkey's terms pleased him, for it tended to justify the war at home and to make it difficult for Austria and Prussia to stay out of the conflict. Russell considered Britain's position now better than ever; Clarendon felt free to consult with France on war strategy before telling Aberdeen.[41] *

Unfortunately, Russia neither declared war nor broke relations when the admirals' instructions were conveyed to her at Sevastopol on January 6. Instead, she requested a clarification of the instructions, indicating that she would accept an occupation of the Black Sea if it served to protect Russia as well as Turkey from attack and allowed her likewise to communicate by sea with her own coasts. Brunnow made it clear that Russia's reply to the January 13 peace terms would depend heavily on the West's response. Buol pleaded with Britain and France to grant Russia the reciprocity she asked, while simultaneously he urged Russia quickly to accept the January 13 peace terms in order to induce the sea powers to do so.[42]

Moreover, France now advocated, as she often had before, that the Allies use their occupation of the Black Sea not to get the war started, but to force Russia to evacuate the Principalities. Both Napoleon and Drouyn were willing to induce Russia to accept the January 13 peace terms by offering her a mutual evacuation of the Black Sea and the Principalities. If the sea powers did enter the war, Drouyn wanted only to defend Turkey's integrity, force Russia out

* Though Clarendon, like the naval experts, was worried about starting a campaign in midwinter, he knew that Russia would have to be provoked into actually fighting the Allies, and he used this fact to answer the peace party's claim that an offensive occupation of the Black Sea would expose the ships to destruction in detail by enemy action. As he told Graham on January 6, the Tsar would not dare attack the Turkish or Western fleets now, when he had declared that he wanted peace and when the sea powers had declared that they wished to mediate between him and the Porte. "This would be pushing perfidy," he said, "far beyond the limits of decency" (Graham Papers Reel 18). The day Clarendon wrote this, the admirals were delivering to Russia the orders confining her ships to port, which Clarendon had sent expressly to provoke a Russian declaration of war and blow up the peace negotiations. He was also discussing with Cowley and others at this same time how to force Russia to fight if she refused to respond even to this challenge. It is not easy to determine what Clarendon's canons of decent, nonperfidious conduct were.

of the Principalities, and make her accept the January 13 terms—war aims Cowley called "vague and meagre."[43] This news, plus reports of secret Franco-Russian contacts through the Saxon minister at Paris Baron Seebach, Nesselrode's son-in-law, frightened Clarendon. "It is terrible," he wrote Cowley, "to think of the dangerous ground on which we are standing," with the French "preparing to back out of the war they have done even more than us to provoke" and Sevastopol reputed to be impregnable. Of course a war would endanger Napoleon's throne, he conceded, but the Emperor himself had "absolutely forced us on in a manner to accelerate if not create the very complications he fears."[44]

France's proposed reciprocal evacuation quickly found support in Britain. Aberdeen's arguments on its behalf were ignored, but Russell, in another of his baffling reversals, favored it as the prelude to an armistice.[45] A real contest arose between Cowley and the French, with the former obliged repeatedly to condemn the French proposal as incompatible with Britain's honor and threaten to proceed alone if necessary. Even so, Cowley could not keep Napoleon from writing an autograph letter to Nicholas on January 29 offering him a reciprocal evacuation as the last chance for peace.[46]

At home, Gladstone refused to take comfort in the thought that Russia had been in the wrong earlier and wanted to know who was in the right now. The issue of war and peace, he insisted, should be clearly joined on the January 13 peace terms, which Europe had approved; their rejection by Russia would justify a strong stand by the sea powers. But the Black Sea question was a separate one, and Russia's request for reciprocity represented clearly "the very greatest effort which Russia could possibly make" to escape her bad position. Gladstone pointed out that Clarendon's proposed answer to Brunnow—that the Allied policy was not reciprocal—"if we put ourselves in the Russian position seems to leave her no alternative but war: certainly enables her with a fair case to escape from the consideration of the Redcliffe note." Even if Britain could not retract what she had said and done, as Clarendon argued, she could meet Russia's request in substance by guaranteeing Russia against Turkish attack.[47]

Clarendon, worried about being abandoned by France and embarrassed by Brunnow's note, wavered momentarily, conveying

Russell's endorsement of a reciprocal evacuation to Cowley.[48] But he never hoped to use Brunnow's *démarche* in order to avoid war; his concern was again over appearances and public opinion. He thought it more manly and honorable to declare war openly than to provoke it from Russia by protecting Turkish aggression on Russian territory. Palmerston, moreover, stiffened his resistance to Buol's and Napoleon's "pacific dodges" with arguments about the cowardice of appearing to back down, the shame of treating Turkey and Russia as equals, and the loss of status that Britain would suffer from yielding to Brunnow's bullying, as Aberdeen cravenly proposed. By January 28, Clarendon agreed with Palmerston's advice to tell Brunnow and Kiselev directly (so as to provoke them to demand their passports) that Britain would explain her instructions more fully if necessary, but would not change them. Clarendon still had worries and doubts—"the worst feature in our prospects now," he commented, "is the growing unpopularity of war" and the danger was great that Napoleon would want to stop at the brink—but he resolved them as always by plunging forward. "The Russians would have swallowed the entrance into the Black Sea," he wrote Cowley, "but having adopted the Emperor's [Napoleon's] proposal made to us le couteau sur la gorge we have arrived rather prematurely to a point from which we shall not recede but where we have every right to find ourselves in French company." Cowley was urged to keep Napoleon up to the mark, and to make France understand that even if she backed out, Britain would fight alone.[49]

This drastic course proved unnecessary. As intended, the British stand struck the vital nerve of Nicholas's honor. It was bad enough for Russia to accept Turkey as an equal; to have her navy bottled up in Sevastopol while the Turkish fleet roamed the Black Sea was too much. The Tsar's reply to Napoleon's letter on February 9 hurled defiance at the sea powers and made war certain.[50]

Thus all obstacles to war, Austria's peace efforts in particular, were pushed aside—but the questions of how, where, and to what ends to fight it were still wide open, and when these were debated, Austria emerged again in the middle of the picture. France had never omitted her from it. After toying, like some other Frenchmen, with using revolutionary means to force Austria into action (a course strongly urged by Cowley), Drouyn adhered to the safer tactics of gradual entanglement. The knowledge that his lures and pressure would at best take time to work and that without Austria the burden of ground fighting would fall upon France, helped make him willing at the last to avoid the war altogether or to limit it narrowly.[51]

In Britain there was no such clarity of view on war aims, but one could discern three groups or tendencies. The old peace party favored virtually a restoration of the status quo ante. It was joined by Russell, who initially proposed an ultimatum for Russia containing terms much more favorable to her in many respects than those of January 13 or even of the original Vienna Note. If Russia accepted these, Russell proposed forcing them on Turkey.[52] * Most of the ministers, however, wanted first to take Sevastopol and sink Russia's Black Sea and Baltic fleets before any further negotiation, thereby destroying her prestige in Europe and the East. After victory they would accept a peace with political losses for Russia, but few or no territorial changes.

Palmerston, enjoying no clear support on war aims within the Cabinet but plenty outside it, wanted Russia crippled both militarily and territorially, and therefore he joined with the second group in demanding, as a start, the capture of Sevastopol. Like them, he was at first buoyantly optimistic, arguing in mid-January that the fleets, aided only by the Turkish army and a supplementary auxiliary force (Newcastle suggested five thousand men), could carry it off. Sobering second thoughts quickly set in. Russell, still amazingly generous toward Russia on war aims,† questioned whether Napoleon could afford to risk a defeat and would commit the thirty thousand men

* Russell's generosity toward Russia, however, was combined with a hostility toward Austria and a conception of international law that, in a former foreign secretary, evokes amazement. He contended that "the Protocol of Vienna [of December 5] gives us a *casus belli* against Austria, if she permits any aggrandisement of Russia in the East, at the expense of Turkey." This is to argue that a state that signs a declaration supporting the principle of the territorial integrity and independence of another state thereby gives her fellow signatory powers grounds for war against her if she fails to prevent other states *not* signatory to the declaration from acting contrary to it—a remarkable doctrine.

† For example, he favored abolishing the rule of 1841 and opening the Straits to warships in peacetime, even though it would give Russia's fleet access to the Mediterranean.

needed. Graham, taking a generally somber view of Allied prospects, insisted that a large landing force would be required and advised simply holding the Dardanelles instead. Victoria and Albert did not see how any great blow could be struck at Russia. Palmerston, conceding that Sevastopol might prove formidable, suggested concentrating on helping Shamil drive Russia out of Circassia and the Caucasus. Out of this uncertainty in British strategic thinking began to emerge some recognition of the levity of provoking a war without knowing how to fight it.[53]

But the perplexity suggested its own solution: get Austria and Prussia to fight the war the West had begun. Clarendon suggested requiring Austria to take her stand as soon as Russia rejected the January 13 terms, warning her that the West would soon turn against her if she tried to stay neutral, "and then gare à Elle." Russell proposed that Austria be urged to send fifty thousand men to help Turkey if Russia crossed the Danube in force. Or, if France preferred an attack on the Vistula, "might not Prussia be called upon at least to furnish a contingent under pain of losing her provinces on the Rhine. . . . Mighty questions, these, and I should like to hear Palmerston's opinion upon them; no one sees so quickly and clearly in these matters." Palmerston did not let Russell down; he promptly wrote Clarendon:

Then [when England and France were at war] it would certainly be necessary to summon Austria and Prussia to declare themselves and to take one side or the other; and in that case they ought not to content themselves with resisting a Russian advance beyond the Danube, they ought to join the Turks in driving the Russians out of the Principalities, and the united forces of the three would accomplish this with ease.

Then the Allies and Turkey could concentrate on the Crimea and Asia, and destroy both of Russia's fleets.[54]

Palmerston did not explain how he would force the German powers to come into the war on the correct side. Bloomfield at Berlin talked of measures against them that would put Sinope in the shade if they tried to stay neutral, and Palmerston's paper, the *Morning Post*, spoke darkly of forcing Austria to take a clear stand by means of Italy. But such talk was bluff, and as Westmorland and Prince Albert pointed out, counterproductive as well. It would be difficult at best to win over Austria and Prussia "after our bluster and abuse of them," said Albert; bullying would only drive them into Russia's arms.[55]

This seemed to leave only France's method of gradual persuasion and entanglement. Supposedly Britain also tried it with Austria, and failed because of Austria's fears and Buol's sterile diplomatic maneuvers. Only public war hysteria, historians have alleged, induced the British government to begin war without first being sure of Austria's attitude;[56] she later tried constantly to win Austria as an ally.

The view is natural but incorrect. The British government not only knowingly pushed Austria's peace efforts aside in order to start the war; once it was begun, while she tried to bring Austria in as her satellite or subsidized mercenary with no conditions attached, she never wanted Austria as a genuine partner or ally and, rather than submit to any Austrian inhibition of British conduct or war aims, preferred to do without her. France looked to Austria as her main continental ally, at least as long as Drouyn was foreign minister; the British consented to deal with Austria as much as they did mainly out of concern for the French alliance. Britain wanted to gain Prussia and Sardinia, not Austria, for the Anglo-French partnership. As Russell said on January 4, ideally the war should be fought by an alliance of Britain, France, Prussia and Turkey. Britain's preference shows clearly in the double standard she applied to Prussia and Austria. Clarendon and Palmerston were always ready to guarantee Prussia's territory as part of an alliance [57] and even, as will be seen, contemplated aggrandizing her territorially. Britain absolutely ruled out any territorial or political guarantee for Austria even when she later actually joined the Western alliance, and British leaders continually contemplated territorial changes in Italy at her expense. London was ready to believe almost any Prussian canard about Austria; it took Clarendon months of disappointment to learn what Manteuffel was like, and he never lost his partisanship for the Prussian liberals.[58] While Austrian suggestions regularly met suspicion and disdain, Prussian initiatives aroused eager expectation, even though they regularly proved worthless. The special mission of Count Pourtalès to London in late December, for example, turned out only to offer Prussia's neutrality, at a price, to Britain. But Russell was not disappointed. "Her role in the play," he said, "is to keep Austria straight by the jealousy she inspires." The British press praised and flattered Prussia while damning Austria.[59]

To be sure, the British finally became extremely bitter when Prussia persisted in a neutrality they claimed was pro-Russian, but even then they pinned great hopes on the Prussian liberals, blamed Prussia's retrograde course on Austria, and wanted still to use Prussia against her. There are doubtless diverse factors involved in Britain's preference for Prussia over Austria.* Whatever its causes, it contributed to the disingenuousness of British dealings with Austria. While Clarendon was praising Austria's policy and urging her to join the West in the coming war, he simultaneously praised Manteuffel for evading Austria's snare of pro-Russian neutrality and urged Prussia to wrest the lead in Germany away from Austria.[60]

Russia, along with the sea powers, now faced a decision on how to fight the war. Her position, though grave, was not desperate. Recent victories at Sinope and in Asia had encouraged her; she could still appeal to the Russian God and the patriotic spirit of 1812. If Austria and Prussia stayed neutral she could hope to fight a successful defensive war on Turkish soil or near her own frontiers.[61]

---

* The most important reasons were clearly political, economic, and ideological. Prussia was a better bet for constitutional liberalism than Austria, did not seem to be competing with Britain for France's attention as Austria was, and in general looked to the British like a better choice to check Russia and France. Along with the Zollverein, she presented better opportunities for British trade than Austria did. But religious feeling and racial sentiment were also involved. Anti-Catholicism, which played so large a role in British domestic politics, was also more important in British foreign policy than has usually been recognzed. The British also felt a racial affinity with North Germans, believing that they shared the Anglo-Saxon virtues of sobriety, discipline, love of freedom, rational prudence, and ability for government lacking in Celts, Latins, Slavs, and other breeds.

One more factor, though much less important, should be mentioned. The British were immensely proud of their institutions, liked to consider themselves as models of orderly progress for the world, and were therefore, like Americans, very susceptible to flattery from foreigners. Liberal Germans, Italians, Magyars, and Poles, and leaders such as Cavour, Kossuth, and Mazzini (even Frederick William!) told the British how much they admired them and hoped to follow their example. No responsible Austrian could say that he saw Britain as a model for Austria and the rest of the world, and Buol, though an Anglophile, did not try.

But a growing Austro-Russian rivalry in the Balkans complicated the task of keeping Austria neutral. Until September 1853, except for the Principalities, there had been fairly harmonious cooperation. Russia helped Austria get the concessions secured by Leiningen executed by Turkey; the two powers both opposed the policies of Serbia's nationalist foreign minister, Ilia Garašanin, and, after his ouster, his equally nationalist successor Jovan Marinović. Russia accepted Austria's precautionary reinforcements on her Serbian frontier from July on, and Buol welcomed the mission of the Russian chargé Fonton to Prince Alexander of Serbia. The sea powers competed more actively than Russia with Austria for influence in this earlier period and constantly demanded explanations of Austria's policy toward Serbia.[62] *

From October on, Austria's worries in this theater increased. Signs multiplied that Turkey and the sea powers would try to make Serbia join them against Russia. The Russian consul Muchin was recalled in November and the Russian consulate closed. Buol heard that Turkey wanted Serbia to allow a Turkish army to cross her soil to get at the Russians in Little Wallachia; Clarendon wrote Westmorland that Serbia had no right to reject a Turkish call for aid against Russia.[63] The evidences of change in Russia's policy were worse still. Fonton's trip into Serbia and the Principalities in the fall was obviously designed to get information on possible anti-Turk risings. Danilo of Montenegro, it was reported, was being encouraged by Russian agents to attack Herçegovina. Despite Meyendorff's warnings, Nesselrode instructed him to try to work out a secret deal with Hess to supply the Serbs with ten thousand rifles; Buol's pedantic ideas about neutrality, said Nesselrode, might get in the way.[64]

Austrian opposition stopped this notion, and some of the other dangerous Russian ideas that cropped up were not actively pursued. General Mikhail Gorchakov, commander in the Principalities, rejected a proposal for actively fomenting a Greek rising in Epirus and Thessaly. But a second Kovalevskii mission to Montenegro in

---

* Buol finally told Westmorland that the West's constant importunity reminded him of the man who assured an acquaintance that he was perfectly confident that the man had never been branded as a thief. Nevertheless, would he please take off his shirt to prove it?

late December and early January was designed, as Austrian agents reported, to prepare both Montenegro and Serbia for revolt when Russia crossed the Danube in the spring. Russia even tried repeatedly to get the loan of an Austrian military engineer, Colonel von Mollinary, to help prepare for her offensive across the Danube. By February, Austria and Russia were openly at odds over Serbia, with Vienna urging Serbia to accept a Turkish firman guaranteeing her privileges in exchange for neutrality, while Russia tried to persuade the Serbs to reject it and keep their options open.[65]

Meanwhile Russia's occupation of the Principalities looked more and more like annexation. After the hospodars left, she appointed officials at will and over boyar protests incorporated the Wallachian militia into the army of occupation for noncombatant duties. Austrian agents reported that Russia was trying to recruit a corps of volunteers for service against Turkey in her spring offensive.[66]

These developments increased the pressure within Austria for adopting a clear policy in the face of the coming war. Francis Joseph, incensed at both the sea powers and Russia, thought of occupying Serbia to cut off Kovalevskii's intrigues. Buol and Bruck were at loggerheads over Buol's refusal either to choose partnership with Russia or to arrange for armed mediation with Prussia and Germany, and Bruck had powerful allies in Vienna.[67] Hübner wanted an open alliance with France and complained to Rechberg that nobody at Vienna had the courage and insight to give the Emperor the true picture. Rechberg in turn warned Buol that the public spirit and order in Lombardy-Venetia were being seriously affected by rumors of an Austro-French breach.[68] Prokesch, still violently anti-English, was worried by the bellicosity of England's language at Frankfurt and by rumors of French plans for war in Italy and on the Rhine. While some of his friends clung to the Holy Alliance for safety, Kübeck believed Austria's situation was virtually hopeless—none of the proposed solutions was likely to do any good.[69]

In January, after long vacillation, Nicholas decided once for all on crossing the Danube and raising the Balkan Christians in revolt in the spring. He recognized the danger of driving Austria over to the West, but believed that there was no other way to distract the sea powers from Russia's Black Sea coast. Besides, he believed that British public opinion would not support a war to overthrow Christian Balkan states that Russia had liberated from the Turks. Count Orlov was assigned the task of persuading Austria to accept this policy and to guarantee her neutrality; the Russian ambassador at Berlin, Count Budberg, received the same assignment for Prussia. The Tsar was again willing to pay Austria handsomely for her neutrality in familiar coin—joint protectorates in the liberated areas, Austrian occupation of Bosnia-Herçegovina, Russian pledges not to allow revolutions and nationalist movements to menace Austria, and promises of Russian armed assistance against the West. Orlov suggested further inducements—a share for Austria in Russia's protectorate over the Principalities or a promise of immediate action to clear the Danube mouth, which Russia had allowed to silt up. But behind them lay the familiar warning that if Austria failed Russia now, Russia would abandon her permanently to her many enemies. Buol knew, moreover, that Orlov, like others before him, intended to work for his dismissal.[70]

Orlov's chances, which he himself considered poor, were in fact nil; Austria's decision was already taken. On January 7, Francis Joseph wrote Nicholas requesting assurances that Russia, in accord with the spirit of Münchengrätz, would not cross the Danube unless forced to by the events of war and would renounce in advance all conquests, raising of revolts, and changes in the status quo. Nicholas sent back his angry rejection with Orlov. The Austrian press, especially the *Austrian Lloyd*, whose editor Eduard Warrens was Buol's protégé, reflected an anti-Russian attitude, warning that Austria could not tolerate a revolutionary policy by Russia. On January 16, Buol advised the Emperor in a *Vortrag* not to promise Russia continued neutrality unless she gave the assurances demanded on January 7 plus her renewed promise not to prolong her occupation of the Principalities unduly. Failing this, Austria should side diplomatically with the West and make an armed demonstration in Transylvania and the Bukovina to force Russia to withdraw, and if Russia openly chose revolutionary war, Austria would have to join the West just as openly. Francis Joseph, at this time fairly confident in Napoleon and angry at Russia, approved the *Vortrag*, and a ministerial council on January 23 unanimously endorsed Buol's policy.[71]

Therefore Orlov's eloquence, though it succeeded in bringing tears to the Emperor's eyes, failed to get him to promise neutrality. Windischgrätz supported Orlov's appeals to 1849 and the traditions of the Holy Alliance and his warnings of what a break with Russia meant, but to no avail. On January 31, another ministerial council unanimously rejected Russia's proposals; at this same time Budberg's efforts were similarly failing at Berlin.[72] Orlov explained his failure as the result of Austria's fear of France (the standard Russian explanation of Austrian conduct for months); the Emperor, he said, tried to conceal it, but Buol admitted it openly. Though Orlov may well have believed this, he was wrong. It was easier and less wounding for Austrians to let Russia think this than to tell them that Austria no longer trusted Nicholas's word and regarded Russia's present policy as more dangerous and revolutionary than France's. Francis Joseph at this time expected France to be moderate as long as Austria adhered to the principles of the December 5 Protocol.[73]

Orlov, however, had good grounds for reporting that Austria, though maintaining an expectant, uncommitted attitude, was not likely to become actively hostile to Russia. Francis Joseph, anticipating Austrian action against Serbia, claimed that Austria's expectant neutrality and the observation corps set up in Transylvania were not measures hostile to Russia, and he indicated that Austria would not necessarily oppose a Russian crossing of the Danube. Buol promoted a twelfth-hour peace proposal through Orlov (to be described later) that was the one faintly hopeful result of the mission. St. Petersburg, not Vienna, closed the door on further peace efforts. Orlov advised trying for a direct agreement with Napoleon rather than dealing further with the German powers, and the Tsar, agreeing with Paskevich that Austria must have worked out her demands with the sea powers, decided to press forward fearlessly even if he had to face new enemies.[74]

Once again this left only Prussia to support Austria's expectant neutrality. The reasons in favor of such mutual support seemed more pressing and obvious than ever—witness the two powers' virtually identical and simultaneous reactions to Russia's offers. Arnim and Thun worked for it, Francis Joseph, Frederick William, and Gerlach favored it, even Buol and Manteuffel were not in principle opposed to it. But the dead weight of mutual aversion and distrust remained immovable; every accusation by Austria met an equal and opposite Prussian charge against her. Buol complained bitterly and with good cause about Prussia's lies and intrigues; the Prussians replied that Austria still had not abandoned Schwarzenberg's policy of trying to mediatize Prussia or to form a separate league against her in Germany. Buol and Thun explained Prussia's trickiness as due in part to Manteuffel's bad character and his extremely weak position; Manteuffel thoughtfully responded with a similar commentary on Buol. Prussia, said Austria, was trying to be a real great power when she was one only by courtesy. Austria, said Prussia, aspired to a leading role in Germany and Europe she could not possibly fill. Buol feared Prussia's advances toward liberal Protestant England; Manteuffel distrusted Austria's rapprochement with ambitious Catholic France. Buol was outraged by Prussia's attempts to get Britain to guarantee Prussia and Germany, leaving Italy exposed to Western attack; Manteuffel charged Austria with trying to trick Prussia into guaranteeing Lombardy and Venetia. Prokesch was an insuperable obstacle to cooperation at Frankfurt, said Berlin. Not so, replied Vienna—Bismarck was to blame.[75]

Under these circumstances it is useless to assess the responsibility for the failure to cooperate. The only points worth making are that Austria at this time was still the suitor, while Prussia played coy and that, in the mutual game of intrigues and dodges, Austria was more sinned against than sinning (later the situation would be reversed in both respects). In early January, when Manteuffel again made a plea for a firm stand by the two powers against French threats and Buol responded by renewing his call for a united policy of expectant neutrality, Manteuffel not only again evaded the issue, but promptly revealed the offer both to St. Petersburg and to Paris and used it to try to displace Austria in the position of favor with the West.[76]

Thus Austria's expectant neutrality was in jeopardy from the time it was resolved upon, even before general war broke out. While a good many governments approved of it—almost all the German states, out of fear of becoming entangled themselves,[77] and Sweden and Denmark, which had just announced their own neutrality in December—no one solidly supported her in it, and Buol already foresaw that circumstances might arise which would make any kind of neutrality no longer possible or desirable.

VII

The March Conferences and
the Austro-Prussian Alliance:
Decision Postponed

On February 2, while Orlov was still in Vienna, the Vienna Conference rejected Russia's unconciliatory answer to the four-power proposals of January 13. Buol did not attempt to defend Russia's reply, but he did try to salvage the January 13 proposal, compromised initially at St. Petersburg by the Anglo-French occupation of the Black Sea. If Orlov on his return could persuade Nicholas to accept the conference's terms and ask Austria to arrange the time and place for negotiations, Austria would work on the sea powers for an armistice, a preliminary peace, and a simultaneous evacuation of the Black Sea and the Principalities to precede the final negotiations. Though obviously a last-gasp effort, the proposal was genuine and (if peace was still one's goal) sensible. Austria made her familiar pleas and exhortations in its behalf at St. Petersburg and in the West.[1]

British suspicions of Austrian treachery, just assuaged by Orlov's failure at Vienna (which the British credited to Manteuffel's firmness against Russian pressure),[2] immediately revived. Clarendon denounced Buol's "detestable suggestions" as "one of the greatest diplomatic outrages I ever heard of." It was not merely irritating that the Buol-Orlov plan should briefly revive the nearly extinct hopes of the peace party,[3] but downright dangerous that it interfered with starting the war and gave France an opportunity for still preventing it. Drouyn, Clarendon noted with grave concern, thought of ending the crisis if Russia accepted the January 13 terms. Clarendon therefore wanted the Buol-Orlov proposal dismissed brusquely to prevent a possible Austro-French peace move.[4]

But Drouyn was only interested in getting Austria and Prussia to sign a four-power convention pledging themselves along with the West to use all means, including force if necessary, to reach a settlement based on the December 5 and January 13 protocols. Bourqueney had told Drouyn that Austria was not ready to consider this, but Drouyn did not wish to ruin his future chances by flatly rebuffing the Buol-Orlov proposal now, and he was reluctant for the same reason to sign a separate convention with Britain.[5] Clarendon also vacillated. At first he endorsed Drouyn's four-power convention and ordered Westmorland to propose it at Vienna. Then two days later he urged that Austria should not be pushed into it. She was already doing all one could expect, he argued, and should not even be called on to support the prospective Anglo-French ultimatum to Russia for evacuation of the Principalities.[6] The reason for the change was partly that Russell advised Clarendon to put off any peremptory and menacing demands on Austria until the war began. If Austria remained passive, said Russell, "We shall *then* have good cause to quarrel with her."[7] But Clarendon mainly was determined to start the war promptly with France alone, so that Austria could not inhibit it or France slip from Britain's grasp.

Therefore while Clarendon declined to try to make Austria sign a convention, he increased the pressure on her over other issues. Westmorland, to his chagrin, was ordered in early February to raise the sequestrations issue again. Pressed by Hudson and Azeglio, Clarendon sent Buol some Sardinian documents proving, he said, the entire innocence of the émigrés and the great "prudence and moderation" shown by Sardinia under Austria's "persecution in its worst form."[8] Simultaneously (and with better reason) Clarendon demanded explanations of Austrian troop movements in the south and called for assurances that Austria would not occupy Serbia or Bosnia. At the same time he admitted privately that Austria was doing all that could be expected of her, he and Cowley repeatedly insisted that even now one word from Austria would stop Russia dead in her tracks.[9] The primary purpose of these tactics was to make sure that if Austria did join the Allies it would be on Britain's terms and that if she did not her refusal could be blamed on her pro-Russian and anti-British bias.*

* This explains, I think, the apparent vagaries and contradictions of Clarendon's tactics. But I confess to being unable to account for Russell's erratic

Austria actually moved steadily toward the sea powers, though slowly and hesitantly by their standards. On February 9, Buol and Arnim signed a new Vienna protocol pledging the four powers to uphold Turkey's integrity and forbidding any separate agreements with Russia inconsistent with this. Then on February 20, Buol told Bourqueney that if the sea powers intended to summon Russia to evacuate the Principalities, Austria would endorse the summons, reserving her freedom on how to support it by material means. If armed action proved necessary, Austria would also need assurances from France on Italy, military pressure by Prussia on Russia, and Germany's endorsement and backing. This initiative, though carefully qualified, broke with Austria's previous refusal to commit herself to anything that might lead to hostilities with Russia. Bourqueney quickly brought forward the four-power military convention he had delayed presenting, and Buol, supported by Francis Joseph, again responded favorably. If (as was all but inevitable) Russia rejected the Buol-Orlov plan and if Prussia also cooperated, Austria would agree to the convention with certain amendments. The amendments Buol proposed were all designed to make the convention less binding on Austria and to make it easier for her to control the war aims of the sea powers. He repeatedly emphasized to Westmorland that Austria insisted on retaining her freedom of action and had no intention of waving the red flag at Russia. But he also gave the impression that only prudential considerations kept Austria from joining directly in the sea powers' summons to Russia to evacuate the Principalities.[10]

Buol's proposal thus worked counter to his ends of controlling and restraining Allied policy. It liberated Clarendon from any fear that negotiations might somehow arise out of the Buol-Orlov project and helped cancel the remaining hesitations of the peace party over the summons to Russia.[11] Clarendon accordingly sent the summons to St. Petersburg via Vienna on February 27, with instructions to hold up the courier there a few hours to give Buol the chance to read and endorse it.[12] The apparent end to uncertainty about Australia's and Prussia's attitude removed Russell's hesitations over war aims, while Clarendon and others were encouraged in their visions

swings in February and March between optimistic trust in Austria and angry suspicion of her. (See Russell's correspondence with Clarendon in Clar. dep. c. 15.)

of a great war to liberate mankind, advance civilization, and gain "great and solid things of the future" for Britain.[13]

As for the agreements with other powers already concluded or contemplated that would stand in Britain's way, Clarendon on February 24 instructed Cowley to try to withdraw the notes already exchanged with France and communicated to Austria and Prussia, containing war goals far too meager for Britain now. Cowley discussed with Drouyn how much the sea powers were committed to the January 13 terms, and he received the assurance that these were only intended to demonstrate the West's moderation and to help bring the German powers into the war. Drouyn proposed several new major aims once hostilities started, and Cowley suggested working them into the proposed four-power convention, though without binding the sea powers to anything specific. Cowley also advised enlisting the Christians in Turkey in the fight against Russia by promising them great postwar benefits if they did so, including a position at least equal to the Turks in the Ottoman Empire.[14]

Nor were Buol's efforts to get French assurances on Italy more successful. Drouyn insisted that French cooperation was dependent on Austria's actually undertaking military operations on the Danube, and even then France would sign only a secret convention on Italy valid solely for the duration. Since Austria and her Italian client states wanted the moral effect of an open entente against revolution, not a secret agreement that temporarily France would hold in reserve her revolutionary weapon, the proposals in February and March for a convention on Italy came to nothing.[15]

So finally did the attempt to reach a four-power convention. All the sea powers' pressure and threats and Austria's arguments could not induce Frederick William to sign. Britain in particular attributed the decision to the King's subservience to Russia, which made Clarendon want "to *kick him to death*." Or, admitting his desire for peace, the British dubbed him "the Pacificator of Putbus" and "the Peacemaker of Potsdam." Clarendon termed Prussia's passing up her chance for liberation suicidal; Albert called Prussia's choice of neutrality "*dumm zum davonlaufen*" (incredibly stupid).[16] In the long view, the West's advice to Prussia was "*dumm zum davonlaufen*," taking no account of the problems and requirements of Prussia's central position or, for that matter, of the dangers that could arise for Europe and for themselves if Prussia took their advice, helped defeat Russia and throw her out of Europe, and thereby established her own greatness and independence.[17]

The dispute between Austria and Prussia was on a higher level, involving two opposed but equally defensible views on how central Europe should cope with the coming war. Buol argued that Germany along with Austria had a vital stake in its outcome. Russia was at present the main culprit and menace, but the sea powers' aims also had to be controlled now, before they began fighting and claimed their rights as belligerents, or the war would ultimately assume revolutionary dimensions. Manteuffel contended that the proposed convention would only draw Austria and Prussia into doing the main fighting and free the sea powers to pursue their special interests.[18] Both were right, and no good compromise between their views was possible.

Anyway, by early March it was clear that Prussia would not sign. Playing a role in the decision at Berlin was the King's discovery that his old friend Bunsen had discussed with Britain the possibility of Prussian territorial gains if she joined the war against Russia—the most shocking thing the King could imagine. He sent General Count von der Groeben to London to investigate, and ultimately recalled Bunsen, replacing him with Count Bernstorff. The fall of Bunsen, an outspoken liberal and Anglophile, combined with the ouster or fall from favor of other liberals in Prussia, marked the victory of the conservative camarilla at Berlin and precipitated an open clash between the King and Prince William. The state crisis that ensued in Prussia took weeks to end.[19]

As for the ideas which Bunsen conveyed to Berlin for redrawing the map of Europe, which caused his downfall, they really derived not from his own fertile imagination, or from Prince Albert, as Bismarck claimed,[20] but from Palmerston and Clarendon. Clarendon of course denied this to Groeben and blamed everything on Bunsen.[21] * The Bunsen affair and its attendant complications produced a deep cooling in Anglo-Prussian relations and marked the beginning of Britain's campaign against the King and the camarilla during the rest of the war.

Frederick William tried to protect himself against reprisal by

* See Appendix B.

another series of special missions to various capitals, which as Manteuffel foresaw only made Prussia appear to be frightened by her own decision.[22] Austria, as she had warned, now turned to the German middle states, telling them she might be compelled to act against Russia and calling for their moral and, if necessary, material support. Manteuffel replied by demanding that Austria explain her intentions in southeastern Europe and by emphasizing Prussia's completely neutral and independent stance before the Prussian diet.[23] The German powers seemed farther apart than ever, and pulling Germany apart between them.

The sea powers now tried to get Austria to forget Prussia and sign an offensive alliance with them; but again their individual tactics differed significantly. France hinted at possible bad results for Austria if she declined; Britain openly threatened her with revolution in Italy or with leaving the Balkans to Russia and fighting only in Asia. Drouyn wanted Austria to agree to secret military talks on the time and manner of Austrian intervention; Clarendon proposed an open military conference, with the Duke of Cambridge, the British commander Lord Raglan, and the French commander Marshal Saint-Arnaud stopping at Vienna to concert military plans with Austria on their way east. Even after Buol rejected this as utterly incompatible with Austria's expectant neutrality, Clarendon still called for a military conference and suggested that Austria begin recruiting a military contingent for herself in Germany. France tempted Austria with plausible advantages—a permanent conservative alliance and concrete territorial and political gains if Austria desired them. Clarendon held out the prospect of liberating Germany and central Europe from Russian "interference," which, he said, had for decades stifled reforms and thus promoted revolution. (The most recent Russian "interference" had been in Hungary in 1849; the reforms Clarendon envisioned were all at Austria's expense.) [24]

The French avoided raising side issues with Austria. Britain, while urging Austria to join the war, continued to voice suspicions, complaints, and demands on matters old and new, some trivial and most unconnected with Austria's stand on the Eastern question.[25] The French at least were willing to talk seriously with Austria about concrete military assistance in a joint Danubian campaign (though they doubtless intended to leave her in the lurch once she entered

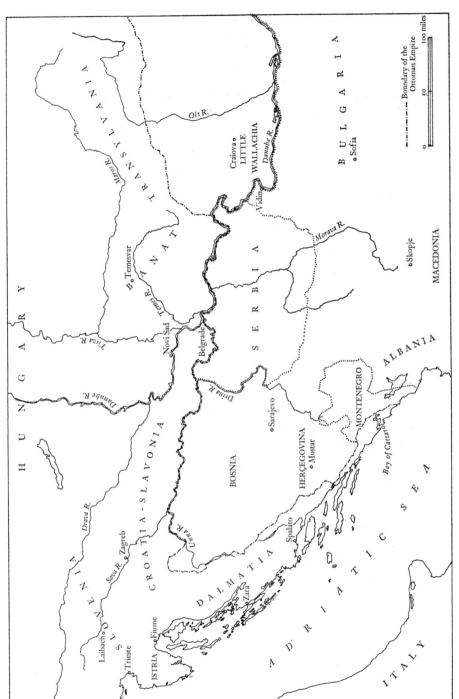

HUNGARY

TRANSYLVANIA

BANAT

B. Temesvar

Maros R.

Tisza R.

Novi Sad

Belgrade

SERBIA

Danube R.

Temes R.

SLOVENIA

Drava R.

Trieste

Laibach

ISTRIA

Fiume

Sava R.

Zagreb

CROATIA - SLAVONIA

Una R.

Drina R.

BOSNIA

Sarajevo

HERCEGOVINA

Mostar

DALMATIA

Spalato

Zara

Bay of Cattaro

MONTENEGRO

ALBANIA

ADRIATIC SEA

ITALY

Olt R.

Craiova

LITTLE

WALLACHIA

Vidin

Danube R.

Morava R.

Skopje

MACEDONIA

BULGARIA

Sofia

Boundary of the
Ottoman Empire

0   50   100 miles

the war). When Buol warned Britain that Austria would not open the fighting under any circumstances, or make any move at all until the Allies were ready to support her on the Danube, Clarendon replied that Austria need not fear; Britain would not stand on the defensive. "Whether it be on the Danube or in the Crimea," he wrote, "we shall carry on *real war* against Russia." This not only ignored the point Buol raised; it tended to confirm his fear that Britain was going to war without knowing where or how to fight it.[26]

No doubt these tactics can be partly explained by Britain's distraction with other concerns more important than Austria and her doubts as to the worth of an Austrian alliance even while she sought it. The most immediate reason, however, was British military strategy. When Bourqueney complained that British indifference regarding Austria hampered his own efforts to win her over, Drouyn pointed out that Britain was interested in the maritime and Asiatic theaters, not the European.[27] In the Allied strategy discussions at Paris from late February on, the French argued strongly for a Danubian campaign as well as a Crimean one, and if Austria and Prussia would actively enter the war, France favored a large-scale joint Allied drive in the Principalities and southern Russia to go along with an Austro-Prussian campaign in Poland. The British, however, were so averse to sharing in any land operations, especially along the Danube, that Clarendon preferred to excuse Austria entirely rather than agree to these plans.[28]

Besides, an alliance with Austria would inhibit British war aims, which soared upward not so much from optimistic jingoism as from the conviction that the grave risks of the war called for aims worthy of Britain's honor and greatness.[29] Palmerston constantly stressed this theme; his goals changed frequently in detail, but never in their aggressive character. His *beau idéal*, embodied in a March 19 memorandum, proposed giving the Aland Isles and Finland to Sweden and "some of the German provinces of Russia on the Baltic" to Prussia; creating "a substantive Kingdom of Poland" as a buffer state against Russia; giving Austria the Danubian Principalities and the mouth of the Danube; either ceding Lombardy and Venetia to Piedmont or making them independent; annexing the Crimea and

Georgia to Turkey; and making Circassia independent or placing it under Turkish suzerainty.[30] *

Some colleagues greeted these ideas with scant enthusiasm and Palmerston admitted their long-range and contingent character, but in general his ideas gained support as time went on. Albert, though doubtful that Turkey could survive the war, was confident that Russia's influence in Europe could be largely nullified through the loss of her western territories. Colloredo reported that such ideas were widespread in Britain. Russell now contemplated liberating Lombardy and resurrecting Poland.[31] Lord Dudley Stuart besieged Palmerston and Clarendon on Poland's behalf, especially advocating Prince Adam Czartoryski's scheme of a Polish Legion for service under the Porte, with separate organizations for Hungarian and Italian émigrés. Clarendon, at Palmerston's behest, instructed Redcliffe to support the idea, though "without any reference whatever to the resuscitation of Poland." Austria's probable objections to such a revolutionary policy were discounted.[32] Hudson, Minto, Lord Shaftesbury, Palmerston's son-in-law, and many others preached the cause of Italy.

In late March, Russell warned Aberdeen that if the government announced that it would seek an early peace consistent with honor, Sir Austen Layard, the noted Assyriologist and enemy of Russia and Austria, would call for war until Russia was crippled, and his amendment might well pass. The next day Russell warned Clarendon not to put anything into the Queen's war message that would commit the sea powers to the existing territorial boundaries of Europe, and Clarendon promptly ordered Cowley to try to cancel the existing agreements on war aims with France. Palmerston fought even harder

---

* While remarks on the rashness of these proposals seem superfluous, two points are worth noting. The first is the strong resemblance between this program and the one allegedly concocted by Bunsen which caused his downfall. The second concerns Palmerston's suggestion of giving Prussia the "German provinces of Russia on the Baltic." There were none such, of course—only Letto-Lithuanian and Estonian provinces with a minority of German nobles and townspeople. Here again one sees a British liberal accepting and supporting dangerous Pan-German claims and aspirations that most Prussian statesmen themselves, including the ambitious Bismarck, would not touch with a ten-foot pole. In fact, in one version of his war aims, Palmerston even contemplated turning all of Russian Poland over to Prussia.

against any self-denying clause in the proposed alliance treaty with France. Redcliffe also proposed a revision of the whole Russian frontier "for the benefit of Poland and other spoliated neighbours to the lasting delivery of Europe from Russian dictation," and saw clearly that if Britain aspired to his kind of settlement, the less she had to do with Austria, the better. A convention with Austria now, he argued, would only embarrass the Allies and serve Russia and "the rump of the Holy Alliance." [33]

Meanwhile, Russia's pressure was exerted on Austria from the opposite direction. The Tsar rejected the Buol-Orlov proposal out of hand and broke relations with the sea powers without bothering to reply to their summons of February 27. His response to their preparations for war and declarations of war and to Austria's placing an observation corps in the Voivodina and Transylvania was to hasten preparations to cross the Danube and seize Silistria. Nationalist and Orthodox sentiment was mobilized at home for the struggle, while revolutionary proclamations went out to the Bulgarians and to the Greeks in revolt in Epirus and Thessaly.[34]

Russia did not ignore the Austrian threat; as Buol once remarked, it probably worried and constrained her more than the Allied fleets in the Black Sea did. Paskevich, named commander of the Danube army on March 5, repeatedly urged evacuating the Principalities before Austria forced Russia to do so.[35] But not even the threat of an Austrian alliance with the West could persuade the Tsar to abandon the offensive, though Paskevich restricted the crossing to the extreme lower Danube and remained ready for quick withdrawal. Nicholas counted on being able to delay an Austro-Western alliance at least till mid-summer, if he could not prevent it entirely with Prussia's help; by that time Russia's position south of the Danube would be consolidated. To gain Prussia's aid in constraining Austria, the Tsar promised Prussia his support in her future bid for German hegemony and sent Duke George of Mecklenburg to Berlin in late March with new Russian peace terms to offer to Austria. Russia finally thought Austria might be diverted from joining the sea powers on the lower Danube into occupying Serbia and Bosnia instead. Though unwilling to risk provoking Austria by encouraging a Serb rising directly, the Russians by late March were hoping for troubles in Serbia that would cause her to intervene.[36]

Prussia's aims coincided with Russia's strategy perfectly. On March 11, Frederick William sent his aide Colonel Edwin von Manteuffel (the premier's cousin) to meet Francis Joseph at Munich with an offer of an Austro-Prussian defensive alliance. The main reasons for Prussia's sudden willingness now to conclude a new alliance after her earlier repeated refusals to renew the treaty of 1851 were two: to keep Austria from joining the West, thus isolating Prussia, and to divert Austrian intervention from the Danubian Principalities, where she would confront Russia, to the western Balkans, where she would draw Western hostility on herself and would be forced to obtain Prussian support to maintain her neutrality. Despite Thun's repeated explanations, the King insisted that what Austria really needed and wanted was Prussian and German backing for an occupation of Bosnia and Serbia against the sea powers' opposition. On March 17, he offered to guarantee to Austria not merely her present territories of Dalmatia and the Littoral, but also "certain Turkish territories" she might feel the need to occupy. As Gerlach explained, these included Bosnia, Serbia, and Montenegro, but *not* the Danubian Principalities. Prussia also offered her services to get Russia to agree to such an occupation.[37]

This Russo-Prussian strategy was the more powerful because it fit the plans of the military men and to some extent of the Emperor himself in Austria. All the previous autumn and winter Buol had had to discourage the idea of a preventive occupation of Bosnia and Serbia. At the ministerial conference of January 31, Hess, while agreeing with the others in rejecting Orlov's proposals, returned to the charge. Russia's projected trans-Danube campaign, he argued, would destroy the Ottoman Empire, revolutionize the southern Balkans, and threaten Austria's southern frontier. Therefore if Turkey could not survive in her present form as a harmless neighbor, the bulk of her European territories, especially Serbia, must come under Austrian rule. Indeed, an immediate occupation of Serbia was a military necessity.[38]

Kübeck remarked in his journal that Hess argued in the same sense as Buol, but "somewhat confusedly." No wonder; while rejecting Orlov's demands and damning Russian policy, Hess advocated in regard to Serbia and other Balkan territories that Austria do exactly what the Russians, including Orlov at that very moment, had been urging her to do: to join Russia in partitioning the Ottoman Empire. Hess's reasons were not mainly pro-Russian, but anti-Turkish and strategic in nature. Like many other generals, he wanted Austria to gain a shorter, more defensible frontier running diagonally from southwest to northeast across the western Balkans by annexing the hinterland to Dalmatia and the Littoral. But his proposal also obviously harmonized with his good friend Bruck's repeated calls for seizing Turkish territories, ostensibly to stop Russia, actually in secret agreement with her to protect Austria's interests. Grünne, usually Hess's jealous rival, supported him, insisting that Austria must not even wait for Russia to cross the Danube before occupying Serbia. The Emperor, summing up the sense of the meeting, concluded that all "had expressed themselves in favor of a prompt (*"demnächstige"*) occupation of Serbia." Buol tried to pour water into the wine, but only by suggesting that Austria move slowly step by step according to developing circumstances.[39]

With the Emperor himself bent on occupying Serbia, supposedly to forestall Russia, the preparations went forward rapidly. In February, 50,000 additional men were assembled; by late March and early April, the disposable forces in the south amounted to 33 infantry battalions, 28 cavalry squadrons, and 88 guns.[40] But Buol worked to ensure that these military moves served only their ostensible purpose of discouraging a Serbian rising promoted from St. Petersburg. While he warned Turkey against trying to enlist the Serbs on her side or fortifying Bosnia in contravention of Austro-Turkish treaties, and supported a strict embargo on the sale of arms and munitions to Serbia, he at the same time rejected Grünne's demand to stop the Turks from rebuilding fortifications the treaties allowed them to restore, and he flatly repudiated the widespread assumption that an occupation was inevitable. Only Russia's unclear intentions necessitated these precautionary measures, he emphasized to General Count Coronini, commander of the forces assembled for intervention. Austria's fundamental principle on Serbia as everywhere else was "the preservation of the status quo in all directions." Coronini should intervene only if anyone attacked Belgrade or some other Serbian territory or clearly threatened to, if Prince Alexander believed his throne threatened by revolt, or if Coronini had "reliable indications" that Russia was about to invade.[41]

As it turned out, Austria's preparations accomplished Buol's purposes rather than those of the military men and the Emperor. Fonton returned from Serbia with little to show for his efforts, and Kovalevskii's mission dragged on fruitlessly. The Russian General Kotzebue complained to Austria's consul at Bucharest, Baron Laurin, that her mobilization in the Voivodina was directly hostile to Russia, robbing her of her best chances for a Christian insurrection and imperiling her plans for the trans-Danube campaign. By late March, to be sure, Russia gave up on the Serbs and would have much preferred an Austrian intervention there to one on the lower Danube.[42]

The Austrian reinforcements naturally created intense suspicion in London and Paris. Supplied with intelligence on the troop concentrations by the French military attaché the Marquis de Chateaurenard, Drouyn persistently demanded assurances that Austria was not going to partition Turkey with Russia.[43] Britain's consul at Belgrade, Thomas de Fonblanque, insisted that such a plot was under way. Redcliffe, also convinced of it, sent the veteran British consul at Bucharest, R. J. Colquhoun, on an extended tour of Bosnia and adjacent provinces to advise the Turks on how to avoid an Austrian occupation. Clarendon even believed the Austrians were encouraging Fonton's intrigues. But by mid-March Clarendon told Redcliffe that he had ample evidence of Austria's good faith, and Fonblanque finally agreed that the presence of Austrian forces had helped restrain the Serbs and would continue to be necessary—though he urged that no Austrian intervention should be allowed until an impartial observer (i.e., Fonblanque himself) considered it advisable.[44]

Thus Buol, aided and spurred by Western pressure, had helped prevent an Austrian occupation of Serbia in early 1854. (Incidentally, Kempen's intelligence reports, emphasizing the fierce national resistance the Serbs would oppose to it, had given Buol some unexpected aid.) [45] But according to both Meyendorff and Chateaurénard, the military men still considered an occupation inevitable. Generals Coronini and Schaffgotsch visited Belgrade in late March in what was more a reconnaissance than a courtesy call. Radetzky, Jellačić, and General Mayerhofer ardently advocated Austrian expansion in the western Balkans, Radetzky even contending that Austria's hold on northern Italy finally depended on it.[46] Hess, now doubtful about occupying Serbia, argued in a memorandum of March 5 that in order to meet the dangers from Turkey's inevitable destruction and to prevent Russian outposts in the form of Byzantine or Slav states from arising in Turkey's place, Austria must strengthen herself politically and strategically by getting control of everything between Samokov and Scutari. To do this, Austria should maintain the status quo in Serbia, preventing any Serbian expansion, and occupy Bosnia and Herçegovina, making them vassal states on the way to their ultimate annexation, setting up an independent Catholic principality in northern Albania under her protection as well. Hess saw some of the problems involved in his program but argued that they could be readily solved. At the same time he was promoting these ideas before the Emperor and within the government, Hess assured Meyendorff that Austria's observation army in the south was directed solely against Bosnia and Serbia—not a man was intended to threaten the Russians.[47]

Meanwhile, others were urging a pro-Western course on Buol, notably Hübner. Some of his arguments for a French alliance plainly missed fire—his warning that Russia was about to attack Austria from Poland, or his plea for a war for "the majesty of the throne, the independence of the state, the universality of the Church!" Buol, who disliked ultramontanes and clerical mingling in politics, had no sympathy especially with the last part of that argument. What did count with Buol, however, was Hübner's report that Cowley and Drouyn had promised that if Austria joined them the sea powers would campaign on the Danube; otherwise they would fight solely in Asia.[48] Colloredo also urged cooperating with the West, though he did so more moderately than Hübner, and he contributed a warning that the sea powers intended to establish their own predominant influence in Serbia if Austria stayed neutral. Clarendon had already brought up the idea of abolishing Russia's protectorate over Serbia in favor of the four powers, and Colloredo had had to dodge it as premature. From what Buol knew of the activities of British and French agents and the pro-Western sympathies of many leading Serbs, the danger of Western predominance was real.[49] Prokesch also now leaned toward the West, though he was not fully converted to war. He argued that at present the greater danger to Austria came from Russia and Prussia, and that if expectant neutrality had to be abandoned, Austria should side with the West on the basis of clear agreements with the sea powers over the Eastern question, Germany, Italy, and Switzerland.[50]

Buol had already reached this conclusion, and presented his case to the Emperor on March 21. Russia, he argued, had made further expectant neutrality impossible. Unless Austria intervened, every course the war might take would cause her intolerable losses and dangers—either a further expansion of Russia's power and influence, or revolutionary measures by the sea powers to force Austria in on their side, or a long, indecisive struggle that would gradually ruin Austria's commerce and exhaust her finances in prolonged military preparedness, or a peace settlement compensating the belligerents at the cost of ruining Turkey and completely isolating Austria. Austria had to seize the present opportune moment to protect her interests in the war and if possible quickly end it; only a carefully planned diplomatic and military intervention on the side of the sea powers could accomplish this. After getting the sea powers to commit themselves to a Danubian campaign, Austria should conclude a treaty with them providing the following:

A mutual pledge against territorial acquisitions.

Joint Allied action at Constantinople in behalf of the Ottoman Christians.

Western intervention with Turkey to get her to entrust Russia's protectorates over Serbia and the Principalities to Austria.

No separate peace or negotiations with Russia until the purpose of the alliance was attained.

A clear military agreement covering the size and nature of the forces each ally would supply.

Finally, an invitation to Prussia to join the alliance either immediately or later.

With this treaty signed and the Western and Turkish armies in position to open the campaign, Austria should make a final peace offer to Russia. If it was rejected, she should summon Russia to evacuate the Principalities. If Russia refused, Austria should move in with Allied and Turkish consent to force Russia out, though assuring Russia that she only intended to clear Turkish soil and would not cross her frontier. If Russia took this as her *casus belli* and declared war or attacked Austria, Austria would then need help from Prussia and Germany. But she could not expect them to join her in the initial summons to Russia and the move into the Principalities; anyway, the back-up help Austria needed from Prussia in case of outright war with Russia was already virtually assured by the alliance Frederick William had just offered. All that was needed was to make the projected alliance more precise, to cover the specific case of a war arising out of Austria's occupation of the Principalities.[51]

A few comments on this crucial proposal: first, Buol was correct in calling it a logical development of the policy laid out by him on January 16 and adopted at the ministerial conferences of January 23 and 31. It harmonized also with his attempt to reach a convention with the sea powers, approved by the Emperor, and with the instructions he and Bach had worked out to guide the Austrian press on the Eastern question.[52] If Buol was to appear reckless in presenting this proposal to Francis Joseph and unprepared for the criticism it met, he had some excuse, for prior to the moment of decision, as Bourqueney and others reported, the Emperor seemed to share and support Buol's views on the role Austria should take in the war.[53]

Second, this was a program inspired far more by the fear of danger than the hope of gain. What almost invariably impressed Buol in the diverse information and advice he received was the perils Austria faced rather than the opportunities she might exploit: not Drouyn's proffered bribe of the Danubian Principalities, but the threat that the sea powers might let Russia keep them or establish their own hegemony there and in Serbia; not the power and prestige Austria could acquire in a successful war at France's side, but the revolutionary war France would fight if Austria stayed out; not the belief expressed by Prokesch that Austria's central position would enable her to get the sea powers to settle the Eastern question and other problems to Austria's advantage, but the conviction that if Austria did not guarantee her essential interests in advance, they would ultimately be trampled on; not the supposition that Prussia's alliance offer put her in Austria's pocket, but the certainty that Prussia was in no case to be trusted. No one of the fears Buol discussed was imaginary or unimportant. Even Buol's appeals to the Emperor to act for the sake of Austria's greatness and independence (a natural appeal to a proud young ruler) do not really say, "Here is a splendid chance for us to grow greater," but rather, "This is a unique opportunity to meet and solve the grave dangers facing us; if we do not seize it, we shall almost surely decline."

Moreover, this was not an expansionist program, as is often claimed,[54] but an alternative to one. Bruck, Hess, and other military men, along with Russia and Prussia, tempted Francis Joseph with the gains he wanted in the western Balkans; Buol worked to fend this off. The proposed protectorate over the Principalities and Serbia was one provision among several designed to protect Austrian interests against both sides, no more or less important than the others, and not even discussed in the two ministerial conferences that followed this *Vortrag*. If territorial or political expansion was Buol's real aim, he would hardly have been so anxious to prevent an occupation of Serbia. Buol really wanted simply what he said—the same rights of protectorate formerly exercised by Russia, only with Western and Turkish consent and cooperation.[55]

The unanswerable criticism of this program is that it could not have worked. The elaborate and highly artificial timetable for action Buol proposed would have broken down even given good will on the part of the sea powers and Prussia, and this was conspicuously lacking. Moreover, Buol could not prove that Austria would be able to control Allied policy by intervening now—his later argument from the analogy of Austria's intervention of 1813 was unconvincing—and his suggestion that Austria could move over to Russia's side if the West went too far hardly presented a plausible alternative. Worse yet, Buol's plan would have risked war with Russia before Austria was absolutely sure of Prussian and German support, even though Austria already had a tempting Prussian alliance offer in hand. The oversight was deliberate and essential to Buol's program; he could not afford to conclude a Prussian alliance until after the decision to act against Russia was taken, for Prussia only intended to hold Austria back. But thereby Buol denied himself the only answer that he, a civilian, could give to his military critics who insisted that Austria dared not challenge Russia militarily with only dubious Western and Turkish support. In fact, Buol himself opened the door to this criticism on March 22 when he said that only the assurance of competent military authorities that the task was beyond Austria's powers would make him change his mind.

Buol's opponents, along with the Emperor and Buol's friend Bach, stormed through these holes in his argument in the March 22 conference, one after another assuming that he was calling for prompt military intervention against Russia (an assumption Buol sought unsuccessfully to refute) and insisting that this was premature and far too dangerous without absolute assurance of Prussia's help. Though no formal decision was reached at this conference, the Emperor announced at its reconvening on March 25 that he was sending Hess to negotiate an alliance with Prussia prior to making any further decision. Hess, meanwhile, had made his own eloquent plea to the Emperor against Buol's policy. While oversimplifying Buol's position, he presented its main point accurately enough: having exhausted every peaceful means of stopping Russia, Austria had to join the West to check her now, or the sea powers and the war itself would ultimately do Austrian interests worse damage than a confrontation with Russia now would cause. Hess replied that while everyone rightly condemned Russia for her present revolutionary policy, Britain's was worse and France's no better. Even if Russia tended to dominate, she had helped fight the revolution for forty years, while Britain protected and promoted it for selfish commercial reasons and France was the chief source and victim of revolutionary ideas. One day Austria would again need Russia's help, while Britain would always be revolutionary and France would be a fit ally only if and when she had the courage to break with the British.

To this Holy Alliance argument Hess added his gloomy appraisal of the awesome military, financial, and political risks of war with Russia. The help of 150,000 Prussian troops was absolutely indispensable, and Austria herself could not be ready before early summer. Should Russia win, she would invade Austria, bringing the revolution with her, and compensate herself and buy off her other enemies with Austrian territory. A Russian defeat would mean almost worse results:

Should Russia lose, Turkey would become purely a side issue. Just as she has been up till now the partial spoils of Russia, she would become entirely the spoil of the three powers who defend her against the former.

Instead, the chief issue would then be the European war with an altered front. Sweden would drive on Petersburg. Poland would rise almost automatically and, thus reborn, would constitute a second revolutionary France in Austria's and the German Confederation's rear. Austria herself, however, they will want to compensate with conquests in the direction of Kiev, if Polish interests allow this, or with protectorates in Turkey, and thereby give Europe a character [*Gestalt*] in which all the conservative elements still existing are sacrificed to a cupidity for territorial aggrandisement. Austria is to be pushed to the East in order to alienate her from Germany, in order gradually to subject the latter to French influence, and out of fear of her to make her [Germany] even more receptive to French purposes, and finally to deliver her entirely into French hands.

Altogether, not a bad reading of Allied intentions. Hess therefore pleaded for a Prussian alliance, the only thing that could give Austria any military help or solid basis for her policy. Until she secured it and was militarily ready (late June at the earliest), she absolutely *must* avoid involvement; even then she ought to stay out unless her interests were far more directly involved than they now were, and finally intervene with Prussia and Germany to stop the war and to "impose our will on France and England as well as Russia." Only if Russia proved absolutely obstinate and the sea powers reversed their policy should Austria come in on their side.[56]

This memoir illustrates perfectly the difference between Buol and his Austrian opponents, and the virtually hopeless dilemma of Austria's position. Each protagonist had the strengths of his opponent's weaknesses, yet the sound points of each argument could not be combined into any viable alternative. Buol was right in stressing the dangers of staying out and allowing the conflict to take its course. Hess was equally right in emphasizing the dangers of getting in and not being able to keep the war from assuming incalculable dimensions. Hess rejected Britain and France as suitable allies and Buol rejected Prussia, at least as an equal partner; from Austria's standpoint, both were right. Either policy might have dealt equally well with Russia—Buol's, to force Russia to back down and accept Austria's terms by joining with the West, or Hess's, to lead Russia back to a conservative policy by adopting armed neutrality with Prussia and Germany. On the other hand, Buol's belief that he could persuade the sea powers to be moderate by offering them Austria's cooperation under carefully controlled conditions, though not unreasonable per se, proved to be wrong, while Hess's idea that Austria, Prussia, and Germany could call a halt to the war and impose terms on the West was naive and would, if tried, almost certainly have proved disastrous for Austria. Buol believed the old Holy Alliance was shattered and hoped to establish a new European balance and a revived Concert based principally upon a Franco-Austrian partnership. Hess and Bruck insisted that the old Eastern alliance was only temporarily deranged and hoped to reestablish it with an Austrian-led central Europe as its fulcrum. Both hopes were visionary.*

In any case, the conference of March 25 found Buol fighting to save what he could by preventing the proposed treaty with Prussia from being a pact to restrain Austria, as both the Prussians and Hess wanted it to be. Buol's instructions to Hess, read to the conference, presented Prussia's policy as basically anti-Austrian and directed toward ultimate supremacy for Prussia in Germany; the King's pro-Austrian sentiments could not alter this fact. Prussia had till now refused to support Austria, hoping to see her driven over to Russia's side, so that Prussia could play the role of Germany's defender and await a favorable chance to join the sea powers. Now Prussia was confused and frightened by the prospect that Austria might act independently to defend her own interests and those of Germany against Russia. This faced Prussia with the unpleasant alternatives either of remaining inactive, and thereby angering the sea powers and alienating German public opinion, or of supporting Austria in a program that could not bring the concessions in Germany which alone would make Prussian support for Austria in the East worthwhile. Therefore Prussia had made her sudden alliance offer simply to constrain Austria from acting against Russia and to compromise her vis-à-vis the West, so as not to lose ground to Austria in Germany. This being the case, Austria must keep two main points in mind during the negotiations: the alliance must not restrict Austria's freedom of action, and the Turkish territories that Austria would be allowed to occupy under protection of the *casus foederis* must in-

---

* This makes it obvious that one cannot prefer Buol's policy to Hess's or Bruck's (as I do) on the ground that it was more viable or promised better results for Austria. My grounds are simply that Buol's policy was safer for Europe, because more free of the tendencies toward expansion and pure power politics that represent the degeneration of conservative policy. Also, Buol seems to me to have been trying hard to do what all statesmen should in a crisis like this—to manage it, to hang onto the wheel and fight for control even when the ship seems headed inevitably for the rocks.

clude the Danubian Principalities. If the *casus foederis* covered only Serbia and Bosnia, Prussia's alliance proposal was simply Orlov's mission in disguise, designed to alienate Austria from the West by making her complicit with Russia in partitioning the Ottoman Empire.[57]

Hess, repeatedly interrupting the reading of these instructions, demanded to know what "reassuring promises" Austria could give Prussia to persuade her to accept a possible armed intervention in the Principalities? Indeed, what legal basis could Austria claim for forcing Russia out, since Austria had earlier accepted the occupation? Obviously this meant war. Buol passionately defended his policy, insisting on its continuity with Austria's whole tradition in the East, denying that Austria had ever accepted the Russian occupation, arguing that armed intervention would not mean war with Russia unless she wanted it, and even appealing to the ghost of Schwarzenberg. But he returned finally to what he called the "question of conscience": which alliance did the other ministers want—one that would protect Austria in an active intervention against Russia in the Principalities, or one that, covering Austria only in Serbia or Bosnia, would, said Buol, "be useless for the protection of Austrian interests in the East"?

This was indeed the issue—and it was not decided. The Emperor saw no essential difference between Buol's position and that of his opponents, agreeing with Buol that the principles and goals adopted by Austria earlier in conjunction with the West should be upheld, but concurring with Hess that intervention automatically meant war with Russia, and wanting to reserve Austria's complete freedom on this score, while assuring Prussia that it would be used only as a last resort. Thus while Buol's plan was temporarily derailed, Hess's ideas of armed neutrality in alliance with Prussia and an Austrian move to the south were not adopted either. The question became one of which goals the alliance when negotiated actually would serve.[58]

Russia, fearful of an immediate Austrian entry into the war, was immensely relieved even at this indecisive outcome. Meyendorff reported the good news on March 24, praising Hess, Grünne, and all the generals. Just as Buol had predicted, the relief from uncertainty encouraged Russia to press forward with the trans-Danube expedition, in the hope that Hess would bring back from Berlin a treaty binding Austria to unconditional neutrality.[59] Meanwhile, Buol concealed as best he could from Bourqueney and Westmorland the full import of what had happened.[60]

In the negotiations that began promptly at Berlin, the same basic issue predominated—whether or not the *casus foederis* would cover Austria in a war arising over her expulsion of Russia from the Danubian Principalities. But each side was divided internally over this issue, and the internal debates were as important as the formal negotiations. Manteuffel, like Prince William, thought that both the German powers would have to line up with the West sooner or later. Regarding participation in the war as more or less inevitable, he was chiefly determined not to be dragged in for Austria's sake. Hence he would accept a *casus foederis* covering the Danubian Principalities if in return Austria would agree to obtain Prussia's consent for any further action, so that he could tie Austria's hands. The King and his chief adviser General Gerlach feared the sea powers most of all, especially France, and were willing despite their dread of war to defend Austria and give her a free hand everywhere, except in the Principalities. Like Hess, Frederick William dreamed of an Austro-Prussian-German armed neutrality that could eventually impose terms on everyone.[61]

Meanwhile, Hess and Thun were not disposed to fight hard for Buol's demands. The idea of a permanent alliance was quickly abandoned. Hess agreed with Gerlach that Russia could not be expected to evacuate the Principalities at this time, and he saw hope for peace in Prussian mediation and in the Russian proposals the Duke of Mecklenburg brought to Berlin. Against his explicit instructions he included the German Confederation as a contracting party in his first draft of the treaty; this of course would have offered Manteuffel welcome help in paralyzing Austria's action.[62] Buol intended to present the alliance to the German states only as a *fait accompli* to which they would have to accede.[63]

Hess led the King to believe that Austria intended to occupy only Wallachia, not Moldavia, and explicitly promised an occupation that would keep out the sea powers and Turkey as well as Russia. He argued that the alliance would help impose an Austro-Prussian solution on both sides and create a new balance of power in Europe, with seventy millions in the center standing between the sixty on each flank—just what the King wanted to hear. Both Austrian envoys agreed with Prussia that Russia's evacuation should be reciprocal with a Western evacuation of the Black Sea, and sympathized with the King's desire for another Prussian or Austro-Prussian mediation effort before Austria sent any summons to Russia. Hess continued to press on Buol, and probably revealed to Prussia, his pro-Russian ideas for a peace settlement.* He even introduced into the proposed military convention a clause restricting Austria and Prussia, in case of war, to defensive action against Russia on or near their frontiers, and he pleaded warmly to the Emperor for this concession.[64]

Buol ultimately curbed these tendencies on Hess's part. Though ready to yield on points of form (for example, he suggested a separate secret article for including the Principalities under the *casus foederis,* to spare Prussia's feelings),[65] he would make no concession on any main point, and the negotiations threatened to break down. Buol hinted that Austria could join the West; the King tried through Hess and a special Prussian emissary Count Alvensleben to appeal to the Emperor against Buol and warned that Prussia might withdraw to her Confederation obligations.

The decisive stage began on April 17, when Hess, arguing Austria's case forcefully despite his own reservations, offered Prussia a new version of the Additional Article. It provided for a joint Austro-Prussian summons to Russia to stop her Balkan offensive immediately and to give binding assurances, not dependent on any third-power actions, that she would evacuate the Principalities soon. If Russia refused, Austria would move into the Principalities under cover of the alliance. This much was clear and in accord with Buol's demands. But in the margin Hess added a paragraph providing that if Russia attached conditions dependent on some third-party action to her assurances, these conditions, if not objectionable, would be supported vis-à-vis the third powers. Moreover, the *casus foederis* would be particularly specified as an attack on the Balkan mountain range

---

* Hess called for an immediate truce, peace negotiations at Vienna or Berlin, and a simultaneous evacuation of the Principalities, the Black Sea, and the Straits. How he expected to get the sea powers to agree to this is nowhere apparent. For Kempen's efforts to lead Francis Joseph in the same direction, see *Kempens Tagebuch,* 322–26.

or a crossing of it. In other words, Hess wanted to commit Austria to supporting Russia's insistence on a reciprocal Western evacuation of the Black Sea and to make only a further extension of Russia's offensive the ground for Austro-Prussian intervention. Along with other evidence it indicates that Hess privately assured Prussia that Austria would act only if Russia refused under any circumstances to evacuate the Principalities or insisted on pressing her offensive farther.

Nonetheless, the King at first still refused to agree; but on the evening of April 18, Manteuffel brought Hess the King's final concession, swearing him to secrecy and warning him against demanding any more. Prussia would accept Austria's Additional Article, though without committing herself to a joint summons to Russia and without stating that Russia's promises must be independent of any third-power action. Hess ardently supported this at Vienna —even a simple defensive alliance, he said, was better than the otherwise inevitable collapse of negotiations—and Buol, seeing that Austria still would have the power to decide whether Russia's guarantees were satisfactory, recommended acceptance. With the Emperor's authorization the pact was concluded on April 20.[66]

Article 1 of the treaty guaranteed both powers' entire territories against attack, while Article 2 provided for the joint defense of German interests against attack even where one party, as a result of an agreement with the other, felt obliged to intervene actively for those interests. Article 3 provided for joint mobilization of a part of each power's armed forces, to be specified in a separate military convention; Article 4 covered the accession of the other German states, and Article 5 prohibited contracting treaties contrary to this one. The Additional Article authorized Austria to summon Russia to stop her offensive and give assurances of a prompt evacuation, and to intervene actively in the Principalities under alliance protection if Russia's reply was unsatisfactory. But Prussia would join in offensive action only if Russia incorporated the Principalities or crossed the Balkan Mountains. The military convention stipulated the circumstances under which Prussia would be obliged to mobilize first 100,000, then 200,00, men on Austria's behalf.[67]

Austria had certainly gained a good deal. Without sacrificing her freedom of action or cutting herself off from the sea powers, she was guaranteed Prussian mobilization and Prussia's support for a partial federal mobilization if the *casus foederis* arose. But she had not gained everything hoped for—a permanent alliance, or immediate Prussian mobilization, or quite as clear a *casus foederis* as Buol wanted—and of course Prussia's aim of holding Austria back remained unchanged. Gerlach and the Foreign Ministry councilor Niebuhr complained that the Additional Article lured Prussia into a trap, and to some extent they were right. Both Hess's explanations of Austria's intentions to Frederick William and Francis Joseph's similar assurances to Edwin Manteuffel and Alvensleben proved misleading in the event. But Buol had been brutally frank with Prussia throughout; the Prussians mainly deceived themselves. The King was naive in believing that the treaty left him completely neutral, and Manteuffel and Gerlach were hardly candid in telling Russia that Prussia had forced Austria to abandon her demand for unconditional Russian pledges of evacuation.[68]

Hess meanwhile displayed the same suppleness on his return to Vienna that he had shown at Berlin, posing as a pro-Westerner to the Duke of Cambridge, as the defender of purely Austrian and German interests to the Emperor, and as the friend of Russia to Meyendorff. Russia, he urged Meyendorff, should use the treaty, a two-edged sword directed mainly against the sea powers, to separate Austria from them and prove to them how helpless they were by themselves against Russia. If Russia maintained a defensive position on the right (i.e., south) bank of the Danube (still occupying the Principalities!) and did not cross the Balkans, Hess promised that Austria would not intervene and that Francis Joseph would then take the independent stance toward the West he really desired. He conceded that Russia could not evacuate the Principalities without an equivalent concession from the West, but he insisted that Austria's support of the Anglo-French ultimatum to Russia was a mistake and that Buol would observe forms in Austria's summons that would satisfy Russia.[69]

Despite these astounding assurances from Hess and others from Prussia, the alliance was a new blow to Russia. She had just received the news that Austria and Prussia had signed a new four-power Vienna Protocol on April 9, containing more pledges to uphold Turkey's independence and integrity. This fact alone, according to

Russia's previous plans and Paskevich's urgent advice, should have led the Russians to begin retreating to the Seret River in Moldavia. But Nicholas insisted upon pursuing the siege of Silistria, and Paskevich yielded, knowing that Austria's army would not be ready for at least six more weeks. Still, the April 20 treaty strengthened the calls for a retreat before it was too late.[70]

As for the sea powers, neither the April 9 protocol nor the Austro-Prussian alliance gave them much cause to rejoice. The protocol had again been France's idea; Austria agreed to it readily, while Prussia and Britain needed persuading. Manteuffel, though greatly relieved that Austria had not joined the Western alliance without Prussia, was worried about how far the sea powers would try to stretch even a purely moral commitment like this protocol. Clarendon at first told Cowley he agreed to France's proposal because "we can't help it"; besides, a Prussian signature on the protocol might help the sea powers force Austria to sign their convention.[71] But Clarendon quickly changed his mind; the war aims stated in the protocol (the January 13 terms) would "fall very far short of public expectation." What Britain wanted was out of reach, he conceded, "and yet one should not like to tie down our hands for the future by agreeing to something reasonable." Therefore Westmorland was instructed to drag his feet at Vienna while Cowley strove to get the offending war aims statement expunged at Paris. Drouyn's insistence, however, finally forced Britain to accept the protocol as it stood.[72]

In any case, it was used by the sea powers only to press Austria to sign their convention and set her date for entering the war. In similar fashion, the April 20 treaty enabled them to argue that Austria, now secure on her left flank, had no more reason not to fight. The great question in the coming months, as Buol saw, would be whether Austria could succeed in forcing Russia out of the Principalities more quickly than the West was able to drag her into the war.[73]

VIII

Austria's Summons to Russia: Decision Taken

In late April, several relatives of Queen Victoria (the Duke of Cambridge, the Duke of Brunswick, Prince Eduard Leiningen) visited Vienna to find out directly from the Emperor and his mother what Austria, now armed with the Prussian alliance, intended to do about Russia. The answer was disappointingly uniform: Austria would fulfill her existing engagements to the West, but she would use military force only if certain conditions were met, that is, if Russia rejected the summons Austria planned to give her to evacuate the Principalities, and if and when Austria herself was militarily prepared and the Allies were ready to support her on the Danube. In the meantime, without trying to mediate, Austria would welcome a Russian proposal to evacuate the Principalities simultaneously with a Western withdrawal from the Black Sea, and would recommend this to the sea powers.[1]

The sea powers reacted in the usual fashion. The French, highly dissatisfied, plied Austria with still more promises and warnings about Italy, the Principalities, and Poland. Clarendon, although he approved of the French tactics, urging Westmorland to imitate them and sending him additional British complaints about Austria for good measure,[2] * nevertheless was content to allow the French to put most of the pressure on Vienna. In fact, for much of April and May, Britain seemed more trustful and patient with Austria than

* A particularly disingenuous complaint was the charge that Buol had repaid Britain's loyalty to Austria by keeping the April 20 treaty terms secret from her. In fact, long before Clarendon made this accusation Buol had communicated both the treaty and the even more secret Additional Article to him through the Duke of Cambridge (Clarendon to Westmorland, 24 May 1854, Clar. dep. c. 129; the Duke of Cambridge to Clarendon, 29–30 April, *ibid.* c. 12).

France was.³ By late May, however, Clarendon was once more thoroughly incensed over Austria's slowness and cowardice. He knew that Austria had many reasons to be cautious (among them her fear of the aggressive war aims of the West), and he recognized that she was still carrying on her announced program in diplomacy and military preparation. What really angered and worried him was the growing fear that this program would not carry Austria willy-nilly into war, as the British often assumed it would, but that it might enable Austria to do just what she wanted and promised to do, that is, force Russia out of the Principalities without war, leaving Austria free then to promote a compromise peace. This policy was what the British denounced as a betrayal of the West and as base subservience to Russia.⁴

Besides, the British realized how difficult and even disadvantageous it would be to cooperate with Austria in war. Though Cabinet debate in late May initially focused on an alliance with Sweden, Austria emerged once more as the crucial factor. Russell proposed this alliance, with the sea powers to offer to subsidize Sweden's war effort, but not to give the Swedes the guarantee of reacquisition of Finland they desired.⁵ Gladstone, attacking the proposal as incompatible with the moral position of the Allies as disinterested upholders of European public law, urged the more honorable course of simply hiring Swedish soldiers as mercenaries and subsidizing Austria instead. Aberdeen, agreeing with Gladstone, urged an expedition to Varna to win Austria over.* Other ministers also attacked the proposal, while the Duke of Newcastle, Colonial Secretary and Secretary for War, defended it on military grounds, and Clarendon termed it "good economy." ⁶ But Prince Albert pointed out its obvious irrelevance to the main issue. Sweden would never join the war unless Austria did so first, and Swedish help would at best be ancillary, while Austria's was vital to the West. Therefore Albert proposed extending the mercenary principle beyond Sweden to other countries including Austria; Britain should "pay for 20,000 Austrians

---

* Even the honest Aberdeen showed a certain disingenuousness here. For while he constantly urged compelling Austria to join the war by means of the Varna expedition, at the same time he told Guizot that his proposed peace congress was a splendid idea, but that Austria, the only power who could arrange it, was unfortunately rapidly becoming the direct enemy of Russia (Ab. Corr. 1852-54, 121, 129-31, 133).

outright and . . . join them to our army (when Austria has declared herself)." [7]

Palmerston intervened in this rather incredible debate over how to buy Britain a Swedish or Austrian army, turning the discussion to the goals, not the means, of war. The worst danger of all, he argued, was Aberdeen's notion of simply expelling Russia from Turkish soil and then making peace. The war would be useless unless it decisively weakened Russia, ultimately by liberating Georgia, Circassia, the Crimea, Bessarabia, and Poland. For the moment, war must be waged in four theaters. In Georgia and Circassia, Turkey herself, aided by a loan and European officers, could throw Russia out. Anglo-French forces with Turkish help could conquer the Crimea and raze Sevastopol. In the Principalities, if Turkey alone could not expel the Russians, "the Austrians will be compelled by a due regard to their own immediate interests to throw their sword into the balance and thus to turn the scale." It was entirely out of the question to subsidize Austria to enable her thus to fight for her own interests. In the Baltic Sea and Finland, Britain needed a land army. She should therefore take Sweden's, merely promising to help subsidize her army and to consult her in the final peace. If Finland came to be conquered, Sweden could have it, but there must be no Allied promises on this score. After all, Sweden would gain most by the destruction of Russia's Baltic fleet and arsenals; she could not ask for more.[8]

Palmerston's advice, which in his typical fashion leaped over obstacles and disdained to tailor ends to means,[9] gave no practical answers to the questions of how to wage the war and lure Austria and Sweden into it. But these questions did not worry him; his main goal was to commit the government to all-out war and total victory unhampered by inhibiting promises to any allies. He could succeed substantially in this purpose, though the other ministers were less radical than he, because he was more representative than they of popular opinion.* As Clarendon said, the British public now hated

* The political risks involved in displaying any sign of moderation or proportion toward Russia were vividly illustrated by Aberdeen's experience in mid-June. When the Tories violently attacked Russia as a constant aggressor and Austria and Prussia as her accomplices in crime, Aberdeen replied very mildly in the House of Lords that in recent decades Russia had not been especially bellicose or land-hungry. Such vicious attacks ensued on him in Parlia-

even to think of ever reestablishing good relations with Russia and would prefer ten years of war to a peace that did not destroy her power. Therefore, he remarked, no matter how reasonable were the peace terms that Austria might propose, Britain would not agree to them.[10]

Thus once more Britain's own military strategy and political goals prevented her from making a serious effort to persuade Austria to join the West. It was just possible, however, that she might be entangled in war through the troubles breaking out in Greece and the southern Balkans in early 1854. Greece had proved a trouble spot for Europe ever since her revolution against the Turks began in 1821. Her independence, established by the Treaty of Adrianople ending the Russo-Turkish War of 1828–1829, had hardly lessened the Greek problem. Greek nationalists who had dreamed of a Greater Greece or a restored Byzantium were forced instead to be satisfied with a petty kingdom that left most Greeks still under Turkish rule, governed by a Bavarian prince, King Otho, saddled with an oppressive debt guaranteed by three protecting great powers (Great Britain, France, and Russia), and subjected to their constant interference and rivalry in its affairs. British and French agents in particular struggled for predominant influence at Athens; France's ascendancy in the middle 1840's promoted a fiery British hatred for Otho, Queen Amalia, and their followers. Palmerston's frequent interventions in Greece (the Don Pacifico case in 1850 being only the most flagrant example) were made less to end Greek corruption and tyranny, as he claimed, than to combat French and Russian influence.[11]

The Anglo-French rivalry over Greece persisted through 1853, with the British constantly assuming a threatening and exigent attitude over against Greece and with France attempting conciliation.[12] But the greater danger soon came to be that of Russian predominance in Greece and a spontaneous or Russian-inspired Greek insurrection against Turkey. Admiral Kornilov's visit to Greece in

---

ment and the press that, pressed by the Queen, Russell, and Clarendon, he had to apologize abjectly to save the ministry. He was especially chagrined that even close friends like Graham failed to come to his defense (3 Hansard, 134, 306–34, 640–65; Russell to Aberdeen, 23 June 1854, Add. ms. 43068; Victoria and Clarendon to Aberdeen, both 26 June, *ibid.* 43048 and 43189; Aberdeen to Graham and Graham to Aberdeen, 26 July, Graham Papers Reel 19).

connection with the Menshikov mission to Constantinople had served to encourage trouble early in 1853, but French mediation helped avert a threatening Turco-Greek conflict in March and April.[13] The general danger remained unabated, however; Epirus and Thessaly were fertile fields for revolt, and the Greek royal couple, inspired by dreams of a Greater Greece, promoted it. Otho persisted in believing, despite repeated warnings to the contrary from Austria, that Europe, the German governments in particular, would support a Christian rising against the Turks. Most of the nation, the army, the parties, and the Greek press supported his actions, though the Cabinet did not. By early 1854 insurrections were under way in Epirus, Thessaly, Western Macedonia, and Chalcedice. With the natives remaining largely passive, Greek volunteers, regular army units, and even prisoners released from Greek jails were used to carry on the movement. The Greek government evaded peremptory Turkish demands to disavow the revolt and help suppress it, and Turkey broke relations with Greece in late March.[14]

This action made some kind of Allied intervention on Turkey's behalf inevitable, but the sea powers were far from united or clear on how to interpret the revolts or handle them. Few in Britain really believed that Russia had caused them, as Theodore Wyse, British minister at Athens, and Sir Henry Ward, High Commissioner of the Ionian Isles, both claimed. (Actually Russian support was largely platonic.) Aberdeen, Clarendon, Cowley, and Russell saw the movement as a genuine national rising against Turkish misrule; Clarendon even thought of trying to persuade the Sultan to make Epirus and Macedonia autonomous principalities like Serbia.[15] While Wyse urged the sea powers to occupy Greece, and Drouyn was prepared for this or other drastic measures (a naval blockade, seizing some Greek islands, confiscating Greek revenues, embargoing Greek shipping, or sealing off Greece's northern border with a military cordon), Britain hesitated. Though Aberdeen did not rule out some kind of naval action, he had conscientious scruples against using British troops against Christians in revolt against Turkey, while Clarendon knew that such a step not only would be quite unpopular but also would require troops that were not available.[16]

Hence, predictably the sea powers called on Austria to quell the insurrection. Drouyn warned that otherwise France would do it herself and would not answer for the consequences. Clarendon hinted that Otho might "dethrone himself" (and Austria knew the British were thinking of getting the House of Savoy to supply his successor). Both sea powers warned that if Austria did not stop the shipments of men and supplies to Greece allegedly going via the Austrian Lloyd at Trieste, they would do so. France's aim, as always, was primarily to entangle Austria and to compromise her further with Russia and Germany, where sympathy for the Greeks was strong. The British simply wanted Austria to supply the troops that Britain did not have for an undertaking which, as Clarendon pointed out, might bring down on Britain the charge that she was doing the same thing as Russia did in the Principalities. There ensued from London the familiar importunate requests that Austria undertake this minor task of suppressing the insurrection, the insistence that if she had spoken a word to Otho earlier the whole affair would not have developed, the intimation that any Austrian failure to act derived from the same cowardice that kept her from fighting Russia.[17]

Meanwhile, Bruck, blaming the revolt on Redcliffe and his agents, wanted Austria to intervene alone to settle the affair according to her interests.[18] Buol was not interested. He had earlier tried to get Bavaria to help restrain Otho,[19] and he now wanted to aid in stopping the revolt. But opinion at home, including the Emperor's, was wary of too much cooperation with the West in this theater, and in Germany the Greek question was a very sensitive one. Frederick William strongly favored emancipating the Christians from Turkish rule, and King Max of Bavaria, Otho's brother, made Greece the touchstone for Bavarian cooperation with Austria in Germany. Besides, Austria could not approve some of the actions the sea powers hinted at, like a total blockade or the overthrow of the dynasty. Finally, Buol did not want to be drawn into war with Russia over Greece or Thessaly.[20]

So Austria chose a middle course, lending a token naval force for surveillance in Greece's western waters and reinforcing her troops in southern Dalmatia, so as to be ready to meet a Turkish request to occupy Albania and Montenegro and stop the revolt from spreading. The government also clamped down on the Austrian Lloyd and restricted visits by Greek warships to Austrian harbors. But Buol refused to participate in an occupation of Greece, advised the sea powers against a blockade, and tried to get France to promise to maintain the dynasty. Thus Buol's claim to Bavaria that his measures were intended to save Otho's throne and spare Greece worse measures was not unfounded.[21]

But Austria's cooperation did not spare Greece an Anglo-French occupation. While the northern insurrection ground to a sorry end in June, suppressed by Turkish troops in fighting marked by the usual atrocities on both sides, the French insisted on occupying at least Athens' seaport Piraeus, and Britain went along mainly out of reluctance to see the French act alone. On May 10–11 the two powers formally demanded that Greece take positive steps to disavow and repress the revolts, and they backed this demand with the landing of six thousand French troops and a British regiment in late May. Otho was forced to accept a new pro-Western ministry headed by his old enemy, Alexander Mavrocordatos.[22]

The Allied occupation and the brutal frankness with which the sea powers proclaimed and exercised their ascendancy in Athens caused Buol further embarrassment. His quarrel with Bruck deepened; Bruck had wanted to use the Greek affair along with other issues to break up the Anglo-French alliance.[23] Bavaria, with Prussian support, proposed that Germany jointly request London and Paris to limit their occupation and end it as soon as order was restored. But Buol declined to join in, and the Prussian and Bavarian requests were swept aside by the West. Austria's cooperation gained her scant thanks in the Western capitals and Turkey; Britain retained her suspicions that Austria was playing a deep game in Greece.[24] But at least the revolt was ended, and Austria had not been brought into war by the back door.

Russia meanwhile had to decide how to meet the growing threat of Austria's armaments and her expected summons to evacuate the Principalities. The Tsar considered the worst conceivable humiliation to be a retreat forced on him by Austria after he had publicly committed himself to the Orthodox cause, and he urged pressing on with the siege of Silistria, insisting that Austria would not dare attack Russia. But if Austria did move into the Principalities, even General Gorchakov, who also wanted to continue the offensive, saw that Russia would have to retreat immediately, and the Tsar himself expected to withdraw for defensive war deep within Russia's frontiers if both Austria and Prussia came into the war.[25] Hence the Russians had to try, despite their bitterness, to neutralize Austria by concessions. Offered directly to Vienna, these proved useless. All Buol would say to Meyendorff's offer to evacuate Little Wallachia and let Austria come in was that if Russia evacuated the Principalities completely and unconditionally, negotiations might still possibly be arranged.[26] Seeing Austria's summons coming, the Russians then promised to evacuate if given something in exchange—for example, a commitment by Austria to protect Russia's southwestern frontier from attack. They also promised to guarantee complete freedom of trade on the lower Danube. Though many in Austria and Germany found these conditions entirely reasonable, Buol insisted that for Austria to demand counterconcessions from the West or to intervene between Russia and her foes militarily was armed mediation. Austria was pledged not to undertake it, and the West would not stand for it.[27]

The Russian promises and offers Austria rebuffed had a considerable effect in Germany, where Austria since April 20 had been trying to line up the German states behind her Eastern policy. Their reluctance to follow her derived not only from fear of involvement and pro-Russian leanings, but also from the aspirations of some middle states for a more independent role in German politics and the European Concert. Saxony's foreign minister, Count Beust, had wanted since June 1853 to organize the middle states' chief ministers into a group that would meet periodically to seek reforms to give the middle states greater power in the Confederation. Initially he made little progress. His ideas were vague, the middle states were incurably jealous and suspicious of one another, and even in combination they were afraid to stand up to Austria and Prussia. But Austria's approach to the West from February 1854 on gave Beust's "third Germany" movement new life and purpose; now the middle states could join Prussia in keeping Austria out of the war. Or, if this proved impossible, King William of Württemberg hoped at least to stop the middle states from being dragged behind Austria.

King Max of Bavaria and his minister-president, Count von der Pfordten, entertained wider aims, much like Bruck's, for the middle states to pursue. Fearing and hating France, and dreading an Austro-

Prussian split that could destroy the Confederation and leave Germany defenseless, Pfordten hoped to form a united central European bloc for armed mediation, which could extort enough concessions from Russia to keep Austria neutral and could then if necessary impose its terms on the West and Turkey. Pfordten wanted Bavaria alone to take the lead in bringing Austria and Prussia together, and he even hoped to get Bavaria admitted as Germany's representative at the peace negotiations. He therefore had little enthusiasm for Beust's proposed middle-state conference. King Max, however, saw an opportunity to gain support for King Otho through it, and insisted on inviting the middle states to a meeting in May at Bamberg.[28]

Already on February 10, Buol warned the German states against doing anything to hamper the German great powers in defending Germany's interests. He did not take the middle states' challenge seriously, however. Prokesch told him that many German states, especially Hanover, really wanted Austria to assert her leadership. In mid-March, after Prussia rejected the proposed four-power military convention, Austria made an initial move to line up the rest of Germany behind her, but the decision of March 25 to seek a Prussian alliance cut short this initiative.[29] After the treaty was signed April 20, Buol with Prussia's reluctant agreement invited all the German states on May 9 to accede to it.[30] The real question for Prussia as well as for the German states was not whether they should accede to the treaty but whether they should support Austria's interpretation and proposed use of it. Manteuffel, Gerlach, and the King put up a stubborn resistance to Austria's demands that Prussia should mobilize to support Austria's demand for an unconditional evacuation of the Principalities and that Germany also should support it without question. Frederick William sent Alvensleben on another special mission to persuade Francis Joseph to be reasonable; the Emperor replied by sending General Mayerhofer to spur Prussia to mobilization measures matching Austria's own.[31]

Meanwhile, Buol again warned the middle states on May 22 against going ahead with their proposed Bamberg conference. The next day Austria and Prussia signed another four-power protocol at Vienna, in which the powers communicated the Anglo-French alliance treaty of April 10 and the Austro-Prussian one of April 20 to each other.* On May 24, Austria and Prussia jointly called on the German states to join their alliance. Despite the pressure, the Bambergers opened their meeting on May 26. Württemberg's foreign minister Neurath advised accepting Germany's accession to the Austro-Prussian alliance and some kind of participation in the coming Austro-Russian war as inevitable; he also urged them to try by negotiation with the German great powers to fix the middle states' obligations as low as possible. But these pessimistic ideas were swept aside. Instead, the conference protocol of May 30 and note of June 3 proposed the conditions under which Germany would be able to accede to the alliance: any summons to Russia to evacuate the Principalities must include reciprocity—that is, the promise of an armistice and a simultaneous evacuation of the Black Sea—and there must be no use of force to drive Russia out.[32]

This looked like a serious defeat for Austria. Actually it was hardly even a setback, for the middle states remained deeply divided. While they all would have liked to get what the note asked for, only Beust supported it wholeheartedly, and even his version did not make it clear whether these were conditions *sine qua non* or only recommendations. Bavaria was supposed to decide whether Austria's and Prussia's answers were satisfactory.[33] Since Austria had no intention of heeding the Bamberg resolution, and Prussia, despite Bismarck's urgings, did not want to risk breaking with Austria for such allies as these, the note had no chance of success.

In fact, its concrete effect was to speed up the very summons to Russia the Bambergers had hoped to prevent or moderate. On May 29, Buol's three dispatches to V. Esterházy, containing Austria's ultimatum, were submitted to a ministerial conference. The first called on Russia to set an early date for evacuating the Principalities and in the meantime to halt her offensive beyond the Danube, with-

---

* After this protocol was signed, Clarendon became convinced that Buol had played a clever trick on Britain and France in making them share in the territorial guarantee of Austria included in the Austro-Prussian treaty. Buol and Bourqueney, astounded at this inference, had to explain patiently to him that the formal communication of a treaty to other nonsignatory powers does not make them party to the obligations of that treaty (Westmorland to Clarendon, 14 June 1854, Clar. dep. c. 12, and 27 June, No. 221, FO 7/428; Buol to Hübner, 19 June, No. 2, PA IX/48).

out making her evacuation dependent on actions by third parties (i.e., no reciprocal evacuation). The second, reserved dispatch warned Russia that this was her only way to escape from the war; the third informed her that Austria would seek a convention with Turkey to occupy the Principalities and would then force Russia out if necessary. The conference accepted the ultimatum with surprisingly little dissent; only Hess still argued for an armistice and a reciprocal evacuation, and the Emperor now agreed with Buol that Austria could not attempt to mediate in this way. He and the other ministers were mainly concerned that Austria might not be militarily prepared to act when Russia's expected rejection came, but Buol replied that the summons still left the exact time and method of Austria's action open. Hess conceded that there would still be time for Austria to wage war this year, though Austria's troop dispositions would not be completed till July. Buol also received authorization to negotiate with Turkey for a convention governing Austria's proposed occupation.[34]

This summons doubtless meant a long step toward war. Most Austrian leaders expected it; Francis Joseph is even reported to have said, "War is inevitable; it is even desirable." [35] But this step was not an attempt to provoke war so as to resume Austria's historic drive to the East.[36] The decision for peace or war was left up to Russia; a refusal was expected but certainly not desired. Nor was territorial aggrandizement the aim; had it been, there were other areas more tempting and at the moment far less dangerous. In saying that war was desirable, Francis Joseph meant what Buol repeatedly said: it was better to accept war now and end it quickly than to let the war continue into next year. By then Austria would be militarily and financially exhausted, and her inability to control the outcome would seal Russia's supremacy in the East and Prussia's triumph in Germany. This was the argument Buol presented in this conference, as in the previous March; he used elements of it, perhaps incautiously, with outsiders as well. He believed he had no other choice. As he told the Bavarian minister Count Lerchenfeld, "We do not want to become hospodars for Russia, and we dare not allow the Western powers to be humiliated in the war that they have somewhat frivolously undertaken." [37]

It is true, as Srbik says, that Buol affronted both Berlin and the middle states by hastily rushing through this summons and sending it off on June 3.[38] Though Alvensleben, Arnim, and Lerchenfeld were informed of the first two dispatches to Esterházy on May 31 and Buol sent Manteuffel a full explanation on June 1, neither Prussia nor the other states were consulted or allowed to request changes. Buol claimed that he had to prevent the Bamberg states from interfering, but Alvensleben claimed that the *fait accompli* was directed at Prussia rather than the middle states. Westmorland supposed that Buol was eager to act while the Emperor was still willing to take strong action against Russia.* Whatever the reason, Buol's tactics were brusque. Yet as he repeatedly pointed out, if Austria wanted to proceed with Prussia and Germany at all, she had to drag them behind her, for their conditions for her ultimatum would simply serve Russia's purpose of keeping Austria from intervention until she was exhausted.[39]

As for Austria's dealing with Russia, the ultimatum itself was clear and frank; the Russians were neither surprised nor in doubt as to its meaning. Hess may again have given Russia private assurances that Austria had no engagements with the West, that a Russian compliance would turn the Emperor entirely toward peace, and that if Russia evacuated the Principalities, Austria would keep the Turks and Allies behind the Danube. These assurances, if actually given, were deceptive. Buol only promised Russia that if she committed herself to an evacuation and began to carry it out, this step, along with a serious request for negotiations, might enable Austria to gain some concession from the sea powers regarding the fleets. True, Buol tried to persuade Russia that Austria would help her obtain an honorable peace at the same time as he was promising the sea powers to help end the Russian menace to Europe. But if the language differed, there was no contradiction in his aim: to confront Russia with a solid European diplomatic coalition and a hopeless military situation, so that she would buy peace now through tolerable diplomatic and political sacrifices and avoid future territorial

---

* There may be something to Westmorland's view. Lerchenfeld reported on May 31 that Buol told him that Francis Joseph had considerably moderated the ultimatum to Russia. In a cipher annex to the same dispatch, Lerchenfeld claimed there had been a serious altercation between the Emperor and Buol over it (GSA, MA I/586). However, I have found no confirmation of this from any Austrian source.

losses.[40] As Bourqueney told Drouyn, no reasoning, threats, or seduction would get Austria to fight if Russia accepted her summons; she would absolutely insist on peace negotiations.

The retreat of the Russians behind the Pruth and the Caudine forks of the conference *à six* seem to the Vienna Cabinet a sufficient lesson for that of Petersburg; it will not be the advocate of a greater humiliation. So much for the question of honor. As for a guarantee against the return of events similar to those that have so profoundly troubled Europe, Austria can be brought to seek them in a new political organization of the Principalities, in a revision of the Treaty of 1841, and in new stipulations on the mouth of the Danube; but she will not go further.[41]

Recognizing Austria's purposes, the sea powers condemned her ultimatum more fiercely than anyone else did. When Buol read it to Bourqueney and Westmorland on June 3, they called it milk-and-water, friendly in tone, and affording Russia wide room for delay and maneuver.[42] Drouyn denounced Austria for suggesting to Russia ways she could escape from the war, and he insisted that France would not grant her any armistice or accept Austria's ideas on the final peace but would at least demand an indemnity for the costs of the war.[43] Until this point Clarendon and Cowley still expected that the momentum of Austria's military preparations and her actions hostile to Russia would pull her into war despite herself. Assuming also that an Austrian entry into the Principalities would automatically involve war with Russia, Clarendon favored an Austro-Turkish convention for such an Austrian occupation, and even rebuked the Turks, Fonblanque, and indirectly Redcliffe himself for putting obstacles in Austria's way.[44] The terms of Austria's summons and, still worse, mounting evidence that she really meant just what she said were a bitter blow to these expectations. Clarendon joined Drouyn in rejecting any thought of an armistice and negotiations, warning Austria that she would rue the day she let Russia escape unharmed to renew her aggressions later. Even Aberdeen told Colloredo that Austria had to join the war now to force a decision if she wanted peace. Both sea powers also accused Austria of additional treacheries. Drouyn claimed that Francis Joseph had made new concessions to Frederick William at Teschen on June 8–9—a plausible enough supposition, though Bourqueney quickly denied it.

Clarendon detected nefarious purposes in the Austro-Turkish convention that Bruck signed on June 14, and he claimed that the May 23 Vienna Protocol had been a clever trap for the West. He also demanded to know whether Austria was planning to occupy the Tuscan island of Elba, an idea which Westmorland said nobody either in Austria or in Tuscany had ever dreamed of.[45]

Buol tried to shrug off these complaints, telling the Emperor that France still considered Austria's aid indispensable.[46] But in fact the summons of June 3 and the convention of June 14 for occupying the Principalities committed Austria to a program, almost a timetable, that made Allied help more indispensable to Austria than Austrian aid was to the West. If Russia yielded, the sea powers also would have to come to the peace table; if Russia refused, their armies would have to support Austria on the Danube. These considerations help explain, if not justify, Buol's obvious appeasing of the Allies in explaining how Austria would respond to the various possible Russian answers to her summons. Most of what he said was clear and straightforward, and entirely in line with Austria's previous policy and declarations.[47] But he was solicitous in meeting Western charges, and too ready to grant the Allies freedom in defining their own war aims and to agree that there had to be effective guarantees against a revival of the Russian threat. He stressed his belief that Russia would probably reject the summons and make war inevitable. Worst of all, he admitted repeatedly that the careful limits he set on Austria's action held good only this year; if the war dragged on, all restrictions would inevitably lapse and territorial changes become inevitable.[48]

This naturally encouraged the West to plan on a war of attrition and to screw their war aims higher. In mid-May, encouraged by Buol's statement to Meyendorff that Russia could no longer re-enter the European Concert without sacrifices, Bourqueney told Buol that any peace settlement would have to settle the questions of the Principalities, the navigation of the Danube and of the Black Sea, and Turkey's ties to the European system. This was the first French suggestion of a program that eventually led to the Four Points notes of August 8, and Buol responded favorably to it. Drouyn then frightened Hübner with hints about major territorial changes, especially a restoration of Poland. When Buol and Francis Joseph protested, he indignantly denied that France meant to restore Poland or reduce Russia to second-class status. She only wanted to contain Russia politically by restoring the balance in the Near East and in the Black Sea. This would involve opening the Black Sea to Allied fleets, possibly providing a base for them on Turkey's Black Sea coast, freeing the Danube mouths from Russian control, and setting up the Principalities on a new basis as a barrier against Russia. On this last point, France expected Austria to take the lead in reorganizing and controlling the Principalities, but if she would not, France would have to.[49]

Drouyn used the carrot and the stick shrewdly, but he did not gain complete agreement from Austria, as he claimed to Cowley.[50] Buol's response on July 2 was a guarded one, suggesting various changes. He argued that once Russia had evacuated the Principalities an armistice on land should be possible, even if the general armistice had to wait until a preliminary peace was concluded. Buol also proposed a European commission to end the obstructions at the Danube mouth and favored European supervision over the Principalities and European guarantees of their new political structure, with Austria acting as Europe's mandatory (far less, from the narrow Austrian viewpoint, than France had offered). Buol pointed out that an Allied naval base in the Black Sea implied a Turkish territorial cession, which certainly should not be forced on her and which would contradict previous Allied pledges against any aggrandizement. Besides, Britain's idea of a general naval limitation seemed more effective. In any case, the Black Sea question should be left open for negotiations, and Austria could not support a demand for a war indemnity.[51]

While Austria and France were at least interested in a general peace program and agreed on its broad outlines, Clarendon wanted only to commit Austria to the destruction of Sevastopol and a severe reduction and limitation of the Russian Black Sea fleet, and instructed Westmorland already in May to sound Buol on these points. Buol tried to convince Britain of the importance of reaching agreement on the Principalities and the Danube, and when Britain suggested opening the Straits to the warships of all nations (which combined with the narrow limitation of Russia's fleet would make Britain master of the Black Sea), Buol reminded the British that

Turkey had some interest in the Straits that she owned and that the 1841 convention should not be altered without her consent after a war ostensibly fought on her behalf. Yet with all Clarendon's indifference to issues other than that of the Black Sea and his suspicions of Austria's selfish designs, he conceded he was "well satisfied with the Austrian bases of peace." Not only would Russia never accept them until she was decisively defeated, but Austria seemed to favor Britain's idea of direct limitation in the Black Sea rather than France's of counterpoise.[52] This being the first of many claims that Austria supported narrow limitation, from which the English were to argue later that she ought to help fight for it, it is worth quoting Westmorland on exactly what Buol said:

Count Buol says there can be no chance of obtaining this without a *great* struggle, it would seem therefore that you have *abandoned* all idea of a *short* war, but he conceives the way in which the proposition might be put forward would be to require as a preliminary to negotiation, that the treaty of 1841 should be *revised*, and when the question came to be discussed, your idea might be produced, by an engagement that all the powers having a right conceded to them of navigating the Black Sea with their ships of war, the *number* that *each* should navigate in the Black Sea including Turkey and Russia should be *limited*. This is merely a suggestion of Count Buol's *in conversation* with me, which I most *confidentially* report to you. It does not supersede the apprehension which he feels, from the immense difficulty of terminating the war in any reasonable or calculable time, *if it is proposed*, but he suggests the *form* of *producing it*, as less likely to put an immediate stop to negociation.[53]

In other words, Buol did not object in principle to a general, multilateral limitation; he was willing to support it diplomatically and to try to find ways of making it compatible with negotiations. At the same time, he disliked and feared the proposal because it tended needlessly to humiliate Russia and prolong the war, and he never remotely considered it an object worth fighting for. Austria's position never changed essentially on this point throughout the war.

Thus by early July, Austria had gained at least tentative Western agreement to war aims that would not automatically exclude negotiations with Russia, while the sea powers had Austria's consent to terms that they thought Russia would not accept and that would tend to draw Austria into war. Austria's most immediate problem, however, was not whether she could arrange negotiations, but whether she would avoid war, which depended mainly on Russia, and whether she would get military help if she became involved, which depended mainly on Prussia.

Though Russia abandoned her siege of Silistria on June 23 and subsequently retreated across the Danube, her answer to Austria's summons promised at first to be wholly unfavorable. Nicholas denounced Austria and Francis Joseph in unmeasured terms in his famous interview with V. Esterházy on July 6, and told Frederick William that he would rather fight Austria than yield to her. Cooler heads talked him out of his initial desire to attack the Austrians as they entered the Principalities, but it still seemed doubtful that Russia would retire behind the Prut without resistance.[54] Nesselrode warned that an Austrian attempt to take over without Russia's consent the part of the Principalities Russia was abandoning meant war.[55] Nonetheless, Russia's actual answer, which Meyendorff's replacement Prince Alexander Gorchakov brought to Vienna, was better than Buol anticipated. Gorchakov indicated that Russia would evacuate both provinces if she was promised a general armistice and given Austria's assurance, ratified by Prussia and Germany, that she would remain neutral and had no more obligations to the West. Buol, recognizing that Russia had some right to request an armistice, conveyed the proposals to London and Paris, arguing that Russia had proved so compliant on most points that in negotiations she might even yield on the Black Sea issue. But he refused to compromise on Austria's original demands to Russia, and he had little hope of a favorable Western response to his appeal.[56]

Thus Russia's conciliatory reply served mainly to increase Buol's difficulties at home and in Germany, as it was intended to. According to Gorchakov, Francis Joseph promised that Austria would occupy the Principalities only to prevent anarchy and to stop a Turkish invasion; she would avoid clashing with Russian troops and might even restrict her occupation to only part of the provinces.[57] Hess, though he continued to prepare the mobilized Third and Fourth Army Corps for war and ordered General Coronini to stand ready to occupy the Principalities, sympathized with Russia's stand and continued to stress the dangers of Austria's position and her absolute need for large-scale help on both flanks if she had to fight Russia.[58] * When Buol argued that the Russian reply as it stood could not be accepted by Austria or forced on the West, Hess concluded that this made an Austrian occupation of the Principalities without war still more unlikely. Hence prompt, large-scale help for Austria from the Allies and Turkey, as well as a Prussian mobilization, were more vital than ever.[59] Buol warned the sea powers constantly that Austria would not fight unless and until their forces were ready to support her.[60]

France was not on principle averse to aiding Austria, though not with the 100,000 men Hess asked for. Bourqueney often promised Buol French cooperation (at the last disingenuously). Aberdeen encouraged Colloredo to believe that the Anglo-French expedition to Varna in June, intended to help Turkey withstand the Russian siege of Silistria, was a prelude to an Anglo-French-Austrian campaign on the Danube.[61] But Clarendon, while eager to give Austria this impression, intended nothing of the sort. Though a large Allied force at Varna would *"set her going,"* he told Cowley, "if once we get her into the field we might then occupy ourselves with the Crimea. Until Sevastopol is taken nothing for war or peace is really done." Palmerston flatly opposed any Danubian campaign, insisting not only, as before, that Britain and France must attack Russia and weaken her in the Crimea, Georgia, and Circassia unless they wished to "lose caste in the world," but also that his strategy would force Austria to do her duty. If the Turks alone could not stop the threat to Constantinople, he told Newcastle, Austria would be forced by circumstances to do so.

Austria has, as usual, been playing a shabby game. When she thought the Russians like to get on, and while she fancied England and France needed hastening, she bragged of her determination to be active against Russia. As soon as she found our troops at Varna, she changed her tone,

---

* Hess's gloomy estimates of the military situation were clearly influenced by his political views; Paskevich was even more pessimistic about Russia's ability to meet any Austrian attack than Hess was about Austria's chances in launching one. Moreover, an able younger Austrian staff officer, Colonel Ramming, contradicted Hess's assessment of Austria's prospects in a Moldavian campaign against Russia at practically every point, and Ramming's estimate (memorandum of 14 May 1854 KA FA 1854/5/6b) seems justified by events. However, the difficulties Hess had to contend with were doubtless great and the risks Austria faced formidable. See Chateaurenard's report of 28 Aug., AMG, Reconnaissances, Autr. 1602/66.

and, according to a despatch which Clarendon had in his hand yesterday, she now says she shall not enter the Principalities, and the Russians must be driven out by the Turks and the English and French. She can hardly think us simple enough to do her work for her; but the best way to force her to act would be to send our troops off to the Crimea.[62]

Though not all members of the Cabinet accepted these typical Palmerstonian distortions of Austria's policy or shared Palmerston's confidence that the Crimean campaign would be over after one main battle and a short siege,[63] Palmerston again got his way. Clarendon told Cowley the next day that despite Britain's "miserably deficient" information on the Crimea and Circassia, the Cabinet felt "we ought not to be hanging about Varna or the Danube" but proceed East as quickly as possible.[64] Military and naval experts had grave doubts about the expedition, and Graham, Wood, and Newcastle shared their fear. But all the ministers accepted the Crimea as the right place to hit Russia; most wanted it attacked immediately, and not one minister, including Clarendon, who mentioned that Austria would react adversely to this move, considered her reaction worth serious consideration. Gladstone agreed with Clarendon that the Allies must not engage in a Danubian campaign; the Crimea was the best target, and Austria and Omer Pasha could take care of the threat to Constantinople. Sidney Herbert argued that it would be stupid and counterproductive to drive Russia out of the Principalities; the Allies should leave her army there to threaten Austria and to be wasted by disease. Sir William Molesworth, President of the Board of Works, concurred entirely; any success the sea powers might have on the Danube would only tend to drive Austria away from joining them.[65]

Thus in mid-June a Danubian campaign was unanimously rejected and the Crimean expedition adopted, even though the official Cabinet decision came only on June 29 and the Allied War Council decision on July 18.[66] The British ministers did not of course really suppose that this decision would not affect Austria's policy adversely, still less that it would force her to join the West, as Palmerston claimed. Clarendon, who knew that the bulk of Russia's ground forces was already concentrated against Austria,* frequently remarked that

---

* Naturally Clarendon denied this to Austria, telling Westmorland that the Austrian claim that the brunt of the Russian attack would fall on her in case of war was simply silly (7 June 1854, Clar. dep. c. 129).

reports of the Crimean expedition were frightening Austria off. So did Westmorland. While Clarendon denounced Austria for a breach of faith for even replying to Russia's first answer to her summons, he admitted to Cowley that the West's decision to send its forces away from Europe might well lead Austria to accept Russia's proposals. Not only Aberdeen, but even Russell (whose erratic policy ideas stemmed partly from genuine, if unpredictable, scruples about dealing honestly and fairly with other powers), understood Austria's position. He said he would consider a Danubian campaign if (as he did not believe) it would bring Austria into the war.[67]

Prince Albert best saw the implications of Britain's policy for Austria. Russia's retreat from Silistria and her evacuation of Wallachia, he wrote his brother Duke Ernest of Coburg, hurt her prestige but improved her military position and made her a greater menace to Austria. Hence Austria had a right to expect an Allied army operating on her right flank, as she had always demanded. But such an operation would be very unpopular in Britain, would expose the armies to heat and disease, and most of all would not yield the spectacular results the British public wanted and Napoleon needed for his prestige; hence the Crimean "diversion" was the right policy.[68]

Albert left the implicit contradiction unresolved. Clarendon, following Palmerston, resolved it by contending that the difficulties Austria faced were strictly her own fault. She had done nothing for the Allies; it was a lie, he told Redcliffe, to claim that Austria had compelled Russia to retreat from Silistria *—want and distress had forced her to it. Since it would be an "extreme imprudence" to expose the Allied troops to disease by pursuing the Russians, the Crimean expedition was the most beneficial strategy possible for Austria, and far better than she deserved. Though Bourqueney and Westmorland pleaded against driving Austria off by openly announcing the expedition, Clarendon, fearing a delay or reversal of the decision, insisted on telling her, even though he claimed that by her own reticence she had forfeited any right to be informed.[69]

---

* Earlier, when Clarendon wanted the siege of Silistria lifted, he insisted that Austria could do it merely "by lifting a finger" (to Westmorland, private, 7 June 1854 Clar. dep. c. 129). Now that it was done, he claimed that Austria had had no part in it. In fact, as he later privately admitted, Austria's pressure had been decisive, though a valiant Turkish defense also helped. Cf. Wimpffen, 76–79.

When Buol announced on July 9 that Austria would move into Wallachia after the retreating Russians to restore order, Clarendon immediately denounced this as somehow a violation of the Austro-Turkish convention because Austria was not driving Russia out by force. Then renewed Turkish attacks on the lower Danube in early July led Russia temporarily to reverse her retreat and concentrate her forces around Giurgevo, and Austria in response held up her occupation, repeating her determination not to fight Russia until the powers were in position to support her. Aberdeen defended Austria's decision, but Clarendon railed at her "sublime baseness." Britain did not regret Austria's retreat, he told Westmorland, since she only wanted to substitute her oppressive occupation for Russia's; but her expectance that the Allies and Turks would do the work of driving Russia out for her was really intolerable.[70] * Already Redcliffe and Bruck were at odds over whether the hospodars should be returned to their posts, as Austria wished, a dispute that gave Britain another stick to beat her with.[71] Once again the complaints about Italy and Switzerland were trundled out and new demands were made on Austria to let the Allies use her territory for military espionage against Russia.[72] All this pressure was supposed to cancel the effect of the Crimean expedition on Austria and to force her to do the only honorable thing—to stop discussions with Prussia, immediately to conclude an offensive alliance with the West, and to attack Russia.† If she did so, said Clarendon, the war would be over by Christmas. The only mention of British assistance was Clarendon's assurance to Colloredo of financial aid, a promise of dubious worth in view of the vagueness of Clarendon's language. Palmerston's opposition to the idea, and Clarendon's and other ministers' qualms about it.[73]

Angry as the British were with Austria, their greatest fear was not that she would refuse to fight but that she might lure France

* Westmorland replied that he too must be a traitor, for he had like Buol expressed the wish to see Allied and Austrian troops joining hands on the Danube (26 July, Clar. dep. c. 12).

† In one of the sporting metaphors that he, Palmerston, and others often used about the war, Clarendon called upon Austria "to hold out the manteau rouge to the bull" and "act the part of matador" against Russia while Europe applauded (to Westmorland, 4 July 1854, Clar. dep. c. 129). Westmorland's response was apt: you urge Austria to take the bull by the horns, forgetting that if she fails to break its neck, its horns will be in her belly, and since the bull cannot swim, we shall escape unscathed (31 Aug., *ibid.* c. 12).

into a campaign on the Danube. Whether this was an actual danger is not easy to say. While France would always choose Britain over Austria in a pinch, Drouyn, Walewski, Bourqueney, and Saint-Arnaud all favored a Danubian campaign, and Napoleon and Marshal Vaillant, Minister of War, at least did not oppose it.[74] In any case, Clarendon was terrified in late July by a report from Westmorland that France, having virtually settled with Austria on the Four Points peace terms, had promised her help on the Danube and ordered some of her troops to prepare to go there. Clarendon saw not only the Crimean expedition in danger, but delays, possible negotiations, and the national disgrace of a patched-up peace looming ahead. Nothing but an unconditional alliance binding Austria to any Allied future operations whatsoever would justify helping her on the Danube now.[75]

Thus Buol entirely failed to ensure any help from the West if Austria entered the war. He had a little more success with Prussia and Germany, though it was far from complete and came only after a bitter struggle. At their meeting at Teschen, June 8–9, Frederick William and Francis Joseph agreed on a joint answer to the Bamberg note and joint pressure at the Diet for unconditional German accession to the Austro-Prussian alliance. The middle states, especially Württemberg, still struggled before submitting. Pfordten and others considered the conditions Russia posed in her initial reply to Austria's summons to be entirely legitimate, and they wanted Austria to arrange new Allied-Russian negotiations over them. But one by one the German states began to give way; a joint Austro-Prussian declaration at the Diet on July 20 forced through a Federal resolution of July 24 bringing all of them except the two Mecklenburgs into line.[76] The fact that Austria and Prussia were agreed on this issue of German accession to the April 20 treaty accounted for its success; the intervention of the sea powers had hindered rather than promoted it and had embarrassed Austria.

On all other questions Prussia remained at loggerheads with her. At Teschen, Frederick William found no differences between Buol and the Emperor to exploit. Francis Joseph refused to promise reciprocity from the sea powers for a Russian evacuation; the King refused to promise prompt mobilization or to admit that Austria alone could decide whether Russia's answer to her summons was acceptable or not.[77] The Austro-Turkish convention of June 14 for occupying the Principalities was another blow to Prussia, momentarily tempting the King to adopt Gerlach's advice and denounce the Austrian alliance. He had hardly recovered and resumed his efforts to delay Austria's action and mediate between her and Russia when Austria announced on June 27 that she intended to move into Wallachia as Russia moved out—the third time in a month the King believed he had been confronted with Austria's *faits accomplis*. Prussia now protested at Vienna against the June 14 convention and the proposed occupation, and Alvensleben hawked the protest around Germany. It was quickly withdrawn at Austria's instance, but Manteuffel insisted that since Austria had not consulted Prussia and did not base her intended occupation on the grounds foreseen in the alliance treaty, if the occupation led to war the *casus foederis* would not apply. Buol insisted just as vigorously that it did.[78]

Even more intense infighting went on behind this open dispute. Hatzfeldt, reputedly the most honest of Prussian diplomats, assured Cowley secretly that Austria had repeatedly told Prussia she had no intention ever of joining the Allies.[79] Bismarck continued skillfully to incite the Diet against Austria and to goad Prokesch, while the King's aides, Edwin Manteuffel and Count Münster, worked at St. Petersburg to inflame Nicholas against Buol and Austria. His own envoys gave Buol trouble. The Mayerhofer mission to speed up Prussian mobilization failed, partly because Mayerhofer made no secret of his pro-Russian sentiments and was easily put off with Prussian evasions. Thun did his duty, but so obviously against his real convictions that in July he asked for leave, confessing his inability to answer Manteuffel's arguments. Buol advised the Emperor to grant it; Thun was replaced by an even more anti-Prussian envoy, Count George Esterházy, on special mission.[80]

What sustained the alliance despite the conflict was Manteuffel's fear of isolation, the desire of some Prussians, including Prince William, to join Austria openly against Russia,[81] * and above all the King's determination to save Austria from herself by restraining her from a Western alliance and war. In some ways he overstepped him-

---

* Bismarck remarked to Prokesch that the King would join Austria in anything but a war of conquest against Russia, and Prince William would join her even in that (Prokesch to Buol, 30 May 1854, No. 62A, PA II/30).

self; in his effort to get a conciliatory answer from Russia to Austria's summons, he clearly encouraged Nicholas in false hopes about Austria's reply. The Russian answer, which Edwin Manteuffel brought back from St. Petersburg,[82] ushered in the worst phase of the struggle over Prussian mobilization and recognition of the *casus foederis*. Prussia, like the German states, contended that she and Austria should use this perfectly acceptable Russian reply as a basis for mediation with the West. Buol denied that the reply from St. Petersburg was satisfactory and insisted that any mediation or infringement on the sea powers' belligerent rights was incompatible with Austria's obligations.[83] The exchanges became more bitter, the differences apparently more irreconcilable. By late July, Buol decided to close with the West first and to force Prussia to follow.[84]

Of course he had been begging the sea powers to consider Russia's answer seriously all the while he was trying to bludgeon Prussia. Why should they not discuss it at another Vienna Conference, he pleaded? Russia might accept the remaining Western demands under Allied and Austrian pressure; if not, nothing was lost. During the conference the sea powers could continue their operations and Austria her preparations. If Russia refused to evacuate Moldavia and resisted Austria when she finally moved into it, Austria would fight —though still to gain a prompt peace. As Buol told Bourqueney, "We desire peace: . . . we desire it to the point of war." [85]

Hopeless though Buol's plea was, the reactions of the two sea powers differed once again. Clarendon refused even to talk to Colloredo about Russia's answer, fearing to state any Allied terms because Russia might accept them before the Allies won great victories or Britain secured her special interests in the East. The only purpose for which he would consider a Vienna Conference was threatening Prussia.[86] Drouyn, though he termed Russia's concessions worthless, agreed with Bourqueney that it would be useful to submit her answer to a Vienna Conference. For one thing, Prussia dreaded doing so, for it would surely be rejected there; for another, this would give the sea powers a further chance to commit Austria to terms that would pull her into the war.[87]

But the strongest inducement for France to agree to another formal conference was Buol's carefully hedged offer on July 21 to conclude a convention on the basis of the Four Points, on which the three powers had practically reached agreement. True, the *casus foederis* for Austria would be only a Russian refusal to evacuate the Principalities, not a Russian rejection of the Four Points, and Buol was still trying in various ways to soften the peace terms for Russia and to make it possible for Prussia to join the alliance. Still, Austria had offered to sign a military agreement without Prussia, and Drouyn wanted speedily to exploit the opportunity.[88]

The British, their mistrust always aroused by any possibility of Franco-Austrian intimacy, suspected foul play.[89] Palmerston, warning that Austria did not really want to cripple Russia, proposed to Clarendon a "safe" treaty that, he said, would "put Austria fairly into our team." There were just three articles in it, binding the contracting powers to wage land and sea war against Russia; to make no separate peace, enter into no separate negotiations, and receive no peace proposals; and to let other states join the alliance—that is, an unlimited alliance for unlimited war. Clarendon quickly dispatched it to Cowley with instructions to make clear to France that even if Austria signed it, Britain would not join France in any promise to help maintain the status quo in Italy even for the duration. "There is no use," he explained, "in being supposed to have made an unpopular pledge." But the British did not really expect this crude device to work. Clarendon soon accepted Drouyn's version of Buol's proposed convention and even consented to certain minor changes Buol requested.[90]

The final version of the convention stated the goal of the alliance as a peace based on the Four Points, which were specified in notes to be exchanged by the powers when they signed the convention. These points were: the substitution of a European guarantee of the Principalities for Russia's protectorate; freeing the Danube mouth for navigation; revision of the Straits Convention of 1841 in the interest of the European balance of power; and a joint European guarantee of Christians' rights in Turkey, within the limits of the Sultan's sovereignty. A fifth point reserved the sea powers' right to raise further demands in accordance with the outcome of the war. The *casus foederis* for Austria was a Russian refusal to evacuate the Principalities; for the West, a Russian attack or declaration of war on Austria.

Palmerston supposed this convention would enable Britain to put together a grand coalition for war aims going far beyond the Four Points. Clarendon considered them vague and flexible enough themselves to necessitate a long war and produce a glorious peace. He assured Redcliffe that Austria had agreed to narrow limitation under Point Three and that Britain would demand the cession of Georgia, Circassia, and the Crimea as her special conditions under Point Five. Russell, though doubting that Austria would really sign the convention and adamant against giving her assurances on Italy, considered the Four Points to be glorious and severe enough to justify and necessitate a long war even without any additions or elastic interpretation. Albert, along with Aberdeen, hoped that Austria's entry into war would end it quickly and prevent Palmerston's war aims from being realized.[91]

But in spite of these divergent views, the British expected that Austria would now enter the war, and everyone except Aberdeen and Westmorland opposed negotiating with Russia now under any circumstances. Though Clarendon angrily consented to let Buol send the Four Points to Russia, he absolutely refused to promise to negotiate upon them even if Russia accepted them unconditionally, arguing, among other things, that "our national honor and dignity forbid it" and that it would be unfair toward Russia:

One great reason . . . why I should object to pledging ourselves to the bases that we have agreed upon with Austria . . . is that they cannot beforehand be clearly explained to Russia, and if she accepted the Bases and found afterwards they implied more than she meant, she might complain of bad faith, and that is what nobody shall accuse England of as long as I have anything to do with foreign affairs.*

Palmerston, to be sure, foresaw a possible use for the Four Points, telling Clarendon that if all the Allied efforts against Russia failed "then we might make an honorable retreat under cover of a protocol." The Four Points, in other words, were to be the basis for peace if the Allies *lost* the war.[92]

---

* What this really says, of course, is that since Britain and France had agreed with Austria on peace terms that appeared moderate, but that Britain intended to interpret in a broad and draconic sense, and since Britain dared not explain to Russia or even to Austria what she really meant by her stated terms, her national honor required her not to present these terms to Russia at all, but simply to fight Russia until she was ready to accept such terms as Britain really wanted but now dared not publicly state.

Britain's refusal to negotiate under any circumstances became an insuperable obstacle to the conclusion of the convention. Minor differences over the text of the Four Points notes could be reconciled. The British government, for example, wanted to word the first point so as absolutely to exclude any special position for any power (i.e., Austria) in the Principalities; Drouyn supported Austria's request for changes. But the key question for Buol, raised time and again, was whether the sea powers would agree to an armistice and begin negotiations if Russia evacuated the Principalities and accepted the Four Points. Drouyn, who really wanted the alliance, tried to answer with evasions, dark hints that Britain would allow no alliance at all if Austria did not sign quickly, and even fantastic arguments that the British were eager for peace but dared not admit it and would settle for less than the Four Points rather than ask for more.[93] Hübner eagerly abetted Drouyn's propaganda, but Buol was not swayed or deceived.* On July 30, he advised the Emperor not to join the sea powers unless France changed Britain's attitude.

Your Majesty could raise justified scruples against proceeding any further with an ally who cannot even speak out openly on the purpose of the war. If England persists in her refusal to negotiate, it will be necessary to make her understand that this could mean the end of the conference and would be bound to promote the Prusso-Russian plan of a third group.[94]

Warning that Austria could be driven into armed neutrality, Buol now began to stall, telling Bourqueney and Westmorland that Austria was willing to exchange the notes immediately, but would not sign the convention until Russia had rejected Austria's renewed demand for unconditional evacuation and had repudiated the Four Points. He argued that Prussia and Germany would only support Austria if it were clear that her aims could not be attained by peaceful means.[95] This was true enough. A storm of indignation had just blown up in Germany over Austria's call on July 28 for mobilization of half the Federal army contingents, and Germany's anger would have been even more justified had Buol demanded this sup-

* Except on British motives. He seems to have thought that their primary concern was getting the negotiations moved to London from Vienna (Buol to G. Esterházy, 4 Aug. 1854, No. 2, PA III/52).

port for Austria while at the same time he was allying Austria to powers who refused to negotiate for peace under any circumstances.[96] Moreover, since Prussia was just at the point of finally yielding to Austrian pressure in regard to mobilization, recognition of the *casus foederis,* and full support at St. Petersburg for an unconditional Russian evacuation and acceptance of the Four Points, Buol could hardly ignore her pleas at least to spare Russia's honor.[97]

But the main point, as both Western envoys reported, was that Francis Joseph, frightened by Clarendon's language, refused to be drawn into a war without limit or goal. The Western envoys in return refused to exchange the notes without Austrian signature of the convention, and in early August the whole affair seemed to have reached an impasse.[98] At this point Russia yielded, handing Buol a handsome victory. Although the military action near the Danube had turned in her favor, in late July she resumed her evacuation of both the Principalities. On August 7, Gorchakov announced to Buol the Russians' intention to withdraw completely, though insisting this was simply a strategic move that would not prejudice Russia's future operations. Drouyn, fearing that Austria would now be reluctant, demanded at London that the Allies exchange the Four Points notes, arguing that the convention would surely follow. On August 8, the three powers exchanged their notes at Vienna.[99]

Buol had apparently by artful diplomacy gained great advantages for Austria with no sacrifices. By proposing a convention he never intended to sign, containing a *casus foederis* for Austria he knew would never arise, he induced the sea powers to commit themselves at least on paper to moderate war aims and gained the reluctant support of Prussia and Germany for Austria's policy and her occupation of the Principalities.[100] This interpretation is natural but misleading; it attributes to Buol a skill and a duplicity he did not possess. The Four Points were Drouyn's program, not Austria's; Austria yielded more than the sea powers in accepting them. Moreover, Buol proposed the convention at a time when a complete Russian evacuation of the Principalities was still far from certain. Westmorland's, Bourqueney's, and Buol's correspondence all show that Buol and Francis Joseph really wanted the alliance and expected probably to have to force Russia to evacuate the Principalities completely.[101] Had it not been for Britain's stand against any negotiations, the convention might have been concluded before Russia's evacuation was officially announced.

Above all, Buol was not really maneuvering between the two sides to gain advantages for Austria. This, in various forms, was what his critics urged him to do. Instead, he displayed a constant loyalty and good faith (his critics said, timidity and appeasement) toward the sea powers. He insisted that Austria could end the war quickly, check Russia's preponderance, and gain a moderate European settlement to the Eastern question only by cooperating with them. To this goal he subordinated all other Austrian interests, including those in Italy, Germany, and the Principalities. Hence Buol did not consider that he had gained much by securing the Four Points notes and Russia's evacuation without tying Austria to the West. As he wrote Prokesch on August 12, Gorchakov had announced Russia's voluntary evacuation hoping to stop the signing of the convention. For Austria to have signed the convention immediately would have been too obvious a provocation; first she would have to present Russia the Four Points. Should Russia reject the terms, however, Austria would have to turn once more to the West, and Russia's realization of this fact might lead her to accept them and make peace.[102]

One other aspect of Crimean War diplomacy—the question of Sweden—needs brief attention before turning to the new phase ushered in by the Four Points notes. It concerned Austria only tangentially, yet here too her policy played a significant role. Sweden's importance in any Baltic campaign against Russia was obvious from the outset. An unsettled quarrel between Sweden and Russia over Finmark, the northernmost part of Norway bordering on Finland, had troubled their relations and led Russia to close her northern frontier to Sweden in September 1852.[103] Strong anti-Russian sentiment prevailed in the liberal Swedish press, in public opinion, and in opposition circles centered in Crown Prince Oscar, but King Oscar I was determined to keep Sweden out of war. On October 26, 1853, Sweden and Denmark announced their intention to remain neutral, but defined their neutrality on December 20 in such a way as to open some of their ports to visit by British and French warships. Russia's complaints went unheeded; Austria and Prussia supported the Danish-Swedish policy and the sea powers accepted it. In fact, France induced Britain by and large to recognize Sweden's definition of neutral rights.[104]

By March and April 1854, Swedish neutrality in any form was in doubt. Austria's minister at Stockholm, Baron Langenau, reported that King Oscar was the only pro-Russian left. Russia's efforts in February and March to get a Swedish promise of neutrality failed, in good part because of the failure of the Orlov mission in Austria. The prospective Allied campaign in the Baltic aroused war fever in Sweden and prompted the Crown Prince to initiate the alliance feelers that France and Britain debated over in the spring of 1854. Sir Charles Napier, commander of the Allied expedition to the Baltic, stopped at Stockholm on April 25–26 to try to conclude an alliance. Neither his visit nor that of a French military envoy, Colonel Blanchard, produced results, mainly because Britain would not meet Sweden's terms, calculating, as Langenau saw, that if Austria joined the war the Allies could get Sweden for nothing. Both the Crown Prince and the King solicited Austria's support for their divergent policies, the King clearly hinting that Austria's entry into war would draw him in as well. But Langenau urged neutrality on the Crown Prince and warned Oscar I against yielding to an ephemeral war fever or being tempted by dubious gains like Finland. Langenau's advice and Austria's declaration that she would be glad to join hands with Sweden if she herself joined the Allies in war, but that Sweden must make her own decisions, bolstered Oscar's neutral policy.[105]

With France taking the lead, Allied pressure on Sweden was renewed more seriously during the summer, despite the advancing season and the relative failure of the Allied Baltic expedition. Drouyn tried to get Austria to exert pressure at Stockholm and dropped hints to the Swedes about regaining the Aland Isles in the Gulf of Bothnia from Russia as well as Finland. At the end of July, Drouyn received a purported offer of an alliance from Oscar I and urged it strongly on Britain. Again Sweden's conditions were the guaranteed acquisition of Finland and Austria's prior entry into the war. General Baragueys d'Hilliers, removed from his ambassadorial post at Constantinople to command the French troops in the Baltic expedition, conveyed France's offer of an alliance to Oscar I on July 29. Their answer, the Swedes made clear to Langenau, rested on Austria's decision. Buol's reply was clear and correct. As Westmorland wrote his wife: "I got a telegraph from Clarendon to-day to know what Buol thought of Grey's country. [W. G. Grey was British envoy to Sweden.] The answer is natural: Should be very happy to shake hands and join, if we respectively want each other; but, till we do, *silence*." Once again, Austria's refusal to join in Western pressure on Sweden helped keep Sweden neutral and earned the thanks of the Swedish government.[106] *

But gratitude, especially that of a small power like Sweden, is not very useful currency in international relations. Buol would need assets much harder than this if, having brought the various powers as far as he had, he was to induce them in the closing months of 1854 to accept the peace settlement he had in mind.

* Cullberg remarks (*Oscar I*, pp. 83–84) that Clarendon was more honest and less importunate in dealing with Sweden than Drouyn, who only wanted to compromise Sweden. In one sense, this is perfectly true—Drouyn, for example, argued that the Allies could hold out the prospect of Finland to Sweden without being bound by it (Drouyn to Walewski, 10 May 1854, AMAE, Mem. et doc. France, 2120). But there was a point at which British policy became more dishonest and compromising than that of France. That is, it was an attempt simply to make Sweden a mercenary satellite in a British-led coalition, without incurring any permanent obligations to her at all. This is illustrated by Clarendon's private letter to Cowley on August 8, condemning Drouyn's ideas for getting Sweden into the war by promising her Finland. Clarendon argued that this promise would tend to prolong the war, make Russia bent on revenge, promise Sweden a dangerous acquisition that would expose her to Russian attack, and prove impossible to impose on Russia militarily. These were all powerful arguments, equally applicable, *mutatis mutandis*, to other British war aims as well. But then Clarendon added that Sweden could not move anyway unless Austria entered the war, and if Austria did, Sweden could be obtained for nothing. Finally he remarked that the Allies should keep Finland in mind, should the Tsar be "driven from St. Petersburg and compelled to take refuge in Siberia" (FO 519/170).

The Desperate Gamble:
Austria's Alliance
with the West

Three days after Russia announced her evacuation of the Principalities, Buol presented Russia with the Four Points for her unconditional acceptance.[1] He could not suppose that his arguments to her and to Germany, that this was in Russia's best interests and would greatly improve her position and promote peace, would be persuasive, but he did hope that the prospect of fighting a defensive war in which even military victory would not help her politically might lead Russia to accept these terms for the sake of peace.[2]

Instead, the Tsar was barely restrained from declaring war on Austria and at least wanted to tell her that war was inevitable unless she changed her ways and proved that she had repented. Still, the Russians knew that war with Austria would only make their situation worse. Paskevich thanked God that the army had escaped unharmed from the Principalities, and even the Tsar recognized that his strategic position was now improved. Alexander Gorchakov proposed exploiting Russia's present defensive stance to punish Austria's treachery by means better than war. Russia should give her neither any good cause to go to war without alienating Prussia and Germany, nor any assurances that would enable her to disarm. This stand would keep Austria in uncertainty until she was financially exhausted, whereupon Russia could dictate the terms for a reconciliation.[3] Some Russians feared this strategy would exhaust Russia as well; nevertheless, the Tsar adopted it. Spurning Prussia's advice to accept the Four Points, Russia sent back an unequivocal refusal to Vienna on September 3, which Gorchakov complacently described as a bombshell. Buol had supposed on the basis of reports from Berlin that Russia would accept at least a part of the Four Points; he still refused to believe that this was her last word.[4]

What Buol had intended to do in case of a Russian refusal is not fully clear. In his private letter of August 31 to G. Esterházy he remarked that it would be vital to make some decisions as soon as the Emperor returned the next day from a three-week vacation. Till now he had preserved Austria's position intact; "now that our policy passes necessarily onto the *field of action* it will have to be defined more clearly in the army and *in the bearing of its chiefs* than in my dispatches." This sentence could mean that Buol intended to recommend a break in relations, mobilization, or even war if Russia rejected the Four Points. But this is inconsistent with the rest of the letter, which dwelt on the importance of getting Prussia really to support the Four Points at St. Petersburg. Besides, Buol knew how unwilling Francis Joseph was to break with Russia, especially without assured Prussian support; he himself admitted that the Russian evacuation had eliminated the April 20 *casus foederis*. He could hardly justify breaking relations or declaring war on Russia if she (as he then anticipated) merely rejected part of a set of terms that had never constituted Austria's *casus belli*. Buol probably intended, therefore, to advise the Emperor in case of a Russian rejection to renew the pressure on St. Petersburg by more negotiations with the West, more efforts to obtain Prusso-German support, and further military preparations.[5]

This advice, if tendered, was not heeded. The Emperor saw no reason to intervene now that Russia had evacuated the Principalities, especially since the Western powers had gone to the Crimea. Buol informed Gorchakov that Austria did not intend to fight Russia, and he explained to the sea powers that a campaign now was out of the question, though Austria would maintain her position and fulfill her present engagements. Now was the time for consolidation, not further risks, he told a disappointed Prokesch.[6]

Austria's mild reaction to Russia's rejection of the Four Points deepened her difficulties with the sea powers. Angry that she had slipped from their grasp in July, they had harangued her all through August. The British insisted that Russia's retreat proved that Austria could have forced her out of the Principalities long ago and made the whole war unnecessary; or, simultaneously, that the evacuation was an Austro-Russian trick designed to give Russia a strategic advantage and imperil the Crimean expedition. Angry as the British were over Austria's cowardice,[7] their chief concern was fear about the Crimean expedition, either that it would never get under way or that it would end in defeat and disgrace.[8] At least at times the salient facts about Austria's stance were clear to British leaders—that Britain herself had kept Austria from signing the convention by refusing to consider negotiations; that the original convention was now obsolete; * and that Austria had never promised to go to war or break relations with Russia over the Four Points. Clarendon admitted that Austria had forced Russia to retreat and that by occupying the Principalities she was protecting Turkey on the Danube and freeing Allied troops for the Crimea, while forcing Russia to amass 300,000 men on her western frontier.[9] He and Russell conceded that Austria's commitment to the Four Points was of some value, even though, according to Clarendon, it would show bad faith toward Russia to negotiate upon them.[10]

Drouyn drew the obvious conclusion from these facts: Austria would not break relations and go to war until financial exhaustion, political uncertainty, and the threat of revolution drove her into the West's arms. Though the British often said the same thing, they found it extremely difficult to sustain a realistic outlook for long; the slightest pretext would occasion another bout of wishful thinking about Austria followed by more bitter recrimination. Clarendon imagined that Austria would not have submitted the Four Points to Russia at all with the intention of swallowing a refusal; hence Russia's rejection revived his and Russell's belief that Austria would now have to fight.[11] Palmerston renewed his advocacy of a restored Kingdom of Poland, something easily accomplished, he said, with Austria and Prussia in the war. Clarendon, thus inspired, asked Prince Albert whether, despite her stupid pride and prejudices, Austria could not be brought to see that an independent Poland would be very advantageous to her. Albert's reply was a crushing refutation of this notion, but Clarendon instructed Westmorland to raise the Polish issue at Vienna anyway. He also resurrected Palmerston's crude offensive alliance proposal of July and sent it off, claiming that Austria had no more excuse for not signing it.[12]

Along with trying every possible argument to justify Austria's

* Bourqueney and Drouyn proposed a purely defensive treaty with Austria as a substitute, but Britain refused it flatly (Clarendon to Cowley, 11 and 12 Aug. 1854, FO 519/170).

refusal to break with Russia,[13] Buol proposed a substitute for the offensive alliance Britain demanded and the defensive alliance France urged: a four-power conference (or three-power, if Prussia refused to take part) held at Vienna for the purpose of defining the Four Points * and for working out with the sea powers the problems likely to arise out of a dual Austro-Turkish occupation of the Principalities. Obviously, as Bourqueney saw, this was simply a device to keep on good terms with the West at a time when nothing would bring peace and one more forward step might plunge Austria into a war she would have to fight essentially alone.[14] Buol's proposal and his arguments only brought more charges of betrayal, lying, conspiracy with Russia, cowardice and stupidity raining down on Austria.[15] Even Aberdeen, though still pro-Austrian, opposed a conference to discuss the Four Points. The proposal was an Austro-Russian trick, said Clarendon, designed to give Austria a pretext to break with the West. "She might seize upon our refusal to consider all terms of peace," he argued, "as such a token of divergent policy as to justify a change in her own." [16]

Once again, the pervasive British suspicions and accusations did not derive mainly from ignorance or caprice, as the French and Austrians supposed. Privately Palmerston, Russell, and Clarendon all recognized, in an oversimplified way, the basic realities in Austrian policy.[17] British policy toward Austria was again a byproduct of the internal debate over war aims, a struggle in which the moderates continued to lose ground. Aberdeen, buffeted by failure and personal bereavement, virtually withdrew from the fight.[18] Argyll was young and inexperienced; Albert, though still opposed to raising the issues of Italy and Poland, favored drastic changes in Germany.[19] Russell, while mainly occupying himself with harassing Aberdeen and planning for electoral reform after the war, played Jekyll and Hyde on war aims, at one time calling for sweeping conquests of Russian territory (capturing the Crimea and Georgia with the aid of German and Piedmontese mercenaries this year, Bessarabia and

---

* This proposal represented Buol's answer to Clarendon's argument that the Four Points were too vague and needed definition and development before they could serve as preliminaries of peace and the basis for an armistice, should Russia accept them unconditionally (Clarendon to Cowley, 29 Aug. 1854, FO 519/170). It infuriated the British to have Buol thus take their argument against negotiating with Russia and use it to propose more conferences with Austria.

Finland with Austrian and Swedish help the next), at another proposing peace terms that, if drastic and impractical in some respects, involved almost no territorial changes.[20] * Redcliffe and Cowley were cool to Palmerston's ideas for redrawing the map of Europe, but insisted on smashing victories for Britain in the East, to ensure her postwar supremacy over France as well as Russia.[21] Palmerston added to his existing program the suggestion that Britain seize Alaska, to "forestall the Bargain between Nicholas and the Yankees," † and wanted Austria committed in advance to any and all territorial changes the war might produce, as requirements of European interests.[22] Clarendon, tempted by every gain and frightened by every danger, remained undecided.

The actual launching of the Crimean expedition focused this diffuse discussion on a single issue: what to do with Sevastopol and the Crimea after their capture. Palmerston first suggested dealing with the anticipated 30,000 Russian prisoners by setting them free to go to Odessa on foot, anticipating that many would starve, die of exposure, or be killed by peasants en route. He then proposed turning the Crimea, with Sevastopol intact, over to the Turks; once Georgia, Circassia, the Sea of Azov, and the Danube mouths were also taken from Russia, the Crimea would link up with Turkish territory fairly

---

* Russell's "moderate" program, typical of much British thinking, deserves a brief comment. Territorially it would have deprived Russia only of the Sulina mouth of the Danube; on principle Russell did not favor partitioning Russia. At the same time, by limiting Russia to four warships of the line in the Black Sea, razing Sevastopol, and opening the Straits to warships of all nations, with other fleets in the Black Sea allowed to be as large as Russia's, he would not only have made Russia defenseless on her southern coasts, but also have deprived Turkey of all control over the Straits which she owned. Thus the greatest naval power, Britain, would have dominated Russia and Turkey alike. Furthermore, in proposing to make the Principalities autonomous like Egypt, with an hereditary prince and no European protectorate, and in wanting to turn the Danube mouth over to Turkey merely on her promise to keep it open for navigation, he either showed a touching faith in Turkish promises and willingness to respect the Principalities' privileges, or he supposed that British and French influence would keep Turkey up to the mark. Finally, in all respects Russell's program simply ignored Austria's rights and interests or trampled them underfoot.

† Palmerston rightly detected a Russo-American deal in the making; the sale of Alaska in 1867 originated in Russian feelers extended at this time (Alan Dowty, *The Limits of American Isolation: The United States and the Crimean War* [New York, 1971], 81–83).

well and Constantinople would finally be secure. "An adverse critic," Palmerston remarked, "might say catch and kill your bear before you determine what you will do with his skin, but I think our bear is as good as taken." [23]

Others, hardly less confident about a quick Allied victory,[24] demurred at returning so much territory to Turkey, some of which she had lost already to Peter the Great. Cowley preferred eventually restoring Sevastopol to Russia with its military installations destroyed; Aberdeen wanted the forts immediately razed and the city evacuated after capture. The Queen suggested awaiting the mature judgment of the generals, while Russell proposed a temporary occupation and an agreement with France to demolish the works if the city were ever returned to Russia.[25]

Clarendon wavered. Though attracted to Russell's idea because it postponed the decision, he also believed that it was extremely desirable that the Crimea, along with Georgia and Circassia, "should be freed from their [the Russians'] yoke and their vicinage." (How he would prevent Russia from being neighbor to lands to be taken from her, Clarendon did not explain.) Yet he knew that giving Turkey these areas would be unpopular in Britain and that they could not survive as independent states, at the same time as he agreed with Palmerston that giving Turkey the Crimea "certainly would be better, if only for appearance sake, than restoring anything to Russia." [26] Finally Clarendon had only one clear idea for the Crimea: to use it for intimidating Austria. With the Crimea in their possession, the sea powers could counter Austria's occupation of the Principalities, nip any Austrian armed mediation or proposed negotiation in the bud, and cast off the Four Points. He told Russell, "Nothing would alarm her [Austria] more than England and France taking up their permanent abode on the shores of the Black Sea, having the command of Constantinople and of the mouths of the Danube and being ready to revolutionize the Slaves [sic] and Hungarians if necessary." [27]

This whole discussion, to be sure, became academic when the Allied victory on the Alma on September 20 led not to the fall of Sevastopol, as was expected and initially reported, but to the start of an arduous siege. Had Sevastopol fallen, many Englishmen would gladly have dispensed with Austrian help; with a winter campaign facing the Allies, her participation again became crucial. Hence the old means for pressing Austria—Italy, Serbia, and Montenegro—were again brought into play. But the chief weapon of the Western powers, and their principal bone of contention with Austria, now became her occupation of the Principalities.

Buol's aims in the Principalities, as noted earlier, were essentially defensive.[28] Getting Russia out was more important to him than getting Austria in. France had been urging Austria to take *de facto* control of them ever since July 1853; only in March 1854 did Buol call for an Austrian protectorate over them and Serbia, and then as one part of a general plan to control and end the war.[29] Austria's claim to want to prevent anarchy and restore order was no mere pretext. Seeds of disorder already existed in the Principalities in the form of a disrupted administration, depleted treasuries, and a countryside stripped by the Russian occupation and war. The hospodars in exile and other Rumanians called on Austria to come in.[30] Austria had to fear not only the usual practical results of a Turkish occupation—border clashes, incursions into Austria, and the flight of refugees onto Austrian soil—but even more its possible political consequences. Omer's army was still full of Polish and Hungarian refugees, and many other émigrés, including Rumanians exiled since 1848, were waiting for the signal to return. The effects of their activity not only on the Principalities but on Transylvania, where the Austrian government had long been worried by Rumanian nationalism, were impossible to calculate.[31] Omer himself was plausibly suspected of aspiring to be another Mehemet Ali, with the Principalities and Bulgaria as his Egypt.[32]

There were also Western ambitions to worry about. The Allied governments, to be sure, were not primarily interested in Serbia and the Principalities for their own sakes, but as bargaining counters used to get Austria into the war or out of Italy. But most of their agents, especially Redcliffe and Colquhoun, were conscious imperialists and strongly anti-Austrian,[33] and the long-range ideas that both Western governments entertained for the Danubian area were highly inimical to Austria's interests. On the surface, France's idea of an independent united Rumanian state ruled by a foreign prince would seem more dangerous for Austria, with her large Rumanian population in Transylvania, than British plans for constitutional representative

government and free trade for the Principalities under the Sultan's
sovereignty or suzerainty. In practice, Britain, more doctrinaire in
approach and more contemptuous of Austria's interests, represented
the greater danger. And even the Russian retreat had not eliminated
Russia as a threat to Austria, for she still hoped to restore her
former preeminence in the Balkans by promoting revolutionary independence movements, hoping later to bring them under her
control.[34]

Therefore all Austrians agreed on the need to control developments in the Principalities. But Buol, to Bruck's anger and disgust,
insisted on proceeding correctly and legally—first a convention with
Turkey, then an occupation with Turkish and Allied sanction and
cooperation.[35] Buol's approach was exploited by France to raise
questions and challenges, to impress on Austria that she had better
not try armed mediation, and to let her know that an Austrian occupation of the Principalities depended finally on her closing with
the West.[36] As soon as the British saw that the occupation would
not automatically bring Austria into the war, they turned against it.
Even an Austrian declaration of war would have brought only a
grudging British consent to Austria's presence in the Principalities,
and no guarantees for the future; Clarendon had always considered
Austria's influence there as bad as Russia's or worse, and it angered
Englishmen intensely that Austria was looking for selfish gains when
her own wider interests ought already to have brought her into the
fray, and when the sea powers were fighting unselfishly in behalf of
European civilization.

When Austria's occupation began in mid-August, Buol quickly
became caught in a cross fire between three groups—Austria's generals and agents, the Turkish authorities spurred on by Redcliffe and
Colquhoun, and the Allied governments—contending over three
main issues. The first concerned the zones of occupation and Austria's interference with Turkish military moves in the Principalities.
Shortly after Austria began moving into Wallachia on August 13,
the Turks, already there following Russia's retreat, occupied Bucharest in force. When Coronini's efforts to get Omer to evacuate almost all of Wallachia in favor of Austria were repulsed, the two
sides agreed after much difficulty and argument on zones of occupation, with a joint occupation of Bucharest and Craiova. Then there

ensued a race for Moldavia, with Hess and Coronini making special efforts to seize the route over which Turkish and Allied forces would have to move if they wished to attack Russia on the Prut River, the key towns being Braila and Galaţi. In the meantime, the Allied commanders in the Crimea, especially Saint-Arnaud, wanted Omer to create a diversion against Russia on the Prut. The news that Austrian generals were trying to dissuade or prevent Omer from doing this brought violent protests and charges of Austrian armed mediation from Constantinople, London, and Paris. Only repeated orders from Francis Joseph compelled Hess to grant the Turks free passage through Moldavia, even relinquishing Braila and Galaţi if the Turks really intended to use them for an offensive into Bessarabia.[37]

No doubt the Turks and Allies had grounds for complaint. The interpretation Hess, Coronini, and Bruck gave to the June 14 convention was untenable, and their aims eminently political. Bruck wanted above all to use Austria's occupation to promote an Austro-Prussian-German armed mediation directed chiefly against the West.[38] So did the generals, who made no secret of their desire to keep the Turks out of Moldavia so that peace negotiations could be started under Austrian sponsorship. The role of "protecting power" they claimed for Austria in the Principalities meant primarily protecting them from the Turks; the generals tried in every way short of overt force to get Turkey to leave and ignored or gave only lip service to Buol's injunctions to cooperate with her and the Allies.[39] Austria's agents, especially Heinrich Lampel, temporary substitute for Laurin at Bucharest, showed some of the same spirit.[40]

But Turkish and Allied motives were no better. The purpose in sending Omer to attack Bessarabia was simply to draw Russia back into Moldavia in pursuit of the Turks, so that Austria would be compelled to fight her; Austria was denounced for failing to fall into the trap. Omer never wanted to go, agreed with Hess that the move was military folly, originally accepted Hess's proposed zones of occupation in Moldavia, and actually began transferring part of his forces to Bulgaria in mid-September. Austria's opposition simply gave him a good excuse for failing to carry out the offensive. When Austrian obstruction was removed, Colquhoun and Redcliffe advised Omer against launching an attack; menacing Russia on the Prut was

Austria's responsibility. Besides, Lord Raglan wanted Omer's troops in the Crimea (though Omer did not want to go there either).[41]

It is more difficult to see Austria as the prime troublemaker on the second issue, Ştirbei's reinstatement as hospodar of Wallachia. Ştirbei was a controversial figure, but his legal right to fill out his term to May 1856 was clear, and so was his experience and talent. Paris-educated and of a leading boyar family, he had played a leading role in Wallachian affairs since 1829, helping draw up the Principalities' basic law, the Règlement Organique, and heading at various times the departments of interior, foreign affairs, cults, and justice. Though his work with the Russians during their occupations of 1829–1834 and 1849–1850 lent color to the charge that he was Russophile, he was actually a progressive nationalist, like his Moldavian colleague Gheorghe Ghica. He had been charged with corruption and had many enemies among the boyars (any strong hospodar was anathema to them), but the opposition would have been relatively impotent had it not been supported and instigated by foreign agents.[42] The specific charge against him, that his delay in leaving his post after the Russian occupation proved him disloyal to the Porte, was clearly a pretext. No charge was made against Ghica, who had done the same thing; the divans of both Principalities had urged it, and Reshid had later sanctioned the action.[43] Since 1849, Redcliffe and Colquhoun had opposed Ştirbei and worked for his downfall because at that time he had cooperated with the Russians while they were protecting the revolutionary émigrés.[44] Colquhoun's protégé and candidate to replace Ştirbei as caimacam, Constantin Cantacuzino, had a much worse record as a Russophile; he had served Russia all through the recent occupation, had been decorated by them, and was appointed head of the provisional government as they withdrew. Besides, Stirbei stood in the way of Redcliffe's and Colquhoun's plans for "reform" in the Principalities, including the abolition of the Règlement Organique, the appointment of the liberal émigré Ion Ghica, Redcliffe's protégé, as Wallachian hospodar, and the naming of Colquhoun's friends to all leading offices. The French agent Eugène Poujade, also in the anti-Ştirbei campaign, was Ion Ghica's brother-in-law. At Paris, meanwhile, the Foreign Ministry hoped to replace Ştirbei with Constantin Ghica, wholly devoted to France.[45]

Buol certainly expected Austria to have a strong influence on Ştirbei, but as he told his agents time and again, Austria did not want an exclusive sphere of influence. Austria was not committed to support Ştirbei if good grounds were found for the Turks to dismiss him.[46] Buol knew that Austria had virtually no party favoring her in the Principalities, and if Bruck, Hess, and others were willing to risk much to create one, Buol was not. His main goals were conservative —preserving the legal order, getting a regular administration with which Austria could work, curbing revolutionaries and émigrés, and holding the door open for an eventual settlement on the Principalities at the peace conference. Neither Ştirbei nor Ghica proved to be Austrian puppets. The generals and Bruck often complained of Ştirbei's weakness under Turkish pressure and his friendship with such dangerous persons as General Władislaw Zamoyski, émigré leader of a Polish legion in Turkish service.[47] Ştirbei retained his nationalist goals of unification and constitutional government, hoping now to achieve them with Austria's support. As for Ghica, he was even more nationalist and eventually became a real thorn in Austria's side.[48]

In any case, Bruck won out in a sharp clash with Redcliffe over Ştirbei's and Ghica's reinstatement.[49] * Fighting to get the decision reversed or delayed, Redcliffe persuaded the Sultan to order an investigation into Ştirbei's conduct as hospodar under Dervish Pasha, Turkish civil commissioner for the Principalities. Colquhoun and Poujade organized a boyar campaign for Ştirbei's recall, amassing evidence that Laurin claimed was nothing but old slanders by political enemies and disgruntled office-seekers. On Ştirbei's return to his post in late September, Colquhoun avoided any relations with him by not officially resuming his own post as British consul, and had the commander of Bucharest, Mashar Pasha (Sir Stephen Lakeman) forbid all public demonstrations in Ştirbei's honor. This set the tone for the vendetta Colquhoun and Redcliffe continued to wage against Ştirbei, even though he and Austria had won the first round.[50]

The third issue was the whole character and purpose of the Austrian occupation. Colquhoun constantly denounced it as unnecessary, immensely unpopular, undisciplined, brutal, despotic, and financially ruinous. His reports, often based on unverified rumor, regularly

---

* Drouyn claimed Ştirbei had won reinstatement by bribing Reshid; Bruck insisted the Sultan wanted to escape from Redcliffe's domination.

became the basis of British protests at Vienna. There was some ground to these charges, as Austrian records show; the most serious incidents and problems of this type will be discussed later. But Colquhoun exaggerated and distorted greatly; his colleague Sam Gardner at Iaşi, who did not share Colquhoun's *furor consularis*, gave quite a different picture.[51] Moreover, Austrian records also reveal the time and effort spent by civilians and military men alike in trying to check or correct these problems, some of them not of Austria's making. There was the chaos inherited from the Russian occupation; constant obstruction and provocation from the Turks, egged on by Redcliffe and Colquhoun; Omer's continual delay in carrying out orders from Constantinople to send away the dangerous elements in his entourage; the refusal of Dervish Pasha to have any dealings with Austria's civil commissioner Eduard Bach (Alexander's brother), on the ground that the Austrian army was simply an auxiliary for the Sultan and Austria had no civil affairs to concern herself with; and the protection of political refugees in the Principalities and encouragement of their anti-Austrian activities by British agents.[52] Nor did Austria lack evidence to support charges she could have raised about the ruinous effects of the Allied occupations of parts of Turkey and Greece or the atrocities committed by the Turks in Bulgaria and Albania.* As Buol remarked, he refrained from doing so for the sake of better relations.[53]

As for the long-range expansionist purposes of the Austrian occupation, there is no doubt that leading Austrians hoped to penetrate the Principalities, tying them to Austria politically, militarily, and economically. Bruck wanted them incorporated in his central European customs union. Coronini promoted schemes for railway, telegraph, and road connections to Austria, and a beginning was made on extending Austria's telegraph network into Moldavia. Hess wanted the Principalities tied into Austria's defenses, with fortresses connecting the lower Danube and the Prut to Galicia and the Bukovina. Francis Joseph and Grünne were particularly interested in leaving behind a native militia organized on Austrian lines. All

---

* Bruck's dispatches are full of such reports, and Redcliffe's own correspondence attests to the scandalous indiscipline of the various irregular troops under British command in the East—conduct so bad that the Turks often protested against it (e.g., Redcliffe to Clarendon, 6 Jan. 1855, No. 14, FO 78/1010).

the commanders became involved in censorship and police affairs; Coronini proposed establishing a secret antirevolutionary police on the Austrian model. Repeatedly there were calls for developing a pro-Austrian party.[54]

Still, what impresses one most in surveying the occupation is not that Austrians entertained such ideas, but how little they accomplished, or seriously attempted. Commanders in the field and officials in Vienna turned their attention first to ordinary military and political routine; next to quarrels with Turkish, British, or local authorities; then to repressive defensive measures like getting the émigrés ousted or suspicious persons watched; and last and least to measures to promote Austria's long-range hold over the Principalities. Coronini could not begin to promote Austrian commercial penetration of the Principalities until the spring of 1855, and by that time Austria was firmly in the Western camp and her days of occupation were already numbered. Even then he constantly complained that only Bruck, who was by that time Finance Minister, supported him. The Emperor's concern over the native militia arose even later, as a product of his fear of disorder after Austria left.[55] The failure to carry out Austria's dreams was not accidental. While Austria had important trade and economic interests in the Principalities, in a real imperialist contest she was too weak, too vulnerable, too poor, too laggard in her own development, too cautious, too narrow and old-fashioned in her ideas, and too inefficient seriously to complete with Britain, France, or Russia. The dreams of Bruck and the generals were always castles in the air.

This is not, of course, to make a virtue out of failure, or to argue that Buol's idea of a limited paternalist Austrian protectorate guaranteed by Europe would have been any more practical than the bolder ideas of his opponents. In the face of Rumanian nationalism and the hostile influence of other powers, even Buol's type of protectorate would eventually have had either to be turned into outright annexation or to be given up.* But there is a virtue in seeing necessity and bowing to it, a sanity in recognizing limitations. For Buol, the main question was always one of controlling, not the Principalities, but the general outcome of the war. Not even his

---

* I am grateful to Professor Barbara Jelavich of Indiana University for stressing this point to me.

rivals would have sacrificed the prospect of peace in order to achieve their goals on the lower Danube. Because Buol was convinced that Austria's larger goals, as well as those in the Principalities, were possible only with Western cooperation and participation, he not merely accepted, but himself offered and promoted, Western control over Austria's actions there and specifically reserved the whole question of the Principalities for European decision in the final peace settlement.[56] Aberdeen saw this quite well, and one may doubt that even the anti-Austrians in Britain believed their own propaganda about Austria's violating the Sultan's sovereign rights and seeking an exclusive protectorate.[57] In fact, Buol constantly defended the legal status quo, Turkey's present rights, and the Principalities' privileges.

In contrast, all the Allied schemes for restructuring them under Turkish sovereignty (Redcliffe and Colquhoun), or making them virtually independent (the French and Russell), or giving them to Austria in exchange for Lombardy-Venetia (Palmerston and Napoleon), or leaving them to Russia in exchange for Asian territory so as to punish Austria (Cowley), or garrisoning them permanently with Turkish soldiers (Clarendon), showed little regard for legality, Turkish rights, the inhabitants' privileges, or the ostensible aims of the war, the preservation of Turkey's integrity and the balance of power.[58] The "aggressiveness" and "selfishness" of Austrian policy consisted essentially in her effort to keep the fate of the Principalities from being settled simply by the sea powers, without Austria and against her interests.[59]

As for Buol's methods, no doubt he awoke to the problems in the Principalities somewhat late (the picture he gave the Emperor on September 18 was misleadingly optimistic, based on Coronini's and Laurin's reports) and he relied too long on exhorting his colleagues to moderation. He did not try to recall Bruck or immediately to rein in the generals on political questions—both moves would have been difficult and risky.[60] But under Western pressure he moved decisively in late September and October, getting Francis Joseph to forbid the generals to interfere with Turkish and Allied military moves and laying out Austria's position for them and Bruck in uncompromising terms. Austria, he asserted, had no obligations toward Russia, which remained her opponent as long as she refused to accept the Four Points. She did have concrete obligations to the sea

powers and Turkey and had no right to an exclusive occupation or
protectorate, or armed mediation. In addition, Buol proposed turning over all questions regarding the occupation that could not be
amicably settled by the parties involved to the ambassadorial conference at Vienna for final decision (here Austria could be outvoted
two to one). Though Hess accepted his orders only under protest
and Bruck's quarrel with Buol flared still higher (especially when
Bruck's instructions were communicated also to Turkey and the sea
powers), by late October the basic problem of divergent policy was
under control.[61]

With Turkey, Buol was both firm and conciliatory. He backed
Bruck's and Coronini's campaigns to get Dervish removed as civil
commissioner and to make Omer remove the émigrés from his entourage, and he warned the Turks against attacking Russia on the
Prut, though Austria would not try to prevent her. At the same
time, while sharply rejecting Turkey's charges of double dealing, he
assured her that Austria respected her rights and would adhere
strictly to the June 14 convention. Moreover, Buol steadily fought
for this policy at home, opposing even his friend Bach on this
score.[62] With the sea powers Buol used more appeasement, carefully considering and patiently answering their most violent charges
and defending their rights before the Emperor and other Austrians,
while actually soft-pedaling Austrian complaints against Allied
agents.[63]

The policy appears both pusillanimous and counterproductive.
But at least it was his *policy*, and not, as has been claimed, a change
in attitude forced on him by Allied victories in the Crimea and by
the embarrassments of Austria's position.[64] On September 23, while
totally in the dark on the outcome of the Crimean expedition, he
wrote Colloredo and Baron Ottenfels, chargé at Paris, to plead for
an answer to his September 14 proposals for a Vienna conference,
insisting:

It is of the most absolute necessity to make known by some kind of
diplomatic accord our determination to remain united in the pursuit of
the same goal. The difference in our positions already gives only too
much leverage to those who are trying to make people believe that we
are going to separate. We must consult on something to fight these
harmful rumors.[65]

Three days later, still ignorant of Crimean developments, Buol made his strongest plea yet to the Emperor for a clear Western alliance. Austria, he argued, had to overcome Western suspicions over the Principalities arising out of "the slanders and distortions from Berlin and the very peculiar conduct and language of our high military authorities." But even careful negotiation over the Principalities could not solve the problem alone. Only a clear treaty relationship with the West would keep the sea powers from trying to embarrass Austria and to force her prematurely into war. Austria's kind of peace could be attained only through the sea powers; a break with them would mean the triumph of Pfordten, Beust, and company, and if Prussia forced Austria to remain passive everyone would be alienated and Austria's vital interests sacrificed. Buol wrote: "We must, as long as Russia will not negotiate for peace, frankly unite with the policy of the sea powers and have the courage to say so on all sides. Only thus will we be able to control their steps and at the same time pursue our own interests." [66] The day after this *Vortrag*, Francis Joseph conceded to Bourqueney that the time for negotiations was past. To Bourqueney's rejoinder that this left only force, he replied, "I understand you, it is a question of the season and the date. I do not want to begin war in October." But the Emperor did agree that a new diplomatic tie was needed now between Austria and the West.[67]

Thus the conflict over the Principalities led back to the terrain of Austria's general relations with the sea powers, which Buol had never deserted. With Bourqueney and Westmorland he worked out a new proposal for a limited defensive treaty, sent to London and Paris on October 3 at Bourqueney's suggestion. The West saw it as no great improvement over Buol's earlier proposal. The sea powers would still have to accept a Vienna conference on the Four Points, agree not to make peace without Austria, and consult her before launching an offensive through the Principalities. Austria, who would be protected against a Russian attack, would have no obligation except to occupy the Principalities against Russia for the duration. Obviously this treaty would serve solely to keep an Austro-Western tie intact through the winter.[68]

Drouyn and Clarendon quickly rejected the proposal; both sea powers continued to denounce Austria's conduct in the Principalities and to threaten to make peace at her expense.[69] But while Clarendon dismissed anything short of a full offensive treaty as worthless, Drouyn, having just publicized Austria's congratulations to France on the falsely reported fall of Sevastopol,[70] wanted further to exploit the Austro-Russian breach. He suggested to Hübner that he would grant Austria her purely defensive treaty for the present if she would set a date for entering the war in the spring. When Hübner convinced him that this was impossible, he proposed to Britain that they follow up Buol's suggestion, earlier rejected by the Allies, of a Vienna conference to deal with the Principalities and the rights of Ottoman Christians (the Fourth Point).[71]

This counterproposal, following the shattering of hopes for quick victory in the Crimea, caused more dispute at London. Aberdeen had favored the original Bourqueney-Buol proposal of a defensive treaty and had even told Colloredo that Austria was not opposing Britain's extravagant war aims vigorously enough. The Queen thought Austria's initiative should not be rejected without a counteroffer.[72] Those who opposed Austria's present proposal were not agreed on why it was bad. Cowley rejected any agreement that would not bring Austria into the war on a fixed date, while Russell, though bitter at Austrian perfidy, would accept a purely defensive treaty with her if only it did not bind England to negotiate or commit her to the Four Points. Clarendon agreed with him; a Vienna conference to define the Four Points was a humiliation the public would not tolerate.[73]

But Drouyn's insistence on returning some counterproposal was hard to resist and the chance to drive a further wedge between Austria and Russia tempting, especially since many informed sources claimed that Austria knew she would have to fight in the spring. For a short time Britain seemed ready to go along with a French project of a modified defensive treaty including, if it could be obtained, a secret article binding Austria to fight by a fixed date in the spring. Cowley, surprisingly, came to favor the treaty even without the secret clause. So did Clarendon, though he was sure Austria would reject the whole project. Even Palmerston proposed only minor changes.[74] Then suddenly Russell changed his mind once more, insisting on an offensive treaty or none and suggesting to this end a separate Austro-British convention binding Austria, as soon as weather permitted, to throw 100,000 men against Bessarabia, this army to receive a subsidy of thirty pounds per man (provided Parliament voted it). Russell explained neither his reversal of view nor his choice of this crude mercenary approach to Austria; presumably he decided to oppose the defensive treaty because Aberdeen favored it.[75] With Clarendon first wavering and then joining Russell, the Cabinet, sharply divided, refused on October 17 to sanction the proposed treaty and definitely rejected it on October 23. The British gave France various predictable grounds for their decision, but the real reason, which a disgusted Drouyn declared he was very weary of hearing, was that the British public would not tolerate the resumption of conferences.[76]

Drouyn now insisted on at least having a Vienna conference on problems in the Principalities, and Clarendon yielded. Buol's offer, he admitted, showed Austria's good faith, and the conference, or, as he called it, the Board of Moldo-Wallachian Claims and Grievances, would serve to control the misconduct of her generals and troops.[77] Redcliffe, delighted that treaty negotiations with Austria had broken down, protested strongly that any conference on the Principalities must be held in Constantinople to protect Britain's predominant influence at the Porte. But Clarendon told him that much as he despised Austria, this was not the time to foster quarrels with her over territories where the Sultan's rights were purely nominal anyway.[78] The conference, meeting from November on in Vienna as problems arose, proved useful, mainly because Buol, despite Bruck's and Coronini's protests, used it faithfully to settle differences and strive for inter-Allied cooperation.[79] Redcliffe and Colquhoun tried continually to bypass and sabotage it, while Clarendon employed it only for registering grievances against Austria, reserving for Constantinople any questions involving the Turkish government, especially the British campaign to replace Ştirbei.[80]

Nor did the Board of Moldo-Wallachian Claims and Grievances stop the sea powers from trying again to trap Austria into war by provoking an Austro-Russian clash in Moldavia. On orders from home, Raglan and Saint-Arnaud pressed Omer throughout November to make a diversion on the Prut. Quite apart from the wretched condition of the Turkish troops, it was militarily absurd to launch an offensive in mid-November in such terrain and everyone knew it; Clarendon, Drouyn, and others clearly expressed their aim of goading Russia into invading Moldavia in pursuit of the Turks. Omer, more eager to fight Redcliffe and Reshid than to attack the Russians, announced and launched his "offensive" in a manner designed to provoke Austrian opposition so as to enable him to abandon it without a direct refusal to the Allies. Coronini and the Austrian General Augustin rose to the bait, refusing the Turks permission because they were demanding areas assigned to Austria by mutual agreement and sending troops into Austrian-occupied zones without notice; Coronini still claimed the right to keep Russia and Turkey separated.[81]

But this time Vienna called the Allied bluff. Hess advised Coronini to let the Turks go ahead; if the Russians beat the Turks and pursued them across the Prut, Coronini should protest, but withdraw northward to avoid a clash. With Omer's invasion route opened wide, Buol, hit with the usual barrage of protests stemming from Colquhoun and Poujade, could prove that there was no obstruction and that the charges showed a clear prejudice against Austria. Bourqueney further reported that Austria had no objection if France wanted to send two divisions to help Omer, though Austria doubted that it was militarily advisable. On December 4 at the Vienna Conference, Austria gave Turkey a permanent invasion route through southern Moldavia—a good way to ensure that she would never use it. Clarendon still insisted that the incident proved Austria's treachery. Westmorland, having supplied abundant evidence to the contrary, ultimately closed the discussion by writing: "As I am convinced that it is as much the object of General Hess as of Count Buol that the most perfect harmony should exist between the Austrian and the Ottoman armies I hope this may be the last occasion upon which I may be called upon to make any observation upon this subject." [82]

Meanwhile, the idea of an Austrian alliance remained alive despite Britain's decisions of October 17 and 23. Drouyn insisted that a treaty could be designed that would stop Austria from falling into armed mediation and that would engage her to fight in the spring without really committing the West to negotiations or the Four

Points. Cowley reluctantly sided with Drouyn. Clarendon, despite his insistence that Austria would never sign anything until Sevastopol fell, produced his own revision of France's proposal, and Russell endorsed it, encouraging Clarendon to inform Palmerston of it and then proceed without Cabinet consent. But Aberdeen wanted Clarendon's draft made more palatable to Austria, especially the sections dealing with the Four Points and the Principalities,[83] while Palmerston objected strongly to any alliance. Once more he insisted that Austria was too weak and cowardly to attempt the armed neutrality with Germany that France feared and wanted to avert. The sole danger was that Austria would entangle the West in negotiations, paralyzing the Allies' military operations and compelling them ultimately either to accept peace on plausible but incomplete terms or to bear the onus of needlessly prolonging the war. Making the Four Points the main basis for peace only heightened this danger, for the Fifth Point, flexible though it was, could hardly be stretched to include such vital British demands as the cession of the Crimea, Georgia, and Circassia. Besides, Article 5 (the *casus foederis*) opened the door to negotiations during the winter by postponing Austria's entry into war until spring. Though insisting that only an unconditional offensive alliance was worth having, Palmerston proposed as a substitute a purely defensive treaty including Turkey, which provided only vague terms for the *casus foederis* and which entailed no Allied military obligation to Austria. Rather than risk negotiations and the possible limiting of British war aims, Palmerston again preferred to dispense with Austrian help.[84]

This time, however, his arguments did not succeed. Clarendon saw little weight in them, and Russell, though Austrophobe like Palmerston, wanted Article 5 retained. In addition, everyone but Palmerston considered Britain's proposed treaty innocuous, almost meaningless, and was sure Austria would not sign it anyway until Sevastopol fell. As Russell remarked, that would be the time to work out terms with France and present them to Vienna.[85]

So the draft treaty was sent to Vienna on November 7, accompanied by the usual accusations, the main one being that Austria was protecting Russia and encouraging her to send reinforcements to the Crimea.[86] * The charge was particularly false at this time, for Austria, as the West knew, had ordered general mobilization on October 22 to put further pressure on Russia to accept the Four Points. Thus Russia was compelled especially now to concentrate on her western frontier.

In reply, Buol once more startled the British by eagerly taking up their proposal, suggesting only minor changes (e.g., not including Turkey in the alliance) and apparently sharpening the *casus foederis* by substituting the end of 1854 for April 1855 as the date at which, if peace were not assured on the basis of the Four Points, the three powers would consult on further measures to achieve the goals of the alliance. He gave up his call for a joint ultimatum to Russia, insisting only that Austria would have to deliver an ultimatum on the peace terms herself, with the sea powers' knowledge and consent, and that if Russia accepted it the sea powers must be ready to negotiate.[87]

Obviously, Buol was trying simultaneously to force Russia to accept the Four Points and to get the sea powers to define them and agree to negotiate on that basis. His reason for moving up the *casus*

---

* An exchange between London and Vienna at this time shows particularly well how anything Buol proposed was twisted into a charge against him. Clarendon's main argument for rejecting Buol's proposed defensive treaty was that as long as battles raged in the Crimea the British public would not stand for any inter-Allied discussion of peace terms. This argument greatly angered the French, for consistently followed it would have ruled out any treating with Austria. Buol, however, calmly replied that if Britain felt this way, the treaty could be postponed, with the sea powers continuing their operations and Austria continuing her pressure on Russia, Prussia, and Germany in favor of the Four Points. Once the season for military operations was past, the three powers could then agree upon terms of peace and sign an alliance providing for an ultimatum to Russia based upon them, which if rejected by Russia would bring the *casus foederis* into play. Buol, in other words, not only accepted Clarendon's objection to discussing terms at that time, but offered to do so later and to sign an alliance then if the British preferred. But Prince Albert violently denounced this offer as proof that Austria would not treat with the Allies until they first took Sevastopol, and Clarendon sent off a rocket to Westmorland condemning him for expressing satisfaction with this shabbiest of all shabby Austrian tricks. Austria only wanted to give Russia another ultimatum because she enjoyed being humiliated, he said; Buol must know that Britain would never participate in such humiliation and bad faith (Bourqueney to Drouyn, 28 Oct. 1854, AMAE Autr. 456; Westmorland to Clarendon, 30 Oct., and Clarendon to Westmorland, 7 Nov., Clar. dep. c. 12 and 130; Albert to Clarendon, 5 Nov., RA G18/93).

foederis date was to force a quick decision from Russia in order to start negotiations in the winter, during the expected lull in fighting, and to end the war before the spring campaign. The big question is, did he think this scheme possible, or was the effort simply an *acquit de conscience* for himself, or a gesture designed to satisfy Austrian and German public opinion when Austria went to war?

The answer is not easy; it involves not merely what Buol said, but the milieu in which he operated, especially his relationship with Francis Joseph. Though there were slight differences, the Emperor basically accepted Buol's policy, supported him, and made the final decisions himself. Both men assumed and repeatedly said that if the war entered a second year, Austria could not stay out (an almost universal assumption); neither took any pleasure in the prospect. Buol knew that Austria's financial condition was bad (though not as disastrous as it has often been painted),[88] and he had to take Hess's gloomy military forecasts seriously. Public opinion in Austria would at best be passive toward a great war. The army and the generals would probably do their duty, but without enthusiasm. Buol, moreover, had always been keenly aware that even an Austrian victory would bring dangers with it.[89] Thus his efforts were probably not mere gestures (or even, as Bourqueney thought, a sign of Buol's determination that war might come as a result of Austrian policy, but must not be its goal), but were another attempt to control an almost unmanageable situation and achieve a quick peace. This was the way Westmorland, Lerchenfeld, and the Prussian minister at Turin, Brassier de St. Simon, who visited Vienna in early November, saw them. To the sea powers Buol expressed pessimism about success, to Prussia and Germany some hope; but he made clear to both that the final effort for peace had to be made.[90]

Meanwhile Hess, dismayed by the mobilization proclamation of October 22, again pleaded eloquently in a *Vortrag* of November 10 against Buol's course, which was leading directly to offensive war on Russia. On November 15 and 17, a ministerial conference met to discuss the issues he raised. No protocol was made; besides Hess's *Vortrag*, the only contemporary sources are a memorandum entitled "Votum" by Alexander Bach, pleading his and Buol's case, and a brief account of the conference in Kübeck's diary. Hess did get further mobilization suspended on November 18, but this hardly meant a defeat for Buol's program. Neither he nor anyone else dreamed of actually fighting before spring under any circumstances; the only purpose of mobilization had been to force Russia to accept the Four Points, and by this time there were many indications that she would probably do so. There is no indication that Buol fought for continued mobilization; according to Kübeck, he argued in the second session that no basic difference existed between the various positions taken. The real issue betwen Buol and his opponents was that of a Western alignment versus Austro-Prussian-German armed neutrality, and Buol won. He and Bach argued at this conference for a Western alliance as the only way to force Russia to peace and to settle the Eastern question permanently on a European basis—exactly the sort of alliance Austria would soon conclude.[91]

Meanwhile, the same reports that Russia was about to yield which enabled Austria to suspend further mobilization caused consternation in the Western capitals. Cowley was especially incensed because Russia's imminent acceptance of the Four Points would convert a trap he had laid for Austria into a snare for Britain. Earlier, Austria had asked what extra demands the Allies intended to raise as belligerents under the Fifth Point, and Cowley had suggested a bargain he was sure Austria would refuse: Austria could receive this information if she accepted a *casus foederis* with a fixed date in the alliance treaty. Austria had not only treacherously accepted this Allied proposal, but actually advanced the *casus foederis* date and so she could now demand this information. To refuse to give it would anger France, wreck the emergent alliance, and risk driving Austria into Russia's arms; to tell Austria what the sea powers really wanted would also risk driving her away, would give the disgraceful impression that the Allies were asking Russia for peace, and would even raise the possibility that Russia might accept the terms.

Somehow this problem had to be met. Even while the alliance proposal was being sent to Vienna on November 7, Drouyn suggested a defense against Russia's possible acceptance of the Four Points: let the sea powers go along in principle with the idea of negotiating with her, but pose new demands on the ground that since the Four Points had been formulated, they had discovered new nefarious Russian plans in the Baltic.[92]

Clarendon, furious that Austria had not rejected the West's alliance proposal, asked Prince Albert how to meet Austria's demand for information on the Allies' extra Fifth Point demands, and was told to stretch the Four Points to include them, so that Austria could not back out. Palmerston, visiting Paris to help Cowley stiffen Drouyn and Napoleon against Austria, pointed out again that Austria was not conspiring with Russia or seeking an excuse to break with the West, as others thought. The danger lay precisely in her policy of bringing the two sides together in "premature negotiation" in the hope "to avoid war for herself and to place herself in the position of a power who by her skill has restored the peace of Europe." Austria's snare, said Palmerston, could be avoided "by a cautious and guarded acceptance of her treaty with suitable reservations." The reservations, to which he claimed Napoleon agreed, simply called on Austria to commit herself in advance to any additional conditions the Allies might raise under the Fifth Point, and to recognize the *casus foederis* if peace were not assured on these additional bases as well by January 1. Moreover, if Russia accepted the Four Points, Palmerston said, the West would have to redefine them so as to make Russia withdraw her acceptance.[93]

Russell suggested instead requiring Russia to prove her sincerity by turning over Sevastopol to the Allies and Ismaila and her fortresses on the Danube to Turkey prior to negotiations. This, he thought, would be a sufficient pledge; "I think asking the whole of the Crimea would be thought by Austria *exorbitant*." Austria's purpose, of course, was "to get her 30 pieces of silver by selling English blood," but his "moderate and reasonable" proposal would give her no excuse to sneak away. Hudson urged rewarding Austria for her eventual participation in the war by getting her to give up Lombardy-Venetia for territory on the Danube.[94]

With all this advice, Clarendon did not know what to think or do in regard to the alliance Buol was so surprisingly willing to sign. He saw that Buol's wish to know the West's terms was perfectly natural, but was sure it must be part of an Austro-Russian plot. Fearing that Russia's accepance of the Four Points was genuine, he insisted it must be insincere, and even hoped that Russia's mocking acceptance would shame Austria into doing her duty. But Drouyn refused all British demands for further commitments by Austria or guarantees by Russia or liberation from Britain's own earlier commitments; Aberdeen and the royal couple urged Clarendon to close with Austria now. Even Palmerston and Cowley conceded that Drouyn's draft of the treaty was as vague as it could be in committing the Allies to specific terms of peace.[95] Querulous and snappish, Clarendon yielded; on November 22, the sea powers notified Austria that they would sign the treaty. The acceptance was hedged with conditions and accompanied by the usual accusations and warnings, but while Clarendon evaded directly promising Austria that Britain would negotiate if Russia accepted the Four Points unconditionally, France gave her promise.[96]

This sufficed for Buol; he believed that Britain dared not openly repudiate negotiations, having committed herself to the Four Points and having accepted the idea of a last Austrian ultimatum to Russia based on them, and he counted on France to overcome British reluctance. However, he made it completely clear to both sea powers that Austria would recognize the *casus foederis* only if genuine peace efforts failed to achieve the peace stipulated in Article I because of *Russian* intransigence.[97] The final negotiations at Vienna on November 26–28 were uneventful; by this time Buol mainly wanted to ensure that a Franco-Austrian agreement on Italy would follow the alliance. Francis Joseph gave his formal consent on November 29; the need to give Prussia two days' prior notice postponed the formal signature until December 2.[98] Although reports were widely circulated at the time and often credited since that Bourqueney and Westmorland had threatened to break relations, and Buol to resign his office, in order to get Francis Joseph's consent, they are without any foundation.*

---

* This story was refuted years ago by Eckhart (pp. 132–34), but Tarle has revived it (II, 321–28), Unckel presents a speculative new version of it (pp. 184–85), and Palmerston's latest biographer, Jasper Ridley (*Lord Palmerston*, 444), has woven it into a completely fanciful account of how peace negotiations ultimately got started. The British and French documents rule out any possible version of it, however, and Bavarian sources enable one to see exactly how the whole canard arose. On December 3, Count Lerchenfeld sent this story in all its colorful detail to Pfordten, having heard it from Gorchakov, who claimed Buol had admitted it to him directly the day before. But then Bourqueney denied flatly to Lerchenfeld that the sea powers had exerted any pressure on Francis Joseph, or needed to; he had decided to sign routinely on November 29. Pressed by Lerchenfeld, Gorchakov now admitted that Buol had told him the true story only "indirectly." When asked to define what

Clearly, the treaty was primarily the result of Buol's efforts.[99] Austria made most of the overtures, granted the main concessions, and accepted all the risks. What had she achieved by it? Had Buol, simultaneously greedy and timid, sought and gained special advantages and securities from all sides, as was widely said at the time and is still sometimes maintained? [100] The special advantages are hard to discover. This treaty did nothing to guarantee Austria's position in the Principalities. Buol saw Austria's problem there, as he had earlier told Bruck, as one of getting the sea powers to forgive her for exercising influence in the Principalities without having joined the war, and Bruck correctly predicted that this alliance would ultimately threaten Austria's position on the lower Danube worse than ever.[101] Britain tried all through the alliance negotiations so to frame the First Point as to exclude Austria entirely from postwar influence in the Principalities, and she intended to continue her efforts. As for Italy, France did pledge herself shortly after the treaty not to disturb the status quo as long as Austria cooperated in the East. But even this hardly overwhelming concession was refused by the British, who during the alliance negotiations secretly promoted a separate alliance with Sardinia, partly to prepare for postwar changes in Italy and to bring Sardinia into the postwar liberal league Britain would head against Russia and Austria.[102]

True, Buol made some progress toward negotiations for peace, but hardly on Austria's terms. The Four Points were Western terms, and if Buol did not completely accept the West's definition of them,[103] he certainly went farther toward their version than they toward his. Moreover, while he frankly revealed his interpretation of them, they carefully concealed their intentions from Austria until the treaty was signed.[104] It could be argued that Buol secured this Western agreement to negotiate at no cost or risk to Austria, since he knew that Russia would accept the Four Points and that thereby the *casus foederis* would be nullified. But in fact he had

"indirectly" meant, Gorchakov said that Buol had told him that he did not wish to add to the existing complications of the situation by provoking a break with the sea powers and that had Francis Joseph refused to sanction the alliance, he would have felt compelled to resign. Lerchenfeld drew the obvious conclusion: Gorchakov had constructed the whole story on the basis of purely hypothetical arguments used by Buol to justify the alliance (Lerchenfeld to Pfordten, 3 and 4 Dec. 1854, GSA, MA I/591).

sought the alliance from late September on, long before he knew Russia would yield; only on November 28 did he know that her acceptance was unconditional, and even then he could not be certain the sea powers would really negotiate. They also went into the alliance aware of Russia's acceptance, but hoping somehow to negate it or persuade Austria it was worthless as a ground for negotiations.[105] The fact that many Englishmen and some Frenchmen, including Napoleon, considered talks with Russia a humiliating concession to Austria indicates the political atmosphere in the West, not the particular advantages Austria gained.

Eckhart's criticism of Buol's policy is correct: he was not selfish or aggressive, but foolish—foolish to suppose he could moderate Allied war aims through loyal cooperation.[106] At the same time, Buol was probably right in believing that the only way to end the war before a second campaign, a goal vital for Austria and Europe alike, was to force Russia to terms set by the Allies with Austrian support. In any case, far from gambling for special Austrian gains, Buol gambled with special Austrian interests (e.g., the Principalities), rendering them more subject to Allied influence and control, in order to gain the alliance, and in so doing gave up weapons (possible rapprochement with Russia or armed neutrality with Germany) that his critics pleaded with him to use in defense of Austrian interests. While he did this to help the sea powers impose on Russia a peace settlement favorable to them, they risked only the "disgrace" of negotiations they intended to evade anyway. Buol's policy may be termed reckless and foolish; but to consider it narrowly Austrian in aim is perverse.

As for France, though her tactics were deceptive, almost as much with Britain as with Austria, her purposes did not contradict the alliance. She did not favor a negotiated peace at this time, but was not absolutely hostile to it, and if she failed to lure Austria into war she did not intend to break with her over it. Even Napoleon wanted to stay on good terms with her for the duration.

Britain's purposes, however, were fundamentally incompatible with the alliance treaty. She had compelling reasons to sign, the military situation being chief among them. The bloody battles of Balaklava and Inkerman in late October and early November, while they had kept the Allied positions from being overrun by Russia and had demonstrated a man-for-man Allied superiority, had not brought Sevastopol's fall any closer or overcome Russia's superiority in numbers, and the ravages of winter, lack of shelter and supplies, and disease were just beginning. Clarendon regularly predicted disaster and even Palmerston contemplated evacuating the troops.[107] Under such circumstances the British could not afford to spurn a treaty that provided a fallback position for the Allies and a means of preventing an Austro-Russian rapprochement. In addition, Britain feared that France might ally with Austria alone if she refused, and she still had some hope of dragging Austria into the war. Completely absent, however, was any intention to abide by the provisions of the treaty in regard to peace negotiations, or any willingness to stop the war short of decisive military victory, whatever the consequences for her alliance partners or the rest of Europe, or any wish to have anything to do with Austria. The alliance treaty, in fact, coincided with the peak of popular hatred of Austria in Britain. Because Clarendon persisted in believing that Austria would not sign the treaty, he told her that her signature might moderate the fierce attacks on her that the public, the press, and Parliament would surely voice. "Be my ally," Britain said in effect, "and I shall try to overlook your crimes and not hate you quite so much as I do." [108]

Austria's diplomacy toward Germany and Prussia had meanwhile been very active. In August and September, Buol worked to get Prussia to accept the Four Points as the indispensable basis for peace, to mobilize behind them, and to help get Germany to do likewise. He also renewed on August 25 his call for a partial Federal mobilization, arguing (disingenuously, in view of his previous admissions) that Russia's evacuation did not end the threat of war for Austria or extinguish the *casus foederis* of the April 20 treaty relating to the Principalities. His efforts got nowhere; until October, Austria clearly was losing ground to Prussia in Germany. Some of Austria's arguments would not hold water—for instance, the claim that Russia still menaced Austria in the Principalities. Prussia and Germany refused to recognize either the general European value or the special importance for Germany that Buol ascribed to the Four Points, and they argued that the West's aggressive war aims constituted the chief obstacle to peace. Above all, they rejected Buol's basic principle that their fitting and beautiful role was to support Austria in what she decided was good for Germany; their idea of a beautiful role was to keep themselves and Austria neutral. If Austria wanted support, she had to grant Prussia and Germany a voice in her policy.[109]

The turning point came when Buol convinced the Emperor in his September 26 *Vortrag* that Austria must openly pursue a Western alignment. Three days later, the Emperor flatly rejected any limitations on his actions, refusing Frederick William's pleas for a promise not to attack Russia. Buol followed this with warnings to Prussia and the German states that Austria would abandon her efforts to persuade them to back the Four Points unconditionally and that, dispensing with their support, she intended to ally with the West. As one Austrian commented, she gave Germany the choice: follow Prussia or us.[110]

The approach worked better than its authors had expected. Manteuffel and Prince William did not believe that Prussia could stay neutral if Austria entered the war, and Frederick William was desperately anxious to prevent an Austro-Western war alliance.[111] As for the middle states, when Apponyi told Pfordten that an Austro-Prussian breach must lead to a Western alliance, Pfordten replied, "Then in the end we'll be forced to go with you also"— and quickly begged Apponyi not to report this admission.[112] In addition, many Germans feared destroying the Confederation and favored supporting Austria. To save Germany from the consequences of an Austro-Prussian breach, Pfordten undertook to mediate between Vienna and Berlin. His program (really that of King Max) called for concessions to satisfy Austria: a renewed Additional Article to the April 20 treaty to protect her forces in the Principalities, and Prusso-German support for the Four Points, correctly defined, as the necessary basis for peace, along with Prusso-German help in forcing Russia to accept them. In exchange, Austria should bind herself not to go beyond the Four Points, and if Russia agreed to them and the West demanded additional concessions, Austria must let the sea powers continue the war on their own.[113]

At Berlin, Pfordten met a favorable reception. Frederick William, frightened further by the Austrian mobilization of October 22, had been thinking along similar lines himself. But at Vienna, Buol made

it clear that this mediation was Bavaria's idea, not his, and declined
to promise to forego offensive action against Russia or an alliance
with the West. He told Pfordten instead that if Prussia refused to
renew unconditionally her support for Austria in the Principalities,
he expected Bavaria to help line up a compact majority against
Prussia in the Diet.

Through extremely angry, Pfordten persisted, banking on general Austrian assurances that she really wanted peace on the basis of
the Four Points and that she would enter into no further engagements with the West without notifying Prussia and Germany. Similar Austrian assurances to Frederick William, plus Pfordten's pleas
to save the Confederation, plus the news that Russia was going to
accept the Four Points, brought Prussia around, which broke the
resistance in turn even of pro-Russian citadels like Württemberg and
Saxony. By late November it was agreed that the Confederation
would endorse the Four Points as the necessary basis for peace; on
November 26, Austria and Prussia signed a new Additional Article
to the April 20 alliance, guaranteeing Austria against Russian attack
also in the Principalities, and the Article was submitted to a committee to prepare a Federal resolution endorsing it.[114] Pfordten
celebrated a personal triumph. Not only had he prevented an
Austro-Prussian breach and averted an Austrian alliance with the
West; he had shown Bavaria to be the tongue on Germany's wagon
and had assured Germany of a powerful and united voice in the
great question of the day.[115]

Two days later, Buol secretly informed Prussia and Bavaria of
his impending alliance with the sea powers.[116] The Germans denounced Buol for lying and deceiving them into supporting Austria
when all the time he intended to join the West. The charges cannot be refuted. Certainly some promises and assurances given by
some Austrians (though not, so far as I can find, by Buol himself)
proved false.[117] And even if Buol did not break explicit promises,
this is hardly the main point, for his policy toward Prussia and
Germany was both hard and deceptive. He allowed others to suppose that his assurances meant more than the letter contained—for
example, that a promise to *notify* Prussia before signing a treaty with
the West meant a commitment to *consult* with her first. And he
engaged at the last in slippery evasion in handling Prussian and

Bavarian suspicions that such a treaty was already virtually agreed on.[118] Buol's tactics stemmed from the assumption that Prussia and Germany should simply be Austria's second and reserve—which they rightly resented. At the same time, Buol's difficulties with the sea powers simply left him no room for concessions to Germany or to Russia.

Deception and hidden motives were not, however, confined to one side. Prussia's purpose remained that of keeping Austria inactive until she was exhausted; Manteuffel still dreamed of an Anglo-French-Prussian entente that would do Russia the service of ending the war and put Austria "into the position right and proper for a sick state." Buol, moreover, was right in claiming that Pfordten finally was working in behalf of Prussia's propositions. Besides, if Buol was deceptive at some points, his main tactic was brutal frankness. He refused repeatedly and emphatically to tie Austria's hands in any way, insisting that any advance pledge by Austria not to go beyond the Four Points or to stay neutral if Russia accepted them would destroy the possibility of bringing the sea powers to a negotiated peace. Manteuffel admitted to Hatzfeldt that the new Additional Article was conceded solely because it was inevitable, with no Austrian *quid pro quo*.[119] Pfordten was convinced by early November that Buol was too committed to a Western alliance to retreat; he only hoped to avert it by giving Austria such open German support that Francis Joseph would find it morally impossible to close with the West and would repudiate Buol. To this end he encouraged Berlin to believe he had received more assurances from Vienna than he really had; his rage was caused partly by seeing his own strategy blow up in his face.[120]

Russia, of course, had the best cause to denounce Austria for the December 2 alliance. This new blow was struck at her just four days after Russia announced her unconditional acceptance of the Four Points, two days after Buol acknowledged it. But the charge of Austrian treachery,[121] though understandable, is not accurate. Instead of luring Russia with false promises, Buol had practically ignored Russia from September on, after coolly refuting her charges about the Four Points and predicting that she would one day reconsider her rejection of them. He was still interested in getting information about Russia's policy, and occasionally he tried to con-

vince her that she had a chance to escape her predicament by accepting the Four Points.[122] But in effect he abandoned to Prussia
and Germany the diplomatic effort of getting Russia to yield,
knowing that their sole reason for pleading with St. Petersburg,
and Russia's for complying, would be to prevent an Austrian alliance
with the West. The promises he gave Gorchakov were the same as
those to the German states: if Russia accepted the Four Points
without condition, Austria would try hard to get real negotiations
started and would not support unjustified Western claims. This
promise Buol fulfilled, at least in his own view.

Moreover, Russia's acceptance was a purely tactical move. Her
desire for revenge on Austria was naturally greater than ever; the
question was whether she should seek it now, invading Galicia and
Transylvania if Austria entered the war, as the Tsar and his Adjutant General Jomini planned, or should postpone her punishment to a better season, as Paskevich preferred.[123] Russia's reverses
in the Crimea (which like the West she blamed on Austria, but with
better reason), and the fear of a great anti-Russian coalition in the
spring, had finally forced Nicholas to swallow the Four Points.
But he still looked for a military victory, and if the moderates welcomed the idea of negotiations, it was in order to split the Allies
and lure one of them, preferably France, over to an entente with
Russia and Prussia, so that Austria would be isolated.[124] Thus Russia
was basically just as opposed to the kind of peace Buol wanted to
achieve as were the sea powers, for the excellent reason that she
would have to pay for it. Though her opposition was less formidable than theirs, her position being worse, it weighed also against
success for Buol in the great gamble for peace to which he committed Austria on December 2.

X

A Fleeting Success:
Peace Negotiations Assured

Immediately upon signing the December 2 alliance, Buol officially communicated Russia's acceptance of the Four Points to the sea powers, telling them that whatever they thought of Russia's move (and Buol argued that it was genuine), it obliged them morally and contractually to test Russia at the peace table. Francis Joseph sent a personal plea for negotiations to Napoleon, while Buol, fearful of a Russian withdrawal of her acceptance in the wake of the December 2 treaty, urged preliminary Allied talks at Vienna to prepare for a prompt meeting with Gorchakov. Of course Austria wanted a glorious peace, he assured Westmorland—the Four Points *were* a glorious peace.[1]

With Clarendon worried about defending himself and the alliance against attacks and ridicule in Parliament (he even suggested keeping the alliance secret for this reason),[2] Drouyn and Cowley had to devise a strategy to meet Austria's call for peace talks. The problem was twofold: how to avoid negotiations altogether or ensure their prompt failure, and how to tell Austria just enough about Allied war aims to get her committed to them, so that she would blame Russia and recognize the *casus foederis* when the talks broke down, but not enough to frighten her away and to give Russia and Germany the chance to accuse the West of destroying Europe's hope of peace. A complicated dialogue developed between Drouyn, Cowley, and the government at London over this delicate task. Drouyn strongly favored keeping the real Western demands under the Third Point secret from Austria (razing Sevastopol, limiting the Black Sea fleet to four ships of the line, and stationing British and French consuls in Russian ports as observers). Austria instead should be induced to state her own peace terms first and in an extreme form, so that she would find it hard to reject the Western demands that would emerge later. Cowley approved Drouyn's tactics, but suspected his motives; he considered him soft on Austria, the Third Point, negotiations, and even peace. Cowley therefore bent his efforts at keeping France "honest"— that is, France should first conclude a separate secret agreement with Britain on peace terms, especially the Third Point, and then cajole and deceive Austria into going along with it in substance. Britain's task was to save France's honor by keeping her up to the mark in this assignment.[3]

Clarendon at first approved Cowley's plan, and the Cabinet, to whom he read one of Cowley's dispatches with this general content, applauded it heartily.[4] * But quickly British sentiment changed to favor a clear statement to all parties of Britain's real war aims and her determination to gain them regardless of the consequences. This would dispel the widespread impression abroad that the December 2 treaty was going to lead to peace talks.† Certainly Austria might be driven off and even France alienated by such publicity; but the risk of falling into negotiations through keeping the aims secret was even greater. As part of the strategy of frankness, Russell proposed requiring Austria to subscribe to Britain's view of Point Three in writing before Britain would go to the peace table. Palmerston endorsed this suggestion and publicized British ideas about peace in the press.[5]

Clarendon also favored frankness with Austria, partly because she might possibly agree to terms that would eliminate negotiations in advance or make them a mere ten-minute formality, and partly because he felt Britain needed to deal honestly with her. As he wrote the Queen, "If the true meaning and object of the 3d Basis is not fairly stated Austria will have the right and will probably avail herself of it to say that she had never intended to go so far and that she must resist the humiliation or spoliation of Russia." This is

* Aberdeen, absent from this Cabinet session, protested sharply to Clarendon, condemning him especially for encouraging Cowley's morbid suspicions of Austria and for letting France suppose that Cowley's unauthorized activities were official British policy. Clarendon returned his usual embarrassed apology, without admitting that he had supported and approved of Cowley's activities.

† Minto remarked that this impression was due to the inexplicable ignorance of international affairs that prevailed in Europe (to Russell, 15 Dec. 1854, PRO 30/22/11F).

the ordinary concept of fair play: if Austria were not informed of Britain's real intentions, she would be entitled later to refuse to go along on a course kept secret from her, to which she had not consented. But simultaneously Clarendon developed and used a second quite different definition of honest dealing. Suppose Austria was really honest toward the West, he told Cowley (and they agreed that no evidence existed of present Austro-Russian collusion):

> It is of the utmost importance to be able to say on the 1st of Jan. to Austria that Russia won't agree to our terms and that she (Austria) must therefore concert active measures with us. Austria (supposing her honest) was at this moment without a pretext for breaking with Russia who has complied with her demand by the acceptation pure et simple. The Bases therefore want to be developed and explained by her [Austria] as well as ourselves to Russia.

Here Clarendon's argument is more subtle. Austria, if she was honest, really wanted war with Russia. But to this end she needed a good pretext to break her promises to Russia, Prussia, and Germany to seek a negotiated settlement. The Allies, in order to deal honestly on their part with Austria, must therefore supply her with that pretext by stating their full demands and stretching the Four Points to include them, so that Austria could present Russia with terms Russia was sure to reject. This definition of honesty is the plain man's definition of treachery; but it, and not the definition used by Clarendon to the Queen, became the operative one for him and other Englishmen. When Cowley later suggested getting Austria to make Russia ask the sea powers for terms, in the hope that Russia would refuse the humiliation and thus negate her acceptance of the Four Points, Clarendon objected that this still would not give Austria enough excuse for war: "My only doubt now is as to not leaving a peg for Austria (*supposing* her honest and bold) to hang a quarrel with Russia on. The bases have been accepted pure and simple. That is what Austria wanted. Can she declare war if Russia refuses to ask us to treat upon them?" He instructed Westmorland to test Austria's sincerity at Vienna—Austria, if she was sincere, must accept an Anglo-French interpretation of the Four Points and send it to St. Petersburg, making its rejection her *casus belli*.[6] Under this definition of sincerity, all the British charges of treachery leveled against Austria become comprehensible and true. She never honestly sought to provoke war with Russia; she never sincerely intended to break her promises to seek a negotiated peace.*

But France would not adopt the British concept of frankness and fair play with Austria. Drouyn insisted that the identic notes interpreting the Four Points, which were to be exchanged between the sea powers and Austria and used with Russia in a meeting preliminary to actual negotiations, should not state how the sea powers wanted to execute Point Three. Britain sharpened the terms and language of these notes, demanding that Russian preponderance in the Black Sea be ended rather than diminished, insisting that Russia ask for peace terms,† and suggesting a territorial cession to Turkey on the lower Danube. While hoping that Russia would refuse to ask for peace terms or would peremptorily reject the identic notes, the sea powers also tried to get Austria to go beyond them, telling Russia what the West really wanted on the Third Point and making Russia's rejection of this her *casus belli*.[7] But as Russell pointed out, neither the December 2 treaty nor the identic notes required Austria to do this; only her difficult position, combined with an Allied warning that if she stayed out of war they would "adopt desperate remedies for a desperate disease," would make her fight. Clarendon understood what was meant by "desperate remedies," replying to Russell, "As to the Austrian regime [in Italy], I suppose we must be silent about that at least till the 1st of Jan. Alors comme alors." [8]

Buol, to Britain's dismay, promptly accepted the content of the identic notes, calling only for a single joint note to Russia instead, to which Drouyn agreed.[9] ‡ Cowley quickly warned against com-

---

* Austria also failed the British test for chivalry, which was that she use the moment when Russia was fighting three other foes to attack her chivalrously and finish her off.

† "Upon that," remarked Clarendon, "must rest our defense with Parliament for such an ugly proceeding as going into the same room with a Russian Plenipotentiary let alone negotiate with him" (to Cowley, 13 Dec. 1854, FO 519/170). Cowley hoped that Russia would refuse to ask the Allies for terms; it would at least postpone the evil day when the sea powers would have to discuss their terms with Austria (to Clarendon, 15 Dec., Clar. dep. c. 18).

‡ The Allied suggestion that Austria respond to their notes with her own identic one, said Buol, smacked too much of the pupil having to recite his lessons before the schoolmaster.

municating this joint note to Russia, for if she asked for an explanation of the Allies' deliberately vague language on the Third Point, any explanation given would provide her with excellent propaganda at home and in Germany. Cowley suggested that Gorchakov simply be told that he must know what Point Three meant and would have to sign without explanation. Or, he proposed later, the Allies could demand that Russia herself state how Point Three should be executed; then they could reject her suggestions. In any case, Cowley assured Clarendon, Napoleon and Drouyn would agree to any expedient for keeping the Allies' intentions secret from Russia, as long as nothing was revealed to Austria until she had signed the joint note and the proposed conference protocol.[10] Clarendon, though tempted, replied that maintaining secrecy toward Russia would have an even worse effect in Germany and would look like bad faith to the British public. Instead, the Allies must first close with Austria on the Third Point and then discuss with her how and when to let Russia know what it meant. If Austria signed the proposed protocol demanding that Russia's predominance in the Black Sea must cease, she must sincerely intend war, and in that case it made no difference what Russia and Germany thought.[11]

This solved the problem of dealing with Russia in good faith. On December 28, the three powers signed their joint note and protocol at Vienna, conveying an extract of the protocol orally the same day to Gorchakov as the official Allied interpretation of the Four Points. The Third Point was left vague, as Drouyn wished. But Britain had already protected herself against the danger presented by this vagueness. Cashing in on promises gained at Paris by Cowley and Palmerston, she had exchanged secret notes with France on December 17 and 19 defining their minimum demands as including the narrow limitation of Russia's Black Sea fleet and the destruction of Sevastopol and possibly other fortresses as well. Thus the terms agreed upon with Austria and conveyed to Russia with a demand for their unconditional acceptance, terms left vague enough to allow room for negotiations, were nullified in advance by a secret agreement on more drastic terms concluded behind Austria's back and designed to make negotiations impossible.

Some dispute has arisen over whether Drouyn or the English were more responsible for this procedure,[12] but the point is not important. What made men who genuinely considered themselves the soul of honor * ignore the implications of this step and many others like it was simply their determination to have military victory at any cost.[13] Aberdeen, never enamored of the war, saw what the Allies' commitments clearly required of them. Denouncing Cowley's schemes as dishonest and childish and noting that he seemed blissfully unaware of his own double-dealing while morbidly suspicious of everyone else, he pointed out to Clarendon that the Four Points were not, as Clarendon claimed, Russian terms. They were Allied terms, worked out and interpreted by them with Austria and conveyed by her to Russia with their permission. Britain and France, having done this, had no right to demand more.[14]

Meanwhile the Austro-French convention on Italy had been negotiated and was signed on December 22. It looked like simply a payment for the December 2 alliance, and for France it was; but Buol, doubtless naively, saw it as part of a general program of conservative Austro-French cooperation,[15] and not designed purely to preserve the status quo. Buol had already joined France in granting a papal request for a reduction in their respective occupation forces, against the opposition of Austrian military leaders.[16] He fought persistently against Grünne's and Radetzky's demands for new conventions with the central Italian states which would require them to contribute fixed contingents of troops in an emergency to Austria's army under Austrian command and empower Austria to garrison certain vital fortresses. Buol's legal and political arguments against this, and his defense of Parma's, Modena's, and Tuscany's right to require a reduction or removal of Austria's auxiliary forces at least persuaded Francis Joseph to postpone the idea, if not drop it entirely.[17] Similarly, Buol's efforts helped promote the evacuation of Tuscany by May 1855. Even Rechberg, a civilian and a moderate, considered him much too liberal, pro-French and optimistic about Austria's Italian position.[18] In any case, the Austro-French convention gained little for Austria. France promised only to help preserve the status quo for the duration; even this pledge was linked to Austrian cooperation in the East. France refused to publicize the agreement and Drouyn downgraded its significance to the British and to his own representatives in Italy.[19]

The Western negotiations with Sardinia, which led to a military

---

* "Anything is better," wrote Cowley to Clarendon December 26, "than that a suspicion of bad faith should rest upon us" (Clar. dep. c. 18).

alliance on January 22, demonstrated the minimal value of the Austro-French convention still more clearly. Cavour's aims were simple. Having vainly worked for a great war of the West versus Austria and Russia, he now had to escape the deadly peril of Austro-French cooperation in Italy by inserting Piedmont between Austria and the Allies, even at considerable cost. The alliance of December 2, instead of turning him away from the West as it did many of his countrymen, made him even more anxious to succeed and more willing to deceive and override anyone, including King Victor Emmanuel II, in the process.

Britain, mainly concerned to secure Sardinian troops, was the prime mover on the other side. Hudson supported the terms Sardinia posed for an alliance in late November: an Allied war loan (not a subsidy, to save Sardinia's dignity); pressure on Austria to settle the sequestrations issue on Sardinia's terms; and a promise to consider Italy at the peace conference. The loan proved no major obstacle, but Sardinia's political conditions raised problems with Austria—though Hudson could not imagine why she would not be willing to make this simple reparation to Sardinia "if they [the Austrians] are honestly bent on joining us in the war against Russia." Russell urged Clarendon immediately to accept Sardinia's "very reasonable" conditions, even at the risk of Austrian defection from the West. He also suggested making Sardinia a partner in the Austro-French convention on Italy and using the impending alliance with Sardinia to frighten Austria into going to war. Anyway, Russell insisted, the Allies would have to take up the Italian question at the peace conference whether or not Sardinia requested it, in order "to clear Tuscany and the Roman states of foreign troops and lay down some principles of government for these states." [20]

Clarendon, though troubled by doubts, was ready to follow Russell, but encountered strong opposition from Aberdeen and the royal couple. Besides, he saw that the sequestrations demand was humiliating to Austria and one that Britain would never comply with herself, and he did not believe that Sardinia was entitled to the role reserved for the great powers at the peace table.[21] The French also urged Britain not to agree to Sardinia's conditions; Drouyn, laying all responsibility for the negotiations on Britain, told Austria that Sardinia had only a minor, purely military significance for France. As a result, the sea powers refused Sardinia's political conditions and Cavour finally signed without them. As Aberdeen saw it, Britain had acquired a new fifteen-thousand-man foreign legion, but Cavour had made further moral conquests among the Whigs. Clarendon praised "the manly straight forward Constitutional Ministers at Turin," telling Austria that Sardinia had given no sign of territorial ambition since Victor Emmanuel had become king. It was sad that Austria refused to recognize Sardinia's friendship and good faith.[22]

Meanwhile, in Germany, Buol suffered his first clear defeat in the wake of the December 2 alliance. While public opinion was fairly favorable to the treaty and to Austria, especially in south Germany, the governments unanimously denounced it, including Bavaria, the one on which Buol counted most. Buol managed some answer to Pfordten's charges of deliberate betrayal and an Austrian sellout to the sea powers, and to his insistence that Austria with Germany's backing could have dictated terms to the West. But Buol could not deny that Austria had preferred a Western alliance to a German one or convince Pfordten that it had been decent to treat Prussia and Germany as he had done. The support previously promised and granted Austria was not withdrawn. The Diet on December 9 endorsed the Austro-Prussian Additional Article of November 26 and adopted the Four Points as Germany's terms for peace, with emphasis on the first two. But this final gain was a hollow one. Frederick William, though quickly thinking better of his original impulse to mobilize against Austria, was so bitter at everything Austria had done and was still doing—for example, inviting him now to accede to her Western alliance after the fact and trying again to mobilize half the Federal contingents against Russia —that he resolutely opposed more concessions.[23]

It would have been wise for Austria to leave Prussia and Germany alone, but Hess, whose political advice continued to be assigned to the files by Buol, insisted on prompt Prussian and Federal mobilization. Dismissing Buol's suggestions for a delay and for different modes of mobilization to meet the political objections of the German states, he demanded the mobilization of 200,000 Prussians within six weeks and the delivery of two Federal corps to the Austrian and Prussian armies as rapidly as possible.[24] Buol, without hope, made the request at Berlin. Manteuffel denied any Russian threat at all and the King warned that an Austrian attack on Russia would destroy the April 20 alliance. Edwin Manteuffel, on another special mission to Vienna, urged his King to stand firm; Austria's lack of German support, combined with Russia's invulnerability to Western attack, would force Austria to Prussia's side.[25]

At this point Buol committed an egregious blunder. On January 14, he sent two circulars to several German courts, excluding Berlin. The first called for a Federal mobilization resolution in the Diet; the second, highly secret, invited the individual German states, in case no such resolution could be reached and the break between Austria and Prussia proved irreparable, to form separate alliances with Austria, placing some of their forces under Austrian command in case of war, in exchange for an Austrian guarantee of their territory and a share in whatever advantages (unspecified) might accrue from the war. This step can be explained, though not justified. Strange as it may sound, it was part of Buol's peace strategy. He considered Prussia's attitude decisive for peace or war in the coming negotiations. If Prussia could be forced by Austro-German pressure to join the anti-Russian alliance and make a real demonstration against Russia, Russia would make peace; otherwise Russia would not. Moreover, Prokesch and others had led Buol to believe that Austria could by this move counter Prussia's efforts to paralyze her through the Confederation. Many states, Prokesch insisted, could be won to individual alliances; Hanover was leaning to Austria and would rather put her whole army under Austrian command than place part of it under Federal control. Pfordten had hinted something similar about Bavaria to Buol and Apponyi.[26]

Nonetheless, Buol had completely failed to read the anti-Austrian temper in the Diet and Germany and to foresee the moral impact of his proposal. No matter how it was qualified, a request to individual states to join Austria in possible war against Russia and to share its "advantages" could only confirm existing suspicions that Austria was ready to destroy the Confederation and imperil Germany for the sake of conquest, or even (as Munich feared) to try to regain the Imperial German crown for Austria. And Buol should never have dreamed that he could keep this move secret from Prussia. Plainly he was blinded by anger and fear that she would succeed in paralyzing Austria and was willing, if the war could not be ended by diplomacy, to see her also in the enemy ranks.[27]

The bitter fruits of this step ripened quickly. Bavaria's reaction, initially cautious, turned wholly hostile. Saxony denounced the secret circular as a demand for the destruction of the Confederation. Someone, probably Beust, communicated it to Prussia, giving her a splendid propaganda weapon. Many Germany states rallied to her, and Bavaria and Württemberg indicated they would prefer isolation or even a link with France to such an Austrian alliance.[28]

Buol's attempt at a defense and counterattack was embarrassing and futile. He could give only worn-out replies to the charge that he was courting offensive war and to the demand that he prove the need for mobilization, and no answer at all to Bismarck's arguments that the sea powers would not be able to impose their peace terms on Russia, and that it was mad to fight Russia for an Anglo-French version of the Four Points when Russia would grant Germany everything worthwhile in them by negotiation. He had an answer to Bismarck's charge that Austria had sold out to the sea powers and wanted to drag Prussia and Germany with her into war for their war aims—but he dared not give it. Only to his envoys and a very few others could he explain privately his strategy of using Prussia and Germany to force Russia to yield, while counting on France to keep Britain reasonable. Publicity would have destroyed this plan in the West, and the gambling nature of the whole scheme would have repelled Prussia and Germany, not attracted them. Faulty as Buol's tactics were, the root difficulty remained that Austria, Prussia, and Germany did not have an equal interest in general peace. As long as Austria and Prussia stayed neutral, the German states were safe and comfortable; as long as Austria did, Prussia was safe, if uncomfortable, in neutrality. But for Austria (or so Buol believed) the position of spectator was intolerable with so many dangers arising out of a prolonged war or a great victory for either side; a moderate general settlement was vitally necessary.[29]

Anyway, he quickly dropped the idea of separate alliances with individual German states. He still sought some kind of military demonstration by the Confederation that would have the moral effect of mobilization on Russia, but he wanted to abandon Austria's mobilization proposal at Frankfurt rather than accept a useless sub-

stitute or face defeat. Bismarck, however, would not let Austria off
easily, and stood Austria's mobilization proposal on its head with a
resolution passed on February 8 calling for mobilization against all
dangers menacing Germany from both sides. This threatened the sea
powers, especially France, rather than Russia and marked a decisive
defeat of Austria by Prussia in the Diet, demonstrating that Austria
could no longer drag Germany behind her if Prussia stayed firm.[30]

Fortunately for Buol, he had already registered important gains
with Russia, whose policy he feared would be adversely affected
by the February 8 resolution. Despite the December 2 treaty, which
Boul confessed had cost him some painful moments to announce
and explain to Gorchakov,[31] Russia did not repudiate her acceptance
of the Four Points. She agreed to a preliminary meeting on December 28 to prepare for negotiations, where, as already mentioned, an
extract of the newly signed Allied protocol interpreting the Four
Points was read to Gorchakov. Again Russia was supposed to accept
it without conditions. Stung by the renewed humiliation and his
failure to separate Austria from the West, Gorchakov began attacking the piece read to him. Buol was able to show that some of
his objections were unfounded or immaterial, but not his main
one to Point Three, which Gorchakov claimed infringed upon the
Tsar's sovereign rights. But he stopped just short of the rejection
the sea powers hoped for, securing a copy of the extract to send
to St. Petersburg, with Russia to reply finally within two weeks.
Bourqueney was confident a rupture was inevitable.[32]

That evening, Boul spent hours trying to convince Gorchakov
that he should have accepted the Allied program as a basis for negotiations, while protesting against language he considered offensive
and reserving Russia's right of interpretation. The next day Gorchakov, apparently convinced, gave Austria a confidential note accepting the Allied declaration with the condition that Russia would
negotiate to end *what was called* Russia's preponderance in the
Black Sea, rejecting anything incompatible with her sovereign rights.
Without some such verbal concession, Gorchakov pleaded, the Tsar
would refuse everything.

Buol had to try to sell this reply to the sea powers, even though
he saw it was designed to split Austria from them rather than to get
negotiations started. Not only Gorchakov, but "the whole native

and foreign Russophile clique" and "the *very extraordinary* Prussian envoy Count Manteuffel," as Buol remarked, were working night and day to get Francis Joseph to declare himself satisfied with what Nicholas offered. Buol warned the sea powers again that Austria was not bound to any particular method of executing Point Three, but only to the program explained in the December 28 protocol; this, moreover, pledged Austria to support its provisions *in* the negotiations, but not to compel Russia to accept them *before* negotiations. Once Russia confirmed her acceptance of the Four Points in their original sense (and Gorchakov had already gone beyond this in conceding the principle of diminishing Russia's naval power), the sea powers were obliged to come to the peace table. At the same time, Buol urged V. Esterházy to do everything possible to keep Russia from returning a fatal negative answer, which would "break the thread and . . . permit the sea powers to escape us."

Once the fatal twelfth of January has arrived, they have the right to reject the bases, which, after all, one must admit are *very elastic.* . . . Petersburg's reply will be *for us at least* the real question of peace and war. A refusal by Russia would deliver our fate to the course of the belligerent powers; an acceptance would be for us our liberty.[33]

The sea powers spurned Buol's argument. Clarendon told Buol, at Palmerston's suggestion, that Britain expected Austria to reply to an unsatisfactory Russia reply with an immediate declaration of war—after which she ought to send an army corps to the Crimea. Drouyn pressed Austria to begin discussions on the military means for executing the *casus foederis* of December 2. Buol requested a delay until Russia's reply was received, and to his surprise and immense relief, Gorchakov announced on January 7 that Russia accepted the Allied terms of December 28 as a basis for negotiations. The next day Buol told France that Austria was ready to exchange military envoys—ostensibly because the danger of war still existed, actually because now that Russia's acceptance made negotiations possible, tangible evidence that Austria took her alliance obligations seriously would help them to succeed.[34] Buol's offer, coming simultaneously with his renewed pleas to Britain for a moderate and therefore more durable peace, bewildered Clarendon; he could not understand why Austria should prepare for war when she seemed eager for peace. But Austria's semiofficial press made Buol's main point very clear; neither side should let national honor and prestige prevent a peace settlement that could spare Europe another Thirty Years' War.[35]

Again London and Paris saw a trick in Russia's acceptance of Allied terms on January 7, and the preparation for another betrayal in Austria's response.[36] Ideas diverged on how to meet the threat. Russell, visiting Paris ostensibly for his health, actually to keep up with Palmerston in playing a role in diplomacy, was happy to find Drouyn still determined to break up the negotiations. Drouyn and Clarendon disagreed, however, over the means. Clarendon now suggested an idea he had earlier dismissed as absurd, namely, communicating the Anglo-French secret agreement of December 17–19 to Austria and requiring her to present its terms to Russia. Drouyn proposed Russell's old idea of demanding a preliminary Russian evacuation of the Crimea. Knowing that Austria would not support this before Russia either, he developed a series of sophistical arguments to contend that this expedient would blow up the conference without alienating Austria. Cowley was convinced and Russell willing to try it.[37]

Clarendon wavered in desperate indecision, at one moment thinking Drouyn's suggestion the best way of breaking off negotiations, at another sure that such a ridiculous demand would only give Russia wonderful propaganda. Yet occasionally he supposed that Nicholas, having yielding much already, might give the Allies what they demanded, or that Austria, knowing negotiations would fail, might be willing to fight. All the same, nothing could compensate for the dreadful contrast between the promised and actual results of the war—Britain's prestige in decline, her "feebleness and incapacity" everywhere derided, John Bright "no longer looked upon as the traitor and coward he was 3 months or even 3 weeks ago." Britain's demands were absurd, Clarendon confessed—like trying to kill a man, failing, and then asking him kindly to cut his own throat. But they were inevitable, and if presented boldly at the outset of negotiations would at least end them quickly. Besides, the impudence of Britain's terms was at least matched by Russia's accepting the Four Points when she must have known the Allies had no intention to negotiate upon them.[38]

Aberdeen, meanwhile, argued strongly for frankness with Austria, so as to end the sea powers' dishonest maneuvers and begin the promised negotiations quickly.[39] * No one would have paid attention, except that Russell partly agreed with him. It was not true, he told Clarendon, that Russia's rejection of the Four Points last September proved her present acceptance of them worthless and insincere (Clarendon's and Prince Albert's argument). Russia had shown less bad faith than Britain, and Austria none at all; against her the only possible charge was "not agreeing to an interpretation of the 3rd Point, which has been purposely hidden from her." Buol should be told what the sea powers wanted, and if he refused to support it, as he had a right to do, they could still avoid negotiations by demanding a prior evacuation of the Crimea.[40]

Clarendon agreed; keeping Austria in the dark was all a short-sighted and dishonest French idea anyway. He therefore sent Westmorland a dispatch on January 20 denouncing Russia's acceptance of the Four Points as worthless and demanding that Austria accept narrow limitation as the necessary means of executing Point Three.[41] Drouyn, protesting that this could only produce a break with Austria and a quarrel with Buol, proposed still another plan. Since Russia had given only a verbal assent to the Allied terms at the conference of January 7, Austria should be required to summon one more conference where Russia would have to sign a protocol attesting her acceptance, and the sea powers could try subtly to insert their interpretation of Point Three into this protocol. Cowley, warmly supporting the suggestion, warned at the same time that if it failed (i.e., if Russia signed even this new protocol), the sea powers would then have to tell Austria what they wanted. If she resisted, they could tell her that it was no use negotiating with Russia when the three powers themselves could not agree on terms. It was all the more necessary to give this ultimatum to Austria, Cowley argued, because Drouyn was still trying to avoid a clean break with her,

* Arguing that the attempt to trap Austria into an agreement without letting her know what was meant was both dishonest and inept, Aberdeen pointed out that by concealing their interpretation of Point Three from her thus far, the sea powers had entitled Austria now to reject their interpretation without relieving them of the obligation to negotiate. Or, he asked, did they intend to give Austria, as well as Russia, an ultimatum on the Four Points? (Cowley, in fact, proposed just such an ultimatum.)

even at the risk of becoming entangled in negotiations. "The question," he cried, "is which is the greater political rogue in the game Drouyn or Buol!" [42] The French protests and Cowley's advice led Clarendon quickly to retreat, wiring Westmorland only to inform Buol of his January 20 dispatch, not press him for any reply. All the while he denounced Drouyn's dishonesty, he became more attracted to Drouyn's idea of avoiding negotiations by demanding Gorchakov's signature on a new protocol.[43]

Thus the sea powers fell over each other in desperate efforts to find a way out of the peace talks; but they cooperated well in putting pressure on Austria. No European guarantees could help Turkey or restrain Russia, insisted Drouyn; an arm or a leg had to be torn off the Tsar's empire. If Austria stayed out, France would make a generous peace and combine with Russia against her. Napoleon appealed to Francis Joseph's chivalry; France could not end the war without military glory.[44] The British applauded these efforts and added their complaints (e.g., that Buol had helped Gorchakov evade really accepting the Allied terms on January 7), with Westmorland almost as much the target of abuse as Buol.[45] Buol remained unmoved. The December 28 protocol was Austria's gospel, he told Westmorland, but she would go no further; the sea powers could not unilaterally expand her obligations.[46]

In late January, Britain's resistance to negotiations began to waver. The change did not result either from Austria's firmness or from political developments in Britain and military events in the Crimea. To be sure, there was widespread dissatisfaction with the government, and the military situation appeared gloomy to all save professional optimists like Palmerston. War fever tended to decline and enlistment was slow and difficult. But the war had hardly begun to strain the resources of the country. A Foreign Enlistment Bill passed by Parliament December 23 promised to produce more troops; so did the Sardinian alliance in January. It was still widely assumed that Austria was bound to enter the war in the spring, and Russia was supposed to be suffering more than the Allies were. The public remained essentially patriotic. Bright's speeches still aroused general execration; his partner, Richard Cobden, was reduced to attacking the war not as morally wrong and foolish, but only as badly managed. Aberdeen was pessimistic about peace, while Greville, now silent, saw no hope for it unless France and Austria dragged Britain to the peace table.[47]

What produced the slight turn toward peace was the final chapter in the long Cabinet crisis. In December the government was again almost broken up by Russell's efforts to get a new War Ministry created, headed by Palmerston, to take over Newcastle's and Sidney Herbert's duties. Defeated, Russell apparently accepted failure and was willing to carry on. But then in the new session of Parliament a group of Radicals led by John Roebuck moved for an inquiry into the conduct of the war. Russell, insisting that he could not face such an inquiry as a member of the present government, abruptly resigned on January 23, and the Aberdeen government collapsed six days later.[48] During another week of political confusion Russell's efforts to form a Whig ministry failed, and Derby, to Disraeli's dismay, declined to try for the Tories.

A Palmerston ministry now was inevitable, and foreign policy, hitherto no factor in the crisis, became important. The desire to end the sorry spectacle Britain was presenting to Europe helped overcome the reluctance many, including the royal couple, felt at accepting Palmerston as prime minister. France intervened directly, Drouyn insisting that no government that did not include Palmerston and Clarendon could carry on the war and maintain the alliance with France.[49] * Above all, Palmerston's reputation for expansive war aims and general recklessness in foreign policy was the chief obstacle to his forming a government. Only by giving many plausible if vague assurances of his moderation and desire for peace could Palmerston, with Aberdeen's magnanimous help, persuade Gladstone, Graham, Sidney Herbert, and Argyll to join him, enabling him to kiss hands on February 6.[50]

Thus a crisis that brought the most bellicose minister in Britain to the helm paradoxically increased the chances for negotiations, if not for peace.[51] Not that efforts to avoid a peace conference were abandoned—Drouyn persisted in his previous tactics,[52] while Claren-

---

* Buol stayed aloof, discounting reports that Britain was in collapse and stating that Austria had no prejudices against any government she would choose—this despite the hatred and fear Austrians felt for Palmerston.

don, though assuring Buol that Palmerston was peace-loving and pro-Austrian,* warned that Britain would fight a Seven or Thirty Years' War rather than surrender her just demands. (He suggested in passing that Austria might be able to satisfy Britain's honor by getting the Tsar to surrender Sevastopol voluntarily.) [53] But with Austria paying no attention, by mid-February a confrontation with Russia at the peace table began to seem unavoidable. Cowley became convinced that Drouyn did not even want to avoid it. To all Drouyn's ideas for blowing up the conference on the first day through presenting new demands to Russia, Cowley replied that Russia might accept them, leaving the Allies in a terrible fix. Cowley urged precipitating matters with Austria by requiring her to make narrow limitation and the razing of Sevastopol her *casus foederis*; Drouyn answered that Britain could do as she liked, but that Austria would refuse, as she had a right to do, and France would not change her relations with her if she did. Drouyn further refused Britain's proposal to take up the Third Point first, insisting on postponing the crisis with Austria by dealing with the Four Points in their natural order.[54]

France's growing stubbornness helped edge Britain toward peace talks; so did domestic conditions. Popular discontent with the war grew in February, and Palmerston's ministry proved little more efficient or less vulnerable than its predecessor. Gladstone, Graham, and Sidney Herbert resigned in late February, ostensibly in protest against the parliamentary inquiry they considered a vendetta against their fallen comrades Aberdeen and Newcastle, but also just as much over their differences with Palmerston on foreign policy. The Cabinet, reformed, was more united but even weaker in its parliamentary base. Under the impact of winter and disease, the military situation continued to worsen, while the death of Nicholas on March 2 removed the chief personal target of British hatred from the scene.[55] Some British leaders began tentatively to think about an outcome other than military victory. Russell distressed Minto acutely by admitting that a military draw might not be too bad. Palmerston conceded privately that Britain could not demand of

---

* Clarendon's exact words, "I am not more anxious than he [Palmerston] is to cultivate the most cordial relations with Austria," were, to be sure, literally true.

Russia the razing of Sevastopol (an argument, to be sure, for Britain's continuing the war and doing the job herself). Cowley began to think that Turkey's security might best be achieved through a European alliance in her favor—apparently wholly unaware that Austria had advocated this for over a year.[56]

Again, however, a fortuitous development did the most to encourage Allied peace sentiment: Napoleon's decision in mid-February to go to the Crimea, taking personal charge of the operations. The pleas and warnings of his ministers and allies, including Austria, seemed to harden rather than dissuade him. Now a negotiated settlement, hitherto a bad *pis aller* for Drouyn, became the best and perhaps only way of preventing Napoleon's voyage and saving the regime. For Clarendon, who termed the idea "insane" and "suicide," it at least made the prospect of negotiations more bearable.[57]

Besides, by mid-February, Clarendon had persuaded Russell, out of office and in some political disgrace, to represent Britain at the Vienna negotiations, thus evading Cowley's and Victoria's dreadful suggestions that Clarendon go himself.[58] The appointment of Russell, a longtime member of the war party who had only recently attacked Austria at Paris and in Parliament,[59] looked like a way of giving the talks an elegant burial. But Russell had turned statesman.* Before accepting the mission he put conditions to Palmerston and Clarendon designed to make success possible. He wanted Prussia admitted to the conference; as a great power she was entitled to it, and should not be left to sulk and intrigue outside. Moreover (in contrast to his recent public display of profound distrust of Austria), he urged a conciliatory approach to Vienna. If the negotiations were either to lead to peace or to a breakdown that would bring Austria into the war, he argued, a frank agreement with her on Point Three was essential.[60]

Though Palmerston and Clarendon told Russell and Aberdeen that they agreed to these conditions, it is plain that they did not do so in substance. Palmerston was willing to let Prussia into the conference, but Clarendon was not, and both repudiated Russell's suggestion of an armistice if the first conference session seemed to

---

* Aberdeen commented wryly that Lord John's wisdom was incontestable but that he had acquired it since he left the Cabinet (to Clarendon, 12 Feb. 1855, Clar. dep. c. 30).

promise success. Clarendon interpreted Russell's call for frank and conciliatory dealing with Austria to mean that Russell would check Gorchakov's impertinence and Buol's backsliding.[61] Yet Palmerston and Clarendon certainly knew that Lord John hoped to bring back peace from Vienna; Clarendon, anticipating military disaster and a great swing in public opinion toward peace, began to think this might not be wholly undesirable, and he gave Russell wide latitude in drawing up his own instructions. While Minto tried to talk Russell out of going, many others, including Aberdeen, who again displayed the magnanimity that was his most attractive trait, wished him Godspeed. When the remaining Peelites resigned, Russell had to be brought into the Cabinet as Colonial Secretary to strengthen it in Parliament. This and his sudden illness threatened to upset his mission, but Clarendon persuaded him to carry on anyway.[62] Buol, who had pleaded for weeks that Britain should name her plenipotentiary, had little ground from experience to rejoice at Russell's appointment, but welcomed it as a sign that Britain took the conference seriously. It proved, Clarendon assured Buol, "that we never intended to avoid the negociation." [63]

The obstacles to successful negotiation remained formidable. Added to the latent disagreement on goals between Russell and Palmerston and Clarendon were differences in tactics between Britain and France, with Russell wanting to proceed quickly to a decision, Bourqueney wishing to spin out the discussions in hopes of a victory in the Crimea. Russell also encouraged Napoleon in ideas about resurrecting Poland, which Drouyn disapproved and which would have horrified Austria.[64] * Austria and the sea powers still had not agreed on military cooperation in case the talks failed. Austria's negotiator, General Count Crenneville, took to Paris estimates of Russian troop strength so high (836,000 men) and requests for assistance so inflated that the French would not take them seriously and tried to avoid helping Austria at all outside the Crimea. Hess insisted that only a great coalition including Prussia could launch the grand offensive needed to bring Russia down. The French claimed

* At Brussels, Russell listened attentively to Leopold's suggestion that a four-power alliance be formed to protect Turkey—something Austria had urged for months (indeed, off and on since 1815) without ever getting Britain's attention. Russell remarked that it might be good to have such an alliance, of limited duration—"say 50 years."

that three or four sharp attacks at various places simultaneously would force her to retreat to the Vistula and accept dictated terms —to which Hess replied that here was where the real war would start. Britain, remaining aloof from these discussions, was concerned only that France, in her laudable efforts to lure Austria into war, must not actually commit herself or Britain to send a single soldier outside the Black Sea theater.[65] In short, by early March, Buol had not improved Austria's position or security in any way, except to ensure that the peace conference would not be wholly fraudulent or absolutely certain to fail.

Meanwhile, other pots were on the boil. In Germany, still hoping to close ranks against Russia, Buol tried to *faire bonne mine au mauvais jeu*, applauding the Federal resolution of February 8 and calling for its implementation, while denying that it could be used against the West or for simple neutrality. But Bismarck and Beust defeated Buol and his interpretation in an exchange of circulars and notes in February and March. Austria's position at Frankfurt improved only because Prokesch was summoned to be second Austrian plenipotentiary at the coming Vienna conferences. Rechberg, his successor, was much better suited to be presidial delegate, while Prokesch was thoroughly conversant with the Eastern question.[66]

To repair Austria's relations with Bavaria, described by Rechberg and Apponyi as very bad,[67] Buol initiated a private correspondence with Pfordten which proved of some value. Buol managed to assuage Pfordten's resentment and apparently convinced him that Austria was really trying for peace. Pfordten assured Buol that Bavaria would not join Prussia in an anti-Austrian combination, as Apponyi and Rechberg feared; she still wanted to mediate between the German great powers, and of the two preferred Austria. But nothing was gained on the main issues. Pfordten refused to admit any Federal obligation to support Austria in any war not provoked by Russia. In fact, he claimed that Russia could call for Federal execution against any German state that joined Austria in an offensive war, thus violating German neutrality. If Austria wanted German help, she would have to make her case before the Diet and give Germany time to decide upon it; in any case, Austria should satisfy herself with a Federal army of reserve to be used in case of Austrian defeat.[68]

Thus Germany could not be bludgeoned into supporting Austria in war unless Russia was plainly the aggressor. As for Prussia, Buol gave up trying to influence her. The Prussian conservatives threatened to resign if she acceded to the December 2 alliance, insisting that Austria did not even want her in it. But Manteuffel and Hatzfeldt joined Prince William and the liberals in favoring accession; isolation was intolerable and it was better to join the West now than be forced to later. The King opposed a simple accession to the treaty as humiliating and still hoped to paralyze Austria, but he also bitterly resented being excluded from the peace conference unless he joined the alliance. To Manteuffel's distress, he again resorted to special missions—E. Manteuffel to Vienna, Count Usedom to London, and, when the French minister Moustier protested that France was being neglected, General Wedell to Paris.[69]

No one, including the special envoys, expected anything from these missions—they brought nothing but the King's tears, as Drouyn cynically remarked—but they served to show the divergence of French and British attitudes toward Prussia. Drouyn, though unwilling to let Prussia join the West in any other way than by simple accession to the December 2 treaty, really wanted her in the alliance and the war, mainly to estrange her permanently from Russia and make her dependent on France.[70] The British, or at least Clarendon, did not want Prussia as presently governed to join the Allies at all. When Bloomfield reported that the King might sign the treaty, Clarendon rejoined, "We shall indeed be ridiculous if this takes place"—Frederick William was an incurable coward and would only be a Russian spy in their midst. Britain's long-range desire was to see the existing German Confederation overthrown, and a change in system at Berlin would be a first vital step.[71] *

The protracted negotiations (early January to mid-March) over

* In late 1854, Albert, spurred on by his brother Ernest and the Gotha liberal party, urged Clarendon to make the dismissal of Manteuffel and the appointment of a liberal ministry in Prussia the price for her return to the European concert. Clarendon, however, was uneasy about too overt interference in Prussian internal affairs, and Aberdeen's opposition prevented any such action (Ernest to Albert, 12 Dec. 1854; Bethmann-Hollweg to Albert, 17 Dec.; Albert to Clarendon, 29 Dec., and Clarendon to Victoria, 30 Dec., RA G20/36, G21/29, 50, and 56; Aberdeen to Clarendon, 1 and 2 Jan. 1855, Add. ms. 43189).

getting Prussia into the alliance had their bizarre aspects. At one point Hatzfeldt, Usedom, and Wedell were all conducting separate and uncoordinated negotiations at Paris. While Prince William pleaded with Britain to help frustrate the Catholic League that Austria was forming to strangle Prussia, he at the same time urged Manteuffel to join Austria for the sake of German unity. Manteuffel tried to convince his rival Gerlach that peace could be reached only by joining France so as to keep the West's terms moderate—the very policy Buol, whom Manteuffel hated, was advocating. While Bismarck fought at Frankfurt to line up Germany against Western pressure and threats, he urged his own government to ally with France and Russia to expel Austria from Germany. Hatzfeldt suggested to Cowley that a little naval intimidation from Britain would help bring his own king around; Bloomfield doubted that even a full blockade would help.[72] So confused and shifting was the situation that a more flexible stand by the sea powers and a better concealment of their boundless contempt for Prussia might have gained her accession; there were frequent predictions of success. But the King never lost his reluctance to become involved in offensive war against Russia, and Nicholas's death in early March made this an unshakable resolve.[73]

As a result, Prussia was excluded from the peace conference, and she blamed Austria for it.[74] Austria's role in this issue was in fact minimal. While Prokesch opposed Prussia's participation and G. Esterházy did not want to ease her return to the Concert, Buol definitely wanted Prussia to accede to the alliance and come to the peace table. Her participation would create a united front against Russia and indicate that Russia was probably willing to make peace.[75] Buol was ready to accept a separate Prussian treaty with the West, to save her pride, and proposed allowing her to sign the December 28 protocol (which the King announced in mid-March he would do) as a step toward her admission. Clarendon flatly refused.[76] But though Buol's proposal proves that he did not want Prussia excluded, he remained bitter with Prussia on all sorts of grounds, and Austro-Prussian relations remained those of cold war.[77]

In one more area trouble ripened for Austria, rendering her vulnerable to attack and pressure at the peace conference—the Principalities. Though accounts based on Western or Russian sources have to be taken with some reserve,[78] troubles in connection with Austria's occupation tended to worsen in early 1855.* The paper money Austria used to pay her soldiers and buy her supplies depreciated rapidly, damaging an already strained economy.[79] Incidents and clashes between soldiers and civilians multiplied. Most of them were minor, but a few, the worst occurring at Craiova in February 1855, were fairly serious and widely publicized in the West.[80] Some army units were demoralized because of bad health and living conditions, pay in depreciating currency, and boredom with routine service in a backward and unfriendly country.[81] Though Austrian army records indicate that most officers tried hard to combat these conditions, there were some glaring examples of cavalier arrogance by officers,[82] and not a few instances of high-handedness by Coronini and other commanders in dealing with the Turks, local officials, and even the hospodars. Buol had to intervene several times to disown their conduct and calm things down.[83] Although Austria had carefully negotiated conventions regulating the provisioning and quartering of her troops, local merchants and authorities continued to complain, while foreign consuls protested that troops were being billeted on their nationals. The Prussian consul in Moldavia, Blücher, proved a special thorn in Austria's side.[84]

All the old quarrels also persisted over Ştirbei, Turkish encouragement of revolutionary plots and sedition, and bad relations between Austrian and Western agents. The details are not important, but on these points the sea powers, not Austria, regularly took the offensive. Colquhoun and Redcliffe hardly bothered any longer to conceal the real aim of their persistent anti-Ştirbei campaign (which Clarendon fully supported): to pave the way, in Colquhoun's words, for "a total and complete remodelling of its [the country's] institutions" or, in Redcliffe's terms, a system of national reform that would tie the Principalities closer to Turkey, seal them off from Russia, and give them "everything to hope from beyond their seaward flank, and nothing to fear from the Carpathian side." [85] The British worked to undermine the ambassadorial conference at Vienna that Buol tried to use to settle disputes. Where

---

* One small gain for Austria, apparently a result of the December 2 alliance, was the removal of anti-Austrian French consuls (Poujade and Ségur) from Bucharest and Belgrade (Nistor, 357–63, 402).

Buol repeatedly urged his agents to avoid conflicts with Western agents, Clarendon encouraged Colquhoun to look for Austrian malfeasance even where Colquhoun failed to suspect it.[86] While even Hess and Coronini now tried to keep out of the Allies' and the Turks' way militarily, the sea powers still attempted to trap or force Austria into a clash with Russia.[87] After Austria had finally got the Turks to remove their Polish Legion from the Principalities, Redcliffe influenced them to send it back. Colquhoun, a close friend of the Polish émigré Czaikowski (Sadik Pasha), promoted his intelligence activities in the Principalities and was at least indirectly responsible for his efforts to promote desertion in the Austrian army.[88]

None of these moves were basically reactions to Austrian misconduct or arose from fear that Austria would cement her hold on the Principalities. Colquhoun, Redcliffe, Clarendon, Russell, Palmerston, and the others who drew up postwar plans for the Principalities never feared that Austria would exercise any real influence, much less control, over what happened on her southeastern frontier.[89] Nor did the proposals concocted at the Quai d'Orsay show much more regard for Austria's voice and interests.[90] Britain and to a lesser extent France bullied Austria over the Principalities, as they did elsewhere, because they knew that she was vulnerable. This knowledge of her vulnerability was one of their biggest assets, and her greatest handicap, in the peace negotiations about to open.

The Vienna Conference:
Peace Defeated

While Russell made his way slowly toward Vienna via Brussels, Paris, and Berlin, with each stop inclining him more toward peace,[1] Buol and Prokesch developed Austria's policy and strategy for the conference.[2] Prokesch concentrated on arguments to refute the West's view of Sevastopol and the Russian Black Sea fleet as the chief danger to Turkey. The war itself, he argued, disproved this; if the sea powers, with their immense naval superiority, had been unable to take one fort of Sevastopol in six months of siege, how could Russia hope to seize Constantinople by a sudden attack? Politically the real threat to Turkey was that of gradual Russian encroachment; this could be halted in the long run only by an Austro-Western alliance for Turkey's defense. Militarily the chief menace to Turkey arose, in this war as in all the previous ones, from the Russian army advancing over the Principalities toward Constantinople; Sevastopol was dangerous chiefly as a supporting base for this sort of operation, and once again the answer to it was Austro-Western cooperation. Prokesch, an experienced general himself, cautiously suggested improving Turkey's defenses in the Balkans by linking her fortresses along the lower Danube and Prut with Austria's defense system (Hess's proposal) or by neutralizing part of Bessarabia and the northern Dobruja. As for the Russian fleet, now largely destroyed by the war, even if rebuilt it could menace Turkey only if she faced it alone in the Black Sea. Several methods of counterpoise would solve this problem—allowing Turkey to summon in friendly fleets if desired, stationing an Allied squadron permanently at the mouth of the Danube, or building an Allied naval base to match Sevastopol on Turkey's coast (again Hess's suggestion). Of course direct limitation of the Russian fleet would be fine, if Russia would accept it, but counterpoise would be no less effective and could be made so disadvantageous to Russia that she would prefer voluntary limitation to it.

Buol accepted all Prokesch's strategic arguments, but this last point was the key one in his diplomatic strategy. Already in January he had begun trying to persuade Russia to adopt a voluntary limitation.[3] Throughout the conference his chief aim would be to devise deterrents that would make it so futile and dangerous for Russia to rebuild her fleet that she would voluntarily renounce the attempt, without being able to claim that her sovereign rights had been infringed.

Austria's ideas and strategy soon subverted Russell. Before long he was convinced that Buol genuinely desired an effective peace settlement and that if Russian stubbornness prevented it from being reached, Austria would honor her alliance obligations. He understood Buol's aims in regard to Point Three and, after some initial skepticism, rapidly was attracted to Buol's proposals.[4] A memorandum Russell wrote, but did not send to London, illustrates his conversion. In it he first rehearsed all the usual British arguments for narrow limitation and against graduated counterpoise. Then, however, he listed seven different ways to protect Turkey without despoiling Russia or maintaining large Allied forces on Turkish soil: (1) empowering the Sultan by treaty to summon the Allied fleets into the Black Sea either if Russia's ships of the line exceeded a certain number, say, fifteen,* or (2) if there was a threat of war; (3) having Austria maintain a warship at the Danube mouth to warn of unusual Russian military preparations; (4) fortifying and garrisoning the Bosporus against surprise attack; (5) guaranteeing Turkey's integrity through a treaty with Russia; (6) pledging Turkey specific armed aid against attack through an Anglo-French-Austrian treaty; and (7) admitting by treaty a specified number of warships of states friendly to Turkey into the Black Sea at all times. Russell then laid out some basic principles that are remarkable enough, coming from him, to be quoted in full:

---

* A surprisingly generous number, since the supposedly preponderant Russian fleet of 1853 numbered only eighteen, and the number afloat at the moment was eight (Admiral Sir Edmund Lyons to Russell, 28 March 1855, PRO 30/22/12D).

In remarking generally on these plans [for defending Turkey] it may be laid down that two conditions must be sought for in any provision of the kind. The first is, that it should not in a state of peace keep up the apprehensions and uncertainties which belong to war; the other and the more important is, that the support to be given to Turkey should be so clearly provided for that it should be forthcoming on the part of Austria, France, and England whenever the occasion shall arise.

If Russia shall find when peace is established that the present alliance is dissolved, she will watch her time, and acting with more rapidity and boldness than in 1852, she will trust to her influence, and to her diplomacy to postpone, or avert altogether the interference of other Powers to prevent the accomplishment of her designs. If, on the other hand, she is convinced that three such powers as Austria, France, and Great Britain will act with promptitude and vigour for the protection of Turkey she will hardly play so hazardous a game.

With regard to the whole question I must observe, that there are certain dangers which rational men ought to provide against; there are others which cannot be provided against at any cost which it is prudent to encounter. Extreme folly and rashness on the part of an Emperor of Russia may at any time produce great calamities to the world; but such a danger could only be guarded against at the expense of a war of many years' duration, which would deprive him of a great part of his dominions. Even the success of such a war might be doubtful, but if it were certain, it is impossible to say what new dangers might arise in the course of the contest. It is better therefore to suppose that the Emperor of Russia will only take up arms with a rational prospect of advantage, to provide against such dangers as may reasonably be calculated upon, and leave to the future to guard against perils, which it belongs to the future to develope.

Proceeding on this principle it might be a sufficient security for Europe to adopt the fourth, the sixth, and the seventh of the measures indicated above. With the forts in the Bosphorus well armed, judiciously placed, and sufficiently garrisoned, with a permission from the Sultan to have a limited number of vessels of powers other than Russia to pass from the Mediterranean to the Black Sea, and above all with a defensive treaty between Turkey, Austria, France, and Great Britain, we might, the other three points being sufficiently secured, put an end to the existing war.[5]

Russell here presented an irrefutable case for precisely the moderate peace settlement Austria had always advocated and Britain had steadily rejected. In fact, he was willing to settle for less counterpoise and deterrent than Buol was ready to sponsor. More important still, the theoretical grounds Russell developed in its behalf—that Turkey's security would be best ensured by a great-power alliance on her behalf, that one must presume some measure of rational behavior in one's opponent and therefore prepare only for reasonable contingencies, that attempts to acquire superfluous security are expensive and tend to create new dangers to replace the old—represent insights that Buol had always upheld and that British policy, as Russell himself expounded and defended it in the first part of his memorandum, repudiated and ignored. While Buol and other Austrians certainly influenced Russell,* this was not an overnight conversion. The memorandum shows rather how difficult it was for anyone willing to look at the Eastern question from a European rather than a narrowly British point of view to avoid coming up with the sort of answer Austria offered.

The hawks at London and Paris quickly became alarmed at the evidence of Russell's softness on peace and at the disturbing course of the Allied preliminary talks at Vienna.[6] There, with Bourqueney's and Russell's support, Buol turned down Drouyn's and Cowley's proposal to force Russia to subscribe to the exact text of the December 28 protocol at the opening conference session. To Cowley's dismay, Drouyn swallowed this defeat and accepted Buol's proposed opening protocol. Worse still, he suggested allowing Austria simply to support the Allied terms on the Third Point as far as she was able, with the sea powers reserving what remained for their special demands under the Fifth Point. Worst of all (though Cowley did not know this), Drouyn told Bourqueney that the Anglo-French exchange of notes represented the West's *maximum* terms on the Third Point; Bourqueney should try to get Buol as close to the maximum as possible.[7]

* Russell also had interesting conversations with Metternich and Prince Paul Esterházy, former longtime ambassador to Britain. To Russell's remark that the British felt Buol was too timid toward Russia, Esterházy replied that Austrians found him too timid toward the West. He countered Russell's warnings of the Russian menace by noting that Austria had lived with this so long it had ceased to frighten her. When Russell suggested a four-power alliance to defend Turkey, Esterházy replied: when will you British show any foresight? I offered you this alliance from Metternich in 1829, and you spurned it! (Russell to Clarendon, 9 and 11 March 1855, Clar. dep. c. 30).

Clarendon could not at first decide whether Buol was merely resisting Britain's admittedly absurd demands or plotting with Gorchakov; Cowley was sure he was doing the latter. In any case, Austria had to be prevented from further corrupting Lord John and seducing the French toward peace.[8] Cowley, Clarendon, Minto, Palmerston, and the Queen all warned Russell against Buol and Prokesch—both of them snakes, according to Clarendon, but the latter notoriously the worst liar and hypocrite imaginable.[9] The best British defense, however, would be to trap Austria into war, and the military convention still being discussed at Paris offered a chance to do this. Austria, still preparing herself militarily, rejected a French proposal of February 28 that would have left the entire Russian central front to Austria; Hess insisted on French support in Galicia, especially if Prussia did not come into the war.[10] The British knew that France could not and would not supply Austria even with the auxiliary help she had promised on February 28. But Palmerston, Cowley, and Clarendon joined in urging France immediately to promise Austria anything she requested. Austria's demands were absurd, clearly a dodge to escape her obligations, Clarendon told Cowley:

However I hope the Emperor will not hesitate to engage that the whole number or *double the number* shall be furnished *by France alone*. Not keeping exactly to the engagement is not what would break a French heart if we could catch Austria in her own trap and drag her into the field besides it would be sound policy and good fun.

In addition, the existence of a secret Allied military convention could prove very useful in the negotiations: "For that reason however it should be kept a profound secret and the Russian plenipotentiary should discover it by accident or the indiscretion of somebody." [11]

Unfortunately, Austria, aware of the usual fate of secret agreements made with the West, declined to sign any convention until the negotiations actually broke down, depriving Clarendon of an opportunity for sound policy and good fun. The next best weapon for defeating Austria's intrigues was the First Point and the question of the Principalities, also discussed in the preliminary negotiations. Among other things, Buol proposed inviting unofficial agents from the three Principalities, including Serbia, to advise the conference on this question. Bourqueney rightly called the proposal "genuinely European." Inviting a Serb agent would open to conference decision an area Austria was often accused of trying to keep as her exclusive sphere of influence; in suggesting that the three Allied consuls at Iași, Bucharest, and Belgrade join in suggesting agents for the Porte and the hospodars to approve, Buol gave the sea powers a majority vote in nominating them.[12] Drouyn was noncommittal. If Austria supported the West unconditionally on the Third Point, she could have whatever she wanted in the Principalities (though not in Serbia); if not, then not. But Cowley denounced Buol's suggestion as "a do—to get us to recognize the Russian powers that be in these provinces. . . . That is what Buol wants, a sop to Russia, to maintain the old constitutions." [13] Along with Britain's prompt rejection of this proposal went more accusations of Austrian conspiracies with Gorchakov and brutality and oppression in the Austrian occupation.[14]

Thus preliminary Allied talks led to no agreement on the Third Point or on military cooperation or on the Principalities. The formal conferences, however, began smoothly enough on March 15. Clarendon, impressed by Buol's opening speech and amused and delighted at Russia's obvious hatred of Austria and Gorchakov's attempts to exclude Buol from the discussions, admitted privately, "We have been mistaken in thinking that Buol was playing booty with Gortchakoff." [15]

The next two sessions on March 17 and 19 brought general agreement on two projects submitted by Prokesch on the First Point. The principles they laid down, that there should be a five-power guarantee of the Principalities' traditional privileges and consultation of the wishes of the people on modifying the Règlement Organique, were vague and harmless or, if anything, favorable to the Allies and unfavorable to a special Austrian protectorate. Nonetheless, Clarendon, inspired by Palmerston, subjected these projects to bitter and prolonged attack. Austria was undermining the Sultan's sovereignty; Prokesch and Gorchakov were combining to restore Holy Alliance tyranny in the Principalities and to stifle all reform and progress. The Principalities now represented England's chief target in her attacks on Austria, and if these were designed mainly to soften Austria up for concessions on the Third Point, the aim of establishing a liberal, pro-British and anti-Austrian regime there remained important.[16]

Drouyn was also dissatisfied with the sessions of March 17 and 19. Criticizing Bourqueney for allegedly allowing Russia to play France's proper role of defender and friend of emerging nationalities, he ordered his reluctant envoy to propose uniting the Principalities and giving them virtual independence in the sixth session on March 26. Gorchakov watched with delight as Britain, Austria, and Turkey joined in rejecting France's proposal as an attack on Turkey's rights.[17] Meanwhile, Austria's policy on the First Point was really one of cautious retreat. In the very first session Prokesch gave up the idea of stationing Austrian as well as Turkish garrisons on the Danube, urging purely native garrisons instead. When Coronini advocated activating quarantine stations in the Principalities under Austria's control to protect the health of his troops (a serious problem), Bruck proposed in an Austrian ministerial conference on March 24 to postpone any such action so as not to disturb the current peace negotiations. Agreeing to this, the conference further resolved to delay a step Bruck felt would be very valuable for Austria's Danubian trade, the uniting of Austrian and Moldo-Wallachian quarantine stations and provisions, until after a general peace was achieved and Austria's occupation ended. These are just two of many indications of Austria's defensive policy and the overriding interest even Buol's opponents had in not sabotaging a possible peace settlement.[18]

The most striking proof of Austria's moderation, however, is Russell's change of view on the Principalities and reform in Turkey. He came to Vienna convinced that Austria's occupation was worse than Russia's and that Austria wanted to do on the lower Danube what she had done in Italy—for him, the worst denunciation possible. Like Whigs generally, he believed all the Principalities needed for prosperity and happiness was closer ties with the Porte, representative institutions, free trade, Western influence, and protection from Austria and Russia. Though he quickly discarded Clarendon's theory that Buol and Gorchakov conspired over the Principalities, his belief that Austria had to be stopped in her drive for an exclusive protectorate persisted. But soon he developed misgivings about

British antidotes—Turkish garrisons and representative institutions, for example—and by late March he was uncertain about all the tenets of British policy. Austria's interests, he now believed, were mainly defensive and easily satisfied. Giving Turkey more control over the Principalities would provoke insurrections; representative institutions probably would not work; constitutional reform might or might not help, but in any case Britain was too far away and should not try too much.[19]

London's sharp criticism of him for failing to fight Prokesch in the conference sessions of March 17 and 19 only turned him more strongly against official British policy. He told Clarendon that his continued allegations of an Austro-Russian plot were sheer non-sense and that the present efforts to avoid a collective guarantee of the Principalities' privileges reversed Britain's previous policy and violated her repeatedly pledged word. Did Clarendon not realize that proposals of his such as increasing the tribute payable to the Porte and allowing Muslims to settle and own property in the Principalities would drive the inhabitants straight back into Russia's arms? Did he want to create by means of Turkish garrisons that same fierce hatred of Turkish soldiers that Britain's vice-consul at Sofia reported the Bulgarians now felt? Buol was right, said Russell, in complaining that Britain did not know what she wanted. At one time she called for a hereditary prince or princes, and these would soon lead to complete independence from Turkey; at another she wanted to increase Turkey's power, which would soon restore to Russia all the popular influence she had lost.[20]

His criticism of the contradictions in British policy finally brought Russell to an insight into the complex and delicate task the Allies had set themselves in the East. The fundamental struggle within the Ottoman Empire, he told Clarendon, was one between the Sultan's authority and the aspirations of his Christian subjects. The Allied aim was to balance these two forces and to exert their influence to preserve and defend Christian privileges, but also to encourage more progressive Turkish institutions. Russia could easily encourage Muslim fanaticism and Christian discontent simultaneously, exploiting the resultant conflict; the Allied task in contrast was extremely difficult: "In giving our support to the Sultan we may offend or alienate his Christian subjects; or on the other hand . . . in promoting liberal reforms we may shake the very foundations of Mahometan institutions." The problem could be solved and the dangers avoided only by building on existing institutions and privileges; using the Christians' patriarchal and local organizations and their existing religious and clan ties to promote their interests; supporting and developing Turkey's present religiously based institutions for her advancement; and *not* trying to erect a single uniform reformed system for the whole Ottoman Empire. Finally, Russell concluded, "A strict and cordial union between France Great Britain and Austria appears to me to offer the only effectual counterpoise to Russian influence. If Austria is thrown into the arms of Russia, it will be difficult to preserve the throne of the Sultan." [21]

There is nothing remarkable about the principles and ideas Russell here enunciated. It is remarkable only that it took him so long and required him to go so far away from London to see truths that Austria had preached from the beginning and that were for the most part self-evident; to recognize, in opposition to everything he and other British leaders had hitherto said and done, that to achieve the goals Britain professed in the East, her policy had to be conservative, not liberal; empirically cautious, not doctrinaire; based on local improvements and the dispersal of power in Turkey along traditional lines, not Empire-wide centralization and modernization; and conducted with and through Austria and Europe, not by Britain alone or with France against the "Holy Alliance." Russell, to be sure, did not remain enlightened long. He was soon defending himself vigorously against Clarendon's charge of insufficient hatred for the Holy Alliance and soliciting advice from Redcliffe on forming popular assemblies in the Principalities, or establishing comprehensive plans for sweeping postwar reform there and in the whole Ottoman Empire.[22] But this relapse is less remarkable than his momentary awakening.

Britain's major concern, much as she opposed Austria on other scores, was of course always Point Three; here a deadlock quickly developed. In private preliminary talks, Gorchakov and his assistant Titov rejected limitation as a violation of Russia's sovereign rights and as depriving her of the defensive naval force she needed to keep Constantinople from falling into hostile hands. Russell, seeing this rejection as proof of Russia's persistent ambitions, considered breaking up the conference. To prevent this, Buol revived Drouyn's proposal of getting Russia to agree voluntarily to limit her Black Sea fleet to the number of ships afloat (the status quo afloat). While telling the sea powers plainly that Austria would not recognize a Russian rejection of this proposal as her *casus belli,* he tried hard to sell the idea to Gorchakov and appeared to have some chance to succeed. Drouyn agreed to the status quo afloat as a basis for limitation; Russell recommended it to London on the ground that Russia would reject it and Austria would be drawn into the war.[23] * Clarendon did not know what to do, writing Palmerston: "It seems impossible to submit to Buol's miserable proposal and we don't even know whether that would be accepted by Russia, yet we must well weigh our chances of success in war before we take a final decision.[24]

Meanwhile, the Second Point (navigation of the Danube) was disposed of on March 21 and 23 with an agreement based on Prokesch's original proposal, with amendments at Austria's expense sponsored by Britain and Russia.[25] This cleared the way for formal discussion of the Third Point, which produced a major explosion on March 26. After Russia rejected direct limitation, Bourqueney, reluctantly following Drouyn's repeated orders, threw a proposal for complete neutralization of the Black Sea onto the table. Russell was taken entirely by surprise, Gorchakov dismissed the idea scornfully, and again the conference threatened to collapse. Buol intervened to propose calling on Russia and Turkey to suggest a method for executing Point Three. The Russian envoys, having nothing to propose, agreed to apply to St. Petersburg for instructions. Thus Buol's suggestion secured a respite for the conference and the disunited allies [26]—but nothing more. Despite Gorchakov's and Titov's urging, the new Tsar Alexander II and his ministers rejected even a voluntary limitation; a personal promise to Francis Joseph not to exceed the status quo of 1853 was as far as Alexander would go.[27]

The March 26 session strengthened London's determination to break up the conference. Palmerston, Clarendon, and others continually reminded Russell that only military victory and a glorious

---

* But at the same time Russell emphasized that Austria would not make this proposal her ultimatum to Russia, and he reported later that Gorchakov thought Russia might agree to voluntary limitation.

peace could save Britain's honor and her alliance with France; Cowley worked equally hard on Napoleon.[28] Even the Emperor's idea of going to the Crimea began to appear less dangerous in view of the threat of an inglorious peace.* British opinions differed over how Austria would respond if Britain now broke up the conference,[29] but all agreed that she should press her original demands, thereby end the negotiations, and continue the war no matter what Austria thought or did.

For Drouyn, however, this policy of deliberately driving Austria into armed neutrality with Prussia and Germany was a horrible nightmare. Improbable as it sounds, he had really hoped that his neutralization proposal might meet the Tsar's objections to direct limitation—which was precisely why Cowley was highly suspicious of it and Clarendon wanted it further sharpened against Russia.[30] Now that his idea had failed in the session of March 26, Drouyn determined to seek a break-through at Vienna personally. Cowley, though afraid of what Drouyn might concoct at Vienna, saw that his absence from Paris would increase his own influence over Napoleon. In addition, if Drouyn were first pinned down to the right terms to be imposed on Russia and then, as was inevitable, failed to make Russia accept them or Austria support them, France would finally have to abandon the Austrian alliance and lean wholly on Britain. Sharing Cowley's hopes and fears, Clarendon insisted that Drouyn first come to England to agree on what he would propose at Vienna. On March 30, in a meeting packed with English hawks, the two powers agreed to demand either direct narrow limitation or neutralization, and to break up the conference if both were refused.[31]

The Allies felt no compunction about reaching this decision without consulting Austria, but they were concerned about how to handle her when she learned of it. Drouyn, foreseeing that Austria would not make either alternative her *casus belli*, opposed trying to coerce her into it. In addition, he hinted to Hübner and Colloredo (without letting them know of the March 30 agreement) that he

* Cowley, eager to visit the theater of war himself, actually encouraged the Emperor to go, while Clarendon confessed that he was beginning to see the Emperor's projected trip "as a sort of dernier ressort to save us from disgrace" (to Cowley, 6 April 1855, FO 519/171).

would try at Vienna in some way to combine the status quo afloat limitation with counterpoise. Thus he was either deceiving Austria or already thinking of evading the agreement with Britain, or both.[32] Clarendon, apparently assuming (without any basis for it) that Austria would have to make one of the Allied alternatives her *casus foederis*, suggested presenting her with both and letting her choose. But Cowley argued strongly for confronting Austria only with neutralization. Not only was the proposal "a good one to break upon," but if they offered Austria a choice, she would reject both plans. If they offered only neutralization, when she rejected it the sea powers might "maneuver so as to get *her* to propose the system of limitation," thus entangling her in war.[33]

Completely ignored in all this discussion, meanwhile, was Russell. Now considered, as Clarendon said, "more completely nobbled by Buol and Co than poor old Westmorland," [34] he received accordingly the treatment he and Clarendon had long given Westmorland. Clarendon not only criticized him severely and unfairly for his handling of the First and Second Points (where, as Russell replied, he was only carrying out his instructions and fulfilling long-standing English pledges), but also sent him arguments to use in which Clarendon himself did not believe.[35] Worst of all, London's backstairs negotiation with France on the main issue of the conference undermined Russell's whole position, especially his efforts to get Russia to volunteer direct limitation.* Only when he learned of these negotiations from Bourqueney and sent a strong protest to London did he receive the March 30 agreement, along with wide-eyed disclaimers from Clarendon, Lansdowne, and Cowley that they ever dreamed of going beyond the Four Points or interfering with his conduct of the negotiations.[36]

Thus Drouyn was pledged to present a neutralization proposal to Austria and Russia that Russell strongly opposed and on which he himself was wavering. After his first interviews with Buol and

---

* These efforts by Russell represented for Clarendon a grave danger to the continuation of the war. As he told Cowley, if Russia accepted a limitation to the present number of ships afloat, "We shall be accused of bad faith if we don't agree. Moreover the question will then be reduced to a difference of 3 or 4 ships and it will be difficult to defend the continuation of the war for such a cause. In short I see nothing but embarrassment ahead" (3 April 1855, FO 519/171).

Francis Joseph on April 6, who characterized the plan as a gratuitous humiliation of the Tsar, he dropped it. But he used his abandonment of neutralization, along with every other tactic and argument, to try to get Austria to make some kind of direct limitation her *casus belli,* instead of merely supporting limitation diplomatically. He especially hoped that Austria had not yet learned what France knew through Berlin, that Russia would reject any limitation at all, and that he could induce her to "pronounce the fatal word" before she found out.[37] Russell, though he joined fully in these efforts, believed that Austria's intolerable isolation, rather than any arguments, would force her to adopt limitation despite herself.[38] Clarendon, while contributing to the pressure on Austria through uncommon rudeness toward Colloredo,[39] doubted that any means would be effective. Occasionally he thought Britain's great patience and moderation with Austria would pay off; usually he reverted to his belief in a Buol-Gorchakov conspiracy.[40]

The relentless Allied pressure failed to change Austria's basic stand. As Prokesch argued in a three-power meeting of April 11, Austria was committed first to a principle, that of attaching Turkey's existence to the European balance, and then to a corollary of that principle, ending Russia's maritime supremacy in the Black Sea. Obviously Russia had no right to a fleet that clearly menaced Turkey; direct limitation might even be the simplest way to solve the problem. But it was not the only satisfactory way, and "in no case will Austria sacrifice the principle to the corollary." [41]

While the conference seemed headed for a breakdown and an Austro-Western breach, the military front continued to be discouraging for the Allies. Massive bombardments and direct attacks on Sevastopol in April proved unsuccessful and were abandoned after heavy losses on both sides. In London plans for a summer campaign were pushed forward feverishly. At Palmerston's behest, Clarendon again urged the Turks to declare Circassia independent, to help gain Britain some Circassian cavalry. Other natives were enrolled as Bashi-Bazouks (irregular auxiliaries) in Britain's new Turkish Legion. Palmerston listened anew to pleas from General Zamoyski and other Poles for a revolutionary program of promoting sedition among Poles in the Russian army—though without any commitment or intention to work for an independent Poland. But nothing promised any immediate results, and at home and at the front the impression in late April was that Russia was gaining strength. The British suspected Marshal Canrobert, Saint-Arnaud's successor, of giving up on victory, and highly placed British officers of doing the same.[42]

Nor did Prussia and Germany give any encouragement to the sea powers or Austria. Buol tried repeatedly to get Prussia to promise Austria military support if she got the sea powers to accept a moderate interpretation of Point Three and presented this as her ultimatum to Russia. Manteuffel, determined to avoid the evil day of commitment as long as possible, would promise nothing to Vienna and continued to send a steady stream of anti-Austrian reports to Paris and London.[43] Buol in turn advocated neutralizing Prussia by means of a French mobilization on the Rhine and a British blockade of Prussian ports if Austria went to war and Prussia turned against her. Russell even suggested requiring Prussia to turn over a fortress each to France and Austria and Danzig to Great Britain as pledges of her neutrality—a proposal the royal couple labeled "monstrous" and blamed on Buol.[44]

But Clarendon had other ideas for Prussia. If Austria ever actually went to war, the Allies could then threaten Berlin at will, he told Bloomfield and Russell; until then, despicable as Prussian policy was, she represented a useful card to play against Austria. If Austria hung back, the sea powers should promote a rapprochement with Prussia; she would quickly unite all of Germany behind her in neutrality. Austria, exhausted, isolated, and threatened on all sides, would then have to fight on the Allies' terms. This strategy of isolating Austria from Germany, which Bloomfield applauded heartily,[45] was more than just a contingency plan. When Palmerston raised the Polish issue in the House of Commons and informed the Bavarian minister at London that Austria wanted to exclude Bavaria from the commission of riverain states regulating Danube navigation, his purpose was to wreck what remained of Austria's position in Germany.[46]

Only one minor development augured well for the conference: the appointment of Turkey's able foreign minister, Ali Pasha, to be her chief plenipotentiary, supplementing the timid Arif Effendi, who could only take proposals *ad referendum*. Redcliffe, hoping to see the conference fail,[47] had worked hard to prevent Ali's coming. From his arrival on April 9 onward, Ali fulfilled Buol's expectation that he would work for a moderate peace.

On April 15, Buol unveiled to the Allies a final Austrian proposal drawn, he emphasized, from earlier Western propositions, especially by Drouyn. This "Austrian ultimatum," as it came to be called, was not really a system of counterpoise, as it was generally considered then and later, but rather of graduated deterrence. What Buol proposed was not to balance Russia's Black Sea fleet with Allied and Turkish forces, but to establish a series of step-by-step responses to every Russian move to rebuild her fleet, to deter her from doing so. If she began to rebuild beyond the status quo afloat, each of the sea powers would be empowered to introduce into the Black Sea half as many ships as the Russians maintained there. If the Sultan saw a danger of war or felt himself menaced by the Russian fleet, he could summon in the entire Allied fleets without opening the Straits to Russia. All the great powers, Russia included, would guarantee Turkey's integrity, and Austria and the West would conclude a military alliance in her favor, the *casus foederis* of which would be either a Russian attack on Turkey or Russia's exceeding the naval status quo of 1853. In addition, the sea powers could if desired station a few ships at the Bosporus, to let Russia know in advance that a descent on Constantinople would put her at war with most of Europe. Austria would present this plan as her ultimatum to Russia, and if it was rejected would recognize the *casus foederis* of December 2.

Buol and Prokesch used every possible argument for their plan, claiming that Austria was violating her basic principle in including any naval limitation at all in the *casus foederis*. Francis Joseph absolutely would not go to war over a certain number of ships; he could not justify it at home or in Germany, and he would not break his word not to deliberately humiliate Russia. They insisted that graduated response was more flexible and therefore better and safer than narrow limitation; it avoided the danger of plunging Europe into war over a single ship, and, in posing a more sensible response to any Russian armaments, it also posed a more credible deterrent. Above all they pleaded for meeting the primary political danger to Turkey by political means (the European guarantee backed by a three-power alliance) and argued that this plan would make fleet expansion so dangerous and futile that Russia might volunteer direct limitation in preference to it.[48]

Drouyn and Russell denounced the limitation to the 1853 status quo as derisory and tried to raise it at least to the status quo afloat, but Buol, backed by the Emperor, held firm.[49] It soon became apparent that neither chief Western envoy really opposed the Austrian ultimatum. On April 15, after vigorously attacking Buol's ideas, Russell cabled Clarendon a plan of his much like Buol's, except for calling on Russia also to cede the islands at the Danube mouth to Turkey and to redefine the Russo-Turkish Asiatic frontier, razing fortresses Russia had abandoned there. Drouyn criticized these additional demands as likely to cause new difficulties, but he encouraged Russell to keep working on his plan, which abandoned direct limitation for some kind of graduated response.[50]

After Russia surprised everyone on April 17 by declining to make any proposal on the Third Point, the three allied delegations agreed among themselves to put Austria's ultimatum to possible use. At the next session, they would first try for direct limitation; if this was refused, then a limitation to the status quo afloat by direct Russo-Turk agreement; and if this also failed, then Buol's ultimatum, improved by adding a provision for stationing Western consuls in Russia's Black Sea ports.[51] On April 19, Drouyn proposed narrow limitation by direct Russo-Turk agreement. Gorchakov hesitated only long enough to ascertain that this plan did not involve the *casus foederis* for Austria and then rejected limitation flatly on April 21, proposing instead to open the Straits to warships of all nations, with the Sultan being permitted to make exceptions and to close the Straits in case of war or attack. Besides putting forward this impossible proposal, the Russians refused to join in any active guarantee of Turkey's integrity. The Western plenipotentiaries now had to either break up the conference or try to gain their governments' consent to the Austrian ultimatum.

Drouyn had already chosen the latter course. His lieutenant Thouvenel urged him strongly to close with Russell on pure counterpoise, which, he said, would save Russia's honor, be safe and effective, satisfy Buol, and garner the plaudits of all Europe. "As for the English Cabinet," wrote Thouvenel, "it appears to me off its head [déraisonné]. Lord Cowley gives free rein to his antipathies against Austria, and nobody calms him down." * Russell had more serious misgivings than the French, fearing at first that Austria would not make even the rejection of her ultimatum her *casus belli*. But on leaving Vienna on April 23 he had become satisfied on this point and convinced of Austria's sincerity, and was willing to sponsor her plan at London. It involved some of the disadvantages of counterpoise, he admitted to Clarendon, and, still worse, would be unpopular at home. However, "it would very nearly attain all the objects of the war" and give Britain a ready-made league to counter future Russian aggression or to meet Turkey's possible dissolution. If Russia rejected it, Austria would enter the war; if the West spurned it, Austria would stay neutral, Russia could send fifty or sixty thousand more men to the Crimea, and the war could go on indefinitely without decision or purpose. Let the Allies fight on, said Russell, if they had good concrete war aims that this proposal would not meet. "But do not let us make the continuance of war depend on a fancied necessity of maintaining our prestige. For prestige depends not on our taking one strong place but on our character and our means. The one is unsullied, the other unimpaired." [52]

Russell's argument required courage. He knew that he would be the prime target of public anger over a cowardly peace, and while some friends urged him to seek peace regardless of any public outcry, most of the advice from those most influential with him went the other way.[53] But his plea went unheard. Austria's ultimatum only strengthened London's determination to break up the conference. Napoleon's visit at this time to the royal couple had not only renewed his enthusiasm for the war and the English alliance, but helped persuade him not to go to the Crimea, removing one of the dangers of continuing the war. Cowley called the Austrian ultimatum mad, a total surrender to Russia; Palmerston termed it a contemptible fraud; the Queen, absurd and incredible; Clarendon, shameful and traitorous. It would only limit the Allies while permitting Russia unlimited naval expansion, said Palmerston. It would positively promote the designs of Catherine the Great, contended

---

* Hübner asked Buol in a private letter of May 9 whether he could explain Cowley's livid hatred of Austria, saying, "I have never seen anyone more implacable and more impassioned in our regard" (PA IX/51).

Clarendon. In two or three months Austria would be back in the Holy Alliance as she desired. But among all the cant and distortions could be found a kernel of truth, one genuine reason for the ministry's attitude. Were Buol's plan adopted, Clarendon wrote Westmorland, we would not be safe in the streets, "and *serve us right.*" [54]

Clarendon therefore considered the conference over as of April 22, while Palmerston wanted a closing session only to get Austria to tell Russia that the sea powers were not bound by any agreements they had made at the conference on Points One and Two.[55] * This raised again the question of whether to summon Austria to recognize the *casus foederis* of the alliance. Palmerston and Napoleon favored doing so; Cowley seems even to have encouraged the Emperor to break relations with Austria if she refused. But Drouyn strongly opposed such a summons and Clarendon wavered. While constantly denouncing Austria, he wanted to do her justice, that is, to recognize that she was base and treacherous because of fears she had and dangers she ran. Besides, he did not know on just what grounds to break with Austria. He wanted to invoke the *casus foederis*, he wrote Redcliffe on April 23, but Drouyn argued that doing so would only enable Austria to make a good case against the Allies as the real obstacle to peace before Europe. Drouyn was perhaps right; moderation toward Austria would make her cowardice and bad faith more evident and embarrassing to her.[56]

At the last minute Buol accepted some slight amendments to the ultimatum, making it still harder to reject out of hand. Now *attaining* the status quo of 1853, rather than exceeding it, would be the *casus belli* in the proposed alliance, and this stipulation would be put in a separate secret article, while the public treaty simply forbade any excessive development of Russia's fleet. Having gained these concessions, Drouyn and Bourqueney pleaded with both Paris and London for acceptance, arguing that Russia would reject

---

* In this same letter Palmerston urged Clarendon to get Holland to abandon her strict neutrality for one favoring the Allies. He admitted this would ruin her good relations and profitable trade with Russia, but she would gain Britain's good will in exchange. "If she refuses," he said, "and in anticipation of her refusal it may be well to take a legal opinion as to our right to seize arms and other contraband of war at the mouth of her rivers and off her harbors and coast." To Palmerston's regret, the legal opinion turned out unfavorable.

it and Austria would be theirs. Bourqueney pointed out how Russell had been converted after coming to Vienna full of anti-Austrian prejudices.[57] Francis Joseph made another personal plea to Napoleon; Buol tried to get Ernest of Coburg to advocate his plan directly to Albert and Victoria.[58] Even Westmorland, knowing his opinions were worse than useless at London, did something to keep the conference alive, holding back from Buol Clarendon's private letter denouncing and rejecting the Austrian ultimatum. Drouyn's account of the French government's attitude, he told Clarendon, differed greatly from what Clarendon told him of it, and Drouyn should have a chance to win both London and Paris to his policy.[59]

The amendments, along with Russell's plea that he be heard in London before a final decision was reached, led Clarendon to suspend instructions to Westmorland on April 24 pending more information.[60] The hawks continued to insist that Austria's plan was designed to ensure Russian preponderance in the Black Sea. Palmerston threatened to resign rather than accept it; Cowley besieged Napoleon with warnings of complete disgrace if the Allies receded an inch from their original terms.[61] Yet what would Austria do when the conference broke up? If she were sincere, said Cowley, she would fight for direct limitation; one or two Allied victories, claimed Palmerston, would bring her in on any terms the Allies wanted. Clarendon, however, was uncertain to the point of incoherence, and the whole French ministry rejected Britain's reasoning.[62]

Worse still, the British could not tell what France might do if they forced her to reject a settlement she favored and continue a stalemated and unpopular war, for the alliance already suffered from serious strains. The French were growing continually more disgusted with Redcliffe and with British policy in the East.[63] The rivalry in Greece remained a sore point.[64] Incensed at the burden falling on her in the Crimea and at British efforts to divert forces to the east coast of the Black Sea, France became extremely angry at Britain's claim that the Sardinian contingent was hers to dispose of, and the British responded with equal irritation.[65] Palmerston's opposition to Ferdinand de Lesseps' project of a Suez Canal, which he insisted was simply a French scheme to get control of Egypt, was already a heated issue.[66] But the main point was France's desire for peace. The British retained confidence only in Napoleon, and even he was erratic. In late April his projected Crimean trip cropped up briefly again, and if Cowley was enthused at the chance to accompany him and see the war, few others were edified.[67]

While Britain hesitated, France still sought desperately to raise Austria's ultimatum to the West's standards. Hübner pleaded with Buol to change the *casus belli* to the status quo afloat; when all efforts to sell the present plan to the sea powers had failed, he wrote, "the moment will have come, I think, for our August Master to say his final word." Buol replied tersely in a marginal note, "He has already said it." [68] Drouyn took a more drastic step. On his return to Paris, he omitted all mention of the status quo of 1853, making the *casus foederis* simply any excessive development of Russia's fleet. If Britain would accept this amended proposal, with the status quo afloat considered the point beyond which development was excessive, he told Russell, he was sure Austria would go along.* Even this did not satisfy the hawks. Cowley objected that Drouyn's amendment was worthless unless Austria was pledged to declare war the day Russia rejected her ultimatum, and Clarendon agreed. He was trying to like the proposal, he told Russell, but simply could not. He wrote, "We may be compelled to accept it but I feel it is too little security for the future, too great an abandonment of all we have been contending for, too manifestly a proof of our military failure and for these reasons too certain to be condemned by public opinion." But Drouyn, too deeply committed to stop at anything, insisted that the ultimatum did make Russian fleet expansion an instant *casus belli* for Austria,[69] and he got Napoleon grudgingly to accept his version, making it almost impossible for Britain to brush aside.

Moreover, some leading Englishmen favored it. Aberdeen, his opinion solicited by Clarendon, argued strongly for peace,[70] while Russell, now a defender of Buol and Francis Joseph and an advocate of a "statesmen's peace," particularly attacked the prevalent British argument that Austria's conduct in this war proved her to be worthless as an ally against Russia in the future. Neither Austria's past record in war as Britain's ally, nor her diplomacy in this crisis, nor

---

* Drouyn had urged this revision of the ultimatum on Buol at Vienna in a note of April 21, but there is no sign that Buol ever accepted it (PA XL/277l).

her present proposal, nor her permanent strategic interest in stopping a Russian advance justified the assumption that she would not honor her commitment. Besides, Russell pointed out, the important consideration was not whether Austria could be trusted to honor the *casus foederis* in the alliance she proposed, but the fact that "the name of such an alliance would probably prevent Russia from making a fruitless attempt at conquest." [71]

Hamilton Seymour, one of the earlier advocates of the war, now favored Austria's ultimatum, mainly on short-range expedient grounds, but in addition because Russia was not the only possible danger, and it might be wise to pave the way for an ultimate Anglo-Russian reconciliation by a moderate peace. Granville also was won over. The most striking change occurred in Prince Albert. On April 25 he attacked the Austrian ultimatum and defended narrow limitation with all the standard British arguments. But on May 3 he circulated another long memorandum which, while still distorting and rejecting Austria's plan, called for diplomatic guarantees to take the place of military ones. An alliance of the four great powers plus Germany against Russia, he now maintained, would give Turkey and Europe adequate security no matter how many ships Russia had in the Black Sea. This insight on Albert's part, it must be said, was not merely tardy, but derivative. What converted him to relying on a political alliance (and a rather crude and excessive one at that) for security against Russia was two memoranda and a letter that his friend and adviser Baron Stockmar sent him and Victoria between April 27 and May 2, all urging (perhaps unwittingly) precisely the case Austria had long made for a moderate peace settlement.[72] Albert's adoption of Stockmar's program merely shows again how hard it was even for someone strongly anti-Austrian to resist her case on political grounds.

May 3 found the British government suspended in indecision. Palmerston, rejecting Albert's arguments, still fought Drouyn's proposal; [73] Cowley threatened to resign and urged Clarendon to do the same rather than dishonor himself by accepting it. But Clarendon wavered, fearing equally the immediate public reaction to a shabby peace and the eventual public revulsion against a prolonged and useless war. The Cabinet as a whole thought Austria's original plan inadequate, but if Austria would accept Drouyn's version and if Napoleon really favored it, Britain would go along.[74]

Thus the decision lay with Napoleon and depended on whether Drouyn or Cowley would possess his soul. On May 4 that issue was fought out. That morning Cowley convinced Napoleon that Drouyn's modifications were really no improvements at all, because even his version of the ultimatum still imposed absolutely no limit on Russian naval expansion.* Though satisfied the game was won, Cowley as a precaution invited himself to Napoleon's interview with Drouyn that afternoon. To his dismay, he arrived to find the Emperor backsliding again. But, as he reported privately to Clarendon, "by great good luck" Marshal Vaillant, the Minister of War, was also there, "and together we soon dusted his colleague's back most handsomely." Vaillant joined Cowley in emphasizing the disgrace of accepting inglorious terms, the worthlessness of the Austrian alliance, and the dangerous impact a peace without victory might have on the army and Napoleon's throne. "In short," Cowley remarked, "he was game to the backbone." Napoleon, again converted, insisted on narrow limitation with Allied fleets equal to Russia's allowed in the Black Sea and consuls stationed in Russian ports; even these were disgraceful terms. "We have beat Drouyn to pieces," exulted Cowley. Drouyn would never forgive him, but that could not be helped.[75]

Cowley's earlier telegrams had given Clarendon hope that the "national humiliation" of Drouyn's plan would be averted; Cowley's private letter raised the expectation that Drouyn himself would be eliminated. Obviously Drouyn had reason to be angry, Clarendon wrote Cowley, "but I am uncommonly glad that old Vaillant shared with you the responsibility of throwing him and the scheme over." Clarendon's joy and relief were not unalloyed; he himself was still troubled by Albert's memorandum and by the military situation, and he conceded that the Cabinet was still divided, with some re-

---

* This argument, used frequently by Palmerston and others as well as Cowley, and important in this crisis, requires a brief comment. It asserts that a fundamental difference in deterrent or limiting force exists between compelling Russia to sign a treaty limiting her ships to a certain number (the British demand) and forcing Russia to accept a peace settlement in which, if she built ships beyond that number, three great powers were pledged to go to war with her (Drouyn's and Austria's ultimatum). Obviously the latter proposal had exactly the same limiting force as the former and failed only to impose on Russia a public humiliation. Britain's argument thus amounted, like so many of hers, to a petty and dishonest quibble. But Napoleon either did not see through it, or was too much concerned with his prestige to care, or both.

gretting discarding a plan that could bring the peace the country seemed increasingly to desire. Nonetheless, Clarendon immediately informed Austria that her ultimatum was rejected and called on her to recognize the *casus foederis* of December 2. A last-minute plea by Bourqueney in behalf of the ultimatum arrived May 5, bearing Austria's renewed assurance that if Russia rejected it Austria would immediately recognize the *casus foederis*. But Clarendon told Albert that the Cabinet saw no need to consider this plea; it was all "a clumsy attempt on the part of Austria to bully England and France into the acceptance of a Russian project." [76]

Thus the peace negotiations to all intents and purposes ended on May 4–5, though, as will be seen, there remained a long and painful aftermath. The margin between ultimate success and failure was not as thin as the tense events of these days might suggest. Without Cowley's intervention, Napoleon would probably have supported Drouyn's plan and Britain would have gone along with it. But Drouyn had arbitrarily altered the *casus belli* of the Austrian ultimatum, and one cannot suppose that he could have imposed his version on Austria. He had tried this tactic before and always encountered a point beyond which Austria would not budge. Everything indicates that Buol's final concession, the attainment of the status quo of 1853, was that point. Hence a different outcome of the May 4 interviews in Paris would probably only have delayed a final breakdown of the Vienna Conference. Nonetheless, the events of May 3–5 are important. Not only would subsequent diplomacy and the Western case before Europe have been substantially different had the conference broken down over the divergence between Drouyn's plan and Austria's ultimatum, but these events make clear the real ground for the West's decision. Napoleon and the British finally rejected even Drouyn's plan simply because it did not satisfy them in terms of national honor, military glory, and personal prestige. This was why Austria's peace efforts failed and the war had to continue. There were of course many arguments made then, and sometimes maintained since, that Austria's plan was insincere, militarily useless, and politically ineffective, and they deserve to be considered briefly. But they turn out to be important mainly for what they unintentionally reveal about those who made them.

The most common contention at the time was that Austria simply wanted to escape from her December 2 commitments and the dangers of her position. According to Clarendon, she would have liked to kick Russia but dared not; according to some writers, Buol wanted to go to war but Francis Joseph prevented him. Hence Austria developed her ultimatum in order to avoid her alliance obligations. One must admire the boldness of this argument. The truth is that Austria never tried to escape from the Western alliance; Buol wanted desperately to stay in it, while Cowley, Palmerston, and others tried to drive Austria out. Austria's ultimatum amply fulfilled every written and oral promise she ever made to the sea powers. Many Englishmen already knew and admitted this (Greville, Russell, Sidney Herbert, Clarendon, even Cowley) and the list would grow as the facts became more widely known. As Westmorland said (and Russell agreed), not Austria's but Britain's good faith and honor were at stake. The government would destroy its reputation for honest dealing if it broke off negotiations and tried to invoke the *casus foederis* of December 2 over a demand (narrow limitation) that it knew Austria had always rejected as binding on her.[77]

Furthermore, there is no serious evidence that at any time before or during the conference Buol switched from wanting war to seeking peace or that the Emperor prevented him from leading Austria into war. His whole policy contradicts this, and his *Vorträge* of March 21 and April 15 and the Emperor's responses directly disprove it. Buol's final proposal represented the kind of peace settlement he had always sought; Prokesch, Rechberg, G. Esterházy, and other advisers warned him not to go beyond it or accept war for any other grounds. Only Hübner urged clinging to France even at the cost of entering the war, and his advice was decisively rejected.[78]

Nor is it true, on the other side, that Austria avoided any risk of war by proposing only what she knew Russia would accept. Clarendon's and Cowley's charge of a Buol-Gorchakov plot over the ultimatum is even more absurd in this instance than usual. Buol kept the ultimatum secret not only from Gorchakov and Russia, but from the highest Austrian officials outside the foreign ministry.[79] Naturally Buol hoped Russia would accept the ultimatum or, better still, volunteer direct limitation in its place; only someone with Cowley's concept of honor would have wanted Russia to refuse. But Austria had no advance knowledge or assurance of how Russia would react, and the available evidence indicates that Alexander would have rejected it.[80] Moreover, Austria prepared seriously to carry through on her ultimatum in case of a rejection. At the last she pressed for a rapid conclusion of the military convention with France. Hess left Vienna to assume command of the army in Galicia. Prokesch had virtually completed the drafts of the ultimatum and the messages that were supposed to go with it to St. Petersburg when Britain's rejection arrived. While Drouyn and Bourqueney deliberately exaggerated the speed and automatic process by which a Russian rejection would bring Austria into the war, Austria clearly would have fulfilled her engagements to the letter and all the way.[81]

The remaining objection is that Austria's proposal would have been ineffective and unworkable. Obviously this could be true even if the sea powers did not actually reject it on this account. Moreover, the argument is in a sense unanswerable, since the plan was never tried and any claim that it would have produced a solid peace must involve a great deal of speculation.[82] But it may be useful to look at the specific criticisms made at that time and since and see what underlies them. The contentions that need to be taken seriously run as follows. (1) Even though Austria's various devices would doubtless end Russia's preponderance in the Black Sea (as Cowley, for example, admitted they would), they would be costly, difficult to maintain, and hence ineffective, for the Allies would soon abandon them after the war. (2) Austria's proposed alliance to defend Turkey would not work because the sea powers would not remain united and the German powers would never fight Russia. (3) After all their sacrifices the Allies had a right to depend on a clear Russian treaty commitment not to rebuild her fleet, rather that her voluntary forbearance, and to expect of Austria not provisions for help in the next war, but measures to prevent it. (4) Giving Turkey the right to decide when she was menaced and could summon European aid would enable her to play the various European powers off against one another to Turkey's profit. (5) Austria's proposals would have led to constant quarrels over interpretation and to other frictions between the West and Russia, with Austria the gainer thereby.[83] *

* The Allies used another common argument against the Austrian ultimatum: since they as belligerents had made all the sacrifices of the war, only they

These arguments all seem plausible enough. But they first of all ignore the whole deterrent purpose of Austria's proposal. It obviously aimed not at giving the Allies help in the next war, which she wanted to avoid as much as they, but at confronting Russia with the prospect of such an overwhelming coalition that she would not start one; not at allowing the sea powers to match Russian naval expansion, but at making such expansion so plainly useless and dangerous that Russia would not try it. Austria's system thus depended not on Russian good faith and forbearance, but on that minimum of prudence and rational conduct that one has to assume if one is ever to make peace with an opponent without obliterating him. Russell saw this, even if his government chose not to. Besides, some of these objections would tell against the Western peace proposals as well, or against any. Every peace settlement or treaty arrangement is only as good as the power and determination available to enforce it. If the Allies would not remain united after the war, a Russian treaty commitment against naval expansion would be little or no better than her voluntary promise; if Austria and Prussia would never fight Russia, their subscription to narrow limitation would be no better than their support for graduated deterrence or counterpoise. As Austria repeatedly pointed out, the powers would be more likely to remain united to support a moderate and flexible settlement than they would to uphold a draconic and rigid one.

These criticisms, moreover, show much of the perversity that results from refusing to accept the logical consequences of one's own position and aims. If Austria proposed allowing two frigates from each sea power to be stationed in the Black Sea, she was imposing a humiliating limitation on the Allies. If she proposed letting Turkey call in their entire fleets in an emergency, she was requiring them to bear in peacetime the burdens of war. Yet plainly the Allies would have to have some means of enforcement—either symbolic forces

---

should determine the terms of peace, not Austria. To that contention, the answer is found in one of Prokesch's notes (PA XL/321): "Our policy is not bent on destruction, and if we find it natural that a state of war brings with it rights that are of its essence, we cannot confuse the rights of war with the conditions of a work of peace." This also, I think, aptly answers Unckel's charge that Buol took virtually no account of the special needs and rights of the belligerent powers (p. 210). Buol in fact took every possible account of their belligerent rights—but not to the point of destroying all possibility of peace for the sake of those rights.

present or superior forces available—to back up any peace settlement. Or again, if Austria refused to guarantee Turkey absolutely against Russia, Austria was abandoning Turkey to her fate. But if the Austrian proposal empowered Turkey to decide when she was menaced and to summon her allies to her aid, she was giving Turkey the power to cause needless trouble. Once again, what did the Allies expect? How could one hope to make a corrupt, declining power secure and independent vis-à-vis a permanently more powerful neighbor, without giving that protected power more opportunity to create trouble on its own? This dilemma explains why Austria had always wanted to make support for Turkey dependent on some measures of European control and restraint.

In effect, a peace settlement, in order to meet these British objections, would have had to protect Turkey and deter Russia without any effort from the Allies and would have had to remain effective whether or not they continued to support it. These requirements are of course contradictory. To meet them, Russia would have had not only to dismantle her fleet but to disappear. The Allies were really calling for safeguards not against a revival of Russian aggression, but against their own anticipated negligence and inconstancy of purpose; demanding not reasonable safety, but that free and absolute security that is an absurdity for any state involved in a multinational system of balance of power.

Probably even the British in their soberer moments did not suppose that they could achieve this kind of security. The fact that the Allies insisted so strongly upon it really indicates again that their objections to Austria's plan were pretexts. They wanted to continue the war because they wanted to continue the war.

One more point: in international relations it is vital to perceive what issues are passed over while others are discussed, and why. In all the furor over the Third Point at Vienna, the real Russian menace to Turkey and Europe was entirely ignored (except by Austria), and no means for meeting it even discussed. What threatened Turkey, in this war as all previous ones, was not the Russian navy descending from Sevastopol, but the Russian army marching over the Balkans. This army, by far the largest and until this war reputedly the best in Europe, was Russia's chief means of pressure and influence on all her neighbors. Everyone knew this, including the British.[84]

Why did no one propose limiting Russia's army? Nothing else could have done as much to curb her power for aggression against Turkey or to relieve her pressure on Europe. True, the demand would have been humiliating and extremely difficult to enforce; yet other demands just as harsh and impractical were considered. The answer is partly that Britain was chiefly concerned about her imperial interests; an end to Russia's Black Sea power would help to curb her expansion toward Persia and Asia and her competition with Britain's empire and trade. But the larger reason for ignoring Russia's army is that far from really considering Austria and Prussia useless as barriers to Russian expansion, as the British claimed they were, the sea powers knew that the German powers could and would check the Russian army because of their own vital interests. The West did not need to block the land route to Constantinople (and in fact could not), but Austria would do it anyway. From the standpoint of Western interests it was thus positively undesirable to limit Russia's land power and to render Austria, Prussia, and Germany more secure from it. They should instead be alienated from Russia, feel threatened by her, and look to the West, especially Britain, for support. Both Palmerston's *beau idéal* of partitioning Russia's Western territories and Redcliffe's idea of surrounding her with independent states assumed explicitly that when Russia recovered her strength and sought revenge, Austria and Prussia would be first in line to feel her wrath.* Both the sea powers, especially France, also always kept in mind the possibility that Russia, once she was alienated from the German powers and held in check by them, would be amenable to a profitable deal over their heads with one or the other of the Western powers.

The point is not to denounce this policy. States possessing a superior position within the international system commonly exploit the insecurity of more exposed states for their own special advantage. Those who consider *sacro egoismo* the only rational rule of foreign policy will consider this perfectly justified. It is only important to be clear on what British and French policy really was. All the rhetoric aside, it never was designed either to secure Tur-

---

* A. J. P. Taylor rightly remarks that the British, in commonly describing Austria and Prussia as Britain's natural allies, simply meant that "they were serving the purposes of Britain's policy without any effort on the British side" ("Crimea: the War that Would Not Boil," in his *Rumours of Wars*, 32).

key from Russian aggression or to relieve central Europe of Russian pressure, but to gain free security for Britain and France at Austria's and Prussia's expense. The implications of this fact for traditional views of Britain's role in the European balance, peace, and Concert must be assessed later.

XII

War Resumed: Austria in Limbo

Logically, the sea powers' rejection of Austria's ultimatum, which was followed by Drouyn's resignation, should have led quickly to a breakup of the Vienna Conference and possibly to a formal breach in the December 2 alliance. That neither of these things happened, at least not immediately, was due primarily to more delay and confusion in the Western camp.

Clarendon, though relieved at escaping negotiations, now feared that Drouyn's resignation would publicize and popularize the peace settlement he had sponsored, making Britain responsible for frustrating peace. To forestall the expected hostile reaction by the public to the failure of the conference, Clarendon told Austria that Britain, while rejecting her proposal, was entirely willing to discuss further propositions on the Third Point—a claim, he confided to Redcliffe, that the growing strength of the peace party in Britain made necessary.[1]

A still worse danger loomed, threatening the life of the ministry.* Russell wanted to resign along with Drouyn, not so much in defense of his policy as because he considered it a matter of personal honor to share Drouyn's fate over a policy they both had advocated. He conceded, however, that if Drouyn had quit because of a personal quarrel with Napoleon, his own honor was not involved.[2] Seizing this opening, Palmerston advised Clarendon to tell Russell that Drouyn had not resigned over the issue of peace or war. Clarendon first told him that the cause of Drouyn's resignation was not known. Then Cowley, criticized in France for interfering in

---

* Colloredo remarked that Clarendon always argued "as if the question for Europe, for England, was the continuance of the Palmerston Cabinet" (to Buol, 28 May 1855, PA VIII/42.

her internal affairs and fearing similar charges at home, corrected the account he had earlier privately given Clarendon and Redcliffe, boasting of his role in overthrowing Drouyn. His first dispatch of May 7, written for a blue book, entirely concealed his part, presenting the resignation as the result of Drouyn's reacting to Napoleon's spontaneous change of mind. The second dispatch, more circumstantial but no less deceptive, charged Drouyn with causing his own downfall by plotting to create a continental league against Britain, while Cowley had simply presented facts to the Emperor at his request. His private letter of May 8 denied even more flatly that he was involved in Drouyn's fall or that it resulted from a split between Drouyn and himself over the question of peace and the maintenance of the Austrian alliance. On the contrary, Cowley assured Hübner in telling him this same story, Britain wanted the Austrian alliance as much as ever and would always listen to any reasonable peace proposal.

Clarendon presented this version to Russell (and to Redcliffe and Austria as well). Russell was thus led to believe not only that Drouyn had resigned over a personal difference with Napoleon, but that Napoleon had rejected Drouyn's peace proposal independently of British advice. This was no doubt naive on Russell's part; but his colleagues' impassioned appeals not to let them and the country down by resigning, and his awareness of what another resignation would do to his own reputation, led him to trust what was told him without much probing. Palmerston and Clarendon heaved a sigh of relief when his resignation was withdrawn.[3]

Meanwhile, France faced once more the problem of explaining why she rejected an Austrian proposal mainly French in origin and favored by most French diplomats and ministers. The new foreign minister Walewski, admitted, indeed emphasized, that politically the ultimatum was wholly satisfactory and provided ample security for Turkey; it merely failed to satisfy the Allies' honor.[4] Bourqueney, who wanted to resign along with Drouyn but was talked out of it,[5] warned that the suspension of the conference left Buol in a position to present his proposal to Russia and that she would seize on it to neutralize Austria and Germany and to stigmatize the West as enemies of peace. Though Buol assured Bourqueney that he had no intention of doing this, Walewski, just as afraid of a

break with Austria as Drouyn had been, immediately proposed renewing the December 2 alliance, with changes to make it a purely
defensive one based on the 1854 protocols. He also instructed
Bourqueney not to press Austria now to recognize the *casus foederis*
of December 2. No sooner had a delighted Bourqueney received
this proposal, however, than a telegram from Paris suspended it—
Cowley, to Clarendon's great satisfaction, had intervened to kill the
initiative.[6]

Austria's reaction to the May 5 decision was one of bitter disappointment and anger. Francis Joseph said that he had been treated
"like the commander of a foreign legion"; Buol's opponents charged
again that the decision proved that Britain was the real enemy of
the whole continent, especially Austria.[7] Buol stood firm on Austria's
ultimatum as her last word, denouncing the West's arguments as
absurd and telling Hübner that while Austria would not try to impose peace on the West, "they will not impose on us a war that is
not commanded by our interests" for the sake of their "private
motives." [8] But Westmorland and Bourqueney could report in mid-
May that Allied fears of an Austro-Russian rapprochement were not
being fulfilled.[9] What led Buol to cling to the Western alliance, as
both his and Prokesch's correspondence show, was not Allied warnings or threats, but simply the conviction that the war would lose
all purpose if the political alignment established to check Russia in
the East were broken up.[10]

In this spirit, and aiming to make Russia rather than the sea
powers responsible for the final breakdown of negotiations, Buol
called for a final conference session, in which he would put forward
the idea of limiting Russia to the status quo afloat and would support it diplomatically, though not as Austria's ultimatum. Russia
would refuse, and the West could make this their reason for breaking off the talks.[11] Cowley immediately protested that Buol was
trying to make the West appear to be suing Russia for peace terms.
On this same ground Clarendon had just vetoed a French proposal
to have Austria sound out Russia once more on the Third Point.
But how could the sea powers plausibly refuse to let Austria
present one of their own proposals to Russia and support it diplomatically? Palmerston admitted that Buol's proposal "seems reasonable"—though adding hastily that the Allies might find the status

quo afloat inconvenient unless they could first take Sevastopol and reduce that status quo to zero. Clarendon only insisted at first on knowing the exact text of what Buol would propose.[12]

Walewski strongly seconded Buol's proposal, arguing that if Russia accepted it the Allies would have admirable terms of peace; if not, Austria was theirs. Once more Clarendon suffered the agonies of indecision, torn between fear of the public reaction to a "cowardly peace" and the even greater fear that the public would finally see that the ministry had thrown away good chances for a satisfactory settlement. Buol's scheme was obviously cooked up with Gorchakov, he insisted; yet without military victory, which was nowhere in sight, Britain could not stand up to France and Austria as she ought. The public would never understand the difference between what Buol wanted to propose and what Britain demanded on the Third Point. Even if Russia rejected the proposal, as Clarendon sometimes supposed she would, Austria would not have to fight; if Russia accepted it, as he often feared, she would appear to have yielded to "renewed entreaties of the allies"—a humiliating prospect. And if agreement was once reached on the Third Point, it would be impossible to continue the war over the Fourth; Europe would never forgive Britain. "If I could but feel sure of the French army," he wrote Cowley, "I would be for throwing over Austria and the Conference completely and once for all"—but the Russians, he feared, were better men.[13] While opposing Buol's proposal at Paris and Vienna, Clarendon asked Palmerston whether amendments designed to frustrate Buol's plot with Gorchakov and to prove Britain's sincerity in negotiations would not be wiser than a flat rejection.[14]

Russell deepened Clarendon's distress by warning him that once Austria closed the conference with this proposal, she would justifiably claim that her alliance commitments had been fulfilled. Clarendon had better prepare to meet that point in Parliament. Worse still, Lord John insisted that Austria's present proposal was neither ineffective nor dishonorable, but a good basis for final peace. He characterized Clarendon's arguments that a balance of forces would promote Russian preponderance in the Black Sea and that Russia wished to lure Western fleets into it as simply absurd. Nothing would ever make Russia consent to the permanent presence of Western fleets in the Black Sea except her present desperate need to keep Austria out of the war. Moreover, Clarendon's "gross insinuation that Austria has all along been playing us false, and trying to impose Russian terms upon us" was gratuitously insulting.[15] Argyll also objected strongly to the grounds on which Buol's proposal was attacked and recognized the real reasons for rejecting it. You believe, he wrote Russell, that the proposal itself is not bad, but that Russia will not accept it: "I think this may be true. But I cannot conceal from myself that a fear lest it *should* be accepted is really at the bottom of the objections of some of our colleagues. They hold, apparently, that it would be a 'dishonourable peace'—meaning a Peace accepted before some military success has been attained." [16]

Once again Palmerston rescued Clarendon, supplying him with arguments to beat down his doubts; tired and baseless though these were, they had the hearty support of the Court.[17] * He also assured Clarendon that Russia was bound to keep a strong army on Austria's frontiers, which would prevent Austria from breaking with the West, and again he threatened resignation before he would cause "our national disgrace" by accepting lower terms.[18] Cowley echoed the same sentiments and warned Clarendon that even informing Russia once more of what the Allies wanted entailed the grave danger of Russia's accepting it: "I should recommend great caution in permitting the word limitation to escape anyone's mouth—for we might be unpleasantly caught." [19]

Cowley's main task, however, was to overcome France's persistent desire to retain some kind of tie with Austria. Even Napoleon still shared to some degree his minister's dread of an open breach with her. Cowley therefore had to work against Walewski as he had against Drouyn,† constantly exposing the differences between Walewski's ideas and the Emperor's impulses and desires. When

---

* Albert even charged Austria with wanting selfishly to "enjoy the advantages of a warlike attitude" without joining the war—an utterly absurd accusation in view of the desperate political, military, and financial straits Austria now found herself in.

† At Walewski's accession, Clarendon wrote Redcliffe that though not very able, the new foreign minister was "an honest man . . . who never lies or intrigues" (7 May 1855, FO 352/42/II/5). Clarendon's and Cowley's confidence in Walewski's integrity lasted about a week.

Walewski under pressure admitted that he considered Buol's (originally Drouyn's) proposal of status quo afloat limitation to be adequate, Cowley went to Napoleon to inquire why he had changed his mind and was abandoning the war. To Napoleon's argument that France merely wanted to trap Austria into fulfilling her obligation, Cowley answered that this tactic had led to Austria's previous betrayals; fear and duress were the only language she understood. Walewski then claimed that the Allies could find a way to continue the war even if Russia accepted Buol's proposal. Cowley replied angrily that Britain's honor would not let her extend terms to Russia on which she herself did not wish to make peace, or enter a conference she did not want to see succeed—one designed in any case solely to enable Austria to escape her obligations. To Walewski's complaint that France was constantly forced to yield to British demands, Cowley answered that, without France, Britain might not now be at war and surely would not be in the present mess. Who was responsible, he asked, for sending the fleets into the Black Sea in midwinter, and for leading the British "to fetter themselves with an Austrian alliance"? [20]

Clarendon warned that Cowley risked undermining his position through too much pressure and unsolicited advice to Napoleon, but Cowley replied as before that he was only performing his painful duty by telling Napoleon truths his ministers tried to conceal. No Frenchman could understand the concept of honor in politics, he declared: the British "must take the honour and interests of France into their safekeeping for there are no men to do it here." [21]

Buol refuted Western arguments and accusations in vain; neither Hübner nor Colloredo was listened to in the Western capitals. Worse still, the fundamental premise of his policy, conservative cooperation with France, was now shaken. As he told Hübner privately, he had never relied on the British ministry with its brutal lust for war; but if Napoleon was turning revolutionary, especially on Poland, Austria would have to reconsider her stance. Yet he still saw a way to save the alliance and proposed it in disregard of Austria's *amour-propre* or his own:

We have had to restrict ourselves to recommending *the reconsideration* of our propositions. To straighten out an affair so fatally ruined, I can only see, by racking my brains, *one means:* but I shall carefully avoid proposing it myself, for that would probably be reason for seeing it rejected. Let them [the French] denounce our propositions, let them say all the evil possible about them. Let them throw the blame for it, if they wish, on the feebleness of our policy. But let them fall back on the counsel of Turkey; let them declare themselves ready to be satisfied if she finds the [Austrian] solution a sufficient guarantee. Let them combine this with some high-flown phrases on the glory and honor of France, to satisfy public opinion. The question would then be one [two words illegible] of finding the person who would wish to run the risk of being its author. Turkey would seize on this with *both hands* if England did not terrorize her, and France would appear to have had its hand forced, and to have yielded out of generous sentiment. . . . This is an idea I suggest to you, and which is inspired in me by the sincere desire to save an alliance that I view as the keystone of the salvation of Europe.[22] *

The suggestion that France let Turkey apparently force her into making peace now, blaming Austria's slackness for the lack of glorious results, was shrewd as well as generous. Ali, returning to Turkey to become Grand Vizier, approved of the Austrian ultimatum and wanted to get out of the war; only Turkey's dependence on the sea powers prevented it. Walewski had already repeatedly admitted that Austria's plan fully met the original purposes of the war. But no one in France was willing or able to carry through any such scheme against British opposition. Persigny, a former advocate of peace, whom Buol suggested as a possible proponent and who still showed himself to Hübner as a defender of Drouyn's policies and the Austrian alliance, actually was now preaching all-out war as new ambassador at London.[23] Cowley continued to defeat every expedient Walewski concocted to meet Austria halfway, threatening to let France attend the final conference session alone rather than degrade Britain by more negotiation. Only his attempt to ban the very mention of limitation at the final session encountered real resistance at Paris. Walewski was willing to ensure that the con-

* Contrast this language of Buol's with Nolfo's explanation of the rift between Austria and the West at this time (*Europa*, 88–89): Buol was "dominated by the will to express always and solely the immediate interest of Austria . . ."; he had a "vision of Austrian interests too explicitly selfish"; his arguments contained "a certain stinginess, which contrasted with the loftily disinterested proclamations which the allies had posited as the basis for their intervention in the East."

ference failed by proposing limitation in its strictest form, but he still wanted to give Austria the chance to tell Germany that Russia had wrecked the negotiations by rejecting it.[24]

The struggle between London and Paris, meanwhile, left the envoys in Vienna in the dark. Walewski at least tried to meet Bourqueney's appeals, but Westmorland's pleas for instructions on how to answer Buol's initiative received only Clarendon's reply that Austria, her knife at Britain's throat, was trying by armed mediation to "drive us into an ignominious peace" based on Russia's terms. Clarendon rejected Buol's proposal for the closing session by telegram on May 24, but the explanation, almost as incoherent as his private outbursts, was not sent till May 29, and only on the thirtieth did Westmorland learn what Britain wanted Buol to do: to close the conferences without making any proposals or even mentioning limitation. Austria should either announce on the West's behalf that Russia's earlier rejection of their terms made the conference pointless or, better still, she should state that "having failed to discover elements likely to be accepted by both parties, she saw no use in continuing the conferences which were therefore closed." [25]

Buol declined politely but firmly.* He told Bourqueney that he would put back whatever the French had dropped themselves and now wanted restored (i.e., Western consuls in Russian ports), but he would not abandon the proposal itself.[26] Thus Britain could not compel Austria simply to close the conference and assume the responsibility for its failure. Worse yet, there were serious differences of opinion over the proposed closing session at home. Albert, though he regarded Austria's policy as pure cowardice while Russia's was intelligent and honorable, warned that ending the conference would enable Austria to escape her obligations. Russell still had grave objections to British policy, while Argyll told Palmerston

---

* I found only one instance, and this not a public one, where Buol's patience with Britain's conduct and tactics broke. In answer to Britain's demand that he simply put the blame on Russia for wrecking the conference, Buol replied that Austria could not consider Russia solely at fault if Russia accepted Austria's peace plan while the West rejected it. Clarendon replied: "England and France being at war with Russia, and having made vast sacrifices, must be allowed to judge for themselves on what terms they could make Peace consistently with their honour. . . ." Someone, probably Buol, wrote alongside this passage the word "*Scheiss*" (Clarendon to Westmorland, 2 June 1855, No. 211, in PA VIII/42).

frankly that he feared Britain was now abandoning the very peace terms that she had worked out with France, for whose sake he had broken with his friends and stayed on in Palmerston's cabinet. But all objections were brushed aside; the one great danger Palmerston, Clarendon, and Cowley saw was that any terms proposed to Russia, no matter how severe, might be accepted and lead to an armistice and an end to the war.[27] Moreover, the Allied landings at Kerch and the destruction of Russian stores on May 24 revived hopes of military victory and increased the desire to end all negotiations.[28]

Cowley finally won in Paris on the very eve of the scheduled closing session; Napoleon ordered Bourqueney not to join Buol in proposing limitation, but, like Westmorland, to declare his instructions exhausted. Thus the conference of June 4 accomplished precisely what Buol had feared and hoped to avoid. He presented his proposal, the sea powers rejected it, and Gorchakov could now safely accept it in principle and declare the conference *de facto* ended by the Western declarations. Bourqueney and Ali in a heated exchange with Gorchakov tried to throw the blame for failure on Russia, but Buol had to concede that the sea powers' positions made further discussion useless.[29] Predictably, Britain accused Buol of conspiring with Gorchakov to produce this outcome. In fact, Buol had deceived Gorchakov if he deceived anyone. The ambassador claimed Buol had made him believe that he would propose only a separate Russo-Turkish limitation agreement and a closure of the Straits with exceptions in favor of the Allies; Buol had then surprised him by demanding limitation to the status quo afloat. There may be something to this story, though it is improbable on certain counts.[30] * In any case, only the West's policy enabled Russia to accept limitation in principle without fearing being committed to it in practice.

This whole interlude could be dismissed as insignificant. The sea powers had rejected Austria's ultimatum originally in order to seek a military victory and a glorious peace; they simply refused to change their minds. Yet the fate of Buol's efforts to give the conference a decent burial and to save the West from embarrassment has some importance. The sea powers handed Russia a gratuitous propaganda

* For one thing, Buol had earlier rejected Prokesch's suggestion of such a separate Russo-Turkish limitation agreement.

victory. They rebuffed Austria, rendered Buol's position even more critical, and burdened his policy of keeping Austria aligned with the West with new difficulties. In order to break the Austro-French connection and make France wholly dependent on Britain, the British compelled their ally to run the risk of facing a central Europe united in hostile armed neutrality while she fought Russia virtually alone on the continent.[31] The British discarded and tried to destroy a diplomatic fallback position Buol was trying to save for them, whose contingent value they had earlier recognized. All this was done for the sake of prosecuting a war whose duration no one could predict, to gain a military victory no one could guarantee, and a military solution whose practical value no one could define. The policy certainly did not spring from optimistic confidence (except perhaps for Palmerston). The military news remained mostly discouraging, and even when it was not, some, like Greville [32] or Clarendon himself, recognized the open-ended character of the war and the virtual certainty that every victory would simply cause British aims to escalate beyond what Allied arms could hope to achieve.* In short, this interlude again shows British policy conducted, to borrow a simile from Bismarck, like a horseman who takes his steed over a high wall in a swampy forest with no idea whether he will come down on solid ground or bottomless bog. Palmerston took the jump jauntily, Clarendon with eyes shut in reckless despair.

Moreover, the arguments Britain in particular used were so shoddy and her tactics so dishonest that she seriously diminished her credit abroad and risked provoking at home the sort of violent, misguided public reaction that often compounds a blunder by forcing policy over to the opposite extreme. The rest of Europe, in-

---

* Clarendon told Redcliffe on June 1 that he could see no logical possibility of obtaining either the diplomatic or military guarantees Redcliffe called for. How could England "take and hold the Crimea, and set free and protect Georgia and Circassia?" What good were diplomatic guarantees in view of Russia's bad faith, her proximity to Turkey, her cherished dreams and traditions, and Turkey's "irremediable corruption and degradation?" These questions haunted him day and night, said Clarendon, and he could find no answer for them. But he fully shared Redcliffe's "horror . . . that Russia should be even partially triumphant" and agreed that "annihilation" would be better for England than wasting away with Europe under Russian hegemony (FO 352/42/II/5).

cluding men fully sympathetic to the Allied cause, saw now that Britain was fighting solely for military honor and prestige.[33] Despite energetic concealment and misrepresentation of the facts by government spokesmen, some in Britain already saw something mysterious and inexplicable in the government's determination to reject Austria's proposals.[34] When the truth did emerge, it proved seriously embarrassing to the government, moving Greville, Clarendon's old close friend, to this reluctant verdict:

> With the greatest regret I am led to the conclusion that the negotiations at Vienna were a sham and a delusion, and that our Government never intended to make peace at all—that from the first they resolved to impose conditions which they knew Russia neither would nor could accept, and then upon one pretext or another they got rid of every proposition or scheme, suggested by any body else, which might by any possibility have led to the conclusion of peace.
>
> . . . It has been a favorite topic of conviction against those who wish for peace, that they are for peace *at any price*, which is neither more nor less than a wilful lie. . . . But it would be more correct to say of others, and of the Government itself that they were for war at any cost, and for peace *at no price* whatsoever.[35]

Rebuffed by the West, Austria had to try to improve her relations with Prussia and Germany. As long as any chance remained to revive the negotiations, Buol refused to try to approach Prussia; only at the very end of May was a feeler for rapprochement extended, to be greeted suspiciously by Manteuffel.[36] Buol also held back from approaching Bavaria or other states, despite warnings from Rechberg and Apponyi that Austria's apparent weakness and indecision were having a very bad effect. Finally on May 24 and 25, he expounded his position fairly frankly, showing how baseless the West's objections to Austria's proposals were, and claiming that if Austria now stayed out of war because Allied aims were immoderate, she at least was entitled to automatic German support and help in maintaining the diplomatic gains already achieved.[37]

The help Buol sought, however, was anything but certain or automatic, for Prussia and Russia had a move under way to force Austria into passive neutrality. On April 30, Nesselrode empowered Glinka, Russian envoy at Frankfurt, to pledge that Russia would uphold her concessions on Points One and Two, those most valuable for

Germany, if Germany would promise to remain strictly neutral. Nesselrode accompanied this *démarche* with convincing arguments in favor of the peace terms Russia had proposed at Vienna; Clarendon called his May 10 circular the ablest paper Russia had produced since the Menshikov mission.[38] At Frankfurt, Rechberg warned that Bismarck might well gain a majority if he presented this Russian offer formally at the Diet and proposed a Federal declaration of neutrality.[39]

Austria managed to escape this danger (for which Buol rightly blamed the West as much as Russia and Prussia), but again not through any arguments or influence of her own. Once more Frederick William's pro-Austrian feelings, Manteuffel's caution, and Bavaria's attitude made the difference. Pfordten believed that merely ensuring Germany's neutrality was not enough; the Glinka *démarche* should be used to promote a separate Russo-Austrian agreement on the Third Point, isolating the sea powers and compelling them to sue for peace. Buol was able to convince Pfordten that the idea was impracticable and incompatible with Austria's engagements, while Prussia, after encouraging the Glinka *démarche*, declined to make a formal proposal to the Diet. By the end of May it had run aground.[40]

Thus Austria escaped isolation in its worst form; yet from early June on, Buol was condemned to watch and wait on events, while the Western alliance to which he clung continued to deteriorate.[41] Figuring in that deterioration was a great debate over the war in the British Parliament, where Austria frequently became the center of controversy. First in early May the government was attacked by Tories and jingo Radicals for flabby conduct of the negotiations and the war. Next John Bright demanded to know whether Austria had made any new peace proposals, and a Radical Member of Parliament, Milner Gibson, moved on May 21 for a reconsideration of Russia's last peace offer of April 26. Clarendon and Palmerston managed to split the peace party and get Gibson's motion withdrawn, doing so by carefully avoiding any reference to Austria's ultimatum, insisting that the conferences were neither closed nor abandoned, and pleading that any debate would spoil the chances of peace. Russell, against his better knowledge and convictions, went along with the government's line, contending that Austria had supported direct naval limitation and had agreed with the sea powers in rejecting Russia's last offer—a misrepresentation of Austria's position by suppressing the truth rather than asserting a falsehood.[42] Disraeli next moved on May 24 to condemn the government for trying to fight and negotiate at the same time, and doing both miserably; he damned Russell's conduct in particular. From the other side, Gladstone and other peace advocates attacked Britain's policy at the conference. Russell, forced to reply, once more defended the government's case for narrow limitation, passed over Austria's ultimatum in silence, and even insisted that her treaty engagements would still compel her to enter the war.[43]

Disraeli's motion lost and a concurrent peace motion by Lord Grey in the House of Lords was easily defeated,[44] but party passions and personal quarrels raised in the debate hung on. Clarendon suspended his correspondence with Aberdeen over the latter's defense of Grey's disloyal speech.[45] Argyll and Gladstone argued heatedly over Russia's peace terms; decades later Argyll would still be incensed by Gladstone's unpatriotic fanaticism at this time.[46] Albert blamed Aberdeen for the pro-Russian conduct of Gladstone and Graham; it reminded him, he said, of the Peelites' disloyal stand on the issue of "Papal Aggression" in 1850.[47] Gladstone and Graham in turn denounced a motion by M. P. Charles Lowe, which blamed the failure of the negotiations on Russia's refusal of limitation, as one more outrageous effort by the government to escape its responsibility. They were now aware of the existence, though not the content, of Austria's ultimatum, "the studied misrepresentation of which," said Graham, "necessarily creates the most suspicious doubts." [48]

The debate on Lowe's amendment, June 4–8, ranks, as Disraeli remarked, among the great ones in House of Commons history. But while both defense and criticism of the government's policy were eloquent,* constructive counterproposals were few, and even these unwittingly came close to Austrian ideas of counterpoise and a European alliance to defend Turkey. In addition, the critics of

---

* The best antiwar arguments came not from semipacifist isolationists such as Bright, Cobden, and Milner Gibson, but from the Peelites and young Tories such as Robert Cecil (the future Lord Salisbury) and Lord Stanley (later fifteenth earl of Derby). Disraeli, whenever he left off his brilliant but irresponsible baiting of Russell, was also very effective. On the other hand, most of the Tories and many of the Radicals were more chauvinist than the Whigs.

the government were hampered by ignorance of Austria's ultimatum, so that debate centered on whether Russia's final offer could have led to a satisfactory peace. The final outcome was again favorable to the government.[49] *

Thus the ministry survived another parliamentary battle; but the subject of the Vienna Conference, just closed, kept cropping up. The June 4 protocol, disclosing the West's summary dismissal of Austria's final proposition, gave the Peelites new evidence of the government's bad faith. Graham was convinced that this proved a satisfactory peace could have been achieved; Gladstone supposed that Palmerston, forgetting his promise made in Parliament to consider any Austrian proposal carefully, had acted to keep himself in office. (He was wrong; Palmerston had never intended to keep his promise and had acted mainly out of patriotism.) Aberdeen learned facts far more shocking. He was told by Persigny that France had actually wanted peace in April and May and had been prevented from reaching it by England. From Russell he learned that after the April 21 conference session Russell had suggested to Gorchakov the very same limitation to the status quo afloat that Austria proposed and the West rejected on June 4, and Gorchakov had promised to support it at St. Petersburg. Moreover, Russell admitted that he still considered Austria's ultimatum a satisfactory basis for peace. Though he tried to defend Britain's blowing up of the conference of June 4 on the ground that Russia would have rejected Austria's proposal anyway, when Aberdeen pointed out the folly of breaking off on such an untested assumption, Russell replied that Clarendon and Palmerston were clearly determined not to

* Three reasons make me believe that a knowledge of Austria's proposal would not have changed many votes in Parliament. First, the mere fact that a proposition originated in Vienna made it anathema, not only to demagogic radicals such as Roebuck and Austen Layard, but also to the average Tory and Whig. Second, the fact that the peace party could make a powerful case against narrow limitation as a satisfactory basis for peace only proved to the other side that no negotiated settlement was any good, but that Britain must fight on till Russia was really crippled by military defeat and territorial losses. Third, the government's case, as presented best by Bulwer Lytton, rested finally on a conspiracy theory of history and a portrayal of Russia as the eternal foe of Britain, infinitely sly, menacing and treacherous, with whom no compromise was possible or honorable. The view was false and it made any durable settlement or sound policy impossible; but the odds against refuting such a view in a popular assembly in wartime are overwhelming.

have peace. Gladstone, comparing this account with Russell's recent defense of governmental policy in Parliament, called it "one of the most lamentable and discreditable pictures that public life can offer" and determined to force a further inquiry into the closing of the Vienna Conference.[50]

He did not have to. Buol, fighting for political survival in Germany and at home, decided finally to reply to the British government's studied misrepresentations of Austria's position. He published documents revealing the terms of Austria's ultimatum and proving that it had been worked out with Russell and supported by him before his departure from Vienna. Under questioning in Parliament, Russell admitted that Buol's disclosures were true. Attacked by advocates of peace and war alike, Russell attempted a defense that actually made a better case for Austria than for his own wisdom and honor. He conceded, for example, that he still believed Buol's plan would have provided "a very fair prospect of the duration of peace," that Austria certainly would have regarded a Russian rejection of her ultimatum as *casus belli*, and that from her standpoint Austria had good reason to believe that she had fulfilled her obligations under the December 2 alliance. He could only defend his own conduct lamely, though with perfect truth, as motivated by the desire not to break up the ministry at a critical time or to increase public distrust of men in office.[51]

His frankness about his beliefs and his unwillingness to blame his colleagues (as he might have done) for his failure to follow his convictions left him defenseless before the merciless attacks of Cobden, Milner Gibson, and Disraeli, while Palmerston sided with him only in very tepid fashion.[52] Greville, seeing that Russell had been maladroit rather than malicious and recognizing that the ministry was still throwing up a smoke screen, predicted that these revelations would make the war still more unpopular on the continent. Bourqueney reported that Lord John had given Austria powerful new arguments for her ultimatum.[53] Cowley, frightened that Drouyn would join with Russell to "play old gooseberry" (make trouble), immediately requested that his ostensible dispatch of May 7 be published to give "the strict truth" regarding Drouyn's resignation and to quell the vicious rumors that he was involved in it. Clarendon and Palmerston quickly agreed to publish documents to exonerate

Cowley and, as Clarendon said, to put the real villain, Buol, "in a state of rabies"—a fit revenge, remarked Palmerston, for the "scurvy trick" he had played on Russell.[54] Then Palmerston demanded that Russell state in Parliament that he now accepted the need to fight to final victory and no longer considered the April proposals satisfactory. Russell did so on July 12 and resigned from the Cabinet the next day.

Under further fire in Parliament, Russell still only hinted at why he had failed to fight harder for the Austro-French ultimatum at home. Unexplained circumstances "quite independent of the merits of the propositions themselves," he said, led him to believe he could no longer urge them—that is, the impression he received from Clarendon that Napoleon had rejected it without British urging. As for Parliament's being left ignorant of this vital proposal all through the May and June debates, Russell replied that it was Clarendon's duty to inform Parliament, and he even defended him for not doing so.[55] G. C. Lewis, now Chancellor of the Exchequer, urged Clarendon to speak in Russell's behalf in the House of Lords, but Clarendon refused. "I could only explain the part Lord John took before he left Vienna and immediately on his return home," wrote Clarendon, "but I have not sufficient confidence in him to do that. He would be as likely to throw me over as not and I should then merely have put myself in a great scrape in order to make matters worse." While some of Russell's friends wrote him to express their personal confidence in him and their shock at the attacks on his character, Clarendon, his own reputation unblemished,* merely undertook to justify himself against Russell's complaints about unfair omissions in the Blue Book published on the Vienna Conference. In his long epistle to Russell, he carefully avoided the subject of Drouyn's resignation, on which Russell was beginning to see the light. What really disgusted him, wrote Clarendon to Cowley at this time, was the opposition's complete lack of national and personal honor; he was almost ashamed of "belonging to a country which is willfully and knowingly sinking itself lower in the estimation of the world." [56]

Angry as Buol was at British tactics throughout this period (his

---

* While attacking Russell, Bulwer Lytton called Clarendon's language and conduct straight, English, and manly.

private letter of June 6 to Hübner is an especially bitter and pene-
trating denunciation of them and warning of their consequences),*
he was even more alarmed that France went along with Britain. If
Napoleon continued to let Palmerston drag him toward revolution,
Buol wrote, Austria could only thank God she was not more
deeply engaged with him.

Rather than allow ourselves to be given the law by a sovereign who in
his turn makes himself the plaything of an English ministry, it would be
better to return to dependence on Russia. The idea that the interests of
the continent have to be deliberated and decided at London is obsolete.
First of all, these are no longer the English of former days; and in addition, we are no longer at all the same.[57]

Bourqueney urgently supported this warning, pleading with Walewski not to invoke the *casus foederis* of December 2, but to
propose some new diplomatic act to save the tie to Vienna. Everyone but Buol, he said, either favored neutrality in order to disarm
and recover financially or advocated armed mediation. Bourqueney
even proposed on his own initiative the renewed defensive triple
treaty that Walewski had earlier suggested and then withdrawn under British pressure. Buol advised Francis Joseph to wait to see if
the French government really backed the initiative.[58]

   Paris did not. Instead, Walewski, his position jeopardized by
Cowley's influence with Napoleon, joined Clarendon in denouncing
Austria and invoking the *casus foederis*, demanding that Austria at
least maintain her armaments to menace Russia and that she publicly
blame Russia for wrecking the peace conference. If she did not, she
could be excluded from all future peace talks and expelled from the
Principalities. Though Clarendon worried a bit over these harsh
demands and threats, and Walewski, still showing signs of what
Cowley termed his stupid hankering after Austria, avoided the un-
truths with which the British invoked the *casus foederis*,[59] † the

____

   * On at least one point, Buol's contention that the West's embarrassment
over the June 4 session was all their own fault, Bourqueney fully agreed. He
complained sharply to Walewski at the humiliating position in which he had
been placed by having to follow Clarendon's orders to Westmorland (5 June
1855, AMAE Autr. 460).
   † Clarendon, for example, claimed that Buol's final proposal did not originate with Drouyn and insisted repeatedly that the Western powers had not
put forward any proposals to which Austria had not agreed and promised to

vital thing was that the sea powers were united against Austria. Cowley in fact considered Walewski's sudden zeal in attacking her a shade excessive, for an open break with Austria was not desirable now. This should wait, as Clarendon said, "until we have obtained very decided military successes." Then Britain could "finish the war off her own bat" without having to consult Austria on terms of peace and end Russia's proponderance in the Black Sea in the right way, by a British expedition sweeping her out of the eastern Black Sea coast as well as the Crimea.[60]

On June 18, the very day Clarendon wrote Redcliffe this, Allied hopes of a quick military victory were dashed by the disastrous failure of an assault on the Malakov Heights.* Moreover, Western efforts to force Austria to maintain her mobilization against Russia were useless in the face of the universal desire in Austria to demobilize her army and cut expenses and losses by disease. Buol did not try to fight this, raising no objection on June 11 in a ministerial conference to sending 62,500 reservists home from Galicia. He sought only to create a diplomatic situation in which Austria could disarm in relative safety without abandoning her engagements or her general policy. On June 10, he asked Russia for informal assurances that she would not invade the Dobruja or repudiate what she had already conceded on the Four Points, at the same time requesting the Turks not to launch any offensive from the Principalities. Both démarches were also conveyed to the sea powers.[61]

Russia readily agreed not to mount an offensive if she were not attacked herself and to maintain the Four Points, with a reservation on executing the Third. But the Turks refused to promise anything and the sea powers protested angrily that Austria was giving formal notice of abandoning her engagements to Turkey. This proved again, said Clarendon, that if the West failed in the Crimea, Austria, a traitor and coward throughout her history, would help Russia

---

support (to Westmorland, 13 June 1855, Nos. 226-27, FO 7/448). It was easy to show not only that these assertions were false, but that Clarendon knew they were, and sometimes privately contradicted them himself (Cowley to Clarendon, 12 June, No. 711, FO 519/4; Russell to Clarendon, 16 June, Clar. dep. c. 30; Colloredo to Buol, 13 June, No. 69A, PA VIII/40).

* Buol's reaction was to tell Bourqueney that if Allied successes made his policy difficult, such a reverse made it impossible (Bourqueney to Walewski, 24 June 1855, No. 98, AMAE Autr. 460).

build her empire on the Bosporus. From June 22 on, the charge that Austria was formally announcing her neutrality in favor of Russia became a standard item in the French repertoire.[62] Vienna was used to such accusations; more disturbing were reports that the Turks under Western pressure would soon ask Austria to leave the Principalities and would undertake new moves to menace Bessarabia with French help. Francis Joseph, in Galicia inspecting the army, was so aroused by these reports he wanted Buol to declare that Austria forbade anyone to undertake war operations in the Principalities, a step Buol felt would have meant revoking the alliance.[63]

This particular storm blew over when Buol succeeded in calming the Emperor and getting statements from Constantinople and Paris that they did did not at present intend to launch an offensive through the Principalities and would inform Austria first if they did. Austrian demobilization proceeded, with Hess's special Third and Fourth Army Command being dissolved in July.[64] But the major political danger remained—the sea powers' determination to get rid of the Four Points. After June 4, first Britain and then France declared the conference agreements actually reached at Vienna nul and *non avenu* and claimed their freedom of action.[65] * Walewski hoped to frighten Austria into a new engagement—perhaps, Hübner supposed, a renewed alliance with a new time limit for Austria to enter the war. Moreover, he still said that the Four Points would play a role in the peace negotiations and claimed freedom for France only *within* the alliance; Austria was to have no excuse to treat separately with Russia.[66] The British simply wanted to get rid of all restrictions on war aims, especially the engagement not to seek territorial cessions from Russia. This was vital, Clarendon pointed out, because Britain had special interests to pursue in Circassia and Asia that she could not defend on European principles and dared not discuss even with France. As for Austria, Palmerston, after weighing the matter, advised against expelling her from the Principalities right now; she was still useful as a limited menace to Russia. But her threats to hold Britain to the Four Points † were in-

---

* Clarendon blandly asked Austria to announce this decision to the German Diet, to spare the Allies any difficulties that Russia might cause by her offer to guarantee the agreements on the first two points.

† The Austrian "threat" to which Palmerston here referred was nothing more than Austria's contention that the Allied agreements of August 8, December 2,

tolerable and should be answered with counterthreats of what would happen to any power that linked up with Russia against the invincible Western powers.[67]

The Malakov disaster of June 18 changed Britain's mood, turning Clarendon again to despair and leading Palmerston to advise him to treat Austria tenderly (as he claimed he had done in 1848–1849). Clarendon responded by defending Austria against attacks on her in the House of Lords.* But with an Allied victory out of reach, he insisted that Austria was certain to declare her neutrality as the prelude to armed mediation or an alliance with Russia, and it was useless to try to stop her.[68] Hence the sea powers continued to repeat their charges. Buol replied with his usual rebuttals, but their language also led him formally to ask both governments whether they still acknowledged the Four Points as their war aims. His purpose and spirit in doing so are clear from his private letter of July 3 to Hübner and Colloredo:

Our relations with London and Paris feel the effects of the ill humor they feel toward us, which, without being at all fair, is perfectly understandable. They are keenly disappointed at not seeing us make real war on Russia alone, so as to leave the field free for them for the sideshow in which they find themselves engaged. They are angry at seeing themselves deceived by illusions which they themselves created as to the attitude we would take. And now finally the sad coincidence of the recent setback before Malakoff! We are too fair not to take this into account and not to abstain from everything which could alter our relations. We have no desire either to recriminate or to bring up their irregularities of language, but we hope that the Allies on their part will sense the im-

---

and December 28, 1854, could not be unilaterally abrograted and remained binding on all parties, including herself.

* The defense Clarendon offered on June 26, however, demonstrated his lack of sensitivity. He knew that Francis Joseph was deeply mortified at being treated by the West as if he were the commander of a foreign legion (Clarendon to Redcliffe, 25 June 1855, FO 352/42/II/5). Yet he defended Austria in Parliament by saying that she had really intended to go to war in December and January, but had not dared to carry out her resolve when Sevastopol had failed to fall to the West. In other words, he portrayed Francis Joseph as acting precisely like the commander of a mercenary legion, ready to run to the aid of the victors for a share of the spoils, but unwilling to fight while the issue was in doubt (3 Hansard, 139, 140–48). This was not only false, but the most insulting falsehood he could have devised.

portance of showing a reciprocal consideration for our delicate position.

While we are waiting, no serious calculation as to the future is possible. They have made it dependent on a deed that admits of no calculation. The sea powers would be very embarrassed to define clearly the *final goal* which they have in view, and still more embarrassed to take into calculation the nonetheless very possible chance that they will not succeed before Sevastopol. In the interest of peace we are reduced to fearing a reverse about as much as a success. I do not see yet how either one or the other will enable us to attain it.

What counts for us is to know accurately what value the powers attach to the Four Points. France's language is not clear and Lord Clarendon has to bring the last phrase of his circular, which sees in them still the basis for future peace, into line with his language to Parliament, which deprives them of all value. We are making superhuman efforts to maintain ourselves on this basis in our relations with the Diet and we would like, whatever happens, to save these Four Points from shipwreck. Let the Cabinets of France and England not then render this task impossible for us, and let them cease their mysterious language. From every side in Germany we hear this objection: how and why do you maintain a principle which the [sea] powers themselves declare abandoned? To tell the truth, we have difficulty finding an answer to that.

Let them not demand the impossible of Austria. Her active cooperation has been sacrificed by the rejection of our propositions. They would have liked having us for the war, without listening to us in the council. Nevertheless we are willing to stay in our *political* position. The powers will again find us there, if they give any evidence of wanting to. But the choice and measure of the means for keeping us there must be left to us. We demand in this respect the same liberty and the same trust that we accord them in the paths they pursue. Our military position, it is true, may be of little use to them in their Crimean expedition. But first of all, what obligation do we have on this point, and further, what could we do? We could ruin ourselves by our efforts and still not arrive at a *threatening* position, which would seriously bother Russia.[69]

Britain responded to this with an angry rejection. He did not wish to snap the last threads of this dead-letter alliance, Clarendon told Henry Elliot, chargé at Vienna, but he would rather let Austria go openly Russian than allow her impudently to tie England to the Four Points after all England had done for her and suffered from her in return. Redcliffe and Colquhoun called constantly for denouncing the Four Points openly.[70] Walewski did not wish to turn

Buol down, but with Cowley denouncing Austria and Napoleon opposed to the Four Points, he went along.[71] The two Emperors exacerbated the quarrel, Francis Joseph by telling the Tsar's aide-de-camp in Galicia that he regarded himself as released from his December 2 obligations, Napoleon by calling on Austria in an address to the Legislative Corps to fulfill her clear treaty obligations by entering the war. A heated press controversy sprang up over both statements.[72] Rumors of an open Austro-Western break flew thick and fast in July.[73]

Only Bourqueney, discouraged and again ready to resign, fought at Buol's side, begging Walewski, "Help me to save the alliance!" Clarendon's brutality and France's indifference, he warned, had nearly destroyed it. Austria could no longer be frightened as before by the hint that she would be excluded from peace negotiations; now all the ministers save Buol were indifferent to this and ready for a direct understanding with Russia. Denouncing the Four Points meant denouncing the December 2 alliance, overthrowing Buol, and freeing Austria to turn to Russia.[74]

Clarendon replied to these warnings that Bourqueney was "quite as twaddly and an Austrian as poor old Westmorland"; besides, his reports and Elliot's similar ones only proved that it was Austria's "inevitable destiny" to throw herself into Russia's arms and that it was useless to try to stop her. He answered Albert's warnings in similar fashion; surprisingly, Victoria seemed to agree with him against her husband.[75] But France was less fatalist. Buol's second, more formal interpellation on July 22, warning that the West's failure to respond would make a direct Austro-Russian understanding inevitable, made Walewski again wish to reassure Austria with equivocal assurances that would not bind the Allies. Cowley opposed this adamantly.[76]

But Palmerston convinced Clarendon that Buol's request to have the Four Points confirmed was really an Austrian trick "to slip out of the treaty." Britain should foil it by telling him that she agreed to the principles of the Four Points and would abide by the engagements of December 2; this would hold Austria in line without fettering Britain.[77] Accordingly, when France on July 25 sent Austria the required assurances, Clarendon tried (too late) to recall his dispatch of July 13 declaring the alliance a dead letter, and fairly gushed assurances for Buol. We do mean what we say, he wrote Elliot; we stand on common ground with Austria, we want to retain the alliance based on the Four Points, we want her in the final peace settlement. We merely cannot endure renewed negotiations before a decisive military success.[78] While Clarendon justified this abrupt change of direction to colleagues with various arguments, inconsistent with one another and in part absurd,[79] he also promised Colquhoun that when peace negotiations did resume, the Allies would be "free and unfettered" by anything that went on at the Vienna Conference—an assurance promptly conveyed to Colquhoun's boyar friends. What Britain's assurances to Austria really meant, as Palmerston interpreted them, was that Russia was still bound to the concessions she had made at Vienna, but the sea powers were entirely free.[80]

Buol accepted the Western assurances, though he knew they represented only a very partial victory rather than a Western retreat, as Hübner claimed.[81] * All that had been accomplished by Buol's and Bourqueney's efforts was some cooling off of the Austro-Western quarrel and the outward preservation of the alliance (though it is worth noting that it was their efforts at this time, and not, as is often supposed, the later Allied victory at Sevastopol, that ensured its survival).[82]

During the rest of the summer no important change occurred in Austria's relations with the West, though quarrels continued to arise with Britain. Clarendon denounced Austria's refusal to allow Britain to set up recruiting depots for her Swiss Legion on Austrian soil as a grossly unfriendly act and as more proof of Austria's cowardice.[83] † Austria protested about British recruiting for their Anglo-Italian Legion just across the Austria border in Sardinia.[84] Coronini and Colquhoun clashed heatedly over the former's proclamation of martial law in the Principalities (a measure provoked

---

* Cowley even suggested secretly letting Russia know how easily the West had brought Austria off, so as to ruin Austro-Russian relations further (to Clarendon, 30 July 1855, Clar. dep. c. 34).

† The governments of the United States, Nova Scotia, and Switzerland also protested against British recruitment practices, and France rejected a British request to recruit on her soil—all presumably acting from this same abject fear of Russia (*Panmure Papers*, I, 277–78; Palmerston to Clarendon, 24 and 25 Sept. 1855, Add. ms. 48579; Cowley to Clarendon, 2 April, Clar. dep. c. 33).

by Sadik Pasha's efforts to incite Austrian soldiers to desert) and over Coronini's accusation that Colquhoun had helped a Hungarian émigré spy named Berczenczey to escape.[85]

Once again the Austrian ultimatum of April 15 became the center of a new peace agitation in Parliament led by Gladstone. He called for a new peace initiative based upon it, which the government countered by again insisting that Austria had never been willing to stand on it herself as her *casus belli*. But this time Russell, who was now coming to see how Clarendon had deceived him in early May, gave the lie to the government story (just as Drouyn did) and revealed further that in April the Turks had wanted to end the war on the basis of Austria's proposal.[86] Naturally, the peace agitation got nowhere, leading only to more disgrace for Gladstone and the denunciation of him and Russell as traitors by Clarendon and others.[87] As for Buol, he again published long, circumstantial proofs that the British government's allegations were false, but the British public and even the ministers continued to believe them anyway.[88]

In a few instances Buol ceased appeasing the British and began taking a firmer line. He virtually told Elliot to mind his own business when the chargé, on Clarendon's orders, sought an investigation into the alleged persecution of three Roman Catholic converts to Protestantism in Moravia,[89] and he similarly rejected his complaints about the conduct of Austria's troops in the Principalities. Clarendon's suggestion that Austria ought to occupy the Sulina mouth of the Danube (which Russia owned), to end the disorders reigning there, was simply ignored.[90] The Austrians managed finally to get Turkey to remove the Poles and other émigrés Colquhoun was protecting from the Principalities and protested strongly against a British-inspired proposal that Turkey induct Christians equally with Muslims into the Turkish army.[91]

But this firmer tone on some questions meant no change in policy. Buol still went out of his way to cooperate wherever he could—in Greece, where the Anglo-French occupation was running into serious trouble,[92] in the proposed building of a canal or a railway in the Principalities from the lower Danube to the Black Sea by a British company,[93] * and especially on the Suez Canal question. Bruck

---

* Thus rather than aiming to combat British commercial activity in the Principalities, as Unckel contends (p. 206), Buol actually promoted British schemes

pleaded with Buol for Austrian pressure on Turkey in favor of Ferdinand de Lesseps' project, which would greatly benefit Austrian trade in the East, but Buol refused to intervene because Britain opposed the idea.[94] All this occurred during the period of Buol's greatest unpopularity at home, when even supporters like G. Esterházy were critical of his pro-Western stance.[95] His policy of appeasement was certainly barren of any good result, but probably no other policy would have worked better. The British government simply was not affected by anything Austria could say or do. Continued military failure and the relative decline of her forces compared to the French only led Britain to try more of the old remedies or concoct new ones even more hopeless.[96] The peace party lapsed into apathy after Gladstone's failure; Palmerston feared only that after Sevastopol fell Austria would again make a try for peace and France would be tempted by it.[97]

Austria's relations with Germany through the summer meanwhile followed the dreary familiar pattern of Austria's demanding support and Prussia and Germany resisting the demand. The main quarrel was over an Austrian-sponsored Federal resolution approving Austria's conduct of the Vienna peace negotiation, intended by Buol to check Germany's drift toward open neutrality. Buol's main difficulty lay in convincing the German states that they ought to help Austria sustain the Four Points, while the sea powers were repudiating them as worthless. He also had a hard time explaining to Bavaria why Austria could not now come to terms with Russia on the basis of the peace offer Austria had made at the closing session at Vienna on June 4, which the sea powers had rejected and Russia was willing to consider. Buol came up with some fairly ingenious arguments, but he did not convince even his own envoy Rechberg.[98] In the end, Austria obtained only a colorless Federal resolution on July 26 thanking her for her peace efforts, and even this was gained partly through a risky and misleading promise to Prussia of participation

that posed a serious potential threat to Austrian commercial interests (cf. B. Marinescu, "Economic Relations between the Romanian Principalities and Great Britain, 1848–1859," *Revue Roumaine d'Histoire*, 1969, 279; and J. H. Jensen and G. Rosegger, "British Railways along the Lower Danube, 1856–1869," *Slavonic and East European Review*, XLVI (1968), 108–12). Here, as on the Suez Canal and many other points, Buol sacrificed commercial interests to supposed political necessity.

in future peace negotiations.[99] As for Russia, once Buol gained the assurance in June that she would not launch an offensive from Bessarabia or repudiate the Four Points, he paid practically no attention to her. Gorchakov's repeated efforts to wean Austria away from the West got nowhere. Elliot explained this failure in typical British fashion: by warning Austria of the danger of Anglo-French preponderance in Europe, Gorchakov had caused Austria to lean toward the stronger side, as she always did.[100]

Thus Buol's diplomacy in the summer of 1855 had succeeded merely in covering Austria's demobilization in the wake of the wrecking of her peace efforts and in preserving a starting point for possible future peace efforts in the form of the Four Points and the Western alliance. More was unattainable, and only time would tell whether even this had been worth doing.

XIII

Austria's Ultimatum: The Struggle for Peace Renewed

On September 8 and 9, the Allies finally took Sevastopol, with the French army storming the Malakov fortress and forcing the Russians to evacuate the city and destroy the remainder of their fleet. The Allied victory had a great political impact, and it caused Buol's stock to rise sharply in Austria. Peace probes began immediately,* some directed at Austria.[1] Gorchakov suggested to Bruck that Austria might now mediate for peace (he had already hinted at this to Buol before Sevastopol's fall). Budberg asked Prussia to intercede to encourage Austrian mediation; King Max of Bavaria instructed Pfordten to see what he could do to promote it.[2] Ali Pasha and the Reis Effendi, Fuad Pasha, hinted to the Austrian chargé Baron Koller that Turkey was now ready to negotiate. The *Morning Chronicle*, under Peelite control, called on Austria to lead Europe back to peace. Prussia offered to join Austria in mediation, and Pfordten and Beust both made trips to Paris in October to try to promote direct Russo-French talks.[3]

Buol's attitude, in contrast, seems to have been curiously lackadaisical. He did not return from his vacation until late September. Austria's official congratulations to her allies on their victory were held up some weeks, to their intense irritation and suspicion.[4] It has often been supposed that Buol was finally galvanized into diplomatic action only by his fear of a direct Russo-French understanding arising out of Pfordten's or Beust's initiatives or the secret

---

* The best study of the whole process by which peace was achieved is Winfried Baumgart, *Der Friede von Paris 1856*. The book appeared too late for me to use it for this study, but I am grateful to Dr. Baumgart for allowing me to read an earlier draft of it.

correspondence entered into by Gorchakov and Morny.* The real explanation for his apparent inactivity is simple. He knew what Russia, Prussia, and Saxony wanted, but never dreamed of going along with their kind of Austro-Prussian mediation—it was contrary to his policy and to Austria's alliance obligations. But he and the Emperor were ready for a joint peace movement with France, and their hopes were aroused by a private letter from Werner to Buol on September 10 reporting hints of one from Paris. A week later, however, Werner dispelled these hopes—Hübner now reported that neither sea power would hear of peace or Austrian mediation. Werner therefore advised Buol not to return to Vienna; if he did, he could not avoid meeting and talking to Gorchakov before the latter left to meet the Tsar in Warsaw. Austria should let all parties know quietly that she favored peace, but otherwise play dumb.[5]

What had happened at Paris to cause Austria's initial hopes to be dispelled was that Walewski, having signaled both Bourqueney and Hübner that France would like to use Austria for a peace move, had then, fearful of Napoleon and Cowley, retracted these feelers in favor of vague hints about what Austria should do as France's ally, not as a mediator. Meanwhile, Napoleon secretly indicated to Ernest of Coburg that he would rather have Prussia mediate, and he actively encouraged secret contacts with Russia through Morny and Gorchakov and semiofficial ones through Beust and the Saxon Minister at Paris, Seebach. He hoped to frighten Austria into still coming into the war, or at least threatening Russia into being ready for peace, so that then France could play the role of mediator and seek a rapprochement with Russia.[6]

As for Buol, he followed Werner's advice, quietly letting it be known on his return that Austria would not mediate, but that she thought the time ripe for a new interallied discussion of peace terms, and hoped the sea powers would be moderate. She also would willingly convey to them any terms Russia wanted transmitted.[7] At

---

* The dates alone, of course, dispose of this theory. By September 30 the groundwork was already laid at Vienna for the Buol-Bourqueney memorandum eventually concluded on November 14, which led finally to Austria's ultimatum to Russia in December. The feelers between Morny and Gorchakov began only in November, and Beust's and Pfordten's mediation efforts at Paris in late October.

the same time, Buol quickly worked out with Bourqueney in extreme secrecy a tentative peace program that Bourqueney took back to Paris on October 1. Cowley learned the essentials of it from Bourqueney: Austria, though still hoping for Allied moderation, would help force stronger terms than those of last May on Russia by breaking relations with her if necessary and trying to get Prussia and Germany to go with her.[8] *

Hübner played no role in promoting this move with Napoleon and Walewski; the task was left entirely to Bourqueney. Buol, who concealed the *démarche* entirely from his other ambassadors, tried to remain calm during the long delay at Paris. By the end of October he was becoming worried, anxious not that peace would be made without Austria, but that Britain might persuade Napoleon to continue the war. Bourqueney returned on November 3, and five days later an agreement was ready for Francis Joseph's consideration. After a brief delay caused by his trip to Trieste, the Emperor gave his consent, and Buol and Bourqueney initialed their memorandum of agreement on November 14, containing the terms Austria would present on the Allies' behalf as her ultimatum to Russia.[9] If Russia accepted them unconditionally, she would get an armistice with these terms as preliminaries of peace; if she refused, Austria would break relations. Once again there were the familiar Five Points, but with changes making them more severe. The first demanded the cession of about half of Bessarabia to Moldavia; the third now demanded neutralization of the Black Sea by a separate Russo-Turkish agreement to be attached to the main treaty; and the fourth, the exclusion of Russia from negotiating the provisions for the protection of Ottoman Christians.[10]

It is easy to see why France would welcome this agreement. It seemed severe enough to induce Britain to come to the peace table,

---

* Cowley even believed from his conversation with Bourqueney that if the Allies joined in a Bessarabian campaign, Austria would enter the war actively. This seems clearly wrong, however; perhaps Bourqueney exaggerated what Austria would do in order to persuade the British. Buol was never willing at this time to enforce an ultimatum by war. As the French chargé at Vienna, De Serre, reported, he evaded committing Austria to any particular means of coercing Russia if she refused the peace terms, and urged the sea powers if they had to continue the war only to wage a *petite guerre* (i.e., a blockade and naval warfare) against Russia.

while Austria would be obliged to force Russia to terms, leaving France free to conciliate Russia. Moreover, as Bourqueney argued, a break in relations with Austria would worsen Russia's position and could lead to further Prussian and German steps against her.[11] But why should Austria have wanted again to assume such risks and responsibilities? Buol argued in his *Vortrag* of November 9 that the terms would free Austria from Russian pressure in the southeast, make the whole Danube virtually an Austrian stream, and thereby restore Austria's prestige and influence in Germany. The terms were fairly hard on Russia, he admitted, but if she accepted the most humiliating one, neutralization of the Black Sea, the Bessarabian cession was also obtainable. Moreover, the plan would not require Austria to go to war.[12]

The *Vortrag*, though clearly slanted to appeal to the Emperor, shows that Buol gravely overestimated the value of Points One and Two to Austria and underestimated the resentment the Bessarabian cession would provoke in Russia and Germany.* At the same time,

* One must agree with the general verdict condemning Buol for the Bessarabian cession, which caused the most trouble at the Paris Peace Congress and afterward. But some mistaken impressions ought to be corrected. First, though Buol finally made the idea his own, it was not originally his. He had never favored the old notion of extending Austria's defensive line to the Dniester, with which Hess occasionally toyed. Earlier Russell, Palmerston, Redcliffe, Clarendon, Drouyn and others had proposed territorial changes on the lower Danube, which Buol discouraged. Palmerston and Clarendon cited his attitude on this question during the Vienna peace conferences as evidence that he and Gorchakov were in collusion (Clarendon to Russell, 13 March 1855, PRO 30/22/12C; Redcliffe to Russell, 27 March, *ibid.* 12D).

Second, even during the fall of 1855 the Bessarabian cession was not simply Austria's idea, as France and Britain would constantly claim. Walewski originally instructed Bourqueney to seek Buol's support for a rectification of the Bessarabian frontier; Palmerston strongly approved. Moreover, Prince Ghica and the Moldavian boyars, supported by Redcliffe, Poujade, and Colquhoun, demanded the cession of all of Bessarabia, something Argyll thought would be desirable (Cowley to Clarendon, 30 Sept. 1855, Clar. dep. c. 34; Palmerston to Clarendon, 9 Oct., *ibid.* c. 31; Argyll to Clarendon, 4 Jan. 1856, *ibid.* c. 48). Buol's fault lay in accepting and expanding this idea instead of restraining it. Had he asked for only the Danube delta instead of half of Bessarabia, even Russia's friends in Germany would not have complained much, and in the end the cession did not much exceed this.

Third, one must not suppose, as others have, that peace would have been easier to reach without this demand. The opposite is true. The one great obstacle to peace in late 1855, it must be emphasized, was Britain's refusal to come to the peace table. Without some territorial cession from Russia, it his main motive was the fear that this chance for peace would be lost and the war might continue indefinitely if Austria took no initiative.

The agreement with France solved only part of the problem; gaining Britain's consent would prove far harder. Her desire for military victory was greater than ever, for the French had captured Sevastopol by storming the Malakov, while the simultaneous British attack on the Redan had ended in disgraceful failure. Clarendon and Palmerston resolutely dismissed any thought of resuming "those horrible negotiations"; at least another year of fighting, perhaps two or three, would be necessary.* The political goals of further war had become no clearer. Napoleon's idea of restoring Poland at least to her 1815 status was met coldly by Palmerston, who only wanted to use the Polish question to gain concessions from Russia elsewhere.[13] The questions of how to preserve Turkey or settle the Eastern question remained unclear; what to do with the Crimea, now expected to fall entirely to the Allies, was unsolved. But the British answer was simply more of the same—more campaigns, despite Clarendon's conviction that Britain was at the nadir of her military fortunes and prestige and that her army would soon be only a contingent of the French; more conquests from Russia, despite his admission to Russell that "no advantage we can gain will be equivalent to the losses and sacrifices we must still undergo—but we are embarked in it and must hope for the best"; more freedom from all commitments on peace terms, despite the inability to conceive of bases better than those now proposed or worth the extra cost.[14]

This Palmerstonian policy of "double or quits," as Sidney Herbert

---

would have been impossible to get her there. Buol knew this, considered some Russian cession inevitable after the fall of Sevastopol, and thought a Bessarabian cession better from Austria's, Turkey's, and Europe's standpoint than one in Asia. He later told Pfordten that the alternative to the Bessarabian cession was to let the war go on indefinitely and endanger the territorial stability of all of Europe (Buol to Apponyi, 31 Dec. 1855, PA IV/23). This was not his only reason for supporting the cession, but it was perfectly true.

* While telling Cowley that it was folly even to think of peace and that he looked forward to two or three more years of war (22 Sept. 1855, FO 519/172), Clarendon wrote Aberdeen his fervent prayer that the fall of Sevastopol might bring peace. "I have not heard that he has endeavoured to give effect to his prayer," Aberdeen later wrote Argyll (Aberdeen to Graham, 23 Sept., Graham Papers Reel 20; Ab. Corr. 1855–60, 110).

called it,[15] involved, inevitably, quarrels with Austria. For the British wanted not only to stop Austria's expected peace move, but also to guard against an entente between France and Austria, which they contended was part of a planned continental league against Britain.[16] * At the moment, the sequestrations issue was less useful than normal for bludgeoning Austria. Even Russell had become convinced at Vienna that Austria really wanted to settle it on a reasonable basis and that the main obstacles lay elsewhere.[17] By fall Buol had brought Bach and the military authorities to accept in principle a new plan for a settlement. The foreign representatives acquainted with it—Elliot, Bourqueney, Walewski, the French minister at Turin the Duc de Gramont, the Sardinian chargé at Vienna Cantono, and even the Sardinian foreign minister di Cibrario —were favorably impressed. At Cavour's urging, Palmerston and Clarendon dismissed the whole idea as a bad joke, Clarendon still insisting that an Austrian apology, restoration of the sequestered property, and compensation to the owners for any losses would make Sardinia Austria's loyal friend.[18] But Britain could hardly push seriously for an amicable settlement, since Cavour did not really want one—it would rob him of his best pretext for a future quarrel.[19]

Fortunately, another Italian issue could be used to make trouble for Austria, the sea powers' quarrel with Ferdinand II, King of the Two Sicilies. In August, two supposedly deliberate insults had deepened the West's hatred of King Bomba and his despotic ways and pro-Russian sentiments: an intimation by the Neapolitan Police Director Mazza to the director of the opera at Naples that he ought not any longer entertain the secretary of the British legation in his theater box, and the failure of authorities at Messina to return a salute from a French naval vessel.[20] Palmerston proposed using these incidents to enforce a long series of political demands on Naples,

---

* Clarendon especially feared that Drouyn might return to power whenever Napoleon tired of Walewski's "pompous ineptitude." To prevent this, and if possible to ruin Drouyn for good, Clarendon conveyed to Cowley information he gained from Stockmar through Prince Albert concerning Drouyn's statements denouncing British policy, and thus indirectly criticizing Napoleon for going along with it (Stockmar to Albert, 8 Sept. 1855, RA G37/66–67; Clarendon to Albert, 26 Sept., and Albert to Clarendon, 28 Sept., RA G38/55 and 71; Clarendon to Cowley, 26 Sept. and 1 Oct., FO 519/172).

backed up by a naval demonstration. Victoria and Clarendon protested against such a dangerous move, whereupon Palmerston, after
instructing Clarendon on the ethical uses of intimidation in international relations,* proposed an alternate plan.[21] Buol should be told
that Bomba's affronts deserved punishment by a naval demonstration; every decent man in Europe would applaud Britain for doing
it. But Britain, profoundly respectful of the House of Habsburg, was
unwilling to cause pain to the Queen of Naples, a Habsburg princess.
Therefore Austria should herself get Bomba to fire Mazza, making
him understand "the disagreeable consequences that would ensue"
if he did not. Clarendon immediately fell in with this suggestion,
telling Austria also that Russia really had contrived the whole difficulty with Naples, in order to promote a Western intervention that
would cause revolution in Italy and frighten Austria back into the
Holy Alliance.[22]

The British of course simply wanted to compromise Austria with
the conservative regimes of Italy; they knew she had no special influence with the morose, fiercely suspicious Ferdinand. But Buol,
who had long urged him to conciliate the West, gave full support to
Britain's demands, and Ferdinand in fact fired Mazza without needing Austria's urgings. The cooperation made no difference in Britain's attitude. Elliot spoke of "the wonderful cowardice of this
government." Clarendon took Austria's help as proof that Britain's
position was absolutely right, brushing aside Buol's pleas that she
modify her inflammatory language on Italy. Palmerston still sought
a pretext for intervention at Naples, and Clarendon warned Vienna
that Britain had not settled with Bomba. Buol must know, he told
Elliot, that a British squadron "would have set Italy ablaze"—"our
forbearance has been very great." [23]

The Casati affair also arose concurrently, again rather trivial in

* To Clarendon's doubts that it was wise to make demands that might require the use of force against a small weak state, Palmerston replied:
"I do not think that your maxim that we ought not to do by a small state what
we should not do to a strong one applies to the present case. . . . The present
question is as to resenting an affront and I apprehend that the only question to
be asked in that case is whether we have or have not the power to do so. If
we have the power, self respect requires that we should exert it; if we have not
the power we may be compelled to pocket the affront" (6 Sept. 1855, Clar.
dep. c. 31).

itself but indicative of British attitudes. In mid-1854, Sardinia had proposed Marquis Antonio Casati—a Lombard émigré, the son of the head of the Milan revolutionary government in 1848, and the author of a recent book calling for Piedmontese annexation of Lombardy and Italian unification under the House of Savoy—as her chargé at Florence. The Tuscan premier, Chevalier Baldasseroni, rejected the nomination as obviously designed to cause Tuscany trouble with Austria. But in July 1855, Turin simply announced Casati's appointment, and Baldasseroni, uncomfortably caught between Turin and Vienna, failed at first to protest. Then the Austrian minister Baron Hügel urged him at least to make clear that Casati could not be received at court by the Habsburg Grand Duke Leopold II, and Buol and Francis Joseph backed Hügel's stand. An intimation by Baldasseroni to Sardinia's minister, Marquis Sauli, that Casati was not really welcome seemed to induce Turin to withdraw the nomination. However, an exchange of violent messages between Baldasseroni and Sauli ensued, leading to a break in relations between Tuscany and Piedmont. Buol, in what Cantono clearly understood was intended as an amicable intervention, took the side of Tuscany, urging Sardinia to respond favorably to the Anglo-French mediation under way and to meet Tuscany's complaints, warning of possible dangerous consequences to which Austria could not be indifferent if the breach went too long unhealed. Cavour immediately denounced this as an Austrian threat, and Cibrario sent off a violent note to Cantono which, had it been presented to Austria, might have caused an open break between Vienna and Turin.

The affair between Tuscany and Sardinia itself, always a tempest in a teapot, was ultimately settled through the mediation of Lord Normanby, British minister at Florence. Normanby's work was assisted by the French chargé Fleauriau, and greatly hindered by the interference of Hudson from Turin, who as usual insisted that Sardinia was quite innocent and that everything Cavour asked for should be granted. The final compromise was favorable to Sardinia; Casati's name was withdrawn and relations restored, with Tuscany having to reopen her legation at Turin, closed since 1849.[24]

In the potentially far more serious Austro-Sardinian quarrel, neither of the sea powers wanted a breach while the Eastern crisis was so serious, but otherwise their reactions differed markedly. De

Serre blamed Sardinia; Paris was critical of both sides, but saw Turin as mainly at fault. Elliot blamed Austria for the basic quarrel, but viewed Sardinia's conduct as gratuitously provocative, and Clarendon agreed that the nomination of Casati was wrong and her note to Austria "needlessly offensive." From London, the Sardinian minister Azeglio warned Cavour not to push matters too far, for Sardinia's case against Austria was defective and fundamentally Britain did not agree with it. There was truth to this, but no danger of Britain's abandoning Sardinia. Shaftesbury, Palmerston's son-in-law, urged Cavour to be "hard and obstinate as a rock" and to "appeal to England, to all Europe, against the vile power of Count Buol." [25] * Clarendon insisted that whatever the merits of this quarrel, the fount and source of all evils in Italy was Austria's "meddling and insolence" and that England had to defend Sardinia against her threatened attack. Palmerston not only insisted that Austria was wholly in the wrong; the very fact that (as he admitted privately) Sardinia's note was unjustified and dangerous made him call it excellent and tell Clarendon: "I envy the man who will have had the pleasure of reading it to Buol. The arrogant insolence of cowards is best met by a rude answer. Civility only encourages them to further insult." [26]

While backing Sardinia against Austria, Britain also covertly encouraged Prussian and German liberals against her. To frustrate any possible Prussian rapprochement with Austria, Clarendon repeatedly ordered Bloomfield to encourage Prussia's ambitions for German leadership and similarly instructed Sir Alexander Malet, envoy at Frankfurt, "to cultivate the national party in Germany." [27] †

* Shaftesbury was drawn to Sardinia's defense chiefly by his zeal to evangelize (i.e., Protestantize) Italy, beginning with Piedmont. Cavour and Azeglio were often annoyed at his queries into alleged Sardinian persecution of Protestants and privately laughed at him, calling him "Grand Priest Shaftesbury." But his sentiments and those of other Englishmen were eminently useful to Cavour in his fight against Rome and Vienna. See *Cavour-Inghilterra*, I, 56–64, 73–75, 77–78, 128–29, 132–33; Marcelli, *Cavour*, 37–77, 85–93.

† Clarendon soon learned the risks of these initiatives—the danger Elliot pointed to from Vienna, that Buol would be overthrown and an open neutralist or pro-Russian take his place, and Clarendon's own discovery that Malet seemed unable to distinguish between the national party and the revolutionary party in Germany. But these experiences made no real difference in his basic policy.

Loftus and other British agents were used in working for liberal constitutionalism against existing regimes, and in particular for the overthrow of Manteuffel and the camarilla at Berlin. Under instructions from London, British agents supported the nationalist propaganda of Prince Albert's favorite publicist, Gustav Dietzel. Duke Ernest's proposal that Britain subsidize a nationalist newspaper to be published by Dietzel was given long and sympathetic discussion by Albert and Clarendon, though apparently no decision was reached.[28] Loftus was told to exploit Protestant sentiment, and especially the Prussian fear of a Franco-Austrian Catholic league in the wake of the Austrian Concordat with the Vatican in September 1855, to make Prussia lean toward Britain in the face of the religious war Clarendon saw looming in the distance.[29]

On a host of other issues Britain showed her readiness to pick a quarrel with Austria. In Greece, where the bitter strife between Otho and the Western-backed Mavrocordatos regime reached a climax in October, Clarendon brushed aside Austria's pleas for moderation. If the sea powers decided to dethrone the King, no one else had a word to say about it.[30] Colquhoun's quarrel with certain Viennese newspapers, and the dispute over the case of Stephan Türr, a deserter from the Austrian army who was arrested by Austrian military authorities at Bucharest while in British service,* provided Clarendon with months of recriminations and demands to Vienna. Almost any ground served to prove Austria's hostility toward Britain—the fact that Austrian vessels obeyed Russia's orders not to transport enemy nationals through Russia's section of the lower Danube;[31] Austria's sale of controlled amounts of lead and nitrate to Russia (a practice Clarendon admitted was far better than Prussia's uncontrolled sale of munitions);[32] a visit by an Austrian general to Varna and Constantinople to inspect the fortifications there; Prokesch's failure to call on the French and British ministers at Athens on his way to Constantinople; or an Austrian error in surveying the Transylvanian-Moldavian border.[33]

The chip on Britain's shoulder became most evident when Hamilton Seymour was appointed to replace Westmorland. Clarendon wrote Elliot that he expected Austria to reject Seymour because he had reported his conversations with Nicholas in January 1853,

* For details, see Appendix C.

and he was prepared for the anticipated affront: "If any such notion were to arise . . . we are not Sardinia, and should not stand any tricks of that kind, and the only consequences of their being attempted would be the cessation of all relations with Austria, and the great applause thereat of the British Public." But Buol declared immediately that Seymour was welcome, and Seymour reported complacently that his reception at Vienna was extremely cordial. Disconcerted, Clarendon replied:

I am very glad Buol received you so well not only on personal grounds but because it manifests a desire to pull well with you through the mud into which he wants to plunge us, or rather France does, for Walewski is more Austrian than the Austrians themselves and quite as Russian as Madame Leiven [*sic*] or the Paris Bourse could desire.[34]

Confused though this passage is, it reveals clearly enough the real ground of British attacks on Austria—not what Austria had done to her, but what Britain wished to do to Austria, namely, to frustrate the Austro-French peace effort. It was over the Buol-Bourqueney memorandum, and the related issues of the Principalities and reform in Turkey, that the main battle with Austria was fought.

The British government, contrary to what it would later claim, was informed about the Austro-French talks from the outset. It could not forbid them and did not even wish to. Palmerston considered Walewski's proposed terms a reasonably good start, agreeing with Cowley that there was little danger they would lead to new negotiations. To improve them, he suggested that Britain exploit Austria's fear of France's desire to redraw the map of Europe, so as to pull Austria into new commitments. Similarly France's wish to restore the Polish kingdom of 1815 should be used to commit her to further vigorous war, without binding England to this impractical aim.[35]

Clarendon, though more afraid that negotiations might ensue, adopted Palmerston's strategy, agreeing that Austria's new-found courage was simply due to the fall of Sevastopol. She would wriggle out of any promises she had made if the Allies met reverses, but if they gained further victories, "we shall be able to beckon her like a cab from the stand and make her go where we please." The peace terms to be drawn up for Austria to present to Russia must include the cession of the Crimea, Georgia, and Circassia. Of course Russia would never accept such losses now, or even tolerate them permanently after crushing military defeat, but "the more we are able to impose the longer Russia will be in shaking them off and the more time Europe will have to prevent her." Palmerston also proposed that the Principalities should be united under a foreign prince, with a money indemnity to Turkey. Austria would have no right to object, and if she did, said Clarendon, "Bourqueney might perhaps stimulate Buol's readiness for a good final settlement by hinting that France would require a remaniement de la carte if we went to another campaign and that the Emperor is the man to indulge France in the caprice." [36] Thus Britain's strategy was clear; to encourage the Buol-Bourqueney talks so as to compromise Austria; to play Austria and France off against each other for purely British goals; to frighten Austria with alleged French territorial ambitions and revolutionary aims; to eliminate anything benefiting Austria in the settlement; and to avoid committing Britain even to the conditions she herself demanded, so that she would be free after an Austro-French agreement was reached to expand it further for the sake of prolonging the war.

With this diplomatic strategy went strenuous efforts to accelerate the war—more recruiting for Britain's foreign legions, repeated demands for another Crimean offensive before winter (though Napoleon wanted to evacuate his army, and General Simpson, the British commander following Raglan's death, considered his forces still under siege),[37] and more plans for a great offensive in the Caucasus next year, despite the admitted failure of every attempt to raise a general Circassian revolt and the imminent fall of Kars.[38] The British urged France to take over ground action in the Baltic and Crimean theaters in 1856, tempting her with hints of a possible offensive in Poland and sweeping territorial changes in Europe. Palmerston told Clarendon that the Germans were "most desirous to get rid of some of their small princes," and territorial aggrandizement for Sardinia would be highly desirable, though how to achieve these goals was not clear. Clarendon's remark to Redcliffe in late December shows how little Britain's aims had been moderated or her strategic planning improved by the lessons of the last two years:

We are bent upon an expedition of our own to Georgia next year and I have no belief in its being interfered with by negotiations, but what I don't see my way very clearly to is how the Allied armies are to get away with *safety* and with *honour* from the Crimea. This all important preliminary step seems to be omitted in all our calculations, English and French, upon the campaigns of next year.[39]

Those Clarendon called the "peacemongers" had no chance of restraining the government. G. C. Lewis stood silent and indecisive in the Cabinet. The Peelites were sure any agitation by them would only enable Palmerston to appeal again to the worst instincts of the British people; Gladstone thought the chances of peace worse in November than in May.[40] Only the changed nature of Anglo-French relations, the fact that Britain now needed France more than France needed her, gave some hope. Evidence mounted daily that Napoleon was slipping from Britain's control. Britain's cool reaction to his ideas on Poland keenly disappointed him; he alarmed London with his eagerness to evacuate the Crimea. The French would have no part of the plan to leave the burdens of Black Sea and Baltic campaigns to her, freeing Britain to promote her imperial designs in the Transcaucasus.[41] France's gains in influence at English expense in the Levant filled Redcliffe with impotent rage,[42] * and the personal clashes between him and Thouvenel grew ever sharper. So did the contest between Cowley, Clarendon, and Persigny on one side, and Walewski on the other. Above all, France was sick of the war; the constant importunities and bellicose counsels of England irritated even Napoleon. Cowley, who had, as Greville remarked, long been functioning more as Napoleon's minister of foreign affairs than as British ambassador, now found himself being left in the dark. The Emperor was newly aloof, offended at him, no longer so accessible to his complaints against Walewski. Cowley could not understand Napoleon's attitude—it had to be caprice, he concluded. But he confessed to Redcliffe, "The sooner that peace can be honorably made the better it will be for the alliance." [43]

---

* Palmerston's standard explanation for France's promoting her interests in the Levant was that this was the kind of conduct to be expected from "so flighty and vain a people as the French at the bottom of whose hearts lie the recollections of all their defeats by sea and by land in the last war with England" (to Clarendon, 17 Oct. 1855, Clar. dep. c. 31).

France's attitude made Clarendon increasingly worried over the Buol-Bourqueney talks and anxious, as he told Palmerston, "before they [the terms] arrive to lay the ground for opposing them." [44] But on studying the actual proposal under the royal couple's influence at Windsor Castle, he found it surprisingly good and sent Palmerston a long defense of it. Russia, he argued, could not possibly accept these demands. Moreover,

the breaking off diplomatic relations la guerre sans la bataille * and concerting together how to compel Russia to accept the terms appears to be very absurd and *Austrian*, but we must remember that from the first she has always said that she would not go to war with Russia unless the Allies were in a position to support her, and if we either get possession of the Crimea or quitted it and thereby had a large disposeable force on which she could rely for aid I think it probable that she would declare war.

Finally, a rejection would seriously endanger the Anglo-French alliance. "If Louis Napoleon for his own interest really wants to slip out of the war," Clarendon argued, "then these propositions may be a godsend." † Victoria and Albert added that if Austria found out how intense peace sentiment was in France and how serious was the rift between her and Britain, she might withdraw this favorable offer.[45]

Attacked by Cowley and Palmerston for imputing sincerity to Austria, Clarendon promptly retreated, agreeing with Cowley that the West "ought to proceed on the *principle* of distrusting Austria." To Palmerston he explained that when he said he thought Austria was sincere, he only meant "that I thought she knew that Russia was exhausted and was therefore sincere in her wish to kick her friend." [46] Still, the terms were so favorable to the Allies (Walewski claimed that if they became known to the public, not one in twenty

---

* This was Buol's phrase to describe what Austria would do if Russia rejected her ultimatum. It is worth noting again that what Clarendon here condemns as "very absurd and *Austrian*" is precisely the essence of sane diplomacy, i.e., using as much persuasion and as little force as necessary to achieve one's goals.

† It is not clear whether Clarendon meant that the Austrian plan would be a godsend in enabling Britain to achieve a decent peace if Napoleon absolutely could not be brought to continue the war, or that it would serve, by its severity toward Russia, to prevent Napoleon from getting peace. Here he probably meant the former; generally the latter.

would reject them) that however Clarendon and Cowley complained, raised objections, bewailed the prospect of negotiations, denounced Austria, and emphasized the humiliation Britain was undergoing for France's sake in even dealing further with Vienna, Britain dared not give Paris a flat negative.[47] So Palmerston again listed the amendments she required: Georgian and Circassian independence, either the cession of the Aland Isles to Sweden or their permanent nonfortification, neutralization of the Sea of Azov and the Dnieper and Bug Rivers as well as the Black Sea, and making neutralization part of the main treaty. At the same time he wrote Persigny charging bitterly (and dishonestly) that Austria and France had negotiated behind Britain's back and were now trying to harry her into an inadequate peace. Rather than accept it, Britain would fight on alone.[48]

Cowley had the main task of getting these amendments adopted by the "Austrian-Russian league" at Paris. Walewski readily agreed to include neutralization in the main treaty, but sharply attacked the other changes. Since the Sea of Azov was too shallow to build or float large vessels, neutralizing it would serve no purpose but to humiliate Russia. France would support Britain on the Aland Isles, but not as a *sine qua non*—just as Britain did with France on Poland.* And since Britain herself did not know what could be done with the territories east of the Black Sea, why raise the question? Napoleon pleaded directly to Victoria that since the sea powers could not destroy Russia unaided, and he did not wish to adopt a revolutionary policy, the only alternative was to join Austria in imposing on Russia a moderate but satisfactory peace.[49] Victoria personally agreed and wanted Austria's proposal accepted with only minimal changes. Even Cowley, surprisingly, thought it safe enough—that is, sure to be rejected by Russia even without Britain's major changes. He also pleaded with Clarendon "for God's sake" not to send a British army into the Caucasus—it would mean another Walcheren. Clarendon was torn by conflicting anxieties. He feared, like the Queen, that Austria might withdraw her offer because of Britain's obstruction, or suspected that France

* Clarendon's reply to this was that Britain would gladly take up the Polish issue and add it to the Buol-Bourqueney terms (Nolfo, *Czartoryski*, 157–58). His idea, of course, was to make a Russian acceptance still more unlikely.

actually wanted Britain to refuse the proposal so that she could make a separate peace and organize a continental league against her. But at other times he was sure Austria was conspiring with Russia over the peace terms, or he dreaded the public reaction to peace talks and the obloquy he would incur by taking part in them. Palmerston, however, assured him that the real danger was that Britain would fall into Austria's "trap" by agreeing to terms she thought Russia would reject, only to find later that Russia accepted them and Britain was bound to negotiate. His hard line continued to prevail.[50]

Buol somehow had to satisfy the British, but without encouraging their belief that Austria still could be dragged into the war. Meanwhile Austrian demobilization was still proceeding, and there was strong pressure at Vienna for further savings in military expenditure. When Bruck in a ministerial conference of November 27 proposed a sharp reduction in the military budget for 1856, Buol strongly supported it. He may have been to some extent bowing to the inevitable, and reluctant to fight Bruck here as he had on so many other issues. But the main point, as he argued repeatedly, was that the reduction would not undercut his policy or the prospects for peace. To Grünne's objection that it would prevent Austria from being able to back up her demands on Russia with armed force if necessary, Buol replied that even if Russia resisted an eventual Austrian ultimatum, she would not dare attack Austria, and purely political means, combined with possible smaller scale military demonstrations, would accomplish Austria's purposes.[51] *

While giving Britain no ground to hope for armed support, Buol went as far as possible to satisfy her politically. He quickly ac-

---

* Unckel (pp. 234–36) agrees with Grünne, criticizing Buol for supposedly yielding to the majority at this conference and accepting a decision for financial reasons that contradicted his main policy. But in fact Buol had no good reason to want Austria's armaments maintained. A reduction would help convince Britain that peace was inevitable. The armaments program was not necessary to protect Austria from Russia—the Austro-Prussian alliance did that—or to bring Russia to terms—for that, a break in relations would probably suffice. Moreover, if such a break occurred, Buol expected and wanted to follow it up not by an armed demonstration but by more negotiations. Walewski, knowing all this, did not even want Austria to respond to a Russian rejection of her ultimatum with a declaration of war (Hübner, I, 360). Where Buol thought an army reduction would hurt Austria politically, in the Principalities, he argued strongly against it.

cepted her demand to put neutralization into the main treaty, asking only for a sop to Russia in the form of a special Russo-Turkish convention on the light coast guard vessels to be permitted. To avoid giving the impression that so mortified the British, that the Allies were suing Russia for peace, he agreed to send the ultimatum to Russia on Austria's initiative, and was willing to use some other expression if the British objected to saying that Austria was "authorized" to do so. Accepting Britain's right to raise additional demands under the Fifth Point, he refused only to communicate these to Russia in advance of actual negotiations, because it would be tantamount to giving her a second ultimatum. Elliot and Seymour reported that Austria was determined to break relations and put all pressure on Russia short of war should she reject the ultimatum. Clarendon told Cowley that Buol's language was perfect.[52]

The British responded with more sermons on their magnanimity in consenting to deal with Austria at all, with denunciations of her for "cramming her ultimatum down our throats rather than that of Russia," with tests of Austria's sincerity, and with reminders of how ill Britain was being compensated for her sacrifices in the war and how much she was giving up in foregoing next year's glorious victories. Clarendon admitted privately that a separate Russo-Turkish convention on coastal vessels would be harmless, but Palmerston reminded him that Parliament would not like it, and so Clarendon denounced the idea to Vienna as either as Austro-Russian trick or pure childishness.* When Austria resisted changes in her ultimatum, she thus proved to the British her collusion with Russia. But when Buol accepted certain changes on the Third Point, Clarendon claimed that he therefore could have no reason to reject changes in Points One and Four as well. Asked why Britain wanted her amendments, he demanded that Austria prove why they should not be granted—a way, he told Cowley, to force Austria to reveal her true animus (this in the same letter in which he described Buol's language as perfect). And there were naturally repeated threats to exclude Austria from the peace settlement if she did not conform.[53]

Yet threats to Austria did not save the British from being pushed

---

* Bourqueney interpreted this as a deliberate effort to prevent peace by making the terms as offensive as possible to Russia; so did Buol, Francis Joseph, and even Victoria.

toward peace by France. Walewski was willing to let Austria be blamed for the rejection of British demands and to make her pay the price of any concessions, but he would not sacrifice the proposal itself, more France's than Austria's in substance.[54] While being dragged toward an agreement, the British watched for possible loopholes. The heart of the Buol-Bourqueney proposal was that the terms of Austria's ultimatum, worked out and authorized by the three powers for presentation to Russia, would if accepted by Russia constitute preliminaries of peace and lead directly to an armistice and prompt final negotiations. This was understood by everyone; without it the plan made no sense. When Austria specifically requested confirmation of this point, Walewski wired Bourqueney, "Austria can loyally promise Petersburg a signature of the preliminaries." Victoria warned that it would be imprudent and dishonest to try to tamper with the ultimatum once Britain had indicated the conditions under which she would accept and be bound by it. In later urging Prussia to support it, Prince Albert specifically assured Prince William that Britain accepted its terms as her preliminaries of peace. Clarendon himself wrote Victoria on November 24: "As it is not *strictly true* that Austria acts on her own account in transmitting her ultimatum to St. Petersburg Lord Clarendon ventures to submit to your Majesty that it is more dignified to avow frankly that Austria is authorized by England and France to propose the conditions to Russia." [55] However, London avoided specifically stating that the terms of Austria's ultimatum constituted Britain's preliminaries of peace. Moreover, in trying to reserve freedom from commitment on the First and Fourth Points of the ultimatum and to get Austria to tell Russia in advance what Britain would demand in addition under the Fifth, Clarendon (how deliberately, it is hard to say) laid a basis for his later attempts to escape from it.[56]

The struggle over Britain's amendments lasted till December 15. Once her wishes on Point Three were met and her attempts to insert her additional territorial demands into Austria's ultimatum were frustrated, Points One and Four became the center of controversy. Britain wanted to exclude Russia not only from helping set up provisions to protect the Christians in Turkey, but from ever participating with Europe in overseeing their execution, and she further wished to exclude both Russia and Austria from helping decide on the future government of the Principalities. The Queen characterized the former demand as needlessly offensive to Russia and failed to understand why Austria should not be involved in the Principalities question. But Palmerston's hatred of Austria was so savage and rabid (Clarendon's words) that the mere suggestion that a radical government in the Principalities might endanger Austria led Palmerston to charge Clarendon with advocating Holy Alliance doctrines.[57]

Bourqueney protested strongly against Britain's tactics, and Seymour warned that Austria's willingness to cooperate could be overstrained. Walewski, though willing to help make Austria yield as long as it cost France nothing, insisted that Britain must accept the ultimatum as it stood if Austria remained firm.[58] Existing personal quarrels deepened in the struggle, with Cowley, Clarendon, and Persigny combining against Walewski, while a new one emerged between Palmerston and Napoleon when Victor Emmanuel repeated to the Emperor some of the language he had heard on his state visit to Britain in December. The French government, Palmerston had said, was a parcel of adventurers collaborating with Austria to hustle Britain into an ignominious peace. But Britain, caring nothing for France, would fight on alone or with Sardinia as her sole ally. Napoleon was deeply hurt; he hated Austria as much as the British did, he protested. Worse yet, Russia heard of the incident and would be sure to exploit the rift at any peace congress.[59]

When Palmerston finally agreed to the Austrian ultimatum, after Austria had made some last-minute concessions,[60] it was not to save the strained Anglo-French alliance. This he always considered a temporary respite in a permanent rivalry, unlikely in any case to outlast the war. Nor was it because his intransigence had isolated him within the Cabinet.* The Peelites were probably right in be-

---

* On November 20 the Cabinet had voted to accept the Austro-French proposal for an Austrian ultimatum to Russia, under various British conditions (Argyll, *Autobiography*, I, 594–97). Argyll took this as a defeat for Palmerston, and several writers have since seen in it a turning point in British policy, the place at which Palmerston and Clarendon had to accept the inevitability of peace. But Palmerston's and Clarendon's strategy was not to refuse to offer Russia peace terms through Austria at all; they simply wanted to screw the terms up so high that Russia would be sure to reject them. The Cabinet deci-

lieving that his popularity was still indispensable for the ministry and that an appeal by him to bellicose middle class patriotism would still quell any opposition. He ceased fighting for harder conditions on learning that both Gorchakov and Seebach insisted that Russia would reject any dishonorable terms, even though she would now accept neutralization of the Black Sea. This news, which heightened Victoria's fears of a separate Franco-Russian peace or an Austrian-Russian rapprochement, only served to convince Palmerston that Russia would most likely reject the Austrian ultimatum because of the Bessarabian cession.[61] To help ensure this result, Palmerston published the general content of the ultimatum in the *Morning Post* before Russia even saw it.[62]

Buol, who had feared total failure, could thus send off the ultimatum with V. Esterházy on December 16. Though not as pessimistic about its chances for acceptance as the Emperor was, he was not very hopeful.[63] Once again Austria began dragooning neutral states into supporting her demands. One neutral, Sweden, had already aligned herself by concluding a defensive alliance with France and Britain on November 21. France was mainly responsible for the treaty, but Austria's choices had again strongly affected Swedish policy. Had Austria entered the war in the spring of 1855, Sweden probably would have followed her.[64] The fall of Sevastopol again revived Swedish war fever to some extent; Count Revertera, Baron Langenau's temporary replacement, reported that Swedish leaders considered her entry into war inevitable if it lasted into the spring of 1856. In fact, a secret clause of the agreement foresaw eventual Swedish participation. But Revertera warned them of the risks of war and encouraged only a defensive alliance.[65]

Of course a friendly and correct policy toward Sweden was easy for Austria; she did not need Sweden. But Prussia now had to be

---

sion left the door open for Palmerston to continue to do this, as Argyll himself saw; Palmerston's and Clarendon's efforts to prevent the ultimatum from achieving peace continued even after Russia finally accepted it in January 1856. Jasper Ridley cites Palmerston's letter to Clarendon of November 23 to argue that Palmerston saw that the negotiations would be serious and practical ones. But that letter, like later ones (e.g., on November 29) really constituted advice to Clarendon on how to avoid Austria's "trap" of successful negotiations. Ridley's account of the origins and development of the peace negotiations (*Lord Palmerston*, 444–53) is otherwise marred by errors.

dragged along after Buol had earlier refused to join her in promoting peace talks [66] and had excluded her from any share in or
knowledge of the Austrian ultimatum. Buol had had his reasons—
the lies Prussia still told the West about Austria,[67] the disarray prevailing at Berlin,* and above all, the need for absolute secrecy if
his plan was to work. The Prussians knew something was going on
and expected to be confronted with another *fait accompli*, even
though Buol instructed G. Esterházy to deny that any negotiations were going on with the West (just as he denied it to various
envoys at Vienna). Only after V. Esterházy left for St. Petersburg
was his cousin authorized to tell Berlin.[68] The secrecy applied
a fortiori to the Germany states. Buol ignored Pfordten's warnings
against presenting Germany with another *fait accompli* and treated
Beust's feverish efforts at peacemaking with sardonic contempt.[69]
A Bavarian-Saxon proposal for reform of the Federal Diet † gave
him a chance to win ground with the third Germany at Prussia's
expense, but Buol made clear that while he favored it, he could not
support it at the expense of Austria's foreign policy, and when
Prussia learned about the proposal, he quickly dropped out rather
than irritate her over a side issue.[70]

Buol, aware of the anger his ultimatum would arouse in Germany
and the *Schadenfreude* that would greet a failure, tried to persuade
Prussia to support it unconditionally by giving her more promises
of a place at the peace conference if she did. Francis Joseph sent
another appeal to the King. But this had little impact at Berlin, especially when the French minister Moustier revealed what Buol had
tried to conceal, that Austria intended to break relations with Russia
if she refused the ultimatum. Moreover, someone, probably Beust,
revealed that Napoleon considered the Bessarabian cession a purely
Austrian demand that he would gladly drop if Russia accepted
everything else.[71] Prussia was not only angered by Austria's tactics
but considered the terms of her ultimatum deliberately designed to

---

* This disarray was highlighted by the revelation in early November that
secret state documents had long been given to the French legation through
bribed servants of Gerlach and Niebuhr (G. Esterházy to Buol, 9 Nov. 1855,
PA III/55).

† The "reform" in question was reactionary in nature, i.e., using Federal
decrees to cut down parliamentary prerogatives in the individual states, especially control over the budget.

provoke a Russian rejection. Frederick William again wanted to save Austria from herself, this time by joining with Saxony to deny her any German help in war.[72] He sent E. Manteuffel once more to work on Francis Joseph and get Austria to back down from her ultimatum. Prussia recommended acceptance to Russia for the sake of peace, but would not endorse its specific provisions.[73] The German reaction to it was the same or worse. Pfordten and King Max denounced the Bessarabian cession in particular. Beust, humiliated again by his failure at peacemaking, claimed that the Federal constitution forbade Germany to support the ultimatum fully. Hanover said she could act only through the Diet; Württemberg insisted again that the lower Danube was a Hungarian, not a German, stream.[74]

Buol tried to convince Pfordten that Austria's terms were valuable for Germany and that the Bessarabian cession was not useless or purely in Austria's interests, but otherwise he paid little attention to German protests. His concern was to break Prussia's resistance. Buol warned E. Manteuffel that Prussia could not long remain neutral, once Austria broke with Russia. If the war was not ended now, he said, next year's main campaign would be in the Baltic; then Prussia would learn what it meant to have a great war going on in her area of vital interests. Under this pressure, first Munich and Dresden and then Berlin gave in and supported the ultimatum fully at St. Petersburg.[75]

But as Buol won this new Pyrrhic victory, Britain again placed the whole peace move in jeopardy. For some time after the ultimatum was sent, Clarendon repeatedly expressed his satisfaction with it and with Austria.* He repeatedly reassured himself and others

---

* For example, he insisted that Britain now had an ultimatum she could be satisfied with; he admitted that Buol had gone as far toward accepting Britain's amendments as he possibly could; he recognized that his suspicions of Austro-Russian collusion had been groundless; he expressed delight and astonishment at Buol's firmness toward Russia and gentlemanly conduct toward the West; and he even grudgingly admitted Austria's probable sincerity. Finding Austria's attitude so much better than France's shiftiness on the Seebach mission, he commented, "It will be strange if after all we should have to look to the assistance of Austria for keeping France strait! [sic]" (Greville Memoirs, VII, 183–84; Clarendon to Cowley, 17, 26, and 28 Dec. 1855, FO 519/172; Clarendon to Seymour, 18 Dec., Clar. dep. c. 134; Clarendon to Palmerston, 27 Dec., Palm. Papers GC/CL/773).

that Russia could not possibly accept such humiliating and dangerous conditions, and he even occasionally felt that Britain was lucky after her military failures to have the chance to exit from the war on such good terms.[76] The government, still determined to restore British prestige by another campaign, continued to plan for it, and welcomed as good news any concrete indication that Russia would decline the terms or that Napoleon would agree to fight on. Even the fall of Kars on November 28 had its good side; Russia, holding this setoff for Sevastopol, would now be even more likely to reject the Bessarabian cession. To hedge against the bare possibility of a Russian acceptance, Clarendon instructed Seymour to make Buol understand that any such acceptance could not possibly be sincere and that if Austria tried more tricks like those of last year with the sea powers, she would never get into the peace conference.[77]

Still, he was not ready to repudiate Britain's commitment openly. When Colloredo asked him on January 1 to confirm that Austria's ultimatum, if accepted unconditionally by Russia, would provide the preliminaries of peace upon which the powers would enter into negotiations (Seymour had specifically acknowledged this at Vienna before the ultimatum was sent), Clarendon answered that the Cabinet had not discussed the question in detail, but "that the beginning of execution already given to the program that it [the Buol-Bourqueney memorandum] contains implies the acceptance of it." This in substance recognized Britain's commitment. That same day, however, Palmerston told Colloredo that he personally felt Britain could not agree to an armistice unless her additional demands were also accepted by Russia in advance—and immediately Palmerston's personal opinion became Britain's official stand. Of course Britain had agreed to the Austrian ultimatum, Clarendon now argued—but only as a basis on which Austria would break relations with Russia if it was refused. Britain had never accepted it as constituting *her* preliminaries of peace and the basis for an armistice; Austria's bad faith in refusing to tell Russia about the additional conditions prevented Britain from doing so. Her stand was dictated solely by a genuine desire for peace and a wish to deal honestly and in good faith with Russia and Austria. If Russia now accepted the ultimatum in ignorance of Britain's special conditions, peace would be frustrated, for then Russia would reject them in the final negotiations. Britain certainly did not wish to raise difficulties, said Clarendon, but Buol "must know that Russia cannot mean to act with good faith." [78]

Sending Seymour a formal statement of Britain's position on January 8 to convey to Buol, Clarendon next appealed to France to support Britain's refusal of an armistice until her extra demands were ensured of Russian acceptance. A decent peace, he conceded, could be made on the ultimatum as it stood; the Buol-Bourqueney memorandum "might have been all well at the time it was agreed to, and we might upon the acceptation pure et simple of the conditions by Russia have signed preliminaries of peace, *if* we had reserved to ourselves the right of not only proposing further conditions but of *keeping them in reserve* until negotiations had commenced." But Britain had not done this; she had stated her special conditions and asked that they be communicated to Russia. Austria's failure to do so was obviously a trick. If Britain was not to be made a fool of, she had to continue the war until assured that Russia accepted the extra conditions also.[79]

In other words: having tried, and failed, to get Britain's additional conditions into the original ultimatum; having not dared to make the communication of these conditions to Russia a *sine qua non* because France would not support it; having agreed upon, and been satisfied with, an ultimatum in which Austria had, as Clarendon admitted, made every possible concession to Britain; having then waited until Austria had engaged herself completely in the *démarche*, so that she now faced a break in relations with Russia and complete isolation from her German allies; knowing and gloating over the fact that Austria was wholly dependent on the West; Britain now sought both to deprive Austria of her one means to persuade Russia to accept the ultimatum, namely, the promise Austria had made in good faith of a prompt armistice and peace negotiations if Russia accepted, and to destroy the hope of peace that alone had led Austria into these exertions and risks.

Seymour, for one, had some comprehension of what his government was doing. He had no desire for peace or any sympathy for Austria; he was eager for another campaign to take Kronstadt and St. Petersburg and thus, as he put it, blow up Russia for good, and he was even more contemptuous of Austrians than of most foreigners. But he was honest enough to know that his government was wrong and prudent enough to see that its policy could lead to serious dangers. At first he tried to dissuade Clarendon by arguing that any blow might topple Buol now, and then Russia and Austria still might get together. Clarendon, however, was delighted at the abuse heaped on Buol by his enemies at Vienna. Seymour next begged for permission not to communicate the fateful dispatch of January 8. If Buol had gone too far in telling Russia that the ultimatum's terms were accepted by the sea powers as preliminaries, it was his fault, Seymour admitted, for he had assured Buol that Britain adhered to the whole plan. Moreover, Austria was still demanding acceptance of the Fifth Point, under which the special British demands would be raised at the peace talks, as *sine qua non* from Russia, though the Russians had just rejected it in their first reply to Vienna. If Britain now in effect told Austria that she had to give Russia a second ultimatum before there could be an armistice, Austria would drop the whole Fifth Point and be reconciled with Russia. Francis Joseph only supported Buol because he thought the West was loyally cooperating with Austria; the communication would prove the opposite. Finally, Seymour told Clarendon privately, if we intended to *demand* that Austria communicate these conditions to Russia (which of course Clarendon had carefully avoided doing), we should have done it sooner. Now this looked like British bad faith and would further embroil Britain with France and unite the continent against her.[80]

Clarendon, feigning surprise that Austria had not communicated the extra conditions to Russia, peremptorily ordered Seymour to give Buol the January 8 dispatch, which he did on January 16, two days before Austria was scheduled to break relations with Russia. It was, he told Clarendon, the most painful duty of his entire life. At the height of the crisis, with Buol under fierce attack from his opponents led by Bruck, he had to give him this British response to Buol's exemplary firmness and loyalty. Moreover, Seymour confessed, he simply could not refute Buol's argument that Britain was bound to the November 14 program. We *did* accept the terms of the ultimatum, Seymour pointed out, and we did *not* insist on our additional conditions being made known to Russia. Having agreed to a compromise, we were now trying to demand the whole loaf. His own admission of Britain's obligation may have been indiscreet, but surely it was not unjustified.[81]

Fortunately for the West, Seymour's and Bourqueney's worst fears were not realized. Though he denounced Britain's stand in measured but very strong language, Buol told Seymour that he had gone too far to change course now. Austria would still break with Russia if it became necessary. However, he counted on France to support his comments on British policy at London and, if Russia accepted the ultimatum, to help Austria compel Britain to keep her part of the bargain.[82] The question was, would France do it? Buol made every possible appeal through Hübner, and Bourqueney, again very angry at Britain's tactics, supported them. The French diplomats and ministers were solidly behind Austria on this question. Cowley's arguments got nowhere with Walewski; even Persigny insisted Britain was absolutely bound. But Cowley still went freely over Walewski's head to Napoleon, who was as Austrophobe and as unscrupulous as he was.[83] The way in which these two, pursuing opposite goals, combined to try to break the agreement with Austria and force her into new sacrifices or isolation forms a fascinating and neglected little episode in Allied diplomacy.*

On January 12, Cowley took Britain's case against the preliminaries and an armistice to the Emperor in private audience. His arguments were typical of him—for example, he contended that the Allies, by refusing Russia an armistice, would be doing Austria a favor. The refusal would precipitate the break in relations Austria must desire now that her relations with Russia had deteriorated so completely. But his main contention was that Austria, by refusing to present and support Britain's additional demands, was herself breaking with the sea powers and setting them free from their part of the agreement. They could now tell Austria that they would take part of Asiatic Russia or the Aland Isles from Russia and forget about Bessarabia, which would frighten Austria into supporting the British demands. Napoleon, although intrigued by the prospect of getting rid of Austria and the Bessarabian cession, replied that the Allies were morally bound to the ultimatum as it stood. But if Russia agreed to everything but the Bessarabian cession, should they not

* Nolfo, for example, says nothing about it (*Europa*, 133–35).

give this up for the sake of peace? Why should they continue the war for Austria, who had done nothing for them? Cowley reported to Clarendon that Napoleon's leanings toward Russia and desire for peace made it more imperative than ever to produce an Austro-Russian breach and to get the additional demands into Austria's ultimatum. The exchange of Kars for Bessarabia suggested by Napoleon, said Cowley, might be used "to put Austria in a cleft stick." Once she broke with Russia, the Allies should tell her, "You've been fair to us, now we'll be the same to you. If you want Bessarabia, we'll support it, but of course we'll require material help." This demand would make Austria back out entirely, and the sea powers could then make peace without her, gaining Britain's additional demands by giving back part of Bessarabia to Russia.[84]

Napoleon meanwhile had heard of Russia's first reply to Austria, accepting the ultimatum except for Bessarabia and Point Five—a reply Buol loyally rejected despite violent German and domestic pressure on him in favor of it. The Emperor now urged Victoria to accept Russia's offer—Bessarabia was purely Austria's demand. Hübner found Walewski going soft on the critical issue, claiming that while the Allies were obligated to sign preliminaries of peace if Russia accepted the ultimatum, an armistice would have to wait till she also accepted the West's special conditions. It was plain not only that Cowley's constant demands that France choose between Britain and Austria were taking their toll, but also that Napoleon, like Cowley, wanted to force Austria, once she broke with Russia, to drop out of the peace negotiations entirely.[85]

At London, Clarendon outdid himself in contradictions and bad faith. He advised the Queen to answer Napoleon noncommittally, but Victoria's reluctance to end the war now with British prestige so low made him even more set against preliminaries and an armistice until the special conditions were accepted. He had to warn her, however, that if Russia really wanted peace it would be impossible to carry on the war, since France had left Britain alone on the path of honor. He abused Buol heartily for treachery and bad faith; at exactly the same time he praised Buol's "straightforward and honorable" conduct to Prussia and tried to make Prussia unconditionally support the very peace plan he was determined to wriggle out of. But the main point is that Clarendon also hoped to oust Austria from the negotiations and to conclude a separate peace with Russia. He wrote Cowley on January 15:

I hope it is true that Seebach has announced the [Russian] desire to treat separately as that will give us a famous hold over Austria. I heartily wish we could wash our hands of Austria and have only to do with Russia for I believe it would facilitate every arrangement, as Russia must hate the idea of concessions that Austria will benefit from more than the true belligerents. However we must not think of what would be shabby but if Austria *frees herself* from her engagements because we have the presumption to want our own terms of peace in addition to hers I should be disposed to let her go her own way because she will at the same time *set us free* and then we might negotiate directly with Russia and pitch all Germany to the infernal regions.[86]

Had Austria broken relations with Russia, it is not likely that Britain would have followed the Napoleon-Cowley-Clarendon plan exactly. For Palmerston refused to cede anything to Russia in exchange for Kars or in order to gain Britain's extra conditions, and insisted that the Bessar..bian cession was not an Austrian, but a British, French, Turkish, and European interest.[87] What the Anglo-French discussions at this time, as well as later developments, make reasonably certain, however, is that had Austria found it necessary to break with Russia, as her part of the agreement required, her allies would then have found some way to sell her out—France so as to form an entente with Russia, and Britain in order to continue the war or get a peace more to her liking. Walewski would probably have opposed this,* but neither he nor the peace party in England

---

* An interesting exchange of letters between Napoleon and Walewski on January 18 demonstrates that at least after Russia's acceptance, Walewski absolutely opposed any further obstruction by Britain. Drouyn had advised Napoleon simply to declare the preliminaries to be the definitive terms of peace, to prevent any failure of the final negotiations. Asked for his advice, Walewski told Napoleon that Drouyn, like himself, Austria, Prussia, Russia, and all of Europe, saw that the matter of the preliminaries was now settled by Russia's acceptance and no longer open to discussion. In addition, France must not make or discuss any more private arrangements with Britain in regard to the coming negotiations independently of Austria. If the Emperor stood firmly on these two points, solidly based on justice, logic, and public feeling, said Walewski, the British ministry would not be sufficiently mad to fight him (Raindre, 491–92).

could have stopped Napoleon or the British ministry from doing it, nor would they probably have tried very hard.[88]

Thus a Russian acceptance of the ultimatum was even more important to Austria than Buol knew. When Russia had seen the ultimatum coming, she had tried to fend it off by communicating a peace proposal that she sent to Paris via Seebach, also to Buol through Gorchakov. At the same time Budberg worked mightily to hold Prussia and Germany to a neutral line against Austria. Neither effort worked. Buol referred Russia's proposal to the West as a useful sign of her desire for peace, but refused to take official notice of it as Gorchakov asked. For France, the Russian move at Vienna was a good excuse to break off the now embarrassing semi-official contacts with Russia through Seebach. He was sent to St. Petersburg officially to support Austria's ultimatum, secretly to let Russia know that Napoleon despised Austria and was willing to support Russia at the peace table if she would swallow Austria's terms now.[89]

When the ultimatum arrived in St. Petersburg, Alexander II was still determined to reject any demands he considered dishonorable.[90] Buol tried to convince Russia that the terms were honorable and to conceal the minatory aspects of Esterházy's mission,[91] but Russia was not deceived. As Buol expected, only more European pressure, isolation, and domestic troubles could make Russia yield. Everyone recognized at a Russian council of January 1 that Russia's military situation was hopeless in the long run. Prince Vorontsev and Grand Duke Constantine wanted to accept the terms as they stood should a Russian counteroffer be rejected. But Gorchakov advised trying a direct approach to France before accepting Vienna's terms, which the Tsar considered humiliating. Therefore Nesselrode sent Gorchakov a counteroffer on January 5, eliminating Point Five and the Bessarabian cession and providing for coastal vessels to *protect* as well as service the Black Sea coasts. Considering Russia's feelings toward Austria, this was a surprisingly conciliatory response; V. Esterházy thought the changes were dictated more by *amour propre* than by an irresistible repugnance to the terms themselves.[92]

Buol, also pleased, was willing to compromise over Bessarabia if a transaction was worked out by the Allies together. Yet despite Russia's rage and Germany's pleas, Austria rejected the Russian counteroffer. Unless Russia yielded unconditionally by January 18, Buol told Gorchakov, Austria would break relations. As Buol wrote Prokesch, he considered such a break possible, even probable—but then more negotiations rather than more war would follow it. Everything depended on Napoleon, but he could be trusted because he really desired peace and needed Austria to achieve it. A ministerial conference endorsed Buol's policy, apparently without dissent, on January 15.[93] Russia may not have expected so firm a stand; in any case, it broke her resistance. On January 15, a ministerial committee unanimously advised acceptance; Esterházy was informed the next day.[94]

This finally assured that the Eastern question would be brought to the peace table, despite some British maneuvers still to come— but not the whole Eastern question. For all the while the struggle over Austria's ultimatum had raged in Europe, Britain was attempting at Constantinople to settle Points One and Four privately with Turkey and France, excluding Austria along with Russia from the settlement. This was of course a long-standing British aim, already much in evidence at the Vienna Conferences. It constituted Britain's main reason for preventing agents from the Principalities from coming to Vienna and for her vetoing any discussion of Point Four, and it figured prominently in her desire to overthrow the Four Points after June 4 and in Clarendon's assurances to Colquhoun that the West would not be bound by any agreements reached at Vienna. Britain's attempt to keep these questions out of any future peace conference did not result solely, or even mainly, from the desire to combat Holy Alliance influence in the Balkans. The reason was rather that no general European conference would approve the kinds of reforms she wanted; they would have to be pushed through by Britain alone, or by Britain and France.*

* Clarendon, though convinced Britain had to vindicate her own humanity and Christianity by doing something for the Christians in Turkey, often despaired of solving the Muslim-Christian problem. But Russell, fully recovered from his attack of caution at Vienna, called for an extensive Anglo-French economic development program and sweeping legal and administrative reforms, arguing that the sea powers must not "despair of seeing men consonant with the institutions of France and England" carry them out. As for Palmerston, he insisted that the Sultan could easily gain the loyalties of what he termed the "Nonconformists" in Turkey by a series of simple reforms: establishing mixed tribunals with Muslim and Christian judges; setting Christian

In August and September, Palmerston and Clarendon discussed the possibility of Turkey's raising an army of five thousand men from the Principalities. Whether they knew this would violate an ancient privilege of the inhabitants is not clear; both agreed that any possible Austrian objections could be ignored. Immediately after Sevastopol fell, Palmerston renewed his suggestion that the Sultan ask Austria to evacuate the Principalities. Victoria objected and Clarendon agreed that politically and strategically this would be unwise, though the inhabitants would be delighted.[95] Britain then proposed to France what Redcliffe and Palmerston had long advocated: that the Sultan establish a new form of constitution and government in the Principalities by decree, following suggestions worked out by Britain and France at Constantinople. Walewski at first wanted to bring Austria into the discussion, but Cowley reported he had persuaded him that she was too pro-Russian.[96]

The trouble with this scheme for Britain was that even cooperation with France had its inconveniences and dangers. She was less systematically hostile to Austrian influence and interests in the Near East than Britain was, and much less interested in imposing "reforms" on Turkey.[97] The less Napoleon had to do with the Turks, the better. Moreover, the sea powers were still basically rivals in the East, and there France was winning. In early May, with Redcliffe away in the Crimea, the Sultan had appointed his and Reshid's old enemy Mehemet Ali to be grand admiral of the Turkish fleet. Reshid resigned, with Ali becoming grand vizier and Fuad Pasha foreign minister.[98] Redcliffe claimed that all this was due to the French chargé Benedetti's intrigues; but French and Austrian sources indicate that these events resulted from internal opposition to Reshid and from the Sultan's weariness of Redcliffe's tyranny

---

officers alongside all Muslim officials, with Christian subjects allowed to appeal to these officers, and they in turn to appeal over the heads of Muslim officials all the way to Constantinople; running integrated Christian-Muslim primary schools in all the chief towns; opening careers to all talents and army service to all Christians; abolishing any punishment for apostasy from Islam, and so on. The Turks, of course, protested violently against all such ideas and all interference in their internal affairs. Prokesch had these sorts of projects in mind when he said that the surest way to destroy the Ottoman Empire was by reform à l'européenne (Clarendon to Russell, 10 April 1855, PRO 30 22/12D; Russell to Redcliffe, 21 April, FO 352/41/I/1; Palmerston to Clarendon, 22 April and 4 May, Clar. dep. c. 31; Testa, V, 156–61).

(as Clarendon also believed). Redcliffe launched a campaign against French influence, and Paris replied by sending Thouvenel, a more formidable opponent, as ambassador.[99] He quickly was on excellent terms with the Porte and with Koller, but Redcliffe, rebuffed in his efforts to oust Mehemet by a direct appeal to the Sultan, became involved in a heated quarrel with Thouvenel, even demanding the removal of some members of the French mission. This time Clarendon refused to back him, though still blaming France for the basic friction at Constantinople.[100] *

The conduct of the war caused further conflict. The Sultan obstructed British plans for Circassia by persistently refusing to renounce his claim to suzerainty over it, while the Russians steadily wore down Shamil's Circassian resistance movement.[101] Clarendon and Redcliffe complained bitterly about Turkey's negligence in sending supplies and reinforcements into eastern Asia Minor and about Napoleon's refusal to let any be diverted from the Crimea.[102] British remedies for the military problems seemed uniformly to backfire. General Williams, sent to help the Turks save Kars, was quickly at odds with Redcliffe and under fire for his strategy.[103] The Bashi-Bazouks serving under Colonel Beatson turned out to be a plague and a disaster; by July, Redcliffe confessed, "The question is no longer how we got into the mess, but how we are to get out of it with honor and safety." In September, French troops had a bloody clash with the Bashi-Bazouks at Gallipoli; in October, with Beatson removed from command, Redcliffe reported that neither he nor anyone else knew where they were.[104] Despite Palmerston's vigorous denials, evidence mounted of crime and other troubles in the Anglo-French occupation of Constantinople, and of some misconduct by British officials.[105]

The proposed Polish Legion, after causing endless propaganda and internecine strife among the émigrés and constant complaints from Austria, ended only in the formation of Cossack "Hundreds," containing Vlachs, Cossacks, Jews, Hungarians, Italians, and especially Bulgars. They were taken into Britain's Turkish Legion under British pay and command in late 1855, but remained much more a

---

* Clarendon remarked privately that Redcliffe's trouble stemmed from his refusal to allow the Sultan to coreign with him.

political football than an instrument of war.[106] Meanwhile the ordinary Turkish soldiers were everywhere despised and maltreated by the French and English.[107]

As instances of military and political failure, these would deserve little attention, other than to note the persistence with which Britain adhered to unproductive tactics and unrealistic goals. It is striking, however, that all these efforts were frankly directed not merely against Russia, but also at one or more of Britain's allies. Clarendon, though bewailing the excesses committed by British-led Turkish irregulars, wanted to build up and support these forces as "the best counterpoise now and hereafter to French aggrandisement in the East." Redcliffe urged a Circassian campaign in the spring both to elevate British prestige and to wrest control of policy in this area from Turkey. Palmerston urged getting Turkey to make land grants available for a permanent military colony of Poles in the Ottoman Empire, both to induce Poles in the Russian army to desert, now and after the war, and to worry and constrain Austria. He similarly wanted the Polish Corps built up and supported, as a powerful instrument of negotiation in Britain's hand. He told Panmure: "It would have a good effect also on Austria. It would be a hint to all those Eastern Powers that peace ought to be made soon, while at the same time it commits us to nothing and gives none of them the slightest ground for remonstrance." [108] *

At this same time Buol was working for cooperation with the West especially on Point Four, as his whole policy at the Vienna conferences and after clearly demonstrates.[109] In mid-September, when Thouvenel suggested preliminary conferences between the three allies and Turkey on the issue, Buol immediately responded favorably and Koller helped get the Turks to agree. This was not an automatic response. Such a conference could easily undermine Austria's treaty rights to protect Catholic Christians in Turkey. Francis Joseph took these quite seriously and insisted on giving his

---

* For these same anti-Russian and anti-Austrian purposes, Clarendon, Redcliffe, and Palmerston tried even after peace was made to keep England's Turkish contingent and Zamoyski's Ottoman Cossacks in existence under Britain's control—with Turkey to foot the bills (Clarendon to Palmerston, 4 April 1856, Palm. Papers GC/CL/851; Clarendon to Redcliffe, 9 May, FO 352/44/1; Temperley, "Last Phase of Redcliffe," 233-35).

personal approval to all instructions sent Koller about them. But he did consent to the proposal, and Buol entered enthusiastically into it.[110] Again this Austrian zeal to cooperate angered Britain. Vigorously denouncing Austria's and Ştirbei's misgovernment in the Principalities, Clarendon and Cowley told the French that good government was impossible unless Austria was excluded.[111] Austria's offer to submit the First Point to the conference and thus subject her alleged ambitions in the Principalities to Allied control made no difference. As a nonbelligerent, said Palmerston, Austria had no right to take part—it was purely selfish of her to want to. The new internuncio, Prokesch, said Redcliffe, would tip the balance against Britain in the conference.[112]

Clarendon's hope "to have fought off from cooperation" with Austria was frustrated, however, by Walewski's support for Austrian participation. Though the French mainly wanted Austria's cooperation in the general effort to bring British to the peace table (the Buol-Bourqueney memorandum was concluded at this time), they also had enough experience with the British at Constantinople to want Austrian support there as well.[113] To get around France's promise to Austria, Clarendon told Redcliffe quickly to work out a direct agreement with the Porte on the new political system to be established in the Prinicpalities and to refer it directly to London and Paris—"then the 2 governments might [one word illegible] of how far it would be expedient to invite the concurrence of Austria." As "the best barrier against Russia and Austria," he urged a union of the Principalities with nominal Turkish suzerainty. Simultaneously he urged Walewski to reject Austria's offer to bring Point One into the proposed conference.[114]

In a further attempt to overcome British suspicions, Buol sent Prokesch's instructions for the conference to the Allies; these were devoid of any hint at an exclusive Austrian protectorate or of any illusion that one was possible.* Clarendon grudgingly admitted to Redcliffe, "I daresay the instructions contain much that is bad but it struck me that there was more good than I expected." [115] But after

* This was true also of Prokesch's private political instructions, which were not communicated to England. These included some special Austrian interests to pursue, but nothing that was not supposed to be gained by negotiation.

a stern rebuke from Palmerston for defending Holy Alliance doctrines in conceding that Austria had a stake in the future government of the Principalities, Clarendon discovered that Prokesch's instructions were a scheme for harmful intervention between the Sultan and his subjects, for fastening foreign tutelage on the Principalities, and for getting the Allies to pull Austria's chestnuts out of the fire. In late December, recognizing Austria's conciliatory tone, Clarendon sent Seymour the plan Redcliffe devised for reorganizing the Principalities, deliberately anti-Austrian as well as anti-Russian in letter and spirit. But Clarendon maintained that it was little different from Austria's own ideas and met all her needs. Apparently he expected her to offer no resistance to it.[116]

Meanwhile, Redcliffe was still working at Constantinople for Ştirbei's ouster, the appointment of Ion Ghica as his successor, and the establishment of a new governmental system by Anglo-French-Turkish fiat. He even tried for a reconciliation with Mehemet Ali, to get Reshid back in power.[117] But the Turks would not listen (Clarendon told him that Turkey had requested his recall three times),[118] and Thouvenel refused any separate Anglo-French agreement. Walewski rejected Palmerston's ideas of parliamentary government and Turkish garrisons in the Principalities as unworkable and hateful to the inhabitants—whereupon Cowley and Clarendon promptly denied that Britain had any such ideas. Frustrated by French resistance and incensed that Walewski insisted on believing his own agent at Bucharest, Béclard, rather than Colquhoun, on conditions in the Principalities,[119] Clarendon in late December thought of trying to settle everything by what he called *"coup de main"*— evidently meaning a Turkish proclamation of a new system without even a prior Anglo-French agreement. As he wrote Redcliffe, it was vital to settle Points One and Four before any peace conference opened, "and I believe it might be done *as easily* . . . by a coup de main as by long conferences which would assuredly give rise to unlimited intrigues, bribes, delays, frauds, and the other paraphernalia of Turkish negotiation." [120]

In other words, a little sharp practice by Britain now would prevent much knavery by others later. But this device would not work in the face of French, Austrian, and Turkish opposition. Redcliffe finally gave up the struggle, and the four-power Constantinople Conference opened on January 9.* Its deliberations and proposals belong with the story of the Paris Peace Congress. Clarendon accepted Austria's participation as a *pis aller*, telling Redcliffe not to display Britain's mistrust of her. Palmerston pointed out the real moral of France's failure to cooperate: the alliance with France was like a "summer season," sure to pass quickly. Britain must never rely on alliances to maintain her interests, but only on her own "strength, energy, and courage." [121]

* Baron Tecco, Sardinian minister at Constantinople, made an unauthorized protest against his exclusion from the conference, which got him a rebuff from Redcliffe and Thouvenel and a summons home by his own government. Walewski insisted on maintaining the previous Allied agreements whereby Sardinia would participate only in questions which directly concerned her regarding the peace, and Clarendon and Palmerston consented (Nolfo, *Europa*, 199–201, 480–86).

XIV

The Paris Congress:
The High Price of Peace

Along with congratulations on Russia's acceptance of Austria's ultimatum, Buol received plenty of reminders that Austria was not out of danger. Hübner warned that Napoleon and Walewski were "at heart . . . both ready to dispense with the Monarchy." Pfordten's shamefaced compliments were accompanied with the prediction that the Bessarabian cession would one day cost Austria dearly, and that France and Russia were already coming together against her. G. Esterházy reported from Berlin that Bloomfield and Clarendon openly proclaimed Britain's anger at Austria for not conveying her additional conditions to Russia.[1]

Remarking that Britain's tactics "can only inspire a profound disgust," Buol was prepared to bear her complaints with equanimity. Her renewed efforts to upset the basis for peace were the real danger. Palmerston, regretfully accepting the inevitability of peace without another campaign, was still determined somehow to get the additional conditions into the preliminaries before signing them or permitting an armistice. His actual demands were in a state of flux. He saw now, for example, that his previous idea of securing Circassia's independence by a Russo-Circassian treaty was impractical because no independent Circassia existed and no representative could be found to sign a treaty for it. But no matter—Britain's firmness had made Russia accept the ultimatum, and more firmness would get the rest of what she wanted, whatever it was. He rebuked Seymour for growing soft at Vienna and admonished him to "put a little starch in your neckcloth" and deal more firmly with Buol's impertinent requests for a prompt signature of preliminaries.[2]

Conditions were not favorable for Palmerston's bluster. Napoleon was disgusted with him. Victor Emmanuel, according to Cowley, had described him "as a sort of rabid animal that all others should flee." Walewski advised the Emperor not even to discuss Britain's contentions. Even the Duke of Cambridge, sent to Paris to participate in a war council planning the spring campaign, admitted that Britain was wrong in wanting to continue the war.[3] Clarendon, though he agreed with Palmerston on the importance of getting the extra demands into the preliminaries, was even more uncertain on how to do it or what they should be and had almost resigned himself to destroying his reputation and career by participating in the peace congress.[4] But once more Cowley concocted a plan to combine France's desire for concessions to Russia with Britain's demand for harsher terms, making Austria pay the price. He had earlier wanted the sea powers to accept Russia's offer of direct negotiations, conveyed through Seebach, and to discard the Austrian ultimatum. Unfortunately, Russia had ruined this idea by accepting the ultimatum. Now Cowley proposed to bypass Walewski and work out a direct agreement with Napoleon to change the preliminaries, introducing a moderated version of Britain's additional demands (still including the evacuation of Kars and the cession of considerable territory in Asia) in exchange for reducing the Bessarabian cession to merely the left bank of the Danube and its fortresses. After all, Cowley contended, Buol was a reasonable man; he must understand that peace would have to come on the Allies' terms, not his.[5]

Walewski and Napoleon agreed heartily on virtually eliminating the Bessarabian cession, even getting Hübner to support them. Bourqueney and Seymour were instructed to get Austria to revise the terms for the preliminaries of peace.[6] This exceeded even Buol's limits of appeasement. Austria had already provided the preliminaries, he told Seymour; she would not run errands or execute commissions for the Allies. Changing the terms now would give Russia good grounds to retract her acceptance of the ultimatum. Bourqueney in desperation wired Walewski that if he carried out his instructions, Austria would abandon the Allies out of an excess of humiliations. Seymour, though explaining Austria's refusal as due to her cowardice, insisted again that Britain should not commit what Austria considered a breach of contract and that Buol was right in considering her morally bound to sign.[7]

Few Englishmen, except for eccentrics such as Aberdeen, considered the argument of moral obligation to Austria worth serious attention, since she had not spent a shilling or shed a drop of blood in the war. Seymour's pleas only further convinced Palmerston that Vienna's atmosphere had corrupted yet another honest Englishman. Clarendon was worried about a possible adverse public reaction to Cowley's scheme, but not about any breach of faith with Austria: "Austria may think us morally bound to sign preliminaries," he told Seymour, "and I am the last man ever to *think* even of eluding a moral obligation; but the nature of the preliminaries must rest with us, and Austria I suppose will not require us to sign conditions of peace which we think insufficient, after all the sacrifices we have made." He revived all his old arguments and added a new one: had not Colloredo himself asked Britain on January 1 whether she agreed to the Buol-Bourqueney memorandum, thus proving that it was entirely distinct from the Austrian ultimatum to which Britain had agreed? * Besides, Britain had only pledged herself, as a favor to Austria, not to go below certain minimum terms; it was absurd to say she could not demand more. And Russia's deceit, as evidenced by her accepting the ultimatum in a dishonest spirit, compelled Britain to protect herself by getting her extra demands accepted now.[8]

Plainly Austria had no way to reason or coerce Britain out of Cowley's plan. But Palmerston helped Buol out by rejecting it because it involved conceding something to Russia in exchange for Britain's additional demands. The Allied equivalent for Kars was not Bessarabia, he told Clarendon, but the evacuation of the Crimea and Britain's foregoing great victories in next year's campaign, like the conquest of Georgia and Kronstadt. Besides, the Russians had not really captured Kars; "it fell into their hands merely by the accident of the garrison not having enough to eat." Thus corrected, Clarendon instructed Seymour not to ask Buol to surrender the Bessarabian cession.[9] Yet Britain still would not sign the preliminaries. Buol, supported by Seymour, tried more persuasion, including promises of support for Britain at the peace table and hints that Austria would

* Thus Buol's final formal precaution taken to make sure that Britain did not try to deny the bargain she had made (a bargain that Clarendon implicitly acknowledged on January 1) was used by Clarendon as proof that no bargain had ever existed. As Buol once remarked, analyzing such arguments as these can only lead one to slander.

trade part of Bessarabia for Britain's demands on the Aland Isles.[10] The response was more denunciation of Austrian treachery and arrogance, further rebukes to Seymour,[11] and a vigorous use of other issues to belabor Austria—the Türr case, Serbia, and the Principalities.[12]

Britain had no such weapons to use against France, however, and Walewski absolutely refused to give Russia a second ultimatum with the extra conditions, now shrunk to the cession or neutralization of the Aland Isles and a consideration of the Black Sea coast. However much Palmerston insisted that "France must give way because we are in the right," continuing the war alone, as Albert said, would be military and political madness.[13] Clarendon, believing it no longer possible to get the extra demands into the preliminaries, suggested on January 21 that Britain would not insist on having them officially conveyed to Russia in advance and accepted by her if France would secretly agree to make them *sine quibus non* at the peace table.[14] Walewski agreed only to let them be communicated unofficially to Russia through Seebach, but refused to make them binding on France; the Black Sea coast demand, he said, was too vague for any possible agreement. Though Walewski went along with Britain on requiring the unconditional evacuation of Kars, he really still hoped to arrange a Kars-Bessarabia exchange.[15]

Even after this agreement, London came up with various devices to escape signing preliminaries without the additional demands. Clarendon proposed inserting the extra conditions into the protocol to be signed at Vienna attesting Russia's acceptance of Austria's terms.* He also suggested that having the preliminaries signed at Paris might facilitate introducing the extra conditions [16] or that preliminaries might be avoided altogether. Palmerston thought it might be possible to *negotiate* the preliminaries at Paris. Cowley hoped against hope that Austria might decide to drop out, declaring her whole "interference" *non avenu*.[17] But all expedients proved fruitless; on January 29, Britain agreed to the protocol that was then signed at Vienna on February 1. Clarendon was gloomy over it, Cowley mortified, Buol immensely relieved and pathetically opti-

---

* He even seriously proposed asking Buol to secure Russia's agreement to this, as a compliment to him for having made Russia accept the main terms earlier.

mistic that the Allies were now on the right path to peace and unity.[18]

Meanwhile the Constantinople Conference had been working on Points One and Four. On Point Four, Redcliffe, Thouvenel, and Prokesch all wanted the Christians in Turkey to enjoy equal property rights, freedom from harassment on account of religion, equal legal status and career opportunities, and similar guarantees. They agreed that much European pressure would be required to extract these from the Porte. Their only serious disagreement arose over the issue on which Clarendon and Walewski had been contending for months: complete freedom for Muslims in Turkey to convert to Christianity. Thouvenel and Prokesch, arguing that few if any European powers would yield to such a demand and that it would undermine the Sultan's religiously based authority, succeeded in watering down Redcliffe's demands to tolerable levels.[19] The twenty-one-point program they completed by the end of January was approved by the Turkish Grand Council and proclaimed as the Hatti-Humayun of Abdul Medjid on February 18.[20] *

Point One involved much greater difficulties, for here each power had a different basic goal and program. Buol and Prokesch, concerned mainly about political dangers for Austria in a liberal or nationalist political settlement for the Principalities, proposed retaining the Règlement Organique, strengthening the hospodars' powers, curbing the boyars' privileges, and carrying out tax and land reforms against boyars and wealthy monasteries to help create a free landed peasantry—a program highly conservative politically, but progressive socially and economically.[21] † France still wanted to unite the Principalities under a foreign prince, as Thouvenel frankly told Prokesch from the outset. But he did not seem adamant on this point, and on other points Austria and France were not far

---

* Buol preferred to delay the public promulgation of the decree, to avoid flaunting Russia's exclusion to the world before the peace congress met, but the sea powers insisted on it and Prokesch supported them. At the same time, Buol's pleas and hopes for a European guarantee of the decree were defeated by Britain. Clarendon recognized that without such a guarantee and supervision the decree would not be executed, but feared it might give Russia a chance for interference (Clarendon to Redcliffe, 15 Feb. 1856, FO 352/44/1).

† As late as 1858, Rumanian nationalists still feared that this program might frustrate unification by distracting the people with social reform (Bodea, 350–52).

apart. The French were at best lukewarm about representative government, and a French memorandum of January 7 advocated Austria's agrarian reforms in Hungary as the model to follow in the Principalities.[22]

Britain's program was purely political in emphasis. It called for a constitution to be decreed by the Sultan, judicial reform, and parliamentary control over taxes and revenues, but said nothing about land reform, the monasteries, the peasant question, or boyar privileges. Even the reforms Britain advocated were to depend entirely on Turkey's initiative, though Clarendon admitted (in opposition to Palmerston) that Turkish administration was as bad as ever and that a decree issued in Constantinople meant little in the provinces.[23] In practice as well as theory British influence was exerted on the side of property and privilege. Colquhoun joined the so-called liberal boyars in trying to get a tax on foreign-controlled monastic lands, which Ştirbei levied and the Wallachian Divan approved, revoked by the Sultan. As Clarendon argued in supporting Colquhoun, this would make the Greek clergy, which drew large revenues from its holdings in the Principalities, look to the West instead of Russia for protection. When Ştirbei emancipated gypsy slaves, Colquhoun attacked him for depriving boyars of their rights. Colquhoun's proposed constitution for the "Grand Duchy of Moldavia and Wallachia" ignored the peasants and would have elevated the boyars into a hereditary aristocracy.[24]

At the conferences themselves, Prokesch proved even more conciliatory than his instructions. Ignoring Coronini's advice on how to advance Austrian interests, he concentrated on cooperating with Thouvenel and strengthening the authority and influence of the Sultan. He failed even to raise the idea of Austrian garrisons along with Turkish ones and agreed to Turkey's replacing the hospodars with provisional caimacams when their terms expired. The one redeeming feature of Prokesch's stance was his concern for social reform; in Thouvenel's words, he "sustained, with a kind of passion, all the reforms that would operate to the benefit of the masses." [25] While Thouvenel worked to promote the union and virtual independence of the Principalities, he cooperated with Prokesch in defeating Redcliffe's attempt to introduce a representative system and in resisting Clarendon's persistent efforts to deprive the peace congress of any voice on the Principalities' future by having the Sultan decree a permanent settlement now.[26] Thus the final decision was left to the peace congress; the program agreed upon at Constantinople on February 11 was only preparatory and advisory.

Nonetheless, it quickly ran into strong opposition. First Werner, acting for Buol who had left for Paris, warned Prokesch against reducing the Principalities' privileges in favor of the Turks and undercutting Grünne's and Coronini's plans for a native militia.[27] Then followed fierce general attacks on the program by Coronini, Ghica, and Ştirbei; and Francis Joseph, much displeased with Prokesch, ordered the whole matter referred to Paris, to which Buol quickly agreed. Since the other powers had reasons of their own to want the Principalities issue raised de novo at Paris, the February 11 program, despite Prokesch's vigorous defense of it, largely went by the boards.[28]

Another question preliminary to the congress also caused Buol embarrassment, this time by his own fault—whether Prussia should be admitted. He wanted to fulfill his promise to get her in, even though he tried to deny that she had really earned it. Francis Joseph insisted on trying for an invitation to Prussia, and Buol, though sure she would oppose Austria, thought she could make even more trouble outside.[29] At the same time, Buol quite indefensibly demanded a second price for Prussia's admission, her support for a Federal resolution endorsing the terms of Austria's ultimatum as the preliminaries of peace. The issue was purely one of prestige, since after February 1 the preliminaries question was settled, but the usual dreary controversy ensued, with Bismarck leading the fight against Austria's proposal at Frankfurt, Buol demanding its acceptance, and Manteuffel grumbling that getting into the congress was not worth the price.[30] Beust's attempts to mediate were again rebuffed by Buol,[31] and finally Frederick William commanded Bismarck to accept the compromise resolution of February 21.[32]

Now Buol could not deliver the invitation to the congress twice promised and paid for. The King was certainly justified in blaming Buol for his mortification, but the actual obstacle was Britain, and more specifically Clarendon. Palmerston was at first grudgingly willing to let Prussia in if she would accept the same obligations as Austria had, but Clarendon persuaded him that her presence would be an unmixed evil. Besides, as Cowley noted, excluding Prussia would elevate British prestige and punish the King as he deserved. As far as the peace settlement was concerned, Cowley told the French that it made no difference whether Prussia agreed to it or not.[33] France, less cavalier about dispensing with the support of a great power for the peace treaty, would have admitted Prussia, but declined Hübner's pleas to make an issue of it at London; she knew Prussia would blame Austria for her exclusion anyway. Britain did recognize the utility of having Prussia, a signatory of the 1841 Straits Convention, confirm those provisions revising it. But as Palmerston told Azeglio, his idea was to bring Prussia in, tell her to sign what was already prepared, and show her the door.[34]

Buol faced further trouble at home over Austrian aims at the Congress. In a *Vortrag* to the Emperor on January 22, Hess sharply criticized Buol's proposed Bessarabian cession as too large and of little military value. He proposed three possible revisions, recommending as the best from the military standpoint a middle line drawing the new frontier roughly diagonally southeast to northwest, from Lake Salsyk to the Shantimir Heights on the Prut. This would return Russia about 207 German square miles of Buol's original cession of 492 square miles (about 10,000 English sq. mi.) But as always, Hess was most concerned to incorporate Moldavia into Austria's defensive system, by fortresses along the lower Danube and Prut manned by Austrian and native troops and connecting to Galician and Transylvanian fortifications. And like Coronini, he still wanted to increase Austria's political influence in the Principalities through the occupation.[35]

Buol did not object to compromising on Bessarabia, but he well knew how hopeless and dangerous it would be to try for these other ideas at Paris. The Emperor, however, ordered Buol, in marginal notes on Buol's draft of his and Hübner's instructions for the congress, to work for Hess's preferred boundary line and for Austrian garrison rights in Moldavia instead of the original cession. Buol, pointing to the danger that Britain would promote Turkish garrisons for all the Danube fortresses, suggested guarding against this by making Moldavia's defense a joint European concern; under this system, and on the basis of the need for patrolling the lower Danube, Austria could try "if possible" to get a garrison right at one point on the Danube. The Emperor found Buol's advice too meager and timid, insisting on trying for an Austrian occupation of Ismaila at the least, and for the free passage of Austrian warships along the whole lower Danube. He also objected to Buol's suggestion of neutralizing the Danube delta and insisted on excluding all but riparian states from the commission to deal with navigation on the Danube *per se* (as opposed to the Sulina mouth). He finally warned Buol sharply against permitting liberal democratic reforms in the Principalities, or letting revolutionary émigrés find refuge there, or giving away Austria's rights to protect Christians in Turkey, or expanding Turkish privileges in Serbia and Montenegro.[36] Obviously the Emperor was much less willing than Buol to trust joint European arrangements to protect Austrian interests.

On February 11, a ministerial conference confirmed Buol's and Hübner's instructions as revised by the Emperor. Francis Joseph also refused to allow Buol to take up the questions of Serbia, Montenegro, or Klek and Sutorina at the congress. But the Emperor did consider undue concessions to Russia dangerous [37] and did not back Bruck's and Hess's ambitious proposals to use the congress to try to open up the whole Near East to Austrian trade and economic penetration. Buol passed silently over these ideas, never having intended to raise them at Paris, and tried to trim down or recast orders for which he had no enthusiasm or hope of success. Accepting Hess's middle line for the Bessarabian cession, he said he would try for a garrison right at one strong point somewhere on the lower Danube, but he warned that it would be very difficult to obtain and that he saw no chance of excluding nonriparian states from the Danube commission.[38]

Buol's pessimism about Austria's chances of promoting particular Austrian interests at Paris would have been even deeper had he known fully what the other powers were planning. Even Nesselrode, about to retire, urged exploiting Austria's isolation and threatening her at the peace table. The Russian plenipotentiaries Orlov and Brunnow were instructed to woo Napoleon and even to pretend to meet the demands of Britain, Russia's worst enemy, in order to force Austria to give up the Bessarabian cession demand. Thereafter Austria could be compelled to join France and Russia against Britain and her extortions. While Nesselrode wanted Russia's anti-Austrian stance to be temporary (still believing that Russia's permanent interests called for the Holy Alliance), Alexander, Gorchakov, and other Russians thirsted above all for revenge on Austria.[39] The French knew this; the Russian vendetta fit their plans perfectly.

The British government continued to argue before outsiders for more war, contending strenuously for another campaign at a joint Council of War at Paris January 10–21;[40] the British public still gave vent to bellicose patriotism.[41] But by early February even Clarendon, Palmerston, and Redcliffe had resigned themselves to peace, though regretting the damage it would do to Britain's prestige and Europe's future.[42] Palmerston's argument now was that Britain must be ready to break up the congress if necessary in order to obtain her full demands. Like all bullies, Russia would back down before enough firmness.[43]

But Clarendon and Albert, knowing this was bluff, considered that everything depended on whether Britain could control Napoleon, and viewed Austria mainly as an instrument to this end (though Clarendon also thought she might be useful for obtaining concessions from Russia, like the cession of the Aland Isles). Encouraged by Seymour to exploit Buol's pro-Western sentiments, Clarendon repeatedly assured Austria that he wanted close cooperation with her during and after the congress. He warned Buol of France's impending betrayal on the Bessarabian issue and promised him loyal British support. At the same time he told Redcliffe that he wished he could arrange a private deal with Russia exchanging most of Bessarabia for territory in Asia, and he urged the French to form a united front with Britain against Russia and Austria, common enemies of the West. As he remarked to Redcliffe in a moment of comparative optimism, "If France and England are really united and that [sic] we play Austria and Russia off against each other I don't *at present* see any reason why we should not obtain as good a peace as circumstances admit of." [44]

The preliminary informal talks at Paris beginning in mid-February quickly made Austria's hapless position clear. The very subjects Napoleon broached with Buol were ominous—he rebuked Austria for staying out of the war, proposed uniting the Principalities, raised the Bessarabian question, and mentioned those of Poland and Italy. Walewski, outwardly friendly, was noncommittal on all issues, while the Russians paraded their hostility and Clarendon flatly rejected Buol's pleas to admit Prussia to the Congress.[45] What went on privately without Buol's knowledge was worse still. Walewski promised the Russians that he would support a Kars-Bessarabia exchange and try otherwise to win Russia concessions, short of breaking with England. He promply tried to persuade Clarendon that Russia would yield on everything else if spared Austria's humiliating demand on Bessarabia. Clarendon resisted, but only in order to get Britain's territorial demand (tentatively, an independent Circassia with Russia's territory stopping at the Kuban River) into the hopper. Walewski's hints that Russia would rather cede territory to the Allies than to Austria clearly intrigued him.[46]

The congress officially opened smoothly enough; no particular trouble arose on February 25, 28, or March 1 over the signing of preliminaries, the declaration of an armistice to last till March 31 (Britain rejected any longer one),[47] and a general review of the main problems before the plenipotentiaries. But a crisis loomed behind the scenes with Russia's refusal to yield Kars without compensation; she tried everywhere to gain Bessarabia in exchange, except by coming to Austria.[48] Buol was empowered to promote a compromise, but as he told Cowley, he would do so only after agreement with the West, not under Russian pressure.[49] Clarendon and Cowley instead urged Buol to stand firm, and in a private meeting on February 27, Walewski even joined the British in insisting on the original cession—adding that if a rupture occurred over it, the sea powers would of course expect active help in the renewed war. Walewski, of course, was simply trying Cowley's old ideas of getting rid of the Bessarabian cession by frightening Austria into backing out of it. The British reasons for urging Austria to stand firm were more complicated—in part the opposition of the British public to any concessions to Russia, in part the belief that this might be a good issue on which to explode the congress and force Austria to break with Russia, but mainly Palmerston's stubborn resistance to concessions. He did not even want to force Austria to fight for Bessarabia, as the Queen did; the sea powers had started the war without her and should finish it that way. Only on March 1 and 2 did he begin yielding to Clarendon's pleas and Victoria's urgings for a compromise, at first telling Clarendon he would exchange most of Bessarabia for the whole Caucasus south of the Kuban, and then empowering him to work out with France (excluding Austria, naturally) any exchange beneficial to Turkey.[50]

Buol, caught between Russia's apparent intransigence and the snares of the sea powers, asked Francis Joseph on February 28 to sanction what he proposed to do. He had flatly refused to participate in the war, he reported, nor did he wish to threaten Russia again with a break in relations. The threat would probably work, but moderation was now called for. He would therefore propose a compromise boundary line, but if Russia rejected even the best concession Buol was empowered to offer, he felt Austria should act according to the November 14 agreement, i.e., break with Russia, rather than yield further. If Austria simply refused to tell the sea powers what she would do in case the negotiations broke down, they would sacrifice her interests to get peace on their terms, and should the war be resumed while Austria stood by and watched, the alliance would be destroyed and Austria left totally isolated. The declaration he proposed would not actually increase Austria's obligations and could gain her once more the honor of saving Europe from further war. It might even help her defend her special interests and "at least be able to mention the wish for a right of occupation on one point of the Danube, on which your Majesty places so much emphasis." [51] *

While Buol awaited the Emperor's reply, the Allies made the expected inquiry through Julian Fane, secretary of the British Embassy at Vienna, now assisting Clarendon. To Buol's promises that Austria would stand firm with the Allies on Bessarabia, Fane replied that this was splendid—but was it Austria's *final* resolution? Britain would welcome a rupture and resumption of the war. Buol immediately replied that if a breakdown of negotiations seemed imminent, he was authorized to propose changes, only the Allies must not leak this information to Russia or concede anything at the end of a session. If Russia remained unyielding through the next session, the Allies should then confer and decide what to offer next.[52] Francis Joseph's reply, though ordering Buol to hold out at least for Hess's preferred boundary line, authorized him as re-

---

* Another indication of how little zeal Buol had for the Emperor's demand, or hope of achieving it.

quested to break relations if Russia refused all reasonable com-
promises.[53] On March 1, however, Orlov, to Buol's and Clarendon's
surprise, conceded in principle the evacuation of Kars and other
territory Russia had conquered without an equivalent. Orlov probably acted on Nesselrode's reiterated advice not to cause a breakup
of the conference and also counted on Napoleon's promise to support Russia when the new Bessarabian frontier was actually traced.[54]

With the Bessarabian issue momentarily defused, conflict arose
over British demands for cessions east of the Black Sea. Clarendon
found himself entirely without support; even the Turks wanted
only the kind of border rectifications Russia was willing to consider.
Clarendon warned Palmerston on March 2 and 3 that the congress
and the Anglo-French alliance were in jeopardy; he had never seen
Napoleon so aroused.[55] Though Redcliffe still urged rolling back
Russia in Asia, Clarendon gave up on March 4, agreeing to a mixed
commission of Russian, Turkish, British, and French representatives
to trace a rectified Asian frontier. Britain's hope to neutralize
Nicolaev and the Sea of Azov also went by the boards, Clarendon
contenting himself with Russia's promise not to construct warships
at Nicolaev.

Buol was delighted at how easily provisional agreement was
reached on the Third Point. Unfortunately, Britain's frustration
found an outlet against Austria in the March 6 session. Buol had
avoided seeking membership for Austria on the Asian frontier
commission, hoping likewise to restrict the Danube navigation commission to the powers directly interested. Walewski and Clarendon
now proposed just what Buol wanted to avoid. According to their
ideas, the original commission on which all the powers would sit,
established to determine the extent and nature of work necessary to
clear the Danube mouth and to lay down bases for the navigation
and policing of the river, would remain in existence indefinitely.
That is, it could be dissolved only by mutual consent, and Britain,
as Clarendon remarked, would never let it be dissolved. Furthermore, the sea powers insisted on giving Bavaria a seat on the permanent commission to carry out the new regulations, and Turkey
vetoed any membership for the Principalities. This meant in effect
that both commissions would be dominated by Austria's opponents
and that international regulation would be extended to the whole

stream, not just its extreme lower course. Buol's counterarguments got nowhere.[56]

The bitterest argument on March 6, however, arose again over Bessarabia. Walewski as usual said nothing in the session itself, while privately pressing hard for sweeping concessions to Russia. Clarendon, still smarting from his previous defeats on Points Three and Five, held out stubbornly; the fact that Turkey was really concerned about Bessarabia far more than about Asia or the Black Sea may have affected his attitude. But by March 8, Clarendon and Cowley decided to yield to save the French alliance, and Palmerston accepted their decision readily enough. Still, it fell to Buol actually to bring about an agreement in the session of March 8. After Russia made two boundary proposals so favorable to herself that even Walewski rejected them, Buol proposed the line advocated in his instructions and the sea powers supported it.[57] Orlov and Brunnow, taken by surprise, reserved judgment until the next session on March 10. There they produced a proposal not too much different from Austria's, and a compromise between the two was agreed upon, with the final tracing to be left to a mixed boundary commission.

This made the final success of the congress certain enough that Prussia could now be invited to join it and ratify the decisions taken.[58] Walewski and Clarendon each credited himself for the achievement, while the Russians praised Napoleon for overcoming Britain's extortions and Austria's selfishness. In fact, Austria's presence and timely mediation had proved indispensable in breaking the logjam. What is more, Buol and Hübner both knew that in so doing they were weakening Austria's already perilous position. They warned Francis Joseph that as long as the possibility of a failure of negotiations and the resumption of war existed, Austria had some leverage with both sides; now that peace was virtually assured, her last weapon was gone and her difficulties would be greater than ever.[59]

The warning was appropriate, for in the March 8 session the Principalities issue was raised in the most ominous way possible for Austria, bringing to the surface in a preliminary way the Italian question as well (though the Italian question as a whole belongs to a later phase of the Congress). In late 1855 the French Foreign

Ministry, discarding its previous thoughts about using an Austrian archduke or a Swedish prince to rule over the united Principalities, adopted Sardinia's suggestion to make the Archduke of Modena their ruler. Then Modena could be given to the Duchess of Parma and Parma be ceded to Sardinia. Cowley objected strongly to uniting the Principalities, urging Palmerston's proposal of separate constitutions decreed by the Sultan instead.* But Napoleon clung to his idea, not merely because Cavour and the Rumanian émigrés at Paris strongly pushed it and because he wanted to do something for nationalism in the Principalities, but especially because uniting them would give him a personal triumph over the Vienna system.[60]

Britain's reaction was ambivalent; Clarendon understated the case when he confessed to Palmerston on March 5 that he still did not see clearly on the Principalities. It would be pleasant and popular for Britain to reward Sardinia with some territory in Italy, but the exchange proposal would hurt Turkey, undermine Britain's plans for the Principalities, and unduly promote French influence. Clarendon still felt a nagging fear that France might join Austria in supporting an oppressive regime on the lower Danube. When Cavour tried to overcome British objections to union by proposing that the rulers of Modena and Parma should rule over the two separate Principalities, with both Modena and Parma going to Piedmont, Clarendon said this would be good for Sardinia but indifferent for the Principalities and bad for the Turks.[61] Palmerston was personally less averse to the exchange plan, but saw grave practical difficulties in it. If Austria retained reversionary rights to Modena and Parma, as he supposed she did, the exchange might give her a claim to the Principalities. Besides, the Sultan would object to it and demand compensation, and Russia and Austria would both oppose it, especially since an independent Rumanian state would certainly try to aggrandize itself later at Austria's expense. Palmerston suggested an easier way to enlarge Sardinia; give the Papal Legations to Austria, wholly or in part, and cede Lombardy to Piedmont. But the next day, March 9, Palmerston withdrew his objections. Azeglio and Cavour were skillfully exploiting Sardinia's

---

* Cowley also urged giving Moldavia all of Bessarabia and stationing Turkish troops on the Dniester—an interesting proposal in view of Cowley's later insistence that the Bessarabian cession was purely a selfish Austrian demand.

popularity in Britain and the British fear of falling behind France in influence at Turin.[62]

Thus both the union of the Principalities and territorial and political revisions in Italy were being considered and promoted by the sea powers without a nod in Austria's direction. All Buol's efforts to prove the dangers of unification to Austria and the legitimate interest she had to take in the fate of the Principalities were fruitless.[63] Moreover, this was an issue where Francis Joseph was really concerned and unhappy. He criticized Prokesch sharply for not fighting hard enough at Constantinople against British and Turkish schemes for increasing Turkish influence on the lower Danube, and he insisted on keeping Russia far enough away from it. The Bessarabian cession, he said, must at least include all of Lake Salsyk. When Buol wrote that he could find no suitable occasion to ask for an Austrian garrison on the Danube,* the Emperor replied that at least the Turks must not get any new rights. Above all, a union of the Principalities would be intolerable.[64]

Though Buol received some warning of France's plan on March 6 when Bourqueney and Napoleon tried to win him over to the idea of an independent kingdom with the Archduke of Modena as its ruler, Buol was nevertheless surprised when Walewski publicly proposed unification on March 8. Clarendon supported it on the ground that the inhabitants wanted it, Russia and Sardinia joined in, and Austria and Turkey were alone in opposition. Heatedly defending the scheme, Walewski even hinted that a majority vote in the congress would decide the issue. Buol and Ali could only gain a delay by pleading absence of instructions. In his pessimistic report of March 9, Buol began mapping a retreat before he had really begun to fight. Austria, he advised, should first wait for the Porte's reaction and argue that the right of initiative belonged to the Sultan, while Prokesch should try to bolster his resistance. But if Turkey proved a broken reed, it would be impossible, Buol argued, for Austria to hold out alone simply on the basis of her interests. The question would then become one "of nullifying as much as possible the dangerous character of this union"—that is, trying to make uni-

---

* Buol actually took up the subject a time or two in private conversations with Napoleon, who gave him some noncommittal encouragement. But Britain's opposition was so strong that Buol never tried to put through a formal proposal.

fication the last rather than first stage in reorganizing the Principalities and to eliminate the elements of popular sovereignty and
nationalism in it. Austria should try to maintain the conservative
senates and Turkey's suzerainty and to install a native prince at
Bucharest or, if this proved impossible, an Austrian archduke. But
Austria must not concede territorial changes in Italy for this purpose.[65]

Francis Joseph ordered Buol to fight against unification; he could
not believe, he said, that Napoleon could fail to see how a Daco-
Roman kingdom would play directly into Russia's hands.[66] Buol
succeeded on March 10 with Clarendon's help in blocking Walewski's attempt to conclude the peace settlement without establishing
any basis at all for reorganizing the Principalities, so as to open the
door to unification. Britain's support for union was obviously lukewarm at best. A committee consisting of Buol, Bourqueney, and
Ali was named to draft articles for the peace treaty on the Principalities. The committee recommended on March 12 that a European
commission sitting at Bucharest work out reforms for the Principalities in cooperation with a Turkish commissioner and the Porte,
with the wishes of the inhabitants to be ascertained through the
election of a divan ad hoc from each province. The committee
proposal was accepted in principle, and unification thus excluded
from the peace treaty. But Buol had gained only a reprieve; he
could get no assurances from Napoleon that the issue would not
be raised later. Buol's policy since early 1854 of trying to solve the
Eastern question in general and the Principalities issue in particular
by cooperation with France had finally reached a dead end. With
France the partner of Rumanian nationalism, Austria turned to the
Turks and to a passive, stubborn obstruction of the union she
dreaded.[67]

Most of the remaining issues to be included in the general peace
concerned Austria only indirectly. The one major exception, the
rules and commissions on navigation and control of the Danube,
came up again on March 12. As Buol had foreseen, Austria's attempt to keep the upper Danube free from international control,
thereby saving the shipping monopoly of the Danube Steamship
Company, made no headway. The next day Buol and Hübner
pleaded for authorization to change their position, telling the Em-

peror that Austria's present stand could not be sold to the congress and was untenable in principle and logic as well. A compromise, Buol suggested, would meet all legitimate objections and still protect Austria's most essential interests: to extend to the whole Danube the principles of freedom of navigation the Congress of Vienna had laid down, but to leave the policing and execution of these principles to the riverain powers, as that congress had also done. In addition, the riverain commission would only begin its work when the original commission to plan the work necessary for clearing the Danube mouth had completed its task and been dissolved, and the riverain states would be allowed time for the transition to free navigation. Francis Joseph approved the proposal, and despite some British objections * it was adopted in essence by the congress on March 27.[68]

In the other disputes, none of great moment, Buol preferred to stay in the background, using behind the scenes what little credit and influence Austria retained. The British delegates, disgruntled at their failures (even their demand for razing of the fortresses east of the Black Sea had to be abandoned), proved more Turkish than the Turks on the number and size of light vessels and unarmed transports to be allowed the riverain powers in the Black Sea. Again left without support by Turkey, France, or Sardinia, Britain had to back down.[69] The entrance of Otto Manteuffel and Hatzfeldt as Prussian envoys on March 18 gave Clarendon another occasion to vent his bile against Frederick William and to make sure that Prussia signed only as little as possible of what had already been decided. Otherwise Prussia's entry merely added to the ranks of those wooing Napoleon and snubbing Austria.[70]

During the last half of March, despite the fact that the main quarrels were settled, there was still much hard negotiating, often over the mere wording of treaty provisions. Sharp disputes broke out, especially between Clarendon and Walewski. Buol played a minor but useful role as conciliator, repeatedly urging the Allies to keep their differences out of the general sessions. He even went to

---

* Britain wanted the proposal rewritten to ensure absolutely free trade; Cowley even proposed warning Buol that Turkey would close the lower Danube to Austria unless the upper Danube was opened (to Clarendon, 12 March 1856, Clar. dep. c. 51).

Napoleon to warn against pushing Britain too far by constantly sponsoring minor concessions to Russia.[71] Clarendon told Palmerston, "Buol has behaved throughout like an *honest gentleman* and from him Cowley and I have always received consistent support." He praised Buol's loyalty similarly to Greville, also at Paris, and claimed that Britain's gains in influence at Constantinople and Vienna far outweighed her failure to extort more concessions from Russia. The thanks Austria gained for her help were the usual British variety. While the general peace treaty was being readied for signature, Clarendon suggested to Cowley that they arrange with France to have only the belligerents (including Sardinia, of course) sign it, calling in Austria afterward to confirm it like Prussia as a signatory of the 1841 Convention.[72]

This idea was perhaps too raw even for Clarendon to pursue; Austria signed the general treaty along with the other powers on March 30. Attached to the main treaty were separate conventions reaffirming the closure of the Straits, regulating the riverain powers' light vessels in the Black Sea, and providing for the nonfortification of the Aland Isles. Just before the signature, however, Clarendon launched an effort to force Austria immediately out of the Principalities, trying, typically, to get France to propose it first. Palmerston strongly supported Clarendon in this idea, proposing also to extend to Serbia a treaty provision barring unilateral intervention in the Principalities except by unanimous great-power consent. This would exclude Austrian and Russian influence from Serbia as well. On March 28, with no warning to Austria, Walewski and Clarendon called in open session for an immediate Austrian evacuation, while insisting on allowing the West six months to evacuate the Crimea and Turkey. The Principalities could not be reorganized, they argued, so long as Austrian troops kept the divans ad hoc from being freely chosen and representing the inhabitants' wishes. Hübner remarked that Allied troops (and their fleets, he might have added) had been influencing the Divan at Constantinople for over two years. Buol pointed out that Austria's rights and obligations in her occupation were regulated just as those of the Allies were, by a convention with Turkey, whereupon Walewski let the matter drop. But the first shot in the Allied campaign to oust Austria had been fired.[73]

The proclamation of the peace treaty brought rejoicing in France, the only power fully satisfied with the settlement. Russia had no cause for joy in the terms, but took satisfaction in her rapprochement with France and Austria's isolation and discomfiture. Sardinia had gained nothing yet, but still hoped for her day for tangible rewards woud come when the congress turned to general European questions.

Cowley was bitterly disappointed, claiming that France had repeatedly played Britain false and even showing some discontent over Clarendon's handling of the negotiations.[74] Redcliffe, as one could expect, was also dissatisfied. But even Palmerston and Victoria were by this time contented on the whole and less fearful of an adverse public reaction. The public in fact greeted the peace calmly or joyfully and tended to blame Austria for any shortcomings in it.[75] As for Clarendon, he was satisfied with his work and prided himself on the magnanimous spirit Britain had shown in consenting to make peace: "If we had continued the war single-handed," he told Victoria on March 30, "France would feel that she had behaved shabbily to us, and would *therefore* have hated us all the more, and become our enemy sooner than under any other circumstances." Besides, there were other popular concerns to turn to now: "If," he wrote Palmerston March 31, "we can now do anything for Italy and for Greece and for Bomba's victims and place an opinion on record about Poland and the expediency of recurring to arbitration before the ultima ratio of war is resorted to we shall satisfy public opinion in England I hope." [76] Greville, aware that this activity was mainly designed to distract public attention from the disappointing results of the war, commented in his customary trenchant way: "The war was founded in delusion and error, and carried on by a factitious and ignorant enthusiasm, and we richly deserve to reap nothing but mortification and disappointment in return for all the blood and treasure we have spent." [77]

As for Austria, Buol knew his role at Paris had been inglorious and that the peace fell short even of his expectations, to say nothing of the Emperor's. He could hardly be surprised that there was little enthusiasm over it at Vienna. Yet he still hoped that what it did for Europe in providing an opportunity for recovery and for Austria in removing the burden of Russian hegemony made it worthwhile.[78] He could not know entirely what Clarendon, Napoleon, and Cavour had in mind for the rest of the congress, but he should have guessed that the worst was yet to come.

XV

The Aftermath:
The Bitter Fruits
of Peace

Prior to March 30 there was little at Paris that was not humiliating for Austria; after it, still less. Buol wanted to leave Paris quickly—indeed, Francis Joseph ordered him to close off the talks as fast as possible.[1] Buol wanted only to conclude the triple alliance in favor of Turkey promised in the Buol-Bourqueney memorandum. But the sea powers had other ideas, none more dangerous to Austria than those on Italy.

Though the Italian question at the Congress and after has been exhaustively treated, no one, even in the most recent scholarship, has seen it from Austria's standpoint or taken her policy seriously. Buol's aim from at least late 1853 onward was to secure Austria's position in Italy by cooperating with the sea powers, especially France, and by conciliating Sardinia. Many military men and some civilians in Austria opposed this policy, of course, and Francis Joseph was not wholly sold on it; yet the evidence that Austria actually maintained a defensive, basically conciliatory stance in Italy is clear. To say this is not to credit Buol or Austria with noble intentions; her vulnerability and her general pro-Western orientation and policy required it of her. It does mean, however, that the threats and offensive measures she is so often supposed to have made were at most the fruitless lunges of the bull at the picadors—responses to the goading of Cavour and the prodding of the sea powers.

Cavour's hopes of driving Austria out of Italy and making territorial gains for Sardinia had been revived by the failure of the Vienna Conference in May 1855, though the war of the West against Austria he desired still failed to eventuate. He quickly took advantage of Western disgust with Austria to demand Sardinia's admission to the final peace congress and obtained it at least for those questions concerning Sardinia.[2] But then the fall of Sevastopol again brought the threat of peace before Sardinia's concrete aims were achieved. Cavour worked feverishly to get Napoleon and the British to agree to include changes in Italy in the peace terms, or at least to force them through at the congress. Napoleon was encouraging but non-committal. Though Hudson assured Cavour that the Emperor only wanted a tie with Austria for the moment so as to use her for purposes of peace now and later to have a pretext to break with her, the Buol-Bourqueney agreement, of which Cavour learned only about ten days after its signature, brought him near despair.[3] While Victor Emmanuel talked rashly of continuing the war with Britain, Cavour, recognizing the probability of peace, set out to procure for Sardinia what was still possible.

His visit to France and Britain with his king in November and December proved useful, especially in Britain, where their reception by the press and the public was enthusiastic.[4] The King was given the Order of the Garter,* and Cavour was able to build up the existing pro-Sardinian and anti-Austrian feeling in Britain. They could not gain any concrete pledges except for Clarendon's promise to defend Sardinia against an Austrian attack, which would only help if Cavour could somehow provoke one. But Napoleon gave Cavour a useful opening by asking him to suggest how the sea powers could help Italy at the congress. Persigny, Prince Napoleon, and Palmerston were strongly pro-Italian; so was Clarendon, with reservations,† and even the Queen, reluctant to despoil Austria and far from enamoured of Victor Emmanuel, came round to supporting the Sar-

---

* Aberdeen remarked of the conferring of the Garter on Victor Emmanuel, "I never could see the sublime effort of virtue in attacking a Sovereign [Nicholas] from whom he [Victor Emmanuel] had received no injury, and with whom he had no cause of quarrel. His disinterested regard for the rights of others, and for the balance of power in Europe, will be best appreciated by those who are best acquainted with the policy of his House" (To Gladstone, 28 Nov. 1855, Add. ms. 44089).

† Marcelli (Cavour, 168 et passim) and to some extent Nolfo (Europa, 231–33, 240) portray Clarendon as pro-Austrian and cold toward Sardinia before and during the Congress. Clarendon sometimes became annoyed at Sardinian claims and the trouble they could cause him, but he shared fully the Whig view of Cavour and Sardinia as models for Italy and the Continent and was in no way sympathetic to Austria.

dinian cause. Only Walewski and to some extent Cowley were unenthusiastic.[5]

Ardently seconded by Hudson, Cavour waged a skillful propaganda campaign, arguing constantly that Austria, having gained enormously on the Danube, would emerge dominant in Europe and a menace to the balance of power unless her usurped and illegal hold on Italy were destroyed or drastically weakened. Both France and Britain knew better, of course; Austria's actual isolation and weakness were apparent. But the theme was plausible to their publics and fit in with their own plans and propaganda. Moreover, the issue of intervention in behalf of Italy split the opposition in Britain. Gladstone, Russell, and many liberals and Radicals strongly favored action on behalf of Italy, while Aberdeen and Graham opposed it, and others were indecisive. Finally, Cavour cleverly exploited the latent Anglo-French rivalry for influence in Sardinia and warned that if Sardinia were not rewarded at the Congress, he would fall and a pro-Austrian and pro-Papal regime come to power.[6]

Though Sardinia was not allowed to sign the February 1 protocol at Vienna, Cavour won a prestige victory in getting her admitted to the Congress as a full participant. Walewski agreed with Buol's argument that this violated the basic distinction between great and lesser powers in the European system, and Clarendon and Palmerston privately recognized the validity of the principle. But Clarendon forced Sardinia's admission through, determined to use her to counter Walewski's "base subserviency to Austria." [7]

Behind the scenes Cavour and his coworkers worked on many proposals for Sardinian territorial acquisitions. The Modena-Parma-Principalities exchange scheme mentioned earlier was developed in several variant forms.* Another idea was to force Austria to evacuate the Papal Legations, secularizing them and turning them over to the Archduke of Modena or the Grand Duke of Tuscany, whose lands would then go to Sardinia. General La Marmora, commander

---

* The most elaborate plan, worked out by Cavour, involved placing the eight-year-old Duke Roberto of Parma on the throne of Wallachia, with his mother, the Duchess Luisa Maria, as regent. She would also marry the Prince of Carignan, Victor Emmanuel's cousin, but since they would probably remain childless, Duke Roberto would eventually take over the throne, and meanwhile Sardinia would get Parma (*Cavour-Inghilterra*, I, 231–34). One may recall in this connection that the most common nineteenth-century liberal charge against the Congress of Vienna was that it had trafficked in thrones and provinces without the consent of the peoples concerned.

of the Sardinian troops in the Crimea, proposed giving Austria the Romagna in exchange for Lombardy up to the Mincio for Sardinia. The British favored the idea, as did Cavour (though Sardinia dared not propose it herself for fear of destroying her reputation in Italy). Napoleon suggested declaring Modena reversible to the Duke of Parma, so that Sardinia could eventually acquire Parma; Palmerston suggested buying out the Duchess of Parma so that Sardinia could have it now. But each plan involved practical difficulties, the worst being that with peace about to be restored, Sardinia and her friends were thrown back on legal means—and legality, Azeglio pointed out, was the greatest barrier to Sardinian ambitions. In addition, the sea powers differed seriously on how best to aggrandize Sardinia. Palmerston and Clarendon were at best lukewarm over the various exchange projects involving the Principalities and wanted to despoil the Pope instead. Napoleon, though willing to help expel Austria from the Legations, did not want to be forced to evacuate Rome or to defy Catholic opinion at home by taking territory away from the Pontiff he was supposed to be protecting.[8]

Moreover, each power had pet ideas about Italy either irrelevant or actually harmful to Cavour's plans. Napoleon already dreamed of forming an Italian Confederation, including Austrian Lombardy, under nominal papal leadership and the actual hegemony of France —the chimera he would pursue for the next decade, which Cavour ultimately destroyed. Palmerston talked of putting the Prince of Carignan on the Greek throne. Cavour considered this useless or harmful to Sardinia, though he would have been glad to use him for some useful throne like Sicily's. Worst of all, at both Paris and London, Sardinia received more talk than commitment or performance. Palmerston's patronizing airs, in fact, got on Cavour's and Azeglio's nerves.[9]

Buol meanwhile worked to settle Austria's quarrel with Sardinia, if possible before the congress. He ran into the usual military-conservative opposition, now augmented at some points by Friedrich Thun, Rechberg's successor as civil adlatus to Radetzky.* Their

---

* Thun especially opposed Buol's efforts to curb Austrian press attacks on Sardinia and France, pointing out that the press in both these states was far more unrestrained in its attacks on Austria and that it was bad to give France the notion that she had a *captatio benevolentiae* where Austria was concerned (Summaries, Thun to Buol, 3 Sept. 1855, and Buol to Thun, 10 Oct., PA XL/3).

differences became evident at a ministerial conference on November 17 called to consider the "reforms" through which Thun proposed to give the Government-General in Lombardy-Venetia a more permanent character, as Francis Joseph desired. Thun's first two recommendations, calling for drawing a curtain over the events of 1848–1849 in considering Italians for appointments and promotion and for strengthening German as the official language of government business (*Amtssprache*), passed without dissent. Thun next called for allowing the émigrés freely to return to Lombardy; Buol and Bach seized on this to argue for a generous settlement of the whole sequestrations issue, and the Emperor ordered a future conference to take it up. But Thun last proposed a formal demand to Sardinia that she control her press and stop her revolutionary propaganda against Austria, supporting the demand if necessary by closing Austria's frontier and embargoing Sardinian exports. Buol attacked this proposal and succeeded in defeating it, arguing that Sardinia's conduct was not motivated merely by her historic enmity toward Austria; she also had a revolutionary element in her midst to worry about if she clamped down on anti-Austrian propaganda. Only by settling the sequestrations issue satisfactorily and creating a better atmosphere between the two states could Austria hope to get her to use the legal means at her disposal.[10]

When Buol and Bach on December 4 presented a sequestrations settlement proposal, to which Buol had won Bach, to a ministerial conference, the other ministers, including Bruck, opposed it as not going far enough and favored simply abolishing the sequestrations. Though Bach insisted on some face-saving provisions, the revised plan approved by the conference on January 29 and decreed by the Emperor on February 8 was almost an Austrian surrender.* It got a very favorable reception from Western representatives, including

---

* The refugees were supposed to decide on and define their future status, either by requesting to return to Austria or by applying for recognition of their foreign citizenship. If they returned, they would be amnestied and enjoy full property rights; if they stayed abroad, they could still have the sequestrations lifted by application. Should any émigrés die abroad during the grace period, their heirs would inherit their Lombard estates. The only exceptions would be specific individuals designated by the Foreign Minister, the Minister of the Interior, and the Police Chief as hardened political enemies of Austria. They would not be allowed to return and would have to sell their estates.

Seymour and the Sardinian chargé Cantono. Walewski congratulated Buol for settling the issue before the congress met, thus proving Austria's desire for good relations with Sardinia through a "testimonial precious for both parties." Buol went to Paris intending to sell the plan to Cavour and work out the details for resuming normal relations.[11]

Cavour could not endure this; as he later told Azeglio, he would resign before he would be on good terms with Austria. With his skill at playing the role of the injured party, he had no difficulty finding grounds to reject the plan. The Sardinian press denounced it as a trick, and Cibrario promptly told Count Paar, Austrian chargé, that it did not satisfy Sardinia's legal grievances or make reparation for the wrongs done her. But Napoleon, Walewski and even Palmerston * thought Austria's proposal sufficient; in fact, the French expected Cavour to be grateful to them for extorting it from Austria. So Cavour reserved judgment, thanked Napoleon for his help, and went through a long interview with Buol on March 7 (which Buol, to Cavour's delight, had to request). Buol's tone and language were reasonable, even benevolent, Cavour admitted; but after considering the matter, he reached the conclusion that Austria's plan only made the original insult to Sardinia worse. She would never surrender the legal rights of even one of her citizens; Austria would have to recognize both the Sardinian citizenship and the full property rights in Lombardy of every single one. It took some hard arguing to get Napoleon, Walewski, and Clarendon to swallow this view, but they did and, by the end of March, Cavour had produced a new Sardinian grievance out of Austria's proposal.[12] †

* One reason why Britain found it difficult to support Sardinia wholeheartedly on this issue was that she herself had long followed a doctrine of inalienable allegiance far stronger than Austria's in regard to British subjects, especially the Irish, emigrating to America. This doctrine played a major role in causing the War of 1812 and in the quarrel over the Fenians and was not eliminated until after the American Civil War (see Jenkins, *Fenians and Anglo-American Relations*, 11–12, 16–19).

† The last chapter in this story came in December 1856, when Austria finally abolished the sequestrations entirely. Cavour, who had always claimed that this would satisfy him completely and lead to friendly relations with Austria, now managed by a series of insults to provoke Austria into breaking relations. Clarendon, irritated with Cavour on other grounds, chided him, in typical Clarendon fashion, for being insufficiently grateful *to Britain* for enabling Sardinia to win a victory in the sequestration question. Cavour insisted that

Thus his *captatio benevolentiae* of the sea powers helped Cavour defeat what he recognized was Buol's desire to get on better terms. (His colleague at Paris, Villamarina, described Hübner's desire for better relations as "insolently conciliatory.") Cavour found many opportunities in the congress to embarrass and isolate Austria, and he exulted in Buol's difficulties and defeats. As he told Azeglio, the universal hatred of Austria he was promoting would bear fruit some day.[13] But not everything went well for him. At Buol's insistence (for reasons Clarendon admitted were sound *per se* and respectful toward Sardinia) Cavour was excluded from strategy discussions of the great powers and kept off the committee to propose provisions for the Principalities. Far worse, the effort to gain anything concrete for Italy seemed hopelessly bogged down; Clarendon wrote Palmerston on March 13 that he saw little chance of achieving anything.[14] To cheer Cavour, Clarendon tried to sell Sardinia's memorandum on reform in the Papal Legations as the basis for an immediate Austrian evacuation. The administrative reforms called for could be easily executed with a little Austrian and papal good will, he told Buol, and would so quickly calm and win over the populace that Austria could withdraw her troops and the Pope could concentrate his around Rome, which would enable the French safely to evacuate their forces. Buol termed the plan "eminently Utopian." "Eminently disingenuous" would have been a better description, since the whole purpose was not to reconcile the Pope with his subjects, but to separate the Pope from his territory and give it to Sardinia. Since Buol refused to cooperate, Clarendon warned that Britain would have to raise the Italian question and record her views on it in the congress, alone if necessary.[15] He also endorsed Cavour's note on conditions in the Papal States for presentation to the congress and eventually to the world.[16]

The worst problem still was that of getting France to raise a question so dangerous for herself as that of the Papal States. A two-hour strategy meeting between Britain, France, and Sardinia on March 19 led to an agreement of sorts, but its results were such that

the end of the sequestrations was no cause for changing his attitude toward Austria or for being grateful to anyone else (*Cavour-Inghilterra*, II, 92, 94–95; *Rel. dipl. Aust.-Sard.*, IV, 285, 291–92, 295–303).

Cavour was tempted, as he would be recurrently during and after the congress, to abandon legality and try to gain something for Sardinia by revolutionary means.* Clarendon not only shared Cavour's discouragement to an extent, but began to be aware of unforeseen consequences to raising the Italian question. To demand that Austria immediately evacuate the Legations would not only embarrass the French at Rome, but also the British and French in Greece. Nor, Clarendon confessed, did he see how either the French or the Austrians could pull out of the Papal States "without a deal of subsequent throat-cutting." [17] Clarendon nevertheless held Napoleon to his agreement to raise the Italian question when the question of evacuating Greece was brought up, and continued to press him to set a date for evacuating Rome. Cavour joined in the pressure, insisting that his proposed reforms in the Papal States would help keep the peninsula free from revolution when at some future date France and Sardinia combined to expel Austria. But the Emperor, agreeable on every other score, refused to commit himself to withdrawing his troops from Rome.[18]

Clarendon's warning to Buol, plus other clear hints of coming trouble, make Buol's attitude on Italy seem incredibly insouciant. Early in the congress Buol assured the nervous representatives of other Italian states that the subject of Italy would probably not come up for discussion and that if it did Austria would protect their interests. He gave Francis Joseph similar assurances just two days before the session of April 8 on which the question was taken up. He certainly knew of Austria's vulnerability to Sardinian and Western attack and propaganda in Italy; a ministerial conference at Vienna on April 2 underlined it. On Radetzky's advice, a papal request to lift the state of siege in Austrian-occupied papal territories was rejected. Werner, substituting for Buol, had earlier argued for the papal request on general political grounds, but here yielded to the generals' and Francis Joseph's insistence that the danger of revolution and the security needs of Austria's troops were more

* At this time the Anglo-Italian Legion was being transferred from Piedmont to Malta, a plot having been discovered among the legionnaires to attack Austria. Cavour momentarily considered seriously the possibility of using it to start a revolution in Sicily (Marcelli, *Cavour*, 201–5; Nolfo, *Europa*, 292–93; *Rel. dipl. GB-Sard.*, V, 242–43; *Cavour-Inghilterra*, I, 224–25).

important.[19] * Buol's relative optimism can only be explained by his determination to view the sea powers' policy through rose-colored glasses [20] and by his wishful belief that somehow his cooperation would pay off in similar treatment from them.

The April 8 session therefore came as a rude jolt, causing Buol to lose the *sang-froid* he had usually managed to retain in the face of previous rebuffs and insults. First Clarendon demanded the suspension of the hospodars in the Principalities so that the divans ad hoc could be chosen and could deliberate freely. Buol opposed this idea and prevented a decision on it, but the conference's sentiments were clearly against Austria. Then Walewski followed with a long, diffuse discussion of issues Austria considered extraneous to the peace congress—a call for reform in Greece so that the Allies could evacuate it, an invitation to Austria to join France in working to end their occupations in the Papal States, a demand for European denunciation of Bomba's regime, and calls for a change in the Belgian constitution and a new code for naval warfare. Clarendon, disappointed with Walewski's vagueness, concentrated on Austria's occupation of the Legations with an attack that, he reported to Palmerston, "completely satisfied Cavour and angered Buol." Cavour, ignoring the French occupation completely, denounced Austria's as rapidly becoming annexation and as posing a growing menace to Sardinia, peace, and the balance of power.

The subject of legal and/or illegal occupations was of course a potential Pandora's box. Hübner pointed out that Sardinia now occupied part of Monaco; Manteuffel raised the issue of Swiss action in Neuchâtel. Austria could have pointed not only to Greece, but to a large number of British occupations, annexations, and punitive expeditions carried on in the non-European world in recent decades, almost all, unlike Austria's, executed against the other governments concerned rather than at their invitation. Again Austria was handicapped by the fact that her position compelled her somehow to maintain the structure of European cooperation in Concert diplomacy, while other powers could play fast and loose with its rules or

---

* The generals' real reason for wanting to maintain the state of siege was to enable them to continue undisturbed the investigation at Bologna into a conspiracy which had led to several assassinations in Parma (Foreign Ministry–Grünne, 25 April 1856, PA XL/88).

even profit by breaking it up. But Buol gave a dignified reply, despite his obvious anger. Austria, though ready to cooperate with France to speed up an eventual evacuation, would make no commitments as to the date, nor would she join in a declaration of principles of government for Naples, Rome, or Athens, particularly since these governments had neither been heard nor consulted on the subject. Walewski therefore contented himself with recording the discussion in a conference protocol (another defeat for Buol). The Russians enjoyed the quarrel as spectators immensely, intervening only to urge the speedy evacuation of Greece.[21] At Orlov's request, Clarendon and Napoleon agreed not to embarrass Alexander II by raising the question of Poland at the congress—a consideration they did not dream of showing Francis Joseph.

The April 8 session had an important moral effect and significance for the future. "Austria," Temperley remarks, "having been placed in the dock by two great powers, was denounced as a criminal by a small one." [22] * Its immediate results, however, were unimpressive. Buol was no doubt overoptimistic in dismissing Cavour's "comédie Parlementaire" as an attempt at compensation for failure to make material gains and in believing that Walewski already regretted his démarche. But Clarendon also believed nothing had been accomplished but to establish a point of departure for the future.[23]

As for Cavour, if he exaggerated his discouragement for British consumption, it was real enough to tempt him again to consider war as a solution. A brief war scare, in fact, grew out of his resolve. On April 11, Cavour warned Clarendon that he would either have to resign in favor of a reactionary regime or find an early opportunity for war with Austria. Cavour claimed repeatedly at this time and later that Clarendon supported the latter choice, promised him British help, openly threatened Austria himself, and privately approved Cavour's plan for provoking war. The occasion seemed ready to hand in Parma, where, after an outburst of assassinations perpetrated by followers of Mazzini in March, a state of siege had been proclaimed and Austrian troops put on the alert.[24] Denouncing

---

* It is harder to agree with Temperley when he concludes that somehow "short-sighted and perfidious Austria" had brought this punishment onto her own head—especially since he sees the inconsistencies in Britain's policies and describes the Clarendon-Cavour-Walewski conspiracy against Austria accurately enough.

these activities as part of an Austrian plan to attack Sardinia, Sardinia concentrated forces on Parma's frontiers, which would, as Azeglio remarked, at least serve to keep up the general rabies against Austria. Cavour hoped to incite Austria to attack by sending Sardinian soldiers by sea to Spezia accompanied by a British fleet—a plan he again claimed Clarendon approved.

Buol was once again caught in the middle. The conservatives and military men at Vienna wanted a strong antirevolutionary stance in Italy regardless of the international consequences, and the Emperor leaned in their direction.[25] But the smaller Italian states, including Parma, wished to appease Italian nationalist sentiment by demonstrating their independence of Austria (even while they needed and desired her military protection), and they wanted desperately to stay out of any Austrian quarrel with Sardinia, France, or Britain.[26] To avoid conflict, Buol again humiliated himself by seeking out Napoleon and Cavour on April 16, the last day of the congress, to plead for their cooperation in preserving peace and achieving better Austro-Sardinian relations. Cavour assured Buol that he also wanted peace and an amicable settlement of differences and valued their personal friendship. That very day he published his memorandum denouncing Austria's occupations in Italy and demanding her immediate withdrawal from the Legations.[27]

Immediately thereafter Cavour left for London, hoping to get a large war loan. With this, Sardinia could prepare militarily and when she was ready could start a war by presenting some unacceptable ultimatum to Austria. If Britain joined in, France would be sure to follow. But instead of support for a war of liberation, Cavour got nothing at London besides the usual promises of moral, diplomatic, and parliamentary support for Sardinia and defense against an Austrian attack. Moreover, Cavour's visit seemed to produce a change in Clarendon's attitude. He defended Austria in Parliament, insisting that she was not threatening Parma, and secured a postponement of a parliamentary inquiry into the peace congress's handling of the Italian question, which Cavour had got the Tory Lord Lyndhurst to sponsor. By May a rift opened between Clarendon and Cavour that would never heal.[28]

Plainly Cavour had at the very least greatly overestimated the amount of specific support Britain would give and had built far too much upon it. There is no trace in Clarendon's private correspondence with Palmerston of his having encouraged Cavour to provoke war,* and whatever he may have said to Cavour, he certainly did not wish to do this. He aimed only to extort enough concessions from Austria to satisfy Sardinia and to save Cavour's position so that he would not be driven to do something provocative.[29] But it is also not correct to say that Clarendon's rift with Cavour came about because of his need for a rapprochement with Austria in order to support Turkey and execute the peace treaty against Russia.[30] That Clarendon was not pro-Austrian during the congress or before has been demonstrated; the April 8 session alone is proof enough. Moreover, Clarendon did not at this time believe that Britain needed Austria's help to execute the peace treaty or uphold Turkey; that insight only broke through sufficiently to influence British decisions considerably later. But even if Clarendon had considered Austria's help in the East indispensable, nothing would have led him to pay for it by supporting her in Italy. Britain had steadfastly refused to do this even when she wanted Austria's help in the war. Clarendon in fact regarded any payment to Austria for services rendered as outrageous blackmail; it is not satirizing his outlook to say that like most Whigs he believed that an ample recompense for any services Austria could render Britain consisted simply of allowing her to associate with Britain. Moreover, Clarendon actually put strong pressure on Austria over the Italian question all through mid-1856, especially just after the congress.

Actually, Clarendon's attitude toward Cavour and Sardinia changed simply because he finally began to see that he had been wrong about them. All through the congress he had continued to believe, despite plain evidence to the contrary, that Cavour was a good Whig—one of the most moderate and practical men he had ever met, he said—whose goal was simply to prevent revolution and promote Italy's national regeneration by peaceful means. His aim therefore was to cheer Cavour up, to keep him from resigning; the promises of British armed support against attack were, like others

* He certainly knew, however, that Cavour was contemplating provoking a war (he would later in 1862 deny that he had had any knowledge of this). Writing on July 23 to Russell of the possibility of an Austro-Sardinian war over Parma, Clarendon said Cavour had told him at Paris that this "might be the best course for Piedmont to take" (PRO 30/22/13B).

made as early as 1853 and many to be made later, designed to keep Sardinia out of France's arms and console Cavour without involving Britain in any real danger, for Austria was obviously (despite British propaganda to the contrary) too weak and vulnerable to attack Sardinia now.[31] With Cavour's surprise visit to London, Clarendon discovered that he was really working to provoke a war with Austria. The previous winter, when Clarendon had wanted the war to continue, this might not have bothered him; * now that he had concluded peace, it was intolerable. Worse still, Cavour committed the grave offense of making trouble for Clarendon in Parliament. Yet even then Clarendon was more disappointed than angry with Cavour. A real breach with him and an approach of sorts to Austria came only when Clarendon later became convinced that Cavour would never be grateful for all he and Britain had done for Sardinia, but would continue to make trouble for him instead.[32] †

The Principalities issue proved almost as traumatic as Italy for Austria in the last stages of the congress. After March 30, the sea powers promptly resumed their calls for immediate Austrian evacuation. Buol replied that this matter strictly speaking concerned only Austria and Turkey and was governed by their convention. But the other powers paid no attention and possessed the means to frustrate the work of reorganization till Austria left. Therefore, on April 4, Buol promised to finish Austria's evacuation before the Allied evacuation of the Crimea and Turkey, though both withdrawals should proceed simultaneously and take no more than six months to complete. In defending this concession to Francis Joseph, Buol again was painfully deferential to the sea powers. It would imperil the

* Clarendon told Hudson on December 20, 1855, in urging the need for another campaign, "The war might then become general et alors comme alors. Out of that might spring fresh territorial arrangements which is the state of things that the King of Sardinia did not disguise his wish for" (Rel. dipl. GB-Sard., V, 192–93).

† In 1862, when Clarendon's reputation as an Austrophile was strongly established, the publication of Cavour's correspondence, with extracts depicting Clarendon as encouraging his warlike projects at the congress, caused a considerable sensation. Prince Richard Metternich, Austrian ambassador at Paris, wrote Rechberg, Austrian foreign minister, "It is evident either that Cavour has lied or that Clarendon is the most false and inconsequent of men. I regret to say that I incline rather toward the latter alternative and I count on profiting from this in the future" (15 Feb. 1862, Problema Veneto, I, 428–29). In fact, each of Metternich's alternative explanations was true.

alliance, he said, if Austria tried to extend the occupation until the work of reorganization was completed. The jealousy and suspicions of Europe needed to be calmed.[33]

Neither this concession nor the evacuation of half of Austria's remaining forces in May, recommended by Buol as a sign of good faith, did any good in this direction. Palmerston congratulated Clarendon for putting Britain in a position to force Austria out of the Principalities immediately, but Clarendon stressed that he merely wanted Austria to know that she was there solely on Allied sufferance. Actually, some Austrian and Turkish troops should be kept in the Principalities for a time to put pressure on Russia. Besides, Orlov had begged Clarendon to force Austria out immediately, and, as Clarendon remarked, "I see no harm in the raw between them being kept up." [34] Nor did Austria's efforts to get Turkish help in preventing dangerous developments in the Principalities accomplish much. While Ali refused to support a British demand for an immediate Austrian withdrawal because of the danger of revolt, the Turks hoped soon to replace Austrian troops with their own and flatly rejected all requests to extend the terms of the present hospodars. On April 8, the congress decided on a provisional regime (caimacamie), and Prokesch could secure no more from the Porte than a vague promise to help turn the divans ad hoc in a conservative direction. As Buol confessed to the Emperor, the Principalities issue was the one most unsettled and unsatisfactory when the congress ended, and a main reason he was glad it was over.[35]

Buol believed that one thing compensated Austria somewhat for all the defeats and humiliations—the secret treaty Britain, France, and Austria signed on April 15, pledging themselves to mutual support of Turkey against Russia. As Buol saw it, this treaty really provided an answer to the Eastern question and the best possible guarantee for European peace. Moreover, as his private journal shows, it was precisely the European, defensive character of the alliance that mattered to him. He insisted that it was not hostile to Russia and compatible with "the most friendly entente among all the powers"; it would only block Russian Panslavist and Utopian dreams in Russia's own true interests and would assure that any new dangers in the East (and there were others besides Russian aggression, as Buol recognized) would be met in common by Europe.

Above all, he saw the treaty as attaching the sea powers to Austria's existence as a great power and protecting her against the nightmare of a Franco-Russian alliance.

> The power the most exposed by its geographic position, Austria had to foresee the possibility that Russia would try to link up with France over Austria's territory. The treaty may thwart [*contrarier*] Russia and cramp [*gêner*] Prussia, but it bears no provocative character at all, and does not exclude the reestablishment of good relations between Russia and Austria.[36]

Buol's belief was sincere, but wholly deluded. His assumption was not unreasonable, that is, that fundamental reasons of state, like the desire to check Russia, defend Turkey, and maintain the balance of power, would lead the sea powers to help keep Austria strong and independent. He supposed that they could not want her otherwise. In fact they both did; both worked to weaken her, during the Crimean War and after, either to eliminate her as an obstacle to their plans or to render her obedient to their purposes. As for the April 15 treaty, France considered it a nuisance, a final token payment on the bargain of November 1855 with Austria. The French frustrated all efforts to make its *casus foederis* clear and precise and quickly informed Russia of it, blaming Britain and Austria for it and assuring Russia it was harmless.[37]

At first Britain wished to make the treaty more automatic and less defensive in character. Cowley, for example, feared that in case of a Russian threat to Turkey the Allies might be committed to try persuasion prior to force in dealing with Russia, which Britain would not tolerate.[38] * The British tried to stretch the *casus foederis* of the alliance to include Russian naval construction at Nicolaev or a military concentration in Bessarabia; Palmerston at first hoped to expand the alliance into an all-European anti-Russian coalition. But Britain's lack of seriousness about the treaty quickly became apparent. On May 2, Clarendon told Cowley that if Walewski blamed the treaty on Britain, he would prove to Russia that it was an Austro-

---

* At the same time that Cowley here wanted to protect Britain against the possibility of having to use persuasion, he and Clarendon, spurred on by peace groups from home, were urging the congress to adopt the principle of using mediation rather than force in international disputes (Protocol No. 23, session of April 14).

French instrument "of which we had disputed the binding force upon us." Palmerston expected the alliance, like the peace settlement, to last only a few years and certainly did not allow it to affect British policy toward Austria. Moreover, while Palmerston blustered and Clarendon complained about the way Russia and France were undermining the peace settlement, the British public, no longer concerned about the Russian menace and tired of the Eastern question, wanted to return to normalcy and had no interest in a treaty to uphold Turkey.[39]

The aftermath of the congress sufficed to destroy even Buol's tenacious hopes and illusions. On the Principalities he still wished, besides averting a political system that would endanger the monarchy, to conciliate the other powers and protect the privileges of the inhabitants. Prokesch was instructed to make sure that the new caimacams (provisional administrators) upheld the Règlement Organique and prevented a Turkish occupation. When half the Austrian forces were evacuated in May, Buol took the opportunity of lodging a sharp protest with the Emperor against the political conduct of the Austrian commanders.[40] But Walewski and the British continued to press Austria to get out, so that Buol had to fall back on his promise to evacuate within six months *if* the other powers did the same.[41] Other headaches developed rapidly. First Prussia and then Sardinia, with Britain's backing, were added to the commission sitting at Bucharest, so that it became solidly anti-Austrian.[42] Prince Ghica broke completely with Austria, working against her economic interests in Moldavia, proclaiming freedom of the press, and agitating openly for union.[43] By late July, Buol admitted in his private journal what Coronini had been saying for months, that French agents with Russian encouragement were spearheading the unification movement.[44]

As for Britain, her policy on the Principalities was inconsistent except for being anti-Austrian. At first Clarendon continued to press Austria hard for immediate evacuation, adding that she should do the same in the Papal States if she wanted good relations with Britain. The Cabinet, he said, could not oppose public opinion on either point, and did not wish to.[45] Yet while certain that Austria's evil influence had to be eliminated, he had no idea whether unification would be good for the Principalities or not. He boasted that Britain would do what Austria would not—respect the wishes of the people; yet he agreed with Cowley that the proposed efforts to determine popular sentiment were useless, the Rumanians being, like all eastern peoples, hopelessly corrupt and open to bribery. The divans ad hoc could not possibly meet, he told Vienna, as long as any Austrian soldiers remained in the country; but he told Cowley that Britain's insistence on "unfettered discussion of freely chosen Divans . . . may be all nonsense and I daresay that intrigue and corruption will be at the bottom of anything that is settled." In fact, he did not much care what happened on the lower Danube. Instructing Cowley to get Bourqueney to press Austria harder about Italy, he said, "That is the European question which most interests *us* just now." [46]

Only in midsummer, when Britain realized that she might need Austria after all, did something like a British policy on the Principalities emerge. Faced with stubborn Russian obstruction and evasions of the peace treaty, the town of Bolgrad and Serpents Isle on the Bessarabian frontier being the chief points in dispute, Clarendon turned to Austria for support. Seymour had painted a vivid picture of Buol's despair at the collapse of his pro-Western policy. Clarendon replied on July 29 that it was Buol's own fault for having tried to create a league with France against Britain. But if he did something about Italy and did not again snub his only friends, Britain would be generous and forgive him. As for the evacuation, Clarendon admitted that Britain had quit the Crimea too soon, and now conceded that "Buol was not so far wrong when he said that the Austrian troops ought not to quit the Principalities until the new frontier was settled."

Two weeks later, when Clarendon had decided that the union of the Principalities was definitely a bad idea, he called for Austrian troops to stay there until Russia fulfilled the peace treaty, adding that Austria ought also finally to recognize that Britain was her only friend and stop treating her shabbily in Italy. On August 26, Clarendon cited Britain's willingness to allow Austria to stay in the Principalities as "a fresh proof of our loyauté towards Austria." One sign from Britain to France or one concession to Russia, he warned, and "there would be a league against Austria in a week." Austria had better therefore draw close to Britain—"not that we want it,"

Clarendon insisted, "as we can manage our affairs singlehanded and I speak only in the interest of Austria." This same spirit of selfless British "loyauté" led Clarendon to inform Buol in late September that as soon as Russia gave up Bolgrad and Serpents Isle, Austria would have to evacuate the Principalities immediately. In the meantime, her troops should now leave Bucharest, for her occupation was quite unpopular in Britain.[47] *

Supported by this kind of British friendship, Austria's stand on the Principalities became increasingly obstructionist, but also more defensive than ever. Buol only hoped now to prevent or delay the execution of ruinous measures. Moreover, his private journal proves that he had no hidden purposes in promising that Austria would evacuate as soon as the peace treaty was carried out. In fact, he admitted privately that as long as the frontier was in dispute Russia had a right to occupy the Turkish territory she still held. The Emperor told Buol that he would like to have Austria's troops remain until the boundary dispute was settled and the commission's work begun. But should that take too long, Austria would prefer to leave the Principalities entirely rather than let herself be pushed out of the capital.[48]

There were more troubles for Austria in Italy after the congress, the result not so much of Cavour's policy as of Britain's. The Peelite charge against Palmerston and Clarendon, that their activity in Italy was designed to cover up their failure to produce results during the war and at the congress, was true. Clarendon had no use for parliamentary debates on Italy, "with vehement abuse of Austria and cock and bull stories about Italian virtues." He also could suggest no remedies himself for Italy, confessing that if he had full powers to deal with the Papal States he would not know what to do. He recognized that no lasting good could come from pun-

---

* While Austria was supporting Britain effectively on the Bolgrad-Serpents Isle disputes, Sardinia went over to France's side, angering Clarendon and Palmerston by her ingratitude. But Hudson suggested a simple solution: win Sardinia's support in the East by getting Austria to agree to let Sardinia have the Po duchies. Austria ought to agree to this "to avoid a free state on her Eastern frontier and the inconvenience of a free press on her Western frontier." Clarendon did not propose this to Austria, but up till November 1856 he did favor giving Sardinia the Po duchies to keep her out of France's arms (*Rel. dipl. GB-Sard.*, V, 326, 342–44, 352–55, 358–59).

ishing Bomba, and much harm might be done. The problem, however, was that Britain could not now fail to act without losing prestige. "We shall cut a sorry figure for having barked at such a wretch as Bomba and then not venturing to bite him." [49] The parliamentary debate on Italy in July, the strongly pro-Italian stand taken by the British press, and the restlessness of Cavour and Azeglio also made some show of action necessary.[50]

Britain began with direct pressure on the offending governments —dispatches to Rome and Naples threatening the Pope and the King with loss of their thrones if they did not meet the wishes of their peoples. A special emissary, Lord Lyons, was sent to Rome to urge Cavour's plan of secularization and reforms on Pius IX. Cowley pressed Walewski to force Austria to evacuate the Legations by pulling out of Rome first. Palmerston suggested that Britain and France set a date four or six months hence after which all occupations or armed interference by anyone into Italy's internal affairs would be forbidden. This would solve the Italian question overnight, compelling sovereigns and people to "settle their differences as best they can without any interference of foreign force, just as the French or English would do." [51] *

But Britain relied mainly on pressure on Austria in order to achieve something for Italy. As Clarendon confessed to Cowley, "It is early to be abusing her [Austria] before the ratifications [of the April 15 treaty] are exchanged," but Parliament would be furious if the Papal States were not soon evacuated. When Seymour reported no success from persuasion and warnings,[52] Palmerston and Clarendon were willing in principle to use stronger means. Napoleon proposed to Cowley on May 23 making Russia a partner in the Anglo-French alliance—an idea so openly anti-Austrian that the Emperor, as Cowley remarked, felt "that there was something of treachery towards Austria in this scheme and he said that it would require tender handling." Cowley was still angry over France's conduct at the peace congress and had lavished praise on Austria for

* Four months later, just when Palmerston's scheme to ban armed intervention should have gone into effect, he was ordering a British naval squadron to the Bay of Naples to prevent Ferdinand II and his subjects from settling their differences in their own way as best they could. The expedition was called off at the last minute because of France's reluctance and opposition at home (Urban, 67–69; Nolfo, *Europa*, 423–30; Moscati, 159–73).

her loyal support of Britain. But he quickly saw the potential gains of Napoleon's proposal—"Germany would be paralysed, and we should be able to dictate our own terms to Austria in regard to Italy"—and had none of the Emperor's qualms about betraying Austria. The only doubt he had was whether the sea powers could get Russia to cooperate in Italy, however much she now hated Austria.[53] Clarendon's caution was equally pragmatic: he was quite willing to bring Russia in, he wrote, as much to curb her as to guide Austria in Italy. But Austria might in sheer despair throw herself into Russia's arms. Palmerston's suggestion was a London conference to impose reforms on the Pope, where Russia might well join Britain, France, and Sardinia "out of spite to Austria." [54]

The British claimed that their tactics were justified by the silent, obstinate, deliberately hostile resistance Buol opposed to their efforts for cooperation in Italy.[55] The fact is that Buol, having no alternative, continued to try appeasement and conciliation of the West on Italy, only to garner more rebuffs and new demands. His plea for cooperation in preventing a conflict over Parma was brushed aside by Walewski, who at the same time, with backing and encouragement from Britain, warned Prussia and the German states not to support Austria or guarantee her possessions in Italy.[56] Clarendon gave Buol another Whig sermon in reply to his plea for help: Buol's unfriendly conduct toward Cavour and his refusal to prepare to evacuate the Legations were the sole causes of Austria's difficulties. Palmerston saw Buol's request as a good chance to teach him another lesson. Buol was too fond of bullying and had to be made to understand that if Austria started a war in Italy, Sardinia this time would not fight alone.[57]

Buol pleaded with Britain not to use a double standard on Italy. Why was she so jealous of the Sultan's sovereignty and so hostile to Pius IX's? Were there not two evils to face in Italy, that of revolutionary agitation and activity as well as that of bad government, both to be weighed on the same scale? If Austria was too indulgent toward bad governments, what about the states which tolerated and encouraged revolutionary attacks on her and other states? Why did only Naples have to be chastised and not Turin? Why did the Legations have to be evacuated immediately regardless of the ensuing dangers, and not Greece? Where would this principle of direct intervention into the internal affairs of sovereign governments, without even formally inviting those governments to confer first on the issue, stop, once it was applied to Italy? Buol fell into what Seymour characterized as his "stupid reserve" only when it became obvious that the sole answers he would receive from Britain were further assurances that there was not "the *slightest indication* of her [Sardinia's] part of a wish to be actively hostile towards Austria," more denunciations of Buol's unfriendliness, and more warnings of isolation if Austria failed to cooperate.[58]

Even then Buol's policy was in no way anti-British. Sympathizing with the aims of the Western powers at Rome and Naples, if not with their methods, he supported the Lyons mission and sent Hübner to Naples in September to support the British and French demands.[59] On Cantono's recall to Turin, Buol pleaded again to be told what Sardinia really wanted; if it was normal relations, why the war of insults? [60] He continued to anger Bruck and Hess by supporting Britain on the Suez Canal, and Kempen by advocating greater freedom for British travelers in Austria. He refused to exploit British troubles in Greece and proposed a center of entente at Vienna to urge Turkey to carry out the reforms of the Sultan's Hatti-Humayun of February, and to consider what to do if internal troubles threatened Turkey. Palmerston and Clarendon denounced this suggestion as another piece of Austrian impudence; even if Austria accepted a London conference on Italy, they would not agree to it.[61] Above all, on the most important issue for Britain, the execution of the Treaty of Paris, Austria gave Britain steady support while France and Sardinia proved wholly unreliable.[62] The British knew that Austria's help was indispensable and even got Austria to send her troops back into Moldavia to put pressure on Russia, always intending, of course, that when the Moor had done his work, the Moor would go.[63]

It was thus not Austria's policy that produced in Britain the attitude toward her which Graham denounced as "this bullying system, with all its dangers and consequences." [64] Nor was it a conviction that Austria had no rights in Italy * and was causing all the trouble

* Palmerston sometimes seemed to think this and to believe that anyone who thought otherwise should keep silent. In expressing his satisfaction that Lacour, "a regular Austrian," was recalled from Constantinople, he wrote Clarendon,

there, or that Austria was useless to Britain. Seymour, in fact, thought Russia would still be able to dominate the Continent if Austria were not there.[65] The British simply knew that they could have Austria's support for nothing, and they felt vastly superior to her in moral and material terms. Reporting on Buol's profound discouragement, Seymour remarked that he would like a rapprochement with Austria as a counterweight to France and Russia, but it would never work. Britain would not be so mad as to abandon gallant little Piedmont, whom Austria had good reason to hate, and besides, "they are a stupid lot these Austrians." But then Britain need not worry; she could do just what pleased her interests in Parliament, "without the slightest regard to those of Kaiser—Pope—or Bomba." Only Britain's French connection needed *ménagement.* "As for these people here—they want us—and we can do very well without them—as with extreme urbanity I contrive occasionally to insinuate." [66]

Clarendon was equally complacent. Though by fall quite disillusioned with Cavour and Sardinia (he described Victor Emmanuel as a "thorough snob" dominated by hatred for Austria and greed for territory) and bitter at France and Russia, he took Austria's cooperation with Britain as proof that Buol had changed and now recognized her as Austria's one true friend. "The only bright spot," he told Aberdeen, "has been the entente really cordiale that we have established with Austria." Aberdeen's reply was apt but probably too subtle for Clarendon: "I congratulate you on your entente with Austria. You will now know more the value of popular opinion. I rejoice for many reasons, and among others, for the belief that you will not now give Lombardy and Venice to our *chivalrous* and *disinterested* ally." [67]

Austria's relations with France after the congress followed a similar path. Flattery and conciliation did no more good with Napoleon and Walewski than with Palmerston and Clarendon; every effort by Vienna to reach a Franco-Austrian understanding on Italy,

---

"The language of La Cour and his wife about Austria is that Austria has as good a right to her Italian provinces as the La Cours have to their estates. This is not the tone that a French minister ought to take. If he thinks so, he might as well keep his thoughts to himself" (27 Oct. 1853, Palm. Papers GC/CL/542).

the Principalities, or executing the peace treaty was ignored or repulsed. Buol tried to convince Paris that the April 15 treaty could give France the leadership of Europe, that it meant "Europe directed in the path of genuine conservative progress by France in the center, giving her left hand to England and her right to Austria." [68] But Napoleon wanted European leadership of a different kind. Even Hübner's hardy illusions about Napoleon died from the chill in Austro-French relations.[69] By early fall the two powers were attacking each other in the press; from late 1856 on, a note of bitterness characterized Buol's journal entries on France that he never sounded against Britain.

In dealing with Russia, Buol hoped for a time that she would decide in her own interest to accept the new situation and patch up relations with Austria. A number of conciliatory gestures were attempted by Vienna to this end, particularly missions by Prince Paul Esterházy to Moscow and by Count Leiningen to Warsaw. But the gestures were fruitless, and Austria opposed Russia on all the issues arising out of the peace treaty. Gorchakov was nominated to succeed Nesselrode and Budberg to succeed Gorchakov at Vienna— both enemies of Austria. Russia openly sought an alliance with France and fought Austria diplomatically and in her press on every issue, including Italy. Plainly Austro-Russian relations were in for a long freeze before any thaw.[70]

The temperature was less arctic at Berlin and Frankfurt. Frederick William was inclined to forgive Francis Joseph (though not Buol), and Rechberg offered a much more difficult target for Bismarck's attacks in the Diet than Austria had represented during the war.[71] But there was little chance for Austria to regain her lost influence in Germany. Reliance on the Holy Alliance was on the wane as surely in Berlin as in St. Petersburg, a process hastened by the King's declining mental powers and by the transformation the industrial revolution was creating in Prussia and Germany.

Only with Turkey were Austria's relations fairly good. Some problems persisted—for example, Klek and Sutorina—for which Buol and Prokesch vainly sought a solution during and after the congress. (Seymour and Clarendon were on the alert to prevent one in any case.) Austria remained suspicious of Turkish efforts to increase her rights and influence in the Balkans and irritated at Turkey's failure to execute her promised reforms. But on the major is-sues, preventing a union of the Principalities and preserving the status quo in southeastern Europe, Austria and Turkey worked to-gether.[72] Yet this very fact was a final humiliation, especially to Francis Joseph and the generals: that after so much effort to try to solve the Eastern question with other European powers in line with Austrian interests, Austria should find her only ally in the despised Turks.

The Outcome for Europe:
Confrontation or Concert

Measured against his goals, Buol's policy was a dismal failure. In fact, he achieved practically everywhere the virtual opposite of what he intended. No one could have accomplished the task Buol set himself or prevented some losses for Austria, but he must bear some responsibility for the dimensions of her defeat. He often failed to handle men well, did not foresee and prepare for others' reactions, displayed at times a wounding sarcasm and stiffness of manner, was excessively concerned for his own and Austria's dignity, and committed serious errors in judgment. He was too hard on Prussia and the German states and concentrated too exclusively on the Russian threat, while at the same time he constantly tended to appease the West. Above all, he prepared no alternative to his policy and persisted in it long after it obviously had failed. Extenuating circumstances cannot alter this verdict much. Though Buol was dependent on the Emperor, who did not always follow his advice, most of the time he enjoyed his support to a surprising degree. The policy Austria followed was distinctively Buol's, and not what it would have been had the Emperor really been his own foreign minister or followed the advice of other Austrians. Buol's opponents, especially the generals, made trouble for him at home and abroad, especially in Italy and the Principalities. Yet he managed to control and thwart this opposition. If Buol was badly served by some envoys, he had put them in their posts or failed to remove them.

Some common charges against Buol and Austria are unfounded, to be sure. He did not pursue a *Schaukelsystem*, that is, one of wavering between East and West with no clear principles or goals. From the beginning he wanted the Eastern question settled in a way that would check Russia through the European Concert, and once the war broke out he sought this same goal solely by cooperating with the West. If anything, he was far too inflexible and consistent in his aims and methods. Nor was his diplomacy, as often charged, too slippery, deceptive, and subtle. Even toward Russia, Prussia, and Germany, frankness was his preferred method, and with the sea powers he bent over backward to be open and fair. Buol was an honest diplomat compared to most of his counterparts. The accusations of betrayal and treachery so often hurled at Austria have some substance or at least an understandable basis coming from Prussia or Russia, but the only interesting thing about these charges as leveled by the sea powers, especially by Britain, is that each time they accused Austria of some plot or trick, they were actually trying to do to her the exact counterpart of what they falsely accused her of doing to them. The charge of grasping selfishness often laid at her door clearly fits other powers better than Austria; so does that of timidity. Of course Austria was cautious; the British or American idea of courage and honor in foreign policy would have meant suicide for her. Buol was not a fighter by nature, and one might wish he had stood up to Western bullying more often. Nevertheless, he repeatedly staked his post and his whole political future on his policy, against great opposition and heavy odds.* Austria twice assumed the obligation to go to war if she could not otherwise secure her interests and Europe's as she conceived them, despite risks greater for her than for any other great power, and she would certainly have fulfilled her pledge had the *casus foederis* arisen. At the same time, she showed civil courage in refusing to enter the war when she believed it could not serve her purposes or Europe's.

In contrast, one cannot survey the consistent pattern of British policy, especially the conduct of Clarendon, without gaining the impression of a clear lack of civil courage and responsibility. Too many British leaders, despite some honorable exceptions, were willing to accept war over a quarrel they knew was inherently soluble for a cause they felt to be unnecessary and even unworthy, rather

* Werner once wrote Prokesch that history would consider Buol one of the most clear-sighted and courageous statesmen of the time. The second part of this encomium, at least, has some foundation (16 Dec. 1854, Prokesch Nachlass; kindly communicated to me by Dr. Rudolf Neck).

than face possible bad political consequences. Nor does it make Britain's case better that while excusing herself on the grounds of public opinion and parliamentary pressures for not controlling her client Turkey and not restraining her own actions, she regularly demanded that Austria, the most vulnerable of the great powers, force Russia, the greatest land power in the world, to knuckle under, and called her cowardly for not doing so.[1]

But these points, if they clear Buol of some unjustified accusations, only reinforce the main criticism: that he allowed the sea powers to make a fool of Austria, exploiting her loyalty to her engagements and Buol's eagerness for a Western alignment and a pro-Western outcome of the war. No wonder a fiery Austrian patriot like Bruck got angry.

It would be difficult, however, to find a plausible alternative course. A Russian alignment would have been disastrous for Austria, and the Bruck-Hess proposal of Austro-Prussian-German armed mediation to force a solution on both sides was not merely, as Buol said, an empty dream, but an ugly and dangerous one, connected with annexationist ideas and pan-German hegemonic aspirations.[2] Nor would the all-out war alliance with the West preached by Hübner and sometimes by Prokesch have been better; Hess was right on the probable disastrous results of this.

One alternative that appears feasible to some historians even today was developed by Metternich. He argued from the beginning that Austria, unlike other powers, had absolutely nothing to gain in the East and a great deal to lose and that her task should therefore be purely European and defensive—maintaining the treaties, preventing war, and preserving the Ottoman Empire. Except for the Leiningen mission and the neutrality proclamation of October 1853, Metternich fundamentally agreed with Austrian policy up to mid-1854. His criticism of Buol during this period was mainly tactical; he wanted Russia maneuvered out of the Principalities, followed by an Austrian occupation, just as Buol did. But thereafter Metternich complained increasingly that Austria was entangling herself with the West for unclear goals when her real task as the central European power was to lead both sides back to peace. If she would stand apart from the conflict in alliance with Prussia and the German Confederation, both sides would eventually grow tired of their "insane hacking away at each other." When they did, Austria could mediate for a peace based as much as possible on the status quo ante, with no special gains for Austria or anyone else.[3]

There are attractive aspects to the kind of neutrality Metternich proposed. If somewhat vague in program, it was genuinely European. He was right on the folly of the war, the worthlessness of victory for its own sake, the absurdity of fighting for slogans like "the triumph of European civilization over barbarism," and the impossibility of Austria's harvesting any worthwhile fruits in the East. It is easy to exaggerate the difference between Metternich's program and Buol's policy and to overlook how much of Metternich was in Buol's,[4]* but there certainly was a difference. Metternich's ideas for ending the war can be compared to Woodrow Wilson's original "Peace without Victory" program in World War I, only they were better thought out and more serious than Wilson's. Buol's policy was like Colonel House's—a pro-Western intervention to help the Allies to moderate victory, so as to keep the war from expanding and causing incalculable damage. Again, Buol's program was far more seriously pursued than House's.

But Metternich's policy also involved illusions and would probably not have worked better than Buol's. As Kübeck wrote after listening to one of the former Chancellor's long homilies, "The Prince spoke wisdom—but it will not work!"[5] His program presupposed a solidarity of interest and principle among the great powers and reserves of good sense and caution that no longer existed. He was wrong in insisting that while revolutionaries wanted a European war over Turkey, all statesmen were bound to abhor the idea. Russia initially courted precisely such a war and revolution. Turkey quickly became ready to fight; Cavour and others actively worked for a great war of West versus East; France was willing to pick up the gauntlet and preferred war to breaking with Britain. Above all, the British war party saw in the Eastern crisis an opportunity for a showdown with Russia and for sweeping changes in Europe that must not be passed by.

---

* Metternich advocated in 1815 and in 1840–1841 the European guarantee and great-power alliance in favor of Turkey that Buol tried so hard to effect. In addition, his program of a Western alliance to stop Russia in 1828–1829 was just what Buol and Francis Joseph tried for at this time, as they claimed.

Nor could Austria, after occupying the Principalities, have dared simply to wait till a bloody military stalemate made the belligerent powers ready to conclude a conservative peace based on the status quo ante reached through Austrian mediation. There was no reason to believe that such a stalemate would develop or that it would have the desired effect on the combatants if it did. Russia by late 1854 was probably frightened out of her dangerous ideas, but it was a temporary cure, and any victory in the war could have revived them. As for the sea powers, invulnerable as they were to real defeat, they simply could not be forced to accept a stalemate; in fact, they would not even accept favorable peace terms acquired without military victory, as the Vienna Conference proved. Moreover, had Austria fallen back on armed neutrality in September 1854 instead of mobilizing and tying up the bulk of Russia's forces in the West, Russia might have been able to overwhelm the Allied army in the Crimea. Then the Russian danger would have been revived, while Britain and France would at least have wanted to try to expand the war elsewhere and force more neutrals into it [6] and might well have decided to gamble with revolution and war against a more vulnerable target, Austria.

Moreover, nothing is more unlikely or difficult to achieve in war than a peace without victory. A military stalemate ordinarily brings political victory to one side or the other. This was the case with Prussia in the Seven Years' War; and had Germany gained a status quo ante peace in 1918, she would have won World War I politically. In the Crimean War, Russia had only to avoid defeat in order to gain political influence and prestige. Everyone recognized this, including the Russians; it was the one good objective reason the Allies had to insist on some kind of triumph and a sound reason for Buol's and Prokesch's insisting that terms must be imposed on Russia that would prove she had lost. Had the West been compelled to accept Metternich's kind of drawn contest instead of Buol's kind of moderate victory, they would have been strongly tempted to renew the contest later. In short, Austria could not afford to stand by and let the war continue uncontrolled. A military stalemate was neither likely nor desirable, while the dangers to Austria of a one-sided victory for either side or an indefinite prolongation of the war were intolerable.

Besides, Metternich's policy gave Austria no hope. If he believed the old Concert of Europe could be restored unchanged, few others did. At best his policy, if successful, would have given Austria a brief reprieve, but it offered no solution to the Eastern question, no answer on Germany and Italy, and no increase in Austria's security. One suspects that Metternich knew this and simply did not believe in any of the proposed solutions. Palmerston accused Metternich of an attitude of "après moi le déluge"; the comment actually indicates Palmerston's superficiality. Metternich's pessimistic realism was not a contemptible point of view. There are historical and social ills that cannot be cured, because the cure will kill the patient; they can only be treated symptomatically and managed. Sometimes a conservative state cannot even, as Metternich urged it should do, outlive its enemies and the evils which beset it. The alternative to Metternich's kind of resignation to these truths is usually 1914—a great last-ditch struggle, with the state going down flags flying in a fight against the inevitable. But Metternich's outlook, if not contemptible, is impractical; political leaders cannot act on it. They must seek answers to problems and believe in their state and its future. Even in Austria, Metternich's view was dismissed by all save a few feudal reactionaries like Windischgrätz (who did not understand it) as weakness, failure of nerve, and a lack of constructive ideas. What an eighty-year-old retired statesman could resign himself to, a twenty-three-year-old Emperor, proud and ambitious, could not.

All things considered, therefore, Buol's policy probably represented the best gamble available for Austria, one worth trying at least up to the breakdown of the Vienna Conferences, when it obviously failed. Then Metternich's kind of expectant neutrality would probably have been better; it still would have meant losses and dangers for Austria, but perhaps less humiliation and damage than actually occurred.*

Yet this conclusion, that Austria failed but that she never had much chance to succeed, is fairly obvious and superficial. The bigger point is to see the significance of Austria's policy and its failure.

---

* To be sure, this leaves unanswered the questions of how the war would then have been ended at all, and whether any direct Allied-Russian peace would not have been even more damaging to Austria.

For all its indecisiveness, the war, as A. J. P. Taylor points out, turned out about as well for Europe and especially for Britain as could be hoped.[7] This was not an accident.* From the diplomatic standpoint, the outcome was largely achieved by Austria, who paid the price for it in her political defeat. While many circumstances contributed to controlling the war, only Austria among the great powers worked effectively and steadily toward this end. She tried to control the Allied war aims in the only feasible way, by cooperating with them; she forced from Russia the concessions that kept the war from getting out of hand and finally ended it; she repeatedly revived its original purpose of protecting Turkey against

* Some have seen the outcome as evidence of the basic soundness of British policy, none more frankly than Michael Hurst (*Historical Journal*, XII [1969], 722–23). The war, he insists, was "a good idea," "certainly justified" in view of the Tsar's aggressive aims and his refusal of the "honorable peace terms offered him by Britain." "Without a reverse that Tsar would be able to restart his little game with impunity later on. A lunge at his underbelly [*sic*] therefore made very good sense and the results more than justified the effort," restraining Russia for two decades in the Near East.
One hardly knows where to begin to comment. Leaving aside the assumptions that Russia needed to be taught a good lesson, that it could be administered only by war, and that the dead and wounded on all sides were a suitable price to pay, and passing over likewise, as Hurst does, the dangers and damage created for all of central Europe in teaching Russia that lesson, let us merely consider the actual results of this war for Britain. It directly created the worst possible danger for her, a Franco-Russian alliance, something she had been concerned for decades to prevent. The fact that this did not primarily turn out to hurt Britain, but rather to help Prussia and Italy and hurt Austria, was due solely to Russia's caution, Napoleon's incompetence, and the usual British luck and margin of safety. If the Crimean War restrained Russia's ambitions in the Near East for a time (and Palmerston and Clarendon surely did not believe it did), it only led her to undermine Turkey (and Austria and the European peace) by a policy far more dangerous than her previous one, namely, the encouragement of Balkan nationalism and revolution. Moreover, the Crimean War led Russia not so much to stop her encroachments as to prepare herself and reorganize her forces better for the next occasion, and it directly spurred her to turn her territorial expansion into those areas (the Far East, the Caucasus, and Central Asia) where British interests were far more vulnerable and directly affected than in the Near East, and where there would be no European coalition available to help stop Russia. The war also promoted serious trouble with the United States over Central America and contributed indirectly but materially to a war with Persia in 1856 and to the British policy of scuttle in the Transcaucasus in the late 1850's. (Cf. Joachim Hoffman, "Die Politik der Mächte in der Endphase der Kaukasuskriege," *Jahrbücher für Geschichte Osteuropas*, XVII (1969), 215–58).

Russia; and she helped spare Europe a great Palmerstonian crusade against Russia ending in a nineteenth-century Peace of Brest-Litovsk.

This claim that Austria's policy worked to the advantage of Europe must seem like a bad joke where Russia, Prussia, and Germany are concerned. Granted, Austria did Russia no favors, and her policy often threatened Prussian and German neutrality. But only her existence and presence made that neutrality possible; had she not been there to take the brunt of Russian and above all of Western pressure, it would have been brought to bear directly on the rest of Germany, and Prussia and the German states surely would have succumbed to it. As for Russia, her bitterness over Austria's ingratitude and treachery was fully understandable. Austrian policy became very anti-Russian, though only after Russia had launched a policy extremely dangerous to Austria and got herself involved in a war that threatened Austria as much as her. Yet if in the long run Russia was lucky to have escaped so lightly from the Crimean War, that good luck was partly due to Austria's presence.* Buol had always worked to make Russia pay a price for ending the war, but a price within reasonable limits. Moreover, it is impossible to see how Russia could have obtained peace and escaped revolution without Austrian intervention. A direct Franco-Russian understanding was highly unlikely. The Morny-Gorchakov and Seebach peace initiatives were simply good devices for France to cozen Russia for postwar purposes; France's peace move with Austria was the only serious one. Napoleon would not have dared to make peace by breaking with Britain, and he could not have dragged Britain to the peace table or satisfied her on the peace terms without Austria's help.

As for the sea powers, Austria's pro-Western orientation both saved them from immense dangers of their own making and rendered them great positive services. France had no effective answer to the threat of Austro-German armed neutrality, Drouyn's nightmare. The talk of withdrawing France's army from the Crimea and starting a war of nationalities on the Rhine was bluff, and sensible

---

* Of course this does not mean that Prussia and Russia should have been grateful to Austria for her efforts, as Prokesch claimed. If she in a sense saved them from the worst possible outcomes of their policies, they did even more to save her from the dangers of her own.

Frenchmen knew it. They could have tried revolutionizing Italy; but this would not have hurt Prussia and Germany and would only have driven Austria into Russia's arms. Drouyn did not want Italy liberated on general principles, and even Napoleon was eventually to learn that it would backfire on France, as Austria always said it would. It was Austria's mobilization and occupation of the Principalities that made the Crimean expedition possible and gave it a chance of success. In the spring of 1855, Austria offered France a chance to end the war on a basis that many sensible Frenchmen (Drouyn, Thouvenel, Bourqueney, Morny) regarded as a godsend. Austria's intervention that fall enabled France to get peace without sacrificing the British alliance; her ultimatum to Russia enabled France to enjoy the position of mediator between all parties at the peace congress.

The Crimean War shows, moreover, that the special providence Bismarck said was reserved for fools, drunkards, and the United States of America operated also for Britain, and Austria was its agent. By April 1856 even Palmerston admitted that future Allied campaigns would probably have been disastrous; he never admitted the role Austria had played in coaxing and wheedling Britain to the peace table and preventing her from sabotaging the peace as it was being made.[8] *

This discussion leads to the main point about the impact of the Crimean War on the European international system. The usual view is that the war was fought to preserve the balance of power in Europe, and that the sea powers' main purpose, especially Britain's, was to restore the balance threatened by Russia and to establish a new liberal Concert to sustain it against Russia, just as the 1815 settlement had established a Concert against revolutionary France.[9] The argument is linked with the general view that peace was maintained throughout the nineteenth century mainly through a stable power equilibrium, which Britain as the leading maritime, naval, commercial, and imperial power was primarily responsible for maintaining.[10] Any examination of this larger view of the balance of power in nineteenth-century international relations is bound to be

* Aberdeen recognized it, however, writing Graham (18 Jan. 1856): "If we obtain it, this will be an Austrian peace, and one certainly not made in collusion with Russia" (Ab. Corr. 1855–1860, 154).

sketchy and oversimplified and to go far beyond the evidence presented here. It must be attempted, however, if the significance of the Crimean War is to be made clear.

To begin with the more general point: European peace in the nineteenth century did not derive to any great degree from Britain's maintaining a continental balance of power while she preserved order in the non-European world (the Pax Britannica). For one thing, she did not perform this task with any consistency. What David Baynes Horn has shown about eighteenth-century British foreign policy, that Britain displayed no consistent concern for the balance of power,[11] applies equally to the nineteenth. She sometimes acted consciously to maintain it, especially where her immediate interests were involved—in Belgium in the 1830's, in Germany and Italy (more disputably) in 1848–1849. But she let the balance be overturned in 1859–1871 without doing anything significant to control the process. She often simply took advantage of the balance on the Continent to promote her own interests elsewhere; she also often, as in the period of Germany's hegemony under Bismarck, paid little attention to the balance, or actually took the side of the stronger group.

Furthermore, British policies and institutions made her ill-suited to the task of maintaining the balance even when she wanted to. From the time of George Canning on, she decided to stand aloof from continental quarrels, intervening only when her direct interests or great European questions were involved, and then with decisive force.[12] In practice she did not even follow this principle consistently. Britain's rejection of alliances and permanent commitments, her insular position and maritime security, her overriding world trade and imperial interests, and her concern for public opinion and Parliament combined to make her policy and her interventions in European affairs even more unpredictable than the principles of Canning necessitated. To serve usefully in preserving peace, an international balance of power, like a national economic plan or an international monetary system, must be a sensitive, mobile mechanism, capable of gradual shifts and adjustments to meet developing situations. It must be given constant attention and timely adjustments to avert major dislocations and conflicts.[13] Trying to operate such a balance from Britain's position by her methods is like operating a jeweler's balance by occasionally throwing weights onto the scales from a position across the room. More than once in the nineteenth century, continental statesmen had to exert themselves strenuously to save the balance from British attempts to maintain it.

But the main point is that a balance of power itself does not necessarily help prevent war. Its main purpose is not to preserve peace but to prevent empire or hegemony, to preserve the independence of the various units within a multinational system. This it sometimes does well. As a peacekeeping device it has grave deficiencies. The very term "balance of power" is so ambiguous that it is virtually useless either as a tool for analyzing policy or a principle for guiding it; almost any policy, including a drive for empire or hegemony, can plausibly be presented as one of maintaining a balance of power.[14] More important is the inherent instability of balance of power politics, the powerful built-in bias within the coalition-forming process itself toward decision rather than balance, the tendency to want to form winning or dominant coalitions rather than balancing or blocking ones. The very process of conducting equilibrist politics therefore easily leads to disequilibrium, promotes dangerous fears and tempting opportunities, and encourages confrontations, conflicts, and even preventive wars.[15] Nothing shows this better than the history of the eighteenth century, where balance of power politics was certainly followed, and out of it emerged repeated wars and great threats to the independence and the very survival of greater and lesser powers alike, culminating in the wars of the French Revolution and Napoleon that destroyed the whole system.*

* This is not the picture one often receives of eighteenth-century international relations. More common are descriptions like Stanley Hoffmann's of the balance of power system from 1648 to 1789:

"The balance operated effectively because the treaties of Westphalia had redistributed territory so as to create a number of major states capable of neutralizing each other and had also removed the poisonous element of religious conflict. Within the main units, mercantilism and absolutism gradually weakened. New transnational ties developed; the 'corporate identity' of monarchs, diplomats, and officers across national boundaries led to a consensus on the legitimacy of the balance, just as the community of European intellectuals produced a consensus on the values of the Enlightenment. The political result was a mechanical balance, frequently disturbed however, either

It was clearly not the balance of power that made the nineteenth century as a whole more peaceful in Europe than its predecessor or successor. It would be easier to argue that various kinds of hegemony kept the peace. Austrian leadership, as long as it lasted, preserved order in Germany and Italy. The absolutist hegemony of the Holy Alliance served to prevent wars over Poland and the Near

---

because a state could never be sure in advance whether or when others would try to curb it, or because of individual ambitions. Hence numerous limited wars occurred: stylized wars of position that only rarely affected the civilian populations."

He describes it further as "a system of increasing moderation," depicts the growth of international law within it, and claims that "the expectation of a harmony of interests [was] . . . fed by the system." "The collapse of that system," he continues, "was a sudden, swift chain reaction" produced by the French Revolution. It tore up the ideological links uniting Europe; French victories destroyed the equilibrium; and Napoleon's ambitions "produced the first modern instance of total power politics" (*The State of War* [New York, 1965], 100–02).

Professor Hoffman is a distinguished scholar; but I wonder whether he and I are thinking of the same century. Does it make sense to speak of worldwide conflicts like the War of the Spanish Succession or the Seven Years' War as limited wars? Can one talk of an expected harmony of interests in a system where the planned partition and destruction of major states, sometimes even great powers, was a common feature of international politics? (Spain, the Low Countries, Sweden, Austria, Prussia, the Ottoman Empire, and Poland were all the objects of such planned or actual partitions.) What moderation or limiting principle does one detect in the aims and ambitions of Louis XIV, or Chatham, or Peter the Great, or Catherine? Can anyone contend that the wars of Louis XIV had no major impact on the civilian population of France, the Rhineland, Upper Germany, and the Low Countries? What of Prussia's inhabitants in the Seven Years' War? Sweden's in the reign of Charles XII? Austria's in the wars of Maria Theresa? Russia's under Peter and Catherine?

Above all, it is a great distortion and oversimplification to believe that the French Revolution came on suddenly, like a snowstorm in springtime, and wrecked a working balance of power system. R. R. Palmer and others have discredited this theory as it relates to the general origins of the revolution, and it works no better in international relations. The fact is that the international system by 1789 had already broken down. The great powers were operating without any restraints, especially in the East. The Eastern war, Hertzberg's Grand Design, and the partitions of Poland all prove it. Moreover, the balance of power had shifted perilously against France. Vergennes's moderation had not paid off; the other powers were delightedly exploiting the weakness caused by her internal troubles. Of course the Revolution added an ideological element to the great struggle for mastery in Europe and helped France to gain that mastery for a time. But the struggle itself rose naturally and inevitably out of eighteenth-century balance of power politics.

East. Germany's continental hegemony after 1871 headed off several threatened wars and restrained international competition within tolerable limits; as soon as the Franco-Russian alliance restored the balance of power, a more dangerous level of competition ensued. British supremacy on the seas and in Africa, American domination of North America and the Caribbean, Russia predominance in the Far East (until Japan's rise) all served to promote peace—a rapacious peace of the stronger, perhaps, but one that avoided great-power confrontations all the same. Obviously it would be as wrong to argue that hegemony per se is the key to peace as it is to claim this of balance of power. What counts is how each in a given situation tends to create international order or disorder—whether it tends to promote insecurity, threats, and dangerously tempting opportunities for members of the system, or contributes to a general sense of security and the willingness to accept restraints and abide by the rules of the system. Balance of power politics has the former effect at least as much as the latter; it often demands the sacrifice of such values as moderation in goals, cooperation, and the consideration of the good of the whole community, supposedly for the sake of keeping the balance.[16]

What accounted for European peace after 1815 was rather a system of international order established upon a balance of power, but going well beyond it. This system rested basically on three elements. The first was the conservative spirit reigning among the great powers, their common determination to maintain the treaties, preserve the status quo, and resist revolutionary wars of aggression or bids by any one for European empire. This element requires little comment, except to note that this spirit of conservative restraint involves not a return to eighteenth-century ideas, but a conscious break with them—a determination to abjure the selfish and reckless policies that had played into the hands of the French revolutionaries and Napoleon and nearly destroyed Europe. Nothing is more striking than the contrast between the land-hungry policies of Austria, Prussia, and Russia through most of the eighteenth century and their policies after 1815. European statesmen had learned that eighteenth-century poker led to Russian roulette and decided to play contract bridge instead.

The second element, the Concert of Europe, is harder to define.

Often statesmen spoke of the European Concert or the Concert of Powers as synonymous with the European state system or the European balance. The Concert had no formal organization; the system of congresses from 1815 to 1823 was only its instrument, and the Concert survived its demise. Nor did the Concert involve a clear-cut ideological or political program. In fact, attempts to give it one—either conservative efforts like those of Metternich and Alexander I in the 1820's or liberal ones like Gladstone's in the 1880's —tended to weaken and disrupt the Concert. Such efforts not only emphasized latent ideological differences between the powers, but also demanded unequally apportioned sacrifices of their individual interests for the sake of a putative general good in which all the powers did not believe, or believe equally. Nevertheless, the Concert did involve some constraint and sacrifice; its members had at least to be willing to cooperate on all crucial European questions and to restrict their purposes to those that would not wreck or undermine the system.

A fair number of Concert rules can be identified, most of them a matter of precedent or general understanding, but some incorporated explicitly into treaties. Like international law in general, their force was moral rather than contractual, but this does not mean they could be broken with impunity. One such rule was that only the five great powers, the Directory of Europe, decided great European questions. Lesser powers had rights that should be protected, and they could be heard on questions that concerned them, but they had no deciding vote. No power could wage war in Europe for territorial gain or promote revolution or unrest within another great power's territory or sphere of vital interest. No international question of vital interest to a great power could be raised without its consent. But if a problem of genuine international import arose, no power could refuse an international conference upon it or exclude any other great power from it. Above all, direct challenges and confrontations between individual great powers had to be avoided at almost any cost, mainly by referring the quarrel to the decision of the Concert. The first and great commandment of the Concert was, "Thou shalt not threaten or humiliate another great power."

Naturally there were strains within the Concert, times when its rules were broken or stretched dangerously, disputes over whether questions were subject to Concert jurisdiction and what form Concert action ought to take. Concert restraints sometimes made the powers restless, especially Britain; Canning's break with the congress system in 1822–1823, though justifiable, was a conscious return to the more unrestrained competition of the eighteenth century. Several of the powers operated without restraint in extra-European areas—Britain especially in Asia; Russia in the Caucasus, Central Asia, and the Far East; France in Algeria—and such operations sometimes rebounded dangerously on the European scene. Especially with Palmerston at the Foreign Office, Britain tended to test the limits of other powers' restraints and to exploit their desire for peace, for the sake of British prestige and interests. All the great powers save Prussia took some actions in Europe between 1815 and 1848 that could be seen as challenges to Concert rules or to other powers, or that at least set bad precedents. Yet all of them, including Britain, generally supported the Concert system up to 1848, which accounts for the fact that questions which in other eras would almost certainly have caused major wars, like the Greek and Belgian and Italian revolutions or the two Mehemet Ali crises, were settled or at least terminated without great-power conflicts.

Almost as important as the Concert for maintaining European peace was the third element, the organization of Germany and Italy into an independent center for Europe under Austrian hegemony. The loose defensive structure of this independent center filled the power vacuum that had been the prime occasion for wars and bids for European empire ever since the sixteenth century. With Austria, the most territorially sated, geographically exposed, and conservative of all the great powers, in charge of the area, central Europe was virtually ensured against wars of territorial aggrandizement and protected from French or Russian encroachment. Furthermore, the whole area served as an ideological and political, as well as military, buffer zone between the autocratic East and the more liberal West. The arrangement helped protect Russia from the threat of dangerous Western ideas and the promotion of revolution, especially in Poland, while it tended to shield the West against the influence of tsarist autocracy. Finally, this system also provided Austria, the power most interested in preserving the status quo, with the position of stage manager of the Concert. Geographically and politically she normally could furnish a *point d'entente et d'union* for the Concert; she could at one and the same time hold dangerous opponents apart and build the bridges to bring them together. She certainly could not do this by force; only in her own sphere could she forcibly repress revolution or violent change, and even here she had to be very careful about how the other great powers would react. The other powers could ignore her efforts at managing the Concert if they wished, and they sometimes did. Nevertheless, Austria's role as the natural center and stage manager of the Concert was often important in preserving peace.

While the revolutions of 1848 obviously weakened all three of these main supports of European peace, they nevertheless survived. There was in fact a revival of conservatism in foreign policy after 1848 just as much as in domestic affairs, out of resignation and lack of alternatives as much as out of conviction. The fact that Concert restraints continued to deter the powers from really exploiting their opportunities for tempting gains accounts for the avoidance of general war in 1848–1850. In many ways the European international system in early 1853 was still that of pre-1848. That Concert diplomacy was still a live option is shown by the rapidity with which centers of Concert entente and action were formed at Constantinople and Vienna as soon as the Eastern question became critical and by the tenacity with which many statesmen clung to a Concert solution as the only possible way out, and acted according to that belief. In other words, it took the war itself to destroy the bases of the long Metternichian peace—the conservative consensus among the powers, the great-power Concert, and the Austrian-led European center. This destruction of the Concert is the main impact of the Crimean War on the European state system.

One might protest that this pictures a phenomenon in terms of cause and effect that is really only two sides of the same coin. To say that the war destroyed the Concert is only to say that the Concert failed to prevent the war; its collapse was a consequence of its own failure. The answer to this plausible argument is that there is an important reason *why* Concert diplomacy failed to prevent European war over a question that, though nasty and difficult, was of the same type that had often before been solved by Concert diplomacy.

Concert diplomacy did not here fail because it was worn out, no longer adequate to the task; it failed because it was prevented from succeeding, its basic principles repudiated and its fundamental rules broken.

It will not do simply to say that the Crimean War resulted from drift and blunder on the part of the great powers. This is of course true in the sense that no great power planned the war or the steps that led to it. But then almost all wars, even those that are "planned," like the Italian war of 1859 or World War II, involve major elements of miscalculation and blunder. Wars, like accidents, are caused. Nor does it answer the question to decide who was to blame for creating the crisis in the first place. No doubt Russia was primarily responsible, with important shares of the blame going to France and Austria. The question is why Concert diplomacy did not succeed in settling the crisis after it arose, and the answer cannot be found simply in miscalculation or public opinion or divided counsels or bad luck. The fact is that every hopeful effort at a Concert-type solution to this crisis—the Vienna Note, the Buol Project, Austria's efforts for an armistice and direct negotiations between Russia and Turkey under Concert supervision, the December 5 protocol, even the January 13 peace terms and the proposed reciprocal evacuation of the Principalities and the Black Sea—was either abandoned before it had a chance to succeed, or rejected at the outset, or sabotaged in operation by a new challenge thrown down by the West to Russia.

Whatever else Russia can be blamed for, she did not cause Concert diplomacy to fail. The last thing she wanted was a confrontation with the West, especially Britain, and the moment she saw she might be caught in such a confrontation, she began backing down, and in the end desperately sought an escape through the Concert. Austria clearly had dangerous ideas and impulses early in 1853, but by midyear she was bending every effort to promote a European solution. France, though she preferred to accept war rather than part with Britain and certainly did her share to escalate the crisis at crucial junctures, would have been satisfied with the kind of diplomatic retreat by Russia which by late 1853 she was eager to make and the Concert could have arranged for her. Even Turkey was not wholly bent on war, as her ultimate acceptance of Redcliffe's December 15 terms attests. The only power that consistently violated Concert rules, rejected or frustrated Concert solutions, and insisted on turning the crisis into a head-to-head confrontation between great powers was Britain. In so doing, she broke the first law of the Concert, "Thou shalt not challenge or seek to humiliate another great power," and thereby helped ensure not only the outbreak of war, but the demise of the Concert itself.

The evidence on this point seems clear and abundant. Yet it has not been seen. The reason is surely not any deliberate concealment or distortion by historians, much less the "falsification of history" with which Soviet historians charge Temperley, Henderson, and Western historians in general. I would suggest that the prevailing assumptions about the balance of power have obscured the picture and prevented the evidence from being seen or appreciated. As long as one supposes that the only effective way to prevent war and preserve the balance of power is to confront an actual or potential aggressor with an overwhelming show of force and compel him to back down, Britain's policy looks normal and right and Austria's timid and irresolute. If no Concert exists, then this procedure may indeed be the only one possible, but its inferiority to Concert methods for purposes of persuasion and conciliation springs to the eye. Surely there is much truth to Buol's dictum that the goal of Concert diplomacy was to bring about a reconciliation of the contending parties and that forceful means are incompatible with reconciliation. The immense psychological and practical advantage of Concert diplomacy is that it confronts an actual or potential aggressor with a group norm that he himself acknowledges, and it promises to reward conformity and punish deviation.

The influence of reigning assumptions about the balance of power can be seen in the form that debate over British policy and the origins of the war has taken. It has centered on two questions: whether Redcliffe was guilty of provoking or luring Russia into war, and whether either Aberdeen's policy of appeasement of Russia or Palmerston's policy of direct confrontation of her would have prevented the war, had either been consistently pursued.[17] Both questions implicitly assume that this crisis was essentially a quarrel between Russia and Britain, or Russia and the sea powers, and that it had to be settled by some kind of British or Western appeasement of Russia, or compromise with her, or challenge to her. The assumption prejudges the question. Once Russia occupied the Principalities, by prevailing nineteenth-century rules and assumptions her quarrel no longer was one with Turkey alone, but became one with Europe as a whole, to be dealt with by the Concert as a group. Of course Britain and France would be vital members of the Concert, perhaps leaders of it and supplying the main coercive force to back it up. No one wanted to rob them of this role, least of all Buol. Nevertheless, the essence of the Concert approach was that if Russia had to be made to back down at all, it must be in favor of a solution all the great powers agreed upon (including Russia, if possible).

The very questions debated, about Redcliffe's alleged war guilt and Aberdeen's policy versus Palmerston's, are best answered in this context. Temperley is quite right in arguing that Redcliffe should not be blamed for the war. The reason, however, is not simply that he preferred a peaceful solution and worked for it (though this is true), but also that despite his ego involvement and frequently high-handed methods he was not basically averse to a Concert type of solution.* If Britain led the Concert in Europe, and he led it at Constantinople, and it served to check Russia and protect Turkey, he would be entirely satisfied. Moreover, he did not originally want to exclude Austria from the Concert, or even to oust Russia from it prior to the outbreak of war. As for Aberdeen, he had no consistent policy, not even one of appeasing Russia; but his very anxiety to avoid commitment and war made him eager for a Concert settlement. The crucial difference in British policy was made by Palmerston's insistence from the outset that Russia had directly challenged

---

* A striking illustration of this fact is an undated memorandum entitled "Objects" found among Redcliffe's private papers (FO 352/36/9), evidently dating from the summer of 1853. Here Redcliffe listed his nine major aims and the progress made so far. The first, to bring about a Russo-Turkish agreement on the Holy Places, was marked "Done." So was the second, to prevent the Porte from accepting Russia's proposed protectorate. The third read: "To bring this about [i.e., the rejection of Russia's protectorate over Turkey] in such a manner as may prevent a quarrel. *not done*." The fifth read: "To energize Austria in the exercise of a legitimate influence independent of others. *Much progress made*." After the last aim, Redcliffe wrote: "Query? Should a kind of general protectorate [of the European powers over the Ottoman Christians] be recommended? *recommended with limitations*."

Britain and France and that they, not the Concert, must force her to back down. Ultimately he proved able to bring the rest of the Cabinet along with him.

It really does not matter whether Palmerston sincerely believed that Russia's policy represented a deliberate challenge to the sea powers. Even if he did (and he had a remarkable capacity for seeing challenges to Britain anywhere and everywhere), the *raison d'être* of the Concert was to transmute even overt and unmistakable challenges from one great power to another into joint European questions and decisions or, failing this, to confront an incorrigible aggressor with a united European front. This was precisely what Palmerston wanted to prevent. He could not tolerate having Russia "grouped," her challenge transmuted, the Concert interposed between her and Britain and France, and a golden bridge thus built for a Russian retreat. This is why he persistently opposed Austrian mediation and was so bent on moving the conference to London. Nor does it really matter whether Palmerston's challenge, laid down by Britain earlier and more forcefully, might have caused Russia to back down and avoid war.* Even if this were granted (and it is at least doubtful, seeing how deeply Nicholas was committed already by late May), the long-range results of Palmerston's policy would have been little less harmful for peace and for the Concert. Another crisis sooner or later would have produced another confrontation before which Russia could not have backed down; no great power can recurrently be challenged and humiliated without resorting to war.

* Jasper Ridley (*Palmerston*, 414–18) argues for this view, and A. J. P. Taylor evidently considers it a fact needing no proof: "Indeed the war would have been avoided if Great Britain had followed the resolute line advocated by Palmerston and Russell—whom Bright blamed for the war. The responsibility for the war lay with the pacific Lord Aberdeen, whom Bright admired; and Aberdeen later admitted it himself" ("Bright and the Crimean War," 513). Taylor is of course entitled to his opinion on the responsibility for the war, though one might wish to know the reasons for his certainty. His implication that Aberdeen later admitted that he had been wrong and Palmerston right is, however, quite false. (He may have fallen into this view through Temperley's misleading account of Aberdeen's remorse—*Crimea*, 385). What tormented Aberdeen's conscience for the rest of his life, as his private correspondence shows, was the feeling that he might have prevented the war had he only fought longer and harder against Palmerston and Russell and not allowed good peace opportunities like the Buol Project to be passed by.

One must not, of course, imply that Britain was the only power in this whole crisis to play fast and loose with Concert principles. Russia's ideas about a private deal with Britain over the Eastern question, Francis Joseph's early notions about partitioning Turkey with Russia, Bruck's proposals to exclude the sea powers from an Eastern settlement—all violated Concert ideas and practices and would have had destructive effects if carried out. Napoleon was an enemy of the existing Concert in many respects, and Cavour even more so. Manteuffel was willing secretly to help Britain exclude Austria from it. These and other signs point to the increasing debility of the Concert system and help explain why many in Britain and outside it were glad to break with it, and few mourned its demise. The fact remains, however, that when the danger of war loomed, the other powers, especially the Eastern powers, clung to the Concert as a means of averting it, and Britain did not. No doubt this was above all because Austria, Prussia, and Russia were more afraid of war and conscious of their greater vulnerability. Virtue in international relations is almost always the daughter of fear and necessity. But this does not change its effects and value or, for that matter, make it any the less virtuous.

It would also be wrong to imply that the reason for Britain's policy was that the whole ministry shared Palmerston's combative views and his desire for a showdown with Russia, or that he won because he had a nation of Palmerstons behind him. Even if one argues, as I do, that Britain repeatedly acted to prevent a diplomatic settlement by posing new conditions it expected and desired Russia to refuse, then using Russia's refusal to justify new Western moves making the challenge to Russia still more unmistakable and unacceptable, one cannot present these tactics as a deliberate design for war. The elements of confusion, divided counsel, fear of public opinion or of political embarrassment, and concern for maintaining the Cabinet in power are all too obvious in the minds of the ministers involved. Russell's changes of mind are almost too swift to follow, much less explain; Clarendon often whirled about like a weathercock in a tornado. Some ministers went along with the policy unwittingly, others with great reluctance.

Moreover, while there is an obvious correspondence between Palmerston's policy of confrontation and what Cobden called "the pugnacious, energetic, self-sufficient foreigner-despising and pity-ing character of the noble insular creature John Bull," [18] it is as much a mistake to regard the pressure of public opinion as decisive for British policy as to ignore or underrate it. For one thing, the ministers' fear of public opinion was fluctuating and equivocal. Clarendon feared just as much that the public would discover what Britain's policy really was and repudiate it as he feared that public opinion would drive Britain into an unnecessary war. He was not the only one to feel this way.[19] For another, public opinion hardly ever dictates policy in the sense of prescribing the exact course a government must follow; it normally simply helps establish the limits of choice available, as it did here. British public opinion un-doubtedly made it impossible for the government *actively* to sup-port Russia against Turkey, or openly to abstain from any intervention, or to accept clear defeat at Russia's hands. There was even something to Palmerston's contention that Britain must be seen to win over Russia. But none of these unacceptable courses were required in order for Britain to participate in Concert diplomacy. All she had to do was simply to stop raising the price of peace her-self, let the other powers in on the process of getting Russia to back down, and exercise enough pressure on her client Turkey to get her to accept a European solution. Such a settlement would even have represented a British victory, of precisely the same kind that Palmerston won over the question of Belgian independence in 1830–1839 and in the Eastern crisis of 1839–1841. Such a victory could have been sold to the public just as the final peace settlement was, with little more effort than went into arousing war fever.

No one will deny that Palmerston's victory owed something to accident, luck, and public opinion. But the element of governmental decision was also present and finally decisive. In the last analysis Palmerston won because enough other ministers came to believe with him that a Concert solution would not do. It would embarrass the ministry at home, would not sufficiently enhance Britain's stand-ing in the world, would not deal Russia an adequate setback, and would even make Britain appear cowardly and unwilling to fight. Thus the ultimate reason the war was begun was the same as would defeat all efforts to end it by negotiation before military victory— British honor and prestige.

Clarendon is an especially fascinating and central figure in this story because, besides typifying what Sir Richard Pares has called "the spontaneous dishonesty of weakness," he mirrored in his internal struggles and vacillations the contradictory pulls of Concert diplomacy and Palmerstonian confrontation. He could not take refuge in Gladstone's highminded but naive belief that the Allies were disinterestedly vindicating European public law against an open aggressor. He knew instead that Britain was pushing other powers, especially Austria, out of her way and demanding British terms or none and that these terms meant the public humiliation of Russia. He knew that Turkey, not Russia, most often represented the major obstacle to a settlement and that the real issue for Britain was not protecting Turkey but openly defeating Russia. The knowledge bothered him, as it did not bother Palmerston; he followed Palmerston, but with a bad conscience. The confused, contradictory, and often logically perverse arguments he developed to justify this policy were at least partly designed to enable him somehow to accept it and live with it himself.

Once again, it could be plausibly objected that there must have been a deeper motive to this policy than a desire for national prestige and honor. The contest with Russia looks instead simply like part of the century-long struggle for commercial, naval, and imperial supremacy, a war to nip a growing Russian naval menace in the bud,* to promote British trade and influence in the Near East, to relieve Russian pressure on the approaches to India, and to elevate British prestige at Russia's expense in all of Asia. One can certainly find these ideas expressed by British leaders. An "imperialism of free trade" was current in Britain at this time,[20] and Palmerston especially believed that Britain, though now supreme in the world, had to respond to every real or apparent challenge, above all in Asia, or face imperial decline. It was this attitude that was mainly responsible for Britain's many confrontations and conflicts in China, Persia, Sind, Afghanistan, and elsewhere.

Nonetheless, the Crimean War was not begun or mainly fought

* This is Wilhelm Treue's thesis (*Der Krimkrieg und die Entstehung der modernen Flotten*, 4–5, 7–11, 32–37). It is more than doubtful, however. British naval supremacy was secure prior to the war, and the British knew it. See C. J. Bartlett, *Great Britain and Sea Power, 1815–1853* (Oxford, 1963), 323–33; *Letters of the Prince Consort*, 191–92.

for these imperial motives; they were important but secondary purposes adopted once it was under way. Britain's attitude toward Austria is partial proof of this. Trade and imperial interests could conceivably have produced war with Russia, but never the running quarrel with Austria. There was no serious trade rivalry with her,[21] no threat to the empire, no naval menace, no thrust toward Constantinople, no conflict of fundamental interest at all. Yet Palmerston, Russell, Clarendon, Redcliffe, and many other British leaders, as well as the general public, were as anti-Austrian as they were anti-Russian. Moreover, given the genuine moral seriousness and idealism of Victorian England (to which Palmerston was in the main an exception),* it is impossible to see Britain launching or fighting a war mainly for commercial gain or manifest self-interest. The British believed—in a sense they *had* to believe—that the war was not justified unless it was fought for a higher purpose, to bring about beneficial changes in Europe commensurate with its costs. The gospel of free trade and liberalism that they propagated undoubtedly harmonized with British interests, but this does not mean that it was not a genuine ideal, and even a relatively unselfish one.[22]

One must therefore take Whig ideology seriously as a major element in forming British war aims, providing the vital idealistic counterpoint to the concern for British honor and prestige that was most responsible for getting her into war and keeping her there. The British desire to promote European progress and ordered liberty against both reactionary despotism and radical revolution, and to replace the old oppressive international order with a new constitutional liberal one built around England, makes sense of many half-serious initiatives cropping up in British policy that had little to do with the war effort or actually impeded it: encouraging liberal parties in Germany and Prussia against the existing regimes; promoting liberalism in the Principalities and Serbia; scolding and threatening bad rulers like the Pope and the kings of Naples and Greece; supporting Sardinia and urging changes in Italy, even if it

---

* Discussing Palmerston as representative of the age, W. L. Burns writes, "What disqualifies him is his lack of the sober, serious, conscious thoughtfulness so characteristic of the age he lived into; and the sense that there was, at the bottom of him, a moral vacuum" (*The Age of Equipoise: A Study of the Mid-Victorian Generation* [New York, 1965], 18).

jeopardized Austria's cooperation in the war. Whig ideology more than particular British interests accounts for the impatient resentment with which British leaders met every attempt by other powers to get them to define their war aims, to remind them of previous commitments, and to insist on the sanctity of treaties. Their reaction was that of the clergyman secretly apostate from the faith and eager to use the church solely to promote social reform who is constantly being reminded by fellow clergymen of his baptismal and ordination vows. Whig ideology helps account for Britain's resistance to a negotiated peace and her disappointment with the results of the war, which served to discredit liberalism at home and abroad instead of spreading its blessings to the Continent. Above all, it explains British opposition to Austria. Catholic in religion, ultramontane in church polity, absolutist in government, feudal in social structure, obscurantist in culture, protectionist in commerce, and imperialist in her relations to her own and other peoples, Austria represented the odious antithesis to Whig ideals as much as Russia did. Her location, moreover, was as annoying as her character was repellent. Russia, a half-Asiatic power, would no longer be able to impede European progress once she was pushed back and her prestige destroyed. But Austria stood in the middle of Europe. A paraphrase of Gladstone's famous statement of 1880, that there was no place on the map where one could put his finger and say, there Austria did good, aptly expresses Britain's mood a quarter of a century before. Everywhere in Europe where Britain wanted to do good—Italy, Germany, Poland, the Balkans, Turkey—Austria was there and standing in Britain's way.

Austria's policy in the war was the most hateful thing of all. It was not only, or mainly, that she betrayed the West by refusing to fight, or that she pursued (according to Britain) purely selfish aims, but that she tried to rob the sea powers of the decisive victory they wanted, and did so in the most frustrating way possible: by cooperating with them rather than siding with Russia. Austria's open enmity might have endangered France, but not Britain; it would have drawn the ideological lines more clearly and given her a vulnerable target welcome to many Englishmen. But instead Austria managed to join the Allies and in her stubborn leechlike fashion to stay with them through a thousand rebuffs, so that time and again when the British wished to act decisively, they found themselves hampered by an ally they despised but could not, on account of her central position, simply cast off or ignore. Repeatedly, down to the final peace, Austria thwarted Britain not by direct opposition but by controlled assistance—by helping her obtain what she claimed to want, thus preventing her from seeking what she really wanted, but dared not openly admit was her aim.*

This was not accident but design. Where Britain wanted a new Europe, Buol struggled to preserve what was essential of the old— not the Holy Alliance, which he neither could nor would restore, nor even the Vienna System (he repeatedly contended that Austria now had to lay a new basis for peace in Europe, as she had done in 1813–1815), but the old Concert in a new form, the old rules and restraints so necessary to Austria, based on a different alignment of the powers. It is misleading to suggest as S. A. Kaehler does that Buol tried to save Austria by reviving the cabinet diplomacy of the eighteenth century and trying a diplomatic revolution like that of Kaunitz in 1756.[23] Austria's desire to check Russia and Prussia with help from the West, especially France, was not at all revolutionary, but a traditional and obvious Austrian policy, expressed by Count Ficquelmont as "always to resist Russia without breaking with her." [24] Although Buol came perilously close to breaking with Russia under the exigencies of war and Western pressure, this remained his basic aim. Metternich had often pursued it before him. One after another, Buol's successors, while denouncing Buol's fatal policy, would actually adopt it themselves, trying to get Western help to stop Russia or Prussia, and failing in this effort as he had done.

* Thus A. J. P. Taylor's critique of Austrian neutrality as "the worst of all policies" is misdirected. "Neutrality," he writes, "like virtue, has its merits if maintained inviolate; it can also be sold for a high price. The one impossible thing it to be up for auction and to remain virtuous at the same time" (*Rumours of Wars*, 36–37). In fact, from April 1854 on, Austria was not neutral, but avowedly tied morally and contractually to the West. Far from trying to sell herself to the highest bidder, she wanted desperately to gain Western co-operation without having to sell her soul and menace her own existence in the bargain. Taylor's principle, however, is sound enough, and could be applied to Britain, where it might read: "Noncommitment has its rewards if maintained consistently; it can also be sacrificed for alliances and added security. The one impossible thing is to want to be allied and uncommitted at the same time."

Even from 1879 to 1914 there were repeated Austrian attempts to turn to the West to check Russia or to escape too great a dependence on Germany.

The reasons for persisting in the policy are obvious enough, and so are the grounds for repeated failure. As long as Austria fulfilled the West's purposes by checking Russia or Prussia, the Western powers saw no need to pay for services they could get for nothing. If she gave up and turned to the north and east for support, she was dismissed as worthless and unreliable. Besides, Britain in particular, at least in critical moments, did not want Austria to resist Russia *without* breaking with her, for such resistance only contained Russia in Europe, freeing her to expand elsewhere in areas of British interests. For both France and Britain, an Austro-German break with Russia was often the real desideratum, freeing them to exploit the break, play *tertius gaudens,* or come to terms with Russia over the head of central Europe.

It was Palmerston who reverted to the eighteenth century, not Buol. Buol's ideas were wholly post-1815: confining potential aggressors within the Concert rather than forming an open coalition against them; fighting wars, if at all, only for clearly defined, rational, calculable ends, and stopping when those ends were achieved; making peace settlements tolerable for the vanquished and enforceable for the victors; providing political rather than military solutions to basically political problems. His main purpose was to save the core of what Metternich had achieved in 1813–1815, which, since 1822, Britain had often opposed and now wanted to destroy: Austria's leadership of an independent center for Europe that would serve both to check Prussian ambitions and Russian expansion and to function as the pivot of the Concert. Buol was not a great man, and perhaps not even an adequate representative of these ideas. But what he stood for deserves respect.

Naturally, he failed. In the short run Austria helped keep the war from getting out of control and contributed greatly to a nonrevolutionary settlement. But that was all. If the Vienna System survived the war for a brief time, the Concert was already in ruins, Few believed in it any more, not even many Austrians; no one listened to the Cassandra cries from Vienna over what would happen if its rules and restraints were discarded. Moreover, Austria exhausted her influence and destroyed her credit by the very methods she had had to use in trying to salvage the Concert. The Crimean War was inevitably her last effort to manage the European system. Her writ had run out; the mandate of heaven had been removed.

There is no ground for regrets and nostalgia here, any more than there is for the gloating over Austria's discomfiture that Cavour and Clarendon indulged in and that one still encounters in the literature. This was Buol's tragedy, perhaps Austria's, but in most respects not Europe's as a whole. The old system Austria represented in Europe was truly worn out and the new version Buol tried to erect proved stillborn. Austria's presence and influence in Europe were still valuable for peace and stability, but probably, at this point in the mid-nineteenth century, at too high a price. She had closed off the best possibilities for her own internal development and long-range stability by opting for neoabsolutism; [25] much the same can be said of Austria's position in Europe. Nowhere was her stand simply one of frozen immobility or reaction, even in Italy, but her concessions and initiatives never went to the core of the problem, nor could they. Austria had to live with her problems, not solve them. Thus if the great questions of Germany and Italy and other national questions were soluble or irrepressible, then Austria had to be pushed aside, and the system and restraints that kept her now unnatural position outwardly intact had to be broken.

But if the Crimean War finally demonstrated Austria's inability to hold the old system together, it exposed even more pitilessly the inadequacy of Western ideas for replacing it and the incapacity of either Britain or France to manage the European state system, even had they been able to reshape it to their liking. What disqualified Britain from leading in organizing Europe for peace was not that she was particularly self-centered in her aims or especially reckless and bellicose. One could certainly argue that she was no more self-centered than any other great power, or than any power has to be, while her recklessness in this war was pretty clearly the result of particular circumstances and personalities, especially Palmerston's, more than any long-range tendency of British policy. What rendered her unfit was rather that Whig ideas on organizing Europe for peace were wrong, and most wrong where the greatest danger lay, in central Europe. British illusions about Italy were plentiful enough, but turned out not to be too important. The Whigs underestimated Cavour's ambitions and failed to foresee the dimensions the Italian question would assume once it was broken open. They took too lightly the risks of general war it entailed and assumed too readily that a new state of northern Italy or all of Italy could easily be fitted into the European state system as a buffer between Austria and France, leaning on Britain for support. But in the end things worked out, by Cavour's doing rather than Britain's. Even a united Italy as a would-be great power did not change the European balance drastically.

It was Whig proposals for Germany and Austria that were potentially, and even in a certain sense actually, disastrous. The British assumed that a unification of Germany under Prussia's leadership was bound to be good for the Germans, for Britain, and for the balance of power, provided only that Prussia turned moderately liberal herself and served as Britain's natural ally in checking Russia and restraining France. As for Austria, she could best meet her internal problems if she surrendered her unnatural position in Germany and Italy and instead concentrated her attention on the Balkans, where she too could act as a barrier to Russian expansion.

No views could have been more mistaken than these, or illustrate more clearly the shortcomings of a crude, mechanical balance of power approach to keeping peace. In fact, a unified Germany was bound to be dangerous to the rest of Europe under any circumstances, and doubly dangerous under the leadership of an ambitious military monarchy like Prussia. Had it followed British ideas—that is, had it been controlled by liberal nationalists and had it followed a policy of joining with Britain against Russia and France—it would have quickly and unfailingly have proved fatal to European peace. Surely it should not have required the twentieth century to prove that the best possible recipe for dividing Europe into armed camps and promoting general war is to have a united nationalist Germany under Prussian leadership challenge Russia and threaten France. The one thing that made Bismarck's Germany tolerable for some decades in Europe—in fact, a force for peace from 1871–1890— was that it did not fit the liberal British prescription for Germany: it was not created or run by liberals, it kept German nationalism

in check, it did not lean openly toward Britain, and above all it
tried to revive and maintain the conservative ties with Russia.

If anything was needed to make the Whig prescription for disaster complete, it was British advice to Austria on how to solve her
problems. Everyone now knows how fatal in the long run for Austria and for Europe were the consequences of her yielding to
Magyar demands, giving up her position in Germany and Italy,
turning for compensation to the Balkans, and thus promoting her
head-to-head confrontations both with Balkan nationalism and with
Russia. What no one seems to notice is that this disastrous course
was exactly what Whigs prescribed as a remedy for Austria's ills.*

Whig ideas about the means for maintaining peace and a stable
international order were equally unwise. It makes sense to destroy
an international system because it obstructs one's own purposes, as
Bismarck and Cavour did, trusting that the international restraints
destroyed along with this system can later be revived under a new
one. It may even be rational to smash such a system because one's
own state is less vulnerable than others and stands to gain in the
general melée (though usually in the long run everyone loses).
Revolutionaries at least argue consistently when they contend
that an existing system must be destroyed because it is corrupt and
oppressive, but that the regenerative processes of revolution can
produce a better order with legitimate rules and restraints. In all
these instances, the actors at least take into account the simple fact
that if one undermines the bases of an international system he also
undermines the rules and code of conduct it has served to enforce.
But to condemn the old order as morally bankrupt, as Britain did;
to encourage others to break its rules in the name of progress; to
demand sweeping reforms and heavy sacrifices from those who
benefit from the system and want to maintain it; and while doing all
this to suppose that its old rules and restraints will remain in effect
and that the old practices of cooperation and mutual accord will
continue to prevail—this is breathtaking inconsistency and illusion.
Not only did Britain help greatly to bring down an international

---

* It is also interesting that the only oppressed nationalities within Austria for
whom Whigs showed sympathy and concern were the master races, the
Magyars and the Italians.

system from which she had benefited along with the other powers, without having any clear idea on how to replace it. She did not even understand what she was doing in this work of destruction. She supposed that she could cut the roots of this international order and that its fruits would continue to grow.

This indicates the gravest fault of British policy, its levity and inconsequence. One can certainly make a case that the old international order represented by Austria was hopelessly decayed and out of date and that it either had to be extensively revised or else overthrown and replaced. Had Britain undertaken seriously to lead in this effort, committing her power and resources to this goal and accepting some responsibility for the final results of her action, one could not criticize her, at least, for her purposes. But this she never seriously undertook; she had a wish, not a policy. She dabbled in promoting liberalism on the Continent, played at substituting a new liberal system for the old conservative Concert, but never worked at it, never finished what she started. The withering criticism Prince Albert directed at Palmerston's policy of "intermeddling" in 1848–1851 * applies even more strongly to this same policy during after the Crimean War, when the British public turned again toward isolation, making it even more certain that British advice would not be followed by commitment or action. Bismarck, it has been said, created a deadlock and called it peace.[26] Perhaps so. Palmerston and Russell sowed chaos and called it progress.

Nor was France much better. If Palmerston was a dangerous man for Europe, Napoleon III was a foolish one for France. The position in 1856 in which France found herself, not principally by her own efforts, was a superb one. Allied with two great powers, she had

---

* "What else does this principle mean," wrote Albert in a memorandum of July 1852, "than the mixing up of the power of England with the internal dissensions, disputes, and quarrels of every country, with the settled purpose, however, not to incur thereby any moral responsibility or the legitimate consequences attaching to it? How sadly are the results of this mode of action illustrated by the present state of affairs in Europe, where the people of almost all countries, after having been led to believe that they would meet with the support of England if they achieved their own liberty and having been thus encouraged to the attempt, have been allowed to be overcome without our stirring a finger on their behalf and are now abandoned to the most cruel tyranny!" (Connell, *Regina vs. Palmerston*, 164–65).

almost every other state, including her recent enemy Russia, ardently seeking her friendship. She had no natural enemies; even sovereigns and ministers who disliked Napoleon had to woo him, and the disruption of the Holy Alliance had dispelled the danger of a hostile coalition against France. All the major questions of the present and future—Germany, Italy, the Near East—were ones in which France could intervene with a decisive voice, to her own profit. Only France in 1856 could have restored the Concert of Europe and led it in a nonrevolutionary but progressive direction. She did not even have to seek this hegemony, but had it thrust upon her. Just as Metternich had tried his best in 1812–1813 to build his system around Napoleon I at the head of a powerful France, so Buol and Francis Joseph in 1854–1856 wanted to be partners with France as a sated, nonrevolutionary power leading Europe. But Napoleon preferred his dream of reorganizing Europe along national lines so that it would somehow also benefit and strengthen France and add glory and permanence to his dynasty. In 1856 he scorned tying himself to a cadaver like Austria. By 1870 his regime was the cadaver to which no one wished to be tied. As an exercise in the dissipation of national power, security and prestige, Napoleon's performance following the Crimean War is almost unparalleled. Compared to it, even Bismarck's successors look good.

Thus the Crimean War not only paved the way for the work of Cavour and Bismarck—this much has always been obvious—but also made their task a European necessity. The reconstruction of Europe was necessitated not so much by the plight of the German and Italian peoples—there were others with far worse national grievances, like the Poles and the Irish, who had to remain unsatisfied—as by the absence of any viable European state system at all. The old one had been destroyed in the Crimean War; the victors had shown themselves incapable of replacing it with anything substantial. The logical and terrible consequence of this should have been a return to unbridled balance of power politics and a concomitant state of international anarchy—that is, a series of inconclusive wars over the German, Italian, and Eastern questions, or a great general war on the international scale, if not the ferocity, of World War I.

No matter what aversion one may feel to Bismarck and Cavour

and their methods, they are responsible for avoiding this. They at least knew what they were destroying, with what they intended to replace it, and how to limit the attendant violence. True, Cavour never could have made Italy the leader or manager of a new European Concert even had he lived longer. She was too small, weak, and generally despised for this. But he did make her large and strong enough to be relatively independent of both Britain and France, and thus assimilable into the balance of power and the Concert, as a satellite state of either of these powers would not have been. Too little attention has been paid to how unsettling and unstable a solution of the Italian question either Napoleon's confederation or Whig-style "liberation" would have been, in contrast to a unified Italy. As for Bismarck, the chief point of his achievement, whatever its bad aspects internally in Germany, is that it accomplished again what 1815 had done and 1856 had undone. It created an independent center for Europe, strong enough to hold its own against East and West, yet not too strong, at least at its inception, for the rest of Europe. Moreover, this European center, as long as Bismarck was in control, was territorially sated, defensively oriented, interested in peace, and, though isolating France, not eager to challenge any great power.

Furthermore, the unification of Germany enabled Bismarck to help revive the Concert and assume the indispensable role of its chief manager. It was, true, a different Concert, with harsher rules, in many ways inferior to the old. Unbridled state interest and raw power were more in evidence. There was more need to divert rivalries and excess energies into extra-European outlets, more call for alliances to deter potential aggressors. The new Concert was much harder on France and more dangerous for her than that of 1815, and not much kinder to emerging nationalities. Yet it was a Concert, the only one practicable, and vastly better than none at all. If the sea powers, especially France, found it uncomfortable, they might have reflected that they not only had helped destroy the old one, but also done what they could to bring Prussia to the very position and power they now found disturbing. All through the Crimean War they had tried to kick and menace her out of neutrality and pacific conservatism; for a long time thereafter they had encouraged her to act boldly to fulfill her destiny as the leader of Germany and as a truly independent European great power. It should not have surprised them that what emerged when Prussia actually followed this course was a formidable semiautocratic military monarchy dominating central Europe and capable of menacing the West as well.

Without moralizing or pressing the point too far, one can see lessons from the Crimean War that all the powers could have learned with profit, and that are not useless even today. For Austria, the chief one would have been that a conciliatory foreign policy and an effort to internationalize dangerous questions cannot by itself compensate for the failure to solve internal problems and meet the challenge of modernization. France might have learned the importance of a power's realizing when it is sated, whether it wants to be or not, and of being satisfied to preserve and enjoy the influence it possesses. But the most important points are those to be learned about the operation of an international system—that it cannot be established and left to run itself, to be set right occasionally by massive interventions. It demands some subordination of private aims to a common purpose, and it requires for successful operation not merely good will and restraint on the part of all its members, but the same kind of patient, prudent, skillful management as the British developed and displayed in domestic politics, which made Britain so superior to most continental states in the handling of her internal affairs. The state best suited to provide this management is not one whose power and position render it fairly independent of the system, able to live without it, but the power dependent on it, compelled by its central position and vulnerability to be a prime investor in its stability and survival.

Such a state may, to be sure, become aggressive, out of fear or greed or opportunity. Austria was certainly tempted repeatedly during this crisis, especially early in 1853, to go after private gains at the expense of the whole system, and without Buol's influence she might have tried it. But to a great extent the necessities of such an exposed state make it virtuous in that it must promote peace; even the more aggressive Austrian spokesmen realized finally that any actions by Austria that would widen the war or tend to dissolve the remaining restraints of the European Concert would make her own situation worse in the long run. Although such states can easily become brakes on progress, as Austria was in many ways, they do so not simply because of internal defects or stupidity and shortsightedness. The cause lies deep in the nature of things. The problem of reconciling order and change has been the bane of every great plan for world peace ever devised. Peace, progress, and justice in international affairs are opposed ideals, in tension if not in contradiction with one another. A call for peace with progress and justice is a demand for sunshine with rain and snow. There is nothing inherently objectionable in taking advantage of an exposed state's vulnerability in order to win concessions from it for the sake of progress, as one sees it, or to avert an impending conflict. It is even justifiable, up to a point, to exploit such a power's insecurity to increase one's own security, for example, to use Austria to block Russia, giving Britain more security and a free hand. Austria was not intransigent on concessions for the sake of peace and stability, and she positively wanted to be used by the West to block Russia. The point at which these procedures become unjustified is precisely the point at which they become counterproductive and dangerous for the system as a whole and for the maintenance of peace—that is, the point at which it becomes evident that the concessions a state is called upon to make are not intended to settle a problem, but to escalate it and pave the way for more demands, or at which it becomes clear that one member in particular is being required to take on more obligations not in order to increase everyone's security within the system, but in order to increase the security of more favored members at the expense of its own.

This is what happened to Austria in the Crimean War and after it. The liberal nineteenth-century statesmen who so frequently operated on the maxim, *"L'Autriche se rendrera—c'est son métier,"* and who dilated with impatient contempt on her refusal to give up gracefully what she ought to realize she could not keep anyway, should have known that no state gives up its great power status or yields to fundamental challenges without a fight. Even the most conservative and pacific state is capable of bringing down the system on which it depends rather than endure the humiliation of having to make all the sacrifices involved in keeping it going. The Crimean War shows how much cooperation can be wrung from a vulnerable power in the interest of maintaining the system; 1859 and 1914 show that there are limits. It does no good at all (in fact, it may do great harm, as empty rhetoric and self-deception do harm) constantly to declare that a state is an essential element of the balance of power, if in fact one lets that state's position constantly deteriorate within the balance or actually helps render it intolerable. One cannot support the balance of power without in some concrete way supporting those states which actually do the most to maintain the balance of power.

These would not have been idle lessons for the latter half of the nineteenth century. The time was bound to come when the Bismarckian system would break down like its Metternichian predecessor, when even the cruder restraints of his Concert would cease to be effective. With the arena of European politics changing from the Continent to the whole world, Britain would become in both a geographic and a political sense central to the new system and its only possible manager. She would face many of the strains, fears, and problems of the sated empire, the central power confronted with the task of the thankless defensive. The peace of the world would largely depend on how much she was willing to invest in the system, how well she actually would play the role she had hitherto claimed to fill—*arbiter mundi*, holder of the balance, manager of the Concert, guardian of peace. But this is another, still more depressing, story.

Appendix A:

The Sichel Case

Thomas Sichel Jr., a member of a Manchester firm, was arrested in Lombardy shortly after the Milan rising in February 1853 on suspicion of spying for Mazzini (apparently because he was carrying a book supposed to be serving as a code book for the alleged spy network). He was first detained, then expelled from Lombardy. Upon British protests, Austria apologized for the incident, reprimanding the officer responsible and removing him from his post. But Clarendon demanded in addition a large monetary reparation for Sichel (at first two thousand pounds, later five hundred), plus a guarantee of future unhindered travel for him and his firm in Austria, the cashiering of the guilty officer from the service, and the punishment of the highest authorities responsible. Buol pointed out that the martial law and military government in effect in Italy made some restrictions on travel inescapable and that such incidents as these, however deplorable, were largely removed from his control. However, he made every effort to gain satisfaction for Britain, incurring the opposition not only of the generals, but also Radetzky's civil adlatus Rechberg, who insisted there was a strong case against Sichel. After the Emperor reprimanded Radetzky and Gyulai, who were finally responsible, Buol asked Clarendon through Westmorland if he really expected Francis Joseph also to administer them a public rebuke. Clarendon insisted on carrying the case to the Emperor himself, who received Westmorland courteously, but would not grant more than Buol had ceded. Though the dispute dragged on through most of 1853, a settlement was finally reached when Sichel was appointed Austria's vice-consul at Manchester.*

* The correspondence between Westmorland and Clarendon on this affair is scattered through FO 7/413, 414, and 419, and Clar. dep. c. 1 and 126. Some of the more important letters are Clarendon to Westmorland, 17 and 31 May and 12 July 1853, Nos. 123, 131, and 204, FO 7/413-414, and 26 July and 23 Aug., Clar. dep. c. 126; Westmorland to Clarendon, 26 July and 7 Sept., *ibid.* c. 1.

Appendix B:

The Bunsen Affair

The point in question here is who initiated the proposal Bunsen sent Manteuffel on March 1 and 2, 1854, calling for Prussia to join the war for the sake of territorial gains in the northeast. It was not Prince Albert, as Bismarck thought. Though Bunsen, a close friend, informed him of the move, Albert apparently did not promote it. He had sternly rejected a similar idea proposed by his brother Ernest in February and disapproved of Bunsen's action. He was glad Bunsen was gone, Albert wrote Ernest later; Bunsen had done him much harm.[1]

Nor was it Bunsen himself. While he did propose an alliance against Russia including Prussia, his proposal contained no hint of territorial compensations for Prussia. His program, given in a secret memorandum to Clarendon on February 16, called for Prussia to enter into the war only after the sea powers and Austria already had done so, and then only after a last effort to get Nicholas to accept the peace terms of January 13 had failed.[2] Bunsen wanted Frederick William lured into the alliance not by territorial gains but by the prospect that the Sultan would emancipate the Christians in Turkey. Clarendon wrote Redcliffe this same day that the "*active* cooperation" of Prussia depended upon this concession. On February 20, Bunsen urged suspending Turkish authority in Epirus, Thessaly, and Macedonia and granting local automony to the Christians there.[3] Frederick William, as the English were well aware, was very enthusiastic about the Greek cause, but very much averse to European territorial changes, especially Palmerston's idea of exchanging the Principalities for Lombardy.[4]

Clarendon, bypassing Aberdeen, gave Bunsen's memorandum to Palmerston, who took it as proof that both Prussia and Austria could now be drawn into war. This would guarantee an easy Allied victory, he wrote Clarendon on February 17. The Allies should make their victory complete instead of merely "tinkering around with the broken fragments of European peace." He proposed his usual type of program for paring Russia down to a suitable size: "Poland, Lithuania, and Samogitia," he said, "would add on conveniently to Prussia"; Austria should get Moldavia and Bessarabia, Turkey should be given Georgia, and Circassia be made independent.[5] Two weeks later, after several private conversations with Palmerston and Clarendon, who also clearly was thinking of giving Russia's Baltic territories to Prussia,[6] Bunsen sent his fatal secret memorandum to Manteuffel, with a copy to Albert. If Palmerston's letter of February 17 leaves any doubt as to where Bunsen's ideas originated, a comparison of his memorandum and Palmerston's *beau idéal* of war aims removes it. Bunsen deserved his downfall, but he was doubtless telling the truth in his later embarrassed defense when he claimed that the proposal for territorial changes—e.g., Lombardy for Wallachia—came from Palmerston. He may even have been led to believe, as he claimed, that these ideas had the approval of the Cabinet.[7] Clarendon's flat denials that he had any prior knowledge of these mad notions of Bunsen have doubtless served to deceive historians.[8]

Appendix C:

The Türr Case

This case demonstrates again the problems Buol faced in being caught between the Austrian generals and the British. Stephan Türr, a Hungarian sublieutenant, had deserted from the Austrian army in Italy and gone over to the Piedmontese enemy in January 1849. Subsequently he was among the Hungarian émigrés protected by Redcliffe at Constantinople, and during the earlier stages of the Eastern crisis he worked for Kossuth in promoting a revolution in Moldo-Wallachia that was supposed to lead to a war between Austria and Turkey. Later he entered British army service as a colonel in its commissariat. On his own initiative, ostensibly to purchase horses and wagons, he entered Wallachia from Bulgaria in September 1855, going to Bucharest (where his former Austrian regiment was stationed) and there making contact with Colquhoun. In view of Türr's notorious past, it is hard to believe Colquhoun's disclaimers of any knowledge of his background or his connections with other revolutionary elements in the Principalities, and easy to understand why many Austrians regarded Türr's presence in Bucharest in British uniform under Colquhoun's protection as a deliberate provocation. But Kempen, who ordered that Türr first be kept under observation and then arrested, also specifically wanted to embarrass Buol and strike a blow at his pro-West policy, and Grünne and Coronini shared in this purpose. Arrested on Coronini's orders at Bucharest on November 1, Türr was charged with high treason and desertion and quickly removed to Austria for questioning and trial.[1]

The French government regretted what Coronini had done, but basically sympathized with Austria.[2] Clarendon confessed to Cowley, swearing him to secrecy about it, that the British Lord Ad-

432

vocate unequivocally stated that Britain had no legal grounds to demand Türr's release. Moreover, Clarendon considered him "a donkey of the first class" for doing what he did and feared that a quarrel over him might promote the anti-British continental league he was sure Austria was trying to form.[3] But Redcliffe immediately began pressing Turkey to seek Türr's release, and Palmerston, though believing also that Türr deserved whatever he got, insisted on the necessity of responding to any challenge such as this, real or apparent, lest Britain lose standing in the world and run into trouble at home. "Next to the determination to force Russia to satisfactory terms of peace," he wrote Clarendon, "the strongest and most general sentiment throughout the nation is hatred of Austria . . . and we shall not fare well in Parliament or with the country if we truckle to the Vienna Government." "These small insults," he argued further, "are attacks upon our outposts, and unless we defend these outposts we shall have to fight for our Citadel." Besides, Austria was weak, vulnerable, and dependent on Britain and should be plainly told that if she insulted Britain now, she would live to regret it.[4]

Thus spurred on, Clarendon launched a campaign to get Türr released. First Elliot and later Seymour repeatedly assured him that Buol was doing all he could, though the army insisted its honor was deeply involved in the case. The general diplomatic situation was a delicate one, the demand for Türr's release coming precisely at the same time (November 1855) as the crucial Anglo-French-Austrian negotiations over amendments to the Austrian ultimatum to Russia. But Clarendon repeatedly insisted that he would break relations with Austria if she did not yield, and he used this threat to get France to put pressure on Austria as well.[5]

While he was fighting the generals at Vienna, Buol complained that Colquhoun was deliberately sabotaging his efforts for a settlement by persuading Turkish authorities in Bulgaria to disobey an order Austria had secured from Constantinople to remove two other Hungarian émigrés, also British agents, from Ruşciuc on the Wallachian border. To his protests and pleas for better cooperation between the agents and governments of Austria and Britain, Clarendon replied with surprise, "One would think from this gravely spoken lecture of Count Buol that we were the offending and

Austria the affronted party." Finally Buol secured Türr's release from the Emperor; he was to be turned over to British authorities, on condition that he never cross Austria's path again. Clarendon, not satisfied, ordered Seymour to demand the restitution of sixty-two ducats confiscated from Türr at his arrest. As for the promise to keep Türr out of Austria's way, it broke down soon after he was turned over to the British at Corfu. He quickly returned to the Balkans and his old revolutionary paths, and Clarendon washed his hands of all responsibility.[6] Later Türr was to take part in the War of 1859 against Austria; to figure in German-Italian diplomacy prior to 1866, when Bismarck considered promoting a Hungarian revolution as part of his campaign to expel Austria from Germany; and to attempt to promote a Russo-Italian war against Austria out of the Eastern Crisis of 1878.

Notes

CHAPTER I

1. *Der Krimkrieg und die österreichische Politik*, 77.

2. For this view of Schwarzenberg, see Friedrich Engel-Janosi, *Der Freiherr von Hübner, 1811-1892*, 65; Franco Valsecchi, *L'Alleanza di Crimea*, 20-23; A. J. P. Taylor, *The Habsburg Monarchy, 1809-1918* (Harper Torchbook ed., 1965), 77; and Kenneth W. Rock, "Reaction Triumphant" (unpublished dissertation, Stanford University, 1969). But compare also the soberer views of Eduard Heller, *Mitteleuropas Vorkämpfer: Fürst Felix zu Schwarzenberg* (Vienna, 1933), 227-28; Rudolph Kiszling, *Fürst Felix zu Schwarzenberg* (Graz-Cologne, 1952); and Friedrich Walter, *Die österreichische Zentralverwaltung*," Part III, Vol. I (1848-1852), 567.

3. Heinrich Friedjung, *Historische Aufsätze* (Stuttgart, 1919), 90-125; Joachim Hoffman, *Die Berliner Mission des Grafen Prokesch-Osten;* and Schwarzenberg to Prokesch, 16 Nov. 1850, PA XL/320.

4. On Buol's policy regarding Germany, see Waltraud Heindl, *Graf Buol-Schauenstein in St. Petersburg und London*, 23-27, and Roy A. Austensen, "The Early Career of Count Buol 1837-1852," 285-344. Buol's rejection in principle of preventive war against Prussia is clear from an undated draft of a reply to a letter evidently from one of the Austrian Archdukes urging this (PA XL/277g).

5. Helmut Böhme, *Deutschlands Weg zur Grossmacht*, 19-50; Buol to Count Friedrich Thun at Berlin, 3 Jan. 1853, PA III/49; Baumgartner to Buol, 8 Feb. 1853, and Baumgarten's memorandum of 19 Feb., PA XL/73.

6. On Napoleon III, see Heinrich Euler, *Napoleon III in seiner Zeit*, Vol. I (Würzburg, 1961). For Austrian attitudes and fears, see Heller, 157-70; Engel-Janosi, *Hübner*, 81-82, 88-94, 96-98, 107-8; and Anton Graf Prokesch-Osten, *Aus den Briefen des Grafen Prokesch von Osten, 1849-1855* (hereafter cited as Prokesch, *Briefe*), 87-90, 114, 283.

7. This account is based primarily on Richard Salomon, "Die Anerken-

nung Napoleons III," *Zeitschrift für osteuropäische Geschichte*, II (1912), 321–66, and the documents published in A. M. Zaionchkovskii, *Vostochnaia voina v sviazu s ei politicheskoi obstanovkoi*, Prilozhenie, I, 190–310. Cf. also Bernhard Unckel, *Österreich und der Krimkrieg*, 26–32; Heindl, 105–9; and Euler, 862–68. There is ample evidence that Buol, though eager for four-power unity, never was much concerned about the numeral "III" *per se* or wanted to make a demonstration against Napoleon; Hübner and King Leopold of Belgium were both far more eager for this than he. See Buol's correspondence with Hübner, Prokesch, and Leopold in Zaionchkovskii, Pril. I, 252–55; Nachlass Prokesch 26/4; and PA XL/277h and l.

8. The British attitude is best illustrated in Ab. Corr. 1852–1854, 12–13; Russell to Cowley, 6 and 8 Jan. 1853, FO 519/197; and Colloredo to Buol, 17 Jan. and 1 Feb. 1853, PA VIII/37 and 38.

9. Buol-Hübner correspondence, January–March 1853, PA IX/44.

10. Heindl, *passim*; A. J. P. Taylor, *The Italian Question in European Diplomacy, 1847–1849* (Manchester, 1934); Kurt Weisbrod, "Lord Palmerston und die europäische Revolution von 1848," 111–47.

11. Unckel, 47–52; Heindl, 55–60; Austensen, 221–26.

12. Heindl, 89–98; Austensen, 354–81.

13. Engel-Janosi, *Österreich und der Vatikan*, I, 70–74; Daniel H. Thomas, "The Reaction of the Great Powers to Louis Napoleon's Rise to Power in 1851," *Historical Journal*, XIII (1970), 242–43.

14. Heindl, 86–87; Buol's private journal (PA XL/277e) shows his Anglophile sentiments clearly.

15. Austensen, 345–54, 391–94.

16. On Palmerston's German policy, clearly pro-Prussian and anti-Austrian, though cautious, see Gunther Gillesen, *Lord Palmerston und die Einigung Deutschlands*, and Weisbrod, 171–89 and 224–51. His Swiss policy is discussed in Ann G. Imlah, *Britain and Switzerland, 1845–1860*, and in Weisbrod, 65–90. Further evidences of his Austrophobia, notorious in England and elsewhere, can be seen in *The Correspondence of Lord Aberdeen and Princess Lieven, 1832–1854*, II, 581, 588; *The Later Correspondence of Lord John Russell, 1840–1878*, II, 18–19, 35–36, 97–99; Brian Connell, ed., *Regina vs. Palmerston*, 84–85, 95–98, 104–20, 131–33, 140–43; and *The Greville Memoirs, 1814–1860*, VI, 171–72. G. H. Henderson gives a good general appraisal of his policy in his *Crimean War Diplomacy and Other Historical Essays*.

17. J. H. Gleason, *The Genesis of Russophobia in England* (Cambridge, Mass., 1950).

18. Austensen, 384–91.

19. *Aberdeen-Lieven Correspondence*, II, 637; Colloredo's private letters to Buol of June to Dec. 1852 and 8 Jan. 1853, PA VIII/36 and 38.

20. J. B. Conacher, *The Aberdeen Coalition, 1852-1855*, 3-27; the Duke of Argyll, *Autobiography and Memoirs*, I, 370-74, 386-87; diary of Sir James Graham, 17-30 Dec. 1852, in Graham Papers (microfilm, Newberry Library, Chicago) Reel 18.

21. Connell, *passim*; see also Sir Theodore Martin, *The Life of His Royal Highness the Prince Consort*, and Frank Eyck, *The Prince Consort*.

22. On Redcliffe's reappointment, see H. W. V. Temperley, *England and the Near East: The Crimea*, 313, and Ab. Corr. 1852-1854, 35. For the origins of Redcliffe's clash with Nicholas, see F. A. Walker, "The Rejection of Stratford Canning by Nicholas I," *Bulletin of the Institute of Historical Research*, XL (1967), 50-64.

23. E. Andics, *Das Bündnis Habsburg-Romanow. Vorgeschichte der zaristischen Intervention in Ungarn im Jahre 1849* (Budapest, 1963); Heindl, 41-52; Austensen, 207-21; and John S. Curtiss, *The Russian Army under Nicholas I, 1825-1855*, 305-11.

24. Heindl, 63-71; Austensen, 221-58. Austria's fears of a Russian penetration of the Balkans encircling the Empire went back at least to the beginning of the eighteenth century—cf. A. V. Florovsky, "Russo-Austrian Conflicts in the Early 18th Century," *Slavonic and East European Review*, XLVII (Jan. 1969), 94-115.

25. Heindl, 78-79; Austensen, *loc cit.*; Theodor Schiemann, *Geschichte Russlands unter Kaiser Nikolaus I*, IV, 252-55, 304, 334-35, 404-15; Radu Florescu, "The Rumanian Principalities and the Origins of the Crimean War," *Slavonic and East European Review*, XLIII (1964), 50-53.

26. Angelo Filipuzzi, *La Pace di Milano (6 agosto 1849)* (Rome, 1955).

27. Walter, *op. cit.*; Friedjung, *Historische Aufsätze*, 24-89, and *Osterreich von 1848 bis 1860*, Vol. I; and Josef Redlich, *Das österreichische Reichs- und Staatsproblem*, I, 324-459.

28. Walter Wagner, *Geschichte des K. K. Kriegsministeriums*, I, 33-93; *Vortrag* by Hess, 1 June 1853, KA, Hess Schriften, VIII, Nr. 58.

29. *Kübecks Tagebücher* and *Das Tagebuch des Polizeiministers Kempen von 1848 bis 1859* (J. K. Mayr, ed.) shed much light on the struggle for control of the secret police and gendarmerie, as does Buol's correspondence with Kempen, PA XL/74. For the economic and fiscal troubles helping to cause the revolution (most of which persisted after it), see Gustav Otruba, "Wirtschaft und soziale Lage Österreichs im Vormärz," *Österreich in Geschichte und Literatur*, X (1966), 161-76, and Julius Marx, *Die wirtschaftlichen Ursachen der Revolution von 1848 in Öster-*

reich (Graz, 1965). For the pre-March problems that made the new gendarmerie necessary, see the same author's "Die öffentliche Sicherheit in den österreichischen Ländern von 1840 bis 1848," *Mitteilungen des Instituts für österreichische Geschichtsforschung,* LXV (1957), 70–92.

30. Oskar Regele, *Feldmarschall Radetzky,* 320–56; Valsecchi, *Alleanza,* 188–94; André Lefèvre, "Les répercussions en Europe occidentale de l'insurrection de Milan en 1853," *Revue d'histoire diplomatique,* LXIX (1955), 330–31; *Rel. dipl. Aust.-Sard.,* IV, 27–39, 46–60, 64–67, 77–85, 88–92. For proof that Buol was taken by surprise by the sequestrations decision, see Bach to Buol, 13 Jan. 1853, and Buol to Bach, 14 Jan., PA XL/74.

31. See Josef Redlich, *Kaiser Franz Joseph von Österreich;* Egon Caesar Count Corti, *Mensch und Herrscher;* Eduard Steinitz, ed., *Erinnerungen an Franz Josef I;* and Friedjung, *Aufsätze,* 493–538. Grünne's remark is in *Kempens Tagebuch,* 35.

32. *Ibid.,* 42–43, 61–70; Corti, 93, 98.

33. Walter, *passim; Kübecks Tagebücher,* 91–102; Paul Müller, *Feldmarschall Fürst Windischgrätz,* 256–81; Helmut Rumpler, *Die Protokolle des österreichischen Ministerrates (1848–1867)* (Vienna, 1970), 17–53.

34. Heindl, 17–23.

35. *Ibid.,* 123–25; Austensen, vi–xi, 404–9; Heller, 172–73.

36. Heindl, 115–20; *Kempens Tagebuch,* 265, 269, 271–73.

37. On Prokesch and his relations with Buol, see A. O. Meyer, *Bismarcks Kampf mit Österreich am Bundestag zu Frankfurt, 1851–1859,* 123–48, 153–60; Hoffmann, *Berliner Mission,* 96–97, 108–10; *Kempens Tagebuch,* 307, 364–66, 368–69, and the Prokesch-Buol correspondence in Prokesch, *Briefe* and in PA XL/321. On Hübner and Buol, see Engel-Janosi, *Hübner,* 105–7; on Thun, Franz Eckhart, *Die deutsche Frage und der Krimkrieg,* 18–20, 27–29; on Maurice Esterházy, Papal Nuncio Cardinal Viale-Préla at Vienna to the Papal Secretariat, 15 May 1856, ASV, NV/326.

CHAPTER II

1. The best discussion is in Temperley, *Crimea,* 280–300.

2. Edouard Thouvenel, *Nicolas Ier et Napoléon III,* 32, 35–46, 74–81; Hübner to Buol, 16 Jan. 1853, No. 8B, PA IX/41.

3. Thouvenel, *Nicolas Ier,* 49–50, 54–56, 74; S. Tatishchev, "Diplomaticheskii raz'rib Rossii s Turtsiei v 1853 g.," *Istoricheskii Vestnik,* XLVII, No. 1 (1892), 165–67.

4. Sess. Papers, 1854 (LXXI), 59–60, 63–66; H. E. Maxwell, *The Life*

and Letters of George William Frederick, Fourth Earl of Clarendon, II, 2.

5. Buol to Mensdorff, 21 Jan. 1853, No. 2, PA X/37; Buol to Hübner, 26 Jan., PA IX/44; Engel-Janosi, *Hübner,* 108–9.

6. S. Nikitin, "Russkaia politika na Balkanach i nachalo vostochnoi voini," *Voprosy Istorii,* 1946, No. 4, 3–4; Temperley, *Crimea,* 221–22; Baron A. Testa *et al.,* eds. *Recueil des traités de la Porte ottomane,* X, 294–97, 373–74.

7. Adolf Beer, *Die orientalische Politik Oesterreichs seit 1774,* 434–37; Buol to Klezl, 27 Dec. 1852, PA XII/44; Buol to AOK, 10 Jan. 1853, PA XL/75; MKSM to Buol, 26 Dec. 1852, and to Jellacić and Coronini, 7 Jan. 1853, KA, MKSM 1853, 53 and ad 53.

8. Protocol of ministerial conference of 11 Jan. 1853, MR Prot. 13; Testa, X, 335–44; Buol to Klezl, 20 Dec. 1852, and Klezl's note to Fuad Pasha, 7 Jan. 1853, PA XII/44 and 46.

9. Denes A. Jánossy, "Die ungarische Emigration und der Krieg im Orient," *Archivium Europeae Centro-Orientalis,* V (1939), and "Die Geheimpläne Kossuths für einen zweiten Befreiungsfeldzug in Ungarn, 1849–1854," *Jahrbuch des Graf Klebelberg Kuno Instituts für ungarische Geschichtsforschung in Wien,* VI (1936).

10. *Kempens Tagebuch,* 270, 272, 274.

11. Leiningen's instructions, 22 Jan. 1853, PA XII/227. An excellent account of the Leiningen mision is Unckel, 57–80.

12. Beer, 436–41; Nikitin, 4–5; Buol to Grünne, 10 and 18 Jan., MKSM 1853/131 and 222.

13. Unckel, 70–74. The documents are mainly in PA XII/227 (some are published in Testa, X, 285–93).

14. See the Klezl-Buol correspondence of February-April 1853, PA XII/46 and 48, and Francis Joseph to Buol, 12 April, PA XL/48.

15. Buol to Hübner, 13 and 26 Feb. 1853, PA IX/44; Russell to Cowley, 1, 3, and 4 Feb., FO 519/197; Colloredo to Buol, 3 and 21 Feb., PA VIII/38; Ab. Corr. 1852–1854, 37–38.

16. Hübner to Buol, 5 and 23 Feb. 1853, PA IX/42.

17. See Klezl's reports all through January and February, PA XIII/46, and Leiningen to Buol, 7 Feb. 1853, No. 5, PA XII/227; Buol to Hübner and Colloredo, 18 Feb., PA IX and VIII/38.

18. Cowley to Clarendon, 28 Feb. 1853, Clar. dep. c. 5; Clarendon to Cowley, 1 and 15 March, FO 519/169; 3 Hansard, 124, 978–99; 125, 153–55; and 126, 371–81; Thun to Buol, 1 and 22 Feb., PA III/48.

19. *Kübecks Tagebücher,* 115; Steinitz, 33.

20. Among those who hold this view are Redlich (*Francis Joseph,*

127–28), Beer (442–43), H. von Srbik (*Deutsche Einheit*, II, 213–14), and Edmond Bapst (*Les origines de la Guerre Crimée*, 335–36).

21. This account is based on the correspondence in PA X/37–38 and PA XII/46 and 227; see also Nikitin, 6–7, and Tatishchev, "Raz'rib Rossii," 723–24.

22. *Kübecks Tagebücher*, 109; Prokesch to Buol, 27 Feb. 1853, PA II/26; Klezl to Buol, 15 May, PA XII/46.

23. Meyendorff, III, 10; Zaionchkovskii, Pril. I, 327–30.

24. Buol to Mensdorff, 23 Feb. 1823, No. 3, PA X/38; Unckel, 79–80.

25. Henderson, 1–14; Temperley, *Crimea*, 270–79; E. V. Tarle, *Krymskaia Voina*, I, 5–7; G. H. Bolsover, "Nicholas I and the Partition of Turkey," *Slavonic Review*, XXVII (1948), 115–45.

26. Zaionchkovskii, Pril. I, 357–58, 582–83, 597–600.

27. *Ibid.*, 359–62; Henderson, 1–14; Nesselrode to Meyendorff, private, 28 Jan. 1853, PA X/38.

28. See Vernon Puryear, *England, Russia, and the Straits Question, 1844–1856*, 34–74, 139–40, on the Anglo-Russian agreement of 1844, which Tarle (I, 105–9) interprets as a conspiracy for aggression against Turkey.

29. Tarle, I, 157–69; Zaionchkovskii, Pril. I, 369–78, 382–85.

30. The best account of the mission is Temperley, *Crimea*, 304–32; a good selection of documents in Zaionchkovskii, Pril. I, 387–437.

31. Meyendorff, III, 14–15; Buol-Prokesch, private, 27 March 1853, PA XL/277a; Buol to Thun, 7 April, PA III/49; Buol to Klezl, 28 March, PA XII/48; Redcliffe to Clarendon, Vienna, 26 March, Clar. dep. c. 10.

32. Buol to Lebzeltern, chargé at St. Petersburg, 6 May 1853, PA X/37; Buol to Klezl, 2 May, PA XII/48; Buol to Hübner, 24 and 31 May, PA IX/44; Cowley to Clarendon, 21 April and 24 May, Nos. 255 and 350, FO 519/1 and 23 May, FO 519/169.

33. See Klezl's reports from March through May (PA XII/46), and Redcliffe to Clarendon, 13 May 1853, Clar. dep. c. 10.

34. Thouvenel, *Nicolas Ier*, 85–87; *Mémoires du Duc de Persigny*, 226–235; Hübner to Buol, 21 March 1853, PA IX/44; Valsecchi, *Alleanza*, 225; Academia Romāna, *Acte şi documente relative la istoria renascerei Romāniei*, II, 53–55.

35. Hübner to Buol, 1, 19, 26, and 29 May 1853, PA IX/44; Cowley to Clarendon, 29 April, 2 and 9 May, Nos. 280, 289 and 305, FO 519/1.

36. Temperley, *Crimea*, 298–300; *Greville Memoirs*, VI, 414–16; QVL, II, 537–38; Russell to Clarendon, 20 March 1853, Clar. dep. c. 3.

37. Clarendon to Aberdeen, 20 and 21 March 1853, Add. ms. 43188; Clarendon to Cowley, 18 and 29 April and 3 May 1853, FO 519/169; Clarendon to Redcliffe, 26 April and 7 May, FO 352/36/1; Clarendon to Palmerston, 11 April, Palm. Papers GC/CL/504/3.

38. Brunnow gave Nesselrode on 25 May a surprisingly accurate portrayal of the situation within the Cabinet—Zaionchkovskii, Pril. II, 22–24.

39. Palmerston to Clarendon, 23, 24, and 28 May 1853, and to Graham, 29 May, Clar. dep. c. 3.

40. Clarendon to Aberdeen, 29 and 30 May 1853, Add. ms. 43188; Clarendon to Redcliffe, 26 May and 1 and 2 June, FO 352/36/1; memoranda by Russell and Lansdowne, 30 May, and Graham to Palmerston, same date, Clar. dep. c. 3; Clarendon to Russell, 31 May, PRO 30/22/11A.

41. Colloredo to Buol, private, 27 Feb. 1853, PA VIII/38; Clarendon to Cowley, 25 Feb. and 8 March, FO 519/169.

42. See D. Jánossy's articles (cited above, note 9); Lefèvre, 329–46; and N. J. Gossman, "British Aid to Polish, Italian, and Hungarian Exiles 1830–1870," *South Atlantic Quarterly*, LXIII (1969), 231–45.

43. Westmorland to Russell, 21 Feb. 1853, and to Clarendon, 27 Feb. and 1 and 8 March, Clar. dep. c. 1; Cowley to Clarendon, 27 Feb., *ibid.* c. 5; Ab. Corr. 1852–1854, 43–60; *Rel. dipl. Aust.-Sard.*, IV, 76; *QVL*, II, 545–46.

44. *Greville Memoirs*, VI, 411–12; *Aberdeen-Lieven Correspondence*, II, 641–42; Clarendon to Cowley, 1 March 1853, FO 519/169; Colloredo to Buol, 15 Feb., PA VIII/38.

45. Evelyn Ashley, *Life of Palmerston*, II, 9–11; Buol to Colloredo, 2 March 1853, PA VIII/38; Westmorland to Clarendon, 11 and 23 March, Clar. dep. c. 1. Austria's complaints did resemble Britain's about America—see Brian Jenkins, *Fenians and Anglo-American Relations during Reconstruction* (Ithaca, N.Y., 1969), 24, 37.

46. *QVL*, II, 534–35; Clarendon to Westmorland, 2 March and 5 April 1853, Nos. 18 and 58, FO 7/412–13, and 1 and 15 March, Clar. dep. c. 125; Clarendon to Aberdeen, 28 and 30 March, and Aberdeen to Clarendon, 29 and 31 March, Add. ms. 43188.

47. *Greville Memoirs*, VI, 408–11; Clarendon to Aberdeen, "Sat. night" [18 March] and 7 April 1853, and Aberdeen to Clarendon, 8 March, Add. ms. 43188; Aberdeen to Victoria, 31 March, Add. ms. 43047; Russell to Clarendon, 4 March, Clar. dep. c. 3.

48. Clarendon to Cowley, 18 March and 8 April 1853, FO 519/169; Clarendon to Seymour, 23 March and 5 April, Clar. dep. c. 125; Russell to Clarendon, 4 and 24 March, *ibid.* c. 3; Cowley to Clarendon, 8 and 17 March, *ibid.* c. 5; Minto to Russell, 3 and 7 April, PRO 30/22/11A.

49. Clarendon to Seymour, 5 April and 3 and 17 May 1853, Clar. dep. c. 125; Nesselrode to Fonton, 7 May, PA X/38.

50. Clarendon to Westmorland, 12 April and 2 and 3 May 1853, Clar. dep. c. 125.

51. 3 Hansard, 125, 446–49; Clarendon to Hudson, 18 April 1853, and

to Westmorland, 19 April and 24 May, Clar. dep. c. 125; Clarendon to Cowley, 15 April, FO 519/169. On the whole sequestrations question, see *Rel. dipl. GB-Sard.*, IV (which publishes many of the documents I used in the archives) and *Rel. dipl. Aust.-Sard.*, IV.

52. Clarendon to Cowley, 9 April and 6 and 27 May 1853, FO 519/169.

53. Hübner to Buol, 24 March and 4 April 1853, Nos. 48C and 54, PA IX/41; Buol to Hübner, 24 March 1853, PA IX/44; Cowley to Clarendon, 17 and 24 March, Nos. 154 and 177, FO 519/1, and 5 and 30 April, Clar. dep. c. 5.

54. Cowley to Clarendon, private, 8, 10, and 13 April 1853, Clar. dep. c. 5, and 26 May, No. 357, FO 519/1; Clarendon to Cowley, 12 April, FO 519/169.

55. Eligio Pometta, *Pagine di storia ticinese nel periodo eroico. Il blocco austriaco (1853–1854)* (Modena, 1943); Hübner to Buol, private, 28 March and 12 and 21 April 1853, PA IX/44; Cowley to Clarendon, 9, 12 and 24 May, FO 519/1; Clarendon to Cowley, 10 and 13 May, FO 519/169; Imlah, 74–88.

56. This point, as well as many others, refutes Tarle's thesis that Britain wanted to lure Russia into aggression against Turkey, so that then Britain could attack Russia in partnership with France and Austria (I, 163–65, *et passim*). Clarendon was in fact more afraid of a quarrel with France than with Russia (to Graham, 24 March 1853, Graham Papers, Reel 18).

57. Russell to Clarendon, 15 and 30 March 1853, Clar. dep. c. 3; Cowley to Clarendon, 19 March, No. 161, FO 519/1; Clarendon to Cowley, private, 18, 19, 22, and 29 March, FO 519/169.

58. Cowley to Clarendon, 19 May 1853, No. 334, FO 519/1; Russell to Clarendon, 29 and 31 May, Clar. dep. c. 3.

59. Westmorland to Clarendon, private, 30 March 1853, Clar. dep. c. 1; Clarendon to Westmorland, 12 April, No. 77, FO 7/413.

60. Friedrich Engel-Janosi, *Graf Rechberg*, 25–28; *Kempens Tagebuch*, 284; ministerial conference protocols of 29 March, 5 April, and 12 August 1853, MR Prot. 12–13; Buol to Rechberg, 22 April, PA XL/75; Francis Joseph to Rechberg and Radetzky, 7 April, PA XL/48.

61. Clarendon to Cowley, 11 March 1853, FO 519/169; Cowley to Clarendon, 1 April, No. 198, FO 519/1.

62. *PAP*, II, 34–35, 37–41; Clarendon to Westmorland, 23 and 29 March 1853, Clar. dep. c. 125; *Letters of the Prince Consort* (Kurt Jagow, ed.), 187–88.

CHAPTER III

1. Zaionchkovskii, Pril. I, 435–38; Tarle, I, 248–69; A. P. Shcherbatov, *General-Feldmarshal kniaz Paskevich*, VII, 49–54; Karl Count Nesselrode, *Lettres et papiers*, X, 225–26.

2. *PAP*, II, 81–88; Shcherbatov, VII, 55–56; Thouvenel, *Nicolas Ier*, 197–200; Nicholas Riasanovsky, *Nicholas I and Official Nationality in Russia, 1825–1855* (Berkeley, 1967), 261–65.

3. Tarle, I, 307–11, 326–27; Zaionchkovskii, II, 32–33; Testa, IV, Pt. 1, 259–65; Meyendorff, III, 54–55.

4. Meyendorff, III, 16–18; Zaionchkovskii, Pril. II, 45–47; Redlich, *Francis Joseph*, 128–31.

5. Meyendorff, III, 39–40, 45–46; Redlich, *Francis Joseph*, 131–34; Russian consul at Belgrade Popov to Nesselrode, 5 June 1853, PA X/38.

6. Nesselrode, X, 242–43, 246–47; Lebzeltern to Buol, 2 June 1853, PA X/38; Buol to Lebzeltern, 22 and 30 June, PA X/37.

7. *Acte şi documente*, II, 130, 146–47; Buol to Lebzeltern, 21 July and 10 Aug. 1853, PA X/37; memorandum by Meysenbug, July 1853, PA X/38; Bruck to Buol, 28 July, No. 18A, PA XII/47; British consul at Bucharest R. J. Colquhoun to Redcliffe, 4, 5, 7, and 10 Aug., FO 78/944.

8. Nesselrode, X, 252–53, 257; Meyendorff, III, 20–24; Lebzeltern to Buol, private, 16 July 1853, PA X/38.

9. Buol's dispatches to Lebzeltern, June 1853, and Francis Joseph to Nicholas, 15 June, PA X/37 and 38; Buol to Klezl, 9 and 27 June, PA XII/46 and 48; Buol to Hübner, 16 June and 2 July, PA IX/44.

10. Meyendorff, III, 49–51; Buol to Lebzeltern, 30 June 1853, No. 2, and Gyulai's instructions, same date, Nos. 1–2, PA X/37 and 38.

11. Meyendorff, III, 34–36, 42, 48–51; Buol to Lebzeltern, 21 July 1853, PA X/37.

12. Meyendorff, III, 19–20; Tarle, I, 317–19.

13. Unckel, 90–91; Grünne to Gyulai, 25–26 and 27 July and 13 Aug. 1853, KA, MKSM 1853/3772; *Mittheilungen des k.k. Kriegsarchivs*, III (1878), 127–40.

14. Buol to Hübner, 21 and 22 June and 2 July 1853, PA IX/44; Westmorland to Clarendon, 11, 17, and 21 June, Nos. 237, 241, and 247, FO 7/419, and 23 June, Clar. dep. c. 1; Cowley to Clarendon, 20 and 22 June, Nos. 452 and 460, FO 519/2.

15. Beer, 448–51; Charles W. Hallberg, *Franz Joseph and Napoleon III*, 50–52; Buol to Thun, 14 June 1853, PA III/49.

16. Buol to Hübner, 14 and 21 June, 2 and 5 July 1853, PA IX/44.

17. Prokesch, *Briefe*, 317–20; unsigned note by Prokesch to Buol, n.d. [mid-1853], Plaz Papers; Buol to Prokesch, 1 July, PA XL/277a.

18. Maxwell, II, 15; Aberdeen to Clarendon, 1 June 1853, Add. ms. 43188; Russell's letters to Clarendon all through June, and Palmerston to Clarendon, 7, 16, 19, and 27 June, Clar. dep. c. 3; Redcliffe to Clarendon, 9 July, *ibid*. c. 10; Redcliffe to Palmerston, 24 June, Palm. Papers GC/CA/245.

19. *Russell Correspondence*, II, 148–51; memorandum by Lansdowne, June 1853; Graham to Russell, 20 June; memorandum by Aberdeen, 21 June; and Aberdeen to Russell, 22 June, all in PRO 30/22/11A; Palmerston to Clarendon, 28 June and 12 July, Clar. dep. c. 3.

20. Clarendon to Palmerston, 17 June 1853, Palm. Papers GC/CL/511; Clarendon to Redcliffe, 18 and 24 June, FO 352/36/1; Clarendon to Cowley, 25, 28, and 30 June, FO 519/169.

21. Clarendon to Redcliffe, 18 June 1853, FO 352/36/1; Colloredo to Buol, 1 June, No. 59A, PA VIII/37; Clarendon to Westmorland, 4 July, No. 189, FO 7/414, and 8 and 15 June, Clar. dep. c. 125–26; Clarendon to Cowley, 17 and 24 June, FO 519/169.

22. Clarendon to Westmorland, 21 June 1853, Clar. dep. c. 126.

23. Sess. Papers, 1854, LXXI, 347–50; Clarendon to Westmorland, 21 June and 4 July 1853, Nos. 168, 174, and 190, FO 7/413–14, and 28 June and 5 July, Clar. dep. c. 126; Westmorland to Clarendon, 27 June, FO 7/419; Clarendon to Cowley, 1 July, FO 519/169.

24. Seymour to Clarendon, 1 July 1853, Clar. dep. c. 8.

25. Clarendon to Westmorland, 28 June and 12 July 1853, Clar. dep. c. 125–26; Westmorland to Clarendon, 22 and 27 June and 9 July, *ibid*. c. 1; Clarendon to Aberdeen and Aberdeen to Clarendon, both 11 July, Add. ms. 43188.

26. Palmerston to Clarendon, 11 June 1853, Clar. dep. c. 3; Clarendon to Palmerston, 11 June, Palm. Papers GC/CL/510/1; Colloredo to Buol, 11 June, No. 63, PA VIII/37; Clarendon to Westmorland, 14 June, No. 150, FO 7/413; Sess. Papers, 1854, LXXI, 316.

27. Colloredo to Buol, 29 June 1853, PA VIII/37.

28. Clarendon to Cowley, 5 VII 1853, FO 519/169.

29. Clar. dep. c. 126.

30. Clarendon's dispatches to Westmorland in June and July are full of these complaints—FO 7/413–14.

31. Martin, *Prince Consort*, III, 28; Prince Albert to Clarendon, 23 July 1853, RA G4/49; Clarendon to Bloomfield, 26 July, Clar. dep. c. 126; Russell to Clarendon, 26 and 27 July, *ibid*. c. 3.

32. *Greville Memoirs*, VI, 431; Russell to Clarendon, 4 and 5 July

1853, Clar. dep. c. 3; Russell to Palmerston, 7 July, Palm. Papers; Russell to Aberdeen, 10 and 13 July, Add. ms. 43067.

33. Ashley, II, 24–35; Palmerston to Clarendon, 15, 27, 28, and 31 July 1853, Clar. dep. c. 3; Clarendon to Aberdeen, 28 July, Add. ms. 43188; *Greville Memoirs*, VI, 437.

34. Clarendon to Westmorland, 26 July 1853, Clar. dep. c. 126; Clarendon to Aberdeen, 28 July, Add. ms. 43188.

35. Clarendon to Cowley, 21 June 1853, FO 519/169; Cowley to Clarendon, 11 July, No. 516, FO 519/2, and 30 July, Clar. dep. c. 6; Drouyn to Walewski, 28 June, AMAE Mem. et doc. France 2120; Colloredo to Buol, 13 June, PA VIII/37.

36. See Hübner's reports throughout June and July 1853, especially 12 July, Nos. 102D, E, and H, PA IX/42; Bourqueney to Drouyn, 6 and 31 July, Nos. 54 and 65–66, AMAE Autr. 451; Cowley to Clarendon, 5 June and 11 and 20 July, FO 519/2.

37. *PAP*, II, 73–74, 113–15; Thun to Buol, 11 June 1853, No. 46, and Buol to Thun, 22 July, PA III/48–49; Prokesch to Buol, 6 July, PA II/26; Frederick William to Francis Joseph, 30 May, and Francis Joseph to Frederick William, 16 July, Kab. Arch. Geh. Akt. 7.

38. Buol to Bruck, 31 May and 9 and 13 June 1853, PA XII/48.

39. Bruck to Buol, 23 June and 14 July 1853, and Buol to Bruck, 4 July, PA XII/48. Bruck was criticized by both sides for favoring the other—which seems to show he tried to be impartial.

40. Hübner to Buol, 22 June 1853, and Buol to Hübner, 21 June, PA IX/44.

41. Testa, IV, Pt. 1, 284–86; Clarendon to Cowley, 29 June and 6 July 1853, FO 519/169; Cowley to Clarendon, 4 and 6 July, Nos. 506 and 511, FO 519/2, and 6 and 7 July, Clar. dep. c. 6; Hübner to Buol, 4, 5, and 6 July, Nos. 94–96, PA IX/41.

42. Buol to Hübner, 2 July 1853, No. 2, PA IX/44; Clarendon to Cowley, 6 and 8 July, FO 519/169.

43. Hübner to Buol, 12 July 1853, Nos. 102B and C, PA IX/42; Clarendon to Cowley, 9 July, FO 519/169; Bourqueney to Drouyn, 8 July, No. 55, and Drouyn to Bourqueney, 9 July, cipher tg, AMAE Autr. 451.

44. Nesselrode, X, 258–59; Buol to Lebzeltern, 14 and 21 July 1853, PA X/37; Buol to Bruck, 18 July, PA XII/48; Bourqueney to Drouyn, 14, 16, and 18 July, cipher tg and Nos. 59–60, AMAE Autr. 451; Clarendon to Redcliffe, 18 July, Clar. dep. c. 126.

45. Bruck to Buol, 18, 20, 22, and 23 July 1853, and Buol to Bruck, 1 August, PA XII/47–48.

46. Drouyn to Bourqueney, 22 July 1853, Nos. 56–57, and Bourqueney

to Drouyn, 25 and 28 July, Nos. 61–62, AMAE Autr. 451; Cowley to Clarendon, 28 July, Clar. dep. c. 6; Clarendon to Westmorland, 28 July, tg, FO 7/414.

47. *Crimea*, 345.

48. Bourqueney to Drouyn, 29 and 30 July 1853, and Drouyn to Bourqueney, AMAE Autr. 451; Cowley to Clarendon, 29 July, Clar. dep. c. 6.

49. Nesselrode, X, 262–63; Russell to Clarendon, 20 July 1853, Clar. dep. c. 6; Clarendon to Aberdeen, 3 Aug., Add. ms. 43188.

50. See my article, "Bruck versus Buol," *Journal of Modern History*, XL (1968), 197–99.

51. Clarendon to Westmorland, 29 and 31 July 1853, FO 7/420, and 2 Aug., Clar. dep. c. 126; Clarendon to Cowley, 30 July, FO 519/169; Clarendon to Redcliffe, 25 July and 3 Aug., FO 352/36/1.

52. Even after the Vienna Note was signed and sent off to St. Petersburg, the British, suspecting that it was somehow Meyendorff's work, were still discussing with Brunnow the possibility of giving Russia her choice between it and Clarendon's proposed Russo-Turkish convention (Ab. Corr. 1852–1854, 178–79, 184; Brunnow to Clarendon, 29 and 30 July and 2 Aug. 1853, Clar. dep. c. 8; *PAP*, II, 123–24).

CHAPTER IV

1. Buol to Bruck, 1 Aug. 1853, PA XII/48; Buol to Hübner, 10 Aug., PA IX/44; Buol to Lebzeltern, 5 and 10 Aug., PA X/47.

2. Nesselrode, X, 267–73.

3. Bruck to Buol, 11, 15, and 18 Aug. 1853, PA XII/47–48.

4. Maxwell, II, 18–19; Temperley, *Crimea*, 347–48; Bruck to Buol, 20 Aug. and 5 Sept. 1853, PA XII/47; Redcliffe to Clarendon, 20 Aug., Clar. dep. c. 10, and to Westmorland, same date, FO 352/36/6.

5. Clarendon to Westmorland, 16 Aug. 1853, Clar. dep. c. 126; Clarendon to Cowley, 9 Aug., FO 519/169.

6. Clarendon to Westmorland, 9 and 17 Aug. 1853, Clar. dep. c. 126; Clarendon to Cowley, 16 Aug., FO 519/169.

7. Aberdeen to Russell, 13 Aug. 1853, and Russell to Clarendon, 20 Aug., PRO/30/22/11A.

8. Clarendon to Aberdeen, 20 and 21 Aug. 1853, RA G5/10 and Add. ms. 43188; Clarendon to Redcliffe, 8, 18, and 24 Aug., FO 352/36/1.

9. To Cowley, 12 and 16 Aug. 1853, FO 519/169.

10. Clarendon to Redcliffe, 24 and 27 Aug. 1853, FO 352/36/1; Clarendon to Cowley, private, 26 and 29 Aug., FO 519/169; Aberdeen to Clarendon, 26 Aug., Add. ms. 43188.

11. Palmerston to Clarendon, 26 Aug. 1853, Clar. dep. c. 3; Russell to Clarendon, 20, 27, 28, and 29 Aug., *ibid.*; Ab. Corr. 1852–1854, 202.

12. Cowley to Clarendon, 29 and 30 Aug. 1853, Nos. 641 and 645, FO 519/2; Clarendon to Cowley, 30 Aug. FO 519/169.

13. Ab. Corr. 1852–1854, 204–6; Clarendon to Cowley, 2 Sept. 1853, FO 519/169; memoranda by Russell and Palmerston, 3 and 5 Sept., PRO 30/22/11A.

14. Aberdeen to Graham, 7 and 12 Sept. 1853, Graham Papers Reel 18; Clarendon to Redcliffe, 8 Sept., FO 352/36/1; Clarendon to Cowley, 6 Sept., FO 519/169.

15. Ab. Corr. 1852–1854, 224–26; memoranda by Russell and Palmerston, 3 and 5 Sept. 1853, PRO 30/22/11A; Palmerston to Clarendon, 5 and 13 Sept., Clar. dep. c. 6; Clarendon to Cowley, 6 and 9 Sept., FO 519/169; Clarendon to Westmorland, 31 Aug. and 6 and 14 Sept., Clar. dep. c. 126.

16. Temperley, *Crimea*, 349; Conacher, 184–85; but cf. also Temperley, "Stratford de Redcliffe," Pt. II, 274–75.

17. Meyendorff, III, 69–70; Westmorland to Clarendon, 14 and 16 Sept. 1853, FO 7/414; Buol to Hübner, 16 Sept., PA IX/44.

18. Hübner to Buol, 12 Sept. 1853, Nos. 141D–F and private, PA IX/42 and 44; Cowley to Clarendon, 12 and 15 Sept., Nos. 679 and 681, FO 519/2; Count Flahault to Clarendon, 6 Sept., and Walewski to Clarendon, 13 Sept., Clar. dep. c. 6.

19. Zaionchkovskii, Pril. II, 63–66; Colloredo to Buol, 7 and 9 Sept. 1853, PA VIII/38; Clarendon to Westmorland, 7 Sept., No. 283, FO 7/414.

20. Clarendon to Redcliffe, 8 Sept. 1853, FO 352/36/1; Clarendon to Cowley, 13 Sept., FO 519/169; Palmerston to Clarendon, 12 and 14 Sept., Palm. Papers GC/CL/523/2 and Clar. dep. c. 3.

21. Ab. Corr. 1852–1854, 226–27; Aberdeen to Victoria, 18 Sept. 1853, Add. ms. 43047; Clarendon to Cowley, 15 and 17 Sept., FO 519/169; Clarendon to Redcliffe, 15 and 17 Sept., FO 352/36/1.

22. Buol to Bruck, 19 Sept. 1853, PA XII/48.

23. Hübner to Buol, 20 Sept. 1853, No. 146B, PA IX/42; Drouyn to Bourqueney, 17 Sept., and Bourqueney to Drouyn, 17 and 18 Sept., AMAE Autr. 451; Cowley to Clarendon, 20 Sept., No. 710, FO 519/2.

24. Buol to Hübner, 17 Sept. 1853, PA IX/44; Bourqueney to Drouyn, 18 Sept., No. 88, AMAE Autr. 451.

25. Westmorland to Clarendon, tgs, 18, 21, and 22 Sept. 1853, FO 7/414 and 421; Clarendon to Westmorland, tgs, 19 and 20 Sept., FO 7/414; Drouyn to Bourqueney, tg, 21 Sept., and Bourqueney to Drouyn,

2 tgs, 22 Sept., AMAE Autr. 451; Buol to Francis Joseph, 21 Sept., PA XL/48.

26. Victoria to Leopold I, 20 Sept. 1853, RA Y98/29; Palmerston to Clarendon, 21 Sept., Clar. dep. c. 3. Clarendon's suspicions about the coming Olmütz meeting were very active and fed from many quarters; but Seymour pointed out to him that at Olmütz Austria might be able to wrest concessions from Nicholas impossible to gain any other way (9 Sept., *ibid.* c. 8).

27. Russell to Clarendon, 12 and 17 Sept. 1853, Clar. dep. c. 3; Russell to Aberdeen, 15 and 17 Sept., and Aberdeen to Russell, 16 and 22 Sept., Add. ms. 43067; memorandum by Prince Albert, 5 Oct., RA G6/1.

28. Clarendon to Cowley, 16 Sept. 1853, FO 519/169; Clarendon to Redcliffe, 17 Sept., FO 352/36/1.

29. Add. ms. 43188.

30. Redcliffe to Clarendon, 19 Sept. 1853, Clar. dep. c. 10; Cowley to Clarendon, 19 and 20 Sept., *ibid.* c. 6; Clarendon to Cowley, 20 Sept., FO 519/169, and to Graham, same date, Graham Papers Reel 18; Seymour to Clarendon, 16 Sept., Clar. dep. c. 8.

31. Colloredo to Buol, 21 and 26 Sept. 1853, PA VIII/38; Hübner to Buol, 28 Sept. and 3 Oct., PA IX/42; Joseph Alexander von Hübner, *Neuf ans de souvenirs,* I, 155–57.

32. Martin, *Prince Consort,* II, 575–76; Aberdeen to Russell, 22 Sept. 1853, PRO 30/22/11A.

33. Clarendon to Graham, 22 Sept. 1853, Graham Papers Reel 18; Clarendon to Cowley, 23 Sept., FO 519/169; Clarendon to Palmerston, 24 Sept., Clar. dep. c. 126; Russell to Clarendon, 22 Sept., *ibid.* c. 3.

34. Palmerston to Clarendon, 21 Sept. 1853, Clar. dep. c. 3; Clarendon to Palmerston (2 letters), 24 Sept., Palm. Papers GC/CL/526–27.

35. Conacher, 188–89; Temperley, *Crimea,* 354; Aberdeen to Graham, 24 Sept. 1853, and Graham to Clarendon, 25 Sept., Graham Papers Reel 18; Clarendon to Westmorland, 24 Sept., Clar. dep. c. 126; Clarendon to Palmerston, 24 Sept., *ibid.* c. 3.

36. Clarendon to Cowley, 23 Sept. 1853, FO 519/169.

37. Cowley to Clarendon, 20, 22, and 29 Sept. 1853, Clar. dep. c. 6; *Russell Correspondence,* II, 153.

38. Cowley to Clarendon, 19 Sept. 1853, No. 693, FO 519/2; Bourqueney to Drouyn, 30 Sept. and 5 Oct., Nos. 95 and 99, AMAE Autr. 451.

39. Hübner to Buol, 21 Sept. 1853, PA IX/44.

40. Palmerston to Clarendon, 21 Sept. 1853, and Russell to Clarendon, 17 Sept., Clar. dep. c. 3; Clarendon to Cowley, 23 Sept., FO 519/169.

41. Martin, *Prince Consort*, II, 513, 519; *QVL*, II, 549; Palmerston to Clarendon, 22 Sept. 1853, Clar. dep. c. 3.

42. Palmerston to Clarendon, 21 Sept. 1853, *ibid.*; Ashley, II, 38–39.

43. *Russkaia Starina*, XV (1876), 165–74; Shcherbatov, VII, 61–62; Zaionchkovskii, Pril. II, 99–111.

44. Tarle, I, 338; Nesselrode, X, 276–80, 286–87; Meyendorff, III, 70–75; Lebzeltern to Buol, private, 10 Sept. 1853, PA X/38; Kurt Borries, *Preussen im Krimkrieg*, 343–46.

45. *Kübecks Tagebücher*, 119; Bruck to Buol, 5 Sept. 1853, PA XII/48; Buol to Francis Joseph, 23 Aug., PA XL/48.

46. Westmorland to Clarendon, 28 and 29 Sept. 1853, Clar. dep. c. 1; Westmorland's memorandum, 27 Sept., and two reports of 28 Sept., Nos. 356–57, FO 7/421; Buol to Hübner, 28 Sept., PA IX/44; Goyon to Bourqueney, 26, 27, and 28 Sept., AMAE Autr. 451.

47. Temperley, *Crimea*, 355; cf. Conacher, 192–200.

48. Clarendon to Westmorland, private, 20 Sept. 1853, Clar. dep. c. 126; Clarendon to Cowley, private, 30 Sept. and 3 Oct., FO 519/169; Clarendon to Russell, 1 Oct., Clar. dep. c. 127 (partly published in Maxwell, II, 25); Clarendon to Palmerston, 3 and 6 Oct., GC/CL/529–30; Palmerston to Clarendon, 3 and 4 Oct., Clar. dep. c. 3.

49. Clarendon to Seymour, 5 Oct. 1853, and Seymour to Clarendon, 14 Oct., Clar. dep. c. 127 and c. 8.

50. Buol to Hübner, 28 Sept. 1853, PA IX/44; Hübner to Buol, 3 Oct., Nos. 151E and F, PA IX/42; Bourqueney to Drouyn, 27 Sept., and Drouyn to Bourqueney, 28 Sept., AMAE Autr. 451.

51. Cowley to Clarendon, 3 Oct. 1853, FO 519/169.

52. Clarendon to Cowley, private, 3 and 4 Oct. 1853, FO 519/169; Clarendon to Aberdeen, 2 Oct., Add. ms. 43188; Clarendon to A. Loftus, 5 Oct., Clar. dep. c. 126.

53. Jasmund, I, 180–82; *Acte şi documente*, II, 243, 246–49; Bourqueney to Drouyn, 4 Oct. 1853, tg, AMAE Autr. 452.

54. Cowley to Clarendon, 5 Oct. 1853, No. 740, FO 519/2, and 9 Oct., Clar. dep. c. 7; Russell to Clarendon, 4 and 5 Oct., *ibid.* c. 3.

55. Clarendon to Westmorland, 5 Oct. 1853, No. 328, FO 7/415, and same date, Clar. dep. c. 127; Westmorland to Clarendon, 9 Oct., *ibid.* c. 1.

56. Buol to Bruck, 26 Sept. and 3 Oct. 1853, PA XII/48. Leopold I of Belgium also argued for retaining the Vienna Note, on the same grounds as Buol (Ab. Corr. 1852–1854, 249–50).

CHAPTER V

1. Borries, 63–65; *PAP*, II, 138–39.

2. Martin, *Prince Consort*, II, 424–25; *Kempens Tagebuch*, 291–92, 294, 298; Westmorland to Clarendon, 18 and 23 Oct. 1853, Clar. dep. c. 1.

3. Unckel, 105–7; *Kübecks Tagebücher*, 127; protocol of conference, 9 Oct. 1853, MR Prot. 13.

4. Bruck to Buol, 30 Jan. 1854, PA XII/52; Redlich, *Francis Joseph*, 135–37.

5. Bourqueney to Drouyn, 16 Oct. 1853, No. 102, AMAE Autr. 452; Marquis du Chateaurénard to the War Ministry, 15 Nov., AMG Reconnaissances Autr. 1602/44; Hübner to Buol, 18 and 22 Oct., PA IX/42; Westmorland to Clarendon, 4 Nov., Clar. dep. c. 1; Shcherbatov, VII, 77–78.

6. Eckhart, 12–15; Jasmund, I, 198–99, 223–25; Prokesch to Buol, 5 and 10 Nov. 1853, Nos. 94 and 97A–B, PA II/27.

7. Count Crivelli to Buol, 10 and 11 Nov. 1853, PA III/48; Prokesch to Buol, 30 Oct. and 14 Nov., PA II/26; Bourqueney to Drouyn, 4 Nov., No. 111 cipher, AMAE Autr. 452.

8. Zaionchkovskii, Pril. II, 248–50; Meyendorff, III, 79–81.

9. Buol to Hübner, 16 Oct. 1853, PA IX/44; Bourqueney to Drouyn, 13 Oct., AMAE Autr. 452; Westmorland to Clarendon, 11 Oct., FO 7/421.

10. FO 352/36/1.

11. 27 Sept. 1853, Clar. dep. c. 3.

12. Minto to Russell, 28 Sept. 1853, PRO 30/22/11A; note by Russell, 4 Oct., and undated memorandum [early Oct.], *ibid.* 11B; Clarendon to Palmerston, 4 Oct., Palm. Papers GC/CL/530.

13. Ashley, II, 41–42; Aberdeen to Graham, 3, 4, and 6 Oct. 1853, and Graham to G. C. Lewis, 5 Oct., Graham Papers Reel 18; Argyll to Russell, 24 Sept. and 7 Oct., PRO 30/22/11A–B (the former letter printed partly in Argyll's *Autobiography*, 465–66); Argyll to Gladstone, 26 Sept., Add. ms. 44098.

14. Conacher, 128–29, 195–99; Aberdeen to Graham, 8 Oct. 1853, Graham Papers Reel 18; Aberdeen to Victoria, 8 Oct., Add. ms. 43047; memorandum by Albert, 10 Oct., RA G6/24.

15. Gladstone to Aberdeen, 12 Oct. 1853, Add. ms. 43070; Graham to Clarendon, 10 Oct., Clar. dep. c. 4; Palmerston to Clarendon, 14 Oct., Palm. Papers GC/CL/1373; Clarendon to G. C. Lewis, 9 Oct. 1853, Clar. dep. c. 532.

16. Clarendon to Redcliffe, 8, 10, and 11 Oct. 1853, FO 352/36/1.

17. Clarendon to Aberdeen, 10, 12, and 15 Oct. 1853, and Aberdeen to Clarendon, 12 Oct., Add. ms. 43188.

18. Palmerston to Clarendon, 11 Oct. 1853, Clar. dep. c. 3; Clarendon to Palmerston, 13 and 17 Oct., Palm. Papers GC/CL/534, 538.

19. Clarendon to Cowley, 7, 8, 10, 14, and 21 Oct. 1853, FO 519/169.

20. Clar. dep. c. 126; Loftus to Clarendon, 30 Sept. 1853, *ibid.*, c. 1.

21. FO 519/169.

22. Clarendon to Bloomfield, 3 Aug. 1853, Clar. dep. c. 126; Clarendon to Westmorland, 8 Oct., *ibid.* c. 127; Clarendon to Cowley, 8 Oct., FO 519/169; *PAP*, II, 131–33.

23. Loftus to Clarendon, 12 Oct. 1853, Clar. dep. c. 1; *Greville Memoirs*, VI, 457–58; Albert's memorandum, 16 Oct., RA G6/44.

24. 11–12 Oct. 1853, Clar. dep. c. 127.

25. Clarendon to Palmerston, 16 Oct. 1853, with Russell's letter to Clarendon, same date, and his draft note enclosed, Palm. Papers GC/CL/536.

26. Palmerston to Clarendon, 17 Oct. 1853, *ibid.* GC/CL/1371; Ashley, II, 49–51.

27. Russell to Clarendon, 16, 19, 22, and 28 Oct. and 5 Nov. 1853, Clar. dep. c. 3; Bunsen to Prince Albert, with enclosure, 21 Oct., RA G6/56–57; Clarendon to Cowley, 18 Oct., FO 519/169, and to Palmerston, 18 Oct., Palm. Papers GC/CL/539.

28. Clar. dep. c. 127.

29. *Ibid.;* Westmorland to Clarendon, 18 and 23 Oct. 1853, *ibid.* c. 1.

30. *Greville Memoirs*, VI, 450–51; Minto to Russell, 12 Oct. 1853, and Palmerston to Russell, 15 Oct., PRO 30/22/11B.

31. Clarendon to Cowley, 1 and 4 Nov. 1853, FO 519/169; Seymour to Clarendon, 18 and 29 Oct., Clar. dep. c. 8; Aberdeen to Victoria, 10 Nov., Add. ms. 43048.

32. Stanmore, I, 231–34; Clarendon to Palmerston, 16 Oct. 1853, Palm. Papers GC/CL/536; Gladstone to Aberdeen, 18 Oct., Add. ms. 43070.

33. Aberdeen to Gladstone, 20 Oct. 1853, Add. ms. 43070.

34. 20 Oct. 1853, Palm. Papers GC/CL/540.

35. Ab. Corr. 1852–1854, 321–22; Russell to Palmerston, 22 Oct. 1853, Palm. Papers; Ashley, II, 49–51.

36. Martin, *Prince Consort*, II, 525–27; Palmerston to Clarendon, 24 Oct. 1853, Palm. Papers GC/CL/541.

37. Clarendon to Aberdeen, 22 and 26 Oct. 1853, Add. ms. 43188; Clarendon to Palmerston, 24 Oct., Palm. Papers GC/CL/542.

38. 24 Oct. 1853, FO 519/169.

39. 28 Oct. 1853, *ibid.*; Clarendon to Redcliffe, 18 and 22 Oct., FO 352/36/1.

40. Westmorland to Clarendon, tg, 25 Oct. 1853, FO 7/415; Buol to Hübner, 27 and 28 Oct., PA IX/44; Clarendon to Westmorland, 28 Oct., Clar. dep. c. 127.

41. Drouyn to Bourqueney, 22 and 29 Oct. 1853, Nos. 76 and 80, and Bourqueney to Drouyn, 25 Oct. and 1 Nov., Nos. 105 and 110, AMAE Autr. 452; Drouyn to Walewski, 1 Nov., *ibid.*, 455; Thouvenel, *Nicolas Ier*, 454–57.

42. Westmorland to Clarendon, 30 Oct. and 1 and 3 Nov. 1853, Nos. 392, 395, and 400, FO 7/421–22; Buol to Colloredo, 31 Oct., PA VIII/38; Clarendon to Westmorland, cipher tg, 1 Nov., FO 7/415; Clarendon to Graham, 29 Oct., Graham Papers Reel 18.

43. 30 Oct. 1853, PA XL/48.

44. PA IX/44.

45. Cowley to Clarendon, 5 Nov. 1853, No. 816, FO 519/2; Colloredo to Buol, 5 Nov., PA VIII/38; Hübner to Buol, 4 Nov., No. 166B and private letter, PA IX/42 and 44.

46. Westmorland to Clarendon, tgs, 6 and 8 Nov. 1853, FO 7/415; Bourqueney to Drouyn, 8 and 12 Nov., Nos. 112 and 114, AMAE Autr. 452.

47. Cowley to Clarendon, 2, 3, and 6 Nov. 1853, Clar. dep. c. 7.

48. Clarendon to Cowley, 8 and 11 Nov. 1853, FO 519/169; Westmorland to Clarendon, 4 Nov., and Clarendon to Westmorland, 9 Nov., Clar. dep. c. 1 and 127. Aberdeen agreed with Drouyn that Palmerston and Clarendon were distorting Austria's position—to Clarendon, 9 Nov., *ibid.* c. 4.

49. Clarendon to Westmorland, 9 Nov. 1853, No. 372, FO 7/415; Clarendon to Cowley, 3 Nov., FO 519/169; Palmerston to Clarendon, 3, 7, and 11 Nov., and memorandum of 3 Nov., Clar. dep. c. 3 and Palm. Papers Russia.

50. Clarendon to Cowley, 4 and 8 Nov. 1853, FO 519/169; Clarendon to Seymour, 9 and 14 Nov., Clar. dep. c. 127; Clarendon to Westmorland, 3 and 16 Nov., *ibid.*

51. Clarendon to Cowley, 1 Nov. 1853, FO 519/169; Colloredo to Buol, 3 Nov., PA VIII/38.

52. Clarendon to Redcliffe, 8 Nov. 1853, FO 352/36/1; Clarendon to Aberdeen and Aberdeen to Clarendon, 9 Nov., Add. ms. 43048; Clarendon to Palmerston, 6 Nov., Palm. Papers GC/CL/544; Aberdeen to Victoria, 10 Nov., Add. ms. 43048.

53. Clarendon argued this to Aberdeen (4 Nov. 1853, Add. ms. 43188),

though even here he mainly stressed the danger of domestic political trouble and embarrassment for Britain abroad.

54. Clarendon to Cowley, private, 10 Nov. 1853, FO 519/169 (partly printed in Maxwell, II, 19); Cowley to Clarendon, private, 11 Nov., Clar. dep. c. 7.

55. Cowley to Clarendon, 11 Nov. 1853, *ibid*.

56. Schroeder, "Austria and the Danubian Principalities," 219–22; Hübner to Buol, 17 Oct. and 25 Nov. 1853, Nos. 156 and 177B and private letter, PA IX/42; Drouyn to Bourqueney, 26 and 28 Nov., AMAE Autr. 452; Cowley to Clarendon, 28 Nov., No. 892, FO 519/2.

57. Cowley, *Paris Embassy*, 32; Drouyn to Bourqueney, 7 Nov. 1853, No. 83, AMAE Autr. 452; Hübner to Buol, 13 and 20 Nov., Nos. 171B and 174C, PA IX/42; Buol to Hübner, 27 Oct., No. 6, PA IX/44; *Rel. dipl. Aust.-Sard.*, IV, 133–34, 140–44.

58. Valsecchi, *Alleanza*, 273–84. Brenier's instructions and reports are in *Rel. dipl. Fr.-Tosc.*, II, 333–34, 348–57, 359–65; the reactions of Austrians and others are shown in *Rel. dipl. Aust.-Tosc.*, IV, 198–218, and *Rel. dipl. GB-Sard.*, IV, 246–47, 252.

59. Bernhard von Mayer to Bach, 24 Nov. 1853, Verwaltungsarchiv (Vienna), Nachlass Bach, IX.

60. Bourqueney to Drouyn, 16, 18, and 23 Nov. 1853, Nos. 117, 119, and 120, AMAE Autr. 452. A good example of such Western distortion is the way in which Buol's conditional promise and plea as reported by Bourqueney on Nov. 18 ("Il ne tient qu'à vous que nous soyons ensemble jusqu'au bout") was changed in Cowley's report to the simple promise, "Nous irons avec vous jusqu'au bout" (*Paris Embassy*, 32–33).

61. Bourqueney to Drouyn, 15 Nov. 1853, No. 116, AMAE Autr. 452; Engel-Janosi, *Hübner*, 110–12; Hübner to Buol, 13 Oct., PA IX/44; Hübner to Rechberg, 8 Oct., PA I/rot 533c; Buol to Hübner, 29 Nov., No. 2, PA IX/44; Cowley to Clarendon, 5 Dec., No. 914, FO 519/2.

62. 29 Nov. 1853, PA IX/44.

63. Drouyn to Bourqueney, 5 Dec. 1853, AMAE Autr. 452.

64. Buol to Bruck, 11 Nov. 1853, Nos. 1–5 and private letter, PA XII/48; Westmorland to Clarendon, 10 Nov., No. 406, FO 7/422; Buol to Hübner, 14 Nov., PA IX/44.

65. Clarendon to Westmorland, 16 Nov. 1853, Clar. dep. c. 127; Clarendon to Cowley, 15, 16, and 18 Nov., FO 519/169; Clarendon to Redcliffe, 18 Nov., FO 352/36/1.

66. Cowley to Clarendon, 14 and 18 Nov. 1853, Nos. 848 and 863, FO 519/2.

67. Buol to Colloredo, tg, 21 Nov. 1853, PA VIII/38; *PAP*, II, 182–83;

Russell to Clarendon, 21 Nov., Clar. dep. c. 3; Clarendon to Seymour, 7 Dec., *ibid.* c. 127; Clarendon to Cowley, 22 Nov., FO 519/169.

68. Drouyn to Bourqueney, 22 Nov. 1853, No. 87, AMAE Autr. 452; Cowley to Clarendon, 20 and 25 Nov., Nos. 869 and 884, FO 519/2.

69. Cowley to Clarendon, 20 Nov. 1853, No. 869 and private letter, FO 519/2 and Clar. dep. c. 7; Clarendon to Cowley, 22 Nov., FO 519/169; Hübner to Buol, 19 Nov., No. 173, PA IX/42.

70. Clarendon to Cowley, 23, 25, and 26 Nov. 1853, FO 519/169. The Nov. 26 letter is particularly revealing: here Clarendon emphasized that he had no hope that this collective *démarche* would do any good at Constantinople; in fact, it would only make it easier for the Turks to drag Britain with them into war. However, the move would help force Austria into closer cooperation with the West.

71. Clarendon to Cowley, 23 Nov. 1853, *ibid.*; Clarendon to Redcliffe, 24, 28, and 29 Nov., FO 352/36/1.

72. Clarendon to Westmorland, 29 Nov. and 7 Dec. 1853, and Clarendon to Loftus, 16 and 29 Nov., Clar. dep. c. 127.

73. Cowley to Clarendon, 4 and 5 Dec. 1853, Clar. dep. c. 7; Clarendon to Cowley, 29 Nov., FO 519/169.

74. Stanmore, II, 238–40; Aberdeen to Victoria, 12, 16, and 26 Nov. 1853, Add. ms. 43048; Aberdeen to Clarendon, 20 and 21 Nov. and 3 Dec., Add. ms. 43188 and Clar. dep. c. 4; Gladstone to Aberdeen, 2 Dec., Add. ms. 43070; Graham to Clarendon, 1 and 5 Dec., Graham Papers Reel 18.

75. Aberdeen to Clarendon, 28 Nov. 1853, Add. ms. 43188; Clarendon to Aberdeen, 28 and 29 Nov. and 1 Dec., *ibid.*; Clarendon to Cowley, 29 Nov., FO 519/169.

76. 4 Dec. 1853, Clar. dep. c. 1.

77. Buol to Hübner, 29 Nov. 1853, PA IX/44; Bourqueney to Drouyn, 28 Nov. and 4 Dec., Nos. 122 and 125, and Drouyn to Bourqueney, 28 Nov., No. 89, AMAE Autr. 452; Clarendon to Cowley, 18 Nov., FO 519/169.

78. Palmerston to Clarendon, 25 Nov. 1853, and Russell to Clarendon, 28 Nov. and 4 and 5 Dec., Clar. dep. c. 3; Clarendon to Russell, 4 Dec., *ibid.* c. 127.

79. E.g., Seymour to Clarendon and Loftus to Clarendon, both 19 Nov. 1853, Clar. dep. c. 8 and 1.

80. Thouvenel, *Nicolas Ier*, 278–79; Zaionchkovskii, Pril. II, 120–21, 194–95; Shcherbatov, VII, 71–72, 76–77.

81. Zaionchkovskii, Pril. II, 273–75, 280–87, 321–26; Shcherbatov, VII, 78–81; Tarle, I, 275–80; Meyendorff, III, 90–91.

82. Nesselrode, X, 304-5.

83. Memorandum by Prince William of Prussia, entitled "Olmütz 1853," n.d., enclosed in Bunsen to Albert, 25 Oct. 1853, RA G6/79.

84. Shcherbatov, VII, 73; Tarle, I, 361-62; Nesselrode, X, 302-3; Nesselrode to Meyendorff, 26 Nov. 1853, PA X/38 (not the letter published in Nesselrode, X, 304-5); Zaionchkovskii, Pril. II, 250-51.

85. Meyendorff, III, 107-111; Zaionchkovskii, Pril. II, 253-54.

86. Buol to Thun, 26 and 28 Nov. 1853, and Thun to Buol, 2 Dec., PA III/49; *PAP*, II, 188-98.

CHAPTER VI

1. Buol to Lebzeltern, 7 and 12 Dec. 1853, PA X/37; Buol to Bruck, 5 Dec., PA XII/48; Buol to Thun, with copy to Prokesch, PA III/49; Buol to Hübner, 8 and 24 Dec., PA IX/44; Buol to Colloredo, 24 Dec., PA VIII/38.

2. Cowley to Clarendon, 12 Dec. 1853, No. 944 and confidential letter, FO 519/2; Clarendon to Reeves, 6 Dec., Clar. dep. c. 535.

3. Drouyn to Bourqueney, 22 Dec. 1853, No. 95, and Bourqueney to Drouyn, 23 Dec., No. 132, AMAE Autr. 452; Cowley to Clarendon, 15 Dec., No. 953, FO 519/2; Clarendon to Cowley, 16 Dec., FO 519/169; Clarendon to Westmorland, 20 Dec., No. 417, FO 7/415.

4. Cowley to Clarendon, 11 and 16 Dec. 1853, Nos. 937 and 957, FO 519/2; Drouyn to Walewski, 13 Dec., AMAE Mem. et doc. France 2120.

5. Temperley, *Crimea*, 370-78; Palmerston to Clarendon, 11 Dec. 1853, Palm. Papers GC/CL/1372; Cowley to Clarendon, 11 and 12 Dec., Clar. dep. c. 7; Martin, *Prince Consort*, II, 431-33; Stanmore, 242.

6. Clarendon to Palmerston, 12 Dec. 1853, Palm. Papers GC/CL/547; Clarendon to Cowley, 13 Dec., FO 519/169; Clarendon to Russell, 13 Dec., PRO 30/22/11B.

7. Clarendon to Redcliffe, 17 Dec. 1853, FO 352/36/1; Clarendon to Cowley, 16 and 17 Dec. 1853, FO 519/169.

8. Ashley, 52-54; Stanmore, 238-40; Aberdeen to Victoria, 6 Dec. 1853, Victoria to Aberdeen, 7 Dec., and Albert to Aberdeen, 9 Dec., Add. ms. 43048. For the dispute over the real grounds for Palmerston's resignation, see Conacher, 215-32; H. C. Bell, "Palmerston and Parliamentary Representation," *Journal of Modern History*, IV (1932), 195-99; and Southgate, 333-34.

9. Russell to Clarendon, 8 Dec. 1853, Clar. dep. c. 3; Russell to Aberdeen, 10 Dec., Add. ms. 43067.

10. Graham to Russell, 11 Dec. 1853, and Clarendon to Russell, 13 Dec., PRO 30/22/11B; Albert to Aberdeen, 9 Dec., Add. ms. 43048; Clarendon to Graham, Aberdeen to Graham, and Graham to Clarendon, all 13 Dec., Graham Papers Reel 18.

11. Aberdeen to Russell, 13 Dec. 1853, PRO 30/22/11B; Graham to Russell, 16 Dec., Graham Papers Reel 18.

12. Aberdeen to Victoria, 17 Dec. 1853, Add. ms. 43048; Clarendon to Russell, 14 Dec., and Russell to Clarendon, 15 Dec., PRO 30/22/11B.

13. Ab. Corr. 1852–1854, 398, 406–7, 413–19; Russell to Graham, 18 and 20 Dec. 1853, Graham to Russell, 19 Dec., and Aberdeen to Graham, 19 Dec., Graham Papers Reel 18.

14. Temperley, *Crimea*, 375–78; cf. also Conacher, 239–42.

15. 16 Dec. 1853, FO 519/169; cf. Clarendon to Palmerston, 25 Nov., Clar. dep. c. 127.

16. Add. ms. 43188.

17. Clarendon to Cowley, 21 Dec. 1853, FO 519/169; Cowley to Clarendon, 19 Dec., No. 968A, FO 519/2, and 17 and 19 Dec., Clar. dep. c. 7.

18. Clarendon to Cowley, 20 and 21 Dec. 1853, FO 519/169; Cowley to Clarendon, 21 and 23 Dec., Clar. dep. c. 7; memorandum by Albert, 26 Dec., RA G8/11.

19. Temperley, *Crimea*, 377–78, 381–82, Appendices VI and VII.

20. *QVL*, II, 570–71; Aberdeen to Clarendon, 21 Dec. 1853, Add. ms. 43188; Aberdeen to Victoria, 22 Dec., Add. ms. 43048; Aberdeen to Graham, 28 Dec., Graham Papers Reel 18.

21. Ab. Corr. 1852–1854, 421–22; Aberdeen to Russell, 20 Dec. 1853, PRO 30/22/11B.

22. FO 352/36/1 and FO 519/169.

23. Clarendon to Cowley, 27 Dec. 1853, FO 519/169; Cowley to Clarendon, 29 Dec., Clar. dep. c. 7 (partly printed in Cowley, *Paris Embassy*, 35).

24. Clarendon to Redcliffe, 27 Dec. 1853, FO 352/36/1; cf. also Clarendon to Cowley, 3 Jan. 1854, FO 519/170.

25. Palmerston to Aberdeen, 23 Dec. 1853, Palm. Papers GC/AB/322; Ashley, II, 21; memorandum by Albert, 25 Dec., RA G8/13.

26. Graham to Clarendon, 13 Dec. 1853, Graham Papers Reel 18; Russell to Clarendon, 19 Dec., Clar. dep. c. 3. Judging by Graham's letter to Russell of Dec. 19 (PRO 30/22/11B), Russell was even contemplating forming a land force to help the fleets ward off a Russian invasion of Turkey.

27. Clarendon to Loftus, 14 Dec. 1853, Clar. dep. c. 127; Clarendon to

Redcliffe, 8 and 24 Dec., FO 352/36/1; Clarendon to Cowley, 27 and 28 Dec., FO 519/169.

28. Cf. Reeves to Clarendon, 16 Oct. 1853, Clar. dep. c. 10; Redcliffe to Clarendon, 21 and 22 Oct. and 5 and 17 Dec., *ibid.*

29. Jasmund, I, 206–11, 215–17.

30. Bruck to Buol, 12, 15, and 19 Dec. 1853, Nos. 59, 60A, and 61, and private letter, 16 Jan. 1854, PA XII/47 and 52; Buol to Bruck, 26 Dec. and 2 Jan., Nos. 1–2 and private letter, PA XII/48–49 and 52; Buol to Francis Joseph, 28 Dec., PA XL/76.

31. Buol to Hübner, 29 Dec. 1853, and Hübner to Buol, 31 Dec., No. 202E, PA IX/44 and 42; Cowley to Clarendon, 29 Dec., Nos. 993 and 996, FO 519/2.

32. Clarendon to Westmorland, tg, 30 Dec. 1853, and private, 31 Dec., FO 7/415 and Clar. dep. c. 127; Clarendon to Aberdeen, 30 Dec., Add. ms. 43188; Clarendon to Cowley, 30 Dec., FO 519/169 (partly printed in Cowley, *Paris Embassy*, 36, but dated Dec. 29).

33. Bruck to Buol, 29 Dec. 1853, No. 64B, PA XII/47; Buol to Bruck, 9 and 16 Jan. 1854, Nos. 1 and 2, *ibid.*, 49; Buol to Hübner, 14 Jan., No. 2, PA IX/48.

34. Bourqueney to Drouyn, 19 Dec. 1853, No. 131, AMAE Autr. 452; Buol to Hübner, 29 Dec., PA IX/44.

35. Bourqueney to Drouyn, 1 Jan. 1854, No. 1, and Drouyn to Bourqueney, 2 Jan., No. 2, AMAE Autr. 453.

36. Bourqueney to Drouyn, 3 Jan. 1854, No. 2, *ibid.;* Hübner to Buol, 31 XII 1853, PA IX/44; Westmorland to Clarendon, 4 Jan., No. 5, FO 7/431, and private letter, Clar. dep. c. 12.

37. Bourqueney to Drouyn, 14 and 17 Jan. 1854, Nos. 9–10, AMAE Autr. 453; Buol to Colloredo, 8 Jan., PA VIII/40; *Kempens Tagebuch,* 314–16; Zaionchkovskii, Pril. II, 254–56.

38. Clarendon to Westmorland, 4 Jan. 1854, Clar. dep. c. 127; Cowley to Clarendon, 9 Jan., No. 27, FO 519/2.

39. Jasmund, I, 227–28, 230–31; Buol to Hübner, 8, 14, 17, and 28 Jan. 1854, PA IX/48; Buol to Lebzeltern, 7 and 13 Jan., and to V. Esterházy, 24 Jan., PA X/38.

40. Redcliffe to Clarendon, 5 Jan. 1854, FO 352/37/I/3; Aberdeen to Victoria, 5 and 12 Jan., Add. ms. 43048 and RA G8/90; Clarendon to Cowley, 3 and 10 Jan., FO 519/170; Clarendon to Westmorland, 11 Jan., Clar. dep. c. 127; Graham to Clarendon, 15 Jan., Graham Papers Reel 19.

41. Russell to Clarendon, 14 Jan. 1854, Clar. dep. c. 15; Clarendon to Aberdeen, 15 Jan., Add. ms. 43188.

42. Buol to Hübner, 24 Jan. 1854, PA IX/48; Westmorland to Clarendon, 23 Jan., Clar. dep. c. 12.

43. Cowley to Clarendon, 13 Jan. 1854, Clar. dep. c. 16, and 26 Jan., No. 87, FO 519/2.

44. Clarendon to Cowley, 17 and 20 Jan. 1854, FO 519/170. .

45. Aberdeen to Clarendon, 20 Jan. 1854, and Russell to Clarendon, 20 Jan., Clar. dep. c. 14–15.

46. Jasmund, I, 241–43; Raymond Lorantas, "Lord Cowley's Mission to Paris," 111–23.

47. Gladstone to Aberdeen (2 letters), 26 Jan. 1854, Add. ms. 43071.

48. Clarendon to Cowley, 20 Jan. 1854, FO 519/170.

49. *Ibid.*, 23, 24, 28, and 30 Jan. and 2 Feb., 1854; Clarendon to Palmerston, 29 Jan., Palm. Papers GC/CL/555; Palmerston to Clarendon, 25 and 29 Jan., Clar. dep. c. 15.

50. Jasmund, I, 245–47.

51. Drouyn to Bourqueney, 27, 28, and 29 Jan. 1854, AMAE Autr. 453; Cowley to Clarendon, 13 and 26 Jan., Clar. dep. c. 16, and 26 Jan., No. 87, FO 519/2.

52. Russell to Clarendon, with enclosed memorandum, 1 Jan. 1854, Clar. dep. c. 15.

53. *Ibid.*, 15 and 17 Jan. 1854; Conacher, 251–56; Martin, *Prince Consort*, II, 564; Newcastle to Russell, 14 Jan., PRO 30/22/11C; Palmerston to Graham, 19 Jan., memorandum by Graham, 22 Jan., and Clarendon to Graham, 22 Jan., Graham Papers Reel 18.

54. Clarendon to Cowley, 17 Jan. 1854, FO 519/170; Russell to Clarendon, 15 Jan., Clar. dep. c. 15; Palmerston to Clarendon, 16 Jan., Palm. Papers GC/CL/552.

55. Thun to Buol, 29 Jan. 1854, No. 5B, PA III/50; *Morning Post*, 4 Jan. 1854; Victoria to Clarendon, 18 Jan., RA G9/19; Westmorland to Clarendon, 8 Jan., Clar. dep. c. 12.

56. Martin, *Triumph of Palmerston*, 216–17; E. di Nolfo, *Europa e Italia*, 73–74.

57. Russell to Clarendon, 4 Jan. 1854, Clar. dep. c. 15; Clarendon to Albert, with enclosure, 16 Jan., RA G9/11 and 18.

58. Loftus's and Bloomfield's private correspondence (Clar. dep. c. 1 and 12) is full of Manteuffel's allegations against Austria, regularly believed both by these diplomats and by the government at London and often made the subject of Clarendon's complaints to Vienna. Bunsen and Victoria's royal relatives in Germany also worked ardently to ruin Austria's reputation.

59. Russell to Clarendon, 11 and 21 Jan. 1854, Clar. dep. c. 15; John M.

Block, "British Opinion of Prussian Policy, 1854-1866" (unpublished dissertation, Univ. of Wisconsin, 1969), 14-16, 29-32.

60. Clarendon to Westmorland and to Loftus, 18 Jan. 1854, Clar. dep. c. 127.

61. Zaionchkovskii, Pril. II, 205-18, 254-56; Meyendorff, III, 97-104; *PAP*, II, 230-34, 244.

62. Nikitin, 20-21; N. Popov, *Rossiya i Serbiya* (Moscow, 1869), II, 346-47; Buol's correspondence with Lebzeltern, July-September 1853, PA X/37.

63. Nikitin, 22-23; Buol to Bruck, 7 and 21 Nov. 1853, PA XII/48; Buol to Grünne, 3 Dec., PA XL/76; Clarendon to Westmorland, 14 Dec., Clar. dep. c. 127.

64. Bruck to Buol, 22 Sept. 1853, PA XII/47; Grünne to Buol, 29 Oct., and Buol to Grünne, 30 Oct., PA XL/76; Nesselrode, X, 308-9.

65. Nikitin, 17-19, 23-28; summaries of Bach to Buol, 31 Jan. 1854 and Grünne to Buol, 28 and 31 Jan., PA XL/2; Baron Anton von Mollinary, *Sechsundvierzig Jahre im Österreich-Ungarischen Heere, 1833-1879* (Zürich, 1905), I, 225-27.

66. Iorga, *Istoria Românilor*, VII, 242-43; Austrian consul at Bucharest Baron Laurin to Buol, 11 Sept. 1853 and 3, 26, and 31 Jan. 1854, PA XXXVIII/103-4; Austrian consul at Iaşi Baron Testa to Buol, 3, 13, and 24 Feb., *ibid.*, 106.

67. *Kempens Tagebuch*, 317-19; Schroeder, "Bruck vs. Buol," 203-05.

68. Hübner to Buol, 10 and 21 Jan. 1854, PA IX/49; Hübner to Rechberg, 6 Jan., PA I/rot 533c; summary of Rechberg to Buol, 23 Jan., PA XL/2.

69. Prokesch to Buol, 31 Dec. 1853 and 25 Feb. 1854, PA II/26 and 29; *Kübecks Tagebücher*, 129, 132.

70. Tarle, I, 407-10, 420-22; Zaionchkovskii, Pril. II, 257, 259-62; Castelbajac to Drouyn, 21 Jan. 1854, PA IX/49.

71. Redlich, *Francis Joseph*, 138-41; Westmorland to Clarendon, 10 Jan. 1854, with enclosures, FO 7/431; Buol's Vortrag, and the protocol of the Jan. 23 conference, PA XL/48; *Kübecks Tagebücher*, 133-34.

72. Eckhart, 31-33; *Kübecks Tagebücher*, 134-35; protocol of conference of Jan. 31, PA XL/48.

73. *Rel. dipl. Aust.-Tosc.*, IV, 208-9.

74. Zaionchkovskii, Pril. II, 262-72; Tarle, I, 424-26, 436.

75. *PAP*, II, 209-11, 225-26, 263, 281, 295-98; Buol to Thun, 20 Dec. 1853, PA III/49; Thun to Buol, 14 Dec., *ibid.*, and 3, 11, 19, and 29 Jan. 1854, PA III/53.

76. Thun to Buol, 3 Jan. 1854, No. 1B, PA III/50; Buol to Thun, 8, 22, and 29 Jan., PA III/52–53.

77. For Wuerttemberg's reaction, more or less typical in Germany, see Götz Krusemarck, *Württemberg und der Krimkrieg*, 13–15.

CHAPTER VII

1. Jasmund, I, 269–71; Buol to V. Esterházy, 5 and 11 Feb. 1854, PA X/38; Buol to Hübner, 7 and 10 Feb., PA IX/48; Westmorland to Clarendon, 19 and 21 Feb., Clar. dep. c. 12.

2. Clarendon to Victoria, 2 Feb. 1854, RA G9/81.

3. Clarendon to Cowley, 10 and 17 Feb. 1854, FO 519/170; Aberdeen to Clarendon, 12 and 21 Feb., Clar. dep. c. 14.

4. Clarendon to Russell, "Monday night" [6 Feb. 1854], "Friday night" [10 Feb.], and 11 Feb., PRO 30/22/11C; Clarendon to Cowley, 14 Feb., FO 519/170; Clarendon to Aberdeen, 20 Feb., Add. ms. 43188.

5. Drouyn to Bourqueney, 12 and 14 Feb. 1854, Nos. 14–15, and Bourqueney to Drouyn, 18 Feb., AMAE Autr. 453; Cowley to Clarendon, 5 and 11 Feb., Nos. 130 and 164, FO 519/2.

6. Clarendon to Westmorland, 31 Jan. and 1 Feb. 1854, tg and No. 49, FO 7/427; Clarendon to Cowley, 2, 3, and 6 Feb., FO 519/170.

7. Russell to Clarendon, 1 Feb. 1854, Clar. dep. c. 15. Bourqueney and Westmorland also urged delay, in order not to cause Buol additional domestic difficulties. Bourqueney to Drouyn, 3 Feb., No. 20, AMAE Autr. 453; Westmorland to Clarendon, 7 Feb., Clar. dep. c. 12.

8. Clarendon to Westmorland, 2 and 13 Feb. 1854, Nos. 50 and 64, FO 7/427; Westmorland to Clarendon, 22 Feb., Clar. dep. c. 12; *Rel. dipl. GB-Sard.*, IV, 256–59, 263, 266.

9. Clarendon to Westmorland, 1, 15, and 18 Feb. 1854, Clar. dep. c. 128; Clarendon to Cowley, 21 Feb., FO 519/170; Cowley to Redcliffe, 17 Feb., FO 352/37/I/5.

10. Bourqueney to Drouyn, 20 and 21 Feb. 1854, AMAE Autr. 453; Buol to Hübner, 25 Feb. and 4 and 7 March, PA IX/48; Westmorland to Clarendon, 25 Feb., Clar. dep. c. 12.

11. Clarendon to Westmorland, 22 and 27 Feb. 1854, Clar. dep. c. 128; Ab. Corr. 1852–1854, 48–49.

12. Clarendon to Westmorland, 25 and 27 Feb. 1854, tg and No. 86, FO 7/427.

13. *Russell Correspondence*, II, 159–60; *Greville Memoirs*, VII, 21–22; Cowley, *Paris Embassy*, 45.

14. Clarendon to Cowley, 24 Feb. and 3 March 1854, FO 519/170;

Cowley to Clarendon, 24 and 26 Feb., Nos. 229 and 245, FO 519/2.

15. Henderson, 16–18; Valsecchi, *Alleanza*, 286–91; Drouyn to Bour-queney, 6 March 1854, and Bourqueney to Drouyn, 12 March, AMAE Autr. 453; Hübner to Buol, 5 March, No. 35C, PA IX/45. For Tuscany's fear of France and desire that Austria guarantee Tuscan neutrality, see *Rel. dipl. Aust.-Tosc.*, IV, 227–28, 244–46, 298–99.

16. Clarendon to Bloomfield, 29 March and 5 April 1854, Clar. dep. c. 128; Clarendon to Cowley, 3 and 7 March, FO 519/170; Albert to Duke Ernest II of Saxe-Coburg-Gotha, 22 March, RA G11/54.

17. Peter Rassow, *Der Konflikt König Friedrich Wilhelms IV mit dem Prinzen von Preussen im Jahre 1854*, 13–16, 19.

18. The most important among very many Austrian and Prussian dis-patches on the convention negotiations are: Buol to Thun, 2 and 5 March 1854, and Thun to Buol, 5 March, No. 13, PA III/52 and 50; and Manteuffel to Arnim, 6 March, No. 27, PA III/53. See also Eckhart, 35–40; Borries, 103–07; and Rassow, 22–24, 26–29.

19. Rassow, 39–46; Borries, 46–49, 110–53.

20. Thun to Buol, 24 March 1854, PA III/53; Prokesch to Buol, 29 and 30 May, Nos. 60A–B and 62C, PA II/30. Though Bismarck was wrong in ascribing the schemes he describes to Albert rather than Palmerston, he was not far off base in describing them as so colossally stupid that they belonged in the nursery rather than in the councils of state.

21. Borries, 121; Clarendon to Bloomfield, 8 and 15 March 1854, Clar. dep. c. 8.

22. Borries, 154–56; Thun to Buol, 9 March 1854, No. 15, PA III/50.

23. Jasmund, I, 286–88; Buol to Thun, 11 March 1854, PA III/53.

24. Hübner to Buol, 15 and 21 March 1854, Nos. 44A and 47A, PA IX/45; Drouyn to Bourqueney, 14 March, No. 29, AMAE Autr. 453; Clarendon to Westmorland, 8 March, No. 109, FO 7/427, and 22 March, Clar. dep. c. 128; Clarendon to Cowley, 7 March, FO 519/170.

25. For example, the British demanded that Radetzky be stopped from his alleged intention to occupy the Piedmontese fortress of Alex-andria; that Austria explain her reported executions in Hungary; that she stop bullying Switzerland; and that the Austrian chargé in the United States cease helping Russia purchase American merchant ships (Claren-don to Westmorland, 29 March, 5 and 12 April 1854, Nos. 129, 133, and 140, FO 7/427; Russell to Clarendon, 24 March, Clar. dep. c. 15).

26. Westmorland to Clarendon, 27 and 29 March and 5 April 1854, Clar. dep. c. 12; Clarendon to Westmorland, 5 April, *ibid.* c. 127.

27. Drouyn to Bourqueney, 7 April 1854, No. 41, AMAE Autr. 454.

28. Memoranda by Cowley, 27 Feb. 1854, and by Newcastle, n.d. [ca.

14 March], RA G10/93 and G11/26; Clarendon to Cowley, 3, 10, 13, and 21 March, FO 519/170.

29. E.g., Redcliffe to Clarendon, 3 March 1854, FO 352/37/I/3.

30. *Russell Correspondence*, II, 160–61; for an earlier version, see Palmerston to Clarendon, 4 March 1854, Clar. dep. c. 15.

31. Lansdowne to Russell, 20 March 1854, PRO 30/22/11C; Russell to Clarendon, 7 March, Clar. dep. c. 15; Martin, *Prince Consort*, III, 12–15; Colloredo to Buol, 3 March, PA VIII/38.

32. Dudley Stuart to Clarendon, 4 March 1854, and various other letters, Feb.–April, Clar. dep. c. 22; Palmerston to Clarendon, 20 March, *ibid.* c. 15; Clarendon to Redcliffe, 7 March and 18 April, FO 352/37/I/1.

33. Russell to Aberdeen, 25 March, and to Clarendon, 26 March 1854, PRO 30/22/11C; Clarendon to Cowley, 27 March, FO 519/170; Palmerston to Clarendon, 6 April, Palm. Papers GC/CL/1375; Redcliffe to Clarendon, 7 April, Clar. dep. c. 22.

34. Jasmund, I, 247–64; Tarle, I, 449–52, 459–62, 496–97; Zaionchkovskii, Pril. II, 312–14.

35. Shcherbatov, VII, 98–102, 125–26, 149–51; Laurin to Buol, 13 and 24 Feb. 1854, PA XXXVIII/103.

36. Nesselrode, XI, 40–43; Meyendorff, III, 136–41; Shcherbatov, VII, 373; Zaionchkovskii, Pril. II, 344–45.

37. Borries, 160–62; Frederick William to Francis Joseph, 11 and 17 March 1854, Kab. Arch. Geh. Akt. 7; Thun to Buol, 13, 15 and 17 March, Nos. 16, 18, and 19, PA III/50.

38. Protocol of conference, 31 Jan. 1854, PA XL/48.

39. *Ibid.*; *Kübecks Tagebücher*, 135; Schroeder, "Bruck vs. Buol," 197–99, 205–7.

40. Unckel, 118–19; Alfons Graf von Wimpffen, *Erinnerungen aus der Walachei*, 34–38, 45–48.

41. Buol to Bruck, 16 Jan. 1854, No. 5, PA XII/49; Buol to Coronini, 2 Feb., and Buol to Grünne, 1, 9, and 19 March, PA XL/78–79; protocol of conference of 21 Feb., MR Prot. 13.

42. Laurin to Buol, 19 and 21 Feb. and 16 April 1854, PA XXXVIII/103.

43. Chateaurenard to War Ministry, 12 and 28 Feb. and 13 March 1854, AMG Reconnaissances, Autr. 1602/47–49; Hübner to Buol, 30 Jan. and 24 Feb., No. 30B, PA IX/49 and 45; Drouyn to Bourqueney, 16 Feb., PA IX/49.

44. Fonblanque to Clarendon, 8, 15, and 21 Feb. and 18 March 1854, FO 78/1008; Colquhoun to Clarendon, 30 March, FO 78/1010; Clarendon to Westmorland, 18 Feb., No. 72, FO 7/427; Clarendon to Redcliffe, 7 March, FO 352/37/I/1; Redcliffe to Clarendon, 26 March, Clar. dep. c. 22.

45. Kempen to Buol, 14 Feb. 1854, PA XL/77.

46. Meyendorff, III, 124–28, 132–33; Chateaurenard to War Ministry, n.d. [April 1854], AMG Reconnaissances, Autr. 1602/54; Steinitz, 31–32; Mayerhofer to Francis Joseph, n.d., KA, FA 1854/13/177.

47. KA, FA III and IV AOK 1854/3.

48. Hübner to Buol, 5 March 1854, No. 35G, and 5 and 15 March, private, PA IX/45 and 49.

49. Colloredo to Buol, 14 Feb. and 3 March 1854, Nos. 21C and 30C, PA VIII/38–39; Drouyn to Bourqueney, 26 Feb., PA IX/49.

50. Prokesch, *Briefe*, 358–61, 363–67, 370–71; Prokesch to Buol, 20 March 1854, PA II/30.

51. PA XL/48 (published in my article, "A Turning Point in Austrian Policy in the Crimean War").

52. Beer, 471–72; memorandum by Bach, "Punktation für die Filial-comités, etc.," 13 Feb. 1854, Verwaltungsarchiv, Nachlass Bach 22; Bach to Archduke Albert, 10 March 1854, KA, FA 1854/13/157.

53. Bourqueney to Drouyn, 22, 23, and 25 Feb. and 14 March 1854, AMAE Autr. 454; *PAP*, II, 370; Cowley to Clarendon, 18 March, No. 339, FO 519/3; *Kübecks Tagebücher*, 137.

54. Steinitz, 38; Unckel, 125–30.

55. See my "Austria and the Danubian Principalities, 1853–1856;" also the reports of the Bavarian minister Count Lerchenfeld to King Max, 23 and 29 May 1854, GSA, MA I/585.

56. Hess's *Denkschrift* of March 25, KA, FA 1854/13/181; cf. also *Kübecks Tagebücher*, 138–39.

57. 25 March 1854, PA XL/48.

58. Protocol of conference, *ibid.*; *Kübecks Tagebücher*, 139.

59. Nesselrode, XI, 45–46; Meyendorff, III, 141–42; Shcherbatov, VII, 121–24, 129–30; Laurin to Buol, 4 April 1854, PA XXXVIII/103.

60. Bourqueney to Drouyn, 26–29 March 1854, AMAE Autr. 454.

61. *PAP*, II, 390–93; Thun to Buol, 2, 3, and 6 April 1854, Nos. 25, 26C–D, and 27A, PA III/50.

62. Thun to Buol, 6 April 1854; Hess to Buol, 30 March and 3, 6, and 7 April; and Hess to Francis Joseph, 9 April, PA III/53.

63. A dispatch drafted for expedition to Count Apponyi at Munich, but not sent, shows that Buol considered seeking support in Germany for his idea of an alliance covering the occupation of the Principalities, but then rejected the notion (PA IV/21).

64. See above, note 62.

65. Buol to Thun, 10 April 1854, and to Hess, 10, 12, and 14 April, PA III/53.

66. *PAP*, II, 402–3, 405; note by Hess, entitled "Projectirte Änderung

des Zusatz-Artikels . . . ," 17 April 1854, and Manteuffel to Hess, 18 April, KA, FA 1854/13/201–02; Hess to Buol, tgs, 18 and 19 April, PA III/53; Buol to Francis Joseph, 19 April, *ibid.*

67. Jasmund, I, 302–5.

68. *PAP*, II, 384, 404, 407–10; Leopold von Gerlach, *Denkwürdigkeiten*, III, 140–41; Rassow, 37–38; Zaionchkovskii, Pril. II, 353–55.

69. Hess to Francis Joseph, 28 April 1854, KA, FA 1854/13/210; Meyendorff, III, 152–54; the Duke of Cambridge to Clarendon, 23 and 25 April, Clar. dep. c. 12. Radetzky showed a similar suppleness, protesting his pro-British sentiments to Westmorland and the Duke of Cambridge and appearing to agree with the idea of sending an Austrian expeditionary corps to Constantinople—and suggesting that to this end Austria must first occupy Serbia! (Duke of Cambridge to Clarendon, 28 April, and Westmorland to Clarendon, 29–30 April, *ibid*).

70. *PAP*, II, 415–17; Shcherbatov, VII, 129–34, 139–49, 374–78; Zaionchkovskii, Pril. II, 348–53, 395–407.

71. Eckhart, 54–56; Drouyn to Bourqueney, 20 March 1854, AMAE Autr. 454; Buol to Thun, 24 March, and Thun to Buol, 3 April, No. 26B, PA III/52 and 50; Clarendon to Cowley, 15 March, FO 519/170.

72. Clarendon to Cowley, 17 and 27 March and 10 April 1854, FO 519/170; Bourqueney to Drouyn, 4 April, No. 61 (with marginal note by Drouyn), AMAE Autr. 454.

73. Clarendon to the Duke of Cambridge, 20 April 1854, and to Westmorland, 20 and 22 April, Clar. dep. c. 128; Buol to Hübner, 1 April, PA IX/48.

CHAPTER VIII

1. *QVL*, III, 30–32; the Duke of Cambridge to Clarendon, 23 and 25 April 1854, and Westmorland to Clarendon, 25 April and 17 May, Clar. dep. c. 12.

2. Cowley to Clarendon, 7 and 29 May 1854, Nos. 614 and 663, FO 519/3; Clarendon to Westmorland, 31 May and 7 June, Nos. 192 and 204, FO 7/428, and 25 April and 9 May, Clar. dep. c. 128.

3. See, for example, Martin, *Prince Consort*, III, 63–64; Clarendon to Redcliffe, 8 and 23 May 1854, FO 352/37/I/1.

4. Clarendon to Cowley, 23, 26, and 29 May and 5 June 1854, FO 519/170. Westmorland tried constantly without success to overcome Clarendon's suspicions; his disgust with Clarendon's arguments and tactics shows up well in his letters to his wife (Priscilla Anne Wellesley

Fane, *The Correspondence of Priscilla, Countess of Westmorland*, 211–20).

5. *Russell Correspondence*, II, 164–66, 169.

6. Gladstone to Graham, 17 May 1854, Add. ms. 44168; memoranda by Aberdeen, 20 May, W[illiam] M[olesworth], 22 May, C[harles] G[reville], n.d., the Duke of Newcastle, 23 May, and Clarendon, 22 May, in PRO 30/22/11D; Clarendon to Cowley, 24 May, FO 519/170.

7. Albert to Clarendon, 29 May, RA G13/67.

8. Memorandum by Palmerston, 26 May 1854, PRO 30/22/11D.

9. Clarendon told Russell that Palmerston's constant redrawing of the map of Europe was "mere child's play unless he can adapt his means to his end which he never attempts to do" (7 May 1854, *ibid*).

10. Clarendon to Cowley, 20 June 1854, FO 519/170.

11. Hans Rall, "Griechenland zwischen Russland und dem übrigen Europa," *Saeculum*, XVIII (1967), 167–72; J. A. Levandis, *The Greek Foreign Debt and the Great Powers, 1821–1898* (New York, 1944), 35–41. On Greek politics, see Hariton Korisis, *Die politischen Parteien Griechenlands* (Hersbruck, 1966); John A. Petropoulos, *Politics and Statecraft in the Kingdom of Greece, 1833–1843* (Princeton, 1968); and Monika Ritter, "Frankreichs Griechenland-Politik," 19–66.

12. Cowley to Clarendon, 24 Aug., 21 Nov., and 1 Dec. 1853, Nos. 629–30, 874, and 904, FO 519/2; Ritter, 66–74.

13. E. V. Nomikos, "The International Position of Greece during the Crimean War," 42–45, 64–78; Ritter, 7–18.

14. Nomikos, 83–118, 244–53; L. Bower and G. Bolitho, *Otho I, King of Greece: A Biography* (London, 1939), 190–239; Ritter, 81–162.

15. Nomikos, 131–49; Ritter, 112–16; Clarendon to Cowley, 7 March 1854, FO 519/170; Clarendon to Russell, 17 April, PRO 30/22/11C.

16. Cowley to Clarendon, 10, 14, and 19 April 1854, Nos. 476–77, 491, and 516, FO 519/3; Aberdeen to Clarendon, 4 and 25 April, Clar. dep. c. 14; Clarendon to Cowley, 21 and 22 April, FO 519/170.

17. Ritter, 189–96; Drouyn to Bourqueney, 6 and 19 April 1854, and Bourqueney to Drouyn, 15 April and 18 May, AMAE Autr. 454; Clarendon to Cowley, 10, 11, 21, and 25 April, FO 519/170; Clarendon to Westmorland, 12 April, Clar. dep. c. 128, and 22 April, No. 152, FO 7/428.

18. Bruck to Buol, 27 March and 3 April 1854, Nos. 26B and 28B, PA XII/50.

19. Buol to Hübner, 24 Oct. 1853, PA IX/44; Buol to Count Apponyi at Munich, 2 March, No. 1, PA IV/21.

20. Borries, 370–71; Apponyi to Buol, 11 April 1854, No. 20B, PA IV/22; De Serre to Drouyn, 1 May, No. 81, AMAE Autr. 454.

21. Testa, X, 390–94; Buol to Hübner, 21 and 30 April 1854, PA IX/48; Buol to Grünne, 27 and 29 April and 4 May, PA XL/79; Buol to Legation Councilor H. von Zwierzina at Munich, 22 April, PA IV/21.

22. Nomikos, 149–226; Ritter, 211–60; Aberdeen to Victoria, 4 and 6 May 1854, Add. ms. 43049; Clarendon to Graham, 2 May, and Graham to Clarendon, 3 May, Graham Papers Reel 19.

23. Schroeder, "Bruck vs. Buol," 204–5; Bruck to Buol, private, 27 April and 11 May 1854, and 4 May, No. 37B, PA XII/52 and 50.

24. Apponyi to Buol, 9 and 10 May 1854, PA IV/22; Lerchenfeld to King Max, 13 May, GSA, MA I/585; Buol to Hübner, 24 June 1854, PA IX/48; Clarendon to Westmorland, 5 June, No. 200, FO 7/428.

25. Tarle, I, 492–95, 521–25; Shcherbatov, VII, 381–89; Zaionchkovskii, Pril. II, 416–18; Barbara Jelavich, *Russland 1852–1871*, 30–32.

26. Nesselrode, XI, 52–58; Meyendorff, III, 166–69; Westmorland to Clarendon, 21 April 1854, Clar. dep. c. 12, and 10 May, No. 181, FO 7/433.

27. Nesselrode, XI, 61–64; Testa, IV, Pt. 2, 133–34; Thun to Buol, 4 May 1854, No. 33C, PA III/50; Apponyi to Buol, 19 May, No. 25B, PA IV/22.

28. Peter Hoffmann, *Württemberg und Bayern im Krimkrieg*, 54–60; W. P. Fuchs, *Die deutschen Mittelstaaten und die Bundesreform*, 12–24, 31–33, 36–40; Krusemarck, 15–18, 20–23, 29–33; Apponyi to Buol, 14 May 1854, PA IV/22; Pfordten to King Max, 11 May, GSA, MA I/585.

29. Buol's circular of 10 Feb. 1854, PA rot 1099; Prokesch to Buol, 27 March 1854, No. 31A–B, PA II/30; Buol to FML Baron von Kellner in Munich, 14 March, PA XL/79.

30. Circular, PA rot 1099. The Prussians protested that Austria's proposed presentation of the treaty was much too anti-Russian—Thun to Buol, 22 and 24 April 1854, and Buol to Thun, 25 April, PA III/50 and 52.

31. Eckhart, 65–67; *PAP*, II, 422–29; Manteuffel to Buol, 14 May 1854, PA III/53; Buol to Thun, 16 May, PA III/52; Francis Joseph to General Mayerhofer, 31 May, PA XL/48.

32. Hoffmann, *Württemberg*, 68–79; Krusemarck, 35–41.

33. Fuchs, 41–46.

34. Protocol of conference of 29 May, PA XL/48.

35. Westmorland, 206–7.

36. Cf. Valsecchi, *Alleanza*, 301–2, and Krusemarck, 56.

37. *PAP*, II, 433–34; Buol to Hübner, 4 June 1854, PA IX/49; Lerchenfeld to King Max, 27 May, GSA, MA I/585.

38. Srbik, *Deutsche Einheit*, II, 237.

39. Eckhart, 73–74; Lerchenfeld to King Max, 2, 3, and 5 June 1854,

GSA, MA I/586; Buol to Thun, 1 June, PA III/52; Buol to Hübner, 4 June, No. 2, PA IX/48.

40. Beer, 479–80, 482; Buol to V. Esterházy, 3 June 1854, PA X/38; Buol to Thun, 9 May, PA III/53.

41. Bourqueney to Drouyn, 21 June 1854, AMAE Autr. 455.

42. Bourqueney to Drouyn, 5 June 1854, AMAE Autr. 454; Westmorland, 212.

43. Drouyn to Bourqueney, 12 June 1854, AMAE Autr. 454; Hübner to Buol, 14 June, PA IX/46.

44. Clarendon to Cowley, 8 June 1854, FO 519/170; Clarendon to Redcliffe, 18 May and 3 and 8 June, FO 352/37/I/1.

45. Colloredo to Buol, 12 June 1854, PA VIII/40; Clarendon to Westmorland, 13 and 20 June, Clar. dep. c. 129; Westmorland to Clarendon, 5 July, No. 258, FO 7/434; Bourqueney to Drouyn, 13 and 15 June, AMAE Autr. 454.

46. Buol to Francis Joseph, 4 June 1854, PA XL/48.

47. See, for example, Westmorland to Clarendon, 1 July 1854, FO 7/434, and Buol's expeditions to Hübner, 4 June and 2 and 21 July, PA IX/48–49.

48. Bourqueney to Drouyn, 30 June 1854, AMAE Autr. 455; Westmorland to Clarendon, 20 June and 18 July, Nos. 234 and 273, FO 7/434–35; Ernest of Saxe-Coburg, *Aus meinem Leben*, II, 200.

49. Hallberg, 72–73; Hübner to Buol, 21 and 31 May 1854, Nos. 78C and 83A, PA IX/46; Bourqueney to Drouyn, 14 May, and Drouyn to Bourqueney, 31 May and 22 June, AMAE Autr. 454–55.

50. Cowley to Clarendon, 26 June 1854, No. 799, FO 519/3.

51. Buol to Hübner, 2 July 1854, No. 3, PA IX/48.

52. Clarendon to Westmorland, 23 May 1854, Clar. dep. c. 129, and 7 July, No. 238, FO 7/429; Westmorland to Clarendon, 31 May and 5 June, Clar. dep. c. 12, and 7 June, FO 7/434; Clarendon to Cowley, 7 July, FO 519/170.

53. Westmorland to Clarendon, 20 June 1854, Clar. dep. c. 12.

54. Zaionchkovskii, Pril. II, 418–22; Shcherbatov, VII, 397–407; Schiemann, IV, 428–29; Beer, 483–85.

55. Nesselrode, XI, 58–59; Buol to Hübner, 2 July 1854, PA IX/48.

56. Jasmund, I, 325–32.

57. Tarle, II, 294–95.

58. Wimpffen, 63–64; Hess to Francis Joseph, 4 July 1854, KA, FA 1854/7/100.

59. Draft of Buol's instruction for Hess, 9 July 1854, KA, MKSM, Separat-Faszikel 63; Hess to Grünne, 15 July, *ibid.*, 1854/2691.

60. E.g., Westmorland to Clarendon, 5 July 1854, Clar. dep. c. 12.

61. Zaionchkovskii, Pril. II, 394; Aberdeen to Victoria, 28 May 1854, Add. ms. 43049; Colloredo to Buol, 19 May, PA VIII/40.

62. Clarendon to Cowley, 16 June 1854, FO 519/170; Clarendon to Redcliffe, 14 June, FO 352/37/I/1; Ashley, II, 61–62, 65–67.

63. Argyll, *Autobiography*, I, 477–78.

64. Clarendon to Cowley, 17 June 1854, FO 519/170.

65. The memoranda cited are in Palm. Papers Russia; cf. also Clarendon to Redcliffe, 18 June 1854, FO 352/37/I/1.

66. Conacher, 447–54.

67. Westmorland, 227–29; Clarendon to Cowley, 11, 12, and 18 July 1854, FO 519/170; Russell to Clarendon, 19 July, Clar. dep. c. 15.

68. Albert to Ernest, 13 July 1854, RA G15/14; Martin, *Prince Consort*, III, 83–86. The aged Tory statesman Lord Ellenborough protested vigorously against the decision to go to the Crimea, on both military and political grounds (to Newcastle, 8 Aug., Palm. Papers Russia). His memorandum was ignored by the Cabinet.

69. Colloredo to Buol, 8 July 1854, PA VIII/40; Clarendon to Westmorland, 27 June and 11 July, Clar. dep. c. 129.

70. Westmorland to Clarendon, 10 July 1854, No. 262, FO 7/435, and 12 July, Clar. dep. c. 12; Clarendon to Westmorland, 22 July, No. 247 and private, FO 7/429 and Clar. dep. c. 129; Clarendon to Cowley, 15 July, FO 519/170; Aberdeen to Clarendon, 11 and 21 July, Add. ms. 43189 and Clar. dep. c. 15; Wimpffen, 81–84.

71. Redcliffe to Clarendon, 15 July 1854, Clar. dep. c. 22.

72. E.g., Clarendon to Westmorland, 21 June and 15 July 1854, Nos. 213 and 241, FO 7/428–29; Clarendon to Cowley, 19 July, FO 519/170.

73. Clarendon to Westmorland, 22 July 1854, Clar. dep. c. 129; Colloredo to Buol, 28 July, No. 81G, PA VIII/39.

74. Westmorland, 224–27; Hübner to Buol, 15 and 22 July 1854, Nos. 101B and 104D, PA IX/46.

75. Clarendon to Cowley, 22 and 24 July 1854, FO 519/170; Clarendon to Russell, 24 July, Clar. dep. c. 15.

76. Krusemarck, 44–55; Eckhart, 74–76; Apponyi to Buol, 18 July 1854, No. 40B, PA IV/22.

77. Borries, 189–90, 194–98; *PAP*, II, 438–40.

78. Borries, 204–5, 373–76; Manteuffel to Arnim, 30 June 1854, PA III/53; Westmorland to Clarendon, 3 July 1854, Clar. dep. c. 12; Buol to Thun, 5 July, No. 2, PA III/52.

79. Cowley to Clarendon, 3 July 1854, Clar. dep. c. 17.

80. Prokesch, *Briefe*, 381–83; Mayerhofer to Grünne, 15 and 30 June, 1854, and Grünne to Mayerhofer, 12 July, KA, MKSM 1854/2515; Thun

to Buol, 16 July, No. 47B, and Buol to Francis Joseph, 18 July, PA III/50 and 53.

81. Borries, 192–94; *PAP*, II, 456–57.

82. *PAP*, II, 440–45, 448–50, 457–59; Shcherbatov, VII, 175–76.

83. Eckhart, 81–84; Buol to Thun, 12 July 1854, Manteuffel to Arnim, 15 July, and Thun to Buol, 16 July, No. 47A–D, PA III/50, 52–53.

84. Buol to G. Esterházy, 30 July 1854, Nos. 1–4, PA III/52.

85. Westmorland to Clarendon, 13 July 1854, No. 272, FO 7/435; Bourqueney to Drouyn, 14 July, AMAE Autr. 455.

86. Clarendon to Cowley, 13 and 14 July 1854, FO 519/170; Clarendon to Westmorland, 26 and 29 July, Nos. 251 and 253, FO 7/429.

87. Bourqueney to Drouyn, 16 and 22 July 1854, and Drouyn to Bourqueney, 27 July, AMAE Autr. 455.

88. Buol to Hübner, 21 July 1854, No. 7 and private letter, PA IX/48; Cowley to Clarendon, 27 July, No. 937, FO 519/3.

89. Colloredo to Buol, 28 July 1854, PA VIII/40.

90. Palmerston to Clarendon, 24, 26, and 28 July 1854, Clar. dep. c. 15; Clarendon to Cowley, 28 and 29 July, FO 519/170; Clarendon to Westmorland, 1, 3, and 5 Aug., Nos. 257–59, FO 7/429.

91. Clarendon to Redcliffe, 8 Aug. 1854, FO 352/37/I/1; Russell to Clarendon, 31 July and 3 and 4 Aug., Clar. dep. c. 15; Martin, *Prince Consort*, III, 84–85.

92. Clarendon to Westmorland, 29 July 1854, Clar. dep. c. 129; Palmerston to Clarendon, 3 Aug., *ibid.* c. 15.

93. Bourqueney to Drouyn, 27 and 29 July and 1 Aug. 1854, and Drouyn to Bourqueney, 28 July and 2 Aug., AMAE Autr. 455; Hübner to Buol, 5 Aug., No. 109, PA IX/46.

94. Buol to Francis Joseph, 30 July 1854, PA XL/48.

95. Buol to Hübner, tg, 3 Aug. 1854, PA IX/48; Westmorland to Clarendon, 5 Aug., No. 292, FO 7/435.

96. Eckhart, 91–92; Krusemarck, 57–59.

97. Buol to G. Esterházy, 1 and 4 Aug. 1854, GA Berlin/112; Manteuffel to Buol, 5 Aug., PA III/53.

98. Bourqueney to Drouyn, 4 Aug. 1854, No. 133, AMAE Autr. 455; Westmorland to Clarendon, 5 Aug., Clar. dep. c. 12.

99. Cowley to Clarendon, 3 and 7 Aug. 1854, Nos. 969 and 980, FO 519/3.

100. Cf. Henderson, 159–67.

101. E.g., Westmorland, 235–36.

102. Buol to Prokesch, 12 Aug. 1854, PA XL/277a.

103. Albin Cullberg, *La politique du roi Oscar I*, 7–20; Paul Knaplund,

"Finmark in British Diplomacy, 1836–1855," *American Historical Review*, XXX (1927), 478–502.

104. Cullberg, 30–40, 58–61, 70–73; Edouard Drouyn de Lhuys, *Les neutres pendant la guerre d'Orient* (n.p., 1868).

105. Cullberg, 41–44, 75–78; Langenau to Buol, 24 Feb., 7 and 18 April, 2 and 18 May, and 1 and 20 June 1854, PA XXVI/12.

106. Cullberg, 82–85; Drouyn to Baudin, French chargé at London, 1 Aug. 1854, Clar. dep. c. 15; Langenau to Buol, 4 July and 1 and 8 Aug., PA XXVI/12; Westmorland, 223.

CHAPTER IX

1. For various interpretations of this move, see Eckhart, 98–99; Henderson, 167–72; and Borries, 212–13.

2. Buol to V. Esterházy, 10 Aug. 1854, PA X/38; Buol to G. Esterházy, 9 Aug., GA Berlin/112.

3. Zaionchkovskii, Pril. II, 365–69; Shcherbatov, VII, 204–5, 407–8; Nesselrode, XI, 74–77.

4. Tarle, II, 299–302; Jasmund, I, 347–49; Westmorland to Clarendon, 29 and 31 Aug. 1854, FO 7/435; Buol to Hübner, 3 Sept., PA IX/49.

5. PA III/53.

6. Franz Schnürer, ed., *Briefe Franz Josephs I an seine Mutter, 1838–1872* (Munich, 1930), 246; Buol to Hübner, 3 Sept. 1854, PA IX/49; Buol to Prokesch, 16 Sept., PA XL/277a.

7. Cowley to Clarendon, 10 Aug. 1854, Clar. dep. c. 17; Russell to Clarendon, 17 and 26 Aug., *ibid.* c. 15.

8. Clarendon to Redcliffe, 29 Aug. 1854, FO 352/37/I/1.

9. Bourqueney to Drouyn, 14 Aug. 1854, No. 139, AMAE Autr. 455; Clarendon to Redcliffe, 8, 12 and 23 Aug., FO 352/37/I/1; Clarendon to Cowley, 14 Aug., FO 519/170; Clarendon to Henry Reeves, 20 July, Clar. dep. c. 535.

10. Russell to Clarendon, 24 Aug. 1854, Clar. dep. c. 15; Clarendon to Cowley, 29 Aug., FO 519/170.

11. Cowley to Clarendon, 18 Aug. 1854, No. 1026, FO 519/3; Clarendon to Cowley, 2 and 18 Sept., FO 519/170; Russell to Clarendon, 4 and 5 Sept., Clar. dep. c. 15.

12. Palmerston to Clarendon, 22 Aug. and 3, 5, and 7 Sept. 1854, Clar. dep. c. 15; Clarendon to Westmorland, 5 Sept., No. 288, FO 7/429, and 14 Sept., Clar. dep. c. 130; Clarendon to Albert, 24 Aug., and Albert to Clarendon, 24 Aug., RA G16/87 and 90.

13. While Buol's arguments were reasonable enough (see his expedi-

tions to Hübner of 3 and 23 Sept. 1854, PA IX/48), the main point was put most frankly by Colloredo when he told Clarendon that it was up to those who declared war to fight it, and not to expect others to do it for them (to Buol, 11 Sept., PA VIII/40).

14. Buol to Hübner, 14 Sept. 1854, No. 1, PA IX/48; Bourqueney to Drouyn, 4 and 14 Sept., Nos. 151 and 158, AMAE Autr. 456.

15. Clarendon to Westmorland, 12, 19, and 26 Sept. 1854, Clar. dep. c. 130; Russell to Clarendon, 15 Sept., and Cowley to Clarendon, 18 and 19 Sept., *ibid.* c. 15 and 18. The main British charge, that Austria was protecting Russia and enabling her to transfer her whole southern army to the Crimea, was false and Clarendon knew it. Cf. Curtiss, 333; Clarendon to Redcliffe, 23 Sept., FO 352/37/I/1.

16. Aberdeen to Clarendon, 29 Sept. 1854, Clar. dep. c. 14; Clarendon to Cowley, 19 Sept., FO 519/170.

17. Palmerston to Clarendon, 19 Sept. 1854, Clar. dep. c. 15; *Russell Correspondence*, II, 170; Clarendon to Cowley, 18 Sept., FO 519/170; Russell to Clarendon, 13 and [?] Sept., Clar. dep. c. 15.

18. Aberdeen to Clarendon, 16 and 23 Aug. 1854, Add. ms. 43189; *Greville Memoirs*, VII, 59, 65.

19. Martin, *Prince Consort*, III, 98–109; memorandum by Albert, 7 Oct. 1854, RA G17/89.

20. Russell to Clarendon, 19 and 30 Sept. 1854, Clar. dep. c. 15.

21. Redcliffe to Clarendon, 27 Aug. 1854, FO 352/37/I/3.

22. Palmerston to Clarendon, 10, 20 and 29 Aug. 1854, Clar. dep. c. 15.

23. Palmerston to Clarendon, 7 Sept. 1854, Palm. Papers GC/CL/570.

24. See, for example, Aberdeen to Russell, 5 Sept. 1854; Clarendon to Russell, 6 Sept.; and Newcastle to Russell, 21 Sept., PRO 30/22/11E.

25. Cowley to Clarendon, 28 Sept. 1854, No. 1178, FO 519/4; Aberdeen to Victoria, 1 Oct., and to Clarendon, 3 Oct., Add. ms. 43049 and 43189; Clarendon to Russell, 1 and 4 Oct., PRO 30/22/11E.

26. Clarendon to Palmerston, 4 Oct. 1854, Palm. Papers GC/CL/577; Clarendon to Redcliffe, 27 and 28 Sept. and 23 Oct., FO 352/37/I/1.

27. 27 Sept. 1854, PRO 30/22/11E; cf. also Clarendon to Cowley, 26 Sept. and 3 Oct., FO 519/170, and Clarendon to Westmorland, 3 Oct., Clar. dep. c. 130.

28. For an opposite view, see Unckel, 146–58 *et passim.*

29. Schroeder, "Danubian Principalities," 219–23; Buol to V. Esterházy, 17 May 1854, and Buol to Bruck, 22 May, PA XII/52.

30. Laurin's dispatches of May and June 1854 are full of such reports and calls for help (PA XXXVIII/103); cf. also Wimpffen, 64–70.

31. Tarle, I, 271; Marceli Handelsman, *Czartoryski, Nicholas I et le*

proche orient (Paris, 1934), 115–16, 119–21; Ion Nistor, "Die Polenlegion im Krimkriege," *Codrul Cosminului*, IX (1935), 71–74. For Austria's concern over Transylvania, see protocol of ministerial conference of 13 Nov. 1853, MR Prot. 13, and *Documente Inedite privitoare la Istoria Transilvaniei intre 1848–1859*, published by Mihail Popescu (Bucharest, 1929), 159–72. On Rumanian nationalism, see Keith Hitchins, *The Rumanian National Movement in Transylvania, 1780–1849* (Cambridge, Mass., 1969).

32. Clarendon to Redcliffe, 23 March 1854, FO 352/37/I/1; Nistor, 374.

33. See, for example, Colquhoun to Redcliffe, 19 July 1854, No. 16, and Fonblanque to Redcliffe, 20 Aug., FO 78/1010 and 1009; cf. also F. S. Rodkey, "Ottoman Concern about Western Economic Penetration in the Levant, 1849–1856," *Journal of Modern History*, XXX (1958), 348–53.

34. Meyendorff, III, 183–84; Tarle, II, 289–91; Zaionchkovskii, Pril. II, 362–65.

35. Buol to Bruck, 8, 15, and 29 May 1854, PA XII/49; Nistor, 5–8, 29–31.

36. Drouyn to Bourqueney, 31 May, 28 June, and 7 July 1854, and Bourqueney to Drouyn, 27 June, AMAE Autr. 455.

37. Wimpffen, 90–138; Nistor, 21–22, 33–34, 93–97, 178–81, 213–14; Hess to Grünne, 17, 20, and 29 Sept. 1854, and to Francis Joseph, 10 Oct., PA XL/78; Francis Joseph to Hess, 21 Sept., and Grünne to Hess, 29 Oct., KA, MKSM 1854, Nos. 3666 and CK 4012.

38. Schroeder, "Bruck vs. Buol," 208–11; Nistor, 126–27.

39. The correspondence between Buol, Hess, Francis Joseph, Grünne, and Coronini can be found in PA XL/78 and KA, FA III and IV AOK/1854/6–9; some of it is published in Nistor, 51–56, 74–76, 79–86, 139–40, 143–47.

40. Lampel to Buol, 13, 16, and 30 Sept. 1854, PA XXXVIII/103.

41. The evidence comes chiefly from Colquhoun's letters to Redcliffe and Clarendon (FO 78/1010) and Redcliffe's to Clarendon, Westmorland, and Colquhoun (FO 352/37/I/3, II/6, and II/9). Cf. also Clarendon to Redcliffe, 13 and 23 Oct. 1854, FO 352/37/I/1; Clarendon to Aberdeen, 6 Sept., Add. ms. 43189; and Poujade to Drouyn, 4 Sept., AMAE Mem. et doc. Roumanie 1.

42. Fréderic Damé, *Histoire de la Roumaine contemporaine depuis l'avènement des princes indigènes jusqu'à nos jours (1822–1900)* (Paris, 1900), 24–25, 35, 77–79.

43. Iorga, *Istoria Românilor*, IX, 241–42; Bruck to Buol, 25 Aug. and 1 Sept. 1853, Nos. 27A and 29B, PA XII/47.

44. Florescu, "Rumanian Principalities," 57–61; Colquhoun to Redcliffe, 4 June 1853, FO 78/944. For Colquhoun's early activity, see Florescu, "R. G. Colquhoun, Ion Câmpineanu and the pro-Western Opposition in Wallachia, 1834–1840," *Slavonic and East European Review*, XLI (1963), 403–19.

45. Colquhoun to Clarendon, 21 Sept. 1853, and to Redcliffe, 19 July and 13 August 1854, FO 78/945 and 1010. Redcliffe's correspondence with Ion Ghica is in FO 352/40/3; with Constantin Ghica, in Clar. dep. c. 10. For the French plan, see an unsigned mémoire of 1854 entitled, "Note sur le prince Constantin Ghika," etc., AMAE, Mem. et doc. Turquie 55.

46. Nistor, 36–41; Buol to Bruck, 31 Aug. 1854, PA XII/49.

47. Nistor, 372–73; Nistor, "Die Polenlegion," 99.

48. "Mémoire remis par le Pce Stirbey," Sept. 1854, PA XII/52; G. Ghica to Buol, 2 Oct., with enclosed mémoire, *ibid*.

49. Bruck to Buol, 6, 10 and 20 July 1854, PA III/50 and 52; Cowley to Clarendon, 25 Sept., Clar. dep. c. 18.

50. See Redcliffe's and Colquhoun's correspondence, August to October 1854, in FO 352/37/II/9–10 and FO 78/1010–11; Laurin's and Lampel's reports for the same period, PA XXXVIII/103–4; and Eduard Bach to Buol, 1 and 31 Oct., PA XII/52.

51. Colquhoun's charges against Austria were regularly relayed by Clarendon to Westmorland (FO 7/429–30). In contrast, Gardner tended to defend the Austrians and even to praise them for protecting Moldavians from Turk arbitrariness (to Redcliffe, 5 Dec. 1854, FO 78/1013).

52. Again the documents in both Austrian and British sources are too numerous to list; some are published by Nistor (44–47, 66–68, 71–73, 129–31).

53. Westmorland to Clarendon, 1 Nov. 1854, No. 409, FO 7/437. The main British-Turkish correspondence over atrocities and misconduct is in FO 352/40/2 and 6 and 41/4; see also Ritter, 298–312.

54. Nistor, 157–60, 168, 188–90, 204–06, 236–39, 267–68; L. Boicu, "Introducerea telegrafiei în Moldova," *Studii și cercetări stiințifice: Istorie*, VIII (1957), No. 2, 279–305.

55. Nistor, 591–94, 642–44, 647–48, 702–3, 745–46, 859–60, 863, 882–83, 899–903.

56. Schroeder, "Danubian Principalities," 216–36, and "Bruck vs. Buol," 208–11.

57. Aberdeen to Clarendon, 1 and 5 Oct. 1854, Add, ms. 43189. Clarendon, Russell, and Prince Albert privately agreed that Austria's main concern was simply repressing revolutionary activity and seeing to the safety of her troops. Albert to Clarendon, 20 and 23 Sept., RA G17/24 and 36; Russell to Clarendon, 11 Sept., Clar. dep. c. 15; Clarendon to Redcliffe, 3 Oct., FO 352/37/I/1.

58. For some examples of these ideas, see Palmerston to Clarendon, 30 Sept. 1854, Palm. Papers GC/CL/1376; Cowley to Redcliffe, 19 Sept., FO 352/37/I/5; and Russell to Clarendon, 17 Sept. and 5 Oct., Clar. dep. c. 15.

59. For evidence of specific British plans to set up the Principalities as a center of Western influence against Russia and Austria, see, for example, Clarendon to Palmerston, 25 Sept. 1854, Palm. Papers GC/CL/573; Undersecretary Hammond (for Clarendon) to Colquhoun, 6 Oct., and Colquhoun to Clarendon, 11 Nov., FO 78/1011.

60. See Buol's correspondence with Hess in August and September, KA, FA III and IV AOK/1854/8–9; Buol to Coronini, 15 Aug. and 17 Sept., KA FA Serbisch-Banater Armee Corps, 326/8 and 327/9; and Buol to Francis Joseph, 18 Sept., PA XL/79.

61. Nistor, 200–4, 213–15, 227–28; Buol to Bruck, 25 Sept., and 16, 23, and 30 Oct., PA XII/49; Bruck to Coronini, 16 Oct., KA, FA Serbisch-Banater Armee Corps 1854/327/X.

62. Wimpffen, 141–46; Buol to Bruck, 18 Sept., 2, 9, and 23 Oct., and 6 Nov. 1854, PA XII/49; Nistor, 281–83; protocol of ministerial conference of 25 June, MR Prot. 13.

63. For example, Westmorland to Clarendon, 27 Sept. 1854, Nos. 362 and 364, FO 7/436, and 11 Oct., Clar. dep. c. 12.

64. Cf. Henderson, 172–73, and Tarle, I, 302–7.

65. Buol to Ottenfels, 23 Sept. 1854, PA IX/48.

66. PA XL/48; cf. Hallberg, 79, and Morrow, 37.

67. Bourqueney to Drouyn, 27 and 29 Sept. 1854, AMAE Autr. 456.

68. Buol to Hübner, 3 Oct. 1854, PA IX/48; Westmorland to Clarendon, 2 Oct., Nos. 365–66, FO 7/436; Bourqueney to Drouyn, 2 Oct., Nos. 168–69, AMAE Autr. 456.

69. Clarendon to Westmorland, 7, 16, and 20 Oct. 1854, Nos. 315, 326, and 333, FO 7/430; Clarendon to Aberdeen, 8 and 14 Oct., Add. ms. 43189; Cowley to Clarendon, 8 Oct., No. 1222, FO 519/4.

70. Hübner to Buol, 10 Oct. 1854, PA IX/49; Hübner, I, 267, 270.

71. Hübner to Buol, 11 Oct. 1854, No. 133A, PA IX/46; Bourqueney to Drouyn, with Drouyn's marginal notes, 8 Oct., AMAE Autr. 456;

Drouyn to Walewski, 11 and 19 Oct., AMAE Mem. et doc. France 2120.

72. Colloredo to Buol, 21 Oct. 1854, PA VIII/40; Aberdeen to Victoria, 6 and 20 Oct., Add. ms. 43049; *QVL*, III, 61–63.

73. Cowley to Clarendon, 6 and 10 Oct. 1854, Clar. dep. c. 18; Russell to Clarendon, 8 Oct., *ibid.;* Clarendon to Palmerston, 7 Oct., Palm. Papers GC/CL/679; Clarendon to Victoria, 8 and 9 Oct., RA G/17/100, 107.

74. Clarendon to Russell, 10 and 11 Oct. 1854, PRO 30/22/11E; Clarendon to Cowley, 10, 13, and 14 Oct., FO 519/170; Palmerston to Clarendon, 15 Oct., Palm. Papers GC/CL/1378; Cowley to Clarendon, 15 and 16 Oct., Clar. dep. c. 18.

75. Russell to Aberdeen, 15 Oct. 1854, Add. ms. 43068; Russell to Clarendon, n.d. [mid-October], Clar. dep. c. 15.

76. Aberdeen to Victoria, 17 and 20 Oct. 1854, and to Clarendon, 23 Oct., Add. ms. 43049 and 43189; Clarendon to Cowley, 17 and 23 Oct., FO 519/170; Drouyn to Bourqueney, 19 Oct., AMAE Autr. 456.

77. Hübner to Buol, 22 Oct. 1854, No. 137B, PA IX/46; Clarendon to Cowley, 23 and 24 Oct., FO 519/170.

78. Redcliffe to Clarendon, 28 Oct. and 10 Nov. 1854, Clar. dep. c. 22; Clarendon to Redcliffe, 9 and 23 Nov., FO 352/37/I/1.

79. See, for example, Hess to Buol, 23 Nov., and Buol to Hess, 29 Nov. and 12 Dec. 1854, PA XL/78; Westmorland to Clarendon, 2, 6, and 13 Dec., Nos. 454, 462, and 469, FO 7/438–39. For Bruck's protests, see Nistor, 104–6, 181–86, *et passim*.

80. Clarendon to Westmorland, 28 and 30 Nov. and 19 Dec. 1854, Nos. 382, 385, and 430, FO 7/430.

81. The documents (very numerous) can be found in Nistor, 231–337, and FO 78/1011 and 1013. The clearest statements of France's and Britain's purposes are in Drouyn to Bourqueney, 28 Nov. 1854, AMAE Autr. 457, and Clarendon to Colquhoun, 29 Nov., FO 78/1011.

82. Hess to Coronini, 15 and 17 Nov. 1854, PA XL/78; Bourqueney to Drouyn, 17, 24, and 25 Nov. and 4 and 6 Dec., AMAE Autr. 457; Clarendon to Westmorland, 30 Nov., No. 389, and Westmorland to Clarendon, 9 Dec., No. 464, FO 7/430 and 438.

83. Cowley to Clarendon, 17 and 19 Oct. and 3 Nov. 1854, Clar. dep. c. 18; Russell to Clarendon, 2 Nov., *ibid.* c. 15; Clarendon to Palmerston, 2 Nov., Palm. Papers GC/CL/580; Aberdeen to Clarendon, 2 Nov., Add. ms. 43189.

84. Palmerston to Clarendon, 2 and 3 Nov. 1854, Clar. dep. c. 15.

85. Russell to Clarendon, 4 Nov. 1854, *ibid.;* Clarendon to Russell, 4

and 6 Nov., PRO 30/22/11F; Clarendon to Victoria, 4 Nov., RA G18/88; *QVL*, III, 64–65.

86. Clarendon to Westmorland, 7 Nov. 1854, FO 7/430; Drouyn to Bourqueney, 6 [?] Nov. 1854, No. 108, AMAE Autr. 457.

87. Bourqueney to Drouyn, 11 and 13 Nov. 1854, AMAE Autr. 457; Buol to Hübner, 13 Nov., PA IX/48; Westmorland to Clarendon, 15 Nov., Clar. dep. c. 12.

88. See Heinrich Benedikt, *Die wirtschaftliche Entwicklung Österreichs ind er Franz-Joseph Zeit* (Vienna, 1958), 33, 35–36. The efforts of some (most recently Unckel, pp. 174–76) to portray Austria's financial weakness as a major cause of her rapprochement with France, and to link the sale of the state-owned *Nordbahn* to a French syndicate with the alliance of December 2, are mistaken. The conference of October 11 which resolved on the sale did not include a discussion of the political side to the transaction; French support for it was solicited (by Bach, not Buol) only after the treaty of December 2 was concluded; and even then Drouyn would give indirect support to it only after all financial negotiations were completed. MCZ 3218.854, MR Prot. 14; Drouyn to Bourqueney, 11 and 19 Dec. 1854, and Bourqueney to Drouyn, 12 Dec., AMAE Autr. 457.

89. See Chateaurenard's reports of 14 and 28 Oct. 1854, AMG, Reconnaissances Autr. 1602/68–69; Hess to Francis Joseph, 26 Oct., KA, MKSM, Fasz. 73, No. 18.

90. Bourqueney to Drouyn, 28 Oct. 1854, AMAE Autr. 456; *PAP*, II, 525–26; Buol to Hübner, 13 Nov., PA IX/48.

91. Unckel, 182–83; *Kübecks Tagebücher*, 161–62; *Kempens Tagebuch*, 348–49; "Votum" by Bach, Verwaltungsarchiv, Nachlass Bach/18.

92. Cowley to Clarendon, 9 Nov. 1854, No. 1347, FO 519/4, and 7, 15, and 17 Nov., Clar. dep. c. 18.

93. Clarendon to Cowley, 17 Nov. 1854, FO 519/170; Clarendon to Albert, 19 Nov., RA G19/77; Martin, *Prince Consort*, III, 163–65; Palmerston to Clarendon, 19 Nov., Clar. dep. c. 15.

94. Russell to Clarendon, 19 and 21 Nov. 1854, Clar. dep. c. 15; *Rel. dipl. GB-Sard.*, IV, 293, 296–99.

95. Clarendon to Russell, 19 and 22 Nov. 1854, PRO 30/22/11F; Clarendon to Cowley, 20 and 27 Nov., FO 519/170; Aberdeen to Victoria, 21 Nov.; Victoria to Clarendon, 22 Nov.; and Clarendon to Victoria, 22 Nov., RA G/19/101, 113, and 124; Cowley to Clarendon, 20 Nov., Clar. dep. c. 18; and Palmerston to Clarendon, 21 Nov., *ibid.* c. 15.

96. Drouyn to Bourqueney, 21 Nov. 1854, PA IX/49; Colloredo to Buol, 22 Nov., No. 104A, PA VIII/39.

97. Buol to Hübner, 27 Nov. 1854, Nos. 4–5, PA IX/48; Westmorland to Clarendon, 22 Nov., Nos. 371–72, FO 7/430.

98. Westmorland to Clarendon, 29 Nov. and 2 Dec. 1854, 2 tgs and Nos. 352–53, FO 7/438; Bourqueney to Drouyn, 28 and 29 Nov., tg and No. 197, AMAE Autr. 457; Buol to Francis Joseph, 29 Nov., PA XL/48.

99. For earlier interpretations, see especially Eckhart, 135–37, and Henderson, 180–81, 183–89. Conacher (429–40) ignores Austria's aims and point of view.

100. Geffcken, 145–46; Agatha Ramm, "Crimean War," in *The New Cambridge Modern History*, X, 481; Unckel, *passim*.

101. Buol to Bruck, 16 Oct. 1854, PA XII/52; Nistor, 411–12.

102. Cowley to Clarendon, 30 Nov. 1854, Clar. dep. c. 18; Clarendon to Cowley, 1 and 2 Dec., FO 519/170. Aberdeen suggested to Clarendon that rather than provoke Sardinia's appetite, he might consider engaging Britain "to protect Lombardy from the much more probable contingency of the renewal of Sardinian invasion" (29 Nov., Add. ms. 43189).

103. As Srbik says (*Deutsche Einheit*, II, 250–51).

104. Clarendon to Westmorland, 24 Nov. 1854, No. 379, FO 7/430; Clarendon to Russell, 27 Nov., PRO 30/22/11F.

105. See, for proof of these points, Buol to Hübner, 13 and 20 Nov. 1854, PA IX/49 and 48; Clarendon to Cowley, 23 Nov., FO 519/170.

106. Eckhart, 135–37, 176.

107. See, for example, Clarendon to Cowley, 10 and 14 Nov. 1854, FO 519/170, and Palmerston to Clarendon, 9 Nov., Clar. dep. c. 15.

108. Clarendon to Westmorland, 22 and 28 Nov. 1854, Clar. dep. c. 130. Hübner, who experienced British hostility directly from Cowley, Russell, and Palmerston, remarked that Britain from the beginning had shown "a truly astounding lack of diplomatic understanding and, alongside a great ignorance of European affairs, a barely disguised malevolence toward Austria" (Hübner, I, 271–72).

109. The best accounts are Borries, 208–11, 221–32; Eckhart, 98–106; and Krusemarck, 59–61. Important documents are in Jasmund, I, 350–63, and *PAP*, II, 489–92, 500–1, and 505. The most important among very many Austrian documents are: Buol to G. Esterházy, 28 Aug. and 14 Sept. 1854, GA Berlin/112; Esterházy to Buol, 3, 8, and 18 Sept., PA III/51 and 53; Buol to Apponyi, 23 Aug., and Apponyi to Buol, 2 and 14 Sept., PA IV/21–22; Count Kuefstein, envoy at Dresden, to Buol, 2 Sept., PA V/21.

110. Jasmund, I, 367–71; Francis Joseph to Frederick William, 29 Sept. 1854, Kab. Arch. Geh. Akt. 7; Buol to G. Esterházy, 30 Sept., PA III/53;

Bernhard von Mayer to Bach, 6 Oct., Verwaltungsarchiv, Nachlass Bach, Briefe/IX.

111. G. Esterházy to Buol, 1 Sept. 1854, No. 14, PA III/51; William to Prince Albert, 2 Nov., RA G18/78; Frederick William to Francis Joseph, 7 Aug., Kab. Arch. Geh. Akt. 7.

112. Apponyi to Buol, 10 Oct. 1854, PA IV/21.

113. Apponyi to Buol, 19 Oct. 1854, PA IV/22; King Max to Pfordten, 11–12 Oct., GSA, MA I/590.

114. Krusemarck, 62–72; Eckhart, 111–24; Jasmund, I, 393–97; Buol to G. Esterházy, 23 Oct. 1854, and Esterházy to Buol, 28 and 30 Oct. and 16 Nov., GA Berlin/112 and PA III/53.

115. Apponyi to Buol, 27 Nov. 1854, No. 71, PA IV/22.

116. Eckhart, 128–31; Buol to G. Esterházy, 28 Nov. 1854, GA Berlin/112; circular of 30 Nov., PA rot 1099.

117. See, for example, Eckhart, 118–19; Krusemarck, 71–72.

118. Buol to G. Esterházy, 23 Nov. 1854, PA III/53.

119. *PAP*, II, 558–63, 576–78; Buol to G. Esterházy, 9 Nov. 1854, PA III/53.

120. Apponyi to Buol, 10 Nov. 1854, PA IV/21.

121. Cf. Tarle, II, 320–24.

122. See, for example, Buol to V. Esterházy, 7 and 27 Oct. 1854, PA X/38.

123. Shcherbatov, VII, 210–24, 228–29, 241–43; Curtiss, 341.

124. Tarle, II, 313–15; Nesselrode, XI, 80–83; G. Esterházy to Buol, 16 Nov. 1854, No. 32B, PA III/51.

CHAPTER X

1. Westmorland to Clarendon, 2 Dec. 1854, Clar. dep. c. 12, and 6 Dec., No. 458, FO 7/438; Buol to Bourqueney, 3 Dec., AMAE Autr. 457; Buol to Hübner, 3 Dec., PA IX/48–49.

2. Clarendon to Cowley, 4 and 5 Dec. 1854, FO 519/170; Clarendon to Westmorland, 5 Dec., Clar. dep. c. 131; Clarendon to Aberdeen, 5 Dec., Add. ms. 43189. For the actual attacks on the alliance in Parliament Dec. 12–13, see 3 Hansard, 212–41.

3. Cowley to Clarendon, 4, 12, and 13 Dec. 1854, Clar. dep. c. 18, and 4, 6, and 13 Dec., Nos. 1459, 1498, and 1502, FO 519/4.

4. Clarendon to Russell, 9 Dec. 1854, PRO 30/22/11F; Clarendon to Russell, 13 Dec., FO 519/170; Aberdeen to Clarendon, 16 Dec., and Clarendon to Aberdeen, 18 Dec., Add. ms. 43189.

5. Henderson, 103–6; Russell to Clarendon, 10, 12, and 14 Dec. 1854, Clar. dep. c. 15; Maxwell, II, 48–49; Greville to Russell, 17 Dec., PRO 30/22/11F.

6. Clarendon to Victoria, 14 Dec. 1854, RA G20/121; Clarendon to Cowley, 11, 15, and 16 Dec., FO 519/170; Clarendon to Westmorland, 7 and 16 Dec., Clar. dep. c. 131.

7. Clarendon to Westmorland, 18 Dec. 1854, No. 422, FO 7/430; Clarendon to Redcliffe, 15 and 18 Dec., FO 352/37/I/1; Colloredo to Buol, 16 Dec., PA VIII/40.

8. Russell to Clarendon, 16 and 23 Dec. 1854, Clar. dep. c. 15; Clarendon to Russell, 17 Dec., PRO 30/22/11F.

9. Bourqueney to Drouyn, 23 Dec. 1854, and Drouyn to Bourqueney, tg, 24 Dec., AMAE Autr. 457; Buol to Hübner, 23 Dec., PA XII/49.

10. Cowley to Clarendon, 20 Dec. 1854, Clar. dep. c. 18, and 24 Dec., No. 1664, FO 519/4.

11. To Cowley, 25 Dec. 1854, FO 519/170.

12. Henderson, 107–12; Warren F. Spencer, "Drouyn de Lhuys," 82–84.

13. E.g., Clarendon to Redcliffe, 22 Dec. 1854, FO 352/37/I/1.

14. To Clarendon, 26 Dec. 1854, Add ms. 43189.

15. Buol to Francis Joseph, 29 Dec. 1854, PA XL/48.

16. Bourqueney to Drouyn, 15 Sept. 1853, AMAE Autr. 451; Buol to Grünne, 9 and 17 Dec. 1853 and 13 Jan. 1854, and Grünne to Buol, 12 Nov. 1853 and 9 Jan. 1854, PA XL/76 and 79; Buol to Hübner, 10 Feb. 1854, No. 6, PA IX/48.

17. The correspondence on the dispute is in PA XL/75–76; cf. also Buol to Francis Joseph, 6 Oct. 1854, PA XL/48.

18. *Rel. dipl. Aust.-Tosc.*, IV, 35–40, 329–31, 333–37, 387–97.

19. Valsecchi, *Alleanza*, 310–13; Drouyn to Bourqueney, 11 and 18 Dec. 1854, and Bourqueney to Drouyn, 20 Dec., AMAE Autr. 457; Cowley to Clarendon, 15 and 18 Dec., Nos. 1511 and 1525, FO 519/4.

20. Valsecchi, *Alleanza*, 346–51, 380–94; O. Anderson, *Liberal State at War*, 219–21; Hudson to Russell, 8 Dec. 1854, PRO 30/22/11F; Russell to Clarendon, 18, 21, and 29 Dec., Clar. dep. c. 15.

21. Clarendon to Russell, 18 and 22 Dec. 1854, PRO 30/22/11F; Victoria to Clarendon, 18 and 20 Dec., RA G21/6 and 15; Aberdeen to Clarendon, 24 Dec., and Clarendon to Aberdeen, 24 Dec., Add. ms. 43189; Clarendon to Hudson, 28 Dec., Clar. dep. c. 131. A very full selection of documents is in *Rel. dipl. GB-Sard.*, IV, 309–63.

22. Valsecchi, *Alleanza*, 395–406; Drouyn to Bourqueney, 2 Jan. 1855, AMAE Autr. 459; Aberdeen to Victoria, 16 Jan., Add. ms. 43050; Claren-

don to Hudson, 31 Jan., and to Westmorland, 31 Jan., Clar. dep. c. 131; Colloredo to Buol, 14 Jan., No. 4D, PA VIII/40.

23. Eckhart, 138–41; *PAP*, II, 580; G. Esterházy to Buol, 2 and 9 Dec. 1854, PA III/53; Apponyi to Buol, 3 Dec., private, and 3, 12 and 20 Dec., Nos. 72A, 73A, and 74A, PA IV/21–22.

24. Buol to Hess, 10, 15, and 27 Dec. 1854, and Hess to Buol, 11, 14, and 18 Dec., PA XL/78; Beer, 519–20; memorandum by Westmorland on a conversation with Hess, 4 Jan. 1855, Clar. dep. c. 27.

25. Jasmund, I, 405–7, 409–11; Borries, 262; G. Esterházy to Buol, 2 and 5 Jan. 1855, PA III/54.

26. Jasmund, I, 413–16; Eckhart, 152–55; Buol to G. Esterházy, 14 Jan. 1855, PA III/55; Apponyi to Buol, 30 Dec. 1854, No. 75B, PA IV/22; Prokesch to Buol, 29 Dec., PA II/30.

27. Srbik, *Deutsche Einheit*, II, 250–51; Westmorland to Clarendon, 24 Jan. 1855, Clar. dep. c. 27.

28. Krusemarck, 78–81; note by Pfordten, 19 Jan. 1855, and Pfordten to King Max, 24 Jan., GSA, MA I/592; Apponyi to Buol, 21 and 29 Jan., PA IV/23; Kuefstein to Buol, 18 Jan., PA V/21; G. Esterházy to Buol, 26 Jan., PA III/55.

29. Austrian circular to German courts, 26 Jan. 1855, PA rot 1099; Buol to Apponyi, 24 Jan. and 1 Feb., PA IV/23; Buol to Kuefstein, 25 Jan., and to Duke Ernest, 7 Feb., PA V/22; Prokesch, *Briefe*, 422; Prokesch to Buol, 4 Feb., PA II/32.

30. Eckhart, 160–62; Borries, 284–89; Apponyi to Buol, 6 Feb. 1855, PA IV/23.

31. Buol to V. Esterházy, 8 Dec. 1854, PA X/38.

32. Buol to Hübner, 4 Jan. 1855, PA IX/51; Bourqueney to Drouyn, tg, 28 Dec. 1854, AMAE Autr. 457.

33. Buol to V. Esterházy, 2, 3, and 5 Jan. 1855, PA X/42; Buol to Hübner, 4 Jan., PA IX/51; Buol to G. Esterházy, 4 Jan., PA III/55; Westmorland to Clarendon, 3 Jan., Clar. dep. c. 27.

34. Palmerston to Clarendon, [?] Dec. 1854, Clar. dep. c. 15; Clarendon to Westmorland, tg, 29 Dec., FO 7/430, and 2 Jan. 1855, Clar. dep. c. 131; Buol to Hübner, 4 and 8 Jan., Nos. 5 and 2, PA IX/51 and 55.

35. Clarendon to Aberdeen, 7 Jan. 1855, Add. ms. 43189; Westmorland to Clarendon, 9 Jan., No. 11, FO 7/451.

36. Henderson, 120–22; Maxwell, II, 54–55; *QVL*, III, 83–84; Clarendon to Westmorland, 9 and 17 Jan. 1855, Clar. dep. c. 131.

37. Clarendon to Russell, 10 Jan. 1855, PRO/30/22/12A; Russell to Clarendon and Cowley to Clarendon, both 11 Jan., Clar. dep. c. 30 and 32; Cowley to Clarendon, 12 Jan., No. 6, FO 519/4.

38. Clarendon to Russell, 12 and 21 Jan. 1855, PRO 30/22/12A; Clarendon to Redcliffe, 12 and 15 Jan., FO 352/42/II/5.

39. Aberdeen to Clarendon, 18 and 21 Jan. 1855, Clar. dep. c. 30.

40. Russell to Clarendon, 17 and 22 Jan. 1855, *ibid.*

41. Clarendon to Cowley, 17, 19, 21, and 22 Jan. 1855, FO 519/171; Clarendon to Westmorland, 20 Jan., No. 21, FO 7/446.

42. Drouyn to Walewski, 20 Jan. 1855, AMAE Mem. et doc. France 2120; Cowley to Clarendon, 19 and 21 Jan., Clar. dep. c. 32, and 21 Jan., Nos. 55–56, FO 519/4; Bernard d'Harcourt, *Diplomatie et diplomates: Les quatre ministères de M. Drouyn de Lhuys* (Paris, 1882), 94–100.

43. Clarendon to Westmorland, tg, 23 Jan. 1855, FO 7/446; Clarendon to Cowley, 24 Jan., FO 519/171, and to Redcliffe, 22 Jan., FO 352/42/II/5.

44. Harcourt, 101–4; Drouyn to Bourqueney, 22 and 24 Jan. 1855, AMAE Autr. 458; Napoleon to Francis Joseph, 26 Jan., PA IX–51.

45. For a sample of Clarendon's complaints and Westmorland's often blunt and effective replies, see Clarendon to Westmorland, 22 Jan. 1855, No. 24, FO 7/446; Westmorland to Clarendon, 10 and 13 Jan., Clar. dep. c. 27, and 31 Jan., No. 53, FO 7/452.

46. Westmorland to Clarendon, 31 Jan. 1855, Clar. dep. c. 27; see also Bourqueney to Drouyn, 29 and 30 Jan., AMAE Autr. 458; Buol to Hübner, 29 Jan., PA IX/51; Francis Joseph to Napoleon, 4 Feb., *ibid.*

47. Conacher, 471–91; *Greville Memoirs*, 93–96, 98–103; Colloredo to Buol, 13 Jan. 1855, PA VIII/42. On the Foreign Enlistment Bill, see Peter Gugolz, *Die Schweiz und der Krimkrieg*, 28–35.

48. Conacher, 494–548. The best primary sources are *QVL*, III, 90–132; Graham Papers Reel 20; and Prince Albert's Papers, especially memoranda he dictated to Victoria (RA G23/1, 5, 24, and 41).

49. Drouyn to Walewski, 31 Jan. 1855, AMAE Mem. et doc. France 2120; Walewski to Albert, 30 Jan., and Albert to Clarendon, 1 Feb., RA G23/55–56; Bourqueney to Drouyn, 6 Feb., AMAE Autr. 458.

50. *Greville Memoirs*, VII, 109–13; exchange of letters between Gladstone, Graham, Palmerston, Clarendon, and Stockmar, 4–6 Feb. 1855, Graham Papers Reel 20; Aberdeen to S. Herbert, 6 Feb., Add. ms. 44089; Argyll to Palmerston, 7 Feb., Palm. Papers GC/AR/5.

51. Henderson, 36–37.

52. Drouyn to Bourqueney, 7 Feb. 1855, AMAE Autr. 458; Hübner to Buol, 10 Feb., No. 18C, PA IX/49.

53. Clarendon to Westmorland, 6, 13, and 20 Feb. 1855, Clar. dep. c. 131.

54. Cowley to Clarendon, 5 and 7 Feb. 1855, *ibid.*, c. 32, and 7, 16, and

18 Feb., Nos. 143, 192, and 198, FO 519/4; Drouyn to Walewski, 19 Feb., AMAE Mem. et doc. France 2120.

55. *Greville Memoirs*, VII, 114–15, 120–23; Fox Maule, Baron Panmure, *The Panmure Papers*, I, 58–60, 65; Gladstone to Graham, 19 Feb. 1855, Aberdeen to Graham, 21 Feb., and Graham to Palmerston, 22 Feb., Graham Papers Reel 20. There is some ground for Henderson's belief (pp. 39–40) that the government grew more warlike after this second crisis. The peace advocates were removed, while plans were pushed forward for a great campaign especially in the Caucasus, to form a belt of independent states to protect Turkey and India from Russia. I think it more significant, however, that Palmerston seems to have moderated his aims, while Clarendon despaired of achieving anything even by the most drastic means. See a memorandum (n.d., but early 1855) by Sir Charles Wood, new First Lord of the Admiralty, Palm. Papers Russia; Palmerston to Clarendon, 3 March, Clar. dep. c. 31; Clarendon to Redcliffe, 23 Feb. and 9 March, FO 352/42/II/5.

56. Ashley, II, 76–78; Minto to Russell, 5 March 1855, PRO 30/22/18; Cowley to Clarendon, 14 Feb., Clar. dep. c. 32.

57. Clarendon to Palmerston, 18 and 19 Feb. 1855, Palm. Papers GC/CL/509–91; Hübner to Buol, 27 Feb., Buol to Hübner, 20 Feb., and Francis Joseph to Napoleon, 8 March, PA IX/51.

58. Maxwell, II, 62–63; *Russell Correspondence*, II, 187–89; Victoria to Clarendon, 19 Jan. 1855, RA G22/57; Cowley to Clarendon, 14 Jan., Clar. dep. c. 32.

59. *Greville Memoirs* VII, 85; *Russell Correspondence*, II, 180–82; Westmorland to Clarendon, 23 Jan. 1855, Clar. dep. c. 27.

60. Russell to Clarendon, 11 Feb. 1855, Clar. dep. c. 30; Russell to Graham, 12 Feb., Graham Papers Reel 20.

61. Clarendon to Russell and Palmerston to Russell, 11 Feb. 1855, PRO 30/22/12A; Clarendon to Cowley, 12 and 14 Feb., FO 519/171; Ab. Corr. 1855–1860, 38–39.

62. *Russell Correspondence*, II, 189–92; Clarendon to Russell, 17 and 22 Feb. 1855, and Argyll to Russell, 22 Feb., PRO 30/22/12B; Clarendon to Aberdeen, 15 Feb., Add. ms. 43189.

63. Bourqueney to Drouyn, 16 Feb. 1855, AMAE Autr. 458; Westmorland to Redcliffe, 19 Feb., FO 352/41/I/1.

64. *Russell Correspondence*, II, 195–96; Russell to Palmerston, 22 and 23 Feb. 1855, PRO 30/22/12B; Westmorland to Clarendon, 28 Feb., Clar. dep. c. 27.

65. Westmorland to Clarendon, 24 Jan. 1855, No. 47, with memorandum by Hess enclosed, FO 7/451; Buol to Hübner, 23 and 30 Jan., and

Hübner to Buol, 10 Feb., No. 18B, PA IX/51 and 49; French mémoire, n.d. [received by Crenneville on 14 Feb.], KA, FA III and IV AOK, 1855/321/II; Cowley to Clarendon, 16 Feb., No. 181, FO 519/4.

66. Jasmund, I, 436–37, 443–44, 450–51; II, 9–12; Prokesch, *Briefe*, I, 434–37; Buol to G. Esterházy, 20 Feb. 1855, PA III/58.

67. Rechberg to Buol, 14 March 1855, No. 3C, PA II/32; Apponyi to Rechberg, 17 March, PA I/rot 533a.

68. Buol to Pfordten, 15 Feb. and 19 March 1855; Pfordten to Buol, 25 Feb.; and Apponyi to Buol, 8 and 22 Feb. and 14 March, all in PA IV/23; Rechberg to Buol, 12 March, PA II/34.

69. Eckhart, 156–57; Borries, 264–66; *PAP*, II, 582–85, and III, 1–3, 5–6; G. Esterházy to Buol, 16 and 21 Dec. 1854, PA III/53.

70. Hübner to Buol, 16 and 19 Jan. 1855, Nos. 5E–F and 7, PA IX/49; G. Esterházy to Buol, 2 Jan., PA III/55.

71. Clarendon to Cowley, 5 Dec. 1854, FO 519/170; Colloredo to Buol, 22 Jan. 1855, No. 6B, PA VIII/40; Clarendon to Aberdeen, 31 Dec. 1854, Add. ms. 43189; Clarendon to Westmorland, 30 Jan. 1855, Clar. dep. c. 131.

72. *PAP*, III, 28–36, 47–50; Prince William to Prince Albert, 22 Dec. 1854, RA G21/30; Cowley to Clarendon, 12 Feb. 1855, No. 163, FO 519/4; Bloomfield to Russell, 29 March, PRO 30/22/12D.

73. G. Esterházy to Buol, 3 and 9 March 1855, Nos. 12 and 13C, PA III/54.

74. Count Fr. Thun to Buol, 15 March 1855, PA III/55.

75. Prokesch to Buol, 12 Jan. 1855, PA II/32; G. Esterházy to Buol, 19 Jan., PA III/55; Buol to Esterházy, 14 and 24 Dec. 1854, PA III/53.

76. Buol to Hübner, 15 Jan. 1855, PA IX/51; Buol to G. Esterházy, 15 and 29 March, GA Berlin/113; Clarendon to Westmorland, 27 March, No. 122, FO 7/447.

77. G. Esterházy to Buol, 16 and 23 Feb. 1855, and Buol to Esterházy, 14 March, PA III/55.

78. E.g., T. W. Riker, *The Making of Roumania*, 48, 52.

79. Nistor, 714–18, 796–97; conference protocols of 25 June and 22 August 1854, MR Prot. 13; Buol to Testa, 13 Feb. 1855, PA XXXVIII/110.

80. On the Craiova affair, see Nistor, 617–19, 621–22, 650–52, 657–59; there is also much material in KA, FA III and IV AOK 1855/332, and in Colquhoun's reports, FO 78/1097.

81. According to a report of 1 April 1855, the 4th Army had lost 3791 men and 17 officers, mainly through disease (KA, FA III and IV AOK 1855/322/6, 6a–b).

82. Nistor, 833–34. The most sensational case was that of Major Count

Stolberg, who formed a liaison with the seventeen-year-old daughter of Prince Ghica, Natalie Balş, and on being caught in *flagrante delicto* by her husband killed him in a duel. Ghica sent his daughter to a convent, while Stolberg went on leave to Czernowitz. What punishment if any he received, I do not know (Nistor, 764; Testa to Buol, 14 June 1855, PA XXXVIII/110).

83. Wimpffen, 160-64; Prince Ghica to Buol, 10 Dec. 1854, PA XII/52; Buol to Hess, 1 March 1855, and to Coronini, 3 March, KA FA III and IV AOK 1855/322/9 and ad 9.

84. Nistor, 111-19, 251-55, 490-97; *Acte şi documente*, III, 1179-83.

85. Colquhoun to Clarendon, 21 April 1855, FO 78/1097; Redcliffe to Colquhoun, 30 Nov. 1854, FO 352/37/II/10.

86. E.g., Buol to Baron von Mihanovich, 8 Oct. 1854, PA XXXVIII/104; Clarendon to Colquhoun, 7 Dec., FO 78/1011.

87. When a minor Russian raid into the Dobruja occurred in early January 1855, the sea powers wanted Austria to take it as her *casus belli*. Colquhoun to Redcliffe, 11 Jan. 1855, FO 352/41/II/5; Clarendon to Westmorland, 12 and 17 Jan., Nos. 12 and 20, FO 7/446; Bourqueney to Drouyn, 13 Jan., AMAE Autr. 458.

88. Colquhoun to Clarendon, 6 and 13 Jan. 1855, FO 78/1097; Nistor, 475-76; Nistor, "Die Polenlegion," 74-88.

89. See, for example, Russell to Clarendon, 27 and 28 Nov. 1854, Clar. dep. c. 15.

90. Various memoirs on the Principalities, to be found in AMAE, Mem. et doc. Roumanie 2 and Turquie 48 and 55, make this point perfectly clear.

CHAPTER XI

1. Russell to Clarendon, 22 Feb. and 2 March 1855, PRO 30/22/12B and FO 7/462.

2. Prokesch's memoranda, position papers, and notes for the conference are in PA XII/218, PA XL/321, and Prokesch Nachlass 26/7.

3. S. Goriainov, *Le Bosphore et les Dardanelles*, 101-3.

4. Russell to Clarendon, 5 and 7 March 1855, Nos. 10 and 12, FO 7/462, and private, same dates, Clar. dep. c. 30.

5. "Memorandum on modes of carrying into effect the 3rd point," n.d., PRO 30/22/12B (a partial draft dated 8 March 1855 is *ibid.* 12C).

6. Russell to Clarendon, 7 March 1855, No. 12, with attached memorandum by Cowley, n.d., FO 7/462.

7. Westmorland to Clarendon, 10 March 1855, No. 102, FO 7/453;

Russell to Cowley, 11 March, FO 519/197; Cowley to Clarendon, 7 March, No. 274, FO 519/4; Bourqueney to Drouyn, 10 and 11 March, and Drouyn to Bourqueney, 7 and 13 March, AMAE Autr. 458–59.

8. Clarendon to Cowley, 9 March 1855, FO 519/174; Clarendon to Palmerston, 11 March, Palm. Papers GC/CL/597; Cowley to Clarendon, 12 and 13 March, Clar. dep. c. 32.

9. Clarendon to Cowley, 14 March 1855, FO 519/171; Minto to Russell, 14, 20, and 27 March, PRO 30/22/12C; Victoria to Clarendon, 14 March, RA G26/49 (not the letter printed in *QVL*, III, 145); Clarendon to Russell, 15 March, PRO 30/22/12C; *Russell Correspondence*, II, 198.

10. Memorandum by Hess, late Feb. 1855, KA FA III and IV AOK 1855/321/II/61; Grünne to Crenneville, 8 March, with enclosed memorandum by Hess of 6 March, KA, MKSM 1855/792.

11. Memorandum by Albert, 6 March 1855, RA G26/2; Cowley to Clarendon, 15 March, No. 317, FO 519/4; Palmerston to Clarendon, 15 March, Clar. dep. c. 31; Clarendon to Cowley, 16 March, FO 519/171.

12. Buol to Hübner, 1 and 14 March 1855, PA IX/51; Bourqueney to Drouyn, 7 March, AMAE Autr. 458.

13. Drouyn to Bourqueney, 22 Feb. 1855, AMAE Autr. 458; Cowley to Clarendon, 5 and 7 March, Nos. 259 and 275, FO 519/4, and 9 March, Clar. dep. c. 32.

14. Palmerston to Russell, 15 March 1855, PRO 30/22/12C (partly published in *Russell Correspondence*, II, 198); Clarendon to Cowley, 7 March, FO 519/171; Clarendon to Westmorland, 8 March, No. 87, FO 7/446.

15. Clarendon to Russell, 20 March 1855, PRO 30/22/12C; Clarendon to Cowley, 16 March, FO 519/171. Jasmund, II, 80–200, contains the Vienna Conference protocols and annexes.

16. Ashley, II, 84–88; Palmerston to Clarendon, 23 March 1855, and memorandum by Palmerston, early April, Clar. dep. c. 31; Clarendon to Cowley, 24 and 26 March, FO 519/171; Clarendon's instructions to Russell from 20 March to 5 April, PRO 30/22/18.

17. Drouyn to Bourqueney, 22 and 25 March 1855, and Bourqueney to Drouyn, 26 March and 2 April, AMAE Autr. 459.

18. Russell to Clarendon, 15 March 1855, No. 20, FO 7/462; conference protocol of 24 March, MR Prot. 14.

19. Russell to Clarendon, 18 and 24 March 1855, Clar. dep. c. 30, and 20 and 28 March, Nos. 25–26 and 41, FO 7/462–63.

20. Russell to Clarendon, 4, 7, and 9 April 1855, Clar. dep. c. 30 and PRO 30/22/12D, and 1 and 11 April, Nos. 53 and 68, *ibid.* 18.

21. Russell to Clarendon, 5 April 1855, No. 55, *ibid.*

22. Russell to Redcliffe, 23 April 1855, FO 352/41/I/1.

23. Buol to Hübner, 21 March 1855, PA IX/51; Westmorland to Clarendon, 26 March, No. 141, FO 7/453; Russell to Clarendon, 21 and 23 March, FO 7/462, and 20 and 26 March, Clar. dep. c. 30.

24. Clarendon to Palmerston, 24 March 1855, Palm. Papers GC/CL/607.

25. Russell to Clarendon, 23 March 1855, FO 7/463.

26. Goriainov, *Bosphore*, 106; Buol to Hübner, 28 March 1855, PA IX/51; Bourqueney to Drouyn, 2 tgs, 26 March, AMAE Autr. 459.

27. Goriainov, *Bosphore*, 106–9, 117–19; Buol to V. Esterházy, 28 March 1855, and Nesselrode to Gorchakov, 29 March, PA X/42.

28. *Russell Correspondence*, II, 199–202; Clarendon to Russell, 27 March 1855, PRO 30/22/12C (partly printed in *ibid.*, 199–200); Cowley to Clarendon, 18 and 25 March, Clar. dep. c. 32.

29. For examples of divergent views, see *Russell Correspondence*, II, 202; Maxwell, II, 82; Bulwer to Russell, 28 March 1855, PRO 30/22/12D.

30. Cowley to Clarendon, 22 March 1855, No. 345, FO 519/4; Clarendon to Cowley, 24 March, FO 519/171.

31. Spencer, 91–95; Henderson, 44–47; Cowley to Clarendon, 27 and 28 March 1855, Clar. dep. c. 32; Clarendon to Palmerston, 28 March, Palm. Papers GC/CL/608; memorandum by Drouyn, 1 April, AMAE Mem. et doc. Autriche 66.

32. Harcourt, 113–25; Hübner to Buol, 1 April 1855, PA IX/51; Colloredo to Buol, 3 April, PA VIII/40.

33. Clarendon to Cowley, 31 March and 2 April 1855, FO 519/171; Cowley to Clarendon, 28 March and 1 April, Clar. dep. c. 32–33.

34. To Cowley, 6 April 1855, FO 519/171. Ironically, Aberdeen, Russell's political rival whom Russell had driven from office, now defended him against the charges of Russell's friend, follower, and Cabinet colleague Clarendon. To Clarendon, 16 and 23 March, Add. ms. 43189.

35. See above, note 20.

36. *Russell Correspondence*, II, 203–5; Russell to Panmure, 28 March 1855, and to Clarendon, 31 March, PRO 30/22/12D; Clarendon to Russell, 3 April, No. 39, *ibid.*, 18; Russell to Cowley, 11 April, FO 519/197; Cowley to Russell, 15 April, PRO 30/22/12D.

37. Harcourt, 125–35; Jasmund, II, 25–31; Drouyn to Thouvenel, 11 April 1855, Bourqueney to Thouvenel, 14 April, and Thouvenel to Bourqueney, 12 April, AMAE Autr. 459 and 462.

38. Russell to Palmerston, 1 April 1855, Palm. Papers; Russell to Clarendon, 10 and 12 April, Clar. dep. c. 30.

39. Colloredo to Buol, 28 March 1855, PA VIII/42.

40. Clarendon to Redcliffe, 13 April 1855, FO 352/42/II/5; Clarendon to Cowley, 13 and 14 April, FO 519/171.

41. Note by Prokesch, n.d., PA XII/218.

42. A. W. Kinglake, *The Invasion of the Crimea*, VII, 135–36, 209–11, 225–28; *Panmure Papers*, I, 118, 160, 163; G. B. Henderson, "Aspirations polonaises en 1855," 103–9; Palmerston to Clarendon, 6 April 1855, Clar. dep. c. 31; Clarendon to Redcliffe, 6 and 9 April, FO 352/42/II/5; Palmerston to Victoria, 9 April, and to Albert, 20 April, RA G28/14 and 89; Lord Raglan to Russell, 26 March, PRO 30/22/12C.

43. *PAP*, III, 101–3; G. Esterházy to Buol, 14 March 1855, PA III/55, and 2, 7, and 19 April, PA III/54; Bloomfield to Clarendon, 11 and 13 April 1855, Clar. dep. c. 27.

44. Russell to Clarendon, 30 March 1855, No. 46, PRO 30/22/18, and 5 April, No. 59, FO 7/463; Victoria to Clarendon, 3 and 11 April, RA G27/120 and G28/29.

45. Clarendon to Russell, 11 April 1855, No. 54, FO 7/461; Clarendon to Bloomfield, 10 April, and Bloomfield to Clarendon, 13 April, Clar. dep. c. 132 and 27.

46. 3 Hansard, 137, 881–82; Buol to Apponyi, 17 April 1855, PA IV/23.

47. Redcliffe to Clarendon, 19 March 1855, Clar. dep. c. 40.

48. Henderson, 51–54; Buol to Hübner, 16 April 1855, PA IX/51; Buol to Colloredo, 16 and 17 April, PA VIII/42; memorandum by Prokesch entitled "Remarques" etc., n.d., PA XII/218; notes by Prokesch, 16 April, PA XL/321 and Prokesch Nachlass 26/7.

49. Buol to Francis Joseph, 15 April 1855, with note by Francis Joseph, PA XL/49.

50. Drouyn to Thouvenel, 16 April 1855, AMAE Autr. 462; Russell to Clarendon, tg, 16 April, FO 7/464; various notes and rough drafts by Russell, ca. 16–20 April, PRO 30/22/18.

51. Drouyn to Thouvenel, 18 April 1855, AMAE Autr. 462; Russell to Clarendon, 18 and 19 April, Nos. 84 and 90, FO 7/464.

52. Thouvenel to Bourqueney, tgs, 17 and 18 April 1855, AMAE Autr. 462; Drouyn to Russell, 22 April, PRO 30/22/12D; Russell to Clarendon, 18, 19, 22, and 23 April, Clar. dep. c. 30; Russell to Palmerston, 23 April, Palm. Papers.

53. See, for example, *Russell Correspondence*, II, 205; Minto to Russell, 8 April, PRO 30/22/12D.

54. Martin, *Prince Consort*, III, 204; *Russell Correspondence*, II, 206–7; two memoranda by Palmerston, 22 April 1855, Clar. dep. c. 31; Cowley to Clarendon, 23 April, *ibid.* c. 33; Clarendon to Westmorland, 24 April, *ibid.* c. 132.

55. *Panmure Papers*, I, 164; Palmerston to Clarendon, 23 and 25 April 1855, Clar. dep. c. 31.

56. Clarendon to Russell, 16 and 17 April 1855, PRO 30/22/12D; Clarendon to Albert, 22 April, RA G28/114; Clarendon to Redcliffe, 16 and 23 April, FO 352/42/II/5.

57. Buol to Hübner, 23 April 1855, PA IX/51; Bourqueney to the Foreign Ministry and Drouyn to the Vicomte de Meloizes, both 23 April, AMAE Autr. 459 and 462.

58. Francis Joseph to Napoleon, [23?] April 1855, Kab. Arch. Geh. Akt. 4; Ernest, *Aus meinem Leben*, II, 257–59. Ernest's actual advice to his brother Albert, in contrast to the unctuous tone he used in writing to Buol, was very anti-Austrian—Ernest to Albert, 15 April, RA G28/68.

59. To Clarendon, 28 April 1855, Clar. dep. c. 27.

60. Tg, 24 April 1855, FO 7/447.

61. Martin, *Prince Consort*, III, 218–19; Clarendon to Cowley, 25 April 1855, FO 519/171; Cowley to Clarendon, 25 April, Clar. dep. c. 33; Palmerston to Clarendon, 26 and 27 April, *ibid*. c. 31.

62. Cowley to Clarendon, 24 and 29 April 1855, Clar. dep. c. 33; Clarendon to Cowley, 23, 27, and 28 April, FO 519/171.

63. Drouyn to Walewski, 7, 15, and 20 Jan. 1855, AMAE Mem. et doc. France, 2120; Clarendon to Redcliffe, 19 Feb., FO 352/42/5.

64. Clarendon to Cowley, 5 May 1855, FO 519/171; Cowley to Clarendon, 23 March, No. 352, FO 519/4.

65. Nolfo, *Europa*, 455–58; *Rel. dipl. GB-Sard*. V, 91–99.

66. Palmerston to Clarendon, 18 March 1855, Palm. Papers GC/CL/1379; Clarendon to Cowley, 21 April, FO 519/171.

67. Cowley to Redcliffe, 29 April 1855, FO 352/41/I/1; Harold Kurtz, *The Empress Eugenie 1826–1920* (London, 1964), 81–82.

68. Hübner to Buol, 30 April 1855, PA IX/49 and 51.

69. Drouyn to Russell, 1 May 1855, and Clarendon to Russell, 3 May, PRO 30/22/12D; Cowley to Clarendon, 2 May, No. 499, FO 519/4; Drouyn to Walewski, 3 May, AMAE Mem. et doc. France 2120.

70. Clarendon to Aberdeen, 2 May 1855, and Aberdeen to Clarendon, 3 May, Add. ms. 43189.

71. Russell to Clarendon, Halle, 25 April 1855, and memorandum entitled "Austria," n.d. [early May], Clar. dep. c. 30.

72. Seymour to Russell, 2 May 1855, PRO 30/22/12D; Lord Edmond Fitzmaurice, *Life of Granville*, I, 103–8; Martin, *Prince Consort*, III, 270–73; Stockmar's memoranda, 27 April and 2 May, and letter to Victoria, 30 April, RA G29/48, 65, and 82.

73. Palmerston to Clarendon, 3 and 6 May 1855, Clar. dep. c. 31.

74. Cowley to Clarendon, 3 May 1855, *ibid*. c. 31; Clarendon to Cow-

ley, 29 and 30 April and 2 May, FO 519/171; Clarendon to Redcliffe, 30 April and 2 and 4 May, FO 352/42/II/5.

75. Cowley to Clarendon, 4 May 1855, Clar. dep. c. 33; cf. also Cowley to Redcliffe, 5 May, FO 352/41/I/1, and Henderson, 53–64.

76. Clarendon to Cowley, 4 and 5 May 1855, FO 519/171; copy of tg, Bourqueney to Drouyn, 3 May, FO 7/455; Clarendon to Albert, 5 May, RA G29/105; Clarendon to Westmorland, 5 May, PA VIII/42.

77. *Greville Memoirs*, VII, 124, 126, 130; Westmorland to Russell, 16 April 1855, PRO 30/22/12D.

78. Even Buol's opponents recognized his sincere search for peace— cf. Meyendorff, III, 198–99, and *Kübecks Tagebücher*, II, 95. Count Lerchenfeld, a strong critic of Buol, wrote King Max of Bavaria later, "Austria has not always chosen the right means to achieve peace; she has, however, always earnestly desired it" (5 Dec. 1855, GSA, MA I/598).

79. Shcherbatov, VII, 323–24; *Kübecks Tagebücher*, 202.

80. Goriainov, *Bosphore*, 117, 121–22; *PAP*, III, 112.

81. Chateaurenard to the War Ministry, 27 April 1855, AMG Reconnaissances Autr. 1602; Bourqueney to Drouyn, 28 April and 3 May, AMAE Autr. 459; Ernest to Albert, 6 June, RA G32/36–38; PA XL/321, ff. 263–74.

82. It is worth noting, however, that Ali Pasha favored Buol's plan for restraining Russia, that Drouyn preferred counterpoise to limitation through most of 1854, and that Redcliffe, however draconic his views on peace in most respects, wanted provisions for the Black Sea remarkably like Buol's (Morrow, 52, 103–6; Bourqueney to Drouyn, 5 May 1855, No. 74, AMAE Autr. 459; Redcliffe to Clarendon, 5 April, FO 352/42/II/7).

83. Morrow, 52–59, 100–1; Martin, *Prince Consort*, III, 262–63; Russell to Clarendon, 30 March 1855, Clar. dep. c. 30.

84. See, for example, *Russell Correspondence*, II, 148–51.

CHAPTER XII

1. Colloredo to Buol, tg, 6 May 1855, PA VIII/40; Clarendon to Palmerston, 13 May, Palm. Papers GC/CL/630; Clarendon to Redcliffe, 11 May, FO 352/42/II/5; Clarendon to Cowley, 4, 5, and 7 May, FO 519/171.

2. Russell to Clarendon, 6 May 1855, PRO 30/22/12D, and 7 and 8 May, Clar. dep. c. 30.

3. Palmerston to Clarendon, 6 and 7 May 1855, *ibid.* c. 31; Clarendon to Russell, 6, 7, and 8 May, PRO 30/22/12D; Cowley to Clarendon, 7 May, Nos. 414–15, FO 519/4, and 7 and 8 May, Clar. dep. c. 33; Clarendon to Cowley, 7 and 9 May, FO 519/171. Drouyn's and Hübner's ac-

counts give further evidence that Cowley lied; see Nolfo, *Europa,* 458; Hübner, I, 326–28; and Hübner to Buol, 9 May, No. 45B, PA IX/49.

4. Walewski to Bourqueney, 10 May 1855, No. 42, AMAE Autr. 459.

5. Bourqueney to Walewski, tg, 9 May 1855, *ibid.*

6. Walewski to Bourqueney, 8 and 11 May 1855, No. 41 and tg, and Bourqueney to Walewski, 10 and 13 May, Nos. 76 and 78, *ibid.*; Cowley to Clarendon, 10 May, No. 528, FO 519/4; Clarendon to Cowley, 11 May, FO 519/171.

7. Westmorland to Clarendon, 6 and 7 May 1855, Clar. dep. c. 27.

8. Buol to Hübner, 8 and 10 May 1855, PA IX/51; Buol to G. Esterházy, 17 May, No. 2, GA Berlin/113.

9. Westmorland to Clarendon, 16 May 1855, No. 233, FO 7/455.

10. Memoranda, Prokesch to Buol, 7, 9, and 12 May 1855, PA XL/321; Prokesch to Rechberg, 17 May, PA I/rot 533c.

11. Buol to Hübner, 14 and 16 May 1855, PA IX/51; Westmorland to Clarendon, 16 May, Nos. 230–31, FO 7/455.

12. Cowley to Clarendon, 14 May 1855, Clar. dep. c. 33; Clarendon to Cowley, 12 May, FO 519/171; Palmerston to Clarendon, 15 May, Clar. dep. c. 31; Clarendon to Westmorland, 2 tgs, 15 May, FO 7/448.

13. Walewski to Clarendon, 18 May 1855, Clar. dep. c. 33; Clarendon to Redcliffe, 18 May, FO 352/42/II/5; Clarendon to Cowley, 16, 17, and 19 May, FO 519/171; Clarendon to Palmerston, 19 May, Palm. Papers GC/CL/632.

14. Clarendon to Cowley, 18 May 1855, FO 519/171; Clarendon to Palmerston, 21 and 22 May, Palm. Papers GC/CL/633–34; Clarendon to Westmorland, tgs, 20 and 21 May, FO 7/448.

15. Clarendon to Russell, 19 and 23 May 1855, PRO 30/22/12E; Russell to Clarendon, 20 and 23 May and 4 June, Clar. dep. c. 30.

16. Argyll to Russell, 23 May 1855, PRO 30/22/12E.

17. Palmerston to Clarendon, 20 May 1855, Clar. dep. c. 31; Martin, *Prince Consort,* III, 222–24, 235.

18. Palmerston to Clarendon, 23 May 1855, Clar. dep. c. 31.

19. Cowley to Clarendon, 17 May 1855, *ibid.* c. 33.

20. Cowley to Clarendon, 17, 18, 20, and 21 May 1855, *ibid.*, and 18, 20, and 27 May, Nos. 570, 584, and 621, FO 519/4.

21. Clarendon to Cowley, 21 May 1855, FO 519/171; Cowley to Clarendon, 22 May, Clar. dep. c. 33, and 20 May, No. 584, FO 519/4.

22. Buol to Hübner and Colloredo, 20 May 1855, PA IX/51 and PA VIII/42; Buol to G. Esterházy, 24 May, PA III/58.

23. Hübner, I, 314–15, 329; Cowley to Clarendon, 11 May 1855, No. 540, FO 519/4.

24. Walewski to Bourqueney, 25 and 27 May 1855, AMAE Autr. 459; Cowley to Clarendon, 21, 23, and 29 May, Nos. 590, 603, and 634, FO 519/4, and 25 and 29 May, Clar. dep. c. 33.

25. Westmorland to Clarendon, 23 May 1855, Clar. dep. c. 27; Clarendon to Westmorland, 22 and 29 May, *ibid.* c. 132, and 24, 29, and 30 May, 2 tgs and Nos. 201–02, FO 7/448; Bourqueney to Walewski, 26 May, No. 84, AMAE Autr. 459.

26. Bourqueney to Walewski, tg No. 87, 2 June 1855, *ibid.* 460.

27. Martin, *Prince Consort*, III, 239–40; memorandum by Albert, 25 May 1855, and Clarendon to Victoria, 26 May, RA G31/26 and 41; Argyll to Palmerston, 30 May, Palm. Papers GC/AR/7; Clarendon to Cowley, 26, 28, and 30 May and 2 June, FO 519/171.

28. Clarendon to Palmerston, 28 May 1855, Palm. Papers GC/CL/641; Palmerston to Clarendon, 31 May, Clar. dep. c. 31; Ashley, II, 94.

29. Cowley to Clarendon, 3 June 1855, No. 658, FO 519/4, and same date, Clar. dep. c. 33.

30. Goriainov, *Bosphore*, 124–27; Clarendon to Victoria, 9 June 1855, RA G32/58.

31. Redcliffe advocated this policy as well as Cowley—Redcliffe to Russell, 28 May 1855, and to Clarendon, 31 May and 10 and 14 June, FO 352/41/I/1 and 42/II/7.

32. *Greville Memoirs*, VII, 132.

33. *PAP*, III, 127; Ernest of Coburg to Buol, 22 May 1855, PA V/22.

34. Aberdeen to Gladstone, 30 May 1855, Add. ms. 43071.

35. Greville to the Duke of Bedford (Russell's brother), 6 Nov. 1855, PRO 30/22/12G.

36. *PAP*, III, 132; Buol to Manteuffel, 8 May 1855, PA III/55; Buol to G. Esterházy, 8 May, GA Berlin/113; Esterházy to Buol, 30 May, No. 30C and private letter, PA III/54 and 55.

37. Jasmund, II, 51–54; Buol to Apponyi, 11 and 24 May 1855, PA IV/23; Apponyi to Buol, 7 and 13 May, *ibid.*; Rechberg to Buol, 9 May, No. 30B, PA II/32.

38. Jasmund, II, 31–42; Clarendon to Palmerston, 19 May 1855, Palm. Papers GC/CL/632.

39. Rechberg to Buol, 9 May 1855, No. 30A, PA II/32; Rechberg to Bach, 13 May, Verwaltungsarchiv, Nachlass Bach/ Briefe XI.

40. Jasmund, II, 54–56, 201–2; Buol to G. Esterházy, 14 May 1855, No. 1, GA Berlin/113; Esterházy to Buol, 21 and 25 May, Nos. 27A and 28A, PA III/54; Buol to Apponyi, 1 June, PA IV/23.

41. Nolfo (*Europa*, 89–96) gives a very pro-Western, anti-Austrian account of this development.

42. 3 Hansard, 138, 18–24, 105–13, 300–2, 836–61.

43. *Ibid.*, 891–97, 973–1010, 1017–91, 1285–95.

44. *Ibid.*, 1093–1175.

45. Clarendon to Aberdeen and Aberdeen to Clarendon, both 28 May 1855, Add. ms. 43189.

46. Argyll to Gladstone, 12, 14, and 17 May 1855, and Gladstone to Argyll, 14 May, Add. ms. 44098; Argyll, *Autobiography*, I, 556–62.

47. Albert to Aberdeen, 3 June 1855, Add. ms. 43050.

48. Graham to Gladstone, 10 May and 2 June 1855, Add. ms. 44163; Gladstone to Aberdeen, 30 May, Add. ms. 43071.

49. 3 Hansard, 138, 1318–96, 1409–86, 1554–1758.

50. Gladstone to Aberdeen, 19 and 26 June 1855, Add. ms. 43071; Aberdeen to Gladstone, 20, 21, and 25 June, *ibid.* and Add. ms. 44089; Aberdeen to Graham, 9 and 21 June, Graham Papers Reel 20; Ab. Corr. 1855–60, 76.

51. 3 Hansard, 139, 297, 563–73.

52. *Ibid.*, 551–59, 573–85, 596–607.

53. Bourqueney to Walewski, 8 July 1855, No. 105, AMAE Autr. 460; *Greville Memoirs*, VII, 141–42, 144–45.

54. Cowley to Clarendon, 8 and 10 July 1855, Clar. dep. c. 34; Clarenond to Cowley, 11 July, FO 519/172; Clarendon to Palmerston, 16 July, Palm. Papers GC/CL/667.

55. Palmerston to Russell, 12 and 13 July 1855, and Russell to Palmerston, 13 July, PRO 30/22/12E; 3 Hansard, 139, 805–6, 889–900, 902–13, 918–31.

56. Clarendon to G. C. Lewis, 12 July 1855, Clar. dep. c. 532; Argyll to Russell and Lansdowne to Russell, July 1855, PRO 30/22/12E; Clarendon to Russell, 22 July, *ibid.;* Clarendon to Cowley, 21 July, FO 519/172; *Greville Memoirs*, VII, 146–50. The Peelites, approving Russell's conduct of the negotiations, blamed him only for staying on afterward in office and attacking those whose views on peace he really shared. Aberdeen to Graham, 11 July, and Graham to Aberdeen, 12 July, Graham Papers Reel 20.

57. Buol to Hübner, 6 June 1855, Nos. 1–3, PA IX/51; Nolfo, *Europa*, 459–60.

58. Bourqueney to Walewski, 3 and 15 June 1855, Nos. 88 and 95, AMAE Autr. 460; Buol to Francis Joseph, 15 June, PA XL/49.

59. Walewski to Bourqueney, 8 and 22 June 1855, Nos. 47 and 51, AMAE Autr. 460; Cowley to Clarendon, 14 and 19 June, Nos. 724–25 and 756, FO 519/4, and 11 June, Clar. dep. c. 33; Cowley to Redcliffe, 19 June, FO 352/41/I/1.

60. Cowley to Clarendon, 24 June 1855, Clar. dep. c. 33; Clarendon to Cowley, 13 June, FO 519/171; Clarendon to Redcliffe, 18 June, FO 352/42/II/5.

61. Ministerial conference protocol of 11 June 1855, MR Prot. 14; Buol to V. Esterházy, 10 June, No. 3, PA X/42; Buol to Koller, 11 June, Nos. 1–2, PA XII/58; Buol to Hübner, 13 June, PA IX/51.

62. Buol to Francis Joseph, 19 and 29 June and 4 July 1855, PA XL/49; Clarendon to Westmorland, 19 June, Clar. dep. c. 133, and 25 June, No. 247, FO 7/448; Clarendon to Cowley, 20 June, FO 519/171; Walewski to Bourqueney, 22 June, Nos. 52–53, PA IX/51.

63. Francis Joseph to Buol, 22 and 24 June 1855, and Buol to Francis Joseph, 23 and 24 June, PA XL/49; Testa to Buol, 25 and 26 June, PA XXXVIII/110; Nistor, 738–39; Buol to Hübner, 22 June, PA IX/51.

64. Buol to Koller, 25 June and 16 and 23 July 1855, and Koller to Buol, 12 July, No. 28A–B, PA XII/58 and 54; Hübner to Buol, 25 and 29 June, PA IX/50.

65. Clarendon to Cowley, 7 June 1855, FO 519/171; Clarendon to Westmorland, 7 and 12 June, tg and No. 223, FO 7/448; Hübner to Buol, 15 June, No. 54B, PA IX/50.

66. Hübner to Buol, 8 June 1855, PA IX/51.

67. *Panmure Papers*, I, 211–12, 232; Clarendon to Cowley, 6 June 1855, FO 519/171; Palmerston to Clarendon, 7 June, Clar. dep. c. 31.

68. Palmerston to Clarendon, 24 June 1855, *ibid.*; Clarendon to Cowley, 30 June, FO 519/171.

69. Henry Elliot to Clarendon, 26 June and 4 July 1855, Nos. 2 and 16, FO 7/456; Bourqueney to Walewski, 29 and 30 June, Nos. 100–1, AMAE Autr. 460; Buol to Hübner, 3 July, PA IX/51.

70. Clarendon to Elliot, 10 July 1855, Clar. dep. c. 133; Redcliffe to Clarendon, 10 and 18 June, *ibid.* c. 40; Colquhoun to Clarendon, 11 July, No. 41, FO 78/1097.

71. Cowley to Clarendon, 3, 8, and 19 July 1855, Clar. dep. c. 34; Walewski to Bourqueney, 12 July, AMAE Autr. 460; Hübner to Buol, 13 July 1855, No. 68B and F, PA IX/50.

72. G. Esterházy to Buol, 29 June 1855, PA III/55; Jasmund, II, 209–11; Cowley to Clarendon, 5 and 8 July, Nos. 885 and 899, FO 519/5; Bourqueney to Walewski, 5 July, No. 103, AMAE Autr. 460.

73. *PAP*, III, 142–43, 145.

74. Elliot to Clarendon, 27 June and 4 July 1855, Clar. dep. c. 27; Bourqueney to Walewski, 14 and 18 July, Nos. 108–9, AMAE Autr. 460.

75. Clarendon to Cowley, 21 July 1855, FO 519/172; Elliot to Claren-

don, 18 July, Clar. dep. c. 27; Albert to Clarendon and Victoria to Clarendon, both 24 July, and Clarendon to Albert, 26 July, RA G35/ 66–67, 83.

76. Buol to Hübner, 22 July 1855, PA IX/51; Cowley to Clarendon, 22 July, Clar. dep. c. 34, and 23 July, No. 979, FO 519/5.

77. Palmerston to Clarendon, 24 July 1855, Clar. dep. c. 31; Clarendon to Palmerston, 31 July, Palm. Papers GC/CL/674.

78. Clarendon to Elliot, 25 and 31 July 1855, Clar. dep. c. 133; Colloredo to Buol, 2 Aug., PA VIII/42; Walewski to Bourqueney, 25 July, No. 58, AMAE Autr. 460.

79. See, for example, the quite different arguments he gave Palmerston (31 July 1855, Palm. Papers GC/CL/674), Cowley (28 July, FO 519/ 172), and Redcliffe (4 Aug., FO 352/42/II/5).

80. Palmerston to Clarendon, 29 July 1855, Clar. dep. c. 31; Clarendon to Colquhoun, 2 Aug., No. 16, and Colquhoun to Clarendon, 8 Sept., FO 78/1098.

81. Buol to Hübner, 13 Aug. 1855, and Hübner to Buol, 3 Aug., PA IX/51.

82. Henderson, 87–88.

83. Clarendon to Westmorland, 3 and 26 May and 1, 5, and 12 June 1855, Nos. 175, 198, tg, 212, and 221, FO 7/447–48, and 5 and 19 June, Clar. dep. c. 132–33; Elliot to Clarendon, 27 June, No. 8, FO 7/456; Buol to Francis Joseph, May 1855, PA XL/49; *Kempens Tagebuch*, 366.

84. Clarendon to Elliot, 27 Aug. and 11 Sept. 1855, Nos. 48 and 62, FO 7/449; Elliot to Clarendon, 5 Sept., No. 91, FO 7/457, and private letter, Clar. dep. c. 27. For evidence that Austria had good reason to fear the Anglo-Italian Legion and its anti-Austrian purposes, see Umberto Marcelli, *Cavour diplomatico*, 106–11, and *Rel. dipl. Aust.-Sard.*, IV, 216–17, 229–30, 232–34. On the recruitment of the Swiss Legion, see Gugolz, 35–48, 72–92, and Imlah, 94–98.

85. The Austrian documents on this affair, too numerous to list, are in PA VIII/42, PA XXXVIII/110, PA XL/83–84, and KA, FA III and IV AOK 1855/322/5–6; some are published in Nistor, 700–63. The British documents are mainly in FO 78/1098–99 and FO 7/448 and 455.

86. 3 Hansard, 139, 1754–74, 1782–1826, 1930–38. Russell's claim that Ali supported the Austrian ultimatum was correct—cf. Bourqueney to Walewski, 24 May 1855, No. 83, AMAE Autr. 459.

87. Gladstone to Aberdeen, 9 Aug. 1855, and Aberdeen to Gladstone, 3 Oct., Add. ms. 43071; Clarendon to Redcliffe, 6 and 11 Aug., FO 352/ 42/II/5; Clarendon to Cowley, 13 Aug., FO 519/172; *Greville Memoirs*, VII, 155–56, 167.

88. Elliot to Clarendon, 15 Aug. 1855, Clar. dep. c. 27, and same date, No. 69, FO 7/457; Argyll to Gladstone, 17 and 22 Aug. 1855, Add. ms. 44098.

89. Clarendon to Elliot, 10 July 1855, No. 11, FO 7/449; Elliot to Clarendon, 18 July, No. 37, FO 7/456.

90. Elliot to Clarendon, 27 June 1855, No. 9, *ibid.;* Clarendon to Elliot, 10 July, No. 9, FO 7/449.

91. Nistor, "Polenlegion," 96–98; Buol to Koller, 21 and 28 May 1855, PA XII/58.

92. Korisis, 48–49; Ritter, 298–312. Buol rejected a Prussian proposal to join in asking the Western powers to end their occupation of Greece (Buol to G. Esterházy, 6 Aug. 1855, GA Berlin/113; Buol to Hübner, 13 Aug., No. 4, PA IX/51).

93. Buol to Hübner, 27 July 1855, *ibid.;* Clarendon to Elliot, 17 July, No. 17, FO 7/449; Clarendon to Redcliffe, 4 Aug., FO 352/42/II/5; Koller's reports, Aug.–Dec. 1855, PA XII/54–56.

94. Ministerial conference protocol, 31 March 1855, MR Prot. 14; extracts of Bruck to Buol, 1 April and 15 Sept., and Buol to Bruck, 16 Oct., PA XL/3.

95. G. Esterházy to Rechberg, 16 June 1855, PA I/rot 533a; *PAP*, III, 161–62; Elliot to Clarendon, 5 Sept. 1855, No. 93, FO 7/457.

96. *Panmure Papers*, I, 324–29, 337–38, 348–49, 359–60; Redcliffe to Clarendon, 28 June and 14 and 20 Aug. 1855, Clar. dep. c. 40–41; Palmerston to Clarendon, 3 Aug., *ibid.* c. 31; Albert to Palmerston, 15 Aug., and Palmerston to Albert, 16 Aug., RA G36/69–70.

97. *Greville Memoirs*, VII, 152; Russell to the Very Rev. W. W. Clark, Dean of Bristol, 18 Aug. 1855, PRO 30/22/12F; Ashley, II, 100–1.

98. Eckhart, 181–83; Jasmund, II, 208–9, 242–51; Buol to Apponyi, 12 and 21 June and 12 July 1855, PA IV/23; Buol to G. Esterházy, 25 and 28 June and 12 July, GA Berlin/113; Rechberg to Prokesch, 20 June, PA II/34.

99. Krusemarck, 85–87; Jasmund, II, 299; Buol to G. Esterházy, 3 Aug. 1855, GA Berlin/113, and 5 July, PA III/58.

100. Jasmund, II, 298; Buol to Hübner, 13 Sept. 1855, PA IX/51; Elliot to Clarendon, 26 July and 29 Aug., Nos. 48–49 and 85, FO 7/456–57. Paskevich explained Austria's policy in exactly the contrary way: she was lying low because she was nearly bankrupt, Russia obviously invincible, and her allies powerless (Shcherbatov, VII, 327–29).

CHAPTER XIII

1. Bourqueney to Walewski, 12 and 18 Sept. 1855, Nos. 131 and 135, and De Serre to Walewski, 12 Oct., No. 145, AMAE Autr. 460–61.

2. Eckhart, 189; Elliot to Clarendon, 12 Sept. 1855, tg and No. 105, FO 7/457; Cowley to Clarendon, 16 Sept., No. 1223, FO 519/5; Bavarian chargé at Vienna von Wick to King Max, 28 Aug., GSA, MA I/597; Max to Pfordten, 23 Sept., *ibid.*

3. Koller to Buol, 20 Sept. 1855, No. 39B, PA XII/55; Austrian chargé at London Count Karolyi to Buol, 21 Sept., No. 105, PA VIII/41; Pfordten to Max, 18 Oct., GSA, MA I/597; François Charles-Roux, *Alexandre II, Gortchakoff, et Napoléon III*, 44–47.

4. Bourqueney to Walewski, 25 Sept. 1855, No. 139, AMAE Autr. 460; Cowley to Clarendon, 15 Oct. 1855, No. 1346, FO 519/5.

5. Werner to Buol, 10 and 17 Sept. 1855, Buol Nachlass (Geneva).

6. Hübner to Buol, 13 and 21 Sept. 1855, Nos. 87C and 89A, PA IX/50; Pfordten to Count Bray at Petersburg, 12 Nov., GSA, MA I/597; V. Boutenko, "Un projet d'alliance franco-russe après des documents inédits des archives russes," *Revue historique*, CLV (1927), 281–83; G. Raindre, "Les papiers inédits du Comte Walewski," *Revue de France*, V, No. 2 (Feb. 1925), 488–90; the Duc de Morny, *Une ambassade en Russie, 1856*, 7–56.

7. Buol to Hübner, 1 Oct. 1855, PA IX/51; Buol to Koller, 1 Oct., PA XII/58; Elliot to Clarendon, 3 Oct., No. 142, FO 7/458, and private, Clar. dep. c. 27.

8. Cowley to Clarendon, 13 Oct. 1855, Clar. dep. c. 34; De Serre to Walewski, 7 and 14 Oct., Nos. 142, 146, AMAE Autr. 461.

9. Hübner, I, 343–44, 349–50, 353–55; Buol to G. Esterházy, 20 Oct. 1855, PA III/58; De Serre to Walewski, 22 and 28 Oct., and Bourqueney to Walewski, 4, 6, 8, 9, 12, and 14 Nov., AMAE Autr. 461.

10. Buol to Hübner, 17 Nov. 1855, No. 1 with enclosures, PA IX/51.

11. Charles-Roux, *Alexandre II*, 56–61; Bourqueney to Walewski, 14 Nov. 1855, No. 160, AMAE Autr. 461.

12. Buol to Francis Joseph, 9 Nov. 1855, PA XL/49; Buol to Hübner, 17 Nov., PA IX/51; Hallberg, 106–7.

13. Nolfo, *Czartoryski*, 47–53, 147–51; Maxwell, II, 93–94; Clarendon to Cowley, 12 and 16 Sept. 1855, FO 519/172; Clarendon to Redcliffe, 17 Sept., FO 352/42/II/5; Palmerston to Clarendon, 16 Sept., Clar. dep. c. 31; Redcliffe to Clarendon, 13 Sept., *ibid.* c. 41.

14. Clarendon to Albert, 20 Sept. 1855, RA G38/20; Clarendon to Russell, 4 Oct., PRO 30/22/12F; Clarendon to Redcliffe, 27 Sept., FO 352/42/II/5.

15. S. Herbert to Graham, 30 June 1855, Graham Papers Reel 20.

16. Clarendon to Cowley, 24 Sept. 1855, FO 519/172; Clarendon to Elliot, 25 Sept., Clar. dep. c. 133.

17. Russell to Clarendon, 24 March and 5 and 23 April 1855, Nos. 35, 60, and 99, FO 7/463 and PRO 30/22/12D.

18. Bourqueney to Walewski, 3 and 6 Sept. 1855, and Walewski to Bourqueney, 22 Sept., AMAE Autr. 460; Elliot to Clarendon, 5 Sept., No. 95, FO 7/457; Hübner to Buol, 21 Sept., No. 89D, PA IX/50; Cowley to Clarendon, 9 Sept., Clar. dep. c. 34; Palmerston to Clarendon, 10 Sept., *ibid.* c. 31; Clarendon to Elliot, 11 Sept., *ibid.* c. 133.

19. For samples of Cavour's tactics in always pressing the sequestrations grievance, but carefully managing to keep it open for future leverage against Austria with the West, see Cavour, *Nuove lettere inedite* (Turin-Rome, 1895), 212–13, 223–25, and 235–37; *Cavour-Inghilterra*, I, 60, 64–69; and *Rel. dipl. GB-Sard.*, IV, 66, and V, 62–63. For an opposing argument, holding that Cavour genuinely sought a settlement and a rapprochement with Austria, but was defeated by Austrian intransigence, see Nolfo, *Europa*, 29–46, 97.

20. *Ibid.*, 410–12; Carlo Baudi di Vesme, "Il Regno delle due Sicilie durante la Guerra di Crimea," *Rassegna storica del Risorgimento*, XXXIX, No. 4 (1952), 395–97, 403; Ruggero Moscati, *Ferdinando II di Borbone*, 154–55.

21. Palmerston to Clarendon, 2 Sept. 1855, and Victoria to Clarendon, 3 Sept., RA G37/42 and 44; Clarendon to Cowley, 6 and 8 Sept., FO 519/172.

22. Palmerston to Clarendon, 9 Sept. 1855, Palm. Papers GC/CL/1380; Clarendon to Elliot, 11 Sept., Clar. dep. c. 133.

23. Moscati, 152–55; Buol to Hübner, 9, 15, and 17 Sept. and 17 Nov. 1855, PA IX/48 and 51; Clarendon to Elliot, 17 Sept. and 2 Oct., Nos. 69 and 85, FO 7/449, and 23 Oct., Clar. dep. c. 134; Elliot to Clarendon, 19 and 27 Sept., *ibid.* c. 27; Palmerston to Clarendon, 24 and 26 Oct., *ibid.* c. 31.

24. Francesco Sidari, *La crisi delle relazioni sardo-toscane nel 1855* (*l'affaire Casati*) (Padua, 1962); Marcelli, *Cavour*, 116–20; Nolfo, *Europa*, 138–39; *Rel. dipl. Aust.-Sard.*, IV, 430–513; *Rel. dipl. GB-Sard.*, V, 132–86; *Rel. dipl. Fr. Tosc.*, II, 474–515.

25. De Serre to Walewski, 15 Oct. 1855, tg and No. 147, AMAE Autr.

461; Cowley to Clarendon, 15 Oct., No. 1351, FO 519/5; Elliot to Clarendon, 17 Oct., Clar. dep. c. 27.

26. Palmerston to Clarendon, 21 Sept. and 14 and 18 Oct. 1855, *ibid.* c. 31; Clarendon to Palmerston, 14 and 16 Oct., Palm. Papers GC/CL/ 709–10.

27. Clarendon to Bloomfield, 17, 25, and 31 July and 7 Aug. 1855, Clar. dep. c. 133; Clarendon to Albert, 2 Aug., RA G36/17.

28. Clarendon to Loftus, 4 and 11 Sept. 1855, Clar. dep. c. 133; memorandum by Ernest, n.d., enclosed in Clarendon to Albert, 11 July, RA G34/56; Clarendon to Albert, 27 Aug. and 14 Sept.; Albert to Clarendon, 28 Aug. and 17 Sept.; and Clarendon to Victoria, 11 Sept., RA G37/3, 13, 87, 120, and 136.

29. Clarendon to Elliot, 6 Nov. 1855, and to Loftus, 23 Oct. and 6 Nov., Clar. dep. c. 134. On the generally hostile reaction to the Concordat at home and abroad, especially in Britain, see Erika Weinzierl-Fischer, *Die österreichischen Konkordate von 1855 und 1934* (Vienna, 1960); Martin, *Prince Consort*, III, 336–39.

30. Ritter, 365–86; Buol to Hübner, 23 Oct. 1855, PA IX/51; Palmerston to Clarendon, 7, 19, and 20 Sept. 1855, and Clarendon to Palmerston, 9 Sept., Clar. dep. c. 31; Clarendon to Cowley, 12 Nov., FO 519/172.

31. Clarendon to Elliot, 23 Oct. 1855, Clar. dep. c. 134.

32. Clarendon to Elliot, 9 and 15 Oct. 1855, Nos. 101 and 116, FO 7/449; *Panmure Papers*, I, 43. Actually, Buol wanted to restrict Austria's export of lead and saltpeter even more sharply for the sake of the Allies, but was defeated by Bruck and Toggenburg (see their correspondence in PA XII/221).

33. Clarendon to Elliot, 26 Oct. 1855, No. 127, FO 7/450; Clarendon to Seymour, 4 and 8 Jan. 1856, Nos. 6 and 12, FO 7/474; Palmerston to Clarendon, 5 Jan., Clar. dep. c. 49.

34. Buol to Colloredo, 5 Nov. 1855, No. 5, PA VIII/42; Clarendon to Elliot, 30 Oct., and to Seymour, 11 Dec., Clar. dep. c. 127.

35. Cowley to Clarendon, 30 Sept. 1855, *ibid.* c. 34; Palmerston to Clarendon, 9 and 16 Oct., *ibid.* c. 31.

36. Clarendon to Cowley, 17, 20, and 22 Oct. 1855, FO 519/172; Clarendon to Elliot, 23 Oct., Clar. dep. c. 134.

37. *Panmure Papers*, I, 425–26, 436–39, 442, 463–65; Clarendon to Cowley, 24 and 31 Oct. 1855, FO 519/172; Martin, *Prince Consort*, III, 317.

38. Cowley to Clarendon, 13 Nov. 1855, No. 1478, FO 519/5; Claren-

don to Cowley, 24 Oct. and 16 Nov. 1855, FO 519/172; Palmerston to Clarendon, 5 Nov. 1855, Clar. dep. c. 31.

39. Palmerston to Clarendon, 26 and 28 Oct. and 22 and 23 Nov. 1855, Clar. dep. c. 31; Clarendon to Redcliffe, 28 Dec., FO 352/42/II/5.

40. Lewis to Graham, 26 Sept. 1855, and Graham to Lewis, 1 Oct., Graham Papers Reel 20; Aberdeen to Gladstone, 19 Oct., and Gladstone to Aberdeen, 3 Nov., Add. ms. 43071; Gladstone to Graham, 13 Nov., Add. ms. 44163.

41. Fitzmaurice, I, 120–23; Cowley to Clarendon, 24 Sept. 1855, No. 1273, FO 519/5; Clarendon to Redcliffe, 3 Nov., FO 352/42/II/5.

42. Redcliffe to Clarendon, 4 Oct. and 4 Dec. 1855, Clar. dep. c. 41.

43. *Greville Memoirs*, VII, 179; Cowley to Redcliffe, 28 Oct. and 3 Nov. 1855, FO 352/41/I/1; Cowley to Clarendon, 11 and 14 Nov., Clar. dep. c. 35.

44. Maxwell, II, 103; Clarendon to Cowley, 12 Nov. 1855, FO 519/172; Clarendon to Palmerston, 17 Nov., Palm. Papers GC/CL/733.

45. *QVL*, III, 191–93; Clarendon to Palmerston, 18 Nov. 1855, Clar. dep. c. 134.

46. Clarendon to Palmerston, 21 Nov. 1855, Palm. Papers GC/CL/737.

47. Clarendon to Cowley, 19, 20, and 21 Nov. 1855, FO 519/172; Cowley to Clarendon, 18 and 19 Nov., Clar. dep. c. 35; Clarendon to Redcliffe, 19 Nov., FO 352/42/II/5. In contrast to Nolfo (*Europa*, 127–28), who thinks the private British documents show a greater readiness on Britain's part to compromise than she displayed publicly, I must agree with Sidney Herbert, who after an interview with Palmerston in November described him as absolutely wild on war and peace terms (Ab. Corr. 1855–1860, 120–23).

48. Ashley, II, 103–4; Palmerston to Clarendon, 20 Nov. 1855, Clar. dep. c. 31.

49. Clarendon to Palmerston, 22 Nov. 1855, Palm. Papers GC/CL/739; Cowley to Clarendon, 22 Nov., No. 1522, FO 519/5, and 21 and 22 Nov., Clar. dep. c. 35; Martin, *Prince Consort*, III, 324–26.

50. *QVL*, III, 195–96; Maxwell, II, 104; Clarendon to Redcliffe, 23 Nov. 1855, FO 352/42/II/5; Cowley to Clarendon, 25 Nov., Clar. dep. c. 35; Palmerston to Clarendon, 23 and 29 Nov., *ibid*. c. 31.

51. MR Prot. 14.

52. Bourqueney to Walewski, 22 and 27 Nov. and 3 Dec. 1855, Nos. 169–70 and 2 tgs, AMAE Autr. 461; Cowley to Clarendon, 25 Nov., No. 1536, FO 519/5; Clarendon to Cowley, 10 Dec., FO 519/172; Clarendon to Redcliffe, 3 Dec., FO 352/42/II/5.

53. Clarendon to Cowley, 28, 29, and 30 Nov. and 10 Dec. 1855, FO 519/172; Clarendon to Elliot, 27 Nov., and to Seymour, 4 Dec., Clar. dep. c. 134.

54. Hübner to Buol, 26 Nov. and 3 Dec. 1855, Nos. 108A–B and 110 and private letter, PA IX/50–51; Cowley to Clarendon, 23, 27, and 28 Nov., Nos. 1525, 1547, and 1551, FO 519/5; Clarendon to Redcliffe, 26 Nov., FO 352/42/II/5.

55. Walewski to Bourqueney, tg, 24 Nov. 1855, AMAE Autr. 461; Clarendon to Victoria, 24 Nov.; Victoria to Clarendon, 29 Nov.; and Albert to Prince William, 30 Dec., RA G40/111, G41/22, and G42/47.

56. Cowley to Clarendon, 5 and 9 Dec. 1855, Nos. 1574 and 1585, FO 519/5; Clarendon to Cowley, 5 Dec., FO 519/172; Clarendon to Seymour, 3 Dec., No. 7, FO 7/450.

57. Victoria to Clarendon, 7 and 14 Dec. 1855, RA G41/43 and 62; Clarendon to Palmerston, 12 and 13 Dec., Palm. Papers GC/CL/758–59; Palmerston to Clarendon, 13 Dec., Clar. dep. c. 31; Maxwell, II, 107.

58. Walewski to Bourqueney, 9 Dec. 1855, No. 76, and Bourqueney to Walewski, 13 and 15 Dec., 2 tgs, AMAE Autr. 461; Seymour to Clarendon, 12 Dec., No. 18, FO 7/460.

59. Nolfo, *Europa*, 156–57; Cowley to Clarendon, 10, 11, and 18 Dec. 1855, Clar. dep. c. 35; Cowley to Redcliffe, 18 Dec., FO 352/42/I/1; Clarendon to Cowley, 14 Dec., FO 519/172.

60. Bourqueney to Walewski, 12 Dec. 1855, 2 tgs, AMAE Autr. 461.

61. Palmerston to Clarendon, 8 Dec. 1855, Clar. dep. c. 31.

62. *Greville Memoirs*, VII, 177–78; Greville to the Duke of Bedford, 17 Dec. 1855, PRO 30/22/12G. For the bad effect Palmerston's disclosures had in Germany, see G. Esterházy to Rechberg, 15 Dec., PA I/rot 533a.

63. Buol to G. Esterházy, 16 Dec. 1855, PA III/55.

64. Guichen, *Crimée*, 342–44; Langenau to Buol, 29 March, 6 April, and 21 May 1855, PA XXVI/12.

65. Count Revertera to Buol, 27 Aug., 29 and 30 Oct., and 2, 5, and 19 Nov. 1855, and Langenau to Buol, 29 Nov. and 18 and 25 Dec., *ibid.*; Buol to Langenau, 22 Dec., *ibid.*

66. Werner to G. Esterházy, 10 and 21 Sept. 1855, GA Berlin/113.

67. Loftus to Clarendon, 22 and 29 Sept. 1855, Clar. dep. c. 27.

68. *PAP*, III, 171–72; Buol to G. Esterházy, 29 Nov. 1855, PA III/58; Lerchenfeld to King Max, 1 and 7 Nov., GSA, MA I/597.

69. Buol to Apponyi, 16 Dec. 1855, PA IV/23; Buol to G. Esterházy, 16 Dec., No. 55, GA Berlin/113.

70. Fuchs, 76–85; Buol to Apponyi, 10 Oct. 1855, PA IV/23; Buol to

G. Esterházy, 17 Nov. and 16 Dec. (No. 3), GA Berlin/113; Lerchenfeld to Max, 7 Sept. and 13 Oct., GSA, MA III/2423 and I/597.

71. Buol to G. Esterházy, 16 and 24 Dec. 1855, No. 4 and tg, GA Berlin/113; Esterházy to Buol, 21 and 26 Dec., PA III/54; Francis Joseph to Frederick William, 10 Dec., Kab. Arch. Geh. Akt. 7.

72. Johann I of Saxony, *Briefwechsel*, 350–59; *PAP*, III, 179–80.

73. *PAP*, III, 176–79; Frederick William to Francis Joseph, 30 Dec. 1855, Kab. Arch. Geh. Akt. 7; G. Esterházy to Buol, 29 Dec., PA III/54.

74. Apponyi to Buol, 26 Dec. 1855, No. 62A–B, PA IV/23; Kuefstein to Buol, 27 and 30 Dec., PA V/21; Buol to Rechberg, 10 Jan. 1856, PA I/rot 533c.

75. Eckhart, 192–201; Buol to G. Esterházy, 10 and 14 Jan. 1856, GA Berlin/114 and PA III/58.

76. Clarendon to Redcliffe, 7 Jan. 1856, FO 352/44/1.

77. Clarendon to Redcliffe, 21 and 31 Dec. 1855, FO 352/42/II/5; Clarendon to Cowley, 31 Dec., FO 519/172; the Duke of Bedford to Russell, 4 Jan. 1856, PRO 30/22/13A; Clarendon to Seymour, 1 Jan., Clar. dep. c. 135.

78. Colloredo to Buol, 1 and 4 Jan. 1856, Nos. 1A–B and 3B, PA VIII/42, and 4 Jan., PA VIII/43; Clarendon to Seymour, 1 Jan., attached to Clarendon to Cowley, 7 Jan., FO 519/173; Fitzmaurice, I, 135.

79. Clarendon to Cowley, 7 and 11 Jan. 1856, FO 519/173; Clarendon to Seymour, 8 Jan., No. 16, FO 7/474, and private letter, Clar. dep. c. 135.

80. Seymour to Clarendon, 7–9 and 15 Jan. 1856, *ibid.* c. 46, and 9, 13, and 15 Jan., No. 19 and 2 tgs, FO 7/480.

81. Clarendon to Seymour, 2 tgs, 15 Jan. 1856, FO 7/474; Seymour to Clarendon, 16 Jan., Nos. 32–34, 39, and 44, FO 7/380.

82. Seymour to Clarendon, 16 Jan. 1856, No. 48, *ibid.*

83. Buol to Hübner, 9, 12, and 18 Jan. 1856, PA IX/54; Bourqueney to Walewski, 13 and 15 Jan., AMAE Autr. 463; Cowley to Clarendon, 10 Jan., No. 62, FO 519/5.

84. Cowley to Clarendon, 12 Jan. 1856, No. 73, FO 519/5, and 8, 9, 10, and 13 Jan., Clar. dep. c. 51.

85. *QVL*, III, 205–6; Hübner to Buol, 13 and 17 Jan. 1856, PA IX/52, 15 Jan., PA IX/54.

86. *QVL*, III, 207–9; Clarendon to Victoria, 15 and 16 Jan. 1856, RA G42/41 and G43/3; Clarendon to Seymour and to Bloomfield, both 15 Jan., Clar. dep. c. 135; Clarendon to Cowley, 14 and 15 Jan., FO 519/173; Fitzmaurice, I, 142–43.

87. Palmerston to Clarendon, 16 Jan. 1856, Clar. dep. c. 49.

88. It would take too long to discuss the views of members of the peace party on the various proposals (the material is found mainly in *Greville Memoirs*, VII, 168–90; PRO 30/22/12G and 13A; Add ms. 43071 and 44098; and Graham Papers Reels 20–21). One point that emerges clearly is that the doves would have been just as willing to break the Allies' agreement with Austria in order to facilitate peace as the hawks were ready to do so to prolong the war.

89. Charles-Roux, *Alexandre II*, 61–63; Tatishchev, *Aleksandr II*, I, 181–82; Buol to Hübner, 11 Dec. 1855, PA IX/51.

90. Tatishchev, *Aleksandr II*, I, 178–79; Rechberg to Buol, 26 Dec. 1855, PA II/34.

91. Charles-Roux, *Alexandre II*, 63–65; Buol to V. Esterházy, 16 Dec, 1855, Nos. 1–3, PA X/42.

92. Tatishchev, *Aleksandr II*, I, 182–85; Jasmund, II, 315; V. Esterházy to Buol, 12 Jan. 1856, PA X/44.

93. Buol to V. Esterházy, 12 and 14 Jan. 1856, PA X/43; Buol to Hübner, 12 Jan., PA IX/54; Buol to Prokesch, 14 Jan., PA XII/60; protocol of 15 Jan., MR Prot. 15.

94. Meyendorff, III, 214–17; Jomini, II, 361–69; Tarle, II, 548–50. The best account of the whole process by which Russia came to accept defeat is in Baumgart.

95. Clarendon to Palmerston, 12 Aug. and 15 Sept. 1855, Palm. Papers GC/CL/678 and 691; Palmerston to Clarendon, 12 Aug. and 13 and 16 Sept., Clar. dep. c. 31; *QVL*, III, 182–84.

96. Cowley to Clarendon, 17 Sept. 1855, No. 1229, FO 519/5.

97. Hübner to Buol, 3 and 5 Sept. 1855, PA IX/50.

98. H. W. V. Temperley, "The Last Phase of Stratford de Redcliffe, 1855–1858," *English Historical Review*, XLVII (1932), 219–21.

99. Redcliffe to Clarendon, 10 June 1855, FO 352/42/II/7; Clarendon to Palmerston, 2 June, Palm. Papers GC/CL/646; Palmerston to Redcliffe, 12 June, Add. ms. 48579.

100. Koller to Buol, 16 Aug. and 6, 13, and 20 Sept. 1855, Nos. 33C, 37C, 38G, and 39C, PA XII/55; Redcliffe to Clarendon, 3, 12, and 29 Sept., and Clarendon to Redcliffe, 3, 10, and 22 Sept. and 20 Oct. 1855, FO 352/42/II/5; Clarendon to Russell, 26 Sept., PRO 30/22/12F.

101. Redcliffe to Clarendon, 24 March 1855, FO 352/42/II/7; Clarendon to Palmerston, 29 June, Palm. Papers GC/CL/662; Curtiss, 169–74, 315–20.

102. Clarendon to Redcliffe, 27 Oct. 1855, FO 352/42/II/5; Clarendon to Palmerston, Paris, 22 and 30 Aug., Palm. Papers GC/CL/684–85.

103. Clarendon to Redcliffe, 2 April 1855, FO 352/42/II/5.

104. Redcliffe to Clarendon, 25 July and 9 Oct. 1855, *ibid.;* 13 Sept., No. 690, FO 78/1086.

105. Palmerston to Clarendon, 30 Aug. 1855, Clar. dep. c. 31; Redcliffe to Clarendon, 26 and 29 Nov., Nos. 977 and 984, FO 78/1092; Koller to Buol, 5 July and 8 Nov., Nos. 27L and 48D, PA XII/54-55.

106. Nolfo, *Czartoryski,* 33-38; Marceli Handelsman, "La question polonaise et les origines du problème bulgare," *Revue historique,* CLXIX (1932), 276-79.

107. Henry Clifford, *Henry Clifford v.c., His Letters and Sketches from the Crimea* (London, 1956), 126, 149, *et passim.*

108. Clarendon to Redcliffe, 23 and 28 July, 12 and 19 Nov. 1855, FO 352/42/II/5; Redcliffe to Clarendon, 15 Nov., *ibid.* 7; *Panmure Papers,* I, 503.

109. The evidence on this point is overwhelming: Austria's efforts to get action on the Fourth Point at the Vienna Conferences; constant correspondence between Buol and Bruck and Koller to settle difficulties between Turkey and the Montenegrins, Bosnians, Serbs, and Albanians (PA XII/55 and 57-58); encouragement to the Sultan to set up a Latin Patriarchate so that no Catholic power, including Austria, could intervene unilaterally on behalf of Catholics; Buol's repeated pleas for co-operation from Western governments and their agents for protection of Christians and promoting reform in Turkey, and so on.

110. Koller to Buol, 13 Sept. and 22 Oct. 1855, No. 38D and 50F, PA XII/55; Buol to Koller, 1 and 29 Oct., PA XII/58; Buol to Hübner, 1 and 5 Nov., PA IX/55.

111. Riker, *Roumania,* 33-34; Clarendon to Cowley, 9 Nov. 1855, with enclosure of Colquhoun to Clarendon, 13 Oct., FO 519/172.

112. Guichen, *Crimée,* 388; Bourqueney to Walewski, 14 Nov. 1855, No. 161, AMAE Autr. 461; Buol to Hübner, 17 Nov., No. 5, PA IX/51; Palmerston to Clarendon, 10 Nov., Clar. dep. c. 31; Redcliffe to Clarendon, 12 and 29 Nov., *ibid.* c. 41.

113. Clarendon to Cowley, 14 Nov. 1855, FO 519/172; Cowley to Clarendon, 24 Oct. and 20 Nov. 1855, Nos. 1399 and 1514, FO 519/5; Koller to Buol, 15 Nov., No. 49B, PA XII/55.

114. Clarendon to Redcliffe, 16 Nov. 1855, FO 352/42/II/5; Clarendon to Cowley, 16 Nov., FO 519/172.

115. Instructions for Prokesch, 30 Nov. 1855, PA XII/58; Buol to Hübner, 3 Dec., Nos. 1-3, PA IX/55; Clarendon to Redcliffe, 10 Dec., FO 352/42/II/5.

116. Clarendon to Redcliffe, 14 and 17 Dec. 1855, *ibid.;* Clarendon to Seymour, 13, 14, and 26 Dec., tg and Nos. 23 and 49, FO 7/450, and 26 Dec., Clar. dep. c. 134.

117. Cornelia C. Bodea, ed., *Corespondenţa politica (1855–1859)*, 39, 45, *et passim;* Koller to Buol, 22 and 29 Nov. 1855, Nos. 50G–L and 52G, and Prokesch to Buol, 27 Dec., No. 3C, PA XII/55.

118. Clarendon to Redcliffe, 4 Jan. 1856, FO 352/44/1.

119. Redcliffe to Clarendon, 27 Dec. 1855, FO 352/42/II/7; Cowley to Clarendon, 31 Dec., Clar. dep. c. 35; Clarendon to Cowley, 1 Jan. 1856, FO 519/173.

120. Clarendon to Redcliffe, 28 Dec. 1855, FO 352/42/II/5.

121. Prokesch to Buol, 3 and 10 Jan. 1856, Nos. 5B and 7A–B, PA XII/56; Clarendon to Redcliffe, 11 Jan., FO 352/44/1; Palmerston to Clarendon, 9 Jan., Clar. dep. c. 49.

CHAPTER XIV

1. Seymour to Clarendon, 22 Jan. 1856, No. 52, FO 7/480; Hübner to Buol, 17 Jan., PA IX/54; Apponyi to Buol, 19 Jan., No. 4A, PA IV/24; G. Esterházy to Buol, 18 Jan., PA III/56.

2. Buol to Hübner, 18 Jan. 1856, PA IX/54; *QVL*, III, 209–11; Palmerston to Clarendon, 17 Jan., Clar. dep. c. 49; Palmerston to Seymour, 24 Jan., *ibid.* c. 46 (partly printed in Ashley, II, 105–7).

3. Cowley to Clarendon, 18 Jan. 1856, Clar. dep. c. 51.

4. Clarendon to Cowley, 18 Jan. 1856, FO 519/173; Clarendon to Palmerston, 17 Jan., Palm. Papers GC/CL/782; Martin, *Prince Consort*, III, 354–55.

5. Cowley to Clarendon, 17 and 19 Jan. 1856, Nos. 89, 96, and 102, FO 519/5, and 17 and 18 Jan., Clar. dep. c. 51.

6. Hübner, I, 383–87; Walewski to Bourqueney, 17, 18, and 20 Jan. 1856, 2 tgs and Nos. 4 and 6, AMAE Autr. 463; Hübner to Buol, 19 Jan., No. 7A–B, PA IX/52.

7. Bourqueney to Walewski, 21 Jan. 1856, 2 tgs and No. 13, AMAE Autr. 453 and 463; Seymour to Clarendon, 21 and 22 Jan., 3 tgs and Nos. 53–54, FO 7/480, and 22–23 and 28 Jan., Clar. dep. c. 46.

8. Clarendon to Palmerston, 20 Jan. 1856, Palm. Papers GC/CL/785; Clarendon to Seymour, 22 Jan., Clar. dep. c. 135.

9. Palmerston to Clarendon, 21 Jan. 1856, Clar. dep. c. 49; Clarendon to Seymour, tg, 21 Jan., FO 7/474.

10. Seymour to Clarendon, 23 and 24 Jan. 1856, Nos. 60, 63, and 66, FO 7/480.

11. Clarendon to Seymour, 25 Jan. 1856, No. 52 and 54–55, FO 7/474, and 29 Jan., Clar. dep. c. 135. For Seymour's defense of himself and Buol, see Seymour to Clarendon, 30 Jan. and 5 and 6 Feb., Clar. dep. c. 46.

12. Clarendon to Seymour, 24, 26, and 30 Jan. and 5 Feb. 1856, 3 tgs and Nos. 72 and 80, FO 7/474.

13. Cowley to Clarendon, 25 Jan. 1856, No. 140, FO 519/5; Hübner to Buol, 26 Jan., No. 13, PA IX/52, and 25 Jan., PA IX/54; Palmerston to Clarendon, 23 Jan., Clar. dep. c. 49; memorandum by Albert, 25 Jan., RA G43/70.

14. Clarendon to Cowley, 21 Jan. 1856, with enclosure of Palmerston to Clarendon, same date, FO 519/173.

15. Cowley to Clarendon, 25 Jan. 1856, Clar. dep. c. 51, and 27 and 28 Jan, Nos. 152 and 154, FO 519/5.

16. Clarendon to Cowley, 24 and 25 Jan. 1856, FO 519/173; Clarendon to Victoria, 29 Jan., RA G43/95.

17. Palmerston to Victoria, 26 Jan. 1856, RA G43/73; Cowley to Clarendon, 28 Jan., Clar. dep. c. 51.

18. Colloredo to Buol, 29 Jan. 1856, No. 9A, PA VIII/42; Cowley to Clarendon, 29 Jan. and 2 Feb., Nos. 164 and 187, FO 519/5; Clarendon to Redcliffe, 4 Feb., FO 352/44/1; Buol to Hübner, 1 Feb., PA IX/54.

19. See Prokesch's reports to Buol, 17 Jan. to 7 Feb. 1856, Nos. 8–12, PA XII/56; Cowley to Clarendon, 31 Jan., No. 182, FO 519/5.

20. Testa, V, 132–37; Temperley, "Last Phase of Redcliffe," 225–31. On the decree itself and its reception in Turkey, see R. H. Davison, *Reform in the Ottoman Empire 1856–1876*, 52–80.

21. Nistor, 870–71; Austrian mémoire, n.d., AMAE Mem. et doc. Turquie 55; convolute entitled "Die Frage der Besteuerung der griechischen Kloster in der Moldau und Walachei," PA XII/213. Prokesch's papers (Prokesch Nachlass 26/8) show a keen interest in social problems in the Principalities, including that of discrimination against Jews.

22. French memoranda on the Principalities, one undated, but late Dec. 1855, the other 7 Jan. 1856, AMAE Mem. et doc. Turquie 55; Prokesch to Buol, 27 Dec. 1855, No. 3A, PA XII/55.

23. Buol to Colloredo, 9 Jan. 1856, No. 4 with enclosure, PA VIII/43; Buol to Prokesch, 14 Jan., Nos. 2–3, PA XII/60; Clarendon to Palmerston and Palmerston to Clarendon, both 22 Oct. 1855, Palm. Papers GC/CL/713 and Clar. dep. c. 31.

24. Colquhoun to Clarendon, 8 Aug. 1855 and 23 March 1856, FO 78/1098 and 1199; Colquhoun to Redcliffe, 10 Jan. 1856, *ibid.* 1199; Clarendon to Redcliffe, 1 Sept. 1855, FO 352/42/II/5.

25. Nistor, 883–88; *Acte și documente*, II, 921–48; Prokesch to Buol 7, 11, and 12 Feb. 1856, Nos. 12E, 13B, and 14A–B, PA XII/56.

26. W. G. East, *The Union of Moldavia and Wallachia*, 40–44; *Acte și documente*, II, 949–54.

27. Jasmund, II, 492–95; Werner to Prokesch, 18 Feb. 1856, PA XII/60.

28. Nistor publishes the most important of many documents on this issue in the Vienna archives (pp. 892–96, 904–7, 929–34, 940–45, 953–59); see also Jasmund, II, 495–504, and Werner to Buol, 25 Feb. 1856, PA XL/277l.

29. Buol to Hübner, 18 and 30 Jan. 1856, PA IX/54; Werner to Buol, tg, 19 Feb., PA XII/220.

30. Jasmund, II, 321; Buol to G. Esterházy, 25 Jan. and 7 Feb. 1856, and Esterházy to Buol, 16 Feb., PA III/58; Buol to Rechberg, 7 Feb., PA I/rot 533c; *PAP*, III, 200–1, 209–10.

31. Krusemarck, 90–92; G. Esterházy to Buol, 5 Feb. 1856, No. 6, and Buol to Esterházy, 3 Feb., GA Berlin/114.

32. John of Saxony, *Briefwechsel*, 359–62; G. Esterházy to Buol, 15 Feb. 1856, No. 8, GA Berlin/114; Eckhart, 204–7.

33. Palmerston to Clarendon, 24 Jan. 1856, Clar. dep. c. 49; Clarendon to Cowley, 28 Jan., FO 519/173; Cowley to Clarendon, 29 Jan., Clar. dep. c. 51, and 5 Feb., No. 204, FO 519/5.

34. Hübner to Buol, 30 Jan. and 6 Feb. 1856, Nos. 12B and 13A–C, PA IX/52; Buol to Francis Joseph, 24 Feb., PA XII/220; *Cavour-Inghilterra*, I, 206–7.

35. PA XII/219 (published in Nistor, 874–77). For Coronini's relentless activity in the Principalities, and complaints of lack of support from Vienna, see *ibid.*, 827–31, 848–50, 959–62, *et passim*.

36. "Punctation für die kaiserlichen Bevollmächtigten bei den Pariser-Konferenzen," 11 Feb. 1856, PA XII/218.

37. Werner to Buol, 28 Feb. 1856, PA XII/220.

38. Protocol of ministerial conference, 11 Feb. 1856, PA XII/219.

39. Tarle, II, 555–56; "K istorii Parizhsogo mira 1856 g," *Krasnyi Arkhiv*, no. 75 (1936), 13–18; Boutenko, 287–89.

40. *Panmure Papers*, II, 56–57, 60–62, 73–80, 92; Clarendon to Bloomfield, 22 Jan. 1856, Clar. dep. c. 135; Palmerston to Victoria, 29 Jan., RA G43/93; Vitzthum, I, 193–97.

41. See *Greville Memoirs*, VII, 193–203, especially his remark of January 22: "What the people of England would really like would be to engage France to continue, and to issue a joint declaration of war against Austria and Prussia" (p. 193).

42. Clarendon to Redcliffe, 11 Feb. 1856, and Redcliffe to Cowley, 13 Feb., FO 352/44/1–2.

43. Palmerston to Clarendon, 25 Feb. 1856, Clar. dep. c. 49.

44. Clarendon to Seymour, 4 and 12 Feb. 1856, *ibid.* c. 135; Seymour to Clarendon, 6 Feb., *ibid.* c. 46, and 10 Feb., No. 120, FO 7/481; Clarendon to Redcliffe, 15 and 19 Feb., FO 352/44/1; *QVL*, III, 223.

45. Buol to Francis Joseph, 20 and 24 Feb. 1856, PA XL/49; Buol and Hübner to Francis Joseph, 24 Feb., No. 1, PA XII/220.

46. *Krasnyi Arkhiv*, 18–23, 27–29; Clarendon to Palmerston, 17, 21, 22–23, and 23 Feb. 1856, Palm. Papers GC/CL/794, 798–800.

47. Clarendon to Seymour, 5 Feb. 1856, No. 77, FO 7/474.

48. Buol and Hübner to Francis Joseph, 26 and 28 Feb. 1856, PA XII/219; *Krasnyi Arkhiv*, 24–26. The Congress protocols are in Testa, V, 47–127.

49. Cowley to Clarendon, 26 Feb. 1856, No. 250, FO 519/5.

50. Buol to Francis Joseph, 26 Feb. 1856, PA XL/49; Clarendon to Palmerston, 24–29 Feb., Palm. Papers GC/CL/802–04, 807–9; Palmerston to Clarendon, 25, 28, and 29 Feb. and 1 and 2 March, Clar. dep. c. 49; Victoria to Palmerston, 25 and 28 Feb., and Palmerston to Victoria, 25 and 28 Feb., RA G45/29–30, 57, and 60.

51. Buol to Francis Joseph, 28 Feb. 1856, PA XL/49.

52. Julian Fane's memorandum, 29 Feb. 1856, enclosed in Clarendon to Palmerston, 1 March, Palm. Papers GC/CL/811.

53. Werner to Buol, tg, 3 March 1856, PA XII/220.

54. Clarendon to Palmerston, 1 March 1856, Palm. Papers GC/CL/810–11; Buol and Hübner to Francis Joseph, 2 March, No. 4B, PA XII/219; *Krasnyi Arkhiv*, 30–31.

55. Maxwell, II, 16–18; Clarendon to Palmerston, 2 March 1856, Palm. Papers GC/CL/812.

56. Redcliffe to Clarendon, 6 March 1856, FO 352/44/1; Buol and Hübner to Francis Joseph, 5 and 7 March, Nos. 5–6, PA XII/219; Clarendon to Palmerston, 6 March, Palm. Papers GC/CL/816.

57. Clarendon to Cowley, 3 and 7 March 1856, FO 519/173; Clarendon to Palmerston, 5 and 8 March, Palm. Papers GC/CL/815 and 818; Palmerston to Clarendon, 8 March 1856, Clar. dep. c. 49; Buol to Francis Joseph, 9 March, No. 2, PA XL/49.

58. Clarendon to Palmerston, 10 March 1856, Palm. Papers GC/CL/820; Buol and Hübner to Francis Joseph, 12 March, PA XII/219.

59. *Krasnyi Arkhiv*, 31–33, 37–43; Buol and Hübner to Francis Joseph, 9 March 1856, No. 7A–B, PA XII/219.

60. East, 54–60, 62–65; N. Corivan, "Deux documents sur le choix d'un prince étranger en 1856," *Revue historique du Sud-Est Européen*, VII (1931), 1–5; various memoranda by Rumanian émigrés, AMAE Mem. et doc. Turquie 54. For Cavour's and Azeglio's activity in behalf of Sardinia's aggrandizement, see *Cavour-Inghilterra*, I, 193–276 *passim*.

61. Clarendon to Palmerston, 5 March 1856, Palm. Papers GC/CL/815; Clarendon to Redcliffe, 19 and 23 Feb., FO 352/44/1; Clarendon to Cowley, 24 Jan., FO 519/173.

62. Palmerston to Clarendon, 1, 7, 8, and 9 March 1856, Clar. dep. c. 49.

63. Cowley to Clarendon, 5 March 1856, No. 279, FO 519/5.

64. Werner to Buol, 25 Feb. 1856, PA XL/277l; Werner to Prokesch, 25 Feb., Nos. 21 and 23, and Werner to Buol, tgs, 5 and 9 March, PA XII/220; Buol to Francis Joseph, 2 March, PA XL/49.

65. Buol to Francis Joseph, 9 March 1856, No. 7, *ibid.;* Buol and Hübner to Francis Joseph, 9 March, No. 7A–B, PA XII/219.

66. Werner to Buol, tg, 9 March 1856, PA XII/220.

67. East, 46–50; Buol and Hübner to Francis Joseph, 12 March 1856, No. 8, PA XII/219; Buol to Francis Joseph, 13 March, PA XL/49; Werner to Buol, 13 March, No. 70, PA XII/59; Julian Fane, "Memorandum of a conversation with Count Buol," 17 March, Clar. dep. c. 46.

68. *Krasnyi Arkhiv*, 35–39; Buol to Francis Joseph, 13 March 1856, No. 1, PA XL/49, and same date, Nos. 9A–C, PA XII/219; Werner to Buol, tg, 16 March, *ibid.;* Buol and Hübner to Francis Joseph, 23 and 26 March, Nos. 12C and 14A, *ibid.*

69. Clarendon to Cowley, 12 March 1856, FO 519/173; Clarendon to Palmerston, 13 and 17 March, Palm. Papers GC/CL/823 and 828.

70. Eckhart, 209–11; Buol and Hübner to Francis Joseph, 19 and 23 March 1856, Nos. 11A and 12A, PA XII/219; Clarendon to Walewski, 21 March 1856, Palm. Papers GC/CL/833; Buol to G. Esterházy, 19 March, PA III/58.

71. *Panmure Papers*, II, 154; Clarendon to Palmerston, 18 March 1856, Palm. Papers GC/CL/829; Buol to Francis Joseph, 19, 23, and 26 March, PA XL/49.

72. Clarendon to Palmerston, 23 and 24 March 1856, Palm. Papers GC/CL/835–36; *Greville Memoirs*, VII, 219–20; Clarendon to Cowley, 16 March, FO 519/173.

73. Jasmund, II, 338–61; Clarendon to Cowley, 16 March 1856, FO 519/173; Palmerston to Clarendon, 26 March, Clar. dep. c. 49; Buol to Francis Joseph, 29 March, PA XL/49; Buol and Hübner to Francis Joseph, 28 March, No. 16, PA XII/219; *Panmure Papers*, II, 166–69.

74. *Greville Memoirs*, VII, 209–17. Cowley offered to resign immediately after the peace treaty, but quickly withdrew the offer at Clarendon's request. To Clarendon, 31 March and 2 April 1856, Clar. dep. c. 51.

75. Martin, *Prince Consort*, III, 470; Redcliffe to Clarendon, 24 April 1856, FO 352/44/1; *QVL*, III, 233; *Greville Memoirs*, VII, 222; Clarendon to Palmerston, 1 April, Palm. Papers GC/CL/847.

76. *QVL*, III, 234–35; Palm. Papers GC/CL/846.

77. *Greville Memoirs*, VII, 218.

78. H. W. V. Temperley, "The Peace of Paris and Its Execution," *Journal of Modern History*, IV (1932), 402–03; Buol to Francis Joseph, 30 March 1856, PA XL/49; Buol to the Foreign Ministry, tg, 11 April, PA XII/220; De Serre to Walewski, 6 April, No. 36, AMAE Autr. 463.

CHAPTER XV

1. Werner to Buol, tg, 6 April 1856, PA XII/220.

2. *Cavour-Inghilterra*, I, 70, 72–73, 86–91, 106–12; Nolfo, *Europa*, 96–107; *Rel. dipl. GB-Sard.*, V, 115–21; *Rel. dipl. Aust.-Sard.*, IV, 205–8.

3. *Cavour-Inghilterra*, I, 126–27, 141, 145–46.

4. M. B. Urban, *British Policy and Opinion on the Unification of Italy*, 18–21; Chiala, *Lettere di Cavour*, II, 375–76; Nolfo, *Europa*, 142–58; Aberdeen to Graham, 5 Dec. 1855, Graham Papers Reel 20.

5. Nolfo, *Europa*, 164–89; Victoria to Clarendon, 7 Feb. 1856, RA G44/40; *Rel. dipl. GB-Sard.*, V, 211; Marcelli, *Cavour*, 151–54.

6. *Cavour-Inghilterra*, I, 47–48, 154–56, 185; *Rel. dipl. GB-Sard.*, V, 200–5.

7. *Cavour-Inghilterra*, I, 160, 164, 177–79, 208–9; Nolfo, *Europa*, 201–5; *Rel. dipl. GB-Sard.*, V, 218–20; Clarendon to Redcliffe, 1 Feb. 1856, FO 352/44/1; Clarendon to Cowley, 5 Feb., FO 519/173.

8. Cavour-Inghilterra, I, 158–276 *passim*; Marcelli, *Cavour*, 123–27, 132–34, 141–42, 178–186, 206–8; Palmerston to Clarendon, 30 March 1856, Clar. dep. c. 49.

9. Istituto Storico italiano per l'Età moderna e contemporanea, *La Guerra del 1859 nei rapporti tra la Francia e l'Europa*, 3d ser., 1848–1860, Vol. I (Rome, 1961), 81–82; *Cavour-Inghilterra*, I, 407–9, 433; Nolfo, *Europa*, 187, 210–13, 219–20.

10. MR Prot. 14; *Kempens Tagebuch*, 379, 423.

11. Elliot to Clarendon, 31 Oct. 1855, Clar. dep. c. 27; ministerial conference protocols, 4 Dec. 1855 and 29 Jan. 1856, MR Prot. 14; Seymour

to Clarendon, 13 Feb. 1856, No. 132, FO 7/481; Walewski to De Serre, 22 Feb., No. 14, and De Serre to Walewski, 14 March, No. 29, AMAE Autr. 463; *Rel. dipl. Aust.-Sard.*, IV, 239–41.

12. *Cavour-Inghilterra*, I, 181–361 *passim*, and II, 63, 67–68; Chiala, *Lettere di Cavour*, II, 407, 420; *Rel. dipl. Aust.-Sard.*, IV, 241–44. Here again Nolfo's account and mine diverge, as do our views of Buol's aims and conduct at the Congress (*Europa*, 239–40, 242).

13. *Cavour-Inghilterra*, I, 187–89, 295, 298–99, 312–13, 323–29, 346, 400–1; *Carteggio Cavour-Salmour*, 86–87, 90–91, 97–98.

14. Clarendon to Palmerston, 21 Feb. and 13 March 1856, Palm. Papers GC/CL/798 and 823; Buol and Hübner to Francis Joseph, 16 March, No. 10B, PA XII/219; Buol to Francis Joseph, 5 March, PA XL/49.

15. Nolfo, *Europa*, 281–90, 498; Marcelli, *Cavour*, 194–201; Clarendon to Palmerston, 27 March 1856, Palm. Papers GC/CL/840.

16. *Cavour-Inghilterra*, I, 372, 383–89, 418.

17. *Ibid.*, 345–46; Nolfo, *Europa*, 500–1; Urban, 25–26.

18. Nolfo, *Europa*, 506–8; *Cavour-Inghilterra*, I, 420–21.

19. Buol and Hübner to Francis Joseph, 26 Feb. 1856, No. 2, PA XII/219; Buol to Werner, 6 April, PA XII/220; ministerial conference protocol, 2 April, MR Prot. 14; Werner to MKSM, 20 Feb., PA XL/88. Hübner denounced Werner as a turncoat for failing to fight the military at this conference (Hübner, I, 416).

20. See, for example, Buol to Francis Joseph, 7 April 1856, PA XL/49.

21. Buol and Hübner to Francis Joseph, 9 April 1856, No. 21, PA XII/219; *Cavour-Inghilterra*, I, 436–41; Hübner, I, 409, 414–15, 419.

22. Temperley, "Treaty of Paris," 413–14.

23. Clarendon to Palmerston, 8 and 9 April 1856, Palm. Papers GC/CL/857–58; Buol to Francis Joseph, 9 April, PA XL/49; *Cavour-Inghilterra*, I, 442, 444–45; Buol Journal, n.d., Plaz Papers. (Though entitled "Suite du Journal du Cte Buol durant les années 1857, 58, et 59," the journal plainly begins in April 1856.)

24. *Cavour-Inghilterra*, I, 451–53, 455–56, 459–67; Pier Luigi Spaggiari, *Il Ducato di Parma e l'Europa (1854–1859)* (Parma, 1957), 40–44; Nolfo, *Europa*, 229.

25. Grünne to the Foreign Ministry, 25 March and 7 and 11 April 1856, PA XL/88; *Rel. dipl., Aust.-Sard.*, IV, 265–69; *Kempens Tagebuch*, 395–96; Nolfo, *Europa*, 388–99.

26. *Ibid.*, 380–84; Spaggiari, 49–63.

27. Jasmund, II, 474–77; *Cavour-Inghilterra*, I, 460–69, 477–79.

28. Nolfo, *Europa*, 317–25; Marcelli, *Cavour*, 219–28.

29. Clarendon to Palmerston, 11, 14, and 15 April 1856, Palm. Papers GC/CL/860, 863–64 (the latter in Nolfo, *Europa*, 509).

30. Urban, 40–41; Nolfo, *Europa,* 297–98, 326; Marcelli, *Cavour,* 229–37.

31. *Cavour-Inghilterra,* I, 273; Nolfo, *Europa,* 171–72; *Rel. dipl. GB-Sard.,* V, 302–3, 335–36.

32. *Ibid.,* 268–70, 272–74, 277, 285–86; *Cavour-Inghilterra,* II, 6–24.

33. East, 65–70; Buol and Hübner to Francis Joseph, 6 April 1856, No. 20A, PA XII/219; Buol to Francis Joseph, 2 April, PA XL/49; Clarendon to Palmerston, 2 April, Palm. Papers GC/CL/848.

34. Buol to the Foreign Ministry, tg, 14 April 1856, PA XII/220; Palmerston to Clarendon, 9 April, Clar. dep. c. 49; Clarendon to Palmerston, 10 April, Palm. Papers GC/CL/859.

35. Cowley to Clarendon, 3 April 1856, No. 357, FO 519/5; Prokesch to Buol, 3 April, No. 28A, PA XII/56; Werner to Buol, tg, 12 April, and Buol to Werner, 13 April, PA XII/220; Buol to Francis Joseph, 15 April, PA XL/49.

36. Buol Journal (entries undated, evidently May–June 1856).

37. Boutenko, 293; *Krasnyi Arkhiv,* 51–56; W. E. Mosse, *The Rise and Fall of the Crimean System,* 38–41.

38. Cowley to Clarendon, 13 April 1856, Clar. dep. c. 51.

39. Mosse, *Crimean System,* 49–50; Temperley, "Treaty of Paris," 523–30, and "British secret diplomacy during the Palmerston period," in *Festskrift til Halvdan Koht pa sekstiardagen 7 de juli 1933* (Oslo, 1933), 292–93; Clarendon to Cowley, 2 and 21 May 1856, FO 519/173.

40. Buol to Prokesch, 21 and 28 April 1856, PA XII/60; Prokesch to Buol, 1 and 9 May, Nos. 36C and 38A, PA XII/56; Buol Journal, n.d. [early June 1856]; Buol to Francis Joseph, 6 April, PA XL/49. For Coronini's continued political activity, see Nistor, 975–82, 1040–53.

41. Hübner to Buol, 7 May 1856, No. 36C, and Buol to Hübner, 12 May, PA IX/52 and 54; Walewski to De Serre, 7 May, No. 25, and De Serre to Walewski, 10 and 28 May, Nos. 47 and 58, AMAE Autr. 463–64.

42. De Serre to Walewski, 6 May 1856, No. 46, AMAE Autr. 463; *Cavour-Inghilterra,* II, 34, 40; *Rel. dipl. GB-Sard.,* V, 299–300.

43. Buol to Prokesch, 26 May 1856, and Prokesch to Buol, 18 and 25 June, Nos. 46E and 47B, PA XII/60 and 56; Bodea, 113–14; Nistor, 1009–11, 1015–31.

44. Nistor, 1034–38, 1040–46; Buol Journal, entry of 29 July 1856.

45. Clarendon to Seymour, 13 May 1856, Clar. dep. c. 135, and many dispatches in May and June, FO 7/475.

46. Cowley to Clarendon, 29 May 1856, Clar. dep. c. 51; Clarendon to Cowley, 28 and 30 May and 2 and 4 June, FO 519/173; Clarendon to Seymour, 1 July, Clar. dep. c. 136.

47. Clarendon to Seymour, 29 July, 12 and 26 Aug., and 29 Sept. 1856, *ibid.*

48. East, 74–75; Buol Journal, various entries, n.d.; Bourqueney to Walewski, 29 Aug. 1856, No. 109, AMAE Autr. 464; Francis Joseph to Buol, tg, 12 Oct., PA XL/49; Nistor, 991–92, 996–1001, 1004–9.

49. Clarendon to Cowley, 21 and 23 May and 9, 25, and 28 June 1856, FO 519/173; *Greville Memoirs*, VII, 223–24.

50. Nolfo, *Europa*, 359–71; Urban, 44–63; 3 Hansard, 143, 741–57; *Cavour-Inghilterra*, II, 44–49.

51. Nolfo, *Europa*, 404–9, 412–23, 522–24; Clarendon to Cowley, 29 April 1856, FO 519/173; Cowley to Clarendon, 27 April, Clar. dep. c. 51; Palmerston to Clarendon, 27 April, *ibid.* c. 49; *Rel. dipl. GB-Sard.*, V, 274–75.

52. Clarendon to Seymour, 29 and 30 April 1856, Clar. dep. c. 135; Seymour to Clarendon, 7, 14, and 28 May, *ibid.* c. 46.

53. Cowley to Clarendon, 23 May 1856, *ibid.* c. 51; Hübner, I, 406.

54. Clarendon to Cowley, 24 May 1856, FO 519/173; Urban, 67–69; *Rel. dipl. GB-Sard.*, V, 294–95.

55. Nolfo agrees with this view (*Europa*, 374–75).

56. De Serre to Walewski, 4 and 14 May 1856, Nos. 44 and 49, and Walewski to De Serre, 22 May, No. 29, AMAE Autr. 464; Buol to Apponyi at London, 19 May, PA VIII/43; Cowley to Clarendon, 20 May, No. 485, FO 519/5; Clarendon to Cowley, 21 May, FO 519/173.

57. Clarendon to Seymour, 26 May 1856, No. 218, FO 7/475; Palmerston to Clarendon, 27 May, Clar. dep. c. 49.

58. Colloredo to Buol, 26 [?] May 1856, PA VIII/42; Buol to Apponyi, 7 and 9 June, PA VIII/43; Clarendon to Seymour, 28 May and 15 and 22 July, Clar. dep. c. 136; Seymour to Clarendon, 9 July, *ibid.* c. 46.

59. Buol Journal, entry of 12 Aug. 1856; Nolfo, *Europa*, 423–30; Urban, 42–43, 59–60.

60. Bourqueney to Walewski, 8 and 16 Aug. 1856, Nos. 93 and 96, AMAE Autr. 464.

61. *Kempens Tagebuch*, 414–16; Ritter, 428–44; Buol Journal, various entries, n.d.; Buol to Apponyi, 1 July 1856, No. 5, PA VIII/43; Palmerston to Clarendon, 8 July, Clar. dep. c. 49; Clarendon to Seymour, 8 July, *ibid.* c. 136.

62. Mosse, *Crimean System*, 55–104; Ashley, II, 117–21. For British clashes with France on other scores (Turkey, Italy, and Spain), see Temperley, "Last Phase of Stratford," 216–59, and W. E. Mosse, "The Return of Reshid Pasha," *English Historical Review*, LXVIII (1953), 546–73 (a destructive critique of Temperley's account); Clarendon to Cowley, 27 June and 23 and 31 July 1856, FO 519/173.

63. Temperley, "Treaty of Paris," 523–33; Seymour to Clarendon, 20 Aug. 1856, Clar. dep. c. 46.

64. Ab. Corr. 1855–1860, 179.

65. Seymour to Clarendon, 3 Sept. 1856, Clar. dep. c. 46.

66. Seymour to Clarendon, 2, 9, and 23 July 1856, *ibid.*

67. *Rel. dipl. GB-Sard.*, V, 326, 352, 374; Clarendon to Aberdeen, 8 Sept. and 4 Dec. 1856, and Aberdeen to Clarendon, 12 Dec., Add. ms. 43189.

68. De Serre to Walewski, 22 April and 14 May 1856, Nos. 40 and 48, AMAE Autr. 463.

69. Engel-Janosi, *Hübner*, 130–33; Nolfo, *Europa*, 356–59; Hübner to Buol, 28 April and 7 and 28 May 1856, PA IX/54.

70. Boutenko, 297–99, 314–23; Mosse, *Crimean System*, 92–95; Buol Journal, 13 June 1856; Buol's correspondence with V. Esterházy and Prince Paul Esterházy, May to Sept. 1856, PA X/43.

71. For the Rechberg-Bismarck conflict, see Meyer, *passim.*

72. W. E. Mosse, "Return of Reshid Pasha," 549–50; Buol Journal, 23 June 1856; Buol to Prokesch, 28 April 1856, No. 3, PA XII/60; Clarendon to Seymour, 18 March and 6 May 1856, Nos. 131 and 165, FO 474–75.

CHAPTER XVI

1. See, for example, Prince Albert's remarks in Ernest, *Aus meinem Leben*, II, 98–99.

2. Schroeder, "Bruck vs. Buol," 214–17.

3. For Metternich's views, the most important source is the Metternich correspondence with Buol edited by C. J. Burckhardt. Other sources are: *Aus Metternichs nachgelassenen Papieren*, edited by Prince Richard Metternich-Winneburg (8 vols., Vienna, 1880–1884), especially Vol. VIII; *Mémoires du Prince de Metternich, lettres inédites du Prince de Metternich au Baron Hübner*, vols. III–IV; *Kübecks Tagebücher;* Prokesch, *Briefe;* and Adolf Beer, ed., *Kübeck und Metternich, Denkschriften und Briefe* (Vienna, 1897).

4. Germaine Lebel, *La France et les principautés danubiennes* (Paris, 1955), 182; Goriainov, *Bosphore*, 93–94; *Russell Correspondence*, I, 16; Eckhart, 198–200; Corti, *Mensch und Herrscher*, 166.

5. *Kübecks Tagebücher*, 133.

6. See, for example, Clarendon to Redcliffe, 30 Oct. 1854, FO 352/37/I/1, and Clarendon to Westmorland, 31 Oct., Clar. dep. c. 130.

7. A. J. P. Taylor, *Struggle for Mastery*, 81–82; see also his "John Bright and the Crimean War," *Bulletin of the Rylands Library*, XXXVI

(1953–1954), 522; and "Crimea: The War that Would Not Boil" in his *Rumours of Wars* (London, 1952), 38–40.

8. Clarendon to Cowley, 22 April 1856, FO 519/173.

9. Henderson, 98–99; Taylor, *Rumours of Wars*, 30–31, 34; Conacher, 138; F. H. Hinsley, *Power and the Pursuit of Peace* (Cambridge, 1963), 226–31.

10. Three different views on how Britain preserved world peace through the balance of power are in Hinsley, 220–27; G. S. Graham, *The Politics of Naval Supremacy* (Cambridge, 1965); and A. H. Imlah, *Economic Elements in Pax Britannica* (Cambridge, 1958), 1–19. Though many political scientists, especially recently, have become skeptical of balance of power theory and practices, most still seem to accept the conventional view of Britain's beneficent balancing and peace-keeping role in the nineteenth century. See, for example, Inis L. Claude Jr., *Power and International Relations* (New York, 1962), 48–49, 59–60, 88–93, and Kenneth N. Waltz, *Foreign Policy and Democratic Politics: The American and British Experience* (Boston, 1967), 1–14. There are, however, at least two major exceptions: A. F. K. Organski, *World Politics* (2d ed., New York, 1968), and Richard Rosecrance, *Action and Reaction in World Politics* (Boston, 1962). Both books reject the conventional view of balance of power as the real peace-keeping mechanism in the nineteenth century, and Rosecrance's view of the actual system is fairly close to my own.

11. David Baynes Horn, *Great Britain and Europe in the Eighteenth Century* (Oxford, 1967), 381–83. (For his account of Anglo-Austrian relations, presenting a good parallel to British policy in the nineteenth century, see pp. 114–18.)

12. The principle antedates Canning, going back at least to Bolingbroke. Arnold Wolfers and Lawrence W. Martin, eds., *The Anglo-American Tradition in Foreign Affairs: Readings from Thomas More to Woodrow Wilson* (New Haven, 1956), 61–62.

13. Herbert Butterfield, "The Balance of Power," in *Diplomatic Investigations: Essays in the Theory of International Politics*, ed. by Butterfield and Martin Wight (London, 1966), 147.

14. See, for example, Claude, *Power and Politics*, 13–27; Martin Wight, "The Balance of Power," *Diplomatic Investigations*, 149–75; J. B. Burton, *International Relations: A General Theory* (Cambridge, 1967); and C. A. McClelland, *Theory and the International System* (New York, 1966), Ch. 3.

15. See W. H. Riker, *A Theory of Political Coalitions* (New Haven, 1962), esp. pp. 147–48, 168–91.

16. For good examples of how the eighteenth-century balance of power system served to encourage brinkmanship and heighten the danger of war, see Patrice Higonnet, "The Origins of the Seven Years' War," *Journal of Modern History*, XL (1968), 57–90, and Herbert N. Kaplan, *Russia and the Outbreak of the Seven Years' War* (Berkeley, 1968).

17. E.g., Conacher, 138, 264–67.

18. Quoted by Martin, *Triumph of Palmerston*, 48.

19. Prince Albert also feared a repudiation of the war by the public (Martin, *Prince Consort*, I, 563.)

20. John Gallagher and Ronald Robinson, "The Imperialism of Free Trade," *Economic History Review*, 2d series, VI (1953), 1–15. But see also Oliver MacDonagh, "The Anti-Imperialism of Free Trade," *ibid.* XIV (1962), 489–501, and D. C. M. Platt, "The Imperialism of Free Trade: Some Reservations," *ibid.* XXI (1968), 296–306.

21. Hedwig Pawelka, *Englisch-österreichische Wirtschaftsbeziehungen in der ersten Hälfte des 19. Jahrhunderts* (Vienna, 1968), 40–49, 164–69.

22. D. C. M. Platt, *Finance, Trade, and Politics in British Foreign Policy 1815–1914* (Oxford, 1968), 95–96.

23. "Realpolitik zur Zeit des Krimkriegs—eine Säkularbetrachtung," *Historische Zeitschrift*, CLXXIV (1952), 436–45, 469–70.

24. To Buol, 29 Jan. 1856, PA XL/277l (quoted in Heindl, 78).

25. However, see A. H. Brenman's dissertation, "Economic Reform in Neuzeit Austria" (Princeton, 1966) for a convincing argument that 1852–1859 was a period of significant economic and administrative reform and modernization.

26. W. N. Medlicott, *Bismarck, Gladstone, and the Concert of Europe* (London, 1956), 337.

APPENDIX B

1. Ernest to Albert, 7 Feb. 1854, and Albert to Ernest, 23 Feb., RA G10/13 and 71; Bunsen to Albert, n.d. [2 March 1854] and 17 March, and Albert to Bunsen, 13 March and n.d. [17 March], RA G10/102 and G11/18 and 33–34; *Letters of the Prince Consort*, 213.

2. Bunsen's memorandum to Clarendon, 16 Feb. 1854, RA G10/42. Bunsen's memoirs (*Christian Carl Josias Freiherr von Bunsen*, ed. by F. Nippold) give Bunsen's aide-memoire for this note (III, 329–30). The content is roughly the same, but even less warlike and binding on Prussia.

3. Clarendon to Redcliffe, 16 Feb. 1854, FO 352/37/I/1; Bunsen to Albert, 21 Feb., with memorandum of 20 Feb., RA G10/60–61.

4. Borries, 351–52; Thun to Buol, 2 March 1854, No. 7B, PA III/50; Bloomfield to Clarendon, 22 Feb. 1854, Clar. dep. c. 12.

5. Palmerston to Clarendon, 17 Feb. 1854, *ibid.* c. 15.

6. Clarendon to Cowley, 9 March 1854, FO 519/170.

7. Bunsen, III, 334–43, 352–56; Borries, 367–69; Reinhold Müller, *Die Partei Bethmann-Hollweg und die orientalische Krise, 1853–1856* (Halle/ Saale, 1926), 59.

8. Interestingly enough, both King Frederick William and his friend and secret adviser Carl William Saegert immediately suspected that Bunsen had fallen into a trap laid by Palmerston. Hans-Joachim Schoeps, *Der Weg ins deutsche Kaiserreich* (Berlin, 1970), 20–22.

APPENDIX C

1. *Kempens Tagebuch,* 377, 380–82, 385; Nistor, 839, 845, 847, 851, 857–58, 860–62; Alexandru Marcu, *Conspiratori și conspiratii in epoca renasterii politice a României 1848–1877* (Bucharest, 1930), 64–67, 77–79; Stefania Türr, *L'opera di Stefano Türr nel Risorgimento italiano, 1849– 1870* (Florence, 1928), II, 6–7, 10–13.

2. Walewski to Bourqueney, 22 Nov. 1855, AMAE Autr. 461.

3. Clarendon to Palmerston, 7 Nov. 1855, Palm. Papers GC/CL/724; Clarendon to Cowley, 26 Nov., FO 519–172; Clarendon to Redcliffe, 26 Nov., FO 352/42/II/5.

4. Redcliffe to Fuad Pasha, 8 Nov. 1855, FO 352/42/I/4; Palmerston to Clarendon, 8 Nov., Palm. Papers GC/CL/724.

5. Elliot to Clarendon, 27 Nov. 1855, No. 218, and Seymour to Clarendon, 6 Dec., No. 4, FO 7/459–460; Clarendon to Elliot, 27 Nov., No. 165, FO 7/450.

6. Elliot to Clarendon, 2 and 3 Dec. 1855, tg and No. 229, FO 7/459; Seymour to Clarendon, 29 Jan. 1856, No. 71, FO 7/481; Clarendon to Seymour, 11 and 15 Dec. 1855, Nos. 19 and 25, FO 7/450, and 7 and 8 April 1856, Nos. 144 tg and 148, FO 7/475.

Selected Bibliography

Published Documents

Academia Romậna, Bucharest. *Acte și documente relative la istoria renascerei României.* . . . 10 vols. Bucharest, 1889–1909.

Curato, Federico, ed. *Le relazioni diplomatiche fra la Gran Bretagna ed il Regno di Sardegna dal 1852 al 1856: Il carteggio di Sir James Hudson.* 2 vols. Turin, 1956.

Great Britain, House of Commons. *Sessional Papers.* Eastern Papers, Vol. LXXI (1854).

——. State Papers, Vols. LXXII (1854); LV (1854–1855); LX (1856); LXI (1856); XVII (1857).

Hansard's Parliamentary Debates. 3rd series. Vols. CXXIV–CLXII (1853–1856). London, 1853–1856.

Istituto Storico italiano per l'Età moderna e contemporanea. *Le relazioni diplomatiche fra l'Austria e il Granducato di Toscana.* 3d series: 1848–1860. Vol. IV (1853–1856). Ed. by Angelo Filipuzzi. Rome, 1968.

——. *Le relazioni diplomatiche fra l'Austria e il Regno di Sardegna.* 3d series: 1848–1860. Vols. III–IV (1849–1857). Ed. by Franco Valsecchi. Rome, 1963.

——. *Le relazioni diplomatiche fra la Francia e il Granducato di Toscana.* 3d series: 1848–1860. Vol. II (1851–1857). Ed. by Armando Saitta. Rome, 1959.

——. *Le relazioni diplomatiche fra la Gran Bretagna e il Regno di Sardegna.* 3d series: 1848–1860. Vols. I–V (1848–1856). Ed. by Federico Curato. Rome, 1955–1968.

Jasmund, Julius von, ed. *Aktenstücke zur orientalischen frage.* 3 vols. Berlin, 1855–1859.

Martens, Fedor Fedorovich, ed. *Recueil des traités conclus par la Russie avec les puissances étrangères.* 15 vols. St. Petersburg, 1874–1906.

Martens, Georg Friedrich von, ed. *Nouveau recueil de traités d'alliance, de paix, de trêve . . . et de plusieurs autres actes servant à la con-*

naissance des relations étrangères des puissances . . . *de l'Europe* . . . *depuis 1808 jusqu'à présent.* . . . 16 vols. Göttingen, 1817–1841.

——. *Nouveau recueil général de traités, conventions et autres transactions remarquables, servant à la connaissance des relations étrangères des puissances et états dans leurs rapports mutuels.* 20 vols. Göttingen, 1843–1875.

——. *Nouveaux supplemens au recueil de traités* . . . *depuis 1761 jusqu'à présent.* . . . Ed. by Frederic Murhard. 3 vols. Göttingen, 1839–1842.

Nistor, Ion I., ed. *Corespondenţa lui Coronini din Principate: Acte şi raporte din Iunie 1854–Martie 1857.* Cernauţi, 1938.

Poschinger, Heinrich Ritter von, ed. *Preussen im Bundestag, 1851–1859: Dokumente der königlichen preussischen Bundestags-Gesandschaft.* 4 vols. Leipzig, 1882–1884. (Publicationen aus den königlichen preussischen Staatsarchiven, vols. XII, XIV, XV, XXIII.)

Raindre, G., ed. "Les papiers inédits du Comte Walewski: Souvenirs et correspondance (1855–1868)," *Revue de France,* V (1925), 485–510.

Testa, Alfred, Freiherr von, *et al.,* eds. *Recueil des traités de la Porte ottomane avec les puissances étrangères, depuis le premier traité conclu, en 1536, entre Suleyman I et François I jusqu'à nos jours.* 11 vols. Paris, 1864–1911.

Memoirs, Diaries, and Collections of Letters

Albert, Prince Consort of Victoria. *Letters of the Prince Consort, 1831–1861.* Ed. by Kurt von Jagow. Trans. by E. T. S. Dugdale. London, 1838.

——. *The Prince Consort and His Brother: Two Hundred New Letters.* Ed. by Hector Bolitho. New York, 1934.

Argyll, George Douglas Campbell, Eighth Duke of. *Autobiography and Memoirs.* Ed. by the Dowager Duchess of Argyll. 2 vols. London, 1906.

Beust, Friedrich Ferdinand, Graf von. *Aus drei Viertel-Jahrhunderten.* 2 vols. Stuttgart, 1887.

Bodea, Cornelia C., ed. *Corespondenţa politica (1855–1859). Documente privind unirea Principatelor,* ed. by A. Oţetea, vol. III, Bucharest, 1963.

Bunsen, Christian C. J. Baron von. *Christian Carl Josias Freiherr von Bunsen.* Ed. by Friedrich Nippold. 3 vols. Leipzig, 1868–1871.

Cavour, Camillo Benso, conte di. *Carteggio Cavour-Salmour.* Bologna, 1936.

——. *Cavour e l'Inghilterra: Carteggio con V. E. d'Azeglio.* 2 vols. Bologna, 1933.

——. *Lettere edite ed inedite di Camillo Cavour.* Ed. by Luigi Chiala. 2d ed. 6 vols. Turin, 1883–1887.

Connell, Brian, ed. *Regina vs. Palmerston: Correspondence between Queen Victoria and Her Foreign and Prime Minister, 1837–1865.* Garden City, New York, 1961.

Cowley, Henry Richard Charles Wellesley, First Earl of. *The Paris Embassy during the Second Empire.* Ed. by F. A. Wellesley. London, 1928.

Ernest II, Duke of Saxe-Coburg-Gotha. *Aus meinem Leben.* 3 vols. Berlin, 1888–1889.

Fane, Priscilla Ann Wellesley, Countess of Westmorland. *The Correspondence of Priscilla, Countess of Westmorland.* Ed. by Rose Weigall. London, 1909.

Franz Joseph I, Emperor of Austria. *Briefe Kaiser Franz Josephs I an seine Mutter, 1838–1872.* Ed. by Franz Schnürer. Munich, 1930.

Friedrich I, Grand Duke of Baden. *Groszherzog Friedrich I von Baden und die deutsche Politik von 1854 bis 1871: Briefwechsel, Denkschriften, Tagebücher.* Ed. by Hermann Oncken. 2 vols. Stuttgart, 1927.

Gerlach, Ludwig Friedrich Leopold von. *Briefe des Generals Leopold von Gerlach an Otto von Bismarck.* Ed. by Horst Kohl. Stuttgart und Berlin, 1912.

——. *Denkwürdigkeiten aus dem Leben Leopold von Gerlachs, General-Adjutanten König Friedrich Wilhelms IV.* Ed. by his daughter. 2 vols. Berlin, 1891.

Greville, Charles Cavendish Fulke. *The Greville Memoirs, 1814–1860.* 8 vols. Ed. by Lytton Strachey and Roger Fulford. London, 1938.

——. *The Letters of Charles Greville and Henry Reeve, 1836–1865.* Ed. by the Rev. A. H. Johnson. London, 1924.

Hübner, Joseph Alexander, Graf von. *Neuf ans de souvenirs d'un ambassadeur d'Autriche à Paris sous le Second Empire, 1851–1859.* 2 vols. Paris, 1904.

Jelavich, Barbara, ed. *Russland, 1852–1871: Aus den Berichten der bayerischen Gesandschaft in St. Petersburg.* Wiesbaden, 1963.

Johann I, King of Saxony. *Briefwechsel zwischen König Johann von Sachsen und den Königen Friedrich Wilhelm IV. und Wilhelm I. von Preussen.* Ed. by Johann Georg, Duke of Saxony. Leipzig, 1911.

Kempen von Fichtenstamm, Johann Franz, Freiherr. *Das Tagebuch des Polizeiministers Kempen von 1848 bis 1859.* Ed. by Joseph Karl Mayr. Vienna and Leipzig, 1931.

Kübeck von Kübau, Karl Friedrich, Freiherr. *Aus dem Nachlass des Freiherrn Carl Friedrich Kübeck von Kübau: Tagebücher, Briefe, Aktenstücke, 1841–1855.* Ed. by Friedrich Walter, Graz-Cologne, 1960.

——. *Kübeck und Metternich, Denkschriften und Briefe.* Ed. by Adolf Beer. Vienna, 1897.

——. *Tagebücher des Carl Friedrich Freiherrn Kübeck von Kübau.* 2 vols. in 3. Vienna, 1909.

Lewis, Sir George Cornewall. *Letters of the Right Honorable Sir George Cornewall Lewis, Bart. to Various Friends.* Ed. by Gilbert Frankland Lewis. London, 1870.

Lieven, Princess Dorothea. *The Correspondence of Lord Aberdeen and Princess Lieven, 1832–1854.* Ed. by E. Jones Parry. 2 vols. London, 1938–1939.

Loftus, Lord Augustus William Frederick Spencer. *The Diplomatic Reminiscences of Lord Augustus Loftus, 1837–1862.* 1st series, 2 vols. London, 1892.

Manteuffel, Otto, Baron von. *Preussens auswärtige Politik, 1850–1858: Unveröffentlichte Dokumente aus dem Nachlasse Manteuffels.* Ed. by Heinrich Ritter von Poschinger. 2 vols. Berlin, 1902.

Meiendorf, Petr Kazimirovich, Baron. *Peter von Meyendorff, ein russischer Diplomat an den Höfen von Berlin und Wien: Politischer und privater Briefwechsel, 1826–1863.* Ed. by Otto Hoetzsch. 3 vols. Berlin and Leipzig, 1923.

Metternich-Winneburg, Prince Clemens Lothar Wenzel von. *Aus Metternichs nachgelassenen Papieren.* Ed. by Prince Richard Metternich-Winneburg. 8 vols. Vienna, 1880–1884.

——. *Briefe des Staatskanzlers Fürsten Metternich-Winneburg an den österreichischen Minister des Allerhöchsten Hauses und des Äussern, Grafen Buol-Schauenstein, aus den Jahren 1852–1859.* Ed. by Carl J. Burckhardt. Munich and Berlin, 1934.

——. *Mémoires du Prince de Metternich: Lettres inédites du Prince de Metternich au Baron Hübner.* Trans. by Constantin de Grunwald. 4 vols. Paris, 1959.

Morny, Charles Auguste Louis Joseph, Duc de. *Extrait des mémoires du duc de Morny: Une ambassade en Russie, 1856.* 4th ed. Paris, 1892.

Nesselrode, Karl Robert, Graf von. *Lettres et papiers du Chancelier comte de Nesselrode, 1760–1850.* Ed. by Anatole Nesselrode. 11 vols. Paris, 1904–1912.

Panmure, Fox Maule Ramsay, Second Baron. *The Panmure Papers, Being a Selection from the Correspondence of Fox Maule, 2nd Baron Panmure Afterwards 11th Earl of Dalhousie.* Ed. by George Brisbane Douglas and George Dalhousie Ramsay. 2 vols. London, 1908.

Persigny, Jean, Duc de. *Mémoires du Duc de Persigny publiés avec des documents inédits.* Paris, 1896.

Prokesch von Osten, Anton graf. *Aus den Briefen des Grafen Prokesch von Osten, 1849–1855.* Vienna, 1896.

Russell, John Russell, First Earl. *The Later Correspondence of Lord John*

Russell, 1840–1878. Ed. by George Peabody Gooch. 2 vols. London, 1925.

Thouvenel, Edouard Antoine. *Nicholas Ier et Napoléon III: Les prélimi-naires de la guerre de Crimé (1852–1854) d'après les papiers inédits de M. Thouvenel*. Ed. by Louis Thouvenel. Paris, 1891.

——. *Pages de l'histoire du Second Empire*. Ed. by Louis Thouvenel. Paris, 1903.

——. *Trois années de la question d'Orient, 1856–1859*. Ed. by Louis Thouvenel. Paris, 1897.

Victoria, Queen of Great Britain. *The Letters of Queen Victoria: A Selection from Her Majesty's Correspondence between the years 1837 and 1861*. Ed. by Arthur Christopher Benson. 1st series. 3 vols. London, 1907.

——. *Letters of Queen Victoria, from the Archives of the House of Brandenburg-Prussia*. Ed. by Hector Bolitho. Trans. by J. Pudney and Lord Sudley. New Haven, 1938.

Vitzthum von Eckstaedt, Carl Friedrich. *St. Petersburg und London in den Jahren 1852–1864*. 2 vols. Stuttgart, 1886.

Secondary Works

Academia Republicii Populare Romîne. *Formarea și consolidarea Orîn-duirii capitaliste (1848–1878). Istoria Romîniei*, Vol. IV. Bucharest, 1964.

Anderson, M. S. *The Eastern Question 1774–1923*. London and New York, 1966.

Anderson, Olive. *A Liberal State at War: English Politics and Economics during the Crimean War*. London, Melbourne, New York, 1967.

Ashley, Evelyn. *The Life of Henry John Temple, Viscount Palmerston, 1846–1865: With Selections from His Speeches and Correspondence*. 2 vols. London, 1876.

Bailey, Frank Edgar. *British Policy and the Turkish Reform Movement, 1826–1853*. London, 1942.

Bapst, Edmond. *Les origines de la guerre Crimée: La France et la Russie de 1848 à 1854*. Paris, 1912.

Bapst, Germain. *Le Maréchal Canrobert: Souvenirs d'un siècle*. 6 vols. Paris, 1898–1913.

Bartlett, Christopher John. *Great Britain and Sea Power, 1815–1853*. Oxford, 1963.

Baumgart, Winfried. *Der Friede von Paris 1856*. Munich, 1972.

Beer, Adolf. *Die orientalische Politik Österreichs seit 1774*. Prague, 1883.

Bell, Herbert F. C. *Lord Palmerston*. 2 vols. London, New York, 1936.

Benedikt, Heinrich. *Die wirtschaftliche Entwicklung in der Franz-Joseph Zeit.* Vienna and Munich, 1958.

Böhme, Helmut. *Deutschlands Weg zur Grossmacht: Studien zum Verhältnis von Wirtschaft und Staat während der Reichsgründungszeit 1848–1881.* Cologne and Berlin, 1966.

Borries, Kurt. *Preussen im Krimkrieg, 1853–1856.* Stuttgart, 1930.

Case, Lynn M. *French Opinion of War and Diplomacy during the Second Empire.* Philadelphia, 1954.

Charles-Roux, François. *Alexandre II, Gortchakoff, et Napoléon III.* Paris, 1913.

Conacher, J. B. *The Aberdeen Coalition, 1852–1855: A Study in Mid-Nineteenth-Century Party Politics.* Cambridge, 1968.

Corti, Egon Caesar, conte. *Mensch und Herrscher: Wege und Schicksale Kaiser Franz Josephs I zwischen Thronbesteigung und Berliner Kongress.* Graz, 1952.

——. *Vom Kind zum Kaiser.* Graz-Vienna, 1950.

Cullberg, Albin. *La politique du roi Oscar I pendant la guerre de Crimée: Études diplomatiques sur les négociations secrètes entre les cabinets de Stockholm, Paris, Saint Petersbourg, et Londres, les années 1853–1856.* Stockholm, 1912.

Curtiss, John Shelton. *The Russian Army under Nicholas I, 1825–1855.* Durham, North Carolina, 1965.

Davison, R. H. *Reform in the Ottoman Empire, 1856–1876.* Princeton, 1963.

Drouyn de Lhuys, Edouard. *Les neutres pendant la guerre d'Orient: Mémoire lu à l'Académie des Sciences Morales et Politiques dans la séance du 4 avril 1868.* Paris, 1868.

East, William Gordon. *The Union of Moldavia and Wallachia.* Cambridge, 1929.

Eckhart, Franz. *Die deutsche Frage und der Krimkrieg.* Berlin and Königsberg, 1931.

Engel-Janosi, Friedrich. *Der Freiherr von Hübner, 1811–1892: Eine Gestalt aus dem Österreich Kaiser Franz Josephs.* Innsbruck, 1933.

——. *Graf Rechberg. Vier Kapitel zu seiner und Österreichs Geschichte.* Munich and Berlin, 1927.

Eyck, Frank. *The Prince Consort: A Political Biography.* Boston, 1959.

Ficquelmont, Count Karl von. *Russlands Politik und die Donaufürstenthümer.* Vienna, 1854.

Fitzmaurice, Lord Edmond. *The Life of Granville George Leveson Gower, Second Earl of Granville K. G., 1815–1891.* 2 vols. London, 1905.

Friedjung, Heinrich. *Historische Aufsätze.* Stuttgart und Berlin, 1919.

——. *Der Krimkrieg und die österreichische Politik.* Stuttgart und Berlin, 1907.

——. *Österreich von 1848 bis 1860.* 2d ed., 2 vols. Stuttgart und Berlin, 1908.

Friese, Christian. *Russland und Preussen vom Krimkrieg bis zum polnischen Aufstand.* Berlin, 1931.

Fuchs, Walther Peter. *Die deutschen Mittelstaaten und die Bundesreform, 1853–1860.* Berlin, 1934.

Geffcken, Friedrich Heinrich. *Zur Geschichte des orientalischen Kriegs, 1853–1856.* Berlin, 1881.

Gillessen, Günther. *Lord Palmerston und die Einigung Deutschlands. Die englische Politik von der Paulskirche bis zu den Dresdner Konferenzen (1848–1851).* Lübeck and Hamburg, 1961.

Gooch, Brison D. *The New Bonapartist Generals in the Crimean War.* The Hague, 1959.

Gooch, George Peabody. *The Second Empire.* London, 1960.

Goriainov, S. M. *Le Bosphore et les Dardanelles.* Paris, 1910.

Gourdon, Edouard. *Histoire du Congrès de Paris.* Paris, 1857.

Gugolz, Peter. *Die Schweiz und der Krimkrieg, 1853–1856.* Basel and Stuttgart, 1965.

Guichen, Eugene Vicomte de. *La guerre de Crimée, 1854–1856.* Paris, 1936.

Hallberg, Charles W. *Franz Joseph and Napoleon III, 1852–1864.* New York, 1955.

Handelsman, Marceli. *Czartoryski, Nicholas I et le proche Orient.* Paris, 1934.

Harcourt, Bernard Hippolyte d'. *Diplomatie et diplomates: Les quatres ministères de M. Drouyn de Lhuys.* Paris, 1882.

Hauterive, Ernst d'. *The Second Empire and Its Downfall: The Correspondence of the Emperor Napoleon III and His Cousin Prince Napoleon.* Trans. by Herbert Wilson. New York, 1927.

Heindl, Waltraud. *Graf Buol-Schauenstein in St. Petersburg und London 1848–1852.* Vienna, 1970.

Heller, Edward. *Mitteleuropas Vorkämpfer: Fürst Felix zu Schwarzenberg.* Vienna, 1933.

Henderson, Gavin B. *Crimean War Diplomacy and Other Historical Essays.* Glasgow, 1947.

Hoffmann, Joachim. *Die Berliner Mission des Grafen Prokesch-Osten, 1849–1852.* Berlin, 1959.

Hoffmann, Peter. *Die diplomatischen Beziehungen zwischen Württem-*

berg und Bayern im Krimkrieg und bis zum Beginn der italienischen Krise (1853–1858). Stuttgart, 1963.

Holbraad, Carsten. *The Concert of Europe: A Study in German and British International Theory 1815–1914*. London, 1970.

Imlah, Ann G. *Britain and Switzerland, 1845–1860: A Study of Anglo-Swiss Relations during Some Critical Years for Swiss Neutrality*. Hamden, Connecticut, 1966.

Iorga, Nicolae. *Istoria Românilor*. 9 vols. Bucharest, 1936–1938.

Jomini, Aleksandr. *Etude diplomatique sur la guerre de Crimée (1852 à 1856) par un ancien diplomate*. 2 vols. St. Petersburg, 1878.

Kinglake, Alexander William. *The Invasion of the Crimea: Its Origin and Account of Its Progress down to the Death of Lord Raglan*. 8 vols. London, 1863.

Kovalevskii, Eg. *Der Krieg Russlands mit der Türkei in den Jahren 1853 und 1854 und der Bruch mit den Westmächten*. Trans. from the Russian by Christian von Sarauw. Leipzig, 1869.

Krusemark, Götz. *Württemberg und der Krimkrieg*. Halle, 1932.

Kunau, Heinrich. *Die Stellung der preussischen Konservativen zur äusseren Politik während des Krimkrieges (1853–1856)*. Halle, 1914.

Lademacher, Horst. *Die belgische Neutralität als Problem der europäischen Politik 1830–1914*. Bonn, 1971.

Lane-Poole, Stanley. *Life of the Right Honourable Stratford Canning*. 2 vols. New York and London, 1888.

Marcelli, Umberto. *Cavour Diplomatico*. Bologna, 1961.

Marlin, Roger. *L'Opinion Franc-Comtoise devant la guerre de Crimée*. Paris, 1957.

Martin, Kingsley. *The Triumph of Lord Palmerston:A Study of Public Opinion in England before the Crimean War*. London, 1924.

Martin, Sir Theodore. *The Life of His Royal Highness the Prince Consort*. 5 vols. London, 1875–1880.

Marx, Karl. *The Eastern Question: A Reprint of Letters Written 1853–1856 Dealing with the Events of the Crimean War*. Ed. by Eleanor Marx Aveling and Edward Aveling. London, 1897.

Maxwell, Sir Herbert Eustace. *The Life and Letters of George William Frederick, Fourth Earl of Clarendon*. 2 vols. London, 1913.

Meyer, Arnold Oskar. *Bismarcks Kampf mit Österreich im Bundestag zu Frankfurt, 1851–1859*. Berlin und Leipzig, 1927.

Moscati, Ruggero. *Ferdinando II di Borbone nei documenti diplomatici austriaci*. Naples, 1947.

Mosse, Werner E. *The European Powers and the German Question, 1848–1871: With Special Reference to England and Russia*. Cambridge, 1958.

——. *The Rise and Fall of the Crimean System, 1855–1871.* London, 1963.

Müller, Paul. *Feldmarschall Fürst Windischgrätz; Revolution und Gegenrevolution in Österreich.* Vienna and Leipzig, 1934.

Müller, Reinhold. *Die Partei Bethmann-Hollweg und die orientalische Krise, 1853–1856.* Halle/Saale, 1926.

The New Cambridge Modern History. The Zenith of European Power, 1830–1870. Ed. by J. P. T. Bury, Vol. X. Cambridge, 1960.

Nistor, Ion. *Ocupaţia austriaca in Principate (1854–1857) dupa rapoartele lui Coronini.* Bucharest, 1938.

Nolfo, Ennio di. *Adam J. Czartoryski e il Congresso di Parigi. (Questione polacca e politica europea nel 1855–56).* Padua, 1964.

——. *Europa e Italia nel 1855–1856.* Rome, 1967.

Parker, Charles Stuart. *Life and Letters of Sir James Graham, Second Baronet of Netherby, P.C., G.C.B., 1792–1861.* 2 vols. London, 1907.

Popov, N. A. *Rossiia i Serbiia: Istoricheskii ocherk russkovo pokrovitelst'va Serbii s' 1806 do 1856 god.* 2 vols. Moscow, 1869.

Puryear, Vernon John. *England, Russia and the Straits Question, 1844–1856.* Berkeley, California, 1931.

——. *France and the Levant, 1820–1854.* Berkeley and Los Angeles, 1941.

——. *International Economics and Diplomacy in the Near East: A Study of British Commercial Policy in the Levant, 1834–1853.* Stanford and London, 1935.

Rassow, Peter. *Der Konflict König Friedrich Wilhelms IV mit dem Prinzen von Preussen im Jahre 1854: Eine preussische Staatskrise.* Wiesbaden, 1960.

Redlich, Joseph. *Kaiser Franz Joseph von Österreich.* Berlin, 1928.

Ridley, Jasper. *Lord Palmerston.* New York, 1970.

Riker, Thad Weed. *The Making of Roumania: A Study of an International Problem, 1856–1866.* London, 1931.

Schiemann, Theodor. *Geschichte Russlands unter Kaiser Nikolaus I.* 4 vols. Berlin, 1904–1919.

Schlitter, Hanns. *Aus der Regierungszeit Kaiser Franz Joseph I.* Wien, 1919.

Schule, Ernst. *Russland und Frankreich vom Ausgang des Krimkrieges bis zum italienischen Krieg, 1856–1859.* Osteuropäische Forschungen, Vol. XIX. Berlin, 1935.

Shcherbatov, Aleksandr P. *General-Feldmarshal kniaz Paskevich, evo zhizn i deiatelnost.* 7 vols. St. Petersburg, 1888—.

Simpson, F. A. *Louis Napoleon and the Recovery of France, 1848–1856.* London, 1923.

Southgate, Donald. *'The Most English Minister . . .': The Policies and Politics of Palmerston.* London and New York, 1966.

Srbik, Heinrich Ritter von. *Deutsche Einheit: Idee und Wirklichkeit vom Heiligen Reich bis Koniggrätz.* 4 vols. Munich, 1936–1942.

——. *Metternich, der Staatsmann und der Mensch.* 3 vols. Munich, 1925–1954.

Stanmore, Arthur Hamilton Gordon, Baron. *The Earl of Aberdeen.* New York, 1893.

Stavrianos, Leften S. *The Balkans since 1453.* 2d ed. New York, 1966.

Steinitz, Eduard, ed. *Erinnerungen an Franz Joseph I.* Berlin, 1931.

Tarle, E. V. *Krymskaia voina.* 2 vols. Moscow, 1950.

Tatishchev, Sergei Spiridonovich. *Imperator Aleksandr II, evo zhizn i tsarstvovanie.* St. Petersburg, 1903.

——. *Imperator Nikolai i inostrannye dvoryi: Istoricheskie ocherki.* St. Petersburg, 1880.

Taylor, A. J. P. *The Struggle for Mastery in Europe, 1848–1918.* Oxford, 1954.

Temperley, Harold W. V. *England and the Near East: The Crimea.* London, 1936.

Treue, Wilhelm. *Der Krimkrieg und die Entstehung der modernen Flotten.* Göttingen, 1954.

Unckel, Bernhard. *Österreich und der Krimkrieg: Studien zur Politik der Donaumonarchie in den Jahren 1854–1856.* Lübeck and Hamburg, 1969.

Urban, Miriam Belle. *British Opinion and Policy on the Unification of Italy, 1856–1861.* Scottsdale, Pennsylvania, 1938.

Valentin, Veit. *Bismarcks Reichsgründung im Urteil englischer Diplomaten.* Amsterdam, 1937.

Valsecchi, Franco. *L'Alleanza di Crimea: Il Risorgimento e l'Europa.* Milan, 1948.

Wagner, Walter. *Geschichte des K. K. Kriegsministeriums.* Vol. I, 1848–1866. Graz and Cologne, 1966.

Walter, Friedrich. *Die österreichische Zentralverwaltung.* III. Abteilung, Vol. I (1848–1852). Vienna, 1964.

Ward, Adolphus William, and George Peabody Gooch, eds. *The Cambridge History of British Foreign Policy, 1783–1919.* 3 vols. Cambridge, 1922–1923.

Wimpffen, Alfons, Graf von. *Erinnerungen aus der Walachei während der Besetzung durch die österreichischen Truppen in den Jahren 1854–1856.* Vienna, 1878.

Zaionchkovskii, A. M. *Vostochnaia voina v sviazu s ei politicheskoi obstanovkoi.* 2 vols. with supplements. St. Petersburg, 1908–1913.

Articles

Anderson, Olive. "Economic Warfare in the Crimean War," *Economic History Review*, XIV (1961), 34–37.

——. "Great Britain and the Beginnings of the Ottoman Public Debt," *The Historical Journal*, VII, No. 1 (1964), 47–63.

Artonne, André. "Le Comte de Bourqueney," *Revue d'histoire diplomatique*, LXVI (1952), 52–66.

Bailey, Frank Edgar. "The Economics of British Foreign Policy, 1825–1850," *Journal of Modern History*, XII (Dec. 1940), 449–84.

Baudi di Vesme, Carlo. "Il Regno delle due Sicilie durante la guerra di Crimea nei documenti diplomatici francesi," *Rassegna storica del Risorgimento*, XXXIX (1952), 395–409.

Baumgart, Winfried. "Probleme der Krimkrieg-Forschung," *Jahrbücher für Geschichte Osteuropas*, new series, XIX (1971), 49–109, 243–64, 371–400.

Bell, Herbert G. "Palmerston and Parliamentary Representation," *Journal of Modern History*, IV (1932), 186–213.

Bilger, Ferdinand. "Grossdeutsche Politik im Lager Radetzkys," *Historische Blätter*, 4 (1931), 3–36.

Bobr-Tylingo, Stanislas. "Napoleon III et le problème polonais (1830–1859)," *Revue internationale d'histoire politique et constitutionelle*, V (1955), 259–80.

Boicu, L. "Incercări Franceze de pătrundere in economia Moldovei in epoca razboiului Crimeii și a Unirii (1853–1859)," Academia Republicii Populare Romîne, *Studii privind unirea Principatelor* (Bucharest, 1960). Pp. 167–98.

——. "Introducerea telegrafiei in Moldova," *Studii si cercetări stiințifice: Istorie*, VIII (1957), 279–305.

——. "Les principautés roumaines dans les projets de Karl von Bruck et Ludwig von Stein pour la constitution de la 'Mitteleuropa' à l'époque de la guerre de Crimée," *Revue roumaine d'histoire*, VI (1967), 233–56.

Bolsover, G. H. "Nicholas I and the Partition of Turkey," *Slavonic Review*, XXVII (1948), 115–45.

Boutenko, V. "Un projet d'alliance franco-russe en 1856 après des documents inédits des archives russes," *Revue historique*, CLV (1927), 277–325.

Charles-Roux, François. "La Russie et l'alliance anglo-français après la guerre de Crimée," *Revue historique*, CI (1909), 272–315.

——. "La Russie, la France et la question d'Orient après la guerre de Crimée," *Revue historique*, CIX (1912), 272–306.

Corivan, N. "Deux documents sur le choix d'un prince étranger en 1856," *Revue historique du Sud-Est européen*, VII (1930), 78–85.

——. "Renseignements sur la conférence de Vienne (1855)," *Revue historique du Sud-Est européen*, VIII (1931), 1–5.

Craig, Gordon A. "Neutrality in the Nineteenth Century." In *War, Politics, and Diplomacy: Selected Essays*. New York and Washington, 1966. Pp. 143–52.

——. "Portrait of a Political General: Edwin von Manteuffel and the Constitutional Conflict in Prussia." In *ibid.*, 91–120.

——. "The System of Alliances and the Balance of Power." In *The Zenith of European Power*, ed. by J. P. T. Bury, pp. 246–73. *The New Cambridge Modern History*, Vol. X. Cambridge, 1960.

Divin, V. A. and N. I. Kazakov. "Ob osveskhenii nekotorykh voprosov istorii Krymskoi Voiny v literature poslednikh let," *Voprosy Istorii* (1957), 141–50.

Florescu, Radu. "British Reactions to the Russian Regime in the Danubian Principalities, 1828–1834," *Journal of Central European Affairs*, XXII (April 1962), 27–42.

——. "The Rumanian Principalities and the Origins of the Crimean War," *Slavonic and East European Review*, XLIII, No. 100 (Dec. 1964), 46–67.

——. "Stratford Canning, Palmerston, and the Wallachian Revolution of 1848," *Journal of Modern History*, XXXV (Sept. 1963), 227–44.

Franz, Georg. "Der Krimkrieg, ein Wendepunkt des europäischen Schicksals," *Geschichte in Wissenschaft und Unterricht*, VII (1956), 448–63.

Georgescu, Elvire. "Sur un projet d'organisation militaire et politique de la Dobrogea en 1855, par Mehmed Sadyk-Pasha (Michel C. Czajkowski)," *Revue historique du Sud-Est européen*, VIII (1931), 161–69.

Gerba, R. "Zur Geschichte der Ereignisse in Bosnien und Montenegro 1853," *Mittheilungen des k. und k. Kriegs-Archivs*, new series, I (1887), 83–159.

Ghisalberti, Alberto M. "L'Alleanza di Crimea e l'opinione publica," *Risorgimento*, VIII (1956), 14–32.

Giarrizzo, Giuseppe. "L'Inghilterra di fronte all'unificazione italiana," *Rassegna storica Toscana*, VI (Oct. 1960), 201–25.

Godechot, Jacques, and Françoise Pernot. "L'action des représentants de la France à Turin et l'intervention sarde dans la guerre de Crimée," *Rassegna storica del Risorgimento*, XLV (1958), 39–56.

Golder, Frank A. "Russian-American Relations during the Crimean War." *American Historical Review*, XXXI (1926), 462–75.

Gonța, Alexander I. "Firmanul pentru Convocarea Divanilor Ad-Hoc și Problema Unirii Principatelor Romîne," Academia Republicii Populare Romîne, *Studii privind unirea Principatelor* (Bucharest, 1960), 281–96.

Gooch, Brison D. "A Century of Historiography on the Origins of the Crimean War." *American Historical Review*, LXII (1956), 33–58.

——. "The Crimean War in Documents and Secondary Works since 1940." *Victorian Studies*, I (March 1958), 271–79.

Goriainov, S. "Les étapes d'alliance franco-russe, 1853–1861," *Revue de Paris*, XIX (1912), 1–29, 529–44, 755–76.

Handelsman, Marceli. "La guerre de Crimée: La question polonaise et les origines du problème bulgare," *Revue historique*, CLXIX (1932), 271–315.

Henderson, Gavin B. "Ein Beitrag zur Entwicklung der napoleonischen Ideen über Polen und Italien während des Krimkrieges," *Zeitschrift für osteuropäische Geschichte*, VIII (1934), 552–67.

Hösch, Edgar. "Neuere Literatur (1940–1960) über den Krimkrieg," *Jahrbücher für Geschichte Osteuropas*, new series, XI (1961), 399–433.

Iorga, Nicolea. "Politica Austriei fața de Unire: Inainte de conferinta de la Paris," *Analele Academiei Romîne*, Memoriile, sectiune istorice, section II, XXXIV, 835–64.

Jánossy, Dénes A. "Die Geheimpläne Kossuths für einen zweiten Befreiungsfeldzug in Ungarn, 1849–1854," *Jahrbuch des Graf Klebelberg Kuno Institut für ungarische Geschichtsforschung in Wien*, VI (Budapest, 1936), 226–302.

——. "Great Britain and Kossuth," *Archivium Europeae centro-orientalis*, III (1937), 53–190.

——. "Die Schweiz und die ungarische Emigration, 1849–1856," *Zeitschrift für schweizerische Geschichte*, XVIII (1938), 438–49.

——. "Die ungarische Emigration und der Krieg im Orient," *Archivium Europeae centro-orientalis*, V (1939), 113–275.

Jelavich, Charles and Barbara. "The Danubian Principalities and Bulgaria under Russian Protectorship," *Jahrbücher für Geschichte Osteuropas*, new series, XI (1961), 349–66.

Kaehler, Siegfried A. "Realpolitik zur Zeit des Krimkriegs—eine Säkularbetrachtung," *Historische Zeitschrift*, CLXXIV (1952), 417–478.

"K istorii Parizhsovo mira 1856 g," *Krasnyi Arkhiv*, No. 75 (1936), 10–61.

Lefèvre, André. "Les répercussions en Europe occidentale de l'insurrection de Milan en 1853," *Revue d'histoire diplomatique*, LXIX, no. 4 (1955), 329–346.

Lorette, J. "Problèmes politiques étrangères sous Léopold Ier: A propos d'éventuelles participations belges à la guerre de Crimée (1854–1856)," in Académie Royale des Sciences d'Outre-Mer, *L'Expansion belge sous Léopold Ier (1831–1865)* (Brussels, 1965), 567–93.

Martini, Angelo. "La S. Sede e la questione d'Oriente negli anni 1853–1856," *Civiltà Cattolica* (1958–1959), anno 109, I, 587–96; II, 149–62; IV, 168–81, 494–507; anno 110, I, 165–74.

Matter, P. "Cavour et la Guerre de Crimée," *Revue historique*, CXXXXV (1924), 161–200.

Mosse, W. E. "The Return of Reshid Pasha, an incident in the career of Lord Stratford de Redcliffe," *English Historical Review*, LXVIII (1953), 546–73.

Nikitin, S. "Russkaia politika na Balkanakh i nachalo vostochnoi voiny," *Voprosy Istorii*, No. 4 (1946), 3–29.

Nistor, Ion I. "Die Polenlegion im Krimkriege," *Codrul Cosminului*, IX (1935), 7–102.

Pingaud, Albert. "La politique extérieure du Second Empire," *Revue historique*, CLVI (1927), 41–68.

Puryear, Vernon John. "New Light on the Origins of the Crimean War," *Journal of Modern History*, III (June 1931), 219–34.

Rall, Hans. "Griechenland zwischen Russland und dem übrigen Europa: Die 'Grosse Idee' der Griechen zwischen 1847 und 1859," *Saeculum*, XVIII (1967), 164–80.

Ramm, Agatha. "The Crimean War." In *The Zenith of European Power*, ed. by J. P. T. Bury, pp. 468–492. *The New Cambridge Modern History*, Vol. X. Cambridge, 1960.

Riker, Thad W. "The Concert of Europe and Moldavia in 1857," *English Historical Review*, XLII, no. 166 (April 1927), 227–44.

Salomon, Richard. "Die Anerkennung Napoleons III: Ein Beitrag zur Geschichte der Politik Nikolaus' I," *Zeitschrift für osteuropäische Geschichte*, II (1912), 321–66.

Schmitt, B. E. "The Diplomatic Preliminaries of the Crimean War," *American Historical Review*, XXV (October 1919), 36–67.

Schroeder, Paul W. "Austria and the Danubian Principalities, 1853–1856," *Central European History*, II (1969), 216–36.

——. "Bruck versus Buol: The Dispute over Austrian Eastern Policy, 1853–1855," *Journal of Modern History*, XL (June 1968), 193–217.

——. "A Turning Point in Austrian Policy in the Crimean War: The Conferences of March, 1854," *Austrian History Yearbook*, IV–V (1968–1969), 159–202.

Seidl, Hauptmann. "Das Mailander Attentat am 6. Februar 1853," *Mit-*

theilungen des. k. und k. Kriegs–Archivs, new series, X (1898), 295–410.

Tatishchev, S. "Diplomaticheskii razryb Rossii s Turtsiei v 1853 g.," *Istoricheskii Vestnik,* XLVII (1892), 153–76.

Taylor, Alan J. P. "Crimea: The War That Would Not Boil." In A. J. P. Taylor, *Rumours of Wars,* pp. 30–40. London, 1952.

Temperley, Harold W. V. "The Alleged Violations of the Straits Convention by Stratford de Redcliffe between June and September, 1853," *English Historical Review,* XLIX (1934), 657–72.

——. "Austria, England and the Ultimatum to Russia, 16 December 1855." In *Wirtschaft und Kultur: Festschrift zum 70. Geburtstag von Alfons Dopsch,* pp. 626–37. Baden and Wien, 1938.

——. "British Policy towards Parliamentary Rule and Constitutionalism in Turkey (1830–1914)," *Cambridge Historical Journal,* IV (1933), 156–91.

——. "The Last Phase of Stratford de Redcliffe, 1855–1858," *English Historical Review,* XLVII (1932), 216–59.

——."Stratford de Redcliffe and the Origins of the Crimean War," *English Historical Review,* XLVIII (1933), 601–21; XLIX (1934), 265–98.

——. "The Treaty of Paris of 1856 and Its Execution," *Journal of Modern History,* IV (1932), 387–414, 523–43.

——. "The Union of Roumania in the Private Letters of Palmerston, Clarendon, and Cowley 1855–1857," *Revue historique de Sud-Est européen,* XIV (1937), 218–32.

——, and Gavin B. Henderson. "Disraeli and Palmerston in 1857, or, The Dangers of Explanations in Parliament," *Cambridge Historical Journal,* VII (1942), 115–26.

Valsecchi, Franco. "Cavour al Congresso di Parigi," *Il Risorgimento,* VIII (1956), 93–109.

Zane, G. "Die österreichischen und die deutschen Wirtschaftsbeziehungen zu den rumänischen Fürstentümern 1774–1874," *Weltwirtschaftliches Archiv,* XXVI (1927, part II), 30–47, 262–81.

Unpublished Dissertations

Austensen, Roy A. "The Early Career of Count Buol, 1837–1852." University of Illinois, 1969.

Lorantas, Raymond M. "Lord Cowley's Mission to Paris, 1852–1856." University of Pennsylvania, 1963.

Morrow, Ian Fitzherbert. "The Black Sea Question during the Crimean War." Cambridge University, 1927.

Nomikos, Eugenia Voyiatzis. "The International Position of Greece during the Crimean War." Stanford University, 1962.

Ritter, Monika. "Frankreichs Griechenland-Politik während des Krimkrieges (im Spiegel der französischen und der bayerischen Gesandtschaftsberichte 1853–1857)." University of Munich, 1966.

Rock, Kenneth W. "Reaction Triumphant: The Diplomacy of Felix Schwarzenberg in Mastering the Hungarian Insurrection, 1848–1850." Stanford University, 1969.

Weisbrod, Kurt. "Lord Palmerston und die europäische Revolution von 1848." University of Heidelberg, 1967.

Index

Abdul-Medjid I, Ottoman Sultan, 342, 351; *see also* Ottoman Empire

Aberdeen, George Hamilton Gordon, Fourth Earl of, British prime minister, 1852-1855

attitude toward Austria, 11, 35-36, 49, 129, 189, 213

efforts to avoid war and commitments, 32-33, 46-47, 49, 62-63, 66, 68, 71-72, 88-90, 96-98, 102, 110, 118-22, 124-26, 130-32, 409-11

fall of his ministry, 247-48

formation of his ministry, 6, 11-12

policy on war aims and peace negotiations, 170-71, 173, 181, 194, 203-5, 216-17, 219, 224, 233, 237-39, 245, 247, 249-50, 252, 275, 297-98, 315, 369-70, 389, 400

Adrianople, Treaty of (1829), 14, 111, 172

Aland Isles, 150, 198, 325, 336, 350, 365

Alaska, 204

Albania, 156, 174

Albert, Prince Consort

on Austria, Prussia, and Germany, 12, 35, 40, 50, 81, 146-47, 188, 203, 220, 252, 269, 292, 320, 430

on British war aims and diplomacy, 135-36, 151, 170-71, 188, 194, 202, 223-24, 238, 245, 276-78, 289, 306, 328, 350, 356

on Eastern crisis, 32, 35, 50, 68, 89, 98, 118-19, 124

on general British politics and policy, 12, 247, 297, 421

Alexander, Prince of Serbia, 138

Alexander II, Tsar of Russia (1855-1881), 265, 280, 339, 356

Ali Pasha, Turkish foreign minister

and premier, 269-70, 291, 311, 341, 362-63, 381

Alvensleben, Albrecht Count von, special Prussian emissary, 165, 167, 177, 180, 191

Anglo-French-Austrian alliance of Dec. 2, 1854, 215-27, 239, 242

of April 15, 1856, 381-83, 390

Anglo-French-Sardinian alliance (Jan. 22, 1855), 237-39, 274

Anglo-French ultimatum to Russia (Feb. 27, 1854), 144-45

Anglo-Italian Legion, 307, 375

Apponyi, Rudolph Count, Austrian minister to Sardinia-Piedmont and to Bavaria, 21, 228, 251, 295

Argyll, George Douglas Campbell, Eighth Duke of, British Lord Privy Seal, 12, 88-89, 98, 203, 247, 289, 297, 314, 329

Arnim, Heinrich Count von, Prussian minister to Austria, 69-70, 141, 145, 180

Austria

appraisals and interpretations of policy, 57-59, 84-86, 112, 114, 158-59, 179-81, 196-97, 212, 220-21, 225-26, 241, 279-81, 314-15, 392-400, 406-8, 412, 416-19, 425-26

foreign policy

on Balkans, 25-26, 28, 138-39, 174-75, 206-15, 351-53, 383-85

on Britain, 8-11, 35-41, 75, 94-95, 195, 213-15, 224-26, 287, 300, 317, 326-27, 336, 387-88, 416-18, 429

conduct of, *see* Buol, Francis Joseph, Hübner, Bruck, Prokesch, Hess, *and* Schwarzenberg

on France, 4-7, 75, 84-85, 104-6,

533

AUSTRIA, GREAT BRITAIN,
AND THE CRIMEAN WAR

Designed by R. E. Rosenbaum.
Composed by Vail-Ballou Press, Inc.,
in 10 point linotype Janson, 3 points leaded,
with display lines in Weiss Roman.
Printed letterpress from type by Vail-Ballou Press
on Warren's 1854 text, 60 pound basis,
with the Cornell University Press watermark.
Illustrations printed by Art Craft of Ithaca.
Bound by Vail-Ballou Press
in Interlaken book cloth
and stamped in All Purpose foil.

Library of Congress Cataloging in Publication Data
(For library cataloging purposes only)

Schroeder, Paul W   .
  Austria, Great Britain, and the Crimean War.

  Bibliography: p.
  1. Crimean War, 1853–1856—Diplomatic history.
2. Europe—Politics—1848–1871.   I. Title.
DK215.S35   947'.07   72-3451
ISBN 0–8014–0742–7